MIKE PRATT
KAREN VAN PEURSEM
MUKESH GARG

AUDITING THEORY & PRACTICE

AUSTRALASIAN EDITION

Auditing Theory and Practice
1st Australasian Edition
Mike Pratt
Karen Van Peursem
Mukesh Garg

Portfolio manager: Fiona Hammond
Product manager: Rachael Pictor / Geoff Howard
Content developer: Stephanie Davis
Senior project editor: Nathan Katz
Cover designer: Alissa Dinallo
Text designer: Rina Gargano (Alba Design)
Permissions/Photo researcher: Debbie Gallagher/Brendan Gallagher
Editor: Paul Smitz
Proofreader: James Anderson
Indexer: Julie King
Art direction: Danielle Maccarone
Cover: Courtesy Stocksy/Clique Images
Typeset by KnowledgeWorks Global Ltd.

Any URLs contained in this publication were checked for currency during the production process. Note, however, that the publisher cannot vouch for the ongoing currency of URLs.

Previous edition published as AUDITING: THEORY AND PRACTICE IN NEW ZEALAND, 7th edition (9780473419363) © 2017 by Karen Van Peursem & Michael J Pratt

This 1st Cengage edition published in 2023

For product information and technology assistance,
in Australia call **1300 790 853**;
in New Zealand call **0800 449 725**

For permission to use material from this text or product, please email **aust.permissions@cengage.com**

National Library of Australia Cataloguing-in-Publication Data
ISBN: 9780170458955
A catalogue record for this book is available from the National Library of Australia.

Cengage Learning Australia
Level 7, 80 Dorcas Street
South Melbourne, Victoria Australia 3205

Cengage Learning New Zealand
Unit 4B Rosedale Office Park
331 Rosedale Road, Albany, North Shore 0632, NZ

For learning solutions, visit **cengage.com.au**

Printed in China by 1010 Printing International Limited.
1 2 3 4 5 6 7 26 25 24 23 22

BRIEF CONTENTS

CONTENTS

Guide to the text

As you read this text you will find a number of features in every chapter to enhance your study of auditing and help you understand how the theory is applied in the real world.

PART-OPENING FEATURES

Understand how key concepts are connected across all chapters in the part by viewing the **Concept map**.

Part openers introduce each of the chapters within the part and give an overview of how they relate to each other.

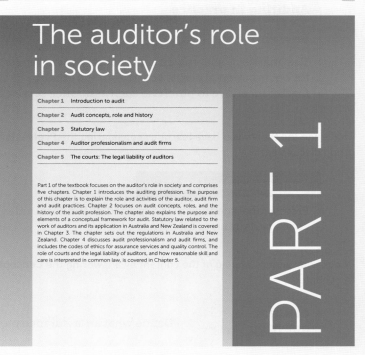

The auditor's role in society

Chapter 1	Introduction to audit
Chapter 2	Audit concepts, role and history
Chapter 3	Statutory law
Chapter 4	Auditor professionalism and audit firms
Chapter 5	The courts: The legal liability of auditors

Part 1 of the textbook focuses on the auditor's role in society and comprises five chapters. Chapter 1 introduces the auditing profession. The purpose of this chapter is to explain the role and activities of the auditor, audit firm and audit practices. Chapter 2 focuses on audit concepts, roles, and the history of the audit profession. The chapter also explains the purpose and elements of a conceptual framework for audit. Statutory law related to the work of auditors and its application in Australia and New Zealand is covered in Chapter 3. The chapter sets out the regulations in Australia and New Zealand. Chapter 4 discusses audit professionalism and audit firms, and includes the codes of ethics for assurance services and quality control. The role of courts and the legal liability of auditors, and how reasonable skill and care is interpreted in common law, is covered in Chapter 5.

PART 1

CHAPTER-OPENING FEATURES

Identify the key concepts you will engage with through the **Learning objectives** at the start of each chapter.

Refer to the **Introduction** for a contextualised summary of the chapter.

CHAPTER 12

12 | Internal control and the auditor

Learning objectives

After studying the material in this chapter, you should be able to:
- describe an appropriate strategy to evaluate a client's control system for audit
- prepare and evaluate documentation methods such as system flowcharts and data flow diagrams using the procedures introduced
- select and describe tests of controls in response to the auditor's evaluation of the client's internal control system.

Introduction

This chapter is about internal controls and when audit tests should be performed on them. Auditing standards define the frame of interest:

For [these] purposes ... the system of internal control consists of five interrelated components: (i) Control environment; (ii) Entity's risk assessment process; (iii) Entity's process to monitor the system of internal control; (iv) Information system and communication; and (v) Control activities. (ASA 315, para 12m; ISA NZ 315, para 12m)

Here, we consider how to incorporate control-testing decisions into the audit strategy and plan (see Figure 12.1). We introduce fundamental controls and consider whether tests of the client's controls allow the auditor to reduce the nature, timing or extent of substantive testing.

This chapter introduces two documentation methods that we ask you to learn to use. Overall, the chapter introduces procedures to understand and evaluate that portion of the client's system of concern to the financial statement auditor.

FEATURES WITHIN CHAPTERS

Analyse practical applications of concepts through **Auditing in practice** boxes.

Auditing in practice

Environmental audits

The 'market' – shareholders, corporate boards, lenders, advisers – may be unwilling to pay for environmental audits because, in the absence of laws that require it to do so, there is little market incentive to purchase such assurance services.

Challenge the theory you have learnt by considering the **Professional scepticism** boxes, perhaps in a group discussion.

Professional scepticism

Professional scepticism is expected of auditors under professional ethical standards and codes pertaining to assurance services.

Check your understanding of the content by answering the **Concept questions** as you progress through the chapter.

CONCEPT QUESTION 1 Define what an 'assurance provider' does and provides.

FEATURES WITHIN CHAPTERS

Short extracts from the AUASB and NZAuASB are covered by **Auditing standards**.

Sufficiency of evidence

Sufficiency (of audit evidence) means the measure of the quantity of audit evidence. The quantity of the audit evidence needed is affected by the auditor's assessment of the risks of material misstatement and also by the quality of such audit evidence. (ASA 500, para 5(f); ISA NZ 500, para 5(f))

END-OF-CHAPTER FEATURES

At the end of each chapter you will find several tools to help you to review, practise and extend your knowledge of the key learning objectives.

Review your understanding of the key chapter topics with the **Summary**.

Study tools

Summary

In this chapter, audit tests were considered, and the types of tests and purposes for them were explained. Differences between *walk-through procedures*, *tests of controls* and *substantive tests* were explained and exampled. Test techniques that enable efficiencies include *sampling*, *dual testing* and *directional testing* were introduced.

Working paper purposes, ownership and protocols were discussed, although each audit firm will vary as to the detail. Working paper hierarchies and examples were also illustrated. This chapter also introduced IT technology tools used by the auditor, such as *automated working papers*, *audit software routines* and *AI expert systems* to improve audit quality. If used wisely, audit technology can enhance audit efficiency and effectiveness.

Extend your understanding with **Case/resources link** relevant to each chapter.

🗃 Case/resources link

CAATs for Classrooms

Accompanying this book is a series of data, integrated worksheets and exercises that are designed to support your learning and give you exposure to hands-on audit decision-making dilemmas faced by auditors in the planning elements of the audit process. Acquire the relevant material for this chapter from your instructor.

Test your knowledge and consolidate your learning through the **Review questions** and **Exercises**.

Review questions

8.1 Define 'testing'. How does this apply to audits?
8.2 What is the difference between the 'sufficiency' and 'nature' of audit evidence?
8.3 What is the difference between 'tracing' and 'vouching'?
8.4 What is a characteristic of 'confirmations' as to evidence quality?
8.5 What is the difference between the 'extent' and 'timing' of audit testing?
8.6 When would it be possible to rely on tests conducted only midway through the year?
8.7 What are the premises, implied or otherwise, that professionals test in an audit?
8.8 Define 'walk-through procedures'.

Exercises

6.1 **RISK:** You must apply your knowledge of risk in relation to a company you have audited previously, when it had strong systems and no problems, but which currently faces challenges because its low-tech market has disappeared and sales have declined. Identify what you believe to be the areas of greatest risk and explain why:
    a overall risk   c control risk
    b inherent risk   d detection risk.
6.2 **RISK MODEL:** Four types of risk are used in the ARM. If you could choose to add 'sampling risk', 'non-sampling risk' or 'technology risk' for a next-stage ARM, what might you add to the model and why?
6.3 **RISK MODEL:** Your audit client is a metal parts manufacturer of significant interest to the community. They fill a unique local market niche but have been hurt by the effects of a falling dollar on raw materials imports. Gross profit margins have held steady.
    Required:
    a Determine whether the following risks are 'high' or 'low', and why:
       i APR
      ii IR
      iii OAR.
    b What does this mean for STR?
    c What are the implications?

Guide to the online resources

FOR THE INSTRUCTOR

Cengage is pleased to provide you with a selection of resources that will help you prepare your lectures and assessments. These teaching tools are accessible via cengage.com.au/instructors for Australia or cengage.co.nz/instructors for New Zealand.

MINDTAP

Premium online teaching and learning tools are available on the *MindTap* platform – the personalised eLearning solution.

MindTap is a flexible and easy-to-use platform that helps build student confidence and gives you a clear picture of their progress. We partner with you to ease the transition to digital – we›re with you every step of the way.

The *Cengage Mobile App* puts your course directly into students› hands with course materials available on their smartphone or tablet. Students can read on the go, complete practice quizzes or participate in interactive real-time activities.

MindTap for Pratt's Auditing Theory and Practice is full of innovative resources to support critical thinking, and help your students move from memorisation to mastery! Includes:
- Pratt's Auditing Theory and Practice eBook
- What do you think? Polling activities
- Concept checks
- Discussion cases with student guide
- CAATs for Classrooms
- Case study: Delos Ltd.

MindTap is a premium purchasable eLearning tool. Contact your Cengage learning consultant to find out how *MindTap* can transform your course.

SOLUTIONS MANUAL

The Solutions Manual provides detailed answers to all review questions and every exercise in the text.

COGNERO® TEST BANK

A bank of questions has been developed in conjunction with the text for creating quizzes, tests and exams for your students. Create multiple test versions in an instant and deliver tests from your LMS, your classroom, or wherever you want using Cognero. Cognero test generator is a flexible online system that allows you to import, edit, and manipulate content from the text's test bank or elsewhere, including your own favourite test questions.

POWERPOINT™ PRESENTATIONS

Use the chapter-by-chapter **PowerPoint slides** to enhance your lecture presentations and handouts by reinforcing the key principles of your subject.

ARTWORK FROM THE TEXT

Add the **digital files** of graphs and flow charts into your learning management system, use them in student handouts, or copy them into your lecture presentations.

DELOS CASE STUDY

The **Delos case** is a comprehensive case study designed to give the learner a full audit practice-like experience from planning to completion.

CAATS FOR CLASSROOMS

CAATs for Classrooms – an Excel subroutine and exercise program for instructors.

FOR THE STUDENT

MINDTAP

MindTap is the next-level online learning tool that helps you get better grades!

MindTap gives you the resources you need to study – all in one place and available when you need them. In the *MindTap Reader*, you can make notes, highlight text and even find a definition directly from the page.

If your instructor has chosen *MindTap* for your subject this semester, log in to *MindTap* to:
- Get better grades
- Save time and get organised
- Connect with your instructor and peers
- Study when and where you want, online and mobile
- Complete assessment tasks as set by your instructor.

When your instructor creates a course using *MindTap*, they will let you know your course link so you can access the content. Please purchase *MindTap* only when directed by your instructor. Course length is set by your instructor.

PREFACE

Welcome to *Auditing Theory and Practice*, Australasian edition. Our book is derived from *Auditing: Theory and Practice,* first published in The United Kingdom by Longman in 1982. It has been continuously in print since then and was first published in New Zealand in 1990. From the outset, the emphasis of the book has been on readability and the why and how of auditing, beyond the recitation of what is to be done.

This Australasian edition is inspired by the ongoing need for a text to reflect Australia's and New Zealand's unique professional and regulatory environments. Furthermore, we believe there is a real need to keep up with changes brought about by updates related to auditing standards and growth in 'other' assurance services, and the expansion of e-business. The explosion in information technology – while providing unmatched global business opportunities – also challenges the integrity of information, necessitating the need for knowledgeable audit professionals.

In this Australasian edition we have expanded some elements, in particular:
* Concept questions throughout to help you check your understanding
* An emphasis on risk, audit judgement and professional scepticism throughout
* Review questions at the end of each chapter
* Exercises for students, also found at the end of each chapter
* Figures, diagrams and examples.

We have also updated and incorporated the most current Standards, requirements, regulations, oversight and professional practices throughout all chapters of the text. We have tightened the content to ensure that it covers, with minimal repetition, the range of topics and material required to understand the theory and practice of auditing. While building on our previous editions, we also take the opportunity to make the material relevant to today's professional and tertiary practices.

To enhance both the accessibility to students and our ability to make changes in accordance with a changing environment, this edition is also available digitally.

Our best thanks go to the Cengage team for their work on presentation to emphasise concepts, and enhance readability and learning.

We have combined a few chapters and expanded support material. We bring other assurance services to the fore, reflect IT changes and highlight recent events.

We have retained our focus on theory and practice in the text and believe that the conceptual framework continues to explain rationales for, and the nature of, audit and assurance. We believe it provides students with the foundational knowledge they need for audit decision-making. Our goal is to help future audit professionals become technically skilled, socially aware and ethically professional members of the business community.

Names used in examples and exercises are fictitious unless specified otherwise, and any resemblance to actual persons or businesses is unintended and coincidental.

ABOUT THE AUTHORS

Dr Michael J. Pratt, D.Com, FCA, was a Professor and Dean at Waikato Management School, University of Waikato, from 1990 to 2008. Before that, he was a Professor of Accounting and Finance at Massey University. Michael holds a doctorate in Finance and has extensive academic, professional, educational, consultancy, governance and leadership experience. He is the author of numerous academic, educational and professional publications in performance improvement, sustainability, strategy, leadership, auditing and accounting.

Dr Karen A. Van Peursem, FCA (CA ANZ), CPA (USA, ret), PhD was a Professor of Accounting at Victoria University of Wellington (2011–2020) and the University of Waikato (2004–2011). Her experience includes over a decade in private accounting firms and industry, followed by a career in teaching, research leadership and graduate supervision. Karen has published numerous academic and professional publications in auditing and professional practice, performance measurement, public sector, education, financial accounting and tax. She is currently a Research Fellow at Victoria University of Wellington.

Associate Professor Mukesh Garg, PhD, CPA (Australia) is an Associate Professor in the Department of Accounting at Monash University. He joined Monash University in 2006 and previously was at Victoria University. Mukesh has teaching experience in auditing, accounting theory, financial reporting, forensic accounting, financial statement analysis and valuation. His areas of research interest include reporting regulations, internal control disclosures, earnings quality, auditing, climate change, cost of capital and valuation of listed companies. He holds a PhD in Accounting and Finance from Monash University and is a qualified member of CPA Australia. He has industry and accounting standard-setting experience with the Australian Accounting Standards Board as Research and Education Principal.

ACKNOWLEDGEMENTS

Cengage Learning would like to thank the following reviewers for their incisive and helpful feedback:
- Angela Hecimovic, The University of Sydney
- Abhijeet Singh, Curtin University
- Quan Nguyen, CIC Higher Education
- Soon Yeow Phang, Monash University
- YH Tham, Curtin University
- Jonathan Tyler, University of Technology Sydney
- Kirsty Meredith, University of the Sunshine Coast
- Chiu Phua, Charles Sturt University.

MILESTONES OF AUDIT

PART 1 THE AUDITOR'S ROLE IN SOCIETY

1 Introduction to audit
2 Audit concepts, role and history
3 Statutory law
4 Auditor professionalism and audit firms
5 The courts: The legal liability of auditors

THE AUDITOR'S ROLE IN SOCIETY

THE AUDITOR'S ROLE IN SOCIETY

PART 2 AUDIT PLANNING

6 Audit risk
7 Audit judgement, materiality and evidence
8 Audit testing and working papers
9 Audit process and analytical procedures
10 Audit planning

PART 3 AUDIT TESTING

11 Principles of internal control
12 Internal control and the auditor
13 Audit sampling
14 Systems testing I: Sales, purchases and payroll
15 Systems II: Warehousing, financing and fixed assets

PART 4 AUDIT COMMUNICATION AND REPORT

16 Completion and review
17 Audit report and opinion

PART 5 SPECIFIC TYPES OF AUDIT

18 Internal audit
19 Social audit
20 Fraud audit

The auditor's role in society

Part 1 of the textbook focuses on the auditor's role in society and comprises five chapters. Chapter 1 introduces the auditing profession. The purpose of this chapter is to explain the role and activities of the auditor, audit firm and audit practices. Chapter 2 focuses on audit concepts, roles, and the history of the audit profession. The chapter also explains the purpose and elements of a conceptual framework for audit. Statutory law related to the work of auditors and its application in Australia and New Zealand is covered in Chapter 3. The chapter sets out the regulations in Australia and New Zealand. Chapter 4 discusses audit professionalism and audit firms, and includes the codes of ethics for assurance services and quality control. The role of courts and the legal liability of auditors, and how reasonable skill and care is interpreted in common law, is covered in Chapter 5.

PART 1

Introduction to audit

Learning Objectives

After studying the material in this chapter, you should be able to:
- describe the nature of audit engagement
- understand the concept of audit
- identify the conditions that call for audit
- understand audit practice in Australia and New Zealand
- describe Australian and New Zealand auditing standards.

Introduction

If you were to ask the average person in the street about the purpose of an auditor's work, you would probably be told that it is to prevent fraud. Were you to press the person further, you might be offered a description of a rather drab individual submerged in a sea of journals and ledgers, surfacing only from time to time to produce sets of figures that are not important and are difficult to understand.

Such is the image of the auditor that has been widespread in the past. However, it is inaccurate and unfair. It is inaccurate because the auditor's primary responsibility is not to produce information, and their interest extends far beyond books of account. It is unfair because auditing is a highly skilled professional task without which the modern economy could not function.

So, what does the auditor do? Through usage, the word *audit* has come to denote the independent checking and validation of information. That information is prepared by and/or claimed to be 'true' by the preparer (client). Understanding the auditor's role and how the auditor carries out this validation through the audit process is the purpose of this text. The auditor provides **assurance** to the users of financial statements.[1]

assurance
'Refers to the expression of a conclusion by an assurance practitioner that is intended to increase the confidence that users can place in a given subject matter.' (CPA Australia, 2019, p. 5)

Professional engagements

Professionals in audit and accounting engage in many revenue-earning activities. They may prepare accounting records, provide tax advice, conduct fraud investigations, or provide business advisory services. They may review forecasts or conduct statutory financial statement audits. Where providing

---

[1] *User* is the term applied to those with direct financial interest in the audited organisation, while *client* refers to the audited organisation or its owners. The term *accountee*, which you will encounter in the next section, embraces a wider group within society who may rely on, and have the right to rely on, the audit assurance.

an opinion on a matter prepared or asserted by others, the audit professional is carrying out a different kind of function and, in such cases, is known as an **assurance practitioner**.

Assurance engagements are thus a particular type of professional service (see **Figure 1.1**). They are sometimes referred to as *reporting engagements* because the assurance practitioner will issue a report on the findings of their investigation.

Figure 1.1 Types of professional engagements

In this text, because of its importance to society and the economy, we concentrate on one type of assurance engagement: the financial statement audit (see **Figure 1.1**). Other engagements are discussed in Part 5: Specific types of audit.

Although professions can profit from providing many different types of services, there is always the risk that clients and auditors have misunderstandings about the engagement. There can be confusion around the duty of care owed or the level of assurance offered. Some professional engagements provide a reasonably high (audit) level of assurance, but many court cases suggest how such confusion can occur. To cite a few examples from Australia and New Zealand:

- Slater and Gordon recently launched an investor class action against Freedom Foods Group and its auditor Deloitte in the Supreme Court of Victoria. The class action alleges that Deloitte failed in its duties in signing off on Freedom Foods accounts each financial year between 2014 and the first half of 2020.
- In the case of *Cam & Bear Pty Ltd v. McGoldrick* [2018] NSWCA 110, the NSW Court of Appeal found that, by failing to provide warnings about the recoverability of assets, the auditor of a self-managed superannuation fund (SMSF) was responsible for 90 per cent of this SMSF's loss.
- In 2017, Fuji Xerox NZ added audit firm EY (formerly Ernst & Young) as a defendant in its case against three former executives over an accounting scandal that saw Fuji Xerox NZ and Fuji Xerox Australia overstate revenues by about A$450 million.
- Deloitte was held to a duty of care to ensure that securities regulations over minimum public subscriptions were met in a non-audit advisory engagement (*Deloitte v. Christchurch Pavilion Ptnshp* [1999])
- The New Zealand Audit Office failed to 'undertake the further obligations set out in its letter of engagement', in addition to the audit, in *Dairy Containers Ltd v. NZI Bank and Others* (1994).

It therefore becomes important to communicate the particular service being provided, so that misunderstandings can be avoided. Distinctions between engagement types are thus categorised in terms of the level of assurance, their scope, and the nature of their users/accountees (see **Table 1.1**).

assurance practitioner
An individual, company or other organisation, whether in public practice, industry or commerce, or the public sector, conducting assurance engagements or related services engagements. (AUASB, 2017)

assurance engagement
'An engagement in which an assurance practitioner aims to obtain sufficient appropriate evidence in order to express a conclusion designed to enhance the degree of confidence of the intended users other than the responsible party about the outcome of the measurement or evaluation of an underlying subject matter against criteria.' (AUASB, 2014)

Table 1.1 Concepts defining professional engagements: Financial statement example

Scope	Users	Level of assurance		
		Reasonable (audit)	Limited (review)	No assurance
Financial statements over a specified period	Shareholders, lenders, investors, others	Financial statement audit	Review of financial statement	Compiling financial statements: Compilation

Level of assurance

The greater the effort (and cost) that goes into gathering evidence – assuming that the effort is efficient – the greater is the assurance it can provide.

The highest level of assurance possible in a reporting engagement is that provided for an audit. While audit engagements will vary from one to another in scope, all audits should express the same level of assurance acquired through the extensive analysis of reliable evidence. Although there is no guarantee that the information is as claimed, even after the audit is completed, reasonable confidence can be placed in it. This is called **reasonable assurance**. An audit opinion requires an examination of a recording of, or claims about, events that have occurred in the past.

The assurance practitioner does not always provide their highest (audit) level of assurance; they can also conduct an engagement in which the assurance is limited. This is referred to as a **limited assurance engagement**.

Other professional engagements, such as compiling financial statements, do not provide assurance (see **Figure 1.1**). No assurance can be provided if the professional is not sufficiently independent to add confidence. Nonetheless, the audit professional, as a member of their profession, is expected to conduct all engagements with care, competence and integrity.

Scope

The scope of an engagement is simply what the engagement includes and what it does not include. For example, the scope of the Australian and New Zealand statutory financial audit includes an assessment of specific financial statements over a fiscal year ending on a particular date. Knowing the scope is important in order to understand the responsibility surrounding that engagement. That is, everyone should agree on what is being done and what is to be reported upon!

This seemingly obvious idea should be taken seriously since there are now numerous court cases in which either the user did not understand or the auditor did not follow through on the expectations of their engagement.

Common engagements include but are not limited to the following:
- the financial statement audit, the scope of which is set out in law (in particular, those statutes referred to in Chapter 3)
- audits of compliance with the law, such as may occur if the auditor is called on to evaluate compliance
- economy, efficiency and effectiveness (EEE) audits, in which the scope has to do with how well management is running the organisation
- reporting on prospective financial statements or forecasts, but not directly on past events – these usually, though not always, also call for a lower level of assurance.

reasonable assurance
The highest level of assurance possible, obtained through an audit engagement where the professional acquires sufficient appropriate evidence to reduce the risk of misstatement to a low level. (ISA NZ 200, para 5)

limited assurance engagement
'An assurance engagement where the assurance practitioner's objective is a reduction in assurance engagement risk to a level that is acceptable in the circumstances of the assurance engagement, but where that risk is greater than that for a reasonable assurance engagement, as the basis for a negative form of expression of the assurance practitioner's conclusion. A limited assurance engagement is commonly referred to as a review.' (IAASB, 2008)

Users of audit report

Another characteristic that distinguishes one engagement from another has to do with who relies on the professional's opinion. For example, management may be the primary beneficiary of a professionally reviewed sales forecast, while the shareholders or regulators may be users of financial audit reports. Knowing the potential user or **accountee** is important to professionals because it helps them plan and target their evidence-collection procedures towards areas that are of greater importance to those users.

accountee
The person or entity to whom information is owed.

CONCEPT QUESTION 1	Define what an 'assurance provider' does and provides.

Concept of audit

A comprehensive definition of an **audit** has been provided by the American Accounting Association (AAA) Committee on Basic Auditing Concepts:

As was noted earlier, an audit provides *reasonable assurance* that the information – in our case, financial statements – is free from material misstatement. According to the International Federation of Accountants (IFAC), a misstatement is considered material if the information is sufficiently incorrect to influence the economic decisions of users of the financial statements. That is, and by definition, an audit provides the highest level of assurance. To achieve this goal, the auditor will gather evidence from documents and records, observing, communicating with managers, and reviewing data and other procedures. This provides confidence that, following investigation, the information is free from material misstatements (IFAC, 2005, Glossary, p. 143).

It is an expensive endeavour to provide 'assurance'. The process of carrying out an audit is time-consuming and requires expertise, planning and care.

audit/auditing
'A systematic process of objectively obtaining and evaluating evidence regarding assertions about economic actions and events to ascertain the degree of correspondence between those assertions and established criteria and communicating the results to interested users.' (AAA, 1973)

What is a financial statement audit?

A financial statement audit is a specific type of assurance-granting engagement. Where required under Australian and New Zealand law, the auditor must come to an opinion as to whether an organisation's financial statements comply with generally accepted accounting principles (GAAP) (see **Figure 1.2**).

The financial statement can be distinguished from other engagements in terms of the scope (financial statements for a specific period), the intended users (shareholders and selected others) and the level of assurance (reasonable). Financial statement audits offer reasonable confidence to those relying on those statements that the information represents a known standard of accounting. Most government organisations, publicly listed companies and entities of public interest must have an annual financial statement audit under law.

Coming to a view on financial statements, even with evidence in hand, is not easy. Determining the valuation of derivatives, for example, involves the estimation of future events; determining the existence of a **going concern** means trying to forecast what may occur in the future; coming to an opinion about contingent liabilities is challenging. As a result, the auditor cannot provide absolute assurance!

going concern
An entity that has the ability to pay its debts as they fall due and that is solvent (assets exceed liabilities).

CONCEPT QUESTION 2	How would you describe a financial statement audit in terms of its scope, users and level of assurance.

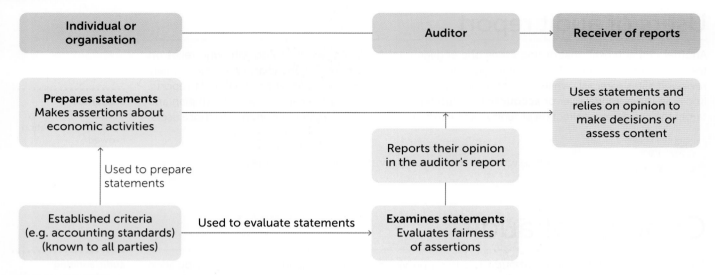

Figure 1.2 Statutory financial statement audit: Process and participants

Theoretical explanations

There are as many different reasons and calls for an audit and other assurance services as there are numbers of users. However, most can be understood in terms of theories explaining the interests of users and accountees. These are informed by:

- neoclassical economics and market assumptions
- social accountability and public theories
- critical theory in terms of its critique of professions (see **Table 1.2**).

Table 1.2 Theories explaining calls for audit

Issue	Neoclassical	Social accountability	Critical
Assumes	• Information is timely, available • Individuals motivated by economic benefit • Managers act in company (or self-) interest	• Imperfect knowledge • Society, stakeholders owed assurance • Law represents societal rights • Market players are not the only stakeholders	• Powerful position held by select few • Power used to further position, status
Explains or predicts	• Market demand for audit • Profession's desire to please the market	• Call for social audits • Third-party liability • Statutory audits	• Self-serving actions that enhance monopoly rights or reduce risk
Views on regulation	• Useful only to ensure unfettered market	• Important to protect society because assurance is a public good	• May be used to retain privileged positions
Role of auditor	• Insurer • Reduces transaction or agency costs	• Protect society from managers (stewards) • Policeman, watchdog, bloodhound for public	• Can create a false or misleading sense of authenticity or fairness

Neoclassical economics

The concepts of neoclassical economics (which informs market theory) are based on economic assumptions grounded in the teachings of Adam Smith. They include assumptions that:

- organisations are profit-maximising
- individual property rights are paramount
- individuals are economically rational
- managers work towards the betterment of their organisation
- perfect knowledge is available to information users
- markets are self-regulating
- market forces tend towards equilibrium – see, for example, Chambers (1966) for a summary of the relationship between economics and accounting.

Proponents of neoclassical economics claim that, for products or services to exist, there must be both demand and supply. Therefore, if audit 'services' – the opinion – are a benefit to market players (such as shareholders), then those players will demand an independent audit through market mechanisms. If the audit is not seen to be particularly useful to market players, they will opt out and the 'supply' will either diminish or the auditor will adjust rents (prices) to make its 'product' more desirable. An implication is that the choice of whether or not to have an audit comes from those who directly benefit from it and who have the resources to pay for it. This interplay can be represented in a typical supply-and-demand curve (see **Figure 1.3**).

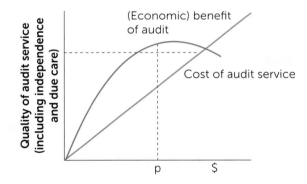

Figure 1.3 Supply and demand for audit services

In **Figure 1.3**, where the lines cross on 'p' is where you find the point at which the greatest economic benefit is achieved by users at the least cost of an audit. Rational purchasers of audit services will only pay for an audit if the perceived benefits exceed the cost of the audit. The 'market' will adjust accordingly if a less-expensive service (such as 'review' or 'compilation') is available that will satisfy the users' needs for verification.

Auditing in practice

Environmental audits

The 'market' – shareholders, corporate boards, lenders, advisers – may be unwilling to pay for environmental audits because, in the absence of laws that require it to do so, there is little market incentive to purchase such assurance services.

Neoclassicist theorists tend to discourage public intervention into, for example, the regulation of industry (or audit) because it would restrict market players from asserting their will. This is essentially a liberal argument that suggests we would all be better off, and equity would be served, if individuals were allowed to work for their own benefit. Concerning audit, this argument suggests that we are better off if we let buyers (e.g., shareholders) purchase audit services at their discretion and in an open market.

Because investors may not be able to judge the quality of audit services unless those services prove to be inadequate via public scandals, the market may also choose to 'purchase' only the services of auditors who are subject to professional standards and obligations. Therefore, the 'profession' itself may well have market value if its leaders can convince the market that its presence improves audit quality.

The perfect information assumptions of neoclassical economics, when taken to an extreme, undermine the very reasons for producing audited financial statements. The efficient market hypothesis, an economics-based theory that became dominant in the 1970s, claims that equity market prices fully reflect all the available information (Fama, 1970). If this were so, then an audit would not be required as share prices are fully informative. Few adopt this pure view today, however. Select interpretations of economics-based theories are found in the following three discussions.

Agency theory

Because acting for one's benefit will not necessarily benefit the business, the principals (board, shareholders) may seek to oversee the behaviour of their managers. They may be willing to incur monitoring costs (such as audit) to ensure that agent-managers do not 'shirk' their work. Agents are, in effect, stewards of company assets, and the auditor is one monitor of their activity.

Auditing in practice

Auditing

Auditing is used to police agent-managers: to uncover instances of illegal or inappropriate behaviour, and to reduce the costs to the business that such fraud would reveal. The political process – and self-serving individuals – generates costs for companies, and some suggest that accounting numbers should be monitored for that reason. Some 'users' believe that auditors should find management fraud and embezzlement in the company because these situations often lead to loss or failure.

Furthermore, the audit would be demanded by (presumably honest) managers so that they can prove their worth to their board of directors and, ultimately, to their shareholders. According to some agency arguments (e.g., Wallace, 1988), managers will thus avoid a downwards reduction in compensation or rewards by principals. Reports that are audited are, in effect, management's evidence of that performance.

Even the threat of audit, which exists before the audit is performed, is likely to improve the quality of the financial information provided by managers, because it is known that auditors will eventually examine their work.

Transactions cost theory

The equity market and its participants are unlikely to have information that is of perfect quality at any point in time. So the assurance that auditors add to financial statements remains useful in the market. Transaction costs are a part of the cost of contracting. Watts and Zimmerman (1990, p. 134) explain that contracting costs arise in conducting market transactions. These include, for example, the legal costs in issuing new shares. They occur in transactions internal to the organisation, such as transfer costs, and in transactions related to politics, such as in meeting additional government contract demands.

Transaction costs include brokerage fees but also the cost of an audit when seen in the light of the benefits that audit brings. The assurance that auditors add to financial statements is useful in reducing those transaction costs that market players might otherwise incur to complete their transactions. Suppliers may be more likely to 'supply' and lenders to 'lend' if they see audited financial statements. An audit is therefore a part of transaction costs (Jensen and Meckling, 1976).

Insurance hypothesis

Financial market players, such as shareholders and finance providers, might also hold out the hope that, should something go wrong, the auditor's 'deep pockets' are available to them. This is the *insurance hypothesis*, an implicit assumption that the audit professional will have to compensate those who relied on the audit opinion and who incurred losses as a result. Such losses often occur when an audited organisation (the client) fails in one way or another, or when fraud or mismanagement has severely depleted its resources. Hence, there is little which can be recovered from that organisation, but the audit firm remains standing.

The insurance hypothesis assumes the existence of a *failed* market in a sense: the user incurring the 'loss' did not have perfect information, at least at the time when a decision should have been made. Nonetheless, suing the auditor in such circumstances, and making assumptions about the auditor's responsibility to compensate for such losses, are more difficult matters. The auditor's service is assumed to be a form of insurance coverage to which users have a right.

It is a difficult hypothesis to prove (e.g., see Brown, Shu and Trompeter, 2009) and, understandably, professional associations do not overtly acknowledge this role. Nonetheless, the nature of some litigation against the auditor would indicate that – at least in the eyes of the victim parties – such an obligation exists.

In common with such variations on neoclassical economics, those with the right to demand an audit are only those who have paid for it. If so, then one has to concede that others – such as the community, third parties (lenders, potential shareholders, employees) and others – do not have those rights and only benefit vicariously as unentitled 'free riders'.

Social accountability and public interest theories

In contrast, public interest theories suggest that regulation should be enacted by the state in public interest. Public interest and social accountability theories assume that regulators can be expected to act in a manner that furthers that public interest. Furthermore, public interest regulation theorists also claim that, without regulation, the needs of only the privileged in society would be served.

For example, those who have few financial resources with which to demand reports and audit would be excluded from access to audited financial statements in a regulation-free environment. Similarly, without regulation, companies may not be inspired to report on their impact on the environment, unless those disclosures present a favourable picture of the business. Hence, given a perspective of public interest regulation, standards and requirements for audit expose a wider range of stakeholders to a wider range of information, as determined through a political process.

Public interest theory rationales are used to justify the existence of the state-mandated audit for public companies. Briloff (1986, p. 4) asserts that

> we consider the total environment in which corporate entities exist, and to which
> they relate: we see them as having compelling responsibilities to a broad spectrum
> of 'publics'. This nexus of publics include: management, shareholders, labour,
> government, customers and consumers, as well as neighbours in the communities in

which the corporation operates. Further, as concern for ecology and the well-being of consumers and posterity intensifies, this responsibility will extend to the total society and environment.

Public interest theory therefore postulates an audience much wider than just shareholders and rests on assumptions that law can be effective in meeting the needs of that audience. An alternative to market-based theories, public interest theory is grounded in Briloff's notion of social accountability (Bloom and Heymann, 1986; Gray, Owen and Maunders, 1987).

Social accountability seeks to bring transparency to the social or environmental effects of the existing economic order so that exploitation can be revealed and thereafter eliminated through the political process. According to Gray, Owen and Maunders (1987, p. 9):

> The purpose of [corporate social accountability] is to discharge an organisation's accountability under the assumption that a social contract exists between the organisation and society. The existence of this social contract demands the discharge of social accountability.

Social accountability theory advocates tend to endorse laws that require the acquisition of audit assurance. Audit is seen as a public good.

As a result, both public interest and social accountability theories suggest that the auditor should design their audit to provide value to a range of users who may be interested in a reliable set of financial statements. It also opens the door to other types of audits, including those that do not have an economic incentive. Environmental or social welfare audits would fall in this category. Examples of how social accountability is represented in audit practice are provided here in the 'Auditing in practice' box.

Auditing in practice

Social accountability

- A social accountability perspective may be useful in explaining legal interference in audit practice, and it may shed some light on a public perception that the auditor should be a 'watchdog' (to use the term immortalised in the judgment in the Kingston Cotton Mill case of 1896) acting on behalf of society as a whole.
- Social accountability may help explain why auditors are defendants in third-party lawsuits. That is, where the plaintiff has a just complaint, some courts hold that it is irrelevant whether their relationship to the auditor lies within or outside specific contractual obligations. The auditor owes the plaintiff due care irrespective of whether that plaintiff 'paid' for the auditor or not (e.g., see *Scott Group v. McFarlane*, an important New Zealand precedent).
- Social accountability would also suggest that audited financial statements should be triple-bottom-line to reveal the social and environmental costs of business.

Advocates of social accountability seek to ensure that organisations discharge their accountability by rendering reports to all groups within society about their use of resources.

Critical theory

> Political economy attributes the division of income or profit to the distribution of power in society and to the social-political and institutional structure that mirrors the distribution of power. (Tinker, 1980)

Another range of theories expresses concern over the potential for self-serving actions and falls under the broad category of critical theory. Drawing in part on the work of the Frankfurt school of critical scholars and philosophers, such as Karl Marx, Michel Foucault and Jacques Derrida, this theory argues that groups who have power, capital and/or prestige manipulate legitimate systems to maintain their privileged positions. So, for example, it may be that the audit profession acts in a self-serving manner to acquire prestige and power.

Although critical theory takes many forms, there is a general concern with the capture of power mechanisms by capitalists. Applying this concern to accounting and auditing, scholars such as the aforementioned have come to suggest that the professions have been active (or at least lucky!) in attaining monopoly rights over the audit, and that they benefit from historical patterns that serve their needs and lobby for self-protection against liability (see, for example, Napier, 1998; Power, 1998; Sikka, 1997).

Auditing in practice

The *Sarbanes–Oxley Act 2002*

The *Sarbanes–Oxley Act 2002* (USA) is an interesting example of what can occur if professional power and privilege are abused. It transferred the power and authority to set standards and regulate the audit profession from the profession itself (the American Institute of Certified Public Accountants [AICPA]) to the government (via the Public Company Accounting Oversight Board [PCAOB]). This had a powerful effect on professions around the world. Similar transfers of authority have since occurred in Australia, New Zealand and elsewhere.

Cousins et al. (1998, pp. 6–7) state that this privileged access to audit has been abused by some members of the profession. However, while it used to be that the audit profession's primary source of revenue came from the audit, this is no longer the case. Furthermore, there are now competing professions in Australia and New Zealand, so monopoly benefits are less likely. Nonetheless, the right to perform the statutory audit may grant a level of respect to the professional who performs it.

Overall, critical theory contributes to an understanding of how social phenomena, and perhaps the darker aspects of human nature, can influence audit regulation, practice and reporting. It provides an important range of explanations for professional and regulatory behaviour, and remains a potent force in holding the profession to account.

CONCEPT QUESTION 3
What is the difference between the transactions cost theory and the insurance hypothesis?
How do each of the following theories help explain the call for audit?
- neoclassical economic theory
- social accountability theory
- critical theory.

Conditions calling for an audit

Where an audit may serve economic, social or personal needs, users may demand, or the law may require, the performance of an independent audit. Theoretical explanations may vary, but generally four conditions are always present when audits are called for:

1 *Conflict of interests*: Financial statements are prepared by managers and they report on management's performance. Managers may be inclined to insert their own bias into their reporting to make the

organisation's performance (e.g., profit) or the financial structure look better than it is. This creates a conflict of interest between the preparers of the financial statements (senior management) and the users of the financial statements (shareholders and bankers). There may also be a conflict of interest between shareholders and outsiders, such as the government or consumers. The independent audit function plays a vital role in ensuring that users are receiving information that is a fair reflection of the organisation's financial affairs.

2   *Remoteness*: For legal, physical, or economic reasons, users of financial statements are generally not able to examine for themselves the accounting data of the organisation in which they are interested. They may have no legal right of access to the entity's books, or they may be physically at a significant distance from the organisation. Because of these challenges, it is necessary that an independent party, with full access to the books and records, should verify that the financial statements provided by management are reliable.

3   *Complexity*: As organisations grow, the volume of their transactions increases. Furthermore, the accounting systems that capture and process them have become more complex. As a result, the auditor must be a qualified person who has both the expertise to understand the business and its transactions, and also the ability to access its accounting system.

   A perfect photograph taken with the best close-up lens available is not essential, but the financial statement auditor should be competent in accounting, systems and law so that they can judge whether the financial information presented meets the standards of accounting practice.

4   *Consequence of error*: If investors and others make decisions based on unreliable information, they may suffer serious financial loss. As a result, they will seek assurance that the information the financial statements contain is reliable and presents a true and fair view.

Where these situations arise, the financial audit can provide a unique service. Where one or more of these conditions are missing, another type of engagement may suffice. So, for example, **small and medium enterprises (SMEs)** may not have an audit. Because such organisations are small and owner-operated, the managers know exactly what is going on in the business. There is no *remoteness*. Yet, should the proprietor decide to sell, they will be in a stronger position if audited financial statements can be produced, as the buyers will indeed be *remote*.

Partnerships, too, can benefit from an audit if the above four conditions exist, although there is no statutory requirement for them in most cases:

*   The independent audit could minimise disputes between partners about the profits or financial position of the partnership – such disputes are a common cause of partnership dissolution. **Conflicts of interest** and the consequences of **misstatement** may loom particularly large.
*   Changes in the partnership may involve complex changes in capital and goodwill. Audited financial statements will ensure that the new partnership sets out on a sound basis, in particular addressing concerns with *complexity*.

The public may benefit from audits of other types of organisation, irrespective of their size, if the four conditions exist. Most banks, insurance companies, co-ops, investment trusts, friendly societies, charities, and solicitor and real estate agent trust accounts require audit under their own rules or statutes, as potential *conflicts of interest*, *remoteness* and *consequence of error* add to the *complexity* of accounting practices.

Audit practice in Australia and New Zealand

Australian and New Zealand audit professionals are employed in the public or private sector – in partnerships and corporations (with some limitations), or as sole traders. Irrespective of their employment structure, as members of audit professions, they are expected to comply with professional

---

small and medium enterprises (SMEs)
Businesses whose personnel numbers fall below a certain threshold.

conflicts of interest
'Occurs when an entity or individual becomes unreliable because of a clash between personal (or self-serving) interests and professional duties or responsibilities.' (Segal, 2022)

misstatement
'The act of expressing a fact that is not correct.' (Cambridge Dictionary, 2022)

rules and codes of ethics. The context in which they work is summarised next and further detailed in later chapters of this text.

Audit professionals

External auditors will be found in accounting firms – such as EY, KPMG and PricewaterhouseCoopers – as either employees, partners, sole traders or (recently) shareholders. In recent times, such companies have been taking on more consulting and internal audit work. Even as they must use caution to maintain their independence, they are possibly best able to be relatively independent of the organisation being audited. As a result, an accounting firm remains the most appropriate entity to conduct a statutory financial statement audit.

Internal auditors serve organisations more directly as an *employee* of that organisation. While they are usually independent of the organisation's middle management, ultimately they are accountable to the organisation leadership itself. External auditors often rely on the work of internal auditors, to an extent that is reasonable under the circumstances, in respect of a client's control systems.

Government auditors are also employees. They may work in the Office of the Auditor-General, or for the Inland Revenue tax department, or central government departments, as the internal auditor. The Australian National Audit Office (ANAO) is the supreme audit institution of Australia, functioning as the national auditor for the Parliament of Australia and the Government of Australia. Audit New Zealand carries out annual audits of hundreds of public entities on behalf of the Auditor-General of New Zealand. Most Australian and New Zealand government departments have internal audit staff.

Audit guidance

In Australia, the Auditing and Assurance Standards Board (AUASB) is an independent, non-corporate Commonwealth entity of the Australian Government, responsible for developing, issuing and maintaining auditing and assurance standards. In New Zealand, the standards for assurance services (audit and review engagements), and ethical standards for assurance engagements, are promulgated by a subcommittee of the External Reporting Board (XRB), namely the New Zealand Auditing and Assurance Standards Board (NZAuASB). The two national standard-setters operate independently of audit firms or professional associations. Current audit standards now draw from international standards issued by the International Auditing and Assurance Standards Board (IAASB).

Standards for non-assurance services and ethical codes for professionals generally are set by each respective professional body, such as Chartered Accountants Australia and New Zealand (CA ANZ) and CPA Australia.

Auditing standards

Let us see how these concepts apply to the standards for the statutory financial statement audit produced by the AUASB and the NZAuASB.

Standards for financial statement audit

Australian Auditing Standards establish requirements and provide application and other explanatory material on the responsibilities of an auditor when engaged to undertake an audit of a financial report, or complete set of financial statements, or other historical financial information; and the form and content of the auditor's report. Australian Auditing Standards and New Zealand Audit Standards are presented in **Table 1.3**.

Table 1.3 Australian and New Zealand auditing standards conceptualised

Concepts	Australian Auditing Standards	New Zealand Audit Standards
Competence	AUASB ASA 100: Preamble to AUASB Standards ASA 220: Quality Control for an Audit of a Financial Report and Other Historical Financial Information	XRB AU1: Application of Auditing and Assurance Standards ISA NZ 220: Quality Control for an Audit of Financial Statements
Independence	ASA 102: Compliance with Ethical Requirements when Performing Audits, Reviews and Other Assurance Engagements	PES 1: Code of Ethics for Assurance Practitioners
Judgement	* ASA 600: Special Considerations – Audits of Group Financial Statements * ASA 610: Using the Work of Internal Auditors * ASA 620: Using the Work of an Auditor's Expert * ASA 710: Comparative Information – Corresponding Figures and Comparative Financial Reports * ASA 720: The Auditor's Responsibility Relating to Other Information	* ISA NZ 600: Special Considerations – Audits of Group Financial Statements (Including the Work of Component Auditors) * ISA NZ 610: Using the Work of Internal Auditors * ISA NZ 620: Using the Work of an Auditor's Expert * ISA NZ 710: Comparative Information ... * ISA NZ 720: The Auditor's Responsibility Relating to Other Information ...
Risk	ASA 300: Planning an Audit of a Financial Report ASA 315: Identifying and Assessing the Risks of Material Misstatement through Understanding the Entity and Its Environment ASA 330: The Auditor's Responses to Assessed Risks	ISA NZ 300: Planning an Audit of Financial Statements ISA NZ 315: Identifying and Assessing the Risks of Material Misstatement through Understanding the Entity and Its Environment ISA NZ 330: The Auditor's Responses to Assessed Risks
Materiality	ASA 320: Materiality in Planning and Performing an Audit * ASA 240: The Auditor's Responsibilities Relating to Fraud in an Audit of a Financial Report	ISA NZ 320: Materiality in Planning and Performing an Audit * ISA NZ 240: The Auditor's Responsibilities Relating to Fraud in an Audit of Financial Statements
Evidence	ASA 250: Consideration of Laws and Regulations in an Audit ... * ASA 402: Audit Considerations Relating to an Entity Using a Service Organisation ASA 500: Audit Evidence ASA 501: Audit Evidence – Specific Considerations for Inventory and Segment ... ASA 505: External Confirmations * ASA 510: Initial Audit Engagements – Opening Balances * ASA 520: Analytical Procedures * ASA 530: Audit Sampling * ASA 540: Auditing Accounting Estimates Including Fair Value ... * ASA 550: Related Parties * ASA 560: Subsequent Events * ASA 570: Going Concern * ASA 580: Written Representations	ISA NZ 250: Consideration of Laws and Regulations ... * ISA NZ 402: Audit Considerations ... an Entity Using a Service Organisation ISA NZ 500: Audit Evidence ISA NZ 501: Audit Evidence – Specific Considerations for Selected Items ISA NZ 505: External Confirmations * ISA NZ 510: Initial Audit Engagements – Opening Balances * ISA NZ 520: Analytical Procedures * ISA NZ 530: Audit Sampling * ISA NZ 540: Auditing Accounting Estimates Including Fair Value * ISA NZ 550: Related Parties * ISA NZ 560: Subsequent Events * ISA NZ 570: Going Concern * ISA NZ 580: Written Representations

→

Concepts	Australian Auditing Standards	New Zealand Audit Standards
Disclosure and communication	ASA 200: Overall Objectives of the Independent Auditor and the Conduct of an Audit in Accordance with Australian Auditing Standards ASA 210: Agreeing the Terms of Audit Engagements ASA 260: Communication with Those Charged with Governance ASA 265: Communicating Deficiencies in Internal Control ... ASA 450: Evaluation of Misstatements Identified During the Audit ASA 700: Forming an Opinion and Reporting on Financial Statements ASA 701: Communicating Key Audit Matters ... ASA 705: Modifications to the Opinion in the Independent Auditor's Report ASA 706: Emphasis of Matter Paragraphs and Other Matters Paragraphs in the Independent Auditor's Report ASA 230: Audit Documentation	ISA NZ 200: Overall Objective in Accordance with International Standards ... ISA NZ 210: Agreeing the Terms of Audit Engagements ISA NZ 260: Communication with Those Charged with Governance ISA NZ 265: Communicating Deficiencies in Internal Control to Those Charged with Governance and Management ISA NZ 450: Evaluation of Misstatements Identified During the Audit ISA NZ 700: Forming an Opinion and Reporting on Financial Statements ISA NZ 701: Communicating Key Audit Matters in the Auditor's Report ISA NZ 705: Modifications to the Opinion in the Independent Auditor's Report ISA NZ 706: Emphasis of Matter Paragraphs and Other Matters ... ** ISA NZ 230: Audit Documentation Firm Policy manuals

Note: Both Australia and New Zealand adopt adaptations of International Standards of Auditing (ISAs).

* Also includes communication, risk and judgement issues.

** Standards included here are current as at January 2022 and primarily relate to financial statement audits.

Standards having to do with 'evidence' are dominant, and their content is often in the form of specific guidance. The number of standards to do with communication issues has grown, which is not surprising given the legal implications of having misunderstandings with your client or with third parties.

Aspects of the planning process have also taken on a more visible role in current auditing standards. Given the focus on 'risk' in audits, this is appropriate, as risk needs to be analysed early in the process in order to be able to decide what tests are important. You can also see that controversial issues usually make it into the standards, such as the auditor's role in detecting fraud or projecting business failure. While these issues may change over time as business or practice itself evolves, the larger (conceptual) issues of evidence and communication remain.

So, while we would argue for a more visible acknowledgement of the role of professional judgement and risk, the current standards for financial audit appear to be broadly inclusive of audit concepts. Credibility issues appear primarily in the professional Code of Ethics. The very existence of standards, guidelines and an ethical code – overseen in New Zealand by the government's Financial Markets Authority from 2011 – is indicative of the auditors' own accountability to their public. The principles and postulates apply to financial audit standards and situations, and to reviews, compilations and other types of engagements in which the professional may become involved.

We also recognise that some concepts can only be realised through intervention by others. So, for example, the growing range of statutes pertaining to audit and legal precedent in the courts holds the assurance practitioner to new forms of account. The professional associations and companies do so for their individual members as well.

International standards

It is not only Australian and New Zealand institutions that follow trends towards independent standard-setting and conceptual foundations. A summary of standard-setting practices elsewhere is provided in **Table 1.4**.

Table 1.4 International standard-setting practices

Source	Standard-setters	Description and authority
International	International Auditing and Assurance Standards Board (IAASB) of IFAC	Representing over 80 nations and issuing International Standards of Auditing (ISAs), which are the basis for those being adapted in Australia and New Zealand. No legal authority, although some nation-states have adopted versions.
United Kingdom	The Auditing Practices Board sets auditing standards and guidelines and issues Statements of Auditing Standards (SAS).	Reviewed by the Joint Monitoring Unit, the Institute of Chartered Accountants of England and Wales (ICAEW), and the UK Department of Trade and Industry (DTI).
United States	The Public Company Accounting Oversight Board (PCAOB)	The PCAOB is a nonprofit corporation established by Congress to oversee the audits of public companies in order to protect investors and further the public interest in the preparation of informative, accurate, and independent audit reports.
European Union	A mix of nation-based regulation. Directives from the European Council of Birmingham (1996) reviewed towards general guidance.	The Union Européenne des Experts Comptables Economiques et Financiers (UEC), an association of European professional accounting bodies, issues non-mandatory statements.
Canada	The Canadian Institute of Chartered Accountants (CICA) issues Generally Accepted Auditing Standards (GAAS).	CICA established the independent Auditing and Assurance Standards Oversight Council (AASOC), which oversees standards and, where necessary, disciplines members.

CONCEPT QUESTION 4

Some audit courses teach from auditing standards. Describe why this approach may be useful for practitioners. Also describe reasons why it may be less useful, in that it limits exposure to:
- professionalism
- audit decision making.

Study tools

Summary

In this chapter, we introduced some concepts and definitions needed for the study of auditing. We also set out the nature of the professional responsibilities concerning assurance and non-assurance services, and we distinguished between them as to the level of assurance provided, the scope, and the user/accountee. Our focus in this text is on reporting engagements, with an even finer lens turned to a particular type of reporting engagement.

We also identified four *conditions* that lead to calls for an audit. We explored the *theoretical rationales* that may explain why someone requires an audit of an organisation with which they have a concern. Economic, social accountability and even critical theories may, to different degrees at different times, serve to explain why 'audit' remains in demand. We also introduced situations in which there may be demand for an audit even when not required under a statute.

We considered the context in which audit operates in Australia and New Zealand, including the nature of the auditor's professional responsibilities. We discussed the structure in which professionals are employed and the effect of that on perceptions of their independence and role.

Until the 1970s, auditing was a somewhat stagnant profession. This is no longer the case, and much revision has been undertaken regarding professional promulgations, financial accounting and taxation. For these reasons, we recommend that you make an effort to read current publications – such as CA ANZ's journal, the *National Business Review* (NZ), the *Australian Financial Review* and daily newspapers – to enlarge and enlighten your perspective on how the profession operates and is perceived.

This introductory chapter provides an overview, and we will explore points in more detail in the chapters to come. It also leaves some questions unanswered: What must be done to conduct a quality audit? How effective is the profession in ensuring quality? How is an audit carried out? What redress does the user/accountee have if the auditor fails? The chapters in this textbook take you, step by step, through the audit process. Finally, this chapter provided a list of auditing and assurance standards based on the AUASB and the NZAuASB.

✍ Case/resources link

CAATs for Classrooms

Accompanying this book is a series of data, integrated worksheets and exercises that are designed to support your learning and give you exposure to hands-on audit decision-making dilemmas faced by auditors in the planning elements of the audit process. Acquire the relevant material for this chapter from your instructor.

Review questions

1.1 How does a 'financial statement audit' relate to 'all assurance services'?

1.2 Name a professional accounting service that does *not* provide assurance.

1.3 How does the assurance provider share their opinion on what they have found?

1.4 Does the financial statement auditor prepare the material they audit? Why or why not?

1.5 How do each of the following theories help explain the call for audit?
   - neoclassical economic theory
   - social accountability theory
   - critical theory.

1.6 Identify and define the four conditions that, together, create a need or call for a financial statement audit.

1.7 Audit professionals may be employed in several contexts. What are they? Which of those contexts is likely to be that in which the external financial statement auditor is employed? Why?

Exercises

1.1 **SCOPE, ASSURANCE, CLIENT:** Discuss how you would classify each of the following in terms of the scope of the engagement, the assurance (if any) and the accountees targeted. Identify other relevant issues as appropriate. Assume that no other services are performed and that each service is independent of the other.

    a   A forecast is prepared for a client based on client data.

    b   An audit is performed, but only on the balance sheet.

    c   Financial statements are reviewed.

    d   The solvency test is performed by the professional for a client.

    e   The internal auditor performs a control assessment.

    f   Compliance with environmental laws is audited.

1.2   **SCOPE, ASSURANCE, CLIENT:** Discuss what type of engagement may be most appropriate for each of the following situations (none include the statutory financial statement audit) and the implications of that choice:

    a   A manager is concerned with whether, and how, revenue, relative to costs, can be improved.

    b   A tax compliance report must be prepared for the partnership Lewis & Hold.

    c   A government agency is concerned that its social goals are not being achieved. It employs an independent professional to look into the issue.

    d   A capital budget must be prepared, and the company requires the services of an independent professional to carry this out.

1.3   **AGENCY THEORY:** Although the shareholders appoint the auditors, the main discussions all take place between directors (members of the audit committee) and auditors. Later in the audit process, the primary communications are between the auditors and the client's managers. A bank, known to the auditor, is planning to lend the client money, but only if the financial statements meet its standards.

    Required:

    a   Does this mean that the appointment process fails to furnish the shareholders with protection from the directors? Why or why not?

    b   Create three different scenarios that describe three different agency relationships possible in this situation. For each, who is the 'principal', who is the 'agent' and what is the 'monitoring cost'?

1.4   **THEORY APPLICATION:** New Zealand's national rail company owns the country's tracks as well as the land beneath the tracks, some of which is leased to power companies for transmission lines. While the government supported its purchase, the rail company must be operated on a profitable or break-even basis, as no more government investment is forthcoming. The government commissioner is concerned that it serves New Zealand's macroeconomic and security interests as well as its domestic and tourism needs. The CEO – who is also the managing director on the company's board – oversees 10 senior managers who manage various divisions within the company.

    Provide two examples each of how the managing director, the auditors, employees or others could be driven from, or subject to, motives grounded in:

a   agency theory

b   social accountability theory

c   economic theory.

Given these motives, how could an audit influence the outcome or costs for each?

1.5　**THEORY PERSPECTIVES:** Discuss the merits of the following statements and their theoretical sources:

　　a　Audit regulation is an aberration in a market economy.

　　b　If the government eliminated all statutes and regulations affecting audit regulations, this would not affect demand.

　　c　Regulatory mechanisms will be 'captured' by political interest groups to maximise their self-interest.

　　d　Auditing provides a means of maintaining existing power structures and domination by power elites.

1.6　**THEORY CASE:** Your former audit client, Tall Capital Ltd, has gone into liquidation 18 months after the end of an audit. Tall Capital's shareholders lost their entire investment. They believe that you should have discovered the solvency problems that existed in regard to Tall Capital and 'flagged' the issues in your audit report. Your audit firm did identify solvency issues – they were clear from the financial statements, which were seen to be compliant with GAAP – but you had not 'flagged' any further or ongoing problems. The complaint against your company claims that, as Tall Capital has failed, you should be held to account. Furthermore, neither Tall Capital Ltd nor its directors could be reached through the courts.

Required:

　　a　Name what theory(ies) appear to be at play here? Explain why.

　　b　How might you respond to such questions by shareholders?

1.7　**AUDIT PARTICIPANTS:** Your audit company is negotiating an audit for TiDee Laundry, which needs the audit to borrow money from its bank. The firm has a hardworking set of owner-directors and has been a successful business. However, the owners know nothing of accounting or finance. The owners prepared cash flow statements and showed that they had reconciled their statements against the bank statements, but they did not prepare accrual entries. They now ask you to do this for them. What do you tell them? Why?

1.8　**CONDITIONS CALLING FOR AUDIT:** Explain whether or not, and why or why not, each of the following has, or does not have, the conditions calling for audit:

　　a　A husband-and-wife partnership has been in business (and the pair have been married) for 30 years. Their business partnership has grown, and they are now adopting complicated manufacturing costing methods to their work-in-progress. They rely on the financial statement to determine whether their ongoing profit is viable, but no-one else is known to be reliant on the statements.

　　b　The financial statements prepared for a local subsidiary will be combined with the offshore statements of the global parent company. Despite its size, the subsidiary is family-owned and no further finance needs are apparent.

　　c　A sole trader has run his plumbing business for 25 years, hiring one or two apprentices and with his wife maintaining the books. He plans to sell the business and retire.

1.9   **AUDIT STANDARDS:** As shown in **Table 1.3** and **Table 1.4**, there are distinct differences in standards for 'audits' and those for 'other engagements'. Consider and evaluate the following:

    a In terms of audit scope/user or assurance, why do such differences exist?

    b In terms of the conceptual framework, do you think each is a relatively complete set of standards? Why or why not?

1.10 **AUDIT STANDARDS:** Review the standards currently set out for 'other engagements' (including any currently under review or in the development stage on the AUASB or XRB websites). Do you think the standards are relatively complete in terms of the conceptual framework? Identify two or three standards that could be developed in this field and relate them to the conceptual framework.

Audit concepts, role and history

Learning objectives

After studying the material in this chapter, you should be able to:
* trace the history of audit
* explain the purpose and elements of a conceptual framework for audit
* explain the role of the external auditor.

Introduction

Auditing as a practice has evolved over 3000 years and as a profession for about the last 150 years. It is only in the past 60 years or so that much consideration has been given to the discipline's underlying theoretical foundations, assumptions and roles. Yet these are important because foundations and roles give the auditor, and the audit process, meaning. If there are shared understandings of what audit is and what auditors do, then misunderstandings are also less likely to occur.

This chapter draws on the history of audit to suggest how events over time have shaped the beliefs, assumptions and expectations peculiar to audit. We set out a conceptual framework for audit to explain broad audit principles, and we consider the role of the auditor and how different views can create different expectations.

The history of audit

In its formative stages, auditing was a practice primarily used for government or feudal control. It was concerned with control and accountability over public wealth (see **Figure 2.1**).[1]

Evidence shows that, more than 2000 years ago, the Egyptians, Greeks, Chinese and Romans all used systems to check the accounting of officials entrusted with public funds. In the Greek and Roman empires, those responsible were periodically required to appear before a government official to give an oral presentation of their accounts. The origin of the word 'audit' (Latin for 'hears') dates from these times.

Pacific island inhabitants appear to have had no equivalent form of accountability. However, it may not have been necessary in the same sense. For example, placing a *tapu* (that which is forbidden) on an action (such as fishing within a certain bay) took on a moral and economic meaning. The Anglo-American culture probably has no equivalent to this – the idea of the separation of church and state is controversial but reasonably well established – and this may be a reason why a more formal structure has had to be put in place in Western-influenced nations.

---

[1] References to 'audit' from this point forward refer to statutory, financial statement audits unless otherwise specified.

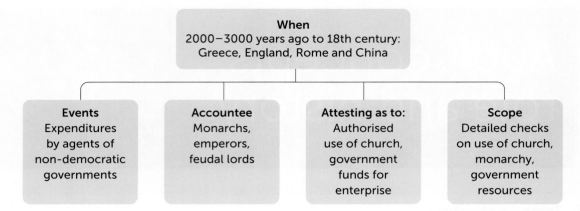

Figure 2.1 Early auditing requirements

Prior to the Industrial Revolution, auditing had little commercial application in European cultures because the conditions necessary for its growth – conflict of interest, remoteness, complexity, and consequence of error – did not exist. However, by the 18th century, costly overseas trading ventures became common. Traders in commercial ventures were required to account for the use of the funds and cargoes entrusted to their care. The accountability obligations for European, Australian and New Zealand settlers were similar. Nelson (New Zealand) settlers, for example, in 1842–52, kept audited accounting records to request funding (Fowler, 2010).

Great fortunes could be won or lost through these ventures, and as a result, audit emerged as an economic necessity. Not surprisingly, a key audit objective was detecting fraud and the misappropriation of funds. To audit for this, accounts were subjected to detailed examination, with a special emphasis on arithmetical accuracy and compliance. The audit was concerned with evaluating only *how* the funds were applied (stewardship), not necessarily *how well* they were applied.

Industrial Revolution, 18–19th centuries

During the Industrial Revolution, conditions changed. Businesses needed large amounts of capital to fund major rail, shipping and manufacturing businesses. The capital requirement was so significant that outside investors were sought and, unlike in the past, they were not the same individuals who managed the business. This created a situation where ownership was distant (remote) from management. A new accountability structure was needed. By the time Australia and, later, New Zealand were widely colonised, a new corporate and statutory regime had been established in Britain, the Netherlands and elsewhere (see **Figure 2.2**).

Little uniformity existed in how audits were conducted, however (Becker, 1980). Today, the standards applying to expected audit performance are far more detailed.

Equity markets also were largely unregulated and speculative, and unsurprisingly, the rate of financial failure was high. Before a change in law, personal liability for company failure was unlimited, and the treatment of debtors, including innocent investors, was harsh. Debtors' prisons and emigration ships (such as those that sailed to parts of Australia) contained many souls who had only made the mistake of investing poorly. It was clear that the growing number of small investors needed some protection.

As a result, the *Joint Stock Companies Act 1844* was passed in Britain, which enabled companies to be formed and officially recognised by registration. Previously, companies could only become recognised by means of a royal charter or a special Act of parliament. The first option was costly and

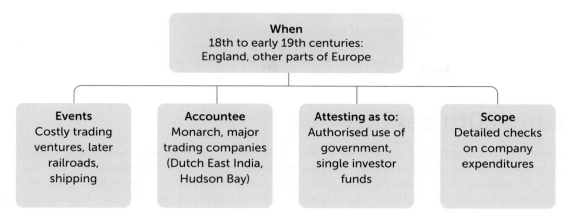

Figure 2.2 Audit in the 18th and early 19th centuries

the latter involved a very slow process. In return for official recognition, companies had to comply with certain regulations:

- Each company's directors had to provide an annual balance sheet to the shareholders that set out the company's state of affairs. No income statement was required, emphasising the focus on asset valuation and solvency.
- An auditor had to be appointed by the company's shareholders. The auditor was empowered to examine the company's records at all reasonable times throughout the year. They were required to report to the company's shareholders as to whether, in their opinion, the balance sheet gave a 'full and fair' view of the company's affairs.

The auditor was not required to be independent of the company's management, nor did they have to be a qualified accountant, as the complexity of the accounts may not have required great expertise. In practice, an auditor was usually appointed by fellow members. Hence, for the first time, and despite its limits, accountability to investors via audit was established.

In 1856, the statutory provisions requiring compulsory audits were repealed. Subsequent events suggest that this move was ill-advised. Of the 88 000 companies registered between 1862 and 1904, more than 50 000 had come to an end. Not surprisingly, compulsory audits were reintroduced in the *British Companies Act of 1900*. This time, and under the auditing provisions of this Act, the auditor had to be independent of management and neither a director nor an officer of the company (i.e., a member of the company's management). Accountability to shareholders was clearly established. The new Act also included the following auditing provisions:

- Auditors were to obtain access to all of a company's books and records that they required to perform their duties. This included access to such documents as contracts and minutes of directors' meetings.
- Auditors were to append a certificate to the foot of the audited balance sheet stating that all of their requirements as auditors had been complied with.

The auditor was now to be a monitor of management on behalf of shareholders, both public and private. The courts later backed this. In the renowned case of *Re London and General Bank (No. 2)* [1895] 2 Ch. 673, the auditor discovered errors in the balance sheet but only informed the directors, not the shareholders. Lindley LJ stated that

> it was not the duty of the auditor to see that the company and its directors acted prudently or imprudently, profitably or unprofitably, in performing their business activities, but it was the auditor's duty to report to shareholders any dishonest acts which had occurred and which affected the propriety of the information contained in the balance sheet.

While making auditors accountable to shareholders, accountability did not yet extend to potential shareholders, lenders or other external users of financial information. This is reflected in the fact that the balance sheet was considered a private communication between management and shareholders. This was changed in law by the *Companies (Consolidation) Act 1908* (UK), which required the auditor to attach a report to a company's annual report; the shareholder remained the primary audit stakeholder.

Early 20th century

Unlike the shareholders of earlier years, who were few in number but closely bound to the companies they owned, 20th-century investors had little interest in the management or fortunes of 'their' companies. These investors were concerned with the returns they could earn, often in the short term. If they thought greater returns could be earned elsewhere, they switched their allegiance (and investment).

With these developments, owners and managers became increasingly separated. Companies' control and management gradually passed to small groups of qualified, professional, salaried managers who might or might not have owned shares in the companies they managed. In this new economic environment, company managers' accountability was extended to the effective and efficient use of funds, and business managers became accountable for generating a return on investments (see **Figure 2.3**).

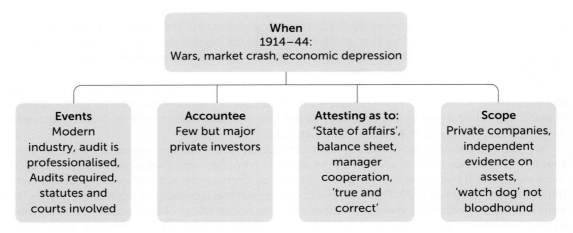

Figure 2.3 Audit in the early 20th century

Net income became a surrogate for a manager's efficiency, and the auditor became accountable, in effect, to the market. This trend accelerated in the 1960s and after, as shareholders became increasingly divorced from 'their' companies, and as companies grew and extended their influence in society.

As stakeholders focused their attention on dividends from profits, the emphasis of users shifted away from the balance sheet, and solvency, towards the income statement and earning power. This shift was led from the United States, but it was dramatically reinforced in Britain by the Royal Mail case (*R v. Kylsant* [1932] IKB 442) that, in the words of De Paula (1948), 'fell like an atom bomb and changed the face of the world of accounting'. This case, more than any other, highlighted the need for the income statement to be subject to audit.

Furthermore, dishonest acts by company directors resulted in corporate collapses in such cases as the Royal Mail case (1932) in Britain and the *McKesson & Robbins* case (1938) in the United States. The 1929 Wall Street crash and the ensuing Great Depression highlighted the power of corporations and the effect corporate failure can have on daily life. These events from the 1920s and 1930s initiated an era in which companies were being held to account in new ways.

Legislators introduced mandatory auditing of the income statement together with the balance sheet in the United States under the *Securities Exchange Act 1934*, and in Britain under the *Companies Act 1948*. The latter was imported into New Zealand as part of the *New Zealand Companies Act 1955*. In Australia, the states and the Commonwealth cooperated in the formation of a uniform national company code which was legislated in each jurisdiction by 1962.

Post-World Wars to present

Recovering from the damage caused by two world wars, Britain was no longer the centre of international commerce. The United States and the Soviet Union were leaders and competitors for economic power, a role now increasingly being adopted by China as well as India. The United States also took a decisive role in professionalising the audit and accounting associations. Auditors' rights and duties were embodied in statute or case law, and professional auditors required university education – both are the basis for practice today.

The unprecedented growth of modern corporations also marked the periods after the First World War and the Second World War. This was accompanied by sophisticated securities markets and credit-granting institutions designed to serve growing economic entities' financial needs. Investment in business entities grew rapidly and became widespread. Company ownership became highly diffused, and a new class of small investor emerged.

There were moves to involve auditors in making directors more accountable. Governing bodies were expected to provide structures that encourage ethical behaviour and quality systems (Cordery, 2007) and in 1993 companies and financial reporting legislation introduced fines for directors' non-compliance. (See **Figure 2.4**.)

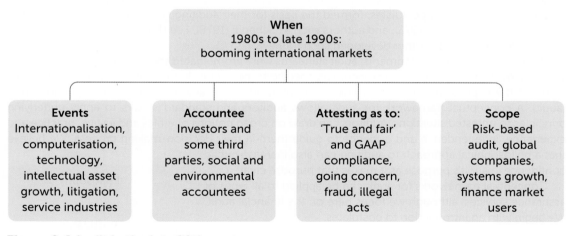

Figure 2.4 Audit in the late 20th century

Our current society is one in which we continue to have explosions in technology, communication systems, online businesses and accounting systems capabilities to match. Macrotaxonomies such as XBRL (eXtensible Business Reporting Language) create information that is never fully collated or reported in standard ways. High-technology companies and global enterprises have primarily replaced large manufacturing industries with difficult-to-value software, algorithms and human-expertise assets. Risks for organisations include global political instabilities, climate change and energy crises.

Collectively, history has established unique practices and expectations as to 'what audit is' today. These understandings are organised in the form of a conceptual framework for audit.

Conceptual framework for audit

A conceptual framework organises ideas around a topic in order to make sense of that topic, to give it meaning. Conceptual frameworks for audit have usually included postulates, concepts, audit standards, codes, guidelines and the relationships between them.

Foundations for meaning, in any discipline, can be said to derive from philosophical traditions. Mautz and Sharaf (1961, p. 4) explain why philosophy is important to an audit discipline in claiming that philosophy:

- gets back to first principles, to rationales behind actions and thoughts that tend to be taken for granted
- is concerned with the systematic organisation of knowledge so that it at once becomes more useful and is less likely to be self-contradictory
- provides a basis on which social relationships may be moulded and understood.

While there is no single philosophy of auditing per se, audit does draw from philosophies of utilitarianism, scepticism, pragmatism and social accountability.

Professional scepticism

Professional scepticism is grounded in the ancient Greek philosophy of the Sceptics – such as Pyrrho of Elis – in which all claims are subject to question and doubt.

In 1961, Mautz and Sharaf made the first serious attempt to develop a philosophy of auditing. It, together with underlying postulates, formed the basis for their auditing conceptual framework. It was later adopted by the AAA (1973), and authors such as Schandl (1978), Lee (1986a), Flint (1988) and Pratt and Van Peursem (1993) further developed such frameworks.

Prior to conceptual developments, audit standards were promulgated somewhat haphazardly. Some were internally inconsistent; others were too specific to be useful. A conceptual framework resolves some of these problems because it links an underlying set of assumptions about a phenomenon (audit). A conceptual framework for audit allows auditors and standard-setters to apply underlying principles to untested situations. Auditors can draw on broad notions of ethics and justice, practice and experience, independence and evidence to guide them in their decision-making process. We believe that a philosophical approach to auditing can also increase public confidence in audit's purpose as it makes that purpose clear.

Conceptual frameworks for audit can be applied to all types of assurance services, although we focus here on the financial audit. We begin with an introduction to postulates.

Postulates in audit

Postulates are the philosophically informed assumptions about what does or does not exist in audit. They take philosophical understandings to the next level. Postulates reveal conditions in which audits are formed and become a starting point for forming concepts and standards (see **Figure 2.5**). That is, they are *a priori*, the basis for concepts and practice standards (Mautz and Sharaf, 1961, p. 41).

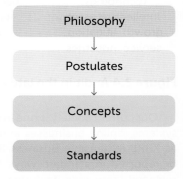

Figure 2.5 Philosophically informed standardised practice

Mautz and Sharaf formed their postulates from a 'careful study of the nature and activities of auditing' (1961, p. 42). Flint (1988, pp. 21–3) and Pratt and Van Peursem (1993) adapted them to consider social and environmental influences as well.

Occasionally, a postulate may change. So, for example, formerly assumptions were made about managers' integrity. Auditors used to produce their report solely *for* management, but now that other stakeholders use audit assurance to, among other things, *monitor* managers, that assumption had to change. Most postulates, however, do not change over time. Postulates are classified here into seven categories (see **Table 2.1**)

Table 2.1 Postulates of auditing

1	*Accountability expectation*	Audit can act as an *element of social control* within the process of corporate or public accountability (Flint, 1971). This postulate asserts that, if there is a need for accountability, there is a need for audit.
2	*Conditions that call for audit*	The second postulate suggests that an audit becomes a necessary part of securing accountability where remoteness, complexity, consequence and conflict exist. This point is raised in Chapter 1.
3	*An independent, unconstrained auditor*	The third postulate identifies independence and freedom from constraint as essential to audit. This follows from the second postulate: in order for all interested parties to have confidence in the audit investigation, the audit must both be and appear to be independent. 'Since the time of Aristotle, it has been an accepted principle that state auditors should be free from direction, influence and intimidation by, and income or reward from, the authorities and persons whose affairs they are called upon to audit.' (Normanton, 1966, p. 298)
4	*Evidence to support an opinion*	The fourth postulate states that the performance of an audit requires that the matter under investigation be susceptible to verification by evidence that is sufficient, reliable and competent. Without evidence, the auditor is unable to express an informed opinion.
5	*Standardisable*	The fifth postulate explains that benchmarks can be set for those who are accountable (e.g., the client), and that their performance can be measured against these benchmarks through the exercise of the auditor's special skills and judgement. In effect, the claims of management and governing boards are both 'measured' and 'measurable'.
6	*Views shared through communication*	The sixth postulate stresses the importance of clear expression and communication of the meaning, significance and intention of audit and the auditor's opinion. Audit opinion is shared via a reporting process. It is also vital that other parties, such as managers, shareholders and others, are served via the communication process.
7	*Benefits produced*	An audit produces an economic or social benefit. In many cases, the auditors will be able to demonstrate a clear benefit by assuring business stakeholders that management-produced financial statements are what they purport to be; that is, in compliance with GAAP. The social benefit is mostly intangible and relates to the reduction of risk to society by ensuring that claims made by governing bodies are legitimate.

Source: Derived from Flint (1988), Mautz and Sharaf (1961), and Pratt and Van Peursem (1993).

Concepts, as explained by Mautz and Sharaf (1961, p. 54), emerge from postulates but serve a different purpose:

> Concepts are abstracted forms … generalised ideas which help us to see similarities and differences and to understand better the subject matter in question. Without concepts, the field of study remains but a mass of unrelated observations. Concepts provide a basis for advancement in the field of knowledge by facilitating communication about it and its problems.

Pratt and Van Peursem (1993), drawing from Mautz and Sharaf (1961) and Flint (1988), offer four audit concepts. It is claimed that the credibility of 'audit' derives from:

1 ethics and ethical behaviour
2 processes incorporating risk, materiality and evidence

3   disclosure through communication and opinion

4   accountability of the audit and audit profession to others.

The conceptual framework for audit incorporates these concepts and the seven postulates into a single framework illustrating the relationships and interactions between concepts and audit standards (see **Figure 2.6**). Each concept is fundamental to the exercise of audit and, for your purposes now, will hopefully enable a deeper understanding of what you will learn about the audit process.

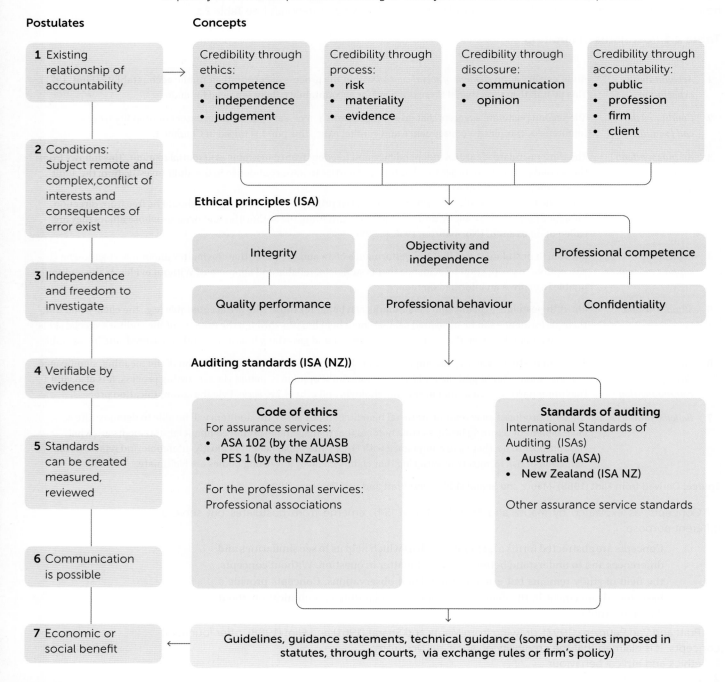

Figure 2.6 A Conceptual framework for audit

Concept: Credibility through ethics

The phrase 'credibility through ethics' refers to characteristics expected of an auditor. As explained by Flint (1988, p. 47):

> The auditor's opinion is no more than an opinion, but it must be believed to be an informed opinion honestly held. It is to the source of that authority and confidence and belief in the capacity of the auditors to give an honest, informed opinion that we must now look.

We concur and conclude that auditors, to retain their professional status, must be perceived to have, and indeed have, the ability to carry out an effective audit in an ethical manner by exhibiting *competence*, *judgement* and *independence*.

Competence

To acquire the confidence of stakeholders, auditors must demonstrate personal skills and relevant knowledge. Auditors need training and experience to assess complex financial subject matter. The auditor should acquire investigative skills towards assessing the credibility of claims. The audit process calls for competence in accounting, mathematics, IT (information technology), behavioural and organisational sciences, law and social practices. It also requires knowledge of the particular client.

Auditing in practice

Audit competency

The auditor is offered an engagement to conduct a financial audit for the subsidiary of an Australian manufacturer. In addition to the usual competencies, the audit firm may need to acquire knowledge of the client's IT system, manufacturing processes, Australian Accounting Standards and global markets. If this knowledge is not 'in-house', the auditor may need to contract in those skills, develop them or simply decline the engagement.

Auditing and accounting have developed as parallel disciplines, but auditing requires competence in a wider range of disciplines.

Judgement

Judgements auditors make lie at the heart of an audit's success or failure. Taking the time and effort to draw informed opinions are of crucial ethical concern. Evaluating the complexity of a business' financial system (postulate 2), and evaluating the evidence against standards and societal expectations (postulate 5), demand that auditors draw on their experience and reasoning throughout the audit.

Auditor judgement is needed to evaluate internal control, materiality, audit risks and disclosure needs, and ultimately to come to an appropriate audit opinion. While there are many aspects to auditor judgement, **professional scepticism** embraces an important subset of this concept.

Both Australian and New Zealand auditing standards require that the auditor exercise professional judgement and maintain professional scepticism throughout the planning and performance of the audit (e.g., AUASB, 2012; External Reporting Board, 2013). How to do that is a challenge for the auditor.

professional scepticism
An 'attitude that enhances the auditor's ability to identify and respond to conditions that may indicate possible misstatement ... This critical assessment is necessary in order for the auditor to draw appropriate conclusions'. (IAASB, 2012, Foreword)

Independence

Professional codes and academicians consistently place primary value on the concept of independence. *Audit independence* refers to the mindset of the auditor, and to the idea that audit decisions should be 'at arm's length'. The auditor should be free from bias. So, for example, an independent auditor should not have an 'interest' in the outcome of the audit and should not be inclined to agree, or disagree, with a client's claim except on the basis of the evidence they gather. Without independence, or its appearance, stakeholders may not believe any assurance offered by the auditor.

Being independent can be challenging. The auditor is challenged should there be pressure on them to 'agree' with an accounting treatment which may not comply with GAAP. Such pressure is known to occur, and the ethical auditor must work, or occasionally sacrifice an engagement, in order to retain their independence.

Independence is a concept long established in law and standards. In *United States v. Arthur Young and Co.* [1984] 52 USLW 4355, Chief Justice Warren Burger put it like this: 'Public faith in the reliability of corporations' financial statements depends upon the public perception of the outside auditor as an independent financial analyst'. This also has implications for professional scepticism.

Professional scepticism

'A sceptical mindset drives auditor behaviour to adopt a questioning approach when considering information and in forming conclusions. In this regard, professional scepticism is inseparably linked to the fundamental ethical principles of objectivity and independence.' (AUASB, 2012, p. 2)

The *appearance* of independence is also important. Flint (1988, p. 57) explains:

> Auditors must be recognised as being without bias or partiality towards any interest. [Without] independence, the audit would be of little value to the individuals to whom accountability was due since there could be little confidence that their opinion added to what was already available.

Professional accounting bodies establish rules of professional conduct or professional ethics designed to protect and enhance the independence of the professional providing an assurance service, but ultimately it is an ethical requirement to which every professional should commit.

CONCEPT QUESTION 1   Why is the independence of the auditor an essential characteristic?

Concept: Credibility through process

The auditing profession derives its credibility from society's perceptions of its auditors' competence, judgement and independence. Perceptions of credibility will ultimately be undermined if the audit is not conducted effectively. We identify three concepts within the audit process: audit risk, audit evidence and audit materiality.

Audit risk

Audit risk is the concern that the auditor may express an inappropriate opinion on the financial statements. Assessing different types of audit risk is an essential part of the planning process, so that auditors can decide upon the nature (type), timing (when) and extent (how many) of audit tests to conduct. Audit risk is a fundamental concept within the audit process since it is directly related (inversely) to the confidence required to come to an opinion about the financial statements.

A thorough analysis of all of the elements of audit risk can thus:
- provide the framework for the development of a detailed audit plan
- assist the auditor in determining the evidence required.

Risk, therefore, provides the conceptual starting point for planning the audit process.

Audit evidence

The auditor's ability to express an opinion on the truth and fairness of financial statements will depend upon the accumulation of sufficient, relevant and reliable evidence. This is a long-recognised postulate of auditing. If the subject matter of the audit is incapable of being verified by evidence, the auditor cannot express an opinion. When the auditor is unable to obtain all of the information and explanations that they deem necessary for those purposes, it will be necessary to issue a disclaimer report (i.e., to decline to express an opinion).

The cost of obtaining evidence can be considered in relation to the economic or social benefit derived from its availability. The additional confidence available from incremental evidence may be matched against its marginal cost, and further evidence may not be obtained if the marginal cost is greater than the marginal utility. While cost should never be primary in selections made in an audit, economic pressures will always exist. This is illustrated by the equilibrium point (p) in the supply-and-demand curve in **Figure 2.7**.

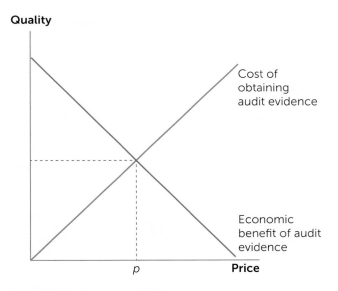

Figure 2.7 Cost-benefit of obtaining further audit evidence

The performance of excessive work (at a greater price to the client) may result in the client, or society, regarding the audit fee as excessive. A significant tension exists here, for the client will naturally be seeking the most economic audit possible. Still, it is imperative that the auditor does not compromise the quality of the audit in an effort to reduce cost.

Professional scepticism

Professional scepticism 'includes a critical assessment of audit evidence. It also means being alert for audit evidence that contradicts other audit evidence or that brings into question the reliability of information obtained from management and those charged with governance' (IAASB, 2012, Foreword).

While clearly the auditor must be responsive to economic pressures to keep costs down, we do not include audit cost-benefit as a concept in light of our view that doing so may compromise audit quality. Therefore, a combination of 'effective' and 'efficient' in an audit will bring about equilibrium in the audit engagement.

Audit materiality

Materiality is a fundamental concept of auditing that will influence the nature, extent and timing of the audit work carried out. The auditor's decision about what is, or is not, material to the financial statements determines what is, or is not, a reportable misstatement. The auditor's decision on materiality is therefore essential.

Flint (1988, p. 129) explains the concept of materiality as follows:

> A statement, fact, item, data or information is material in accounting if, giving full consideration to these surrounding circumstances as they exist at the time, it is of such a nature that its disclosure (or omission), its misstatement, or the method of treating it, would be likely to influence the decision or action of the users for whom the statement, etc. is prepared.

CONCEPT QUESTION 2 Define 'materiality' as we are concerned with it in the audit of financial statements.

If an account, or amount, is material, then more or more-reliable evidence must be gathered. If the auditor fails to do so, the risk of audit failure increases.

The auditor's decisions about what is 'material', about what is 'sufficient and appropriate evidence', and about what level of risk they accept, influences the audit process. Each decision also influences the level of each of the other two process concepts, as illustrated in **Figure 2.8**.

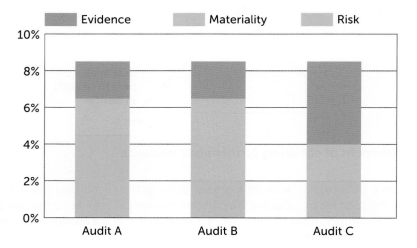

Figure 2.8 Interactions between audit evidence, materiality and risk

Assuming that 95 per cent overall confidence is required in each of these audits, then:
- In Audit A, the auditor accepts a relatively high risk that they will fail to find errors in the accounts.
- In Audit B, a greater level of error is material, or 'tolerated'.
- In Audit C, an exceptionally high level or quality of evidence will be collected.

Concept: Credibility through disclosure

'Communication' is fundamental to audit. So, for example, without an audit opinion about the accounts' compliance with GAAP, the discoveries made by the auditor have no meaning. Communication involves both internal and external interaction. Internal communications usually occur between the auditor and the client's board, management and employees. External communications involve stakeholders such as those relying on the audit opinion, government regulators, or even the judiciary. Typically, the auditor may communicate as to:

- the negotiation of audit contracts and fees
- decisions about the scope, level of assurance and intended user of the opinion
- obtaining access to the client's documents and records
- what comprises the client's responsibility and what is expected of the auditor
- how to improve the client's processes or systems
- situations in which the auditor must share their findings.

   Communications include both formal and informal documents, and those written, oral or online. The ultimate expression of the auditor's responsibility is a report stating their opinion as to the quality of the financial statements (or other matters) under review.

Credibility through accountability

To fulfil their responsibilities, the assurance professional must also be held to account. We agree with Flint (1988) that the effort made to achieve audit goals would be in vain if there were no mechanisms to ensure that professionals are held to account. That is, to be trustworthy, auditors are accountable to those in their firm and their profession, to their client, and to other stakeholders who rely on the audit opinion.

To the firm

The auditor has a professional duty to exercise due care at all times, and to conduct audit work to a standard that does not betray the legitimate expectations of society. The firm can also demand the accountability of the auditor. An audit firm's system of quality control can provide assurance that standards are followed by its members.

To the profession

If individual practitioners fail to meet professional standards, they may find themselves exposed to sanctions imposed by their professional body. Professional sanctions may include public notification (through their professional journal), or temporary or permanent expulsion (and loss of livelihood). Individual practitioners may, of course, conduct their work to more exacting standards than those presumed by the profession. However, audit professions generally oversee standards of care (through ethical codes) that are expected of auditors.

To the client

Ironically, although it is the client – the party *being* audited – that pays for the engagement, assurance is also for selected external stakeholders such as known lenders or investors. Nonetheless, the client is not to be forgotten. One of the most critical responsibilities assurance practitioners owe to their client is maintaining *confidentiality* of the information they acquire during the audit process. Confidentiality expectations are normally set out in professional ethics codes and sometimes in law. Auditors also owe an obligation to provide an assurance service under contract, although, in a statutory audit, many of the terms are set out in statute.

To the public

Statute and case law tend to be the vehicles that most closely reflect social expectations. The courts can impose significant financial penalties on auditors who fail to exercise due care. Based on concerns over setting their own rules, a number of professions have lost their right to set auditing standards for assurance services. In Australia, the AUASB is responsible for developing, issuing and maintaining auditing and assurance standards. In New Zealand, and following international trends, the XRB and its subcommittees facilitate this change.

Standards do tend to lag behind developments in the courts. Plaintiffs in a court of law may seek to prove that existing auditing and assurance standards should be more exacting (Willekens, Steele and Miltz, 1996). This is why we see professional bodies and standard-setters respond to court rulings, to meet such public expectations.

It is incumbent on practitioners to be aware of courts' findings as to what constitutes reasonable care and skill, to limit the risk of audit failure, and to satisfy social expectations. Failure to do so will expose the auditor to charges of negligence.

A conceptual framework for audit: Summary and considerations

In summary, the conceptual framework for audit, drawing from its forerunners in conceptual theory, employs seven underlying postulates, or assumptions as to the fundamental purpose and nature of audit. From these postulates are derived four audit concepts setting out the conditions that must exist for audit to be a meaningful endeavour. From these relatively stable elements (see **Figure 2.6**) are derived standards, codes and guidance statements that help the auditor to address specific and known situations. Standards, codes and guidelines – detailed in other chapters in this text – tend to undergo frequent change as technology, practices and client processes change. There should be little change in either concepts or postulates, however, deriving as they do from fundamental principles.

We do wish to point out that, in some frameworks, there is a *confidentiality* concept; that is, the understanding that a client's information is confidential. We believe that retaining the information of a client is extremely important, to respect the client's privacy and to give them confidence in the auditor's professionalism. Retaining all matters confidential in all circumstances is controversial, however. Questions arise as to whether clients' behaviour should remain undisclosed if, for example, the client commits fraud or engages in unethical employment practices. The question of 'confidentiality' is considered in discussions as to the role of the auditor.

The role of the external auditor

People rely on auditors' opinions to make financial decisions, and businesses rely on the public's trust in those statements to attract investors. The auditor's *role*, therefore, is to provide confidence. We take this opportunity to introduce the idea of 'roles' in general and the auditor's role in particular to explain public expectations of auditor's behaviour, and what happens when expectations conflict. First, a definition from Davidson (1975):

> A *role* is the sum of cultural and behavioural patterns associated with a particular status within a society ... [it consists of] attitudes, values and behaviour ascribed by society to any and all persons occupying this status.

That is, a role comprises what we do and are expected to do. It can be understood as behaviour in response to expectations. The auditor's role has to do with how they should behave, with what they know or understand, their relationships with others, and how they are to perform their work. Factors that determine the auditor's role can include business norms, social or legal rules, and personal values. Auditors' behaviour, decisions and actions are judged in terms of the role expected of them.

The auditor's role has changed somewhat over time and will probably continue to do so to some degree simply because societal expectations change. We now evaluate the auditor's role as it has evolved and what it means for audit. Unless specified otherwise, you can assume that we are now referring to the Australian and New Zealand statutory financial audit. We begin with the influence of role senders.

Auditing in practice

Requirements for an audit committee

The Australian Securities Exchange (ASX) Corporate Governance Council's Best Practice Recommendations (S4.1) require listed entities to have audit committees comprising at least three independent (non-executive) board members. Audit committees are also required under the New Zealand Exchange's (NZX) rules (2003). Other jurisdictions (e.g., the United States and the United Kingdom) require independent audit committees to be part of large public organisations. This is now common practice and creates important connections between governing boards and the external (financial statement) auditor.

Role senders

Those who influence auditors' behaviour are referred to as **role senders**. As Davidson (1975) states, role senders can have legal, contractual or cooperative relationships with the auditor (see **Figure 2.9**). Those most visibly influential are termed 'formal role senders' because their views are set out in a formal and recognised form. For example, Australian and New Zealand statutory law requiring audit is 'formal' because it is both known and authoritative. Formal role senders for the Australian and New Zealand statutory audit include the following:

- *Shareholders*, or other 'owners' of the client's business – They influence via their contractual relationships with an audit firm. Shareholders are represented by their governing board and, within it, usually an **audit committee**.
- *Parliamentarians* – Through formulating and passing statutory laws which establish mandatory audit for some organisations.
- *Professions* – Professional organisations such as CA ANZ, which are recognised by the Financial Markets Authority (FMA) in New Zealand and the Financial Reporting Council (FRC) in Australia.
- *Regulators* – Regulators as committees on the XRB, or as established by the FMA or FRC, that regulate auditors and/or the audit profession.
- *Courts* – Courts have taken a leading role in determining the finer points of that which is considered to amount to due care and diligence by the auditor. The courts have also had a strong hand in determining those to whom the auditor is accountable.
- *Professional firms* – The audit firm trains its staff; establishes quality control, working paper and review procedures; and manages other formalised modes of operation.

role senders
Those who influence auditors' behaviour and can have legal, contractual or cooperative relationships with the auditor.

audit committee
Subcommittee of a governing board. Despite its title, it is the client, *not* the external auditor. Audit committees represent shareholders' interests and liaise with auditors on issues of strategy, governance and audit. They are usually composed of 3–7 members, some or all of whom are independent of management.

Some role senders may be more or less powerful at any point in time. For example, prior to the introduction of audit committees, shareholders were not well represented in regards to audit decisions. Those less formal, or powerful, may include the following:

- *Potential lenders and investors* have not always been formally recognised but may be influential in guiding auditors' behaviour because of the threat of such recognition through the courts.
- Although the independence of an auditor is valued, it may be difficult for an auditor to remain independent of *managers* and other employees with whom they work on a daily basis.
- Concern about how the *media* or *educators* portray auditors may be a source of influence.
- *Unions* may call for the verification of information of interest to employees.

Together, these influences shape how auditors perceive their duty, how and why they gather evidence, and the shape that their opinion takes.

Formal role senders	Informal role senders
• Shareholders • Parliament • Courts • Firms • Regulators • Professions	• Media • Lobbyists • Unions • Lenders • Educators • Managers

Figure 2.9 Role of the auditor: Formal and informal role senders

Role conflict: The expectation gap

Recalling audit theory, the audit potentially:

- satisfies the demand for social accountability by those entrusted with resources
- responds to a free-market demand for assurance of financial information produced by management
- is a contracting cost necessary to protect shareholder-principals from the self-serving actions of their agent-managers
- serves privileged members of society, such as professionals, to help them retain their rights and status in an audit.

Because of these different interests, the auditor's role shifts, and auditors may come into conflict with certain of their stakeholders at different times and in different circumstances. Furthermore, audit role senders may not convey clear messages, lag behind needs in practice, or offer contradictory requirements. When this occurs, the result is a gap between what the public thinks the auditor should do and what the auditor does. This is referred to as the *audit expectation gap* (Koh and Woo, 1998) (see **Figure 2.10**).

The audit expectation gap may arise from a number of sources, some of which can be explained from audit theory:

- *Principal* board members may expect auditors to monitor manager-agents closely.
- *Economic* players may seek a fast turnaround and quick response to market conditions so that they can make buy/sell decisions.
- Stakeholders may expect the auditors to provide *insurance* for their losses.
- *Social accountability* advocates may expect auditors to identify social inequities.
- *External stakeholders* may expect the auditor to discover fraud or errors.

What the auditor does	←————————————→	What the user expects the auditor to do

Figure 2.10 The audit expectation gap

Conflicting or unrealistic expectations	Poor auditor communications	Negligent audit practice	Inadequate standards

Figure 2.11 Sources that may contribute to the audit expectation gap

Source: Selected elements derived from Porter, Ó hÓgartaigh and Baskerville (2012).

These and other sources result in a 'gap' that comprises one or more of the problems shown in **Figure 2.11**, which are frequently observed in practice.

There will always be expectation gaps because there are always different needs and views, and because laws and standards typically lag behind discovering the need for them. The negligent audit practice is something to avoid, and professional requirements for education, training and ethical behaviour endeavour to reduce its incidence as much as possible. Standard-setters have been trying to address 'communication' problems with new standards and new forms of audit reports. Nonetheless, the public expects a lot from auditors, as it should, and there will always be debate around the auditor's role. Issues that repeatedly emerge are discovering and reporting client fraud, the likelihood of company failure, and a client's illegal acts.

CONCEPT QUESTION 3	What is the audit expectation gap?

Fraud detection

Management fraud involves either the misappropriation of an organisation's assets (such as stealing equipment) or the manipulation of accounting information (such as overstating asset valuation). The requirement to identify and disclose fraud discovered during an audit has always been a part of the auditor's role, but 'how much' a part has never been agreed. The very existence of management fraud is usually of concern because what is found may only be a portion of the fraud.

For some users, any fraud should be discovered and reported. For others (and particularly from the auditor's point of view), only *some* can be discovered, and of those, on only *some* occasions should that discovery be disclosed publicly. This is the substance of this expectation gap.

In Australia, the *Corporations Act 2001* (s 1308) states that a person commits an offence if a document is required under or for the purposes of this Act; or is lodged with or submitted to the Australian Securities and Investments Commission (ASIC); and the person makes, or authorises the making of, a statement in the document; or omits, or authorises the omission of, a matter or thing from the document; and the person knows that the document is materially false or misleading because of the statement or omission.

In New Zealand, the *Companies Act 1993* (as amended to 2017) states that anyone who 'knowingly makes a materially false or misleading statement in any document ... required by the Act will be criminally liable' (s 377, 1(a)). Therefore, an auditor commits an offence if they make a false disclosure, or fail to disclose matters of which they have knowledge and which should be disclosed in the audit report.

Auditors may also be criminally liable under section 380 of the same Act. This section states that any person who is 'knowingly a party to a company carrying on business with intent to defraud ... or for a

Management fraud
An intentional act by one or more individuals among management – those charged with governance, or employees or third parties – involving the use of deception to obtain an unjust or illegal advantage. (ISA NZ 240, para 12(a))

fraudulent purpose, commits an offence' (s 380, 2(a). Potentially, an auditor may therefore be liable if they are implicated in business carried out by a client in a fraudulent manner.

Predicting company failure

Company failure as an audit began after securities regulations in the 1930s brought the professional accountant/auditor more firmly into the role of regulating markets. After the First World War, and given the experiences of the Great Depression, investors and the business community began to look to auditors for assurance as to company solvency (Becker, 1980). Studies show that by 1973, 81 per cent of shareholders expected assurance about financial soundness (Lee, 1986b, p. 294; MacDonald Commission, 1988, p. 2.20), and this is probably still true today.

Portrayed in the accounting standards as a *going concern* issue, predicting company failure is a unique task for auditors who are not usually called upon to *predict* future events (see **Figure 2.12**).

Is this an unreasonable ask? No, probably not. In an Australian study, Carey, Geiger and O'Connell (2008) found that of the 60 surviving companies receiving a going concern modified opinion, 24 per cent switched auditors the year after receiving an 'Emphasis of matter' modification, and 11.4 per cent switched the year after receiving a qualified opinion. Auditors could have done better. Also, predictions of failure are reasonably possible for

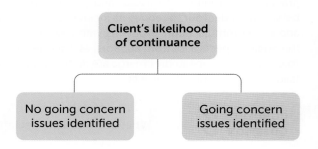

Figure 2.12 Auditors can be called upon to predict a going concern issue

the short period of time. Nor are the search requirements onerous. A New Zealand study revealed that only 20 per cent of companies failing between 1987 and 1991 received qualified opinions (Pratt, 1993).

The Australian Auditing Standards' ASA 570: Going Concern (July 2020, para 6) and the New Zealand guidance in ISA NZ 570: Going Concern (October 2015) highlight the responsibility of the auditor to

> obtain sufficient appropriate audit evidence regarding, and conclude on, the appropriateness of management's use of the going concern basis of accounting in the preparation of the financial statements, and to conclude ... whether a material uncertainty exists about the entity's ability to continue as a going concern.

Usually, this involves audit procedures designed to identify particular risks, such as a large debt becoming current or the threat of litigation. Auditors must consider the appropriateness of the use of the going concern assumption when planning and performing audit procedures, evaluating the results, and remaining alert for audit evidence, which may cast significant doubt on the ability to continue as a going concern (ASA 570; IFAC, 2005; ISA NZ 570, paras 3, 6).

The going concern assessment should not be confused with the Australian and New Zealand *solvency test* requirements. For companies within the scope of the solvency legislation, the test should be applied each time dividends are paid (see the High Court ruling by Justice Heath in 2002 on *Kitchener Nominees Ltd*).

Oddly, the change to international going concern standards somewhat reduces the requirements placed on auditors. Under the international standard, the auditor, in assessing GAAP, must come to an opinion as to whether the company should revalue its assets and liabilities as a result of a likelihood of failure within 12 months of the balance sheet date (IFAC, 2005; ISA NZ 570, para 18). Formerly, the requirement was for them to assess going concern up to 12 months from the *report date*.

The courts have not appeared to expect unreasonable predictive skills from the auditor, but they seem to come down harder on the audit firm when audit negligence is apparent. There is clearly a public concern, and the profession and companies would be wise to keep this in mind.

CONCEPT QUESTION 4	What is the auditor's responsibility for predicting company failure?

Detecting and reporting illegal acts

Traditionally, the auditor has not had a duty to discover or disclose illegal acts by the client when not specifically contracted to do so. When the employers of the audit were also the only users, it was unlikely that they would have wanted their indiscretions to be disclosed.

Times have changed, however, and in an open society, there is public interest in, and the right to know about, how a company conducts its business. The auditor's duty to identify and disclose illegal acts is a relatively recent responsibility. However, events such as the Watergate scandal which inspired the US *Foreign Corrupt Practices Act 1977* have raised public expectations about what the auditor should identify and disclose. Our audit standards indicate that the auditor has some responsibility to understand and respond to the legal environment (IFAC, 2005; ISA NZ 250; ASA 720).

ASA 250 and ISA NZ 250 point out that management's (and the governing board's) responsibility is to comply with the law. Nonetheless, they do distinguish between laws and regulations that have a direct, material effect on the financial statements and those that affect the likely continuance of the client. As to the first:

> The provisions of those laws and regulations generally recognised to have a direct effect on the determination of material amounts and disclosures in the financial statements such as tax and pension laws and regulations. (ASA 250, para 6(a))

For these matters, the auditor should obtain sufficient appropriate evidence, as would be expected for any potentially material amount on the financial statements.

As to the second, the reference is to, for example, situations in which the client may be subject to:

- operating licence or certification laws
- solvency requirements
- employment or environment regulation
- anti-money-laundering requirements.

In this case, procedures should be adopted to determine compliance or non-compliance because 'compliance with such laws and regulations may ... have a material effect on the financial statements' (ASA 250, para 6(b)). Generally, if the legal requirement is unlikely to affect the financial statement, the less likely the auditor is to become aware of it or the need to act upon it. However, it is a new area of standardisation, and the fine points are yet to be worked out in the law.

Nonetheless, this is a far cry from the expectation to find all activities that are against the law. The auditor cannot be expected to find all breaches of employment or environmental law, contract or international law. The professional can contract to a broader scope to look for such violations (at, of course, a higher price), but the statutory financial auditor is to remain focused on the potential for misstatement in the financial statements.

Determining or finding that a client is engaging in illegal activity can place the auditor in a problematic situation. Where incidents are found that do *not* have a material effect on the financial statements or the client's going concern, auditors are caught in an ethical dilemma: should they break the bonds of confidentiality that exist between themselves and their clients, or should they serve a public good by notifying authorities of illegal transactions?

Traditionally, professions have held out for the former, as illustrated in the form taken by the standards. In Australia, the APES 110: Code of Ethics for Professional Accountants (including Independence Standards) issued by the Accounting Professional & Ethical Standards Board (APESB) requires

> the auditor to take steps to respond to identified or suspected non-compliance with laws and regulations and determine whether further action is needed. Such steps may include the communication of identified or suspected non-compliance with laws and regulations to other auditors within a group, including a group engagement partner, component auditors or other auditors performing work at components of a group for purposes other than the audit of the group financial report. (ASA 250, para A8)

In New Zealand, the statement Reporting Non-Compliance to Regulatory and Enforcement Authorities (ISA NZ 250, para A19) explains:

> The auditor's professional duty to maintain the confidentiality of client information may preclude reporting identified or suspected non-compliance with laws and regulations to a party outside the entity. However, the auditor's legal responsibilities vary by jurisdiction and, in certain circumstances, the duty of confidentiality may be overridden by statute, the laws or courts of law.

In the United Kingdom, a number of statutes (*Financial Services Act 1986, Banking Act 1987, Building Societies Act 1986*) establish many circumstances where an auditor should report matters of public interest. Australia and New Zealand offer fewer opportunities.

So, if discovered, should the auditor disclose a client's illegal acts in a public forum? With a few specified exceptions, and assuming that the act has no effect as raised in the two categories above, the answer is generally 'no'. The auditor's *confidentiality* obligations to the client come to the fore.

Whether the disclosure is appropriate or not, the auditor should act in a manner creditable to the profession.

> In exceptional cases when management or those charged with governance do not take the remedial action that the auditor considers appropriate in the circumstances and withdrawal from the engagement is not possible (see paragraph A25), the auditor may consider describing the identified or suspected non-compliance in an Other Matter paragraph in accordance with ASA 706. (ASA 250, para A26.1)

> In exceptional cases, the auditor may consider whether withdrawal from the engagement ... is necessary when management or those charged with governance do not take the remedial action that the auditor considers appropriate in the circumstances, even when the non-compliance is not material to the financial statements. When deciding whether withdrawal from the engagement is necessary, the auditor may consider seeking legal advice. (ISA NZ 250, para A18)

That is, it may be better to withdraw from an engagement – even if there has been significant time spent – should they run the risk of being associated with illegal or fraudulent acts. Other issues have created role conflict as well, at least in the past:

- Should the auditor find *all* errors and misstatements? No, only material misstatements.
- Is the financial auditor responsible for analysing the client's control systems? No, only those used to determine auditability and financial statement material misstatements.
- Should the auditor come to a precise valuation of all assets? No, that is not possible with respect to estimated amounts, nor is it any longer expected.

Such issues have generally been resolved in the courts and subsequently clarified in auditing standards and guidelines. **Table 2.2** shows expectation gap positions.

Table 2.2 Role conflict: Expectation gap positions

Three sources of role conflict and expectation gap		
Going concern problems? Some obligation on the auditor to determine, and if material, report	*Client's illegal acts? Some obligation related to the effects on the financial statements or under specific legislation*	*Client fraud? Some obligation to engage in an active search for material misstatement resulting from fraud and to investigate suspicions, with a limited obligation to report*

So, where does this leave the auditor? Essentially, these are circumstances that call for the auditor to make the hard call and apply a professional – and personal – code of ethics. Doing so may involve sacrificing income or losing a client, so it is not easy. Nonetheless, making the right decision is, in the long run, essential to the client, their stakeholders, the credibility of the profession, and society.

Also, and depending on the cause of the conflict, further resolutions may be sought:
- audit report changes – to 'explain' the auditor's role more fully or clearly
- improve the audit process – an obvious solution for auditor negligence
- independently regulate professions – this now occurs in Australia and New Zealand
- reduce auditor conflicts of interest – it may be necessary to forbid the auditor from having other interests in the client, a controversial topic.

Study tools

Summary

In this chapter, the history of audit and the idea of 'role' were introduced, accompanied by a discussion of influences on the auditor ('role senders'). We saw how audit has evolved and changed over time, emerging from simple practices of measuring stewardship to today's complicated processes for a complex international financial market.

We believe that the development of audit concepts can lead to a more informed discussion of the controversial issues that face the auditing profession, by providing a holistic view of events and expectations. Although we have applied these concepts to external, statutory, financial audits, they are also relevant to other types of assurance services. Gathering evidence, assessing risk, and identifying what is important (material) are as relevant to, for example, reviews of forecasts, internal audits, environmental disclosures and internal controls as they are to financial reports, though the forms they take will vary.

We have illustrated how a conceptual framework can be used as a tool of analysis. Each of these concepts and how they are put into practice, in turn, is discussed in the chapters that follow. While the audit process may change, and procedures will vary by audit firm and client, we believe the conceptual framework provides a deeper understanding of the principles that guide audit practice.

Role conflict – or the expectation gap – examines the auditor's responsibility to predict company failure, and to identify and disclose management fraud and illegal acts of the client. It is noted that, while the profession is in an often difficult position of having to respond to the sometimes conflicting or unreasonable demands of the stakeholders, in other instances, it is apparent that professional members have let their standards fall, to the detriment of those in the profession and outside. Further details of the statutes, cases and standards referred to in this chapter can be found in the chapters to follow.

🔗 Case/resources link

CAATs for Classrooms

Accompanying this book is a series of data, integrated worksheets and exercises that are designed to support your learning and give you exposure to hands-on audit decision-making dilemmas faced by auditors in the planning elements of the audit process. Acquire the relevant material for this chapter from your instructor.

Review questions

2.1   Why do we need a philosophy of auditing?

2.2   Name and describe the postulates modified from Mautz and Sharaf, and Flint.

2.3   Discuss why each of the postulates may, or may not, apply to today's environment.

2.4   Using the Pratt-Van Peursem conceptual framework:

    a   Name and describe the four categories of concepts.

    b   Identify the 'concepts' within each category and describe why they are in that category.

    c   Name and describe the ethical standard categories in the framework (and also in current auditing standards).

    d   Identify the categories of current auditing standards for Australian/New Zealand audits.

    e   Describe the ways in which these concepts and standards are formed.

2.5   Discuss the importance of auditor accountability and highlight the importance of this to the audit company, client, profession and the public.

2.6   Drawing from Flint's work, concepts are classified into four broad groups. How might the absence of these concepts affect practice?

2.7   Detail why ethics is important for professional auditors.

2.8   What is the meaning of 'independence' in terms of the relationship between the external financial statement auditor and their client? Why is it important?

2.9   What is the meaning of the 'cost–benefit' of audit evidence? What are the implications for the audit process?

2.10   How are 'materiality', 'risk' and 'evidence' related to each other?

2.11   Provide three examples of 'disclosure' required through or within the audit engagement.

2.12   If the client pays the auditor for their services, explain why there is an accountability to:

    a   the firm

    b   the professional association

    c   the public.

2.13   Certain expectations are attached to social positions and are referred to as 'role senders'. Provide three examples with respect to Australian/New Zealand statutory audit.

2.14 Describe the difference between 'formal' and 'informal' role senders, using examples.

2.15 Explain why each of the formal role senders named fits that description.

2.16 What is the auditor's responsibility for detecting fraud? What is their responsibility for reporting fraud?

2.17 Compare early 'events' with 'events' affecting audit today.

2.18 Compare early 'clients' (and users) with those of today.

2.19 Describe how the 'scope' of audit has changed over time and why.

2.20 Name and describe three different statutes that have influenced audit today. Describe those influences.

2.21 What is the auditor's responsibility for detecting management fraud?

2.22 What is the auditor's responsibility for predicting other illegal acts?

2.23 What is the auditor's responsibility for reporting each of the issues of:
   a predicting company failure
   b management fraud
   c other illegal acts.

2.24 State four potential causes of the 'audit expectation gap'.

2.25 What has been the emphasis for audit in each of the following eras?
   a formative years
   b Industrial Revolution – 18th–19th centuries
   c early 20th century
   d post–world wars era.

Exercises

2.1 **STANDARDS:** Evaluate the following audit standards, guidelines, guidance statements or exposure drafts (i to vii) in detail to determine which of the following they relate to:
   a philosophical guidance
   b postulates or unprovable assumptions, conceptual in nature
   c standard-like
   d guideline-like.
      i guidance on the auditor's responsibility to detect and report fraud
      ii guidance on independence
      iii guidance on the auditor's report
      iv guidance on the auditor's responsibility with respect to detecting going concern problems
      v guidance on relying on the expertise of others
      vi guidance on skills and competence needed for a forecast engagement
      vii guidance on how to live life in a meaningful way.

2.2 **AUDIT STANDARDS:** As shown in Chapter 1, there are distinct differences between standards for 'audits' and those for 'other engagements'. Consider and evaluate the following:

a   In terms of audit scope/user or assurance (see Chapter 1), why are such differences needed?

b   In terms of the conceptual framework, do you think each is a relatively complete set of standards? Why or why not.

2.3 **STANDARDS AND GUIDELINES:** You are conducting a review engagement for a business client who repairs watches and makes keys in a shopping mall. She needs the assurance for a bank loan. The client has already looked at the standards which you follow and has asked you to explain how the *evidence* for a 'review' engagement might be different from that for an 'audit' engagement.

Required:

a   Explain how the evidence concept can exist for both types of engagements.

b   Explain where those differences may be found in standards/guidelines and why they are not in the concepts.

2.4 **AUDIT STANDARDS:** Review the standards currently set out for 'other engagements' (including any currently under review or development on a professional website or the AUASB or XRB websites). Do you think the standards are relatively complete in terms of the conceptual framework, or in terms of practical needs on the ground? Identify 2–3 standards that could be developed in this field and relate to them using the conceptual framework.

2.5 **CONCEPTS AND PRACTICE:** Your audit client has asked you to complete the preparation of his set of financial statements before you audit them, because he is not well versed in accounting and does not know how to prepare the adjusting entries. He also explains to you that, as the audit is just for his own purpose, and he does not plan to give the accounts or audit report to anyone else, this should not be a problem.

Required:

a   Explain to him, using terms from the conceptual framework, why this would be inappropriate and why.

b   At what point should this communication occur and why?

c   What might you suggest to the client before proceeding?

d   What might you discuss and what might you ask the client in terms of his needs for assurance?

2.6 **CONCEPTUAL FRAMEWORK FOR AUDITING:** Explain why the structure shown in **Figure 2.13** would not work well. Consider the purpose of each element, and why placing them 'out of order' might have particular effects on the auditor's frame of mind or their logic.

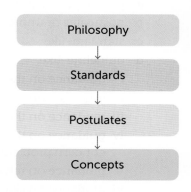

Figure 2.13
A questionable conceptual framework

2.7 **EXPECTATION GAP:** Take and defend a position as to whether the following situations represent deficient performance by the auditor, deficient standards, or unreasonable expectations on the part of the non-auditor:

   a   Loan receipts from an overseas financier were recorded as sales.

   b   Inventory (stock) of unprocessed and processed lamb products were grossly overvalued.

   c   There was no mention of going concern problems in the auditor's report.

   d   Fortex was expanding too fast for its market and this information was not disclosed.

2.8 **ILLEGAL ACTS:** The auditor has a growing obligation with respect to anti-money-laundering expectations in the current environment. Investigate the Australian/New Zealand auditor's current obligations. On that basis, decide what the auditor should do if they discover that their client's chief financial officer was involved in overseas investments (legally, with the company's spare cash) concerning financial derivatives in the United States and in the United Kingdom.

2.9 **AUDIT HISTORY:** You have just encountered Rip Van Winkle, who has woken up from a 200-year sleep. He was an 'auditor' in his day, and he claims that the only thing he needs to do for an audit is to ensure that the money given to his client by the government, and a few large shareholders, was spent for purposes set out in the company's charter. That is, he would only investigate the cash flow. What is your response and, in the context of modern expectations, why?

2.10 **DISCLOSURE:** Evaluate how disclosure legislation, or ethics requirements, might impact the following situation. The auditor discovers that their audit client is employing overseas labour at $5 per hour. These individual employees are brought into the country illegally and they are being paid less than 30 per cent of the minimum wage in the country. This has no material effect on the financial statements.

2.11 **PERFORMANCE AND GOING CONCERN:** The auditor has discovered that their client, Near Misses Ltd, has filed a lawsuit against them because one of their outdoor equipment devices failed and caused a fatal accident. What is the issue here and do you think the auditor should have identified the problem?

2.12 **ROLE SENDERS:** The auditor is a pivotal aspect of the conceptual framework. Discuss the role of the auditor in society and highlight some expectations of the auditor as a 'role sender'.

2.13 **ROLE:** What has brought about the increase in the auditor's social accountability? Provide a case law example. How might this apply to an audit of, for example, Air New Zealand or Qantas.

2.14 **HISTORY:** Auditing, to maintain its important role in society, must be capable of adjusting to society's demands. What adjustments have auditors made to the audit process over time, and what inspired these changes? Apply this to Australia/New Zealand.

2.15 **ROLE SENDERS:** Using **Figure 2.9**, identify all role senders relevant to the audit of a public utility which is partly government owned and partly private shareholder owned.

2.16 **HISTORY:** Your client is the CEO and owner of a family-owned business who does not understand why he, as well as his employees, should be subject to audit (and professional scepticism). The CEO's understanding is that the audit is for the purposes of seeing the financial position so that he can make reasonable finance decisions, and he knows that his bank will be interested in it as well as he has an ongoing loan with the bank. The CEO contributed all of the original equity to the business so he questions why he is under review.

a   Explain to the CEO how, over time, the role of the auditor with respect to management has changed.

b   Explain to him why, in his particular circumstances, professional scepticism must be applied to him no less than to his employees.

Statutory law

Learning objectives

After studying the material in this chapter, you should be able to:
- identify how stakeholders, users and the public are served by statutory law and the auditor
- understand auditor–client relationships in statute
- describe the applications of statutory law in Australia
- understand auditor and client requirements in Australia
- describe the applications of statutory law in New Zealand
- understand auditor and client requirements in New Zealand.

Introduction

> Where professional standards lag behind public expectations, the latter may serve as the basis for determining legal liability and ethical judgments. (Burton, 1972, p. 49)

As you have learned, there are a number of formal audit role senders:
- statute from parliamentary law
- regulators
- shareholders
- courts
- accounting firms
- professional associations.

While we will be discussing each of these role senders during the course of the book, the first two – statutory law and regulators – are considered in this chapter. In particular, we examine the statutes that most powerfully guide the financial statement audit in Australia and New Zealand, and we study a number of legislative influences on audit practice. The content of this chapter on statutory law and its influence on external audit is based on the Australia and New Zealand contexts.

The **statutory audit** refers to engagements in which the audit is conducted primarily *because* it is imposed under Australian and New Zealand statutory requirements. The reasons for such requirements are usually:
- *to serve a public good*, such as to assure stakeholders who may not have a direct economic interest in, or authority over, an entity, ensuring that they receive the benefits of audit
- *to compensate for the effects of imperfect markets*. So, for example, in audit professional practice, the auditor may work with the client's management and be compensated from an agreement made with the governing body, even though they owe accountability to a larger group such as shareholders. However, shareholders and others with economic interests may be distant from the auditor in practice. So laws imposed upon audit practice may better serve those wider interests.

statutory audit
Engagements in which an audit is conducted primarily because it is imposed under Australian or New Zealand statutory requirements.

49

CONCEPT QUESTION 1   What is a 'statutory audit' and why is it called that?

Statutory law and the auditor

Statutes are those Acts of parliament that have been passed into law. Collectively, statutory law is referred to as 'legislation' because it is created by 'legislators' or by 'parliamentarians'. Criminal and/or civil penalties may be imposed should its requirements in law not be met. Audit professionals are subject to mandates set out in statutory law, as well as to the **regulations** which are related to them.

regulations
Authoritative rules or orders, usually dealing with details or procedures. They may, or may not, have the force of law, but when established under statute, they are likely to be required in law.

As with other industries and individuals, audit practitioners and professionals in Australia and New Zealand are subject to a growing range of statutes and regulations. These have their foundations in the English common law system, and British governance systems and parliamentary structures continue to be influential today. However, each country's own particular economic history also influences statutory law, as illustrated by, for example, mining industries in regard to Australian law, or corporate law changes following financial scandals in New Zealand.

British and US statutes of the 19th and early 20th centuries also led to expectations that the Australian and New Zealand auditor would be a trained and licensed professional, fulfil ethical duties, and be active in approved professional associations.

Further influences originate in US law in – for example, the *Securities Exchange Act 1934*, which established oversight over financial systems; and the *Sarbanes–Oxley Act 2002*, which called for more disclosures in the annual and audit reports.

Essentially, these events laid the groundwork for statutory law that either imposed requirements on a governing body intending to submit its accounts to audit, or on the auditor and what the auditor does. Statutory law of concern to the Australian and New Zealand practitioner is summarised in **Table 3.1**.

Table 3.1 Statutes and for-profit audit

Australia		New Zealand	
Title	**Regulates**	**Title**	**Regulates**
Corporations Act 2001 (Cth) (*Corporations Act*)	Registered companies	*Companies Act 1993* (*Cos Act*)	Registered companies
Australian Securities and Investments Commission Act 2001 (*ASIC Act*)	Administers ASIC, established independent standard-setting boards under the Australian Accounting Standards Board (AASB), conducts (under CLERP 9) audit inspections	*Financial Markets Authority Act 2011* (*FMA Act*)	Established the FMA to regulate entities of public interest, conducts oversight
		Auditor Regulation Act 2011 (revised 2014) (*ARA*)	Recognises authority of XRB and FMA
Corporate Law Economic Reform Program (Audit Reform & Corporate Disclosure) Act 2004 (*CLERP 9 Act*)	Established AASB and legal authority for standards, more disclosure and independence requirements	*Financial Reporting Act 2013* (*FRA*)	Grants legal authority to the XRB and its subcommittees
Australian Prudential Regulation Authority Act 1998 (*APRA Act*)	Protect interests of depositors, insurance policy-holders, certain retirement funds	*Financial Markets Conduct Act 2013* (*FMCA*)	Protects interests of stakeholders in entities of public interest (including companies)

Such law is not always specifically designed for audit, but it does influence audit practice. The focus on corporate legislation reflects the fact that the primary form of public interest accountability was historically concerned with overseeing companies. Demand for greater independence for standard-setters and for regulating other types of organisations led to other laws affecting the audit process. Overall, these statutes set out who must prepare information for audit, who is allowed (or required) to perform the audit, and which authorities regulate audit, set standards and conduct oversight.

Professional scepticism

Audit practice reviews by Australia's ASIC and New Zealand's FMA have raised concerns about whether auditors show appropriate levels of scepticism in, for example, their collection of evidence (ASIC) or in their consideration of users/stakeholders (FMA) (CA ANZ, 2022).

Statutes and regulating authorities tend to be unique to each nation-state. However, regarding Australia and New Zealand, the activities and institutes that both countries regulate share similarities, as illustrated in **Figure 3.1**.

Statutes of primary interest to auditors	Authority to accredit and oversee professions, to enforce statutory independence requirements	Authority to set (NZ) or oversee (AUS) standards and codes of ethics for assurance services	Tasked with performing audit, and each profession's own entry and ethical rules, overseeing its own members
• Australia – *CLERP 9 Act* (2004), *ASIC Act* (2001), *Corporations Act* (2001) • *New Zealand – FMCA* (2013), *FMAA* (2011), *Cos Act* (1993), *FRA* (2013), *ARA* (2011)	• Australia – ASIC, FRC • New Zealand – FMA	• Australia – FRC oversees standards formulated by accounting (AASB) and audit (AUASB) standard setters • New Zealand – NZAuASB under the XRB formulates standards • IAASB formulates ISAs for audit	• Australia – accredited professional bodies such as CA ANZ, CPA Australia, Institute of Public Accountants (IPA) • New Zealand – accredited professional bodies such as CA ANZ

Figure 3.1 Audit oversight authority and regulators

The AUASB (Australia) and NZAuASB (New Zealand) standard-setting bodies, along with similar authorities in, for example, Fiji, Malaysia, Indonesia and Samoa, work to ensure their standards conform with the ISAs. It is noted, however, that without nation-based statutory authority, international bodies such as the IAASB cannot impose their promulgations. The nature of statutory influence is discussed next.

Auditor–client relationship in statute

The governing board of the organisation being audited has a responsibility both to prepare the annual report and financial statements in accordance with accounting standards, and to employ and work with an appropriate and independent audit professional.

The audit firm is responsible, in statute, for meeting certain ethical requirements, and for planning and conducting the audit in accordance with auditing standards. The statute does vary depending on the organisation and on the nation-state in which it is based. However, the broad concerns surrounding these practices are shared.

Essentially, organisations that serve a large number of remote members of a public – such as public companies or certain financial, insurance or superannuation schemes – are called upon, under statute, to lodge (or 'file') their annual reports with a state-based regulatory authority. Those annual reports, including financial statements, must usually be subjected to an independent audit.

Most annual reports must be accompanied, also in law, by the auditor's report, which includes the auditor's opinion on the claims made by the organisation's management.

CONCEPT QUESTION 2	What conceptual framework 'concepts' are served by requiring an audit report and opinion to be published and lodged with statutory authorities?

Organisations requiring audit under statute make up a large segment of both the Australian and New Zealand economies. As an example, a 2014 Australian study revealed that 222 of the country's statutes required an audit (Bessell, Powell and Richardson). Statutory law in Australia and New Zealand imposes a number of requirements as to who can be the auditor; what are the contractual and communication arrangements between the auditor, the client organisation and its shareholders (or stakeholders); and how the auditor must report.

Approval of the auditor or audit firm must, under the relevant Act, be made by shareholders/owners/trustees at their annual meeting. There could be further disclosure requirements for some organisations.

Auditor's appointment

The auditor is charged both with being appropriately professionally qualified, and with performing in a manner expected of a professional. Statutory law imposes a number of restrictions as to who can take up the role (see **Table 3.2**).

Table 3.2 Appointment of the auditor

	Australia	New Zealand
Who is the auditor?	Registered company auditors (RCAs) ('reviews' separate); company registration. Competence, experience (i.e., via accreditation)	'Qualified auditor' or chartered accountant or eligible member of accredited and registered company, licensed under *ARA*
The auditor cannot be:	Director, employee, liquidator	Director, employee, liquidator
Lead auditor rotation requirements	The APESB specifies audit partner rotation requirements (especially affecting public interest entities) – normally five years.	NZX rules require lead auditor to retire every five years
How is the auditor selected?	Approved at annual meetings, provisions for a short-term role	Approved at annual meetings, provisions for a short-term role

'Qualified' refers to the qualifications of the auditor and/or their firm. The statutory auditor cannot normally have such obligations as would damage their independence from the client. Typically, the auditor should not be a:

* director of the client's business
* employee or partner of the client
* liquidator or receiver of the client.

Requirements as to the rotation of lead auditor staff are imposed in both New Zealand and Australia as a further means of strengthening independence. The rotation of audit firms is not required, although it has been introduced in a few countries (e.g., the Netherlands).

These processes and requirements are important for providing some assurance to shareholders and other stakeholders that the *ethics of the auditor*, in particular their independence and competence, meet basic standards of quality.

Audit firm: Legal form

The legal form of an audit firm, and the potential liability of the firm's owners or partners, is a controversial matter. Under earlier legislation, the audit firm could only be a sole trader or an unlimited partnership. This enacted direct financial *accountability* of the auditor, which could be very costly in the event of audit failures. Audit partners were subject to **joint and several liability** in which each audit partner could be subject to financial penalties in regards to aggrieved parties, which could put their business *and* personal assets at risk. Although such risk could be insured against, the professional auditor was highly exposed to expensive litigation under such regimes.

The auditor is often included as one of the defendants in corporate failure lawsuits partly because of their 'deep pockets'; that is, the auditor may be the only defendant left with assets when company failure occurs. The cost of insurance premiums for such extensive exposure can be prohibitive. After many years of lobbying by auditors, this came to be seen as placing an unfair burden on the auditor. Recent legislative changes have reduced this risk and recognised that a limit to the auditor's liability is needed (see **Table 3.3**).

joint and several liability
Arises in contract 'when two or more persons jointly promise in the same contract to do the same thing, but also separately promise to do the same thing'. (Thomson Reuters, 2022)

Table 3.3 Liability of auditors under statute

Australia	New Zealand
Australia adopted a proportionate liability scheme in 2004 under which the auditor (or audit firm) is responsible for only that proportion of the damage or loss attributable to the firm's responsibility for that damage or loss. State statutes also operate; for example, New South Wales caps the liability at 10 times the audit fee for large audits.	Under a 2014 legislative amendment, which became effective in July 2015, New Zealand auditors can incorporate – under certain restrictive conditions. While still liable to some determinable extent, this has enabled auditors to be partially protected by the corporate veil.

Such modifications to statute mean that audit firms are less subject to prohibitively costly judgments. They also reduce the *accountability of the auditor* to its stakeholders, although action may be needed to reduce audit litigation costs. Australia and New Zealand are not alone in this, as described by the ICAEW (2008):

> The current position in Europe varies. In Germany, for example, there is a statutory cap of a fixed monetary amount, though these caps do not apply for deliberate breaches of duty. In France, by contrast, the auditor's duty arises in tort and cannot be limited by contract or otherwise …

In the U.S., auditors cannot limit liability for their own negligence and, in the wake of corporate collapses and the introduction of the Sarbanes–Oxley Act, reform of auditors' liability was not on the agenda for some time. However, a U.S. Treasury Committee has looked at the issue (without coming to any real conclusion) but discussions are taking place between U.K. authorities and the SEC about the latter accepting U.K. LLAs [limited liability agreements].

Statute law has therefore been enacted to allow an audit firm to structure itself in ways that protect its members from unlimited liability, while still holding firms accountable to those who may suffer damage due to auditor negligence.

Working with the auditor

Audit fees are set once they have been approved by shareholders at an annual meeting. Fees are negotiated between the client's board or its audit committee and the audit firm prior to the beginning of audit work. Fee-setting is a commercial, not a statutory, issue. Under current legislation, the auditor can be reappointed unless they are no longer qualified or withdraw.

Allowing the auditor access to all information they deem necessary is an essential condition in ensuring that the auditor can acquire the *evidence* they need. This right to 'access' is found in most statutes where audit is required. The decision to remove an auditor is also a delicate *communication* process that tends to be guided by statute. (See **Table 3.4**.)

Table 3.4 Auditor's access and removal

Australia	*New Zealand*
(*Corporations Act 2001*, ss 329, 327D and RG26)	(*Cos Act 1993*, s 207P-W; *FRA 2013*, s 38-9; *FMCA 2013*)
Making information available to the auditor	
Access to all records, explanations and information. The audit committee must review non-audit services (*Corporations Act 2001*). An audit 'independence' declaration should be found within the directors' report.	Access to all records, inquiries and meetings are required under *Cos Act 1993* (s 194) and *FMA Act 2013* legislation.
Restrictions on the removal of an auditor	
For public companies, a meeting to remove the auditor follows the filing of 'intention' to remove (see *Corporations Act 2001*, s 329, RG26)	Shareholders must give the auditors 20 working days' notice of the proposal to replace them.
On notification, and for public companies, the auditor has the opportunity to make representations to its members (see *Corporations Act 2001*, s 329 and RG26).	On notification, the auditor must be given an opportunity to 'make representations on the proposed change to the shareholders'.
Consent to resign is available unless concerns are raised about disagreements with the client's management or board (*Corporations Act 2001*; see RG26.17-2.59). (Similar requirements apply to other organisations.)	An auditor who does not wish to be reappointed must give written notice and may provide additional information that the board must circulate to shareholders.
The entity must normally notify ASIC of a new auditor appointment.	The entity may be required to notify the regulator of the appointment of an auditor to the company.

The concern regarding auditor resignation is that the client may wish to remove an auditor who has discovered, or intends to disclose, an unremedied discrepancy in the accounts. So, for example, the auditor may decline to agree with the client's overstated asset valuation, and, for this reason, the governing board may wish to remove that auditor and seek a less-informed alternative. For this reason, audit statute law invariably contains careful provisions in regard to auditor retirement or resignation.

CONCEPT QUESTION	3	What would be at risk if clients could end their contract with the independent auditor without explanation and at any time during the audit?

Audit committees

The audit committee is a subcommittee of the client's governing board. Committee members address, and are available to communicate, matters to do with financial reporting, audit and internal control on behalf of the client organisation. An audit committee is a useful *communication* mechanism through which the auditor can raise concerns with the governing board. So, for example, if the independent auditor has concerns about management fraud, this issue can be raised directly with the audit committee.

CONCEPT QUESTION	4	Audit committee members need not be professionally qualified auditors/accountants. Should they be?

While not generally mandatory in statute, audit committees are imposed under stock exchange rules. The NZX requires certain listed companies to have an audit committee. Similarly, the ASX's listing rules specify that entities large enough to be in the S&P All Ordinaries Index (large companies) and certain others must have an audit committee. Furthermore, all Australian listed companies must explain whether an audit committee exists and 'if not, why not'.

Audit report

The auditor's report includes the audit *opinion* on whether the financial statements (or other matters audited) are true and fair. Any such report must also include information as required under each specific statute and/or as required under auditing standards. The auditor's report should, in most cases, be sent to ASIC in Australia. In New Zealand, it should go to the Registrar of Companies and to the XRB if *Companies Act 1993* requirements have not been met. The content of the audit report is, to some extent, set out in statute by virtue of the mandatory auditing standards.

Auditor ethics

Ethical requirements of the auditor are generally set out in auditing standards (e.g., ASA 102) and in codes imposed by professional bodies (e.g., CA ANZ). Given Australia and New Zealand's moves to impose accounting and auditing standards in law, these standards are effectively statutory requirements. Fundamental principles of professional ethics, as set out in ISAs, have now been adopted in many Pacific-rim nations. They can be seen as organising principles and generally include integrity, objectivity, professional competence, due care, confidentiality and professional behaviour.

Maintaining the *confidentiality of the client* and the client's information is addressed in statute as well as in code. Generally, the professional should not reveal information about their client, as the auditor should protect the information to which they have unique access. Situations in which the confidentiality between the audit professional and their client can or should be broken are very few and generally limited to those in which either the client gives permission to disclose, or where information is made available to other professional members for quality review. These situations are also guided in statute.

Audit and Indigenous tradition

The very term 'audit' is a reference to 'auditory'; that is, audit was originally organised as a speaking and listening process by which someone is orally held to account. A particular feature of indigenous communities – including Aboriginal and Torres Strait Islanders, New Zealand Māori and other Pacific island peoples – is their own reliance on oral, not written, tradition. So it might be reasonable to think that audit would be compatible with indigenous practices. Nonetheless, the right to the protection of cultural data, traditional knowledge and expression was only recently recognised, in a 2015 promulgation – 'Data sovereignty for Indigenous people: Current practice and future needs' (Taylor and Kukutai, 2015) – by First Nation scholars, representatives of indigenous organisations, and government leaders from Australia, New Zealand, Canada and the United States. And such protection, or its audit, is not always present in law.

Exceptions include certain aspects of Māori *tikanga* or customary values, which are akin to customary law in the English legal tradition. *Tikanga* has been recognised by the New Zealand Law Commission and aspects have been incorporated into New Zealand common and statute law. Aboriginal and Torres Strait Islander organisations and agencies in Australia have certainly been subject to performance and finance audits under, for example, the *Aboriginal and Torres Strait Islander Commission Act 1989*. The incorporation of Australian Indigenous values and views into law continues to be a challenging process, but it did benefit from the advisory work of the National Indigenous Council (2004–08).

Specific applications to Australia and New Zealand are discussed in the remaining sections of this chapter.

Statutory law: Applications in Australia

Early Australian statutes were influenced by British precedent, including, for example, the *Limited Liability Act 1955* (UK) as to limitations on an investor's liability, and the *Mining Companies Act 1871* (Victoria) as to the no-liability audit company. The *Companies Act 1862* (UK) offered a framework for consolidating English corporate law, which Australia looked to in addressing its own diverse state-based statutes in the 1870s. By 1970, each state had enacted uniform company legislation that ultimately emerged in the form of Australia's *Corporations Act 1989* (Cth), which itself has been superseded by the *Corporations Act 2001*.

While there are many statutes and authorities in Australia, those that have the most significant influence on current audit practice include the following:

- *Corporations Act 2001* (Cth)
- Financial Reporting Council
- *Australian Securities and Investments Commission Act 2001 (ASIC Act)*
- *Corporate Law Economic Reform Program (Audit Reform & Corporate Disclosure) Act 2004 (CLERP 9 Act)*.
- Australian Prudential Regulation Authority.[1]

Each of these is outlined in the sections to follow.

---

[1] There are also relevant regulations related to these Acts.

Corporations Act 2001 (Cth) (*Corporations Act*)

The *Corporations Act 2001* (Cth) is an Act of the Commonwealth of Australia and is the principal legislation regulating companies at the federal and state levels. It sets out the laws dealing with business entities in Australia and regulates matters such as the formation and operation of companies. The *Corporations Act* is the primary basis of Australian corporations law and also regulates other entities, such as partnerships and managed investment schemes. Australian Auditing Standards are made under section 336 of this Act.

Financial Reporting Council (FRC)

The FRC is responsible for overseeing the effectiveness of the financial reporting framework in Australia. Its key functions include oversight of the accounting and auditing standards-setting processes for the public and private sectors. The FRC provides strategic advice as to the quality of audits conducted by Australian auditors, and advises the relevant minister on these and related matters to the extent that they affect the financial reporting framework in Australia.

The FRC also monitors the development of international accounting and auditing standards, and works to further the development and adoption of a single set of such standards for worldwide use. It is a statutory body under part 12 of the *Australian Securities and Investments Commission Act 2001*.

Specific accounting and auditing standard-setting functions for which the FRC is responsible include, among others, appointing the members of the AASB and AUASB (other than the chair); approving and monitoring the AASB and AUASB's: priorities; business plans; budgets; and staffing arrangements (including level, structure and composition of staffing); determining the AASB and AUASB's broad strategic directions (see **Figure 3.2**).

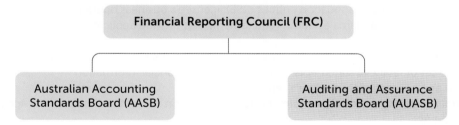

Figure 3.2 Australian accounting standard-setting

Under the strategic direction given to the AUASB by the FRC, the AUASB is required, inter alia, to develop auditing standards that have a clear public interest focus.

Australian Securities and Investments Commission Act 2001 (ASIC Act)

The FRC operates within a framework set out in the *Australian Securities and Investments Commission Act 2001*. This Act sets out core objectives for accounting and auditing standard-setting in Australia. ASIC regulates compliance with the financial reporting and auditing requirements for entities subject to the *Corporations Act* and, in some circumstances, provides relief from those requirements.

The AUASB is a non-corporate Commonwealth entity of the Australian Government established under section 227A of the *ASIC Act*, as amended. Under section 336 of the *Corporations Act*, the AUASB may make auditing standards for the purposes of the corporations legislation. These standards are legislative instruments under the *Legislation Act 2003*. ASIC and the *Corporations Act* have now replaced much of the previous corporate law statutes in Australia.

Corporate Law Economic Reform Program (Audit Reform & Corporate Disclosure) Act 2004 (CLERP 9 Act)

The *CLERP 9 Act* implemented recommendations made by the 2001 Ramsay Report into corporate and audit practice. It was a significant legislation, making compliance with the standards issued by the AUASB mandatory; it also strengthened audit independence. It was inspired by a series of major company failures, including HIH, the second-largest insurer in Australia, with costly effects on most sectors of Australian society (see Joint Committee of Public Accounts and Audit, 2002).

Australian Prudential Regulation Authority (APRA)

APRA is an independent statutory authority that supervises institutions across the banking, insurance and superannuation sectors, and promotes financial system stability in Australia. Australian financial services (AFS) licensees must also lodge financial statements under section 989B of the *Corporations Act*. Prudential Standard SPS 310 Audit and Related Matters sets out APRA's requirements in relation to the audit of registrable superannuation entities (RSE) licensee's business operations.

Australian Auditing Standards establish requirements and provide application and other explanatory material in regards to:

* the responsibilities of an auditor when engaged to undertake an audit of a financial report, or complete set of financial statements, or other historical financial information
* the form and content of the auditor's report.

In Australia, auditing standards are primarily found in section 336 of the *Corporations Act*, but some lie outside the Act.

Auditor and the client: Requirements in Australia

Although all companies should keep financial records to ensure they understand how their operations are faring, some types of companies need to keep these records for the purposes of preparing and lodging financial reports with ASIC. Generally, Australian public companies and selective other organisations (referred to as 'reporting entities') must prepare financial statements and submit (lodge) them with regulators where there are substantial sums of money involved, the general public has invested funds with the company, or the company exists for charitable purposes only and is not intended to make

a profit.[2] Section 292 of the *Corporations Act 2001* (Cth) requires the following entities to prepare financial reports:
- all disclosing entities
- public companies
- companies limited by guarantee (with exceptions)
- all large proprietary companies that are not disclosing entities
- all registered managed investment schemes
- small proprietary companies that are foreign-controlled
- small proprietary companies that have one or more crowd-sourced funding shareholders at any time during the year.

CONCEPT QUESTION 5	What are 'reporting entities'? Provide examples.

The following entities may also be required to prepare financial reports:
- small proprietary companies directed to prepare financial reports
- small proprietary companies that shareholders direct to prepare a financial report
- small companies limited by guarantee subject to a member direction (*Corporations Act*, section 294A). AFS licensees must also lodge financial statements under section 989B of the *Corporations Act*.

Financial reports prepared in accordance with the *Corporations Act* generally must comply with accounting standards (see section 296). Australian Accounting Standards now conform with International Financial Reporting Standards (IFRS) requirements, which Australia adopted in 2003. Section 601CK of the *Corporations Act* requires registered foreign companies to lodge balance sheets, profit-and-loss statements, cash-flow statements and other documents with ASIC.

Lodging requirements: Australia

Entities in Australia must lodge documents, reports or audit opinions based on whether certain conditions are met. What must be lodged or audited depends on the statutory requirement for each type of industry or business. General requirements can be found under *ASIC Act* sections 294, 295(1–4), 296(1), 298–300(A), 301 and 308. In most cases, and at a minimum, the following audited statements should be lodged:
- Statement of Financial Position
- Statement of Profit and Loss
- Statement of Cash Flows
- Statement of Changes in Equity
- Notes to the Financial Statement (e.g., see *Corporations Act*, section 60).
There may also need to be a **directors' declaration** that the financial statements:
- comply with accounting standards
- give a true and fair view
- show the firm will be able (on reasonable grounds) to pay its debts
- have been made in accordance with the *Corporations Act* (section 295(4))
The directors' report also includes the *auditor's independence declaration* (sections 298–300A), a somewhat unique requirement in Australian law.

directors' declaration
A declaration by the directors on the financial statements and the notes.

---

[2] If a company is a charity registered with the Australian Charities and Not-for-profits Commission (ACNC), then it must comply with the reporting requirements of the ACNC. Charities' annual reporting obligations are dependent on their size – small, medium or large. They fulfil these reporting obligations by submitting an annual information statement, as well as an annual financial report (if medium or large in size).

Statutory law: Applications in New Zealand

Companies legislation, again influenced by British legislation, was introduced in New Zealand in 1908, with major amendments occurring in 1955, 1993 and 2011. New Zealand does not have the separate 'state' problem experienced by Australia, so legislation was not complicated by state-based diversity. Following colonisation by the British in the 19th century, New Zealand developed a legal system based on English common law, but this was also influenced by developments in other countries, particularly the United States and those in the Commonwealth.

New Zealand's audit-related legislation reflects patterns found overseas, although distinctive New Zealand events were also influential. So, for example, the *Companies Act 1993* was a move to make directors more accountable following the financial crash of 1987–91, in which the New Zealand share market lost two-thirds of its value. Governing bodies are now expected to actively encourage ethical behaviour and better systems of internal control (Cordery, 2007) – and in good part, this is addressed via 'audit'.

Criminal and/or civil penalties may be imposed should statutory law requirements not be met. Those statutes that have had the most significant influence on audit practice include the following:[3]

- *The Companies Act 1993* (2013) (Cos Act)
- *The Financial Markets Conduct Act 2013* (FMCA)
- *Financial Markets Authority Act 2011* (FMA)
- *The Financial Reporting Act 2013* (FRA)
- *The Auditor Regulation Act 2011* (2014)(ARA)

Each of these is outlined in the sections to follow.

Companies Act 1993 (Cos Act)

The *Companies Act 1993*, and amendments such as part 11, and recent amendments to it (e.g., 2013), regulate New Zealand corporate entities, in particular those listed on the NZX. The *Cos Act* includes a number of sections relevant to financial audit. Some pertain to the client's governing board's obligations, and others to what the auditor must do. Together, the *Cos Act* and the *Financial Markets Conduct Act 2013* impose requirements on organisations that form the backbone of New Zealand's private-sector enterprises.

Financial Markets Conduct Act 2013 (FMCA)

The *Financial Markets Conduct Act 2013*, effective for periods beginning after April 2014, oversees a wide range of New Zealand organisations offering financial products and services, including, but not limited to, companies. This Act spreads audit requirements more widely, as it came about in response to problems that occurred when New Zealand business organisations – in particular private finance companies – could avoid a statutory audit by simply not forming as a 'company'. Businesses of public interest now organised as 'partnerships' or 'trusts', or using structures, can no longer avoid the public scrutiny provided by independent audit, as all *FMCA* reporting entities must make disclosures and be subjected to audit.

---

[3] There are also relevant regulations related to these Acts.

FMCA reporting entities include those with or presenting as:

- debt securities
- equity securities
- managed investment products and derivatives
- large NZX-listed companies
- trustee companies
- life insurance companies
- unit trusts
- banks
- non-bank deposit takers
- entities that service the finance industry
- Internal Affairs Department-regulated institutions (casinos, moneychangers, trusts and company service providers – see part 7 of the Act).

The *FMCA* thus regulates a wide range of organisations in New Zealand and adds to the requirements already in place for large New Zealand-listed companies.

Financial Markets Authority Act 2011 (*FMA Act*)

The *Financial Markets Authority Act 2011* created, among other things, the Financial Markets Authority (FMA), a government entity that reports to the Minister of Commerce. Its members have regulatory functions formerly delegated to the Securities Commission, the Companies Office and CA ANZ. The FMA's mandate is primarily to help identify illegal transactions such as money laundering, insider trading and securities transaction interests by directors and managers.

Of interest to auditors, the FMA is responsible for independent oversight of the accounting and auditing profession(s) in New Zealand. It is the government body that accredits professional institutes such as the CA ANZ. This is a role formerly held by the profession itself.

Financial Reporting Act 2013 (*FRA*)

The *Financial Reporting Act 2013* established the XRB, which promulgates accounting as well as auditing and assurance standards through two boards: the New Zealand Accounting Standards Board (NZASB) and the NZAuASB. The NZAuASB promulgates standards for audits and reviews (see **Figure 3.3**).

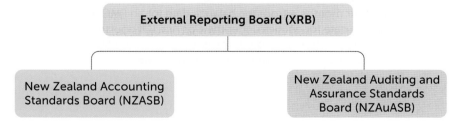

Figure 3.3 New Zealand accounting standard-setting

As per the *FRA*, auditing and assurance standards are required under the law. This gives auditors the authority to demand applicable accounting standards from clients (the auditees) and their governing boards.

Auditor Regulation Act 2011 (ARA)

The *Auditor Regulation Act 2011* recognises the standard-setting authority of the XRB and the authority of the FMA to license audit firms and register auditors. This bridges several pieces of legislation as to the role and authority of auditors and governing boards.

Auditor and the client: Requirements in New Zealand

The governing board obligations of, primarily, FMA-classified New Zealand entities are set out here. Most of the for-profit organisations requiring audit under statute fall under either *Companies* or *FMCA* legislation.

The auditors' clients (the organisations being audited) are also subject to statutory obligations, some of which are relevant to an audit. Specific audit-related requirements for them are set out in, for example:

- *Cos Act* (amended 2013)
- *FMCA* (for FMC reporting entities)
- *Partnership Act 1908* and *Limited Partnerships Act 2008*.

The client's governing body has responsibilities regarding how and when they file information, and how they engage with the independent financial statement auditor.

Lodging requirements: New Zealand

Under both the *Cos Act* (sections 194–211) and the *FMCA* (part 7) in regards to FMC reporting entities, governing boards must file financial reports and submit them for audit. These, together with the *FRA*, require governing boards to:

- keep accounting records from which the financial position can be determined
- ensure compliance with the *FRA*
- provide explanations and information to the auditor
- ensure compliance with applicable financial reporting standards (i.e., GAAP)
- produce and maintain auditable records[4]
- ensure they employ qualified auditors and audit firms (*FRA*, section 36F).

Financial statements must be completed, and audited statements *must be filed*, within three months plus 20 days – essentially four months – from the balance date for an FMC reporting entity, and within five months from the balance date for entities under the *Cos Act*. (Of course, many of these companies are also FMC reporting entities, so the audited returns would have to be filed within the four months.) Reporting, filing and audit requirements are summarised in **Table 3.5.**

---

[4] For example, see the *Cos Act*, section 194, and the *FRA*, sections 38–39. Smaller entities (with revenue less than NZ$30 million or assets less than NZ$60 million) can use a reporting framework which is not compliant with GAAP. Registered charities, however, must prepare reports in accordance with GAAP if payments equal or exceed NZ$40 000 and must be audited by a qualified auditor if expenses are at or exceed NZ$500 000, under *Charities Act* provisions amended from April 2014.

Table 3.5 Audit and financial reporting requirements

Organisation type	Statute	Filing required?*	Audit required?
FMC reporting entities	*FMCA*	Yes, within 3 months + 20 days	Yes
Companies (large)	*Cos Act*; *FRA*, s 45	Yes, within 5 months of balance date	Yes (unless 95% of shareholders opt out)
Subsidiaries/businesses of overseas companies	*FRA*, s 45; *Cos Act*	Yes, within 5 months of the balance date	Yes
SMEs (> 9 shareholders)	*Cos Act*, s 201	Yes (unless 95% of shareholders opt out)	Yes (s 206; unless 95% opt out)
SMEs (<10 shareholders)	*Cos Act*, s 201	No (unless 5% of shareholders opt in)	No (unless 5% of shareholders opt in)

* Tax reporting or filing requirements not considered here.

Study tools

Summary

Statutory law regulates auditors, and governing boards, in circumstances where an unfettered market may otherwise fail to serve company shareholders or other stakeholders. Statutory law mandates conditions that auditors, and audit firms, must meet in order to conduct statutory audits. The statutes also regulate certain ethical behaviours and impose expectations on professional associations. They set out some means of communication between the auditor and shareholders.

The client's governing body is also, to some extent, regulated in Australian and New Zealand statutes. Essentially, it is their responsibility to provide information in a timely manner, using acceptable systems and reporting standards. In some circumstances, clients must also form an audit committee which enhances communications with the auditor. ISAs now form the basis for statute-mandated auditing standards in Australia, New Zealand and some other Pacific-rim nations such as Fiji and Malaysia.

🔗 Case/resources link

CAATs for Classrooms

Accompanying this book is a series of data, integrated worksheets and exercises that are designed to support your learning and give you exposure to hands-on audit decision-making dilemmas faced by auditors in the planning elements of the audit process. Acquire the relevant material for this chapter from your instructor.

Review questions

3.1   Name the relevant statutes affecting Australian/New Zealand audit.

3.2   For each of the statutes named, describe the general purpose.

3.3   What is the standard-setting body for Australian/NZ assurance services?

3.4   What determines the organisational form which audit companies may take?

3.5   Who regulates non-assurance professional services?

3.6   For what types of organisations is audit required in Australia/NZ? Under what conditions?

3.7   To conduct an audit of a reporting entity, what requirements must the auditor meet?

3.8   How is an auditor selected? What is the process?

3.9   How can the auditor be removed from performing an audit for a client?

3.10   There are certain roles which the statutory auditor must avoid under the statute. Name four.

3.11   Why is it useful to have an audit committee should you have concerns that senior management is committing fraud?

Exercises

3.1   **STANDARDS:** The local audit professional association is accustomed to setting standards for New Zealand auditors. The firm's founding partner, who has been conducting audits since 2005, says there is no need to change to the new standards. The prior standards are adequate as they allow more flexibility, and the audit firm can make more of their decisions using them.

    a   Identify why the audit partner should not be doing this, and why.

    b   Consider why the audit partner may be justified in this view, even though it may not be acceptable.

    c   Explain to the audit partner the difference between standard-setting bodies authorised by the (sole) professional association and those now set by the XRB. Identify the implications of failing to follow both.

3.2   **STANDARDS AND STATUTE:** The client, a small partnership, wishes you to perform a review engagement of their financial statements for the year ended 30 June 2021. They want the review because the bank from whom they wish to borrow will accept a review, and you have advised them to proceed.

    a   What responsibilities do you, the assurance professional, have under the statute for such an engagement?

    b   What standards should be followed?

    c   What codes should be followed?

    d   What is the role of financial reporting regulators and the professional association with respect to such an engagement?

3.3 **STANDARDS AND STATUTE:** What if the partnership client in Exercise 3.2 wanted a compilation of the financial statements rather than a review? What would change? Why and how?

3.4 **REPORTING:** The financial statement audit for your client for the year ended 30 June 2021 is almost complete. However, on contacting their legal adviser to obtain information about the client's potential liabilities in late August, you find out that the adviser has just gone on holiday for the next three months. What are the implications, and what should you as the auditor do?

3.5 **AUDITOR:** A professional firm conducting a statutory audit is 'registered'. However, the usual partner in charge is unwell and has asked you to conduct the audit. While the partner in charge is 'qualified', you have not yet achieved your qualifications. It is a medium-sized audit firm, and an important client. What should you do, and why?

3.6 **AUDITOR REMOVAL:** Consider what would occur, under Australian and New Zealand laws and regulations, in the following situations:

    a   Directors recommend to their shareholders that an auditor be removed.

    b   An auditor has performed the same engagement year after year for the last decade.

    c   A professional company has decided to withdraw from statutory financial statement audit work.

3.7 **AUDITOR REMOVAL:** Despite an auditor's representations, shareholders pass a resolution to remove them and replace them with a new company. What actions should the departing auditor take? What actions should the new auditor take? Why?

3.8 **STATUTE AND THEORY:** In terms of economic and social accountability theories, provide separate explanations as to why it may be important to impose an audit under the statute. Be specific.

3.9 **AUDITOR LIABILITY:** Your senior partner has decided to incorporate the company under new legislation. What should the partner investigate, and how, before they make any assumptions about whether the resulting company can continue to perform statutory audits. What might they need to have or know?

3.10 **AUDITOR LIABILITY:** Select one or two major companies in Australia/New Zealand and determine, from their websites, the form of business they currently employ for audit. What are the implications of their choices for auditor liability and obligations?

3.11 **CONFIDENTIALITY:** How is the auditor's responsibility to retain the confidentiality of the client and their information challenged in statutory law? Should you discover a situation found in the statute which requires the disclosure of client information to a regulatory authority, how would you go about communicating and carrying out this process?

4 | Auditor professionalism and audit firms

Learning objectives

....

After studying the material in this chapter, you should be able to:
- identify key events in the history of the audit profession
- explain requirements of the code of ethics for assurance services, and their relationship to fundamental principles
- distinguish between internal quality control and the peer review of audit firms
- identify the means by which a firm can manage its accountability exposure through its legal and other forms.

Introduction

This chapter considers how accounting and auditing professions evolved and what that means for practice today. We identify the fundamental ethical principles involved and describe the behaviours and practices expected of assurance providers. We consider why ethics is important to clients, to society and to the profession. Independence 'risks' are set out, as are the means by which they can be mitigated, including the process of peer review and quality management. The legal structures and protections by which professional firms can form conclude the chapter.

History of auditing profession

The professionalism of auditing and accounting is a relatively recent event, being less than 175 years old, even though auditing has itself existed for longer. It is usually professionalism that distinguishes the principled expert from the trade technician, and this distinction is essential in the audit profession. To professionalise a group with trade skills, such as financial auditors, implies that its members also have shared values, ethical boundaries and a real commitment to do their best. A professional may also be expected to act for greater public good and to do what is 'right', even if doing so is not always easy.

To demonstrate professionalism, the following characteristics will need to be shown to exist in an association. Its members should:
- enjoy a particular range of *technical skills*, such as in accounting and systems
- establish and maintain *ethical standards*
- demonstrate high *standards of entry* and for continuing membership

- establish performance standards and procedures that *serve the public good*
- be subject to a process by which those who have failed to maintain professional standards are *disciplined*. They may be issued fines, the infraction may be published (such as in CA ANZ's *Acuity* magazine or CPA Australia's *In The Black*), or they may have their licence to practise retracted.

The legitimacy of accounting and auditing professional associations has been challenged at times. This has tended to occur when audited organisations fail, or when it is discovered that practitioners have not adhered to ethical standards – as described by Pasewark, Shockley and Wilkerson (1995, p. 77):

> Current events and circumstances are symptomatic of a legitimation crisis facing the auditing profession – the profession has violated, or is perceived to have violated this code. This study's results suggest that in-charge auditors, when confronted with 'powerful' client employees, will, with some likelihood, compromise the profession's objectivity claim.

Ethical behaviour is crucial to the credibility, and even to the continued existence, of professional associations. Essentially, if we cannot trust the professional to do their job and behave ethically, we cannot rely on them to give an informed, fair and honest audit opinion.

Audit litigation occurring through the courts (see Chapter 5) reveals several situations where an audit failure made its way before a judge and into the public arena. Other damaging situations have occurred when a member disappoints in their private life. The public furore over the misappropriation of funds by a former New Zealand auditor-general in the 1990s is an example of what a professional association does not want to see. Negative publicity is of great concern to the accounting and auditing profession as it can harm many: the clients, users and accountees, professions and professional members. Fortunately, most are seen to serve a higher purpose most of the time (Van Peursem and Hauriasi, 1999).

CONCEPT QUESTION 1	What are the 'characteristics' of a professional association?

The following traces how professionalism developed in audit (and accounting) in developed countries and how the profession's members have, and attempt to demonstrate, the ethical practices expected of them.

Professional history

The first accounting profession was established in Scotland in 1854, followed by professional formation in the United States (1887), New Zealand (1894), Australia (1885 in Adelaide, incorporating in 1907) and Canada (1902). The ICAEW grew from the merger of three separate associations in 1951. Auditing was always a major, if not the defining, activity of professional accounting. Legislative requirement made it even more so.

Australian company legislation drew from England's *Companies Act 1862*. As in Britain, the Australian statutes of 1864 (Victoria), *Companies Act 1862* (South Australia) and *Companies Act 1874* (New South Wales) were passed with no audit requirements. The *Companies Act 1896* (Victoria), however, did distinguish between public companies and proprietary companies, and it required, in respect of public companies, compulsory audit. Also as in Britain, auditors were initially laypeople such as shareholders. The Australian Office of the Auditor-General was created by legislation in 1901 and provides for the conduct of a range of audit functions across the Australian Government sector.

In New Zealand, the initial *Companies Act* (1860) also failed to require audit. However, this too changed due to the influence of the UK companies legislation.

Early professional associations were important in regulating and monitoring those who were to perform audit on what were now large industrial organisations. The Incorporated institutes of accountants (1886 in Victoria, 1894 in New Zealand) were the first of these.

Australia has multiple professional associations that are recognised in the national legislation:

- Chartered Accountants Australia and New Zealand (CA ANZ)
- CPA Australia (not associated with the US AICPA)
- Institute of Public Accountants (IPA).

CA ANZ was formed with the 2014 merger of the Institute of Chartered Accountants Australia (formed in 1920) and the New Zealand Institute of Chartered Accountants (NZICA). By 1982, the Institute of Chartered Accountants Australia, which was originally called the Commonwealth Institute of Accountants, offered workplace-oriented entry exams for graduates of accredited university courses. In 1947, a merger resulted in the Australian Society of Accountants (ASA), which in 1990 became the Australian Society of Certified Practising Accountants (ASCPA), and in 2000 CPA Australia. The IPA (formerly the National Institute of Accountants), which first formed in 1923, constitutes a third recognised Australian professional society.

By 1908, New Zealand professional associations had combined into a single professional body, as established by the *New Zealand Society of Accountants Act*, and in 2014 it combined with CA ANZ. Together with CPA Australia, CA ANZ is a recognised professional association in New Zealand. A profession's recognition is important because its qualified members are permitted to conduct statutory audits.

Court cases indicate that, by 1920, auditing had developed as a discipline and required the technical skills of qualified accountants and the ethical status of professionalism. By the 1930s, academic degrees specialising in accounting and auditing had been incorporated into US university curricula. This led to a growth in research in accounting and auditing, and it lent a professional 'status' to the profession's associations. Australian and New Zealand universities then introduced qualifications as well. By the 1970s, the profession's role in audit standard-setting and performance was well established.

Professions' roles in standard-setting

Until recently, professional associations produced *and* approved all auditing standards and ethical codes. This changed, however, in response to growing public concern that those performing an audit should be independent from those creating the relevant standards. The Australian *Corporations Act 2001* requires auditors to provide an 'independence declaration' with the audit report, and reform under the *Corporate Law Economic Reform Program Act 2004* followed on the heels of various corporate scandals.

As a result, in Australia, audit standard-setting authority now rests with the AUASB; in New Zealand, it lies with the NZAuASB. A similar pattern has occurred regarding professional ethical codes. Codes produced by professional associations – such as CA ANZ, CPA Australia and the IPA – must now be compatible with Australia's Accounting Professional & Ethical Standards Board (APESB) or New Zealand's NZAuASB. ASIC monitors compliance standards.

The APESB was formed in 2006 from a combination of professional associations. The board issues ethical and professional standards, some of which are enforceable in law where they are part of auditing standards, such as the APES 110: Code of Ethics for Professional Accountants.

Standards and codes in Australia and New Zealand draw heavily from international codes, specifically IFAC and its International Ethics Standards Board for Accountants (IESBA). As a result, guidance for professional and assurance practice is less country-specific and further removed from the practitioners who perform this practice.

Professional members, whether they conduct assurance services or not, must still comply with the codes and standards of their professional association. Associations such as CA ANZ, CPA Australia and IPA set standards for non-assurance engagements (e.g., compilations, budget preparation, system developments). In a non-assurance engagement, the practitioner can be wholly guided by their professional standards and whatever contractual agreements have been reached with the client. But in an assurance service (audit or review), due to the greater public responsibility involved, legislated requirements of the APESB and NZAuASB are imposed primarily in regard to issues of 'independence' (see **Figure 4.1**).

| If offering a non-assurance service, follow your professional association's code | + | ... but if it is *also* an assurance service ... | = | ... then also follow APESB (Australia) or NZAuASB (NZ) ethical standards and codes |

Figure 4.1 Ethical standards for professional services

This is also illustrated in the next section in **Table 4.1**, where part IV applies specifically to assurance services and are in addition to those required of professional engagements generally.

As other professional associations start to receive approval to conduct Australian or New Zealand statutory audits, a competitive environment among these organisations emerged (Mataira and Van Peursem, 2010). Professional associations have their own as well as public interests, and independent standard-setting is seen to reduce some of the negative impacts of this.

CONCEPT QUESTION 2 How does the concept of 'independence' apply to the oversight of professional associations?

Code of ethics for assurance services

Acting ethically can be described as doing 'good' or 'right' (Velasquez, 1988, p. 1). A person's ethical character is tested when faced with a choice of whether or not to do the 'right' thing when doing so could result in personal loss. Everyone has to make such decisions throughout their lives, but in the case of professionals, these decisions take on an added dimension because professionals are put in a position of trust.

You'll recall from the conceptual framework for audit that applying ethics (an audit concept) is fundamental to the auditor's work. Where the auditor exhibits *competency*, *judgement*, *integrity* and *independence*, their opinion has social and economic value. The concepts of 'independence' and 'confidentiality' are commonly represented in professional codes. In recent years, a particular emphasis has been placed on what are considered to be the five 'fundamental ethical principles'. As derived from APES 110 (para 110.1 A1), they are:

- *Integrity* – referring to personal characteristics such as honesty and straightforwardness;
- *Objectivity* – not to allow bias or conflicts of interest to compromise professional decisions;
- *Professional Competence and Due Care* – referring to having and maintaining an appropriate body of professional knowledge and skill; and to act 'diligently' (with 'due care') in accordance with professional standards;
- *Confidentiality* – to respect the confidentiality of information acquired as a result of professional and business relationships;
- *Professional Behaviour* – to comply with law and to act in a way that does not discredit the profession.[1]

These fundamental principles were developed by the International Ethics Standards Board for Accountants (IESBA) and adopted in the Australian and New Zealand codes.

---

[1] All APES references in chapter are reproduced with the permission of the copyright owner, Accounting Professional & Ethical Standards Board Limited (APESB), Australia.

CONCEPT QUESTION 3	Why are ethics important for auditors?

We believe that 'due care' and 'professional competence' encompass two different ideas ('taking care' and 'competence'). Also, there are – albeit rare – exceptions to the 'confidentiality' requirement, some of which are discussed later in this chapter. Finally, we suggest that the principle of 'professional behaviour' may have a self-serving as well as a social benefit. Nonetheless, these principles generally make sense and are used extensively to explain professional ethical standards for assurance practitioners (see **Table 4.1**).

Table 4.1 Ethical code structures for assurance services

Australia: APESB's APES 110 Code of Ethics for Professional Accountants	New Zealand: XRB's PES 1 Code of Ethics for Assurance Practitioners (in parentheses)
Part I: Complying with the Code, Fundamental Principles and Conceptual Framework Part II: Members in Business (Professional Accountants in Business) Part III: Members in Public Practice (Application of the Code ...) Part IV: Independence Standards (International), parts 4A and 4B	

1   *Part IV (4A): Independence Standards (Int'l), para 400–79, for Audit & Review Engagements*
2   Fees (and contingent fees)
3   Compensation & evaluation (performing non-assurance services to clients)
4   Gifts & hospitality
5   Actual or threatened litigation
6   Financial interests
7   Loans & guarantees
8   Business relationships
9   Family & personal relationships
10 Recent services with an audit client
11 Services as director or officer of an audit client
12 Employment with an audit client
13 Temporary personnel assignments (Aus)
14 Long association with an audit client (including rotation)
15 Provision of non assurance services (including accounting, bookkeeping, administration, valuation, tax, internal audit, information technology, litigation support, legal, recruiting, corporate finance)
16 Reports on special purpose financial services that include a restriction on use and distribution (audit and review engagements), para 800–899
17 *Part IV (4B) Independence for Assurance Engagements Other than Audit & Review*

Portions mandatory for public interest entities. Parts 4A and 4B in Australia and New Zealand are largely consistent with ISA standards. Codes, or portions of them, are current at date of publication. Elements may be effective on different dates due to transition rules (none later than 2022). Refer to https://apesb.org.au or https://www.xrb.govt.nz for current standards and details.

Sources: APESB (2018); XRB (2021).

In Australia, the AUASB has issued ASA 102: Compliance with Ethical Requirements when Performing Audits, Reviews and Other Assurance Engagements. The following identifies particular issues of concern raised in these standards for assurance services, and sets out how they are addressed.

Independence

Someone approaching a project with an independent mind would not be inclined towards one outcome or another, but would make their decisions solely based on the facts of the situation. Independence is sometimes described as the cornerstone of auditing because, without it, the audit report lacks authority and consequently value (Flint, 1988, p. 54).

This idea is not new: the AICPA (1950, p. 25) described independence as the 'foundation of the public accounting profession'. Even today, associations are establishing separate regulatory bodies whose only purpose is to ensure audit independence; for example, the Public Company Accounting Oversight Board (PCAOB) created by the US Securities and Exchange Commission (SEC), and the Joint Monitoring Unit in the United Kingdom. Indeed, independence is so fundamental that external auditors are also known as independent auditors – it has always been recognised as a fundamental concept of audit.

Independence: Actual and appearance

> No major firm escapes the net. The individual professional determines his or her own personal reputation; the appearance of firm-sanctioned or widely practiced unethical activity determines the reputation and status of the profession. (Pasewark, Shockley and Wilkerson, 1995)

The auditors' ethical standards and strength of character are determinants of whether they can maintain an independent state of mind. This idea is conveyed in APES 110: Code of Ethics for Professional Accountants (including Independent Standards) (para 400.5), p. 109.

Barriers to performing ethically may inhibit compliance, however. Professional scepticism plays a role in meeting ethical standards as well.

Professional scepticism

Professional scepticism is expected of auditors under professional ethical standards and codes pertaining to assurance services.

Both the UK Audit Inspection Unit (AIU) and the US PCAOB 'cited a lack of professional scepticism as a serious problem for auditors' (Murray, 2012, p. 37). There may be unintended influences on the auditor which place their professional scepticism skills at risk (see **Figure 4.2**).

Independence is linked to the principles of objectivity and integrity. It comprises, as noted in APES 110 (para 400.5):

> (a) Independence of mind – the state of mind that permits the expression of a conclusion without being affected by influences that compromise professional judgement, thereby allowing an individual to act with integrity, and exercise objectivity and professional scepticism.
> (b) Independence in appearance – the avoidance of facts and circumstances that are so significant that a reasonable and informed third party would be likely to conclude that a Firm's, or an Audit or Assurance Team member's integrity, objectivity or professional scepticism has been compromised.

If the public perceives, erroneously or not, that auditors go unpunished for unethical acts, then all members, and the credibility of the profession as a whole, is threatened.

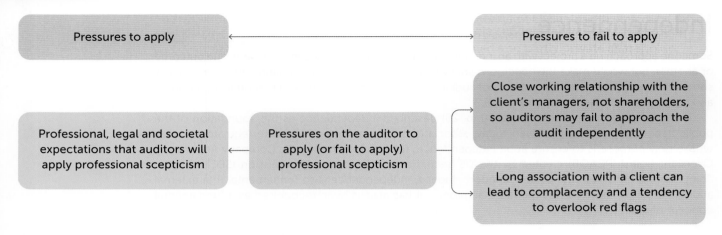

Figure 4.2 Professional scepticism: Pressures and influences

Source: Derived from Murray (2012, pp. 36–9).

Auditing in practice

Ethical scandals

These have long been serious concerns about auditors' ethics. This has been indicated by a number of widely publicised scandals, including those documented in an SEC PricewaterhouseCoopers report that revealed more than 8000 violations of existing ethical rules, including violations by more than 1300 partners who reported an average of five violations each (Cox, 2000).

Threats to independence

The preparer of the financial (or other) statements (the client) may have an interest in how the financial position and operations are being portrayed. Although their task is to create financial statements in accordance with GAAP, managers in an agency risk the anger of their shareholders if the statements show poor outcomes. Consequently, they may tend to present this information in a way that highlights (or exaggerates) their accomplishments.

Directors may also have reason to distort financial outcomes. For example, should they wish to attract buyers with their asset base or seek to raise funds from a share issue, they have an incentive to manipulate the content of the financial statements.

The conflict that results places the auditor in an uncomfortable position between those who pay their fee (the client) and those who benefit from their services (the public, suppliers, consumers, shareholders, employees and others). The auditor is expected to resist self-serving temptations and remain independent of their client.

ISA-inspired classifications of what comprises a threat to the independence of the auditor are set out in **Table 4.2**.

There are many situations that create threats. More examples can be found in the standards themselves: APES 110 (Australia) and PES 1 (New Zealand). Nonetheless, there are said to be acceptable **safeguards** that, if applied, provide an acceptable response.

safeguards
Actions, taken individually or in combination, that effectively reduce threats to compliance with the fundamental principles to an acceptable level. (APES 110, para 100.2(c))

Table 4.2 Threats to independence

Threat	Example(s)
Self-interest threat	A firm or someone working on the assurance team benefits from a financial interest in the client A firm or partner is in a position to be personally, or financially, at risk should they lose an assurance client
Self-review threat	When a member of the audit team or the firm: 1 is involved in an assurance engagement on material or claims they had a part in producing 2 produced the system on which the information being audited was created 3 exerted influence over the subject matter under review
Advocacy threat	If a member of the audit team becomes an advocate for or against an audit client's position in a court of law
Familiarity threat	Because of a relationship or long association with an audit client, an audit team member becomes sympathetic to their interests Having conducted the audit for many years, the auditor is complacent about gathering sufficient evidence to support their opinion
Intimidation threat	An audit team member may be threatened in litigation by a client, or with dismissal There is untoward pressure to reduce fees or audit quality

They fall into two broad categories: (a) safeguards created by the assurance practitioner's profession, legislation or regulation; and (b) safeguards within the firm's own systems and procedures (PES 1, para 100.13). Irrespective, their application is said to eliminate, or mitigate, the threats to independence that might otherwise occur. They are designed to help ensure the auditor both acts and appears to act in a manner in which they retain their objectivity and independence from the client. Examples of 'safeguards' might include:

- procedures, systems and complaint mechanisms established so that the professional is guided towards reporting, and expected to report, ethical concerns as appropriate to senior members within the firm
- a clear separation of the departments that perform assurance from those providing management advisory services – this will not address all circumstances related to the threat of 'self-review' or 'self-interest', but it may reduce some concerns with 'familiarity'
- rules created by legislation, regulation, the profession or firm to guard against such risks.

There are some situations for which no safeguard can provide sufficient protection, some of which are discussed later in this chapter. Under various guises, much of the ethical codes are to do with trying to ensure that the assurance professional takes an independent and unbiased approach to their work, and that they appear to do so as well.

CONCEPT QUESTION	4	What does it mean to have 'threats to independence'?

Financial interests and conflicts

Conflicts that can emerge from the auditor having **financial interests** in the client are a central audit independence concern.

financial interest
A situation in which there is a financial interest between the auditor or audit firm and the client's organisation, other than the current fee for the audit engagement.

Auditors initially have a financial interest in the client by virtue of being paid by the client for the audit. They can also have financial interests through having invested in the client's shares, through loans and loan guarantees, or through other means.

The problem with relying on their clients for revenue is that auditors provide a service not only for the client organisation but for the users of its financial statements. This leads to what Goldman and Barlev (1974) call the 'auditor–client conflict'. Because the auditor will almost certainly want to retain the client in the future, the audit client has coercive power over the auditor by, for example, threatening not to re-engage the auditor. Even if the audit client has not expressed such a threat, the possibility of a change of auditor may be in the auditor's mind, and this could sway their judgement.

The nature of the auditor–client relationship clearly gives the client the opportunity to influence the auditor's judgement – a situation that gives the public ample reason to doubt the independence of the auditor.

The extent to which a financial matter is seen to be significant, or *material*, is essentially left to the auditor's judgement. Aspects of financial interest commonly addressed by professional codes include fee dependence, lowballing, fee determination, auditor rotation and management advisory services.

Fee dependence and lowballing

fee dependence
If the fees from one audit client make up a large proportion of an audit firm's revenue, then that audit firm may have – or may be seen to have – a vested interest in the outcome of the audit.

lowballing
Occurs where the audit contract price is cut to such an extent that the fees received are less than the costs incurred by the professional. Auditors are willing to do this because they expect to earn 'quasi-rents' (lower costs resulting from auditing a previously audited client) by keeping the engagement for a number of years. In addition, they may anticipate lucrative consultancy projects as a spin-off from the audit.

Any significant **fee dependence** on the client is a risk to the auditor's independence and to the appearance of their independence.

While Australia and New Zealand do not set a revenue amount or proportion at which independence would be seen to be impaired, other jurisdictions have done so. UK standards, for example, recommend that such proportions should not exceed 15 per cent of revenue. New Zealand prescriptions leave the decision to professional members, stating that they should not have 'undue dependence' (section 200.4), but that it is 'impracticable to define and prescribe all situations' (section 120.2) that the professional may encounter.

One way for a firm to attract clients is to reduce its audit fees for a new client to secure the engagement. An extreme form of this price-cutting is known as **lowballing**.

Lowballing, while difficult to measure, does appear to exist in practice (Beattie and Fearnley, 1998) and reflects a form of neoclassical economic (competitive) theory. Lowballing results in a potential loss of independence because the auditor is essentially committed to keeping the client. If the client takes an unethical stand, or places unwarranted pressure on the professional to comply with their interests, the lowballing professional may be dependent on their fees. This could cause them to be reluctant to withdraw from the engagement if, in other circumstances, they should do so. This is a potentially serious threat to the auditor's independence.

When a client has failed to pay fees for the professional service they have received, or are consistently late in settling their bill, a fee dependence situation can be inadvertently created. Generally, a firm should have collection policies and follow up promptly on late payers, as they would normally be motivated to do. In some circumstances, however, the client can owe so much that the professional comes to have a financial interest in ensuring that the business continues until their debt is settled. The situation can lead to either an 'intimidative' and/or 'self-interest' risk; irrespective, it can create an unintended fee dependence situation.

Contingent fees

Contingent fees refer to the practice of receiving fees that are 'contingent' on the nature of the outcome of the engagement. The concern with contingent fees is that, should the auditor's remuneration be dependent on the opinion type, then the auditor would be inclined to give an 'unqualified' opinion because they would be financially rewarded for doing so. PES 1 makes it clear that 'professional fees must be a fair reflection of the value of the professional services performed for the client' (para 240). For assurance services such as audit, this code makes it clear that there is nothing the auditor can do to safeguard against the independence threat that contingent fees introduce. It is not allowed for assurance services (APES 110, para R410.9; PES 1, para 240.9).

Commissions

A related concern is the potential for professional members to receive commissions for having carried out particular services. *Commissions* refer to the practice of receiving fees for referring clients to other service providers or the like.

For example – and of particular concern – is the idea that the professional refers a client to someone in another industry and receives a commission from that person for doing so. Independence, or its appearance, could be impaired if the client assumes that the professional's advice is unbiased when in reality the professional is acting in their own self-interest. Commissions, as with contingent fees, are unacceptable for assurance services *(APES 110, para AUST R330.5.2; PES 1, para 240.9).*

However, for non-assurance services, commissions may be possible depending on the circumstances. According to APES 110 (para AUST R330.5.1), a member in public practice who is undertaking an engagement in Australia and receives a referral fee or commission shall inform the client in writing of:

- the existence of such arrangement;
- the identity of the other party or parties; and
- the method of calculation of the referral fee, commission or other benefit accruing directly or indirectly to the Member.

This reinforces that providers of assurance services are held to stricter standards.

Incompatible services

Should the professional auditor also offer their services in another capacity, there is the risk that these roles could be incompatible. There are roles that auditors are prohibited from undertaking for their audit clients.[2] It is conceivable that, should the auditor engage in speculative business finance arrangements, or in illegal enterprises, damage to the reputation of the profession could result. APES 110 (para R115.1) refers to the fact that

> A Member shall not knowingly engage in any business, occupation or activity that impairs or might impair the integrity, objectivity or good reputation of the profession, and as a result would be incompatible with the fundamental principles.

What this might be is left to the judgement of the auditor, although they would be wise to be informed of court precedent in this matter (e.g., *Dyck v. Roulston* [1997], a British Columbia, Canada case in which the professional was also a financial adviser).

Auditor rotation

Rotation offers a safeguard to the concern that arises if the auditor audits the same client year after year. 'Familiarity' or 'self-interest' threats to independence can result with respect to a client with whom the auditor becomes close. Audit rotation can apply to the firm as a whole or to rotation of the lead auditor (partner) within a firm. Both Australia and New Zealand have adopted the International Code of Ethics for Professional Accountants (including International Independence Standards). The PES 1 is the standard

---

[2] Refer to https://apesb.org.au/wp-content/uploads/2020/08/APES_110_Prohibitions_Audit_Clients_12_Aug_2020.pdf for details of current prohibitions (APES 110 Code Prohibitions applicable to Auditors for all Audit and Review Engagements).

issued in New Zealand. The Australian equivalent is APES 110 and includes auditor rotation requirements for public interest entities. This complements existing companies legislation and listing requirements in both countries. In summary, by 2023, for Public Interest Entities (PIEs) engagement partners must be rotated after a time for a period of seven years in New Zealand (5 years for Australia), with a 'cooling off' period of at least five years. The Engagement Quality Control Review (EQCR) can have a three year cooling-off period. Other key audit partners have a 2 year cooling-off period. The other key audit partner can also have a 7 year time on period.[3] Rotation can be costly, as it is expensive to give up the knowledge acquired over years of working with a client (Jackson, Moldrich and Roebuck, 2008).

Australia and New Zealand are moving towards stricter requirements for audit partner involvement and further changes are possible. Audit firm rotation is not currently required, but consideration is encouraged of changing auditor firms at least every 10 years.

Management advisory services (MAS)

One of the most controversial issues to do with auditor independence is whether an auditor, or the auditor's firm, should be allowed to conduct other types of services for their assurance client. These non-assurance services are generically referred to as **management advisory services** or MAS.

There are many types of MAS, ranging from the compilation of records to systems analysis, to design and fraud investigations. It may be that the client asks the audit firm to conduct the audit *and*, given their familiarity with the accounts, design a payroll accounting system for them as well. Should they do it?

Conducting MAS along with the audit is a potential independence threat because the auditor could have an interest in maintaining or supporting that client's business. That is, conducting both MAS and the audit can result in an 'advocacy', 'self-interest' or 'self-review' threat to the auditor's independence.

Non-assurance services (NAS) provide significant revenue to audit firms, however, professionals are reluctant to give them up. Research on the matter indicates that independence may be retained by the firm if certain restrictions are put in place, but that the *appearance* of independence can still suffer. This leaves the auditor in somewhat of a dilemma as to whether, or when, to agree to provide NAS.[4]

Standard-setters have also been reluctant to forbid NAS, but most place restrictions on their nature. The ICAEW and the PCAOB require disclosure of non-audit work, an increased role for audit committees, and strict limitations on what NAS the auditor can provide.

In Australia, APESB has put restrictions on providing non-assurance services to their audit clients. Firms and Network Firms might provide a range of non-assurance services to their audit clients, consistent with their skills and expertise. Providing non-assurance services to audit clients might create threats to compliance with the fundamental principles and threats to Independence (APES 110, para 600.2). Guidance is provided in broad terms accompanied by lists of examples (APES 110, para R600.8):[5]

> To avoid assuming a management responsibility when providing any non-assurance service to an Audit Client, the Firm shall be satisfied that client management makes all judgements and decisions that are the proper responsibility of management.

Management responsibilities may involve any or all of the following (APES 110, para 600.7 A1):

> … controlling, leading and directing an entity, including making decisions regarding the acquisition, deployment and control of human, financial, technological, physical and intangible resources.

management advisory services (MAS)
Refers to the practice of performing non-assurance services for an assurance client.

---

[3] Refer to https://apesb.org.au/wp-content/uploads/2021/01/APESB_Audit_Partner_Rotation_QAs_Nov_2019_web.pdf for further details on the rotation requirements in Australia.

[4] APESB have recently issued and exposure draft which proposes revisions to the NAS provisions in the Code. The changes are expected to come into effect from 1 July 2023.

[5] New Zealand has long required the disclosure of 'other services' performed by the auditor. The code and standards on the issue are the same as cited for Australia.

So, it may be possible to put safeguards in place to reduce independence risks. Audit firms may have 'internal walls', they may conduct regular internal reviews of contracts and services provided to assurance clients, or they may advise clients to simply use another firm.

Audit firms usually benefit from providing NAS for audit clients; after all, the additional fees are tempting and the auditor already knows information about the client that helps them provide a better service. And from the client's point of view, the auditor is in an excellent position to provide advice.

A critical view, however, would have it that standards leave too much to professional judgement, particularly as commercial pressures on auditors are so great. Zeff (1988) claims that, where this occurs, it leads to a consulting mentality rather than an independent, professionally sceptical mentality. On our part, we believe that auditors should be free to provide NAS. However, in order to enhance independence, it would be best if these services were not provided to audit clients.

Personal relationships and conflicts

Personal relationships between audit firms and client firm members can also cause independence problems, either in fact or in appearance, due to 'familiarity' or 'self-interest' threat. It is, after all, unreasonable to expect an auditor to be unbiased when investigating reports prepared by a spouse, parent or former partner.

In addition, if the public finds out about the relationship, the appearance of independence is damaged. One of the catalysts for forming a separate independence body in Australia was the questionable practice of placing former audit firm partners on company boards (Ravlic, 2001).

In Australia, under 'Prohibited Interests, Relationships and Actions', the APESB prohibits the participation of an auditor in an audit team if an immediate family member (spouse – or equivalent – or dependant) is, or was, during the engagement period, a director or officer of the client or an employee able to exert significant influence over accounting records or financial statements of the client.

The New Zealand code identifies the threat of 'family and personal relationships' and offers a harder line when it comes to those issues already restricted under statute: disallowing such parties to be a director, officer or employee of their audit client (see PES 1, paras 290, 126–127). While exceptions are allowed, again, most audit firms will have a strict policy that prevents those working on an assurance engagement from having close involvement with the client.

Confidentiality

The auditor cannot, and should not, conduct the audit unless they have full access to information held by and about the client. Yet much of that is 'private' and potentially commercially sensitive. Moreover, if the client does not trust the professional with their information, they are unlikely to make it all available to them, rendering the audit impossible. So, for these and related reasons, ensuring the **confidentiality** of client information is both an important and controversial element of the ethical code.

Confidentiality issues entail a broad brush, as they are not just expected during employment but also in casual encounters and even following employment. Confidentiality does not just refer to specific information but also to circumstances in which it may *appear* that the member is using their knowledge for self-interest. Generally, client information should always remain confidential.

Nonetheless, there are circumstances (albeit they are rare) when it may be allowable, and in the public's interest, to disclose something the auditor learned during their investigation. If the Member in Public Practice determines that disclosure of the non-compliance with laws and regulations (NOCLAR) or suspected NOCLAR to an appropriate authority is an appropriate course of action in the circumstances, that disclosure is permitted pursuant to paragraph R114.1(d) of the Code. Such circumstances (APES 110, para R114.1(d)) are generally limited to circumstances when:

- the client's permission is specifically given for disclosure
- under professional peer review situations, the person examining a firm's working papers is *also* required to maintain confidentiality
- there is a legal or professional duty or right to disclose specific information.

confidentiality
'To respect the confidentiality of information acquired as a result of professional and business relationships [and therefore not disclose such] information outside the firm or employing organisation without proper and specific authority … to disclose, nor use, the information for the personal advantage of the assurance practitioner or third parties.' (APES 110, para R114.1; PES 1, para 100.5d)

The auditor's working papers (evidence of their work) can be subpoenaed, creating a legal obligation; or a specific statute may call for specific types of disclosure to specific parties. Disclosing anything about a client is, however, usually unethical, and such a decision should only be made after careful consideration of the circumstances – consideration that may include acquiring expert legal advice.

To conclude, it is noted that while many rules and examples exist in the standards and codes, they cannot match the number or variety of circumstances that the assurance professional will encounter. Applying audit judgement, and having a working knowledge of the principles and rules around ethics, will best serve the auditor.

Credibility through accountability

Peer review (external oversight) and quality control (internal oversight) are two means by which the professional company is held to account for the quality of the work it performs. Accountability of the firm is also achieved through the legal form it adopts, and the extent to which that form causes it to be held to account – or liable – and to whom. These three applications of this audit concept are considered in the sections to follow.

Peer review

Peer review is a process in which an independent peer group (usually another firm) conducts a review of a particular firm's policies and procedures. The objective is to express an opinion on whether the peer-reviewed firm's system of quality control policies and procedures provides reasonable assurance that its members are conforming to professional standards.

Past practice has been to review both general policies and specific procedures in a peer review. Usually, a sample of the firm's working papers is examined in detail to determine whether an audit was conducted with care and is well documented in the audit working papers.

Today in Australia and New Zealand, peer review is conducted on a regular basis. Most eligible Australian members are subject to a full review, which is normally conducted with the assignment of an experienced reviewer familiar with the engagement types conducted by the practice. In New Zealand, under the *Auditor Regulation Act 2011*, there must be a regular review of systems, policies and procedures. Past practice tends to indicate that, if a review team finds problems, they are likely to return to the firm within a short period of time to ensure that they have been resolved.

The Australian National Audit Office (ANAO) and the New Zealand Office of the Auditor-General have a long-standing arrangement to conduct reciprocal performance audit peer reviews. These focus on the performance audit for public sector organisations and are conducted on a rotating basis.

Evidence has shown that firms are keen to have their practices reviewed, as long as they are able to promote that fact to their prospective clients. Doing so may be a way to distinguish their audit 'quality' from that of other firms. However, the use of peer reviews to self-promote, as indicated by US practice, can be controversial as it does challenge the question of whether doing so could place the profession into disrepute.

Quality management

APES 320 Quality Management for Firms that Provide Non-Assurance Services states that:[6]
- the non-assurance practices of firms are required to apply APES 320; and
- assurance practices of firms are required to comply with APES 210 Conformity with Auditing and Assurance Standards, which includes the quality management standards issued by the AUASB (ASQM 1, ASQM 2 and ASA 220).

---

[6] APES 320 Quality Control for Firms was superseded on 1 January 2023. The revised APES 320 Quality Management for Firms that Provide Non-Assurance Services became effective from 1 January 2023.

Table 4.3 A selection of quality-management review topics

Contents include guidance with respect to, for example:
1   Leadership responsibilities within the firm
2   Personnel, training, assignment and supervision of staff
3   Ethical requirements and practices
4   Accepting and continuing engagement policies
5   Performance expectations
6   Documentation of the quality control system.

Source: Selections derived from: ASQC 1: Quality Control for Firms that Perform Audits and Reviews of Financial Reports and Other Financial Information, Other Assurance Engagements and Related Services Engagements (2021) and PES 3 (2016).

Quality-management practices comprise the firm's own policies and procedures to ensure audit quality. An audit firm tends to examine such practices as per **Table 4.3**.

Having a quality-management and review system in place is believed to enhance the quality of the audit by ensuring that practices are assessed by independent parties within the firm. In Australia, ASQC 1: Quality Management for Firms that Perform Audits or Reviews of Financial Reports and Other Financial Information, or Other Assurance or Related Services Engagements (ASQM 1) establishes the firm's responsibilities for its system of quality management and requires the firm to design and implement responses to address quality risks related to engagement performance. Such responses include establishing policies or procedures addressing Engagement Quality Reviews in accordance with ASQM 2 Engagement Quality Reviews (ASQM 2). In New Zealand, PES 3 (of the same name), offer standards that conform with international expectations.[7]

As with other professional activities, the assurance provider is called on to make considered judgements based on the facts before them (PES 3, para 15):

> … because circumstances vary widely and all such circumstances cannot be anticipated, the firm shall consider whether there are particular matters or circumstances that require the firm to establish policies and procedures in addition to those required by this Professional and Ethical Standard to meet the stated objective.

It is expected that a firm's quality-control practices will be followed by each individual member as well as by the firm taken as a whole. The *communication* concept, along with other subtle references to audit judgement, is well represented in quality control (AUASB, 2020b):

> … each individual has a personal responsibility for quality and is expected to comply with these policies and procedures. Encouraging firm personnel to communicate their views or concerns on quality control matters recognises the importance of obtaining feedback on the firm's system of quality control.

Compliance is mandatory for an assurance service. References to independence and threats to independence are a common theme throughout the standards.

CONCEPT QUESTION 5	Who is served by 'quality control' and 'peer review' in audit practice, and how?

---

[7] International Standard on Quality Control (ISQC) 1: Quality Control for Firms that Perform Audits and Reviews of Financial Statements, and Other Assurance and Related Services Engagements, issued by the IAASB.

Managing a firm's accountability

The auditor's credibility also depends on the extent to which they, or their firm, are held to account for their actions, and this forms a fundamental part of the conceptual framework (see Chapter 2). If they fail in their duty, there should be a cost. One of the ways in which professionals are held to account is through **professional liability** for their actions.

professional liability
Refers to how the auditor is or can be legally held to account for the quality of their work.

Arguments for and against

Ultimately, the auditor's responsibility is determined by the courts and by those who may litigate against them. With an increase in the number and size of claims, the cost of defence and rising insurance indemnity premiums are seen by some to have become unreasonably high over the years.

Yet, the assurance provider is there, after all, to provide 'assurance'. If they fail to fulfil their duties, then there should be a cost. Those who may face loss due to an auditor's negligence should, it seems, be able to reach the auditor to receive compensation for that loss.

In the closing decades of the 20th century, two major international firms were forced to dissolve due to the cost of litigation, but all as a result of their own negligence: Laventhol and Horwath in the 1980s, and Arthur Andersen after the Enron scandal in the 1990s. These were major failures in their time and an indictment on professional quality. But should the cost have been that high? Are annual premiums exceeding, for example, $500 000 per audit partner excessive?

The challenge is to find a structure that balances the interests of users and accountees, who need to have recourse to holding auditors to account, against the reasonable interests of the assurance provider, who needs some protection from unreasonable claims. The way in which professionals are held to account through the structure of their firms is one method of achieving this. Indeed, practices have changed in recent years to try to reset that balance.

Firm structure options

Audit firms can be structured and regulated in different ways. The general advantages and disadvantages of different structures include the following:

1 *Sole traders* and *simple partnerships* may provide the greatest protection to clients and other users of assurance because the sole trader or partner is subject to joint and several liabilities. That is, their business interests may be reached should they be seen to have breached professional standards, and their personal assets can be reached as well. This can be unfairly punitive to the professional, however, particularly those partners not directly involved with the engagement under litigation.
2 *Limited partnerships* in accounting and auditing professions limit personal liability to those partners most directly involved with a particular client's work. This serves to provide some protection to partners not involved in the engagement. Such arrangements usually have indemnity insurance requirements.
3 *Incorporation* of an assurance firm protects the assurance provider the most because only the corporate assets can be reached in claims against the firm. To protect clients and the public users of assurance, restrictions are usually placed on a registered assurance provider adopting the corporate firm.

Legislated restrictions

It may be possible to restrict the extent to which the audit firm, and the auditor, are held to account through law. This has been offered in, for example, efforts to allow the following:

1 *Statutory caps* set financial limits as to the maximum amount to which a firm can be held to account on any one individual engagement. Those objecting to it point out that the loss incurred from

an auditor's negligence may far exceed the statutory cap, and that would be unfair to those who actually suffer because of an auditor's negligence. It nonetheless protects the audit firm from liability in excess of that capped amount, and allows them to plan their risk more carefully.

2   *Insurance coverage* can be legislated or optional. As a condition of allowing the corporate form, insurance is generally mandatory to protect the firm and the aggrieved party. That is, through insuring through a third party, the audit firm may both reduce the impact of litigation against themselves, and the client or third parties can be assured of having access to compensation should the judgement be against the auditor. Again, the level of risk can thus be known, but it may fail to fairly represent the effects of auditor negligence should this occur.

Large firm benefits

Today, most statutory audits are performed by staff and partners in major, often international firms. There are several reasons for this, as large, international firms:

*   have *expert resources* with which to support auditors and they may be vertically integrated. For example, information systems specialists, legal advisers and industry specialists may be useful or necessary to support the knowledge base of the audit team.
*   enable one organisation, with a common training program, corporate culture, working paper format and procedures, to carry out the *audit of international organisations* and their overseas subsidiaries. This strengthens audit consistency. Many audits performed in Australia and New Zealand are for such subsidiaries, the parent companies of which are based overseas. The local office of an international firm will carry out the audit of the local subsidiary and submit its findings to the overseas office.
*   benefit from *educational economies of size*, and as a result are appealing to new graduates, who will be performing much of the fieldwork in their learning years. The attraction of such firms lies in their training capabilities, travel possibilities and opportunities for promotion.
*   are recognised by a public that tends to believe that major firms will provide a better audit. This is not necessarily the case, as small-firm partners are equally subject to litigation. However, the insurance hypotheses of audit may play a role here. That is, should the business fail and go into bankruptcy, the deep pocket of the international audit firm is a tempting litigation target for those who have suffered a loss.

These are serious matters. Protecting clients and those who rely on the auditor's assurance, while providing reasonable space in which professionals can operate, is proving to be a challenging balance to achieve.

National practices

A review of professions and laws here, and Western-nation precedent overseas, indicates how these issues are currently addressed in law:

*   Australian professional bodies have lobbied for limits (statutory caps) to the auditor's liability. From 2005, corporate law reform has permitted professional firms to *incorporate* under certain conditions. *Proportionate liability* is also allowed, to shift responsibility for the cost incurred by negligent audit firms away from the common law principle of joint and several liability to responsibility only for the proportion of losses attributable to the auditor. This is a complex area of law, additionally complicated by the fact that the details vary between states. Some states also limit the auditor's liability in the courts.
*   In New Zealand, statutory financial statement auditors may be organised under the corporate form. However, there are limitations relating to the qualifications and liability of some partners and indemnity coverage (see Chapter 3). This is a relatively new allowance in New Zealand, so the rules are evolving.
*   In the United Kingdom, auditors can also operate in the *corporate form*, as long as they maintain professional liability insurance. The Professional Oversight Board is an agency under the secretary of the Department of Trade and Industry (DTI), and it oversees professional practices and self-regulatory conduct.

- In the United States, starting on a state-by-state basis, auditors can now operate under *Limited Liability Partnerships* (*LLPs*). The professional body is the AICPA, while the PCAOB approves Statements on Auditing Standards (SAS). The PCAOB is an agency of the federal government and answers to the powerful SEC, which administers securities' legislation. Removal of the AICPA from standard-setting occurred in response to market failures resulting from cases such as Enron and WorldCom.
- Canadian law and practice vary to some extent from province to province. Alberta and the Yukon territory, for example, permit professional incorporation, while in British Columbia, professional corporations can exist with liability insurance. CICA is the primary professional association.

In summary, the potential for loss to auditors from litigation is less in Australia and New Zealand because class actions and contingent legal fees are restricted, and because the auditors here can form structures that offer some protection from unlimited liability.

Study tools

Summary

In this chapter, we learn how auditors, over time, have played a trusted role in society and occupy a position for which they must be held to account. We outlined the range of responsibilities and the business structures through which auditors operate. We reviewed elements of the ethical codes to which they are subject.

Society expects assurance providers – auditors – to have high ethical standards. The most important ethical issue is the auditor's independence because of the conflicts that are inherent to assurance work. We discussed the reasons why it is important for auditors to possess both an ethical state of mind and its appearance, if they are to fulfil their obligations.

We then looked at particular issues in ethics and independence, threats to and safeguards for independence, and particular applications of the ethical code for assurance services. By submitting to peer review, members of the profession can maintain social status and demonstrate their commitment to quality. Quality-control procedures, managed by the firm itself, provide comfort that quality audit is maintained. It is important to bear in mind, though, should you become an auditor, that no amount of regulation can make ethical decisions for you. These decisions will ultimately depend on your personal beliefs and approach to what you value.

🔗 Case/resources link

CAATs for Classrooms

Accompanying this book is a series of data, integrated worksheets and exercises that are designed to support your learning and give you exposure to hands-on audit decision-making dilemmas faced by auditors in the planning elements of the audit process. Acquire the relevant material for this chapter from your instructor.

Review questions

4.1 Name and describe four statutes that are important with respect to the formation of the audit profession and its association(s) in Australia or New Zealand.

4.2 Explain the role and positioning of the AUASB/NZAuASB.

4.3 Auditors have a responsibility to behave in a professional manner. Explain why this is important.

4.4   Name and define sources of pressure on the auditor to comply (or not comply) with professional ethical standards.

4.5   Name all of the fundamental principles in the Code of Ethics and define them.

4.6   Explain the difference between independence 'in appearance' and 'in fact'. Why is the distinction important?

4.7   For each of the five threats to independence, identify one possible 'safeguard'.

4.8   What is the meaning, in terms of these ethical codes, of an auditor's:

    a   financial interests   d   incompatible occupations

    b   fee dependence   e   personal relationships.

    c   lowballing

4.9   Describe the following terms, distinguish between them, outline how they potentially compromise audit independence, and describe the restrictions around them for assurance services (threats and safeguards, if any):

    a commissions

    b contingent fees.

4.10   Define 'management advisory services', then provide three examples and describe the threats and acceptable safeguards (if any) for each.

4.11   Confidentiality is an expectation that can create issues. Provide examples of such issues and discuss the appropriate actions.

4.12   Describe commonly employed firm structures, as well as the advantages and disadvantages for the audit firm and for users-accountees.

4.13   Why are larger firms more active in performing statutory audits?

4.14   Describe the different firm structure practices found in Australia, New Zealand and other countries.

4.15   Compare and contrast accounting profession and firm practices in: Australia, New Zealand, the United Kingdom, the United States and Canada.

4.16   Compare and contrast 'peer review' and 'quality control'.

4.17   Explain the environment which places pressure on the auditor's inclination to apply professional scepticism in a repeat engagement.

Exercises

4.1   **COMMUNICATION:** A commercial bank employed a major audit firm to perform its annual financial audit on its 2021 statements. The firm concluded that the provision for doubtful debts was understated by a material amount. The firm and the board of directors came to an agreement as to a 'true and fair' amount. An unqualified report was rendered. In 2022, the board employed a different firm. You are the managing partner of the new firm. What communications should you have before accepting the engagement?

4.2   **ETHICS:** While playing golf with Bill Sims, the manager of Traders Ltd, Tom Lurk (ACA) suggests to Bill that Traders Ltd would save money by appointing him (Lurk) as auditor. He promises to do just as good a job as the present auditor for half the fee. He also points out that, given his investment in Traders Ltd, he would be more conscientious in carrying out his duties. Furthermore, Lurk understands that Sims has just lost his accountant, and he points out that he can do all the accounting until Bill finds a suitable replacement. What ethical breaches have been made by Tom Lurk?

4.3 **PROFESSIONS:** In terms of whether a profession is likely to have the characteristics, and be seen to enjoy the characteristics, of a true 'profession', consider the following associations, then rank each of them on a scale of 1 ('high' professionalism) to 3 ('low'). Explain why and/or under what conditions your ranking would occur?

What is the most important ethical issue for a member in each of these?

  a   general practitioner: medicine
  b   surgeon
  c   plumber
  d   health ministry manager
  e   internal auditor
  f   accountant (who does statutory financial audit)
  g   accountant (no audit work done)
  h   Air New Zealand pilot
  i   scientist
  j   barrister and District Court judge
  k   nuclear physicist
  l   minister of parliament.

4.4 **ETHICS:** Your client does not understand why your profession is concerned with professional ethics. He believes that your job is simply to review what he has done and report on it – why are ethics required? Explain.

4.5 **PROFESSION:** Explain why it is important that the organisation that promulgates standards for audit professional work is separate from the professional organisation itself. How does this relate to the 'independence' concept you have learned?

4.6 **CONFIDENTIALITY:** You have been in contact with potential shareholders for your audit client. They believe that the information and evidence you acquire should *not* be kept confidential, that they should know exactly what you have found and any problems you encountered when auditing the client.

Required: Explain the need for retaining the confidentiality of the client's information, even from shareholders, and for what purpose. Explain to them those circumstances in which information about the client may be made public.

4.7 **ETHICS:** For each situation below, explain how these actions might indicate an 'independence in mind' and/or an 'independence in appearance':

  a   The auditor declines to accept an engagement in which his old friend is the CEO.
  b   The auditor declines to accept an engagement with the managing director's wife's business, for which she asked him to produce a budget.

4.8   **ETHICS:** An auditor encounters the following situation. Her client is a partnership operated by a husband-and-wife team. The couple has struggled to pay their current debt over the last couple of years and are relying on the audit to obtain a loan from a second bank. This year, you have helped them produce a budget and forecast that they have used with their first bank. You have also advised them on a payroll package that you have used and recommend, but you did not purchase or operate it for them. You have known the couple socially for the last five years, and you want to help them with their business. Unfortunately, you have helped them, but they have not paid you for the last two years.

Mid-year, the couple split up under the pressure of the business and both husband and wife have asked you to conduct the audit for their use in divorce proceedings.

Required: Identify the various types of threat this situation represents and recommend the sort of safeguard, if any, that may enable the auditor to continue.

4.9   **ETHICS:** Name and describe each ethical situation below and how you might safeguard against it.

a   Your client offers to pay you a bonus if you get them out of a dispute with the NZ Inland Revenue Department.

b   You bid against a competing firm to obtain the audit of Client X, and you win the bid, having submitted the lowest offer – an offer which may be below cost.

c   You, as a partner, and your small firm have faithfully served the client for the past eight years.

d   You recommend a barrister to your audit client to advise them on their upcoming litigation. The barrister returns the favour.

e   You authorise the purchase of capital equipment for your audit client, but you do not have any part in recording the transaction.

4.10   **PROFESSION AND ETHICS:**

PwC will lose its most lucrative audit contract among NZX-listed issuers when Fonterra ends a 15-year relationship that's earned the auditor $94 million. This week Fonterra recommended KPMG be appointed the new auditor for the financial year ending July 2020. PwC's appointment was challenged by farmer and former director Greg Gent at this year's annual meeting, who said the relationship had become too close.

Fonterra's current audit agreement with PwC concludes at the completion of the FY19 statements, it said. If approved, KPMG will also likely be auditor of the Fonterra Shareholders' Fund, said John Shewan, chairman of the fund's manager.

In the financial year to July 31, PwC was paid $7 million by Fonterra – $6 million to audit the financial statements and $1 million for other services, such as advisory services. In that year Fonterra reported its first loss after writing down the value of its Beingmate investment by $405 million from the original $750 million paid and compensating former customer Danone with $183 million over the 2013 recall triggered by a botulism scare at one of its plants. In the prior financial year, PwC was paid $6 million. The contract represented around 25 per cent of its total auditors' fees in 2017 when they reached $25 million, according to NZX data.

Fonterra's annual report consistently says the company 'operates a rigorous selection process to appoint its auditors and has a policy of rotating its lead external audit partner in accordance with best practice', yet it has only changed auditor once before, appointing PwC in 2004. A year before the appointment, former PwC veteran Roger France was appointed a Fonterra director, having retired from the accounting firm in 2001.

Other PwC alumni include current Fonterra directors Bruce Hassall and Brent Goldsack. PwC's 2018 audit report notes the board decided Hassall, who chairs the audit committee, wouldn't be involved in the auditor appointment or setting audit fees for three years. It also said Goldsack was never involved in providing audit services to Fonterra during his time as a PwC partner.

When asked why the cooperative is changing auditors, chief financial officer Marc Rivers told BusinessDesk: 'It's good practice to have a change now and again and have a fresh pair of eyes to look at things.' He acknowledged Fonterra hasn't introduced new eyes regularly, and that PwC held the role for a 'very long time, pretty much since inception'. However, 'I think across other companies, other cooperatives, it would be good practice to look at that,' he said.

KPMG was Fonterra's first auditor, signing off on accounts for the 2002 and 2003 financial years, for which it was paid $8 million and $10 million respectively. The auditor switch comes after a leadership shuffle, with both the chair and the chief executive standing down at the same time. John Monaghan was appointed chairman and Miles Hurrell as interim chief executive. The dairy giant is also in the process of carrying out a major strategic review in a bid to address the poor financial results.

Earlier this week Fonterra confirmed it will pull out of the joint venture with Beingmate and take back full ownership of the Darnum plant by the end of the year. It said ownership of ice cream maker Tip Top is under the microscope and that its under-performing Chinese farms are a source of 'heightened focus'.

Source: Newsroom (2018).

Required: Consider the professional and ethical implications, including 'independence' and the 'appearance of independence', of the decisions made in this case.

The courts: The legal liability of auditors

Learning objectives

After studying the material in this chapter, you should be able to:

- describe an auditor's duty of care under contract law
- describe common law liability history to third parties under the law of tort
- explain how 'reasonable skill and care' is interpreted in common law
- explain when an auditor might use contributory negligence as a defence.

Introduction

An important means of holding the auditor to account is to ensure that stakeholders have legal recourse should the auditor fail in their duties. It is only through common law – lawsuits – that negligent auditors encounter those directly affected by their mistakes. It is also where, over time, principles, standards and statutes have come to be influenced by judiciary who make decisions about new or particularly egregious situations.

In effect, common law is the means by which society expresses its expectations of, or disappointments in, the auditor. If negligent in the conduct of an audit, the cost to firms can be high. In 2012, for example, the Federal Court in Melbourne approved Australia's biggest-ever settlement in a class-action suit, a A$200 million deal for Centro Properties Group shareholders, including A$67 million payable by the audit firm. It can also be costly to defend lawsuits if the argument of the **plaintiff** is weak, so it is important to consider their impact.

This chapter looks into circumstances in which litigation against the auditor (the **defendant**) is most likely to be successful, or unsuccessful. We focus on situations in which the auditor is accused of 'negligence', unintentional error, not where they are accused of fraud or criminal acts.

> Plaintiff (client or third parties) ⟶ Defendant (auditor)

plaintiff
A party or person that brings a case against another in a court of law.

defendant
The person or other party about which a complaint is being made in a court of law.

'To whom': The auditor's duty of care

The duty of the auditor to apply 'reasonable care and skill' has set the primary principle by which we still operate today. In 1895, Lindley LJ observed regarding *London and General Bank (No. 2)* [1895] 2 Ch. 673:

> Such I take to be the duty of the auditor: he must be honest – i.e. he must not certify what he does not believe to be true, and he must take reasonable care and skill ... What is reasonable care in any particular case must depend on the circumstances of that case.

In the 1896 *Kingston Cotton Mill* case, Lopes LJ coined another phrase still used today, by observing that the auditor 'is a watchdog, but not a bloodhound'. He explained that, in the absence of suspicious circumstances, the auditor is not obliged to 'sniff out' all fraud and error. Bordering on the idea of 'professional scepticism', Lord Denning in 1958 reflected on *Fomento (Sterling Area) Ltd v. Selsdon Pen Co. Ltd*:

> What is the proper function of an auditor: to take care to see that errors are not made, be they errors of computation, errors of omission or commission, or downright untruths. To perform this task properly, he must come to it with an enquiring mind – not suspicious of dishonesty ... but suspecting that someone may have made a mistake somewhere and that a check must be made to ensure that there has been none.

We thus consider cases that help explain litigation against the auditor and when it may be more likely to succeed. Overlaying the discussion is the important distinction between litigation that may be brought against the auditor under 'contract' and, by contrast, litigation under the law of 'tort'. Regarding this, we will be using **Figure 5.1** throughout the chapter to provide perspective.

The subject of those 'to whom' an auditor owes a duty initiates the discussion. Those individuals to whom an auditor owes a duty of care can be seen to have a relationship with the auditor under contract, or they may have a relationship as a third party. Third parties are not parties to the contract, nor do they (directly) pay for the assurance service. Third parties are those who are *foreseen* or who are *reasonably foreseeable*. These types of plaintiffs are represented in **Figure 5.2**.

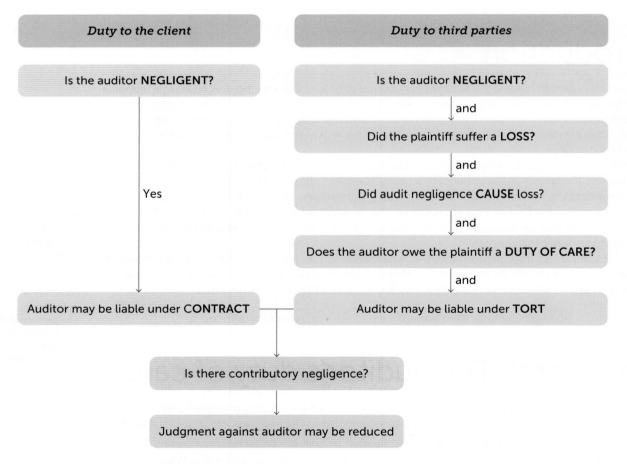

Figure 5.1 The auditor's liability through the courts

Under the law of *contract*, the auditor has obligations to the client with whom they have agreed on a contract for audit. Other plaintiffs, those who are 'third parties', may bring their cases under the *law of tort*. This relationship between 'auditor-defendant' and 'plaintiff' determines how the court will interpret their obligations to each other. That is, auditors may have a contractual obligation to the client, but there is also a social–economic obligation to selected others. These distinctions are discussed below.

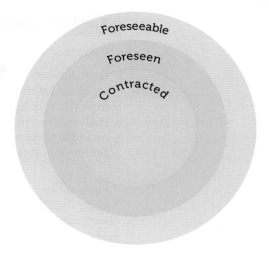

| CONCEPT QUESTION 1 | What is the meaning of 'reasonable care and skill' in the context of an auditor? |

Duty of care under contract

The statutory financial statement auditor is under a contractual duty to conduct the audit with reasonable care and skill. The contract is with the organisation as a whole. There is no contract with individual stakeholders (e.g., shareholders) or obligations, for example, should the value of an organisation (e.g., the share price) simply decline. Such was established in *Caparo Industries PLC v. Dickman & Others* (discussed later in this chapter). Auditors are liable to their clients due to their relationship under contract law. In the case of *Simonius Vischer & Co v. Holt & Thompson* [September 1979], NSW Court of Appeal, Sheppard J stated:

Figure 5.2 When an auditor may owe a duty of care

> An auditor is bound by contract, in consideration of the fee which his client agrees to pay him, to carry out the obligations imposed on him ... Further, in my view, where the defendant has protection under a contract, it is not permissible to disregard the contract and allege a wider liability in tort.

For an action by the audit client against the auditor to succeed, negligence must be proven. An auditor would probably not be held negligent for failure to detect a fraud that was immaterial; however, they are responsible for taking reasonable steps to identify material fraud and to follow up on suspicions raised during the investigation.

Auditing in practice

Management fraud

Auditor Arthur Young was held liable for loss consequent upon fraud by a senior executive of a client. The loss (A$58 704) was not material, but it followed a failure by the auditors to inform the directors of suspicious circumstances encountered in the audit (*WA Chip & Pulp Co. Pty Ltd v. Arthur Young* [1986] 12 ACLR 25).

If the fraud is material to the accounts, liability may still be avoided if detection could not reasonably have been achieved.

Auditors may also be held liable in statute for certain breaches of duty, such as failing to comply with standards (many of which themselves were inspired by case law). In most Australian jurisdictions, the standard of care for auditors is first determined by civil liability Acts. EC Audit Pty Ltd and its auditor faced criminal prosecution for an alleged failure to comply with such standards (see the 'Auditing in practice' box).

Auditing in practice

Criminal charge against an auditor

On 8 June 2021, criminal charges were laid against EC Audit Pty Ltd, and its director and registered auditor, Robert James Evett, for breaches of auditing standards. ASIC brought three charges against both the firm and Mr Evett relating to the 2016–18 financial audits of Halifax Investment Services Pty Ltd. The defendants pleaded guilty and were subjected to financial penalties. They were the first auditors in Australia to face criminal charges and be sentenced under section 989CA of the *Corporations Act 2001*.

In other respects, however, common law is the first guide. We note the 1997 Canadian case *Kripps v. Touche Ross* 35 CCLT (29)60, where the auditor followed existing standards (GAAP), despite their questionable appeal to a 'true and fair' view. Canada's Court of Appeal stated that GAAP may be a guide, but auditors are retained to form an opinion on the fairness of the financial statements. In other words, the court expected them to *make an exception* to standard compliance. While diverting from standards would be extremely ill-advised, this does show the fluid nature of law over time and over varying jurisdictions.

Duty to third parties

Neither company nor contract law provides redress for third parties in respect of audit negligence. Third parties may, however, be able to recover damages under the law of tort. For some time, liability to third parties existed in respect of physical injury (*Donoghue v. Stevenson* [1932] All ER Rep 1), but no liability for financial loss was available, which was damaging in financially distressed times (Lys and Watts, 1994).

Third parties include those who may have relied on the financial statements, but who are not contracted to the auditor. Whether the auditor owes a duty of care to third parties is an idea long exercised in the courts. The relationship between the auditor who negligently issues an inappropriate audit opinion and a user of the financial statements who suffers loss through reliance on it, is less clear. Cases from the 1950s onwards began to test this principle.

Foreseen parties: *Candler v. Crane* and *Hedley Byrne*

As late as 1951, the case of *Candler v. Crane, Christmas and Co.* [1951] 2 KB 164 confirmed that there could be no liability for financial loss in the absence of a contractual relationship. In this case, accounts were negligently prepared by the defendants (by their own admission). A Mr Candler was induced to invest money in the company on the strength of these accounts, and he subsequently lost his investment when the company was wound up.

As a prospective investor, rather than an existing one to whom contractual duties would have been owed, he failed in litigation against the auditors. A majority verdict found for the auditor, although there was one dissenting judge, Lord Denning:

> Accountants owe their duty, of course, to their employer or client and also, I think, to any third person to whom they themselves show the accounts, or to whom they know their employer is going to show the accounts so as to induce him to invest money or to take some other action on them. I do not think, however, the duty can be extended still further so as to include strangers of whom they have heard nothing and to whom their employer, without their knowledge, may choose to show their accounts. Once the accountants have handed the accounts to their employer, they are not, as a rule, responsible for what he does with them without their knowledge or consent.

Lord Denning's views were upheld some 12 years later in the case of *Hedley Byrne and Co. Ltd v. Heller and Partners Ltd* (1963) 2 All ER 575. Heller and Partners were sued in respect of losses that resulted from their negligent issuance of a customer reference in their capacity as merchant bankers. They escaped liability only through a disclaimer clause, but Lord Morris stated:

> If someone possessed of a special skill undertakes, quite irrespective of contract, to apply that skill for the assistance of another person who relies upon such a skill, a duty of care will arise.

Later, in *Hedley Byrne & Co. Ltd v. Heller & Partners Ltd* [1964] AC 465, His Lordship stated the principle even more broadly:

> If in a sphere in which a person is so placed that others could reasonably rely on his judgement or his skill or upon his ability to make careful enquiry, a person takes it upon himself to give information or advice to, or allows his information or advice to be passed onto another who, as he knows or should know, will place reliance upon it, then a duty of care will arise.[1]

Examples of occasions when an accountant may run the risk of incurring liability to third parties under the *Hedley Byrne* doctrine include the following.

- in preparing financial statements or a report for a client when it is known, or ought reasonably to be expected, that such documents are intended to be shown to and relied upon by a third party.
- in giving references regarding a client's creditworthiness, or assurance as to their capacity to carry out the terms of contracts (e.g., leases), or giving any other type of reference on behalf of the client.

The ICAEW obtained counsel's advice as to the extent of potential liability following the *Hedley Byrne* decision. It was considered that the following circumstances must apply for liability to result (see **Figure 5.1**):

1   The auditor-accountant must have been negligent.
2   The third party must have suffered a financial loss.
3   The loss must have occurred as a result of the accountant's negligence.
4   There must have been what has come to be called a **special relationship**.

A number of cases in the 1970s and 1980s led to a broadening of *Hedley Byrne*'s special relationship principle (see **Table 5.1** and **Table 5.2** for summaries).

Foreseeable parties

In *Jeb Fasteners Ltd v. Marks, Bloom & Co.* (1981) (UK), and related cases, the auditors were aware of the company's liquidity problems and had a discussion with the plaintiffs at the time of takeover negotiations. Jeb Fasteners subsequently purchased the company, but the takeover was not a success, and Jeb sued the auditors on the grounds that they were misled by misstated financial accounts.

Justice Woolf applied a 'reasonable foresight' test, as opposed to the 'special relationship' test of *Hedley Byrne*, based on a ruling by Lord Wilberforce in *Anns v. London Borough of Merton* (1978) AC 728 House of Lords, in which it was held that:

> First, one has to ask whether, as between the alleged wrongdoer and the person who has suffered damage, there is a sufficient relationship of proximity or neighbourhood such that, in the reasonable contemplation of the former, carelessness on his part may be likely to cause damage to the latter, in which case a prima facie duty of care arises.

special relationship
Occurs when the auditor knows the purpose involved, and the specific person or class of people who will be relying on their opinion.

---

[1] An exception appears in *Moore Stephens v. Stone Rolls Ltd* (2010) UKHL 39 (UK), in which the plaintiff was essentially a single manager-owner and perpetrator of a fraud, which the auditor had failed to find. Per Lord Mance: 'an auditor cannot ... defeat a claim for breach of duty ... by attributing to the company the very fraud which the auditor should have detected'.

Second, if the first question is answered affirmatively, it is necessary to consider whether there are any considerations which ought to negate or reduce or limit the scope of the duty or the class of person to whom it is owed or the damages to which any breach of it may give rise.

Justice Woolf's ruling has some authority, but it left the extent of that unknown third-party liability unconfirmed. A New Zealand case opened the door further, however. In *Scott Group Ltd v McFarlane* (1978) 1 NZLR 553 Court of Appeal was found a precedent for expanding those to whom an auditor owes a duty of care. Although not binding outside New Zealand, it established an expansion of the auditor's liability in law. The original ruling was ultimately reversed in the Court of Appeal, as reliance (cause) was not proven. Nonetheless, it did suggest that the auditor was obligated to those who were not just 'foreseen' but also 'foreseeable' (see **Figure 5.1**).

Per Justice Woodhouse:

> A duty of care is owed by auditors who could, or should, reasonably foresee that a particular person or group of persons will rely on the audited financial statements for a particular type of investment decision.

These rulings grew in influence under *Twomax Ltd and Goode v. Dickson, McFarlane and Robinson* (1983) SLT 98 (Scotland). Twomax Ltd acquired a controlling interest in Kintyre Knitwear Ltd, of which Dickson, McFarlane and Robinson were the auditors. Twomax, and joint plaintiffs Gordon and Goode, stated that they had relied on the audit opinion of Dickson et al. in purchasing their respective interests. There were mistakes in the audited financials, and the plaintiffs claimed that, had they been aware of its true position, they would not have been interested in Kintyre.

Lord Steward relied on the *Jeb Fasteners* case and decided that, although the auditors were not aware of the specific intention of the plaintiffs, they were aware of the fact that Kintyre needed capital. This made the situation *foreseeable*, and the judge accordingly ruled in favour of the plaintiffs. This expansion of those to whom an auditor owes a duty of care was significant, as anyone who relied on the auditors' work, and lost 'as a result', could make a reasonable claim against them (see **Figure 5.1**)

CONCEPT QUESTION 2	What is the difference between a 'foreseen' party and a 'foreseeable' or 'reasonably foreseeable' party in case law?

It is noted that Australian courts, as exampled by *R Lowe Lippman Figdor & Franck v. AGC Ltd* (1992) and *Esanda Finance v. KPMG* (1994), may have looked to a smaller range of potential third parties, such as those the provider of information *induced* to rely on their information. The risk of expanding that range to 'reasonably foreseeable' plaintiffs loomed large.

What then? *Caparo Industries* (UK)

The decision in the UK case of *Caparo Industries PLC v. Dickman & Others* (QB division, December 1987) addressed the issue of third-party liability and, to some extent, reversed earlier decisions. The case was brought after Caparo Industries purchased a controlling interest in the public company Fidelity. In doing so, Caparo relied on the audited financial statements, which reported a profit of £1.3 million. Caparo alleged that there should have been a reported loss of £460000 and that the auditors were negligent in failing to discover this misrepresentation.

The High Court found that the auditors owed no duty of care to Caparo as an investor or potential investor. The Court of Appeal then reversed this decision on the grounds that the auditor, Touche Ross, knew of the reliance of those particular parties on its work. The decision was appealed in the House of Lords, which came to three conditions that must be met to establish a duty of care to third parties (*Caparo Industries PLC v Dickman* [1990] UKHL 2). They are:

1 Should the auditors reasonably have foreseen that economic loss would result from any failure to perform the audit with due care?
2 Was the relationship between Caparo and the auditors sufficiently close and direct to establish knowledge of Caparo as a person or a member of a limited class of persons who would be likely to rely on their report?
3 Would the imposition of liability or economic loss be fair, reasonable and just in the case's specific circumstances?

The second condition indicated a reluctance on the part of this court to cause auditors to be liable to all injured parties where those parties are unknown. It was also found that, as the auditors' statutory duty extends to the body of shareholders as a whole, no duty of care is owed to individual shareholders or potential shareholders. The latter was affirmed in a Canadian case, *Hercules Management v. Ernst & Young* (1997) 31BLR(2d) 147.

The House of Lords' thus concluded that the auditors did *not* owe a duty of care to Caparo and reversed the Court of Appeal decision. In giving its decision, the House of Lords referred to and *disapproved* of the New Zealand Court of Appeal decision in *Scott Group Ltd v. McFarlane*. It also abandoned the two-step test and returned to the 'special relationship' (foreseen) of *Hedley Byrne*.

The House of Lords' decision regarding Caparo was warmly received among auditors, as you can well imagine. However, a subsequent New Zealand case has shown that the Caparo outcome cannot be assumed (see the upcoming **Table 5.2**). **Table 5.1** traces this history.

Table 5.1 Persuasive court cases: Auditor's liability 'to whom'

Case	Significance
Ultramares Corp v. Touche (1931) (UK)	Accountants' liability should not be extended to third parties: it can only arise under a contractual relationship.
Donoghue v. Stevenson (1932) (UK)	A duty of care is owed to third parties where it can be reasonably foreseen that failure to take care may result in physical injury.
Candler v. Crane, Christmas & Co. (1951) (UK)	No duty of care is owed to third parties in the case of financial loss. Lord Denning's dissenting opinion set a precedent for 'special relationship'.
Hedley Byrne & Co Ltd v. Heller and Partners Ltd (1963) (UK)	A duty of care is owed to third parties for financial loss, where it can be shown that a 'special relationship' exists; i.e., where the auditor knows, or ought to know, that someone is going to rely on those accounts for some specific purpose.
Anns v. Merton Borough Council (1977) (UK)	Introduced the concept of 'within the reasonable contemplation' of the person giving advice, in place of 'knowledge' that 'someone will rely …', and replaced 'special relationship' with 'a relationship of proximity or neighbourhood' – thus potentially extending the third parties regarding whom a duty of care arises.
Jeb Fasteners Ltd v. Marks, Bloom & Co. (1981) (UK)	Woolf J's judgment extends liability, as did the previous *Scott Group Ltd* (NZ) case and the foreseeability concept, to circumstances in which any form of financial support appears likely to be needed. The judicial ruling in *Twomax Ltd and Goode v. Dickson, McFarlane and Robinson* (1983, Scotland), of the same era, extended the view.
Caparo Industries PLC v. Dickman and Others (1987) (UK)	Appeal to the House of Lords held for defendants and that auditors were liable to neither potential nor individual shareholders, among others.

It would appear safest to assume that negligently prepared or audited financial statements can result in lawsuits from clients and third parties alike.

Australia and New Zealand

The Australian courts have gestured towards empathy with the auditor's position in their tendency to rely on the principles of 'foreseen' or 'reasonably foreseeable'. Even as early as 1971 (*MLC v. Evatt*), the 'special relationship' was generally limited in the Australian courts to those known to be relying on the advice, and to those giving it in their professional capacity. In *Esanda Finance v. Peat Marwick* (1997), for example, the High Court ruled that the auditor owed a duty to a third party only if it were known that such reliance would be made – a finding similar to that made in the Australian case *R Lowe Lippman Figdor and Franck v. AGC Advances Ltd* (1992).

In contrast, the Caparo decision was not consistently upheld in New Zealand. In *South Pacific Manufacturing v. New Zealand Security Consultants and Investigators Ltd* (1992) 2 NZLR 282, Richardson J found that the ultimate question in such a case is whether it is just and reasonable to impose a broad duty of care in light of all the circumstances. He cited *Anns v. Merton Borough Council* with favour and stated that the existence of policy considerations that tend to negate or restrict – or strengthen the existence of – a duty is important, as is foreseeability between parties. Highlighting the sociocultural distinctions found between Australia and New Zealand in law, Casey J explained:

> Questions of whether liability ought to be imposed in particular situations are likely to be influenced by current perceptions of community attitudes and goals. It may well be that, in the United Kingdom, society has moved rather more quickly than we have in New Zealand towards a more robust view that people should be responsible for their own protection, with the consequent retreat from the more expansive view of liability implicit in Anns and the cases which followed it.

It would appear unwise for an auditor to rely on *Hedley Byrne* to restrict liability. A few key cases pertaining to the auditor's liability to third parties in Australia and New Zealand can be found in **Table 5.2**.

Table 5.2 To whom: An Australian-New Zealand comparison

Australia	New Zealand
Alexander & Ors v. Cambridge Credit Corporation (1987) 5 ACLC 587 Auditors negligent for failing to require trust deed debt provision in the accounts; liable to shareholders but, as cause not proven, not to selected third parties.	No indication of Australian/New Zealand differences on the nature of auditor's contractual obligations.
MLC v. Evatt (1971) AC 793 For a special relationship to exist, those giving the financial advice must not only know that someone is relying on it, but must be giving it in his/her professional capacity. Similar finding as to inducing or being aware of reliance in *Esanda Finance v. Peat Marwick*. Affirms 'foreseen' view of Australian courts.	*Scott Group Ltd v. McFarlane* (1978) 1 NZLR 553 Established a duty of care by auditors who could reasonably foresee that persons will rely on a particular decision. *Hedley Byrne* principle extended to test of reasonable foreseeability.
R Lowe Lippman Figdor and Franck v. AGC Advances Ltd (1992) Supreme Court of Victoria rules that without an implied attempt to induce a third party to an action, a duty of care did not arise. No indication of Australian courts taking auditor's liability to 'foreseeability', although may be closer to 'restatement' rule.	*South Pacific Manufacturing v. New Zealand Security Consultants and Investigators Ltd* (1992) 2 NZLR 282 While not pertaining to auditors, affirms the court's support for a 'foreseeability' test.
Esanda Finance v. Peat Marwick (1997). Broadly supports the foreseen principle as expressed in Caparo. Consistent also was *Cam & Bear Pty Ltd v McGoldrick* [2018] NSWCA 110 and *Ryan Wealth Holdings Pty Ltd v Baumgartner* [2018] NSWSC 1502 – poor disclosure to those to whom they owed a contractual duty of care.	*Allison v. KPMG* (1998) The New Zealand High Court returns to a view closer to *Caparo*.

In our view, if company law wants auditors to have a duty of care to creditors and others, it should clearly say so. Tort should not be used as a back door for creating unknown levels of liability. Within Australia, there are moves to define the auditor's liability more in statute, but time will tell. On the grounds of equity, and due to the costly nature of litigation, it is questionable whether the auditor should, in fact, be held responsible for the financial loss of every potential user of those accounts.

'For what': Reasonable skill and care

Occasionally, a member of the judiciary takes opportunities to summarise the specific duties of auditors and to remind us of general principles. 'Reasonable skill and care', for example, remains the theoretical measure of whether auditor negligence has occurred. Lopes LJ 'general standard' in *Kingston Cotton Mill Co. (No. 2)* (1896) Ch 279 continues to be applied.

What the courts expect

Towards the end of the 19th century, judgments by the courts made it clear that reasonable care and skill involved more than merely a check on the audit client's books. In the case of *London Oil Storage Co. Ltd v. Seear, Hasluck & Co.* (1904) 31 Acct LR 1, it was held that the auditor was liable for damage sustained by a company that resulted from their failure to verify the existence of assets included in the balance sheet. It was established that the auditor, in ensuring that the information given in the audited balance sheet corresponded with the books, was not merely to check the arithmetical accuracy of the entries but also to examine its source. They were also required to ensure that the data in the books represented fact rather than fiction. Thus, and for the first time, the auditor had to go beyond the books and management representations for their evidence.

Other precedents developed through a series of prominent court cases:

- In *Arthur E Green & Co. v. The Central Advance and Discount Corporation Ltd* (1920) 63 Acct LR 1, the court held that the auditor was negligent in accepting a schedule of bad debts provided by a responsible officer of the company when it was apparent that other debts not included in the schedule were also irrecoverable. The case established that not only was the auditor required to go beyond the company's internal documentary evidence, they were also required to relate it to evidence obtained from different sources.
- Particularly because of court decisions in such cases as *London Oil Storage Co. Ltd v. Seear Hasluck and Co.*, a new emphasis was placed on physically observing assets claimed to exist, including cash and inventory.
- The *McKesson & Robbins* case (1938, US) illustrated the extent to which fraud can occur if auditors fail to apply professional scepticism to their work. The owner, a former bootlegger and twice-convicted felon, created entire departments to produce false invoices and they ultimately overstated sales by a cumulative US$340 million. The complacent auditors 'appreciated' the client's help to confirm debtor validity, which of course was falsified.

It is now clear that, where reasonable, the auditor should obtain outside evidence which is as independent of management control as possible. Accepted benchmarks for due care are summarised in **Figure 5.3**.

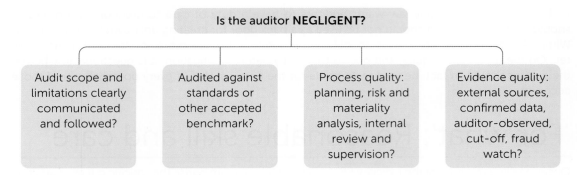

Figure 5.3 What is auditor negligence?

Principles tested: 1970

The principle of 'reasonable skill and care' remains roughly intact. A renowned 1970 Australian case in the NSW Supreme Court reiterated, and reminded us, of the criteria which it represents. *Pacific Acceptance Corporation Ltd v Forsyth & Ors* (1970) 92 WN (NSW) 29 was the first case since *Re London and General Bank* to substantially consider the expectations of the auditor in a modern environment. In his extensive judgement, Moffitt J offered comprehensive guidance on auditors' duties and responsibilities. Some of the important legal principles he confirmed or established were as follows:

1   When auditors accept an engagement to conduct a statutory financial audit, they can be taken to have promised to conduct such examination as necessary to form their opinion and exercise due care and skill in doing so.

2   Auditors' duties are not confined to an examination of the audit client's books and records at balance date but extend to an audit of the client's financial affairs in general and for the whole of the relevant financial period.

3   The duty to audit involves a duty to pay due regard to the possibility that fraud may have occurred. The audit program and audit procedures should be structured so that the auditor has a reasonable expectation of detecting material fraud if it exists.

4   Auditors have a duty to make prompt and frank disclosure to the appropriate level of management regarding material matters discovered during the audit. This includes a duty to report promptly to the client's directors if suspicious circumstances are uncovered.

5   The auditors' duty to report includes a duty to report to shareholders at their annual general meeting any material matters discovered during the audit process. This responsibility cannot be shirked on the grounds that it involves an adverse reflection on the board, a director or a senior executive, or on the pretext that public disclosure may damage the company.

6   The auditor has a paramount duty to check material matters for themselves. However, reliance may be placed on inquiries from others where it is reasonable to do so. Nevertheless, reliance on others is to be regarded as an aid to, not a substitute for, the auditor's own procedures.

7   The use of inexperienced staff or the failure to use an adequate audit program do not, of themselves, establish negligence. However, if audit failure occurs (that is, if a material misstatement in the financial statements is not uncovered by the audit), then the use of such staff and/or the absence of a satisfactory audit program may be taken as evidence that the failure occurred as a result of negligence. This position was reaffirmed in an Australian case (*Duke Group Ltd v. Pilmer* [1998] 27 ACSR1) in which auditors, Nelson Wheeler, 'conceded that [a] valuation was undertaken incompetently. The work was delegated to staff with insufficient experience, and their work was not adequately supervised' (Ross, 1998b, p. 77).

In his judgment, Moffitt J noted that professional standards and practices must change over time to reflect changes in the business environment. He also observed that the courts, in trying to ascertain what qualifies as 'reasonable skill, care and caution', are guided by professional standards and best auditing practices of the time.

Nonetheless, the courts will not be bound by these standards. If they see fit, they will make their own decisions. It is the courts that determine what is 'reasonable skill and care' in the circumstances of each case. Furthermore, a number of these points have now been incorporated into Australian, New Zealand and international auditing standards. Justice Pennycuick, in *re Gerrard (Thomas) & Son Ltd* (1968) Ch 455, stated that it was

> not clear that the quality of the auditor's duty has changed in any relevant respect since 1896. Basically, that duty has always been to audit a company's accounts with reasonable care and skill. The real ground on which *re Kingston Cotton Mill* ... is, I think, capable of being distinguished, is that standards of reasonable care and skill are upon expert evidence, more exacting today than those which prevailed in 1896.

In *Gerrard (Thomas)*, the auditor failed to evaluate stock. In *Twomax*, the auditors failed to make physical checks at inventory count or conduct a debtor's circularisation. They were adjudged 'negligent', and there would be few auditors today who would disagree. Precedent up to this point is summarised in **Table 5.3**.

Table 5.3 Reasonable care and skill, 1895–1970

Case	Specific duty of care arising from case
1896 *Kingston Cotton Mill Co. (No. 2)* Ch 279 (UK)	General standard laid down in terms of *reasonable skill, care and caution*, '*watchdog not a bloodhound*'.
1904 *London Oil Storage Co. Ltd v. Seear, Hasluck & Co.* 31 Acct LR 1 (UK)	Auditors to *verify the existence of assets* reported in the balance sheet. First time courts clarified that auditors were expected to go beyond the books and records of the client for evidence.
1920 *Arthur E Green & Co. v. The Central Advance and Discount Corporation Ltd* 63 Acct LR 1 (UK)	Not only was the auditor required to go beyond the company's internal documentary evidence, they were also required to relate evidence obtained from different sources.
1938 *McKesson & Robbins* case (USA)	Massive fraud over time; auditors should *verify assets on balance sheet*, including, in this case, *accounts receivable and inventory*.
1970 *Pacific Acceptance Corporation Ltd v Forsyth & Ors* 92 WN (NSW) 29 (Australia)	Confirmed or established specific duties of the modern auditor. Inspired the call for *developing and strengthening auditing standards*.

Principles in the modern era

Applications of 'reasonable skill and care' continue to be refined. Common law started to address the challenges of modern audit practice in the 1980s, including the auditor's responsibility to gather different and/or more sophisticated types of evidence, and to better understand and analyse the client's computerised systems. A number of cases have been instructive in this regard, the following among them:

- *H E Kane v. Coopers and Lybrand* (1983) 44 NBR 2D 374 (Canada) was concerned with irregular accounting practices employed in relation to a customer of an air travel business. The plaintiffs contended that if the special accounting practices relating to that customer had been identified by the auditor, corrective measures would have been taken, and H E Kane would not have suffered a loss. Hoyt J, finding against the defendants, stated that the defendants had failed to carry out sufficient detailed testing, and in particular had failed to conduct any form of detailed cut-off test or year-end ticket reconciliation.

- In another Canadian case, *Revelstoke Credit Union v. Miller, Berry* (1984) WWR 2 297, the importance of the systems audit and detailed testing came to light. It centred on losses from unauthorised loans made by the manager of Revelstoke Credit Union. The systems audit for the company in 1977 was conducted on only one day's transactions. On the basis of this testing, the auditor wrote that 'no unusual items were noted, supporting documentation and proper approvals received. Conclusion: good control in this area'. McEachern CJSC found that this level of testing was wholly inadequate, especially when compared to the 25 complete loan files that were checked in the previous years. The judge further considered that the balance sheet confirmation of outstanding loans and the review of transactions from the confirmation date to the year-end were not properly conducted. Although ultimately the 'except for' rule led to a ruling for the defendants, both the systems audit and the year-end review were deemed inadequate to form an opinion.
- In Australia's *AWA Ltd v Daniels Deloitte Haskins & Sells* (1992) (and related litigation), the auditor's responsibility for assessing the client's system was again at issue. A young officer of AWA Ltd (Koval) made risky and unauthorised foreign-exchange transactions over a period of several years, overall leading to a A$49.8 million loss. It went to the NSW Supreme Court, where Rogers J found auditors negligent in relation to their failure to advise the client's board of their own audit test findings which indicated failures in the client's internal control systems, and their role in detecting fraud.
- A New Zealand case, *Jagwar Holdings Ltd v. Julian* (1992) 6 NZCLC 68,040, found that Jagwar used information from a 1986 financial profile to make an investment in Fullers Corp. Although auditor PwC escaped liability through a court position that a duty of care does not arise when a statement made for a particular purpose is used for another purpose, negligence was established. Specifically, the auditors did not comply with standards regarding the nature of the review with Fullers, and they:
  1 did not review the quality of data presented
  2 labelled the report as an 'audit' when it was in fact a 'review'
  3 labelled the balance sheet as covering a 'period of', not a 'point in' time
  4 failed to consider the opening position in accounts.

  This all appears to be very sloppy work and represents a series of audit failures.

A number of company failures occurred in the last two decades of the 20th century, including Enron and WorldCom in the United States; Polly Peck, BCCI and Barings Bank in the United Kingdom; and Parmalat in Italy. New Zealand alone lost two-thirds of its market value between 1987 and 1991 due to corporate failures. Professional scepticism seems to have been in short supply.

Professional scepticism

'To succeed in avoiding detection [the fraudster] needed a good deal of luck, not the least of which was the good fortune not to have [an auditor] alert to the possibility that his human frailties might embrace dishonesty.'

Source: Justice Thomas, ruling on the 1979 New Zealand case *Dairy Containers Ltd v. NZI*, in which ongoing management fraud was not detected by the auditors.

These events shook market confidence and led to new audit regulations, including the *Sarbanes-Oxley Act* in the United States, the *Financial Markets Authority Act* in New Zealand, and new corporate law in Australia. The Australian HIH Insurance company failure loomed large among these and is worthy of closer scrutiny to see how corporate and watchdog failures can come to cause damage to the economy at large as well as to shareholders and other stakeholders.

HIH Insurance (Australia), 2001

At the start of the 21st century, HIH stakeholders suffered losses amounting to A$5.3 billion – by 2000, liabilities had exceeded assets by A$4 billion (Mak et al. 2005). HIH CEO and co-founder Ray Williams and his team were found to have committed gross mismanagement, failing to provide for future claims, hiding or under-reserving future liabilities, and expanding into the US and UK markets too quickly.

Williams was a powerful influence on HIH practices, and the company's board failed to appreciate the problems that were probably knowable by mid-1999. Ultimately, two million policyholders were denied the opportunity to withdraw and save their invested premiums, and 27000 shareholders lost their entire investment. The case thus affected all levels of Australian society.

The blame was said to be attributable to multiple sources, including the failure of the board to act, and the failure of APRA or ASIC to intervene. The auditor, Arthur Andersen was implicated as well.[2] A Royal Commission set up in the aftermath of the crisis found that the auditor failed to do enough testing. Arthur Andersen was also found to have joined the cover-up, signing off an unqualified audit in October 2000 despite cash outflows that year of A$678 million from operations.

The Royal Commission concluded that the failure was due, in part, to a lack of auditor independence, and that they may have been protecting other sources of income from HIH. This highlights many questions concerning whether an auditor should be performing 'other' services for the audit client. Justice Neville Owen concluded that Arthur Andersen maintaining an ongoing relationship with HIH management led to practices that its own audit manual would not have supported.

Other, more recent Australian cases (e.g., *Centro Properties Group*, 2012; and *Premium Income Fund*, 2015) have shown that the auditor's due care continues to appear before the courts. HIH and related events inspired the creation of Australian Professor Ian Ramsay's 2001 report into auditor practice (Ramsay, 2001), including oversight of professional independence practices and 'going concern' disclosures in the audit opinion. Some of these examples are summarised in **Table 5.4**.

Table 5.4 Reasonable care and skill, 1971 to present day

Case	Specific duty of care arising from case
1968 *re Gerrard (Thomas) & Son Ltd* Ch 455 (UK)	Reaffirmed the concept of 'reasonable care and skill' and extended that idea to the evaluation of a client's inventory (stock).
1983 *H E Kane v. Coopers and Lybrand* 44 NBR 2D 374 (Canada)	Highlights the danger of relying on letters of representation, that the courts will pay attention to expert evidence, and the *importance of confirmations and cut-off tests.*
1984 *Revelstoke Credit Union v. Miller, Berry,* WWR 2 297 (Canada)	Systems audit and year-end review were inadequate, emphasising the necessity of *examining the client's system and controls, and the importance of year-end reviews.*
1992 *AWA Ltd v Daniels Deloitte Haskins & Sells* 10 ACLC 933 (Australia)	Highlighted need to keep client's governing board aware of system concerns discovered in the audit, possibly emphasising the importance of the Letter to Management (see Chapter 17 of this text).
1992 *Jagwar Holdings Ltd v. Julian,* 6 NZCLC 68,040 (New Zealand)	Duty does not arise when a statement made for a particular purpose is used for another purpose. *Emphasises need for engagement letter and internal reviews by which the audit process is evaluated.*
2003 HIH Insurance (Australia)	Massive losses, and part of what led to independent oversight of auditor independence. Established importance of 'going concern' opinion.
2012 *Centro Properties Group* (Australia)	The Federal Court (Melbourne) awarded A$67 million to plaintiffs in relation to PwC negligence as to a short-term A$2 billion guarantee liability (2006–07), *highlighting the importance of reviewing significant transactions and potential misclassifications in the accounts.*
2015 *Premium Income Fund* (Australia)	Unit-holders settled a case against KPMG (Australian Federal Court). Judge Perram said the fund had entered into loss-making transactions, and KPMG allegedly failed to detect their questionable validity. *Highlights the potential impact of related party transactions.*

[2] Arthur Andersen went bankrupt not long after, following other accusations of negligent and complacent audit practice. It is the largest failure to date of a Big Five (now Big Four) audit firm.

Contributory negligence

In the event that auditors are proven negligent, it may be possible for them to invoke the defence of contributory negligence, such that the judgment against the auditor would be reduced (see **Figure 5.1**). Such a defence was allowed in *H E Kane v. Coopers and Lybrand* (1983) and in *Revelstoke Credit Union v. Miller, Berry* (1984).

Gwilliam (1987b) explains that 'in order to succeed in a defence based upon contributory negligence, an auditor, being sued by a corporate client, has to overcome three specific obstacles':

1   The directors of the company must have been negligent.
2   Contributory negligence must be available as a defence to actions under contract.
3   Contributory negligence must be arguable in the particular circumstances of an audit designed to give an opinion on a set of financial statements.

Gwilliam explains that the courts have traditionally been reluctant to hold directors who have acted in good faith to more than minimal terms of duty. This principle is established in a number of cases, including the previously discussed *Revelstoke* case and, to some extent, in the statute. The UK 1945 *Law Reform (Contributory Negligence) Act* allows for apportionment to reduce the actual amount of any damages awarded, and this appears to have been influential, but not until about 40 years later.

Even as relatively recently as 1979, as illustrated in the Australian case *Simonius Vischer & Co. v. Holt & Thompson* (1979) 2 NSW LR 322, this was not a clear course of action for auditors. The logic is explained by Moffitt J:

> Where the action for professional negligence is against an auditor, it is difficult to see how a finding of contributory negligence, according to the usual concepts, could be made. If, as where the audit is of a public company, the audit contract or the undertaking of an audit is found to impose a duty to be exercised so as to safeguard the interests of shareholders, it is difficult to see how the conduct of any servant or director could constitute the relevant negligence so as to defeat the claim against the auditor, whose duty it is to check the conduct of such persons, and, where appropriate, report it to the shareholders.

So, the availability of this defence was controversial. Although the 1945 UK *Law Reform Act* established contributory negligence as a defence under tort, whether the same applied under contract was not yet clear.

In the *Revelstoke Credit Union* and *H E Kane* cases, however, the contracted defendants sought to claim contributory negligence. In *H E Kane*, the defendants contended that 'Harold Kane's complete lack of supervision of the travel division and (his son) Charles Kane's wilful concealment of unreported tickets amounts to conduct by the company which should reduce an award'. Similarly, in *Revelstoke Credit Union v. Miller, Berry* (1984) WWR 2 297, the defendants argued that the directors and managers of the credit union had been negligent. Both cases involved the law of contract. Hoyt J, however, stated:

> In my view as the consequences flowing from the former distinction between actions founded in tort or contract is becoming blurred, the award must be reduced because of the company's conduct.

In the Australian case *AWA Ltd v. Daniels Deloitte Haskins and Sells* (1992) 10 ACLC 933, it was also found that the argument of contributory negligence was available to the auditors under both contract and tort. Justice Rogers ruled on the matter and defined contributory negligence as follows (Ross, 1992, p. 66):

> [A] plaintiff's failure to meet the standard of care to which it is required to conform for its own protection, and which is a legally contributing cause in bringing about the loss.

Other jurisdictions, such as New Zealand also followed; for example, in the 1992 *Mirage Entertainment v. A Young* case, the auditor's liability was reduced by 40 per cent.

Contributory negligence is now established as a defence to reduce judgments against the auditor. However, *H E Kane* could be seen as restricting such actions to small proprietary companies and, as in the *Revelstoke Credit Union* case, judges appear to place a lower standard of skill and care on directors and managers than on the auditors. Nonetheless, the auditor has an opportunity to reduce judgments against them should the blame be rightfully shared.

When auditors are complicit

While not the primary topic of this chapter, statutory and criminal law can also be imposed should an auditor (or anyone!) commit illegal acts or be associated with crime. As discussed by Chung et al. (2010), Australian law directly addresses this:

> It is possible for a third party to sue an auditor for misleading or deceptive conduct under the *Trade Practices Act 1974*, the *Australian Securities and Investments Commission Act 2001*, and the State and Territory Fair Trading Acts.

It would also bring the profession into disrepute. Needless to say, the auditor should not commit, or in any way be associated with, the conduct of a criminal act.

CONCEPT QUESTION 3	What is 'contributory negligence' and how can an auditor invoke this defence?

Study tools

Summary

This chapter traced the legal liability of auditors through case law in Australia, New Zealand and influential cases in other countries. Included are a selection of the cases that have seen judicial decisions over the years, and a few of these have established lasting principles which guide practice today.

Those to whom the auditor owes a duty of care were considered, including those contracted with the auditor. We also considered those third parties who can be reasonably foreseen by the auditor and those who, although unknown specifically to the auditor, may be foreseeable. That which the plaintiff must prove was also discussed.

Practices that comprise an auditor's 'duty of care' or its absence were identified. Contributory negligence to reduce judgments against the auditor was also discussed. While the precise extent of liability remains uncertain, there is a growing trend to 'blame the auditor' through litigation against them when something goes wrong.

Nonetheless, while it may appear intimidating, audit disputes do not often lead to the courtroom – though when they do, the costs can be staggering. The best way to avoid litigation is through clearly defined and communicated engagement terms, and by applying competence and due care.

🔗 Case/resources link

CAATs for Classrooms

Accompanying this book is a series of data, integrated worksheets and exercises that are designed to support your learning and give you exposure to hands-on audit decision-making dilemmas faced by auditors in the planning elements of the audit process. Acquire the relevant material for this chapter from your instructor.

Review questions

5.1   Who came up with the concept of 'reasonable care and skill'?

5.2   Discuss whether the auditor should be a 'watchdog' or a 'bloodhound'.

5.3   In the cases examined here, are we concerned with the auditor as 'plaintiff' or 'defendant'?

5.4   In some of the cases examined here, are we concerned with the auditor's or the client's 'illegal or fraudulent' behaviour?

5.5   Describe the circumstances in which an auditor may be held liable to clients under contract law.

5.6   Describe the circumstances that could give rise to liability to third parties under the law of tort.

5.7   Name two important cases in relation to liability to foreseen third parties, and explain the significance of each case and findings relative to audit concerns.

5.8   Name two important cases in relation to liability to foreseeable parties, and explain the significance of each case and findings relative to audit concerns.

5.9   Explain what constitutes reasonable skill and care. Identify key cases and their significance to this standard.

5.10 Explain how auditors may be able to reduce their liability by demonstrating contributory negligence by managers or directors of client entities.

5.11 Explain the significance of, and points made in, the *Pacific Acceptance* case.

5.12 Compare Australian and New Zealand common law history with respect to the auditor's duty of care to third parties.

5.13 Explain how selective cases since 1980 have addressed practice issues that may not have existed in the 19th or early 20th centuries.

Exercises

5.1   **AUDITOR'S LIABILITY:** AX Ltd advise you that they require your audited financial statements to support an application to the bank for a loan. Without your knowledge, the statements were shown to W, who, on the basis of the reports, invested a large sum in AX Ltd. AX Ltd subsequently became insolvent and W suffered considerable financial loss. What is your legal liability to W?

5.2 **AUDITOR'S LIABILITY:** Consider the legal implications of the actions of the external auditor in the following circumstance. Indicate whether or not, in your opinion, the auditor is liable for negligence, and, if so, in what manner. Where relevant, state alternative actions that should have been taken by the auditor.

Smart is an officer of Lenders Ltd. Early in a financial year, he embezzled $10 000 from the company to cover a temporary financial problem. Just before the balance date, he repaid the stolen money together with interest at the company's standard rate and forged documents that purported that the loan was made to a fictitious person. The audit clerk noticed that the loan had not been authorised in the normal manner. However, as the loan had been repaid and the profit position had not been affected, she decided to keep quiet about it and the subsequent audit report was therefore unqualified.

5.3 **CASE LAW IMPACT:** Describe how the outcome of the *Pacific Acceptance* case may have had an impact on audit practice and specific standards pronouncements in Australia, New Zealand and/or overseas.

5.4 **AUDITOR'S LIABILITY:** T was the auditor for Company L, which wished to borrow money from a private investor: I. The financial statements received an unqualified ('clean') audit opinion, but Company L failed within three months of the end of the audit, and the private investor received none of their investment back. Under each of the following circumstances, who is most likely to be liable?

a I requested the audit from the CEO of Company L. As a result, the CEO contacted the auditor but did not tell the auditor why the assurance was needed.

b I met with the CEO of Company L and T prior to the beginning of the audit engagement.

c Same as (b), except that the financial statements clearly and appropriately disclosed the going concern risk in accordance with GAAP.

5.5 **THEORY AND LIABILITY:** Aaron was the auditor for Business B. Those who relied on Aaron's (clean) audit opinion included the existing partners of Business B, potentially new partners of Business B, and the CEO of Business B in regards to demonstrating to the partners what an excellent management job she had done. For each of those reliant on the opinion:

a state, in terms of theory (see Chapter 1), why they are likely to be interested in the audit opinion

b whether, under contract, the auditor has some obligation to that user

c whether, under tort, the auditor has some obligation to that user.

5.6 **AUDITOR NEGLIGENCE:** The auditor declined to conduct an audit of the client's financial statements because he did not have the audited beginning balances for the statements. The client was able to convince the auditor to conduct a 'review' engagement, however. The auditor's opinion was (inappropriately) unqualified. What recourse does the client have, and under what circumstances are they most likely to succeed?

5.7 **AUDITOR'S LIABILITY:** The auditor completed their annual audit for Company R, and on the basis of the auditor's opinion, Bill committed funds. Company R failed, and Bill lost all of his money. Determine under which, if any, of the following circumstances Bill may recover from the auditor. Consider each situation independently:

a   While Bill eventually recovered his money, the auditor failed to test Company R's inventory, which was material to the financial statements.

b   The auditor failed to test R's (material) inventory, and Bill lost his entire investment, but Company R intentionally kept Bill's use of the opinion secret from the auditor.

c   The auditor failed to test R's (material) inventory, but Bill could have recovered his money from Company R if the auditor had not ignored a notice made in the local paper and brought it to Bill's attention.

5.8 **AUDITOR'S LIABILITY:** The auditor, having completed the audit for Company R, was unaware that the company's senior manager was misappropriating funds of a material amount by creating false purchase invoices, a process that led to the authorisation of cheques. These cheques were not sent to Company R's suppliers, but rather to the senior manager's personal account. The auditor conducted appropriate tests on the controls but, through bad luck, did not happen to test the accounts that may have identified the problem. Furthermore, the senior manager did quite a good job of hiding his actions and of ensuring that the invoices that would have shown the problem were kept from the auditor.

a   Is the auditor liable under contract? Explain.

b   Is the auditor liable under the law of tort? Explain.

c   If the auditor had a judgement made against him under contract, would he have any further recourse? If so, what?

d   If the auditor had a judgement made against him under the law of tort, would he have any further recourse? If so, what? And what would this affect?

5.9 **FUJI XEROX CASE:** A financial scandal involving Fuji Xerox New Zealand (FXNZ) and Australia (FXA) emerged on the disclosure by KPMG to Japanese shareholder FujiFilm that revenues and valuations were incorrect. It was estimated that accounts were overstated by NZ$450 million (2011–16). The case had local, regional and international implications.

An independent report implicated a 'sales at any cost' culture led, in part, by incentives that rewarded employees on revenue. Common practices included bringing estimates of future revenue forward. False revenues may have comprised, at one point, up to 30 per cent of FXNZ's revenue. Favoured or family-member employees benefited from large salary bonuses and NZ$25 000 holidays, feeding a culture of greed. Changing auditors in early 2017 to KPMG seemed to mark the end of this, as the new firm raised concerns about revenue recognition and potential fraud with FujiFilm.

A series of actions followed. A report commissioned by FujiFilm found 'inappropriate accounting' in both Australia and New Zealand. The Australian Government began parliamentary inquiries into major-firm practices for federal entities. The New Zealand professional disciplinary board censured and suspended

Fuji Xerox's audit team leader, who acknowledged negligence. Four Japan-based senior managers and directors resigned and court actions were taken against three of them. Finally, and more recently, former accounting firm EY was added to the list of defendants (Slade, 2019; Wide Format Online Magazine, n.d.).

Required: Identify the types of court action possible against the former auditors by any of the various stakeholders in FXNZ, FXA or FujiFilm. Set out what would have to be proven for each suit to be successful. Consider the implications of 'adding' the auditor to the list of other 'defendants' in this case, and why litigants may choose to do so.

5.10 **ONLINE CASE RESEARCH: HIH, HARRISSCARFE, ONETEL OR FONTERRA:** Consider one of the following cases: Australia's HIH, HarrisScarfe or OneTel; or New Zealand's 2005 Fonterra case.

Required:

a Conduct library or online research to see what you can find on the selected case.

b From your findings, see if you can identify the potential for applications of the *insurance hypothesis*, *agency theory*, *transaction cost theory* or *social accountability*. Describe why.

c Explain in your own words who or what could have been done to prevent such situations in statute, standards or practice.

MILESTONES OF AUDIT

PART 1 THE AUDITOR'S ROLE IN SOCIETY

1 Introduction to audit
2 Audit concepts, role and history
3 Statutory law
4 Auditor professionalism and audit firms
5 The courts: The legal liability of auditors

PART 2 AUDIT PLANNING

6 Audit risk
7 Audit judgement, materiality and evidence
8 Audit testing and working papers
9 Audit process and analytical procedures
10 Audit planning

PART 3 AUDIT TESTING

11 Principles of internal control
12 Internal control and the auditor
13 Audit sampling
14 Systems testing I: Sales, purchases and payroll
15 Systems II: Warehousing, financing and fixed assets

PART 4 AUDIT COMMUNICATION AND REPORT

16 Completion and review
17 Audit report and opinion

PART 5 SPECIFIC TYPES OF AUDIT

18 Internal audit
19 Social audit
20 Fraud audit

THE AUDITOR'S ROLE IN SOCIETY

PLANNING

Audit planning

Part 2 of the textbook focuses on audit planning and comprises five chapters. Chapter 6 discusses audit risk, specifically the auditor's financial risk and approach to audit planning. Chapter 7 details the issues and challenges in applying audit judgement, materiality and evidence. Working papers and the purpose of audit testing are covered in Chapter 8, which sets out the regulations in Australia and New Zealand. Chapter 9 features the audit process and analytical procedures, discussing the evidence gained, and the nature, extent and timing of analytical procedures. The procedures used in the initial and detailed planning processes, scope-defining issues, and the engagement letter are covered in Chapter 10.

PART 2

Audit risk

Learning objectives

After studying the material in this chapter, you should be able to:
- define audit risk at the 'financial' and 'assertion' levels
- describe a 'risk approach' to audit planning
- apply a risk model approach and explain the resulting interactions among risks
- identify and explain indicators of misstatement and fraud risk.

Introduction

> The objective of the auditor is to identify and assess the risks of material misstatement, whether due to fraud or error, at the financial report and assertion levels, thereby providing a basis for designing and implementing responses to the assessed risks of material misstatement. (ASA 315, para 1.1)

Even if an audit is performed with competence and due care, there is still a chance – or 'risk' – that the audit opinion will not reflect the true condition of the financial statements. This is known as *audit risk* and will always exist to some degree simply because the auditor, despite their best efforts, cannot know everything:

> Audit risk [is] the risk that the auditor expresses an inappropriate [unmodified] audit opinion when the financial statements are materially misstated. (ISA NZ 200, para 13(c))

Risks at the *financial report* level refer to 'management override of internal control ... lack of management competence or lack of oversight over the preparation of the financial report' (ASA 315, paras 122–124). Risks at the *assertion level* refer to implied claims by management that are useful in selecting audit tests. Management assertions include occurrence, completeness, accuracy, classification, existence, rights and obligations, and valuation (see Chapter 7 for more details).

It is the financial report level, misstatement risks and their elements, and risk models for audit planning that are considered in this chapter.

A risk approach

> The risk assessment procedures shall include ... (a) Enquiries of management, of appropriate individuals within the internal audit function; (b) Analytical procedures; (c) Observation and inspection. (ASA 315, para 14; ISA NZ 315, para 6)

The *risk approach* is one in which the auditor carries out a number of procedures to study aspects of the client organisation that are more likely to suffer from material misstatement. A risk approach helps the auditor decide what evidence may be more or less important based on where material misstatement is more or less likely to occur.

In the past, audits consisted of a fixed set of fairly predictable actions, such as re-performing calculations and confirming assets irrespective of whether the risks warranted it. But the 'old way' did not capture the unique concerns associated with each engagement, nor did it consider how particular risks could lead to material error (Eilifsen, Knechel and Wallage, 2001). Furthermore, with predictable testing procedures, savvy (and fraudulent) managers could avoid detection, as they knew what the auditor was likely to test.

Essentially, prime reasons to adopt a 'risk' approach are that it focuses audit planning and (ultimately) testing on the areas most likely to reveal a material misstatement – if it exists. A risk approach is even more important in today's environment, for the following reasons:

- *Global businesses* are complex and their systems can create information overload for the auditor, unless the auditor can focus on important areas of concern.
- *Digital business environments* and potential data breaches are concerns. Risks lie in complex communication systems and data storage networks. Large businesses may be vulnerable to ransomware attacks, while small businesses with online transactions and cloud data may not be able to afford sophisticated protections.
- *Information taxonomies* such as XBRL and enterprise resource systems such as SAP use data bits which are decoupled from reports (such as financial statements) and which create the need for ongoing risk analyses within **continuous audits**.
- *Litigation defence* can be improved if the auditor can show that they logically approached the audit process and took audit risk into account (see Chapter 5).
- *High costs of audit* can be logically reduced by using a risk approach. Audit firms must maintain quality when reducing costs. One way of doing so is to collect more or better evidence from areas seen to be at higher risk.

A risk assessment approach is also expected under auditing standards:

> The auditor shall design and perform risk assessment procedures to obtain audit evidence that provides an appropriate basis for (a) The identification and assessment of risks of material misstatement, whether due to fraud or error ... (ASA 315, para 13)

Furthermore, there is a direct relationship between risk assessment, planning and professional scepticism – a relationship raised extensively by Australia's AUASB.

continuous audit
Refers to a situation in which audit functions are ongoing and where audit tests are carried out on a system as that system is operating. A continuous audit usually employs automated procedures that test, and report, whether data is being captured, processed and stored appropriately throughout the year.

Professional scepticism

Professional scepticism 'includes being alert to conditions that may indicate possible error or fraud, and to circumstances that suggest the need for [additional] audit procedure [in, for example,] accepting the engagement; [assessing the] integrity of owners, management and directors; [and conducting the] initial risk assessment procedures'.

Source: AUASB (2012, pp. 2–3).

Hence, the planning process must involve the auditor grasping each client's system, industry and business so that they can assess this risk. They must understand the client's obligations, pressures and governance. The auditor should have a sense of where management's and employees' actions could lead to material misstatements, whether intentional or otherwise. The key to a risk analysis approach is to help auditors focus on areas where the greatest risks of misstatement arise.

> Risk assessment procedures – the audit procedures performed to obtain an understanding of the entity and its environment, including the entity's internal control, to identify and assess the risks of material misstatement ... (ISA NZ 315, para 4(d))

There are many circumstances that might indicate risk (see ASA 330 and ISA NZ 315 for examples), but how the risk approach is to be conducted is left to the professional.

Audit firms put weight on auditor business, audit risk and client business risk. Firms may use the weighted risk score for each assessed client. For example, KPMG uses KRisk, an innovative client acceptance and computerised decision aid developed by the risk management unit of the firm (Bell et al. 2002). Avoiding audit business risk is most important for auditors. Auditors may adapt to the client acceptance risks by using three strategies (Johnstone, 2000):

1 screening clients based on their risk characteristics
2 screening clients based on the audit firm's risk of loss on engagement
3 adapting more proactively using strategies that include adjusting the audit fee and making plans about the necessary audit evidence.

Overall audit risk

....

overall audit risk (OAR)
The impact of an inappropriate audit opinion – that is, of audit failure – and the costly outcomes that could occur as a result. Such an outcome could be, for example, a third party's unjustified reliance on an opinion to purchase a business that, had that opinion been appropriate, they would not have bought.

'Audit risk' is a broad concept but can be made more operable by segmenting it into examinable elements. A key element is the concept of **overall audit risk (OAR)**. The source of OAR in each engagement is important for the auditor to understand.

Auditing in practice

Audit testing

- If the auditor knows that forecasted earnings will be used to value the business for sale, audit testing may focus on the accuracy of the company's earnings.
- If the auditor determines that controls over payroll are absent, it may be appropriate to increase tests over the validity of employment data.

A return to audit theory gives us a sense of how OAR can lead to audit failure, as described in the 'Auditing in practice' box titled 'Overall audit risk: Implications for users'.

Auditing in practice

Overall audit risk: Implications for users

- From an agency point of view, OAR arises from a failure of the auditor (as a monitor) to discover or inform the board of directors or shareholders (principals) of the quality of their managers' stewardship.
- From a neoclassical point of view, OAR arises from market players who may have relied on a 'clean' opinion concerning misstated financial statements to make a lending or investment decision. In macroeconomic terms, loss of trust in the auditor's opinion could lead to the inability to operate a viable equity market.
- From a social accountability perspective, audit failure can have an effect on society at large. So, for example, there may be a cost to employee trade unions if they relied on (unreliable) financial statements to negotiate their pay packets.
- Taking a critical view, one implication is the possibility that, as a result of public audit failure, the firm or audit profession itself is brought into disrepute, and their work and opinions may be less trusted.

OAR is thus an important element to assess.

CONCEPT QUESTION 1   Define OAR and discuss the factors it is influenced by.

Employing OAR and other elements, we now introduce an audit risk model similar to one formerly used with standards, to show how a risk approach can guide audit planning.

Audit risk models

A risk-based approach does not stop with OAR. An **audit risk model** helps determine the level of evidence that should be gathered relative to risk embedded in the systems and environment of a client's business. So those systems and that environment must be evaluated by the auditor.

The ARM is an audit-planning device. Using an ARM encourages the auditor to assess the confidence gained (and risk remaining) at each stage of the audit process. It creates a reasoned and systematic approach to audit. Despite being somewhat mathematical, a basic ARM is not rigid but rather a framework to guide audit judgement.

Numerous models are used in audit firms. We have selected one that is relatively simple and that illustrates the relationship between risk and evidence. To use our ARM, the auditor first selects an 'acceptable' level of OAR. Keep in mind that if OAR is low, then more audit testing will be required.

> **audit risk model (ARM)** A mathematical expression of the relationship between an acceptable level of overall audit risk (OAR) and the risk particulars of an organisation, system, industry or economy that increase or reduce that risk.

Auditing in practice

Low OAR

If the auditor knows that the financial statements will be relied on by those intending to purchase the client, they may select a low OAR, such as 2 per cent.

Together with OAR, risks of material misstatement can be introduced into the ARM. The two risk types often used to explain how financial statements may be materially misstated (ASA 200, para 13.2(n); ISA NZ 200, para 13(n)) are referred to as *control* and *inherent* risks. Inherent risk also classifies risks sourced in the client's 'business', 'industry' and 'management'. These are defined in **Table 6.1**.

Table 6.1 Non-controllable risks of misstatement

1	*Control risk (CR)* – the risk that a misstatement that could occur in an assertion about a class of transaction, account balance or disclosure and that could be material, either individually or when aggregated with other misstatements, will not be prevented, or detected and corrected, on a timely basis by the entity's internal control (ASA 200, para 13.2(e(ii)); ISA NZ 200, para 13(n)).
2	*Inherent risk (IR)* –the susceptibility of an assertion about a class of transaction, account balance or disclosure to a misstatement that could be material, either individually or when aggregated with other misstatements, before consideration of any related controls (ASA 200, para 13.2(e(i)); ISA NZ 200, para 13(n)). IR is usually considered a function of: a *Business risk* – a risk resulting from significant conditions, events, circumstances, actions or inactions that could adversely affect an entity's ability to achieve its objectives and execute its strategies, or from the setting of inappropriate objectives and strategies (ISA NZ 315, para 4(b)). b *Industry risk* – relevant industry factors include ... conditions such as the competitive environment, supplier and customer relationships, and technological developments (ISA NZ 315, para A25). c *Management risk* – the risk that management may intentionally distort the financial statements or a portion of them.

Collectively, inherent and control risks are known as *non-controllable risks*. As the term implies, the environment and controls of the organisation are outside the external auditor's control. If inherent and control risks are high, the auditor must look elsewhere for their evidence. In particular, they will have to rely more heavily on **substantive tests** to reduce the only type of risks over which they have control.

The final category added to the ARM, therefore, involves the risk that an auditor's own substantive procedures will fail to identify material misstatements. This is the risk that is determinable, or 'controllable', by the auditor (see **Table 6.2**). For the purposes of our planning model, this is divided into analytical procedures the auditor carries out, and substantive procedures.

substantive tests
The audit evidence-collection procedures that determine whether account balances, or transactions that lead to account balances, comply with GAAP.

Table 6.2 Controllable detection risks

> 3   *Detection risk (DR)** – the risk that the procedures performed by the auditor to reduce audit risk to an acceptably low level will not detect a misstatement that exists and that could be material, either individually or when aggregated with other misstatements (ASA 200, para 13.1(e); ISA NZ 200, para 13(d)). DR is the only risk that the auditor can fully control. It can be divided into two testing procedures:
> a   *Analytic procedures risk (APR)* – the risk that audit procedures to estimate an account balance will fail to identify a material misstatement in the account or the assertion being tested. APR refers to, in particular, risks reduced by conducting analytic procedures.
> b   *Substantive testing risk (STR)* – the risk that substantive tests of transactions, or direct tests on balances, will fail to identify a material misstatement in the account, or the assertion, being tested.

* Acronyms are used to facilitate formulas later in this chapter.

Therefore, in a high-risk environment, an auditor will probably have to do more extensive substantive tests than they would in a low-risk environment. Similarly, they will require more *confidence* from their substantive procedures should confidence from the control and inherent environments be low.

CONCEPT QUESTION 2   What are 'substantive tests' and why are they used?

Audit confidence is the conceptual complement (or reciprocal) of audit risk.

Auditing in practice

Audit confidence

If the auditor decides that an OAR of 5 per cent is acceptable, then the overall audit confidence required is 95 per cent (100 − 5). Hence, the auditor can be 95 per cent 'confident' but not 'absolutely sure' that they came to an appropriate audit opinion.

Audit confidence can also be derived from an analysis of inherent risk (IR), control risk (CR), analytical procedures risk (APR) and substantive testing risk (STR). Confidence increases if those risks are low or lowered (see **Figure 6.1**).

Figure 6.1 Confidence–risk relationship

As IR and CR are observable but not controllable, the auditor can only increase confidence (or reduce OAR) by increasing the nature, timing or extent of the STR and APR. This becomes important in applying these concepts to the audit risk model.

Applying an audit risk model

During the planning stage, the auditor will use a risk model to decide what level and type of substantive testing they must conduct in order to bring the OAR down (or overall confidence up) to an acceptable level.

Broad qualitative values (e.g., 'high', 'medium', 'low'), or more precise quantitative values (e.g., a percentage), can be ascribed to each of the elements of the risk model. It is difficult to precisely measure risk, however. It is hard to know whether the risk of a business failing is 'precisely' 50 per cent or 80 per cent. That said, the auditor may have a sense that it is 'high' rather than 'medium' or 'low'. So, while precise measurement may be desired, broad measures are usually more practical and are employed in practice.

A degree of risk will always be associated with any audit. Even examining all transactions and balances will not enable the auditor to avoid the risk of an understatement, because some transactions may not have been recorded. Therefore, auditors must decide on the level of confidence they deem necessary. Most audit firms expect at least a 95 per cent confidence level, but there are exceptions. Other principles apply, too:

- *Substantive tests must always be carried out* because auditors report on the substance of financial statements, not on the system that produces them.
- There is a *limit to the confidence from internal control* that can reasonably be derived. Much beyond 40 per cent confidence would seem high.
- A client's *failure to provide fundamental internal controls may prevent auditability*. This is because it may be impossible to gain sufficient confidence from other audit procedures, and the risk from understatement (missing information) may be significant. Assessing such problems by, or before, the planning stage is important.

Quantitative aspects

While different formulations are possible, the relationship between the components of audit risk can be expressed as shown in **Figure 6.2**.

$$OAR = IR \times CR \times APR \times STR \text{ or } OAR = f(IR, CR, APR, STR), \text{ where}$$

IR   = inherent risk

CR   = control risk

APR = analytical procedures risk

STR = substantive testing risk

Figure 6.2 An audit risk model: Quantified

The auditor wishes to solve for the risk they can control – STR – to find out the risk allowable (or confidence required) from substantive testing. Hence, and using a little algebra, the above formula becomes:

Solving for controllable risk:

$$STR = OAR/(IR \times CR \times APR)$$

What we want to know – STR – will vary for each client, for each subsystem and for each assertion. STR can be reduced by expanding the substantive audit tests, or it can be increased by conducting fewer or less reliable substantive tests.

Everything on the right-hand side of the formula (except for APR) is non-controllable but hopefully measurable. Once determined, they will drive the decision of what STR must be.

IR and CR are determined by the client's situation and systems, respectively. Measuring APR – using ratios and other procedures that the auditor employs – is usually a low-cost part of audit testing, so irrespective of other risks, APR tests should usually be performed.

Let's look at a specific ARM example. Assume that:

Acceptable overall audit risk (OAR)   = 5%

Inherent risk (IR)   = 70%

Confidence from controls   = 40% (thus, CR = 60%, or 100 – 40)

Confidence from analytical procedures = 40% (thus, APR = 60%)

Using the formula:

$$STR = 0.05/(0.7 \times 0.6 \times 0.6) = 20\% \text{ (to nearest 1\%)}$$

Therefore, to achieve the maximum level of OAR, the auditors must derive 80 per cent (100 – 20) confidence from substantive tests.

Qualitative aspects

For an audit in which the acceptable OAR risk is 5 per cent (the confidence required is 95 per cent), the auditor will have been able to rely on other aspects of the client's system or environment to reduce the effort they have to put into substantive tests of detail. **Figure 6.3** illustrates the non-controllable risks that have to be assessed for this purpose.

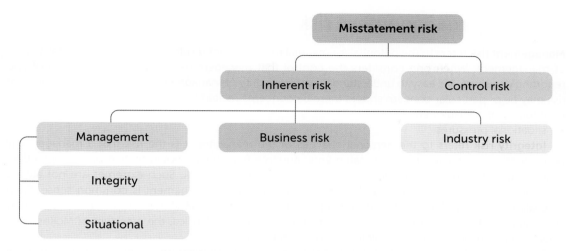

Figure 6.3 Risk of material misstatement (non-controllable risk)

Determining an appropriate weighting for each risk is often a matter of making a qualitative assessment of the client's situation. Some guidance follows.

Assessing control risk

As shown in **Table 6.1**, CR occurs when a material misstatement may not be prevented or detected by the client's system of internal control. It would be difficult to conduct any audit without being able to rely on the client's own systems. The external auditor will not be onsite or have access to the client's system at all times, so some reliance on their system is inevitable.

Auditing in practice

If there is no control ...

The client is a community bazaar in which all sales are via direct debit or cash. If there is no control to ensure that all transactions are recorded, then it would be difficult, or impossible, for the auditor to be confident all sales are recorded in the books. They cannot, therefore, rely on the client's sales-completion controls.

Assessing CR is a challenge for the auditor, which is covered in later chapters of this book. At this point, it is simply important to know that CR may be assessed as 'high', 'medium' or 'low' for the ARM based on the quality of the client's system.

Assessing inherent risk

IR has to do with the environment surrounding the client organisation and the pressures on management as they decide how to prepare their financial statements. Being non-controllable, the auditor can observe and analyse these factors, but they cannot change them. IR can be associated with management directly, or with the business/industry environment in which an organisation operates.

Assessing management risk

management risk
The potential for material misstatement resulting from the intentional actions of management.

Management risk refers to the potential for material misstatement resulting from the intentional actions of management. When one considers the control that managers have over business, financial and reporting decisions, it is easy to understand why the integrity of management is so critical. Management risk may be of particular concern should there be concerns related to:

* integrity of management
* situational pressures.

integrity risk
The risk that a manager may be inclined to distort the financial statements.

Integrity risk refers to the personal qualities of the managers. It is the risk that a manager may be inclined to distort the financial statements. Auditors have been known to hire private detectives to investigate the integrity of clients in order to assess integrity risk. Such extremes are not always appropriate, although evaluating a client before accepting an engagement is common sense. Such an evaluation may well have alerted the auditors in the famous 1938 McKesson & Robbins case (Barr and Galpeer, 1987), discussed earlier in this text, in which Philip Musica, the president of McKesson & Robbins, had previously been convicted of commercial fraud.

situational pressure
The risk that management will misstate the financials as a result of pressure they may be under.

Situational pressure refers to the risk that management will misstate the financials as a result of pressure they may be under. Pressure on managers can arise from a missed profit forecast, an impending takeover or 'going concern' problems. It may be tempting to misstate the financial statements in such circumstances, not necessarily for personal financial gain but 'for the good of the company'. An evaluation of the potential for misstatement due to situational pressure centres on the identification of external pressures. An example from New Zealand is given here in the 'Auditing in practice' box.

Auditing in practice

Situational pressure

Economic restructuring, the collapse of local manufacturing and cheap imports saw New Zealand unemployment rise dramatically during the late 1980s, hitting a national high of 10.7% in 1992. R. W. Saunders, Ltd, a clothing manufacturer, came under pressure because the market had 'gone soft', eventually leading to redundancies.

Source: Matthews (2021).

Much litigation against auditors involves situations in which managers – due to their access to controls and authority – are in a position to present a less-than-compliant picture of the financial position or operations.

Assessing business and industry risks

Business and industry risks are those associated with peculiarities inherent in the client's business and the industry in which it operates. Some businesses/industries are comparatively low risk, while others may be highly sensitive to changes in pricing, competition, consumer trends and/or technology. Other risks pertain to how the organisation is structured or operates. An engagement that is likely to receive publicity, and make the auditor's actions more visible, may also attract a higher risk premium (e.g., see Botica Redmayne, Bradbury and Cahan, 2010).

Industry risk

The risk of stock obsolescence would be high in the fashion industry because only the most up-to-date stock is likely to sell and, therefore, have value. In contrast, the gold bullion dealer could reasonably rely on the likelihood that stock will not become obsolete, although it could be volatile, so there is some, but not the same level of, risk.

A business risk will be more specific to the organisation being audited.

Business risk

Growing competition in the client's region may place pressure on the survival of the organisation. So, if an appliance store has enjoyed a monopoly position in a region for many years and, in the current year being audited, a strong competitor has emerged, there is a risk to the organisation's survival or profitability.

The evaluation of business and industry risks can influence the nature and extent of audit tests by directing attention to areas where the potential for misstatement is high. Examples of situations that may indicate the presence of business or industry risk, as well as management integrity risk, are illustrated in **Table 6.3**.

Table 6.3 Indicators of risk examples

Management integrity risk	Business risk	Industry risk
Criminal history	Supply chain changes	Market changes
Extensive related parties	System or IT changes	Exchange rate changes
Unusual management-approved adjusting entries	Business sale/purchase planned	Volatile market exposure
High or unrealistic management incentives	Complex alliances and related parties	Declining demand for product or service
History of misstating	Poorly skilled staff	Export/import cost changes
Questionable ethics	Key personnel changes	Climate change impact
Management fraud history	Cash flow problems	Natural disasters

Assessing detection risk: Sampling and non-sampling risk

Substantive testing risk is assessed from procedures we often associate with auditing: re-performing data entry, conducting reconciliations and recounting stock. Statistical sampling is employed in many of these tests, where it is appropriate to do so. Therefore, STR is often seen to be attributable to at least two sources related to the sampling process:

- sampling risk
- non-sampling risk (see **Figure 6.4**).

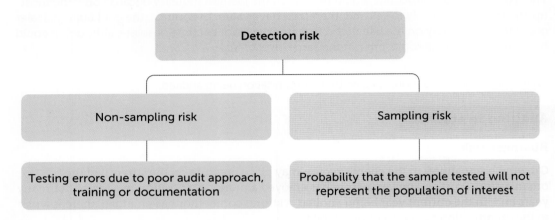

Figure 6.4 Sampling and detection risk

sampling risk
The risk that the auditor's conclusion, based on a sample, may be different from the conclusion that would be reached if the entire population were tested.

non-sampling risk
The risk that the auditor uses inappropriate procedures or misinterprets evidence and, as a result, fails to recognise an error.

Sampling risk means that the auditor's conclusion, based on a sample, may be different from the conclusion that would be reached if the entire population were tested. For example, a test of some invoices will not identify errors that only exist in untested invoices. Sampling risk can be reduced by requiring a high level of confidence, or a low tolerable error, in the sample plan.

Non-sampling risk is the risk that the auditor uses inappropriate procedures or misinterprets evidence and, as a result, fails to recognise an error. So, for example, inexperienced auditors may test for understatement when the situation calls for a test of overstatement. Reducing non-sampling risk relies on planning, careful conduct and oversight of auditors. Quality-control procedures help ensure that non-sampling risks are minimised and that the audit is performed to an acceptable standard of due care.

It is not usually the case that non-sampling risk is incorporated into the ARM because the audit firm would hope to reduce that risk to near zero, as sampling risk indicates a poorly conducted audit. More guidance on audit sampling, and other methods used to conduct substantive tests, is provided in later chapters in this book.

CONCEPT QUESTION 3	Define 'sampling' risk and 'non-sampling' risk.

Misstatement sources and risk

A way of understanding the impact of risk is to consider the reason for misstatements. That is, the impact of misstatements may be more or less material depending on whether there is *intent*, *non-intent* or *misunderstandings* as to how to treat particular data. The following sections look at examples of sources of misstatements.

Errors

By definition, errors are unintentional. Most audit problems arise from errors made by the client's staff when making judgement decisions or when recording transactions. Errors may result from making incorrect entries, a failure to make entries, making incorrect calculations, posting to a wrong ledger account, or bad judgement. For example, the double payment of an account may result from staff erroneously presenting the same invoice twice for payment, or staff may make incorrect calculations regarding the year-end stock valuation. In either example, the auditor could be at risk of non-discovery if the items in question are material. Usually, a sound system of internal control will prevent material errors from occurring.

Employee fraud

Greater risk lies in employee fraud, especially in smaller companies, whereby the client's assets are somehow misappropriated. Agency theory principles would suggest that interest by principals in employee fraud would be high, even without the evidence of frequent occurrence.

> **Auditing in practice**
>
> **Employee fraud**
>
> According to a study by EY (Sherwin, 1998), over half of those surveyed had suffered from at least one (known) fraud incident in the previous 12 months. It was also revealed that most frauds are carried out by employees who have been with a company for at least several years; that is, they are 'inside jobs'.

Some auditors still seek comfort from the *Kingston Cotton Mill* judgment of 1896, where Lopes LJ ruled that it was not the auditor's specific duty to detect fraud. But to rely on this case is naive. We all recognise that the auditor's prime responsibility is to report on annual financial statements. Financial statements can be misstated through fraud; however, if the misstatement is material, it should be looked for and discovered by the auditors. If suspicious circumstances were noticed, or should have been noticed, the auditor is obligated to probe those circumstances to the full.

Distortion

Distortion means manipulating accounts to present a more favourable picture than is actually the case. Off-balance-sheet financing disclosed as sales would be one type of distortion. The effects can often be material: in the United Kingdom, more than half of serious frauds are committed by directors and management (Sherwin, 1998). Distortion may be much more difficult to detect than either error or employee fraud because it is senior managers who are creating the distortion, and the auditor may have to consider such wide-ranging 'indicators' as the pay incentive system or the buying habits of managers (Galpin and Van Peursem, 1994).

Pressure on management may result from the unsatisfactory performance of individual managers or the organisation as a whole, or from specific circumstances in which the organisation finds itself. Any one or combination of these factors would serve to increase audit risk (see **Figure 6.4** for examples).

Distortion is most likely to be achieved by:

- altering valuations of non-monetary assets or provisions
- capitalising items that should be charged against profit
- manipulating the cut-off procedures at the balance sheet date.

It follows that these are the areas of increased audit risk, and in these areas, substantive testing should not be reduced.

In larger organisations, distortion will seldom be achieved by fictitiously creating or concealing numerous transactions (though the Equity Funding Corp fraud in America, which first came to light in 1973, was an exception). In smaller proprietary companies, distortion may be more possible. Where there is no separation of ownership and control, such as could occur in a small business, controls can be overridden, making distortion easier. For example, the owner-managers of small companies may understate profits (by suppressing cash sales, for example) to deceive taxation authorities, or overstate profits by overstating stock to deceive bankers who are being approached for a loan.

Misstatement characteristics

Different categories of misstatement have different degrees of audit risk associated with them. Risk from management fraud usually is more significant than that from employee fraud, which is, in turn, generally more significant than that from error. Also, each category of misstatement is more likely to occur in certain audit areas than in others. For example, distortion is unlikely to happen in the area of wages but is possible in the area of stock.

Moreover, the misstatement can be expected to be in a particular direction, depending on the audit area and the nature of the misstatement. For example, employee fraud in the area of wages would almost certainly result in an overstatement of wages. **Table 6.4** depicts some more-common causes of misstatement and assesses the effects on the financial statements that may result.

Table 6.4 Risk situations for distortion and fraud, implications and responses

Situation assessed as the risk of misstatement	Potential misstatement if distortion results	Reasonable auditor response
Declining trends in trading income or market share	Overstated revenues	Assess high industry risk; increase revenue and sales returns accounts tests
Signs that demand for client products or services on the decline	Overstated stock, overstated receivables	Assess high industry risk; increase stock valuation and receivables valuation audit tests
Cash-flow or liquidity problems	Going concern assumption not modified	High-risk audit, reduce acceptable overall audit risk; carefully examine solvency and liquidity
Past performance of the organisation significantly better than the industry norm	Any distortion possible (e.g., overstated revenues or assets, understated costs or liabilities)	Assess high integrity risk; increase tests that senior management concerned could override on these accounts
Loan or equity stock to be issued shortly	Profit picture overstated, debt understated to impress investors	Assess high situational risk; increase tests on relevant transactions (e.g., journal entries) and accounts
Manager is enjoying a lifestyle apparently above their means	Management fraud potential; distortion could result from capitalising on stolen assets	Assess high integrity risk; increase tests on convertible or monetary (susceptible) assets
Contest for control of the organisation appears likely	Distortions to meet expectations of internal candidates	Assess high business risk; increase tests on relevant accounts accessible to relevant managers
Remuneration is based on profit performance	Overstated profit (overstated revenue, understated costs)	Assess high situational risk; assess adjustments to revenues or expenses by manager

Study tools

Summary

Ultimately, an analysis of risk helps the auditor decide whether to accept an engagement. Once accepted, it is useful to anticipate the sorts of outcomes that could result should the worst (audit failure) occur. Knowing what contributes to that risk is useful because that knowledge can assist the auditor in planning the audit so as to focus on those areas most susceptible to material misstatement.

Risk analysis, and forming a risk model such as that illustrated in this chapter, help the auditor make important decisions as to the nature, extent and timing of audit procedures appropriate to a client, a system and each assertion.

The chapter ends with an explanation of the nature of, and distinctions between, errors, distortions in the financial statements, and fraud or misappropriation. Examples of situations were shown that may increase the potential risk of material misstatement due to fraud or distortion, together with reasonable audit responses.

Case/resources link

CAATs for Classrooms

Accompanying this book is a series of data, integrated worksheets and exercises that are designed to support your learning and give you exposure to hands-on audit decision-making dilemmas faced by auditors in the planning elements of the audit process. Acquire the relevant material for this chapter from your instructor.

Review questions

6.1 What does it mean to apply a risk approach to an audit? How does this differ from past practice?

6.2 Describe the nature and source of guidance provided to the auditor with respect to the auditor's responsibility for applying the risk approach.

6.3 Distinguish between audit risk at the 'financial' and 'assertion' levels as defined in auditing standards.

6.4 Name and describe five reasons for moving to the audit risk approach.

6.5 The audit risk model is an approximate mathematical model. Why would it be used, and at what point in the audit? Is it precise regarding actual risk?

6.6 Define and distinguish between each of the following:
   a   detection risk
   b   inherent risk
   c   control risk.

6.7 Define and distinguish between each of the following. Include in your analysis the 'type' of risk each one is:
   a   analytical procedures risk   d   industry risk
   b   substantive testing risk   e   management risk.
   c   business risk

6.8 Identify some limitations to the extent to which an auditor can, or should, reduce each of the following risks:

    a substantive testing risk

    b internal control risk.

6.9 Explain why we tend to solve for STR.

6.10 Explain how each of the other risks in the ARM is determined.

6.11 Explain the difference between risks associated with integrity and situational pressures. What larger category do they fall within?

6.12 Is 'sampling' risk or 'non-sampling' risk controllable by the auditor?

6.13 Distinguish between the meanings of each of the following, and describe why these differences may be relevant to the auditor – misstatements from:

    a errors

    b employee fraud

    c distortion.

6.14 Describe how audit risk and audit confidence will inform the planning of an audit.

Exercises

6.1 **RISK:** You must apply your knowledge of risk in relation to a company you have audited previously, when it had strong systems and no problems, but which currently faces challenges because its low-tech market has disappeared and sales have declined. Identify what you believe to be the areas of greatest risk and explain why:

    a overall risk   **c** control risk

    b inherent risk   **d** detection risk.

6.2 **RISK MODEL:** Four types of risk are used in the ARM. If you could choose to add 'sampling risk', 'non-sampling risk' or 'technology risk' for a next-stage ARM, what might you add to the model and why?

6.3 **RISK MODEL:** Your audit client is a metal parts manufacturer of significant interest to the community. They fill a unique local market niche but have been hurt by the effects of a falling dollar on raw materials imports. Gross profit margins have held steady.

    Required:

    a Determine whether the following risks are 'high' or 'low', and why:

        i APR

        ii IR

        iii OAR.

    b What does this mean for STR?

    c What are the implications?

6.4 **RISK TYPES:** What risk is most closely affected by each of the following?

a A client has implemented a subroutine in their payroll records program that casts and cross-casts all daily journal entries and postings.

b Unfortunately, the company's senior systems manager has a habit of overriding this feature and making her entries.

c After investigating, you find that all the senior managers have similar 'habits', and you decide that it may result from their incentive-based pay contracts.

d This year, the client has contracted with the government to provide a monopoly service – the provision of energy power lines in a fast-growing regional city.

e Inventory turnover is very low this year: 86 days on average, compared with 74 days on average last year.

6.5 **RISK TYPES:** What type of inherent risk might be indicated by each of the following for Laundry Ltd, a dry-cleaning and clothing repair business:

a It is venturing into financial investment activities.

b Customers are finding it cheaper to ship their clothing offshore for repair, as the South-East Asian market has opened up.

c The exchange rate on the company's investments has become more volatile.

d The long-time manager is leaving.

6.6 **RISK TYPES:** What type of inherent risk might be indicated by each of the following for an auto repair shop:

a The CEO is trying to increase the products completed per day to meet board incentives.

b Some of the customers have been paying later than usual.

c The senior manager has noticed that cash receipts per day have suddenly trended down.

d New diagnostic equipment has been purchased to improve efficiencies, and a large loan has been taken out on it.

e The senior manager is to receive bonuses based on throughput.

6.7 **RISK TYPES:** What types of risks, of all possible kinds, are suggested by the following events occurring for the audit of Bybee Ltd:

a The company produces aeroplane parts that may soon become obsolete.

b It relies on the high-level skills of its engineering team.

c There is no lock or protection on the warehouse that contains the completed parts.

d Its process for recording 'cost of sales' and 'work in progress' confuses beginning inventory with processed goods.

e The business is relying on getting a loan from a bank based on this audit.

f Junior audit staff failed to follow standard procedures to identify and collect the random group they are using for testing.

g No-one keeps track of cash in the business.

h The auditor cannot test all of the transactions, so they must rely on the results of a test of some of them.

6.8   **RISK MODEL:** For the client being audited, and due to the implications of audit failure, an auditor requires a very low OAR, and assesses their CR as very low (45 per cent) and the inherent risk as high (90 per cent). To what level of confidence must they conduct their substantive tests? Explain.

6.9   **RISK:** For each of the situations below, determine whether it would lead the auditor to increase, decrease or not change the nature, timing and/or extent of their testing:

    a Anyone in the business can enter sales information into the accounting information system.

    b The manager is under pressure to show a profit.

    c The client has been audited previously by your firm, and there is little to suggest that anyone you know of will rely on the financial statements.

    d The stock manager carefully updates stock records according to the client's policy.

    e Your audit firm has new staff who are unaccustomed to the firm's policies.

    f You are aware that several potential buyers are relying on financial statements to make significant investment decisions.

    g The client continues to have steady growth and a customer base.

6.10   **BUSINESS AND INDUSTRY RISK:** Use **Table 6.3**, and the risk examples within it, to:

    a conclude why each type of risk is classified as either a 'business' or 'industry' risk

    b describe how these types of risks are different from each other, and what that may mean for determining how they should be classified.

6.11   **RISK DECISIONS:** **Figure 6.5** illustrates possible outcomes of different audit decisions related to risk:

    Required:

    a Explain why each box on the right is classified as 'high', 'medium' or 'low'.

    b If later tests of controls reveal that controls over the *completeness* of transfers from inventory to cost of sales are inadequate, what would be the effect? Show that effect on this model.

    c If later tests reveal that the manager of stock control had a history of stealing stock, a risk originally assessed as 'low', what effect would this have on this model? Explain why, and show that effect on this model.

6.12   **RISK TYPES:** Review **Figure 6.6**.

    Required: Explain what has occurred in the analysis of each situation and what this means for substantive testing.

6.13   **RISK:** Consider the information in **Table 6.4** and identify:

    a why each of the distortion or fraud occurrences might occur in the situation described

    b why the auditor response may (or may not) be reasonable in all circumstances.

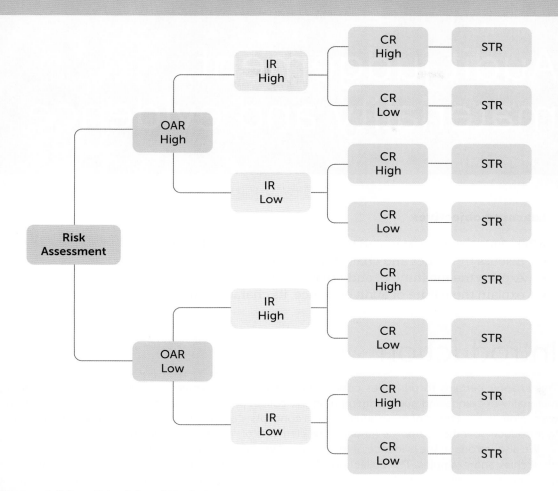

Figure 6.5 Possible risk-related outcomes

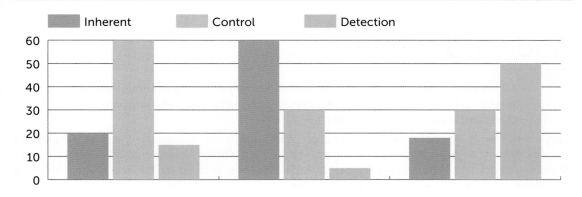

Figure 6.6 Inherent, control and detection graph

Audit judgement, materiality and evidence

Learning objectives

After studying the material in this chapter, you should be able to:
- discuss the issues and challenges in applying audit judgement
- explain the meaning of audit materiality and how it is applied in planning
- explain the nature of audit evidence, its characteristics and distinctions.

Introduction

This chapter pertains to principles concerning auditors' employment of their audit risk evaluations, materiality decisions and audit judgement in the collection and evaluation of evidential matter. Here, we explore the last three of these audit process concepts – audit judgement, materiality and evidence – to introduce how they comprise fundamental elements of modern audit practice.

We also introduce the evidence of the auditor's work and judgements, and provide an illustration of hierarchies and examples. The collection of evidence with which to make audit considerations is the fundamental activity of audit. When you see auditors gathering and checking invoices, observing stock counts, reviewing bank reconciliations or sending out letters of confirmation, you are observing the evidence-collection process by which an opinion can be made.

Audit judgement

> We consider audit as a process of critical thinking, analysis, and careful evaluation. The mechanical procedures, although necessary, must be performed with a large context of thoughtful inquiry. (Greenawalt, 1997)

Judgement lies at the heart of any profession, and audit is no exception. It involves a person's capacity to form an opinion or make a decision based on a careful weighing up of evidential matter. While regulators and standard-setters can provide guidance, it is up to the professional to apply thoughtful consideration and ethics, and consider what to examine and how, and how to interpret the results.

Audit judgement is often associated with *professional scepticism*. The latter is, in effect, 'a way of looking at things' such that the auditor achieves a capacity for making more appropriate decisions.

> ### Professional scepticism
>
> Professional scepticism means an attitude that includes a questioning mind, being alert to conditions which may indicate possible misstatement due to error or fraud, and a critical assessment of audit evidence (ASA 200, para 13(L)).

Applying auditor judgement – and a professionally sceptical 'attitude' – is necessary at every stage of the audit process, hence its classification as an audit 'concept'. There is no auditing standard solely dedicated to 'judgement', though it permeates all standards to some extent. There is, however, growing regulatory guidance for applying professional scepticism, as illustrated by the following example (ICAEW, 2018, p. 5):

> It's far easier to question someone if you remember that the client isn't the person in the suit standing in front of you; it's whoever served you your latte before you came into work, because it's their pension fund that has shares in the company you're auditing.

This chapter looks at what it means to employ judgement in the performance of an audit, how it is regulated, and ways in which audit decisions might be improved.

CONCEPT QUESTION **1**	When is 'judgement' used in the audit process?

Influences on audit decisions

The following sets out practices and policies that are said to comprise and potentially improve audit judgement. They include education, audit firm's policies, addressing heuristics/biases and decision styles.

Education

Learning programs affect how auditors approach the audit process (e.g., IAESB, 2017; Van Peursem and Julian, 2005). The Australian and New Zealand accounting professions recognise the importance of education in their requirements for pre- and post-qualification education, including the use of conceptual theory to put the complexities and details of the audit process into the larger socioeconomic and ethical contexts.

Audit firm policies

Audit firms form policies on planning, supervision and in-house training, all of which can influence the quality of auditor judgements. Such policies may include:

> (a) Discussion of significant matters with the engagement partner; (b) Review of the financial statements and the proposed auditor's report; (c) Review of selected audit documentation relating to the significant judgments the engagement team made and the conclusions it reached; and (d) Evaluation of the conclusions reached in formulating the auditor's report. (ISA NZ 220, para 20)

These may be important. While experience counts, there is no guarantee that senior audit staff always come to *better* decisions. Kent and Weber (1998) found that auditors who considered themselves to be experts were more *confident* but not necessarily more *precise* than their less experienced colleagues.

Auditors specialising in an industry may be more effective but not necessarily more efficient (e.g., see Moroney, 2007). Competitive bidding can also lead to time pressure on the job, making it difficult for the auditor to give concerns that have been raised and the attention they may deserve. This suggests to us the importance of adopting policies to benefit from experience, team intellect, review practices and ethical understandings when making audit decisions.

Heuristics, bias and cognition

Auditors, and those who rely on audit opinions, like to think those audit decisions are objective, fair and free from bias. However, the nature of a judgement process does not lend itself to complete objectivity because judgement relies on views of, and reflections on, the evidential matter. Even the way in which we select evidence is a form of bias that can lead to either appropriate or inappropriate testing.

Auditing in practice

Suspicion and additional tests

An auditor who knows their client's purchasing manager well after three years on the engagement, has come to assume that the purchasing manager is honest. As a result, the auditor fails to perform additional tests needed to discover why there appears to be a suspicious number of missing purchase invoices.

Cognitive processes merit further consideration. People may not be aware of their own biases and how such biases affect their decisions. Cognition, a topic in the psychology literature, has been applied to auditor judgement situations. Tversky and Kahneman (1974), in particular, offer insights into three important heuristics, or biases, of concern to auditors: anchoring and adjustment, availability, and representativeness.

Anchoring and adjustment

Under this heuristic, new information is evaluated by reference to existing information. This will occur if the auditor assumes that the 'true' value of an account or the 'true' information provided is proximate to information that management has provided.

Auditing in practice

Anchoring and adjustment

Let's say the inventory of a company is reported at $100 000, and that the auditors assume that the true balance is somewhere near that amount, and they anchor their tests on that assumption. As a result, the auditor may search for errors in the inventory listed by the client. If, in fact, the inventory is totally fictitious or not owned, then the auditor's assumptions may not prompt them to look for the real problem of false entries, missing a material misstatement.

Anchoring and adjustment have been detected in studies as to how an auditor operates, and efforts have been made to mitigate this effect (e.g., Presutti, 1995). Anchoring and adjustment are, therefore, riskier starting points for auditors.

Availability

Availability refers to when a decision maker considers the probability of an event occurring in relation to the ease with which similar events are brought to mind. As a result, it is likely that recent or highly sensationalised events become disproportionately influential. These are also referred to as 'recency effects', and there is evidence to suggest that auditors are influenced by these considerations (e.g., see Chan, 1996).

Auditing in practice

Availability

Suppose an auditor encounters undisclosed liabilities in a previous engagement. Recalling this event, they may be inclined to spend additional time on undisclosed liabilities in the current engagement, irrespective of whether they carry similar risks.

Representativeness

Under this heuristic, the likelihood of misstatement is based on a situation's similarity to other known patterns. The auditor may have a series of stereotypes, or 'templates', relating to past experiences, and they will match a current situation to those stereotypes, reducing the complexity of a situation but possibly resulting in misinterpretation.

Auditing in practice

Representativeness

An auditor recalls that credit agencies tend to have more uncollectable debts in densely populated neighbourhoods. As a result of this stereotype, the auditor selects a sample in two strata, representing the two groups, and tests one more heavily.

Applying *representativeness* can have several effects. It could either:
- *reduce audit cost* and increase audit efficiency, because the representative knowledge may reflect the true audit situation before them; or
- *lead to complacency* and potentially an inappropriate opinion, if the auditor is not alert to unexpected risks of misstatement.

The representativeness heuristic can therefore be valuable, but it also has the ability to reduce professional scepticism. So auditors should be alert to unique situations as well as those which follow a known pattern.

Decision styles and theories

Cognitive decision styles can also influence the judgements auditors make, as exemplified by the following two approaches:

- *intuitive approach* means being attentive to a 'gut feel' about a situation. While potentially valuable, it is an insufficient source of evidence, or confidence, on its own.
- *analytical approach* relies on technical models and quantitative information to highlight issues of concern. The use of data-driven programs and expert systems can identify concerns which the auditor should follow up with further testing. Audit expert systems, for example, are programs that prompt the user (auditor) for facts about a client and analyse those facts based on a predetermined algorithm.

A combination of the 'intuitive' approach, achieved through reflection and communication among the audit team, and 'analytical' knowledge, using models and expert systems, is probably the most effective in most cases.

Decision styles can also draw from critical theory, in which the auditor's motives or abilities can be questioned. Examples include the following:

- *Image theory* (Beach and Frederickson, 1989) is the idea that decisions are the result of the decision maker's self-image, values and morals – also called a trajectory image. The decision maker comes to a view looking through this lens.
- *Structuration theory* (Giddens, 1984) argues that an overly analytical approach limits audit. Judgement may be impaired if auditors are too busy following fixed processes or are perhaps less open to the evidence in front of them. Whether they know it or not, auditors (and others) may look for evidence that supports the decisions they have already unconsciously made. This has been shown to occur (Bamber, Ramsey and Tubbs, 1997; Brody, Golen and Reckers, 1998).

Firms do generally seek a consistent, highly documented approach via which to facilitate review and ensure a common basis for analysis. There may be some justification for doing so, but 'fostering an appropriately independent and sceptical mindset' (IAASB, 2019) is vitally important to uncovering the potential for material misstatement.

Summary of audit judgement

In summary, it is important to convey that the audit is an investigative process requiring the thoughtful collection and evaluation of evidence. Audit judgement employs elements of subjective, as well as objective, decision making. The policies of the firm, conscientious audit leadership, analytical tools, and the efforts of the audit team all play an important role in coming to the best audit judgements possible. A framework illustrating these processes, along with one example, can be found in **Table 7.1**.

Table 7.1 Auditor judgement processes: An example

Approach to auditor judgement	Valuation of accounts receivable example
Ask clarifying questions and identify client assumptions.	Credit or payment policies or control weaknesses lead to an overstatement.
While avoiding being rude or cynical, take a critical attitude towards the client's claims.	Acquire independent evidence about debt values; e.g., ageing lists and correspondence indicating a reluctance to pay.
Examine client practice by performing select audit tests.	Infer from debtor inquiry if management and valuation claims seem fair.
Decide on appropriate action in response to the results of tests and inquiries.	Gather further evidence if needed, coming to a conclusion about whether an account is materially misstated or needs adjustment.

One important decision that auditors make concerns the selection of materiality levels.

Materiality

According to IFAC (2005):

> Information is material if its omission or misstatement could influence the economic decisions of users taken on the basis of financial statements.

The auditor is responsible for discovering and assessing the impact of material financial statement misstatements on potential users. The audit firm is thus charged with conducting an audit investigation that is likely to identify any misstatements which exceed a tolerable level.

In economic terms, materiality can be understood in terms of the potential loss of market confidence should a particular type or magnitude of error exist, undiscovered, in the financial statements. Materiality is fundamental to an audit and is a concept that permeates the auditor's thinking throughout their investigation. Australian and New Zealand auditing standards (ASA 320, para 4; ISA NZ 320, para 4) offer further explanation of the auditor's role in terms of materiality:

> The auditor's determination of materiality is a matter of professional judgement, and is affected by the auditor's perception of the financial information needs of users of the financial report.

Essentially, the auditor makes materiality decisions early in their process so that, once testing begins, they have a benchmark against which to compare any errors found or suspected. That is, this particular decision determines how the investigation will proceed and what will be considered important. The auditor's materiality decision thus:

- assists in the determination of the nature, extent and timing of audit tests
- provides a basis for deciding whether accounting errors should be corrected or can be left until the subsequent period
- provides a benchmark to determine how important it may be to disclose an event or misstatement in the financial statements
- influences the auditors in relation to the issuance of a qualified opinion should the material misstatement not be remedied.

CONCEPT QUESTION 2   Define 'materiality' and summarise how it affects audit decisions.

Two types of 'materiality' are recognised: accounting materiality and audit materiality.

Accounting versus audit materiality

Accounting materiality refers to the minimum monetary amount of omission, misstatement or non-disclosure that would influence the judgement of the reasonable user of financial statements (e.g., see Jacoby and Levy, 2016). Accounting materiality is determined to prepare the financial statements and decide what level of precision would lead to the necessity of adjusting the balances or disclosures.

A particular account and its amount may be material because of its importance or its magnitude (size).

Auditing in practice

Value of intangibles

If it is known that banker-users and manager-users of a particular set of accounts have little interest in the value of intangibles and discard them in their calculations, then small errors or omissions in that account would be considered immaterial.

Audit materiality also relates to users' interests, but it is concerned with planning the audit and audit testing. Audit materiality has to do with decisions about the scope of the investigation aligned with the risk of failing to find material errors. The selection of one type of test over another may be done on the basis that it will provide more risk-relevant or material information. If an overstatement of debt is of particular concern in an engagement, then additional and costly procedures to identify external debt-holders may be justified in terms of audit materiality.

So, the auditor makes decisions about 'materiality', but not with quite the same concerns or focus as would the client preparing their own accounts. Audit materiality refers to the fact that an auditor must use their decision to:

- help determine the nature of audit risks
- identify risks of material misstatements
- determine the other audit procedures needed as a result (see ASA 320, paras 5–8).

Auditing and accounting materiality are related, therefore, but not identical. They are both concerned with 'users', but one or the other may be higher, lower or simply different.

Auditing in practice

Accounting materiality

An auditor decides that *any* amount of misstatement in Business A's ending stock is 'material' because of a concern with stock fraud. So, any error above 0 is material in *audit materiality* terms. *Accounting materiality* is $10 000 related to its relative size.

An accounting materiality decision for Business B is highly precise with respect to a loans account, but because the auditor-perceived relevance and cost to test this do not justify that level of precision, the auditor selects a larger amount for audit materiality.

This distinction is a fine point, but it is important because it illustrates how the auditor must come to their own assessments and conclusions about what is material to the audit, and not simply rely on the client's materiality assessment.

We will now take you through some practices to illustrate how materiality decisions can be derived.

Determining audit materiality

In the planning phase, auditors determine a broad – termed *overall* or *planning* – level of materiality. Then they disaggregate that among accounts, assertions or systems prior to audit tests being performed. At later stages, misstatements found in audit tests will be collated and compared with these materiality amounts. Decisions will then be made as to whether the statements are, or are not, materially misstated in compliance with GAAP. The general process is illustrated in **Figure 7.1**.

| Select overall materiality | Disaggregate and allocate | Obtain audit evidence | Compare evidence found to materiality |

Figure 7.1 Materiality and evidence relationship

The selection of materiality is a professional decision. Although audit regulators have issued guidance on how to derive materiality, there is a reluctance to specify quantitative criteria. The reasons for such reluctance include that:

- fixed amounts could be used as an excuse to replace professional judgement
- as user needs are unknown or vary, materiality is not a fixed concept

- GAAP can be ambiguous, not lending itself to quantitative measures
- unique client circumstances make it difficult to produce standardised criteria.

Despite these challenges, past Australian and New Zealand standards provided some quantitative guidance. Although now replaced, they suggested that misstatements in excess of 10 per cent of the true value were presumed material, and that less than 5 per cent were presumed immaterial, unless there was evidence to the contrary (amounts in between 5 per cent and 10 per cent being unclassified).

Again, these guidelines no longer exist in standards; however, we think they offer a benchmark that gives readers a general sense of where the starting points for determining materiality can reasonably lie. The first challenge, therefore, is to determine an appropriate overall or planning materiality for the client.

Overall (or planning) materiality

Overall materiality, sometimes termed *planning materiality*, is selected early in the process by the auditor – usually the senior in the firm. In coming to this important decision, and later on, in relation to disaggregation decisions, the auditor must decide what is most important for them to discover.

Overall materiality is selected by using both qualitative and quantitative methods, benefiting from both intuitive and analytical forms of judgement. As to the *quantitative* methods, auditors should consider the particular circumstances of the client and the risk that a certain amount of undiscovered errors or omissions will pose.

The auditor should also consider *qualitative criteria*, such as whether or not an unusual error would send a different message to the user. For example, if a $5000 error (on the surface, small) turns a company's profit into a loss, then the $5000 may well be material. So, the auditor might ask themselves whether a certain type or magnitude of misstatement would:

- lead users to reach different conclusions on liquidity, solvency or profitability
- be highly unusual, indicating unknown or previously unassessed risks
- appear to be sourced in management distortion or misappropriation
- contravene a statutory requirement that permits little room for error
- be unlikely because the precise measurement is possible
- be likely because the precise measurement is not possible, as in some estimates
- hit a critical point, such as 'insolvency', or change a 'profit' to a 'loss'
- have an effect on reportable segments, parents or subsidiaries.

Sometimes several overall materiality levels are set in order to establish one for Statement of Financial Position values and another for net income. So, for example, if assets exceed $10 000 000 and net income is only $150 000, then it is likely that a material amount for those assets will be far too large if used for the smaller net income.

The auditor begins the process by using a select combination of accounts as a basis for overall materiality, and then a level of precision. Typical bases and proportions are shown in **Table 7.2**.

Table 7.2 Typical bases and proportions

Basis	Typical percentage
Profit	8–10% of average net income
Sales	1–3% of gross sales
Total assets	1–2% of total assets
Working capital	8–10% of working capital

Income and sales bases may be more appropriate for trading, manufacturing and service companies, whereas asset ratios may be more appropriate for investment and property companies. Ratios that consistently reflect operations or positions have good potential as a base for planning materiality because they form an expected pattern. The auditors should look for the most suitable of these. An example is presented in the 'Auditing in practice' box.

Auditing in practice

Example: The auditor must select an overall materiality amount for Basil Ltd

Client information:	Client account balance	Audit firm policy: Range
Total revenue	$500 000	2–5%
Total assets	$200 000	2–5%
Income before taxes	$50 000	5–10%

The auditor must select one amount as overall materiality. In this case, total assets are selected because they have been consistent over time and are strategic to Basil's success. Applying audit firm policy (above), overall materiality must be between $4000 (2 per cent of total assets) and $10 000 (5 per cent) of total assets. Because the auditor believes users would tolerate a large range of error, and for cost considerations, they select 5 per cent or $10 000.

If there is user tolerance for larger errors, then overall materiality can be increased. If the user tolerance for misstatement is low, then overall materiality should be small. These judgements will have a direct effect on the amount and type of evidence and testing needed. This relationship is illustrated in **Figure 7.2**.

Is materiality level small? Testing must be to a higher level of precision.	←——→	Is materiality level large? Testing can be to a lower level of precision.

Figure 7.2 Materiality decision and testing

If the cumulative net impact of known errors exceeds overall materiality, the auditors must consider whether to insist on the correction of the accounts by the client or, if not corrected or correctable, qualifying their audit opinion.

Disaggregating overall materiality

Overall materiality is determined in respect of the financial statements taken as a whole. The auditor also disaggregates overall materiality and allocates the resulting amounts to smaller components so as to better assess the results of audit tests. While amounts can be allocated in various ways – to accounts, systems or individual tests[1] – we use the 'allocation to accounts' method. Each allocation comprises the auditor's decision as to what a **tolerable misstatement** would comprise for each account.

tolerable misstatement
The amount of error or omission the auditor is willing to tolerate and still conclude that the account (or account group) shows a true and fair view.

---

[1] Other methods include: monetary unit sampling to avoid the disaggregation problem, as the sampling process selects the larger (and possibly more important) accounts; different materiality amounts for each set of tests or account groupings; combining the effects of different account errors; and incorporating cost-benefit considerations (Dutta and Graham, 1998). These methods are left for advanced study.

For this, the auditor can divide overall materiality by the number of account balances and allocate that to each account. Although easy to do, it fails to consider the different risks that may accrue to different-sized accounts. Nor does it consider that the risks associated with one account may fundamentally differ from those associated with another.

The following illustrates a modified version of an *allocation to accounts* method:

- Overall materiality is first allocated to different accounts based on each account's balance relative to the total. This is only a starting point, however.
- Adjustments to each allocation may be made for the risks identified as associated with each account.

This method takes into consideration both the size of the account balance and any particular risks. An ongoing example is introduced in the 'Auditing in practice' box.

Auditing in practice

Basil Ltd

An audit firm is performing an audit of Basil Ltd. **Table 7.3** illustrates its account balances at year-end, preliminary and adjusted allocations. The auditor has selected planning materiality of $14 500, using 2.9 per cent of revenue as the basis.

Overall materiality is initially allocated on a relative monetary amount but is then adjusted for qualitative reasons. The cash allocation is adjusted to zero because of the importance of testing cash controls, and because it is easy (low-cost) to test cash to precision. On the other hand, accounts receivable and inventory testing is costly. In this particular case, the auditors also decide that the risk of error in these two accounts is not particularly high and therefore increase the allocation. Lenders are relying on the cost-of-goods-sold valuations for their use, so the latter's tolerable misstatement is reduced to ensure greater precision in that account.

In Basil Ltd, no misstatements in cash are tolerated. This may be because errors in cash indicate errors in a large range of other accounts, or because it is cheaper to audit (via a bank reconciliation review). Assessing user interests and costs, the auditor tolerates up to a $2000 misstatement in accounts receivable (see **Table 7.3**).

Table 7.3 Basil Ltd accounts

Description	Account ($)	Allocation ($)	
	Balance	Preliminary	Adjusted
Cash	1000	10	–
Accounts receivable	120 000	1200	2000
Inventory	79 000	790	1000
Accounts payable	39 000	390	100
Long-term debts	252 000	2520	900
Shareholder equity	9000	90	1000
Revenue	500 000	5000	5300
Cost of sales	420 000	4200	3900
Operating expenses	30 000	300	300
Totals	1 450 000	14 500	14 500

The adjusted amounts become the auditor's 'tolerable misstatements'. Normally, such decisions should not change over the course of an audit. Otherwise, it could appear that the auditor is manipulating the criteria in order to fit the data.

The allocation-to-accounts method is appropriate for a risk-based approach because the emphasis is on risks to individual accounts. Risks associated with 'anchoring and adjustment' are a potential bias with this method, since the tolerable error is anchored on the balance sheet or income statement amount.

Audit evidence

Audit evidence is any information obtained or used by auditors in the formation of their opinion. Audit evidence, or the evidential matter from which it is derived, may be acquired from sources within, or external to, the organisation being audited (ISA 500, para 3*)*.

Auditing in practice

Sources of evidence

Sources of evidence from the client may include data from or about systems or databases, documentation, or discussions with managers and employees. Sources of evidence outside the client may include documentation from customers, suppliers, lenders, banks and the client's solicitors, as well as discussions with external parties. Audit test results, using information from within or external to the client, are also a form of audit evidence.

Evidence for an audit opinion is not, however, the same as evidence for legal or scientific purposes (see **Figure 7.3**). The scientist is concerned with the formulation of scientific laws and hence will conduct experiments to ensure the consistency of the results.

Figure 7.3 Evidence in audit, law and science

In the (Western) legal context, courts of law want to obtain evidence whose veracity is beyond reasonable doubt and which is legally admissible. By contrast, auditors require only such evidence as to enable the auditor to reach an opinion or reasonable conclusion.

> The auditor's objective is to design and perform audit procedures in such a way as to enable the auditor to obtain sufficient appropriate audit evidence to draw reasonable conclusions on which to base the auditor's opinion. (ASA 500, para 4; ISA 500, para 4)

That does not make it easy, but it enlarges the range of evidential matter that can be used to develop audit evidence. Standards provide further guidance to this concept in terms of 'professional scepticism'.

Professional scepticism

Professional scepticism 'includes being alert to, for example, audit evidence that contradicts other audit evidence obtained … questioning contradictory audit evidence and the reliability of documents and responses to enquiries and other information … a belief that management and those charged with governance are honest and have integrity does not relieve the auditor of the need to maintain professional scepticism or allow the auditor to be satisfied with less-than-persuasive audit evidence …' (ISA NZ 200, paras A20–A24).

The *cost* of evidence is also a consideration, although it should not interfere with the requirement to obtain 'sufficient, appropriate' audit evidence. Nonetheless, audit is a commercial activity, and, in economics terms, the auditor needs to make cost–benefit decisions. The auditor will be aware that the costs of obtaining all the evidence may exceed its economic or social benefit. For example, seeking all possible evidence on 'going concern' or 'client fraud' could absorb limitless costs. The auditor must find that balance between obtaining sufficient, appropriate evidence and knowing when doing so may be impossible or outside the scope of an audit investigation.

While evidence can be acquired from observation, testing, and a range of methods (set out in the chapters to follow), as a concept, all audit evidence should be sufficient, appropriate and reliable to be persuasive. These characteristics are now considered.

Sufficiency of evidence

> Sufficiency (of audit evidence) means the measure of the quantity of audit evidence. The quantity of the audit evidence needed is affected by the auditor's assessment of the risks of material misstatement and also by the quality of such audit evidence. (ASA 500, para 5(f); ISA NZ 500, para 5(f))

One factor to consider is the magnitude of evidence. *Sufficiency* refers to 'amounts': how many invoices to examine, how many tests to perform, how many confirmation letters to send, and so on. Having more evidence about a matter will usually provide a better understanding of the underlying phenomenon.

This is not always the case. Irrespective of how many purchase authorisation documents the auditor gathers, it will not answer whether there were undocumented authorisations. Nonetheless, sufficiency is important, as was indicated in the influential 1970 Australian *Pacific Acceptance* case, in which Moffitt J was highly critical of the tiny volume of evidence collected. Auditors must clearly offer a sufficient magnitude of independent evidence to offer a persuasive argument for their views.

Appropriateness: Assertions

Evidence must also consider all reasonable risks, hence the use of *assertions*, which are

> representations, explicit or otherwise … which are inherent in management representing that the financial report is prepared in accordance with the applicable financial reporting framework. (ASA 315, para A1; ISA NZ 315, 2016, para 4a; ISA NZ 315, 2020, para 12(a))

In particular, because clients make certain claims about their financial statements (that they comply with GAAP, for example), then these claims – or assertions – offer a useful framework for the auditor's investigation.

> Assertions are used by the auditor to consider the different types of potential misstatements that may occur when identifying, assessing and responding to the risks of material misstatement. (ASA 315, para A1; ISA NZ 315, 2016, para 4a; ISA NZ 315, 2020, para 12(a))

Practice has shown that it is useful to classify assertions into categories related to what the auditor investigates, in particular as to:
- the client's accounting information systems and controls
- the account balances in the financial statements
- information as presented or disclosed in the financial statements.

With respect to the first – systems – relevant evidence should be a measure of whether system controls prevent or detect (material) errors in the financial statements. With respect to the second – balances – relevant evidence should be acquired to ensure that assets, liabilities and equity exist; that they reflect true ownership or obligation; and that they are valued appropriately. The third – presentation and disclosure – has it that relevant information is disclosed in accordance with accepted practice.

Auditing in practice

Recording transactions

Financial statement auditors want to determine whether the accounting information system has captured all sales transactions that have occurred, whether those captured and recorded represent valid sales transactions, and whether their classification within the accounts, notes and policies to the statements comply with GAAP.

So, auditors must determine whether the implied assertions of management are met. Depending on the auditor's risk assessment, they may need to consider *all* assertions for *each* transaction or balance. That is a lot of work and testing. In practice, risk analysis will usually indicate that a greater risk of material error is more associated with some assertions than others for each particular situation, account or system.

Assertions about classes of transactions

Management assertions as to their transactions and control systems are as follows:
- *Occurrence* (also referred to as *validity* or *occurrence-validity*) – the claim that recorded transactions represent those that actually did occur and/or that they represent transactions which were authorised to occur
- *Completeness* – the claim that all transactions that occurred in the business were recorded by the system; that none were missed or excluded, or understated
- *Accuracy* – the claim that those amounts that go towards making up financial statement balances, or amounts that are transferred from one form to another, are arithmetically correct in their calculations and are transferred accurately
- *Classification* – the claim that the transactions recorded are appropriately classified within the accounts to which they belong.[2]

---

[2] A full list can be found in the standards summarised in **Figure 7.4**. While we use all concepts, we avoid repetition (i.e., completeness which is repeated) and those which are not assertions (i.e. cut-off is a test which looks at completeness and/or validity).

Classes of transactions (assertions)

- Have all the income and expenses been recorded? (completeness)
- Have expenses been accurately calculated and posted? (accuracy)
- Did the sales transactions represent real sales? (validity–occurrence)
- Have the employee expenses been approved? (validity–occurrence)
- Have they been posted to the appropriate expense accounts? (classification)
- Are end-of-year sales captured in current-year transactions? (completeness)
- Are next-year sales excluded from current-year transactions? (validity–occurrence)

Assertions about account balances

Other audit test objectives are concerned with management assertions as to the balances in the financial accounts or the transactions that lead to those balances. These are tested using substantive tests of balances. So, in addition to the assertions named above for transaction processes, there are additional assertions for ending balances:

- *Existence* – the claim that assets physically exist as claimed. For example, stock, copyright, brand names or customer databases can all be checked for their 'existence'. 'Existence' is also the concern that the assets may have been lost or stolen
- *Rights and obligations* – the legal status as to ownership of assets at the balance date, and of obligations and liabilities such as collateralised equipment or long-term debt.
- *Valuation* – refers to the carrying value of an account for which an estimate is used. Examples are the value of assets not publicly traded, the realisable values of depreciated assets, and the collectable values of accounts receivable. 'Valuation' involves looking at a reasonable range where historical cost is not GAAP.

Assertions about presentation and disclosure

There are also *presentation* assertions to do with the quality of accounting disclosure. This may include how the accounts are listed, disaggregated, classified or disclosed in the notes and accounting policies to the financial statements.

Account balances, presentation and disclosure assertions

- Are leasehold automobiles on hand? (existence)
- Is goodwill at an appropriate net carrying value? (valuation)
- Is the machinery used owned by the client? (rights–obligation)
- Are there debts owed on fixed assets purchased under contract? (rights–obligation)
- Are mining-depletion expenses sufficient to represent declines in value? (valuation)
- Is fixed-asset depreciation policy disclosed appropriately? (presentation)
- Has the long-term portion of goodwill been disclosed as long-term? (presentation)

To illustrate the importance of addressing all assertions, imagine the misstatement that could occur if all sales listed were accurately calculated, posted and included in the trial balance, but were never, in fact, sales at all. They were the proceeds from shareholder loans. That is, *completeness* and *accuracy* assertions were supported, but *classification* was not: potentially a material overstatement of net profit and an understatement of liabilities.

Likewise, if an item of stock was *complete, accurate, presented, had occurred* and was *owned* by the client, but was stolen, then the failure to test *existence* would result in an overstatement of assets. We will use this framework of assertions in this text (see **Table 7.4**).

Table 7.4 Framework of assertions

Systems and transactions	OCAC	Occurrence–Validity, Completeness, Accuracy, Classification
Account balances and presentation	ERV+P	(above +) Existence, Rights-Obligations, Valuation, Presentation-Disclosure

It may be a valuable exercise for you to learn these assertions now at this stage of your studies.

Finally, and as ever, professional scepticism plays an increasingly visible role in audit discourse, and this applies to the characteristics of audit *evidence*.

Professional scepticism

'ASIC's focus in their 2019 audit inspection report requires audit firms to consider: "Whether appropriate professional scepticism is exercised about the sufficiency and appropriateness of audit evidence, accounting treatments and accounting estimates."'

Source: CA ANZ (2022).

Reliability of evidence

The auditor is called upon to make a judgement on the quality, or persuasiveness, of the evidence they obtain, and one aspect of that quality is its reliability. That is, given its source, is your evidence more or less likely to represent the true situation? Accordingly, the reliability of audit evidence is influenced by whether it is from:

- *External sources:* For example, confirmations received from a third party, or a separate department within the client's organisation, are more reliable than those obtained from the original records because that information producer is relatively independent from those whose system is being tested.
- *Tested systems:* Evidence obtained from the entity's records is more reliable if you are confident that the related control system operates effectively; so, performing tests of controls prior to substantive testing provides that benefit. Relying on any tested system to estimate a balance in an untested system may also strengthen reliability.
- *Auditors directly:* Evidence obtained directly by the auditors is more reliable than that obtained from someone within the entity, reflecting the idea that information obtained from independent sources is less likely to be influenced by the manager or employee who has an interest in the audit outcome.
- *Documents and written representations:* Written evidence is more reliable than oral evidence. Written evidence can include emails and websites if traceable to the author.
- *Original sources:* Original documents, such as deeds, trusts and minutes, are generally more reliable than copies. Online signatures can pose a reliability challenge, but *digital signatures* – given the controls around them – may be more reliable than *e-signatures*.

In evaluating the reliability of evidence, auditors should also consider whether there are inconsistencies; for example, if inventory documents show different information than purchase invoices. Consideration of evidence taken 'as a whole' is an important part of the auditor's review process, as inconsistencies can indicate material problems. **Table 7.5** illustrates these points.

Table 7.5 Potential reliability of audit evidence

Source of evidence	Oral evidence quality	Written, directly obtained evidence quality
Internal evidence:		
Same cycle	Nil	Low/nil
Independent cycle	Low	Medium
Audited, independent cycle	Medium	High
External evidence	Medium	High
Auditor-developed models	n/a	Medium/high

The assertions set out in Australian and New Zealand standards are presented in **Figure 7.4**. More details about them can be found on the respective regulator websites.

Assertions about classes of transactions and events:	
(i) Occurrence	
(ii) Completeness	
(iii) Accuracy	
(iv) Cut-off	
(v) Classification	
Assertions about account balances and related disclosures at the period end:	
(i) Existence	
(ii) Rights and obligations	
(iii) Completeness	
(iv) Accuracy valuation and allocation	
(v) Classification	
(vi) Presentation	
Assertions about presentation and disclosure:	
(i) Occurrence and rights and obligations	
(ii) Completeness	
(iii) Classification and understandability	
(iv) Accuracy and valuation	

Figure 7.4 Assertions listed in standards: A complete list as of October 2021

Sources: ASA 315; ISA NZ 315.

CONCEPT QUESTION 3   Define 'audit evidence'.

Study tools

Summary

Factors influencing the exercise of professional audit judgement were considered in this chapter. The process of audit decision making was characterised as pragmatic, with reliance based on heuristics and decision styles as well as risk-based decision models. The role of decision models was acknowledged, but we encourage auditing students to remember the critical role of auditors' judgement throughout the audit process.

Materiality decisions, including planning materiality, bases and disaggregation into tolerable misstatements, rely on the auditors' judgement quality. Two theoretical concepts of materiality – accounting and auditing – were considered. The allocation-to-accounts method of disaggregation was explained.

This chapter also discussed the nature, timing and extent of the audit evidence required to come to an audit opinion on the financial statements. Sources and types of audit evidence were described, as was the reliability of different types of evidence. Management assertions, about which the auditor must come to a view on each material account, were set out and employed in discussions and examples.

🔗 Case/resources link

CAATs for Classrooms

Accompanying this book is a series of data, integrated worksheets and exercises that are designed to support your learning and give you exposure to hands-on audit decision-making dilemmas faced by auditors in the planning elements of the audit process. Acquire the relevant material for this chapter from your instructor.

Review questions

7.1   Describe the relationship between audit judgement and professional scepticism.

7.2   Define and describe each of the following types of heuristics or biases:
   a   anchoring and adjustment
   b   availability
   c   representativeness.

7.3   Describe each of the following decision theories and name their proponents:
   a   image theory
   b   structuration theory.

7.4   Explain how company policies and education can improve auditor judgement.

7.5   How is 'auditing materiality' different from, or similar to, 'accounting materiality'?

7.6   Why are standard-setters reluctant to set fixed materiality levels for the auditor to use? What do current standards say about the auditor's role with respect to materiality?

7.7   Define overall (planning) materiality.

7.8   When overall materiality is set at a low level, what does this mean for testing?

7.9   What are the bases usually used to set overall materiality?

7.10 When might one base be more appropriate than another?

7.11 What does it mean to say that the auditor wishes to 'disaggregate' overall materiality?

7.12 What is the *allocation-to-accounts* method of disaggregation, and why is it useful?

7.13 What is the meaning of *tolerable misstatement*, and how does it apply to the disaggregation process?

7.14 Using the allocation-to-accounts method:

    a Describe the difference between the 'preliminary' allocation and the 'adjusted' allocation.

    b Describe how each is arrived at? By whom?

    c What criteria are used?

7.15 Describe the auditor's obligation with respect to audit evidence as set out in the standards.

7.16 Distinguish between evidence that is persuasive, scientific and legal. Why are these differences important to the auditor?

7.17 What is the difference between 'sufficient' and 'appropriate' evidence?

7.18 Name and define the management assertions as to transactions and control systems.

7.19 Name and define the additional management assertions as to balances in the accounts.

7.20 Define the meaning of management assertions as to 'presentation and disclosure'.

7.21 List five factors that influence the reliability of audit evidence.

Exercises

7.1 **MATERIALITY:** Assume the following information about your audit client, Te Wanui Ltd, a wholesale boat products firm. The industry has prospered this year, but you are concerned about Te Wanui's generous credit policy. Ending account balances are as follows:

Assets ($)	
Cash	18 000
Receivables	1 450 000
Stock	10 000 000
Liabilities	7 500 000
Total revenue	4 000 000
Net income	700 000

Required: What questions might you ask before determining the percentage and basis for planning materiality? Why did you ask those questions? Assume your firm decides that planning materiality should be $500 000.

a   Allocate this to balance sheet accounts, using the allocation method.

b   Allocate this to a test of debtors' accounts, using the basic allowance method (advanced).

c   Set out your assumptions and rationales in coming to such disaggregation.

7.2   **MATERIALITY AND ALLOCATION:** You are performing the current statutory audit for a company identified by your instructor. You are asked to calculate a tolerable error for each balance sheet account. Assume that an overall materiality level of 5 per cent of net income before taxes has been chosen. Consider the impact of your decisions.

7.3   **MATERIALITY AND TOLERABLE ERROR:** An auditor finds the following errors in the books of Jonas Industries:

a $10 000 provisions for doubtful debts not recorded

b $8000 payable to a supplier accrued twice

c $23 000 of recorded sales are in next year's invoices

d $5000 should be written off as a bad debt (provision method).

Required: Jonas does not wish to adjust for these errors. Prepare a schedule showing the impact of them on the financial statements and on key ratios of concern. The following accounts have unadjusted balances:

Accounts receivable (net)	$1 043 000
Accounts payable	$85 000
Sales	$959 000
Expenses	$940 000
Net income	$19 000
Working capital ratio	(2340/1170)

7.4   **MATERIALITY:** Address the steps posed in **Figure 7.1** for an organisation such as:

a   a public primary school

b   a smart phone provider

c   rail (government-owned)

d   online payroll record provider

e   a large fishing corporation.

7.5   **MATERIALITY:** Consider examples (in this chapter) for Basil Ltd. What would be the effects on overall materiality, the base used for overall materiality, disaggregation decisions or tolerable misstatement (if any) for each of the following independent decisions:

a   Net sales turns out to be a relatively stable and important account for Basil's users.

b   The inventory value precision is highly important because it will be relied on by a new potential owner.

c   The inventory value precision is easier to measure than originally anticipated.

   d The cost of sales can be precisely measured along with the inventory balance.

   e Long-term debt values are not being relied on by anyone known to the auditor.

Use the following case for the next three exercises:

As the auditor conducting the financial statement audit for her client, Interface Ltd, Leanne discovers indications that a manager is possibly overstating the value of sales. They do not appear to misstate any other account. Leanne addresses her concerns to that manager and to his immediate manager, the CEO. Both say that they believe the account has been stated correctly. However, rather than 'delay the audit', both managers ask Leanne to reduce the scope of her investigation and conduct an audit of the Statement of Financial Position only.

7.6 **JUDGEMENT:** Apply the judgement processes in the left-hand column of **Table 7.1** to the aforementioned situation. Assume no further changes are made by the client. Where does this lead Leanne? What, as a result of her evaluation, will she be doing next?

7.7 **JUDGEMENT:** What heuristic (of those discussed in this chapter) may be indicated by each of the following independent situations:

   a Leanne received a request only last month to conduct a 'Balance sheet only' audit. She produced the engagement letter with that restriction on scope and completed the audit. On that basis, she decides to do the same for Interface Ltd.

   b Leanne decides to conduct additional tests for the sales account. While these tests do not consider accounts receivable or verify sales documents, the work she performs convinces her that the account has not been misstated.

   c Leanne remembers a similar situation in which someone tried to reduce the scope of an engagement to avoid problems. On the basis of that recollection, she declines to follow the managers' suggestions and withdraws from the engagement.

   d Leanne remembers a similar situation in which a client tried to reduce the scope of an engagement to avoid problems. On the basis of that concern, she investigates other activities and adjustments performed by the managers and makes further inquiries as to their characters.

7.8 **JUDGEMENT:** How might each of the following approaches identify a concern as to the potential for fraud, or an auditor's failure to find it, in Interface Ltd:

   a intuitive approach   c image theory

   b analytical approach   d structuration theory.

7.9 **JUDGEMENT:** Design a training program for new audit trainees. It should be designed to improve their audit judgement. Decide what elements it should include, how teams may be structured for learning, and the sort of content it might include.

7.10 **EVIDENCE AND PERSUASIVENESS:** On a scale of 1 (low level) to 3 (high level), where would you place the following sources of evidence in regards to their persuasiveness? Explain why.

   a watching the end-of-year stock count

   b re-adding a page of the client's sales journal, which an employee has downloaded for you

    c checking the sales journal data you added up against the original sales invoices

    d contacting the client's lawyer, with permission, to ask about a case in progress

    e opening a box of stock after it has been counted to see if it has all of the items claimed

    f talking to the manager about the system changes that have occurred

    g reviewing whether the current portion of the debt has been revealed in the current liabilities section of the Statement of Financial Position.

7.11 **EVIDENCE TYPE:**

Required: Complete both (a) and (b) below:

    a For each of the issues listed in Exercise 7.10, name the reliability of the evidence being used.

    b For each of the issues listed in Exercise 7.10, identify the primary management assertion being tested. In most cases, there will only be one, although exceptions can exist.

7.12 **EVIDENCE:** What management assertions may be of particular risk in each of the following circumstances?

    a There is a concern with theft in the stock warehouse.

    b Items for sale in a tourism shop are all there on consignment.

    c The school charity bazaar accepts cash for its sales, and no receipts are issued.

    d Sales in the first few days of the next year are captured in current year accounts.

    e An unintentional program error turns positive amounts into negative amounts between journal and ledger entries.

    f The depreciation policy is unknowable from the financial statements.

7.13 **EVIDENCE:** Classify each of the following situations in terms of their *sufficiency* (enough or not enough), their *relevance* and their *reliability*.

The auditor:

    a examines 400 purchase invoices in order to understand whether all purchases have been recorded

    b inquires of the client's (only) solicitor as to whether there are any customers threatening to sue the client

    c calls the payroll manager to confirm whether payroll withholdings for PAYE are authorised by payroll records

    d drives out to three of the five building sites to ensure that the construction is going on – the two sites not examined were too far away to drive to easily

    e examines all purchase documents in the fixed asset online file to ensure that the correct amounts have been included in the financial statements and that they are all purchases and not leases.

Audit testing and working papers

Learning objectives

After studying the material in this chapter, you should be able to:
- explain the purpose of audit testing; and when, where and how it is applied
- describe testing methods that improve audit efficiencies and effectiveness
- create audit working papers, and describe their purpose and characteristics
- explain how auditors use and benefit from this and computerised audit systems.

Introduction

In an assurance engagement, the auditor is employed to determine whether the claims of another are justified in fact. In a financial statement audit, management asserts that the financial statements are a fair presentation in compliance with GAAP. Other types of audit may determine the legality of tax deductions or the efficiency of management. However, it is common across audits for tests to be carried out to collect evidence as to whether these claims can, or cannot, be supported. Audit testing is thus fundamental to the audit process.

Documenting the auditor's evidence, test results and decisions is equally important. The auditor's documentation for each engagement – which can number in hundreds of pages – is called the audit **working papers**. Working papers are evidence of the auditor's work, and they are prepared to describe what occurred and what decisions were made. This chapter discusses working paper protocols, styles and ownership, and provides examples.

Computerised (or information technology (IT)) audit assistance programs round out this chapter on audit testing. IT systems and audit firm networks and formats are invariably used in each engagement. They help the auditor conduct tests and, if used properly, improve the efficiency and effectiveness of the audit. Automated working papers, data-extraction software and artificial intelligence (expert system) packages are some of the tools employed. This chapter covers these and provides examples.

To begin with, we introduce the detailed procedures that are associated with the public's view of what an audit is: fieldwork, and testing methods and their documentation. We will start with audit testing, its principles, and the methods by which it is achieved.

working papers
Auditor's documentation for each engagement. It is evidence of the auditor's work and describes what occurred and what decisions were made.

Audit testing

Audit testing refers to the techniques that auditors use to gather evidence. With respect to the financial statement audit, 'assertions' are, in effect, management's claims about the quality of the client's information system and the compliance of its accounts with GAAP. It is these implied assertions that are audit-tested.

....

testing
To 'test' is to analyse the validity of a premise, such as a client's claim that the statements comply with GAAP, by subjecting all or a portion of that claim to a process by which information or processes are examined in support of that claim. (Toba, 1975)

Testing is an often time-consuming part of the audit process, taking up much of the auditor's work in the field. When auditors are vouching or tracing invoices, downloading and manipulating client databases, recasting ledgers and journals, or observing the stock count, they are, in fact, performing audit tests.

In the following sections, we consider each element of this thoughtful definition with reference to the financial statement audit process.

'To analyse the validity'

This brings us back to the idea of audit evidence and judgement. The purpose of an audit is to obtain sufficient, appropriate evidence to enable the auditor to analyse a claim and form an opinion. To achieve this, auditors pay particular attention to those areas of greatest risk and the level of misstatement they decide to tolerate. The analysis of audit evidence also calls for a level of professional scepticism:

Professional scepticism

The auditor should nurture the following attitudes and approaches:
- 'Have the self-confidence and strength of character to maintain an enquiring mind.
- Suspend trust: rationally and logically consider all the likely options, not just the one that is being put in front of you.
- Resist the temptation to just accept the easy answer.
- Go beyond simply providing evidence to support disclosures. Consider alternative disclosures or viewpoints as well.'

Source: CA ANZ (2022).

Structurally, auditors decide on the nature, extent and timing of the audit tests necessary to increase the likelihood of uncovering the potential for material misstatement.

Nature: Type of test

Audit tests must be designed to provide appropriate evidence, whether testing a client's control system or examining invoice prices. It may be important in some to conduct extensive tests on account balances; in others, extensive tests of controls may be more appropriate. The *nature* of the procedures will vary with the circumstances of the engagement.

The challenge, then, is to match the type of test to the assertion of concern, its risk of material misstatement and tolerable misstatements – while still achieving audit efficiencies. Many different procedures can be performed, some categories of which are as follows.

- *Inspection* – to examine accounting records, documents or tangible assets. The reliability of the inspection will depend on the nature and source of the items examined. Inspection of tangible assets will provide reliable evidence as to their *existence*, but not as to their *rights-obligations*, *accuracy* or *valuation*.
- *Observation* – observing a procedure being performed by client staff. Observation can provide reliable evidence as to satisfactory performance only at the time of the observation. So, for example, stocktaking procedures may be carefully conducted while the auditors are watching, but less so as soon as the auditors depart.
- *Confirmation* – seeking information from knowledgeable and usually external source. Confirmations are usually sent to a sample of the client's debtors, creditors, and all of its solicitors, bankers and lenders. Confirmation is not limited to outsiders: independent internal managers can provide reliable confirmation if they are independent of the system or decisions being audited.

- *Inquiry* – asking a knowledgeable person about a process, intent or fact. In assessing its reliability, auditors should consider the respondent's competence, independence and integrity. In some cases, such as to organisational plans for the future, client inquiry may be the only form of evidence available. So, while less reliable generally, inquiries may be, on some occasions, the only source of information.

Auditing in practice

Competence, independence and integrity

As to *competence*, a purchase manager is unlikely to be aware of IT program controls. As to *independence*, an accounts manager may be reluctant to tell you the true value of account sales used to calculate their earnings. A bookkeeper who has misappropriated funds in the past may lack the *integrity* necessary to rely on their claims.

- *Re-performance* – the process of repeating a procedure or calculation that has been performed by the client. Re-performance tests the quality of that original activity. It may be done to ensure that the action was performed *accurately* or in an authorised (*valid*) fashion. Re-adding numbers on documents or walking through transactions from start to finish (or vice versa) are types of re-performance. Re-performance is generally a reliable form of evidence as long as the base data is accurate. Re-performance can involve *tracing* or *vouching* when reviewing a transaction from initiation to completion (or vice versa).

Auditing in practice

Payroll data

The auditor downloads the client's payroll data from the client's database and re-calculates (re-performs) the payroll withholdings and net payroll. They then compare that to what the client actually recorded and paid. The auditor then vouches for the ending payroll balance back to the authorised employee records.

- *Tracing* – testing transactions forward from a transaction source towards the (concluding) financial statements. Tracing is useful for testing transactions for *completeness* (if the source is complete).
- *Vouching* – testing accounting transactions from the financial statements back to their source. It is useful to test for *occurrence-validity* (see **Figure 8.1**).
- *Analytical procedures* – auditor conducts analytical procedures to compare expected patterns or trends with actual disclosures in the statements. The purpose is to identify and subsequently investigate unusual variations that could lead to material misstatements. So, for example, an unusually high sales figure may indicate that there is an overstatement in sales. Unusual patterns in asset valuation could indicate management distortion.

Figure 8.1 Tracing and vouching

A variety of methods are used to perform analytical procedures, from simple ratios to complex models, and they are an important tool for the auditor. (For more detail on this type of method, see Chapter 9.)

Auditors are not limited to particular techniques or evidence. They will choose or be guided by the audit firm's policy, risk assessment and materiality understandings, and the necessary level of reliability needed for each management assertion.

Extent: How many?

Extent has to do with the number or volume of tests to conduct. The extent needed is dictated by the degree of risk, materiality and audit efficiencies. Obtaining 2–3 confirmations from a client's customers may be too little, while obtaining 1000 may be more than what is needed to come to a reasonable conclusion and take too much time. Inquiring of *all* of your client's solicitors may be important, but if an account is immaterial (and you are not concerned with understatement), no tests may be needed. If it is economical to download your client's database, it may be more efficient to test the entire population than to select a sample. So risk, materiality and audit efficiencies factor into the decision of 'how much' to test.

Timing: When?

The *timing* of audit tests takes efficiency into account as well as audit effectiveness. Some tests can only be conducted at certain times, such as observation of the client's stock count. If, however, it is possible to conduct tests of detail prior to the client's fiscal year-end (and thereby reduce or eliminate such tests at year-end), then efficiencies can be gained. This should only occur if:

- the system of internal control can be relied upon
- you are confident the client implemented those controls throughout the entire year.

Testing prior to the balance date can be appropriate where there is heavy demand on the audit staff at year-end, or where delays in control tests will lead to costly errors later on. A loss of the **audit trail** may occur because people 'forget' what happened earlier in the year: they failed to record changes to the system, or forgot the negotiations undertaken.

In systems that have undergone recent changes, it is essential that the auditor is on hand to observe and possibly test the procedures by which a system is established or changed. Otherwise, it may be 'too late' to come to a view on the client's control system.

------

audit trail
The ability to determine the source, the processing and/or the conclusion of a transaction by referring to accounting records.

'A premise'

'A premise' refers to the claims which are subject to investigation. A 'premise' is that the financial statements are a fair representation and comply with GAAP. Testing, by its nature, and using Toba's (1975) definition, does one or more of:

- establishing a premise, such as is common to scientific endeavours where testing helps to establish relationship among variables
- corroborating a premise, such as requiring a statement from an independent witness to support an accused's alibi
- refuting a premise, such as when a taxpayer presents receipts for payments to refute the tax authority's premise that deductions from income taken are unjustified.

In the statutory financial audit, management *assertions* as to the statement disclosures,[1] and the systems that drive them, are corroborated or refuted through the collection and evaluation of evidence.

------

[1] You'll recall, in terms of assertions, that accounts represent what has *occurred* and are *valid, complete, accurate, valued, classified* appropriately, *exist, owned* and meet presentation standards.

International, Australian and New Zealand standards define two types of engagements, the latter of which also *establishes a* premise.

The difference seems to lie with the client's engagement with a claim. In a **direct engagement** asking whether operations are efficient, for example, the auditor may be the one to establish the premise to be tested (by defining 'efficiency') and the basis on which it is to be measured.

The financial statement audit is an **attestation engagement** because, like other attestation engagements, the auditor is presented with the claim and its measure by an outsider (i.e., GAAP, claimed by the client). The distinction affects how the auditor approaches the engagement and will be discussed under 'other' engagements later in this text (see Part 5 of this text).

Examine or subject to a process

To carry out audit tests, auditors must conduct procedures on an accounting system, documents or other evidential matter. You will recall that auditors may inspect, observe, re-perform, confirm, inquire or perform analytical procedures. These are all types of 'tests'. Broader categories of tests are also worth knowing about (see **Figure 8.2**).

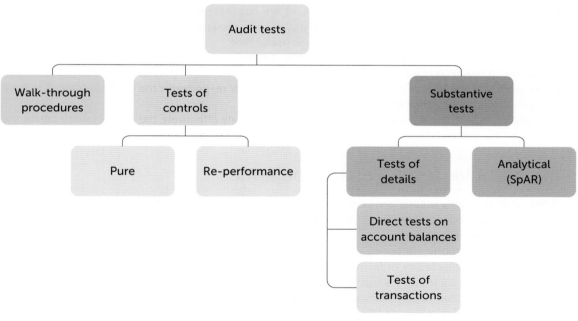

Figure 8.2 Audit test types

Terms from ASA 330 and ISA NZ 330.

Walk-through procedures

Walk-through procedures are a process by which the auditor traces one example of each transaction from inception through the client's system. The auditor might take a sales document, for example, and follow it from capture (the sales point) to data input, processing (journalising/posting) and output (financial statements). The purpose is to see how the system and its controls function, and how that process leads to recording in the financial statements.

direct engagement
The assurance practitioner measures or evaluates the subject matter against criteria, obtains appropriate evidence, and evaluates the subject matter against the criteria. (AUASB, 2020a, paras 12–13; NZAuASB, 2014, paras 12–13)

attestation engagement
A party *other than* the assurance practitioner measures, offers and usually presents the subject matter to the assurance practitioner (the auditor). The assurance practitioner addresses whether (it) is free from material misstatement. (AUASB, 2014)

Depth testing

Depth testing is an extended and distinct form of walk-through procedure. While a walk-through procedure helps the auditor *understand* a system, depth tests are conducted to *test* that same system. Depth testing refers to all the tests used to obtain evidence about how transactions move through a system, such as a 'sale' or a 'purchase'.

Depth testing may include tracing and vouching for *completeness* or *occurrence*, casting and cross-casting for *accuracy* ('casting' means adding up a column of figures, while 'cross-casting' means adding up the separately computed totals from each column to ensure they agree with the overall total), re-performing actual or test entries to test controls, reconciling to bank records, or inspecting 'exception reports'. It comprises the tests needed for an auditor to be convinced that the system works 'as promised'. The auditor will usually pay particular attention to higher-risk accounts or transactions in designing their depth test.

Tests of controls

Tests of controls are performed by the auditor on the client's internal control system. The purpose is to determine whether controls of concern are, or are not, operating effectively throughout the year. Auditors will test only those controls that are designed to prevent or detect errors that could lead to material misstatements. Some definitions may be useful here:

- *Pure tests of control* are those in which only the indicator of the control is reviewed (such as observing the existence of a check).
- *Re-performance tests of controls* occur when the auditor re-performs the controls claimed to have been carried out by the client.

If one of these internal controls does not appear to operate effectively, the auditors will increase the nature, timing and/or extent of their substantive testing.

Substantive tests: Tests of balances

Substantive tests/procedures are concerned with testing balances or the transactions that lead to balances in the accounts. The focus, therefore, is on 'balances', not 'controls'. These procedures involve the following (see **Figure 8.2**):

- *Tests of transactions* – a test to ascertain whether data moves properly through the system to be appropriately reflected in, or from, the account balances
- *Direct tests on balances* – a test examining balances or portions of them directly. Re-performing depreciation schedule calculations is one example.
- *Specific analytical review (SpAR)* procedures – a type of analytical review test used as a substantive test (for more on this topic, see Chapter 9).

'All or a portion of that claim'

This calls to mind the idea that it would be impossible to test all the transactions or all of the controls for all assertions in any cost-effective way. How does the auditor select the appropriate tests? What elements of the system require more-rigorous testing? How can audit efficiencies be achieved? Several audit-testing methods can reduce the audit cost while still ensuring audit quality, namely:

- dual testing
- directional testing
- sampling.

Dual testing

Dual testing means conducting multiple tests using the same data or documents (see **Table 8.1** for several examples). Dual testing avoids duplication and saves time as the data or document download time is reduced. However, auditors should be careful to ensure that the objectives of both tests can be separately met using the same sample.

Table 8.1 Dual testing examples

Document tested	Control test	Substantive test
Sales invoice	Inspect for authorising signature	Re-perform computation of sales prices, or review sales program
Stock record	Inspect for reviewer's initials	Confirm cost from purchase records
Debtors' ledger	Observe reconciliation evidence	Confirm validity of balances

Directional testing

To save time, the auditor can conduct directional tests. *Directional tests* exploit the double-entry basis of accounting by assuming that it would be unnecessary to test both sides of a journal entry, just the higher-risk side. If one part of an entry is shown to be correct, the assumption is that the other side is also correct.

Auditing in practice

Overstatement and understatement

Satisfactory evidence from audit tests designed to test debtors for overstatement may also indicate that credit sales have not been overstated. Similarly, testing for understatement in accounts payable will also test for the understatement of purchases.

Although all accounts are susceptible to overstatement and understatement, some may be more likely to be misstated in one direction or the other. So, for example, if senior management distorts accounts, they are likely to do so by overstating assets or understating liabilities. On the other hand, employee theft is more likely to be concealed by the understatement of assets (i.e., cash stolen) or the overstatement of expenses. This gives the directional-tester a place to start. **Table 8.2** illustrates these general principles.

Table 8.2 Principle and corollary tests

	Purpose of the primary test	Resulting corollary test: U – Understatement; O – Overstatement						
	Test for:	Assets		Liabilities		Income		Expenses
Assets	Overstatement	–	or	O	or	O	or	U
Liabilities	Understatement	U	or	–	or	O	or	U
Income	Overstatement	O	or	U	or	–	or	O
Expenses	Understatement	O	or	U	or	U	or	–

It follows that auditors can design primary tests to check for the most likely misstatements. However, this system is not fully endorsed in auditing practice, and some words of caution are in order:

- If we use the double-entry principle in this way, we are dependent on the trial balance; consequently, the usual tests on the trial balance become crucial.
- Care must be taken to test all debit balances for overstatement and all credits for understatement, since an omission of one affects more than just that account.
- Underlying assumptions about the 'other side' of the double-entry transaction can make this cost-cutting measure risky if unexpected entries are actually made.

Cost-cutting measures, such as directional testing, should always be used with caution.

Sampling

> Audit sampling is designed to enable conclusions to be drawn about an entire population on the basis of testing a sample drawn from it. (ASA 500, para A56; ISA NZ 500, para A56)

Sampling is a common method of achieving audit efficiency. One need only consider the thousands of transactions that occur monthly or even daily in large or medium-sized businesses to get a sense of the enormity of testing all transactions. Audit resources are limited, and there are constraints on the size of the audit fee, yet audit quality must be preserved. Sampling a portion of the records is an accepted part of the audit process, to preserve this quality.

Sampling may be applied either to tests of control or substantive tests, or both. The usual method would be for auditors to select a random sample from the population being tested and use the sample results to conclude on all similar transactions or balances. Sampling is most appropriate in an audit where the following conditions apply:

- *Many similar transactions.* There is a large number of similar transactions, documents or control occurrences. Do not sample if the cost of sampling exceeds the cost of confirming the whole population by some other means.
- *Individually immaterial, in combination material.* When transactions are individually immaterial (small) but together significant, they can, in combination, lead to material misstatement. There is no purpose in testing transactions that lead to an immaterial balance unless there is a risk of understatement (or fraud). Also, individually material transactions should be subject to testing. Where there are many small transactions, however, sampling is often appropriate.
- *Cost-effective.* If it is less expensive to sample than to examine the entire population, and doing so would not sacrifice audit quality, then it would seem wise to sample. In some cases, computer-assisted auditing techniques and client utility programs make testing all the transactions easier and less costly, so each situation differs.

Much of the work of audit sampling lies in planning. Decisions must be made about the purpose of the test, selecting a sample, and treating errors found or unavailable sample documentation. Decisions must also be made about how or whether to extrapolate the results to the population. Common uses for sampling are found in cycles such as:

- inventory and stock control
- accounts receivable and sometimes accounts payable
- sales and purchase transactions
- payroll transactions.

CONCEPT QUESTION 1   Define 'sampling' and state why it may be useful in an audit.

Testing strategies

Building on your knowledge to this point, it may be possible to see how decisions about audit risk can inform the auditor's strategy. That is, the level of testing required *responds* to the auditor's assessment of overall, inherent and control risks (see **Table 8.3**).

Table 8.3 Evidence, risk and judgement matrix

Source of risk	Audit evidence implications of an assessment of:	
	Low risk	**High risk**
Inherent risk: management integrity	Reduced likelihood of distortion; lower-cost audit possible	Distortion concern; need to obtain reliable and independent sources of evidence, perform additional substantive procedures
Inherent risk: business or industry	Reduced likelihood of pressure on management to distort balances	As above, analytical procedures may be useful to identify unusual relationships
Control risk (after tests of controls)	May reduce nature, timing, the extent of substantive tests	1 – auditability concern; 2 – may increase nature, timing, the extent of substantive tests, increased risk of employee fraud
Overall audit risk	Conduct audit with the usual due care and skill	May require additional procedures given particular sensitivity of the engagement
Substantive tests: specific analytical review	Gives comfort on income statement; possibly reduces other substantive tests	May require a different type of, or more extensive, substantive testing to identify the source of the concern raised by this risk
Substantive tests: of balances or transactions leading to balances	An auditor-controllable risk; must be low if the auditor cannot rely on the inherent environment or controls	A controllable risk; higher risk acceptable if high reliance on inherent risk and controls achieved – cost efficiencies also considered

So, the auditor may decide to conduct a *response* that either focuses on 'tests of controls' or 'substantive tests'. See if you can follow the response logic in **Table 8.3**. You will note that should control risk (CR) be high – that is, where controls are absent or not working – they cannot be relied upon. Inherent risk (IR) and overall audit risk (OAR) assessments also guide the audit response. See ASA 330 and ISA NZ 330: The Auditor's Responses to Assessed Risks for more examples and applications.

Selecting evidence is not the end of the story. Compiling the findings to form an opinion is a challenging and somewhat subjective task, one addressed in the chapters to follow.

> **CONCEPT QUESTION 2**   Name and define seven ways of testing.

Working papers

An important means of ensuring audit quality and accountability is through the production of **audit working papers**.

audit working papers
A 'record of audit procedures performed, relevant audit evidence obtained, and conclusions the auditor reached'. (ASA 230, para 5; ISA NZ 230, para 5)

The profession requires the preparation of working papers, and well it should, for working papers are evidence of their work, logic and decisions. They form a defence should a firm be accused of failing to apply due care.

> The objective of the auditor is to prepare documentation that provides: (a) A sufficient and appropriate record of the basis for the auditor's report; and (b) Evidence that the audit was planned and performed in accordance with Auditing Standards ... (ASA 230, para 5; ISA NZ 230, para 5)

Completing audit working papers is an ongoing process throughout the audit. All working papers together are evidence of audit quality (or a lack of it). They are held in the audit firm's files and databases for years afterwards:

> Firms are required to establish policies and procedures for the retention of engagement documentation. The retention period for audit engagements ordinarily is no shorter than five years from the date of the auditor's report or if later, the date of the group auditor's report. (ASA 230, para A23; ISA NZ 230, para A23)

Working papers do *not* belong to management, shareholders or the public: *they are the auditor's property*. As such, working papers are not normally available to others. This is important because they contain information about the client, and client confidentiality should be maintained. While there are exceptions – the working papers may be subpoenaed in a court of law, or quality reviewers would look at them – they generally are available only to the audit firm that owns them.[2]

Auditing in practice

Case law

In 2001–02, senior audit partners at Arthur Andersen LLP, auditor of the (later bankrupt) Enron Corporation, had staff destroy working paper material, other than basic data, presumably to protect the firm from having to produce these papers in court. Andersen, to its credit, fired the key managers involved, but one wonders whether reputational damage had not already occurred (e.g., see Fisher, 2002), and why those managers would have taken such an unethical stance in the first place. This and similar cases led to the dissolution of this major audit firm.

Working papers are important, and not only to the auditors. They serve the auditor, the client and the public because they:
- record the work done for the purposes of the partner review
- record who performed the work (and so provide a possible indicator of experience)
- provide evidence of the work done in the event of subsequent legal proceedings
- help ensure a methodical approach to the work
- facilitate the transfer of work in the event of new staff being engaged in the audit
- assist in planning the subsequent year's audit.

Working papers may be pre-formatted to make online completion easier. Once complete, they are usually reviewed by the audit manager and, towards the conclusion of the audit, by the audit partner-in-charge. Audit working papers thus include a great deal of information. See **Table 8.4** for an example of a working paper.

---

[2] Although prior Australian and New Zealand audit standards claim rights of ownership of working papers to the auditor, such ownership claims are currently being challenged in the British courts. It remains to be seen whether Australia and New Zealand will feel the impact of such changes should they occur.

Table 8.4 Working paper example: Fixed asset schedule

Fixed asset schedule					Prepared by JL	Reviewed by BA			C030.1.3	
Acme Office Supplies – 30.06.22					Date 17.07.22	Date 03.09.22				
	Equipment basis (000s)				Accumulated depreciation					
Fixed assets	Beg. bal.	Purch.	Disposal	End bal.		Beg. bal.	Deprec. expense	Acc. dep. disposals	End bal.	
Building	1325			1325	√	308	44		352	# √
Loader	64			64	√	32	16		48	# √
Truck: FtBd		128		128	√	112	8	120	0	# √
Truck: 4×4	113		113	0	√	0	21		21	# √
Forklift	235			235	√	118	47		165	# √
Totals	1737	128	113	1752	√	570	136	120	586	# √
√		√	√	x √		√	√	√	x √	
				Findings: no errors Conclusion: accurate, complete, exist						

Key: √ cast, cross-cst x trace to WTB, # examine

Working paper structures

A clear working paper format and structure enables the audit managers and, later, the audit partner to review them quickly. While that format will vary by company, there are shared characteristics. In particular, each audit working paper will include the:

- client's name
- title of the working paper
- balance date
- working paper code
- audit preparer's signature or initials and date
- audit reviewer's signature or initials and date
- other elements.

The structure of working papers – that is, how they are ordered and referenced – is also important for review purposes. Managers and partners can then follow how the logic in one working paper leads to another. See **Figure 8.3** for an illustration of how working papers flow and interact with each other.

That 'flow' is enabled if each account (or system) is assigned a code; usually, this is an initial or a number. In **Figure 8.3**, all *sales*-related working papers start with the letter 'S'. Using a code and subcodes results in a 'hierarchy' of working papers. The main working paper for an account or process is usually called the 'lead schedule'.

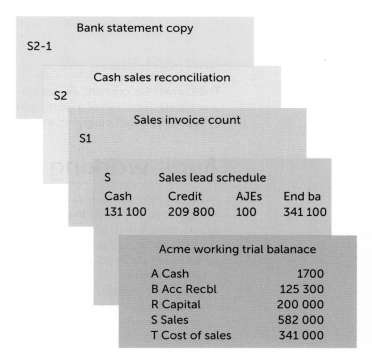

Figure 8.3 Hierarchy of audit working papers

Audit working papers can be classified to a *permanent file* for those that are of continuing significance. A *current audit file* is for working papers that are only of relevance to the current year's audit. A filing index may exist for both permanent and current audit files, indicating the location of each type of file (an example appears in **Table 8.5**) and its subsets. A standardised structure facilitates subsequent review by the audit manager and senior partner.

Permanent file

The permanent file contains information of long-term interest to the auditor. As such, it may be used by new audit team members to familiarise themselves with the client organisation, or by ongoing auditors to review the client's situation. Having a permanent file can also reduce the likelihood of irritating the client by asking the same questions year in, year out.

The following items would normally be contained in the permanent file:
- a copy of the client's founding documents, such as memorandums and articles of association, partnership agreements and club rules
- copies of documents such as long-term leases, debenture deeds, and major contracts of continuing significance
- details as to the nature of the business
- details of the physical location of factories, offices, shops, warehouses etc.
- names and addresses of the client's advisers, including attorneys, bankers and other consultants
- a copy of the letter of engagement
- an organisation chart of the client's staff, with particular emphasis on those employees with whom the auditor is likely to have regular contact
- account manuals, charts of account, system flow charts and data flow diagrams
- details of the financial history of the client and schedules of significant events
- copies of previous reports to management
- copies of previous points on accounts.

Current file

The current file contains everything else: essentially all the working papers that relate to the current year's audit. A portion of a working paper index is shown in **Table 8.5**.

Illustrative audit programs and working papers are found throughout this text.

Audit working paper principles

Audit files should record all of the decisions made during the planning process as well as during testing, along with all of the information obtained from testing and conclusions reached. When drafting working papers, ensure that they show:
- the *audit procedures* used to avoid omissions
- *sufficient detail* to enable an experienced auditor with no previous connection to the audit to evaluate them
- *significant matters* that may require the exercise of judgement, together with the auditor's conclusions. If difficult questions arise, the auditor should record the relevant information received and summarise both the management and audit conclusions. This is important because a third party who has the benefit of hindsight may subsequently question the auditor's judgement. It is crucial to be able to show what facts were known at the time of the auditor's decision, to be able to demonstrate that, based on these facts, the conclusion was reasonable
- *signatures and dates,* including the dates on which documents were received from the client

Table 8.5 Audit working paper: Index example

Audit working paper index A3			
Acme Office Supplies – Year ended 30 June 2021			
Section	Subsection	Contents	Prepared by Date Reviewed by Date
A		**Client and contract documents**	
	A010	Last working trial balance (WTB) and adjustments found	
	A020	Incorporation documents	
	A030	Letter of representation	
	A040	Engagement letter	
	A050	Governing board minutes	
B		**Planning documents**	
	B010	Risk analysis	
	B020	Management integrity checklist	
	B030	Business and industry risk checklist	
	B040	Fundamental controls checklist	
	B050	Overall analytical review schedule	
	B060	Materiality assessment schedule	
	B070	Audit plan: Budget and staffing	
	B080	Internal control questionnaires and evaluations	
S		**Sales subsystem**	
	S010	Accounts receivable lead schedule	
	S020	Sales returns and allowances lead schedule	
	S030	Credit sales lead schedule	

- *references* to the financial statements, the summary schedules or an index
- *comparative figures* for account balances
- the *extent and detail of audit work*, or reference *supporting audit working papers*
- *explanations* of any audit ticks, marks and footnotes used on the working paper
- *findings,* where the working paper pertains to evidence or tests performed
- *conclusions,* indicating whether the results of the tests or other evidence meet expectations and, where they do not, its implications. So, for example, missing sales documents could indicate either overstated sales or poor records.

Copies of the client's schedules can also form part of the working papers, either permanent or current. These days, working papers are usually found in pre-formatted databases, although preserving hard copies as a backup is not unusual.

IT and computerised testing support

The audit profession is under pressure from its clients to reduce audit fees. Yet, the risks of doing so are high: if costs are cut at the expense of audit quality, then litigation, loss of professional status, and socioeconomic costs to users and others can result. Therefore, efficiency improvements must derive from improved evidence-collection techniques that do not sacrifice quality.

IT is an essential tool for these reasons. IT programs for audit tend to be procedures, or algorithms, that deal with data in particular ways. IT support helps the auditor to achieve the following:
- Gain audit efficiencies in high-volume or repetitive tasks. Audit is a staff-intensive business – once it has been set up, IT support can reduce staff costs. Efficiencies occur from:
  — high volumes of testing
  — accurate calculations (although programs must be right.)
  — consistent working paper documentation.
- Train, motivate and attract staff by using new technologies
- Increase flexibility by client-specific design and on-the-spot change response
- Use tests that are otherwise too costly to perform (i.e., analytical review)
- Impress clients and potential clients with the use of technology
- Expand into new revenue streams (i.e., internal audit or systems development)
- Support decision making.

Given the availability of notebooks, mobile devices, cloud and network capability, IT support offers the added convenience of communications interface between the auditor in the field, firm programs, firm expertise, and other audit team members. Firms, through local area networks (LANs) have real-time and onsite capabilities available to audit teams. Firms will probably be equipped with software packages such as for writing reports and accessing policy. Proprietary statistical packages may be available.

This section is concerned with the specifics of how the auditor uses IT to support the audit process. Computerised and IT audit assistance is only limited by the imagination of those who create systems, but in general, they can be categorised as:
- automated working papers
- audit software routines
- data-extraction software
- Artificial intelligence (AI) and expert systems.

Automated working papers

Imagine that, while clearing review notes at the end of an audit, two new adjusting journal entries (AJEs) are needed: the financial statements must be redone. Accomplishing this task manually would probably result in a costly delay.

If, however, the engagement uses an automated working paper program, the auditor can enter (authorised) adjustments and thereby update all records in a moment (see **Table 8.6**). Time is saved and expenses are reduced. (Keep in mind, however, that while the auditor controls their working papers, the client must authorise changes to their accounts.)

Table 8.6 Working paper example: Working trial balance and errors found

Client working trial balance + adjustments	Acme Office Supplies – Year ended 30 June 2022		Prepared by Date	Reviewed by Date		A10
	Per client		AJEs – errors found	W/P ref	Adjusted balances	
Cash	2000				2000	
Accounts receivable	87 600				87 600	
Provision for BD		1000				1000
Inventory	189 400				189 400	
Fixed assets	270 000				270 000	
Accum. depreciation		150 000				150 000
Accounts payable		30 300	9325	P10.3		20 995
Payroll tax payable		13 100				13 100
Interest payable		2700	9325	P10.3		12 025
LT debts payable		100 000				100 000
Share capital		200 000	1520	S10.4		198 480
Retained earnings		30 000				30 000
Sales		305 900				305 900
Sales returns	4000		1520	S10.4	5520	
Cost of sales	150 000				150 000	
Wages	60 000				60 000	
Rent expense	13 000				13 000	

An automated working paper program is a general term for software that collates and documents information, such as the client's WTB, financial statements and other auditor schedules. There are two approaches to the automation of working paper programs (see **Figure 8.4**):
- hard-coded
- template.

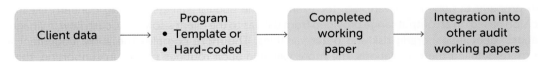

Client data → Program • Template or • Hard-coded → Completed working paper → Integration into other audit working papers

Figure 8.4 Working paper programs and integrated systems

Hard-coded programs are written using a formal programming language and are structured. The user responds to input screens and produces a report based on a standardised format. This approach can be inflexible in that users may not be able to modify or add to the existing programs, and the input screens do not necessarily fit in with that required for a particular client. But hard-coded programs usually require less expertise on the user's part and typically contain more error-trapping routines. They can be used, as an example, for fixed internal control questionnaires.

Template working paper programs are designed around software such as spreadsheets or fourth-generation programs, which do not comprise a programming language in the traditional sense. However, they do offer significant programming features, particularly the flexibility to design working papers specific to the client. Creating templates requires experience and knowledge, so this is usually left to more senior audit team members.

Irrespective of the program type, most audit data today is recorded on integration-based working paper systems (see **Figure 8.4**). In such systems:

- audit decision support tools can be made available and documented via the firm's LAN
- cloud-based data capacity may be available for extensive data loads
- access to professional literature, such as standards, court judgments or industry data, can be incorporated directly into the working papers
- auditors' tablets or laptops, with wi-fi support, can be used to coordinate teamwork decisions in real time
- evidence from clients' databases can be downloaded and saved, or manipulated for tests, and made available for additions to the auditor's working papers
- working papers can be reviewed and 'signed off' electronically
- a system can be programmed to inform the partners about the performance of the audit team against the budget at any particular point in time.

Audit firms would be wise to apply the same controls to their systems that they expect of their clients.

Audit software routines

The term *audit software routine* is used to describe software programs that assist the auditor in specific audit decisions and evidence-gathering routines. Typical routines include:

- data extraction and analysis software
- flowcharting
- internal control evaluation
- audit program design
- test design and sample size determination
- random number generation and sample selection
- going concern analysis
- materiality calculation
- ratio analysis for overall analytical review
- regression analysis for use in specific analytical review procedures.[3]

The auditor will be prompted by on-screen instructions to make and document their judgements with properly designed software. So, for example, the auditor selects a going concern likelihood decision based on an output range provided from data as to the client's solvency, cash flow, managerial changes, debt ratios, credit risk and other variables. The more complex the audit judgement and the more detailed the calculations, the more valuable audit routines can be in supporting, though not replacing, a decision. The advantages, in addition to calculation efficiencies, include working paper consistency and training potential. The audit decision process is documented in the audit working papers.

The parts of the audit process that involve repetitive calculations, data manipulation and standardised documentation lend themselves to automation. Time and budget data can usually be

---

[3] A number of these functions can be found in the CAATs package accompanying this text.

efficiently maintained. Ratio analysis and models can be performed. Software packages produce lead schedules, trial balances, adjusting entries and financial statements, and are capable of downloading and manipulating client data for testing.

Table 8.7 illustrates a portion of an audit software routine designed to determine sample size for audit tests. A feature of all audit tools should be that they provide a standardised and step-by-step approach to specific audit functions or decision problems. They should prompt the user for the appropriate audit judgements.

Table 8.7 Working papers: Credit sales test design

Credit sales tests of controls Acme Office Supplies – 30.06.22			Prepared by Date Reviewed by Date S030.01		
Assertions	**(Analysis)**	**Occur-valid**	**Complete**	**Accuracy**	**Classification**
Auditor decisions					
IR assessment		Hi	Lo	Lo	Hi
Sampling unit		Cust. invoice	Sales orders	Program	Sales > $10 000
Materiality/data source	Materiality $2000	Debtor Ledger accts	Customer sales docs	Program download	Sales ledger accounts
Time budget	3 hrs prep	3 hrs	2 hrs	2 hrs	2 hrs
Model recommendations					
Sample size needed	95% confid.	177	103	Sale prog.	Sales > $10 000
Substantive response expansion if		Any exception	> 3 errors	> 2 errors	Any exception
W/P reference	S030.01.02	S030.01.02	S030.01.03	S030.01.04	S030.01.05

Clients, as well as audit managers, expect high-technology audits. Given the common use of IT tools, it is likely that the courts will expect auditors to use those at their disposal. The use of computerised and IT audit software is an accepted audit practice.

Data-extraction software for substantive testing

Technology is also available to 'download' files from the client's database to the auditor's system for testing. This enables the auditor to manipulate and interrogate the files using their own inquiry packages, such as *key word*, *unusual amount* or *repetitive amount* recognition software. So, for example, the package may identify accounts receivable accounts with credit balances for re-performance, or 'new creditor' names for authorisation testing. In addition to taking less time to conduct and freeing up staff time, data-extraction software supports:

- *Independence* – interrogations can be made independently of the client's systems and programming staff. Often, the client's own system and employees will assist, although it is essential for the run to be totally under the auditor's control.
- *Ease of access* – the offline interrogation of files saves client computing time and gives the auditor greater flexibility.
- *Extent of work* – in a more manual audit, it is unlikely that the whole population would be tested in detail; however, a computer program can test an entire population. So for example, all debtors' transactions can be re-performed by a system on downloaded data, while doing so by hand would be too time-consuming.

Extraction programs can generally be used for carrying out many different types of substantive or control testing procedures, including those for specific analytical reviews and tests of transactions leading to balances, such as:

- preparing graphic analyses or reports using software and downloaded data
- statistical sampling, or extracting random samples from client downloads – an audit software routine can be used to calculate the sample size required, select the sample, and evaluate the sample's test result
- testing client data after first selecting and downloading the data.

Auditing in practice

Data downloads, tests and assertions

- Recalculating journal balances (accuracy).
- Performing limit tests; for example, identifying credit authorisations that are in excess of a predetermined amount (occurrence-validity).
- Performing sequence checks to identify missing data; for example, identifying missing cheques from a cheque number listing (completeness).
- Comparing the data held on two different files; for example, comparing vendor names with an authorised vendor list (occurrence-validity).
- Searching for unusual data, such as undepreciated assets (valuation).
- Searching for fraud indicators, such as scanning client records to see if multiple payroll payments went to the same bank account (occurrence-validity).
- Searching for management distortion indicators, such as small tool amounts debited to capital accounts (classification).

Computer audit extraction software can be designed in such a way that it does not require computer experts to operate it. This will, however, depend on the client's system as well as the audit firm's, so setting up the process can be time-consuming. Extraction software may not work, it may be too costly, or it may not operate with the audit firm's program. In such cases, its use may not be cost-effective or feasible.

AI and expert systems

The automated routines discussed above apply step-by-step algorithms to each situation. Artificial intelligence (AI) is a 'step up' from this (Joshi, 2016):

> The field of artificial intelligence (AI) is concerned with methods of developing systems that display aspects of intelligent behaviour ... to imitate the human capabilities of thinking and sensing.

AIs respond to particular situations in unique ways, thus simulating human decision making through complex string structures. An audit expert's reasoning can be, to some extent, simulated in AI knowledge-informed system, termed an *expert system*. Data is input to an *inference engine,* or logic chain, that subsequently offers a 'decision' or a 'reasonable decision range'. Audit expert systems are an early use of AI, and firms have developed sophisticated models for a range of complex audit decisions, including planning, fundamental internal control analysis and audit program development.

Typical audit expert systems consist of a series of questions that request facts about a client. Once the auditor has entered this information, the system applies its knowledge base to that data to form a decision recommendation. An expert system typically will be informed by international audit seniors who have access to extensive audit datasets from previous engagements, and a depth of experience (see **Figure 8.5**).

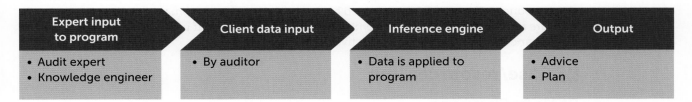

Figure 8.5 Expert system structure

Expert systems are a valuable audit tool as they make international expertise available to local firms and to each individual auditor. They can handle complex information and can provide educational value to less experienced auditors.

A risk of using expert systems, and to a lesser extent any audit tool, lies in the possibility that auditors will treat them as mechanical replacements for judgement. Provided expert systems are well designed; they can *supplement* auditor judgement, but not replace it.

Auditing in practice

Materiality decisions

Materiality decisions made during the planning process can benefit from a firm's expert system. The auditor answers a list of questions related to the client's inherent, overall and control risks, as well as other factors such as location, industry type or age. The expert system then can calculate a 'relevant range' in which planning materiality might reasonably lie.

CONCEPT QUESTION 3 Define 'automated working papers' and name their benefits to the auditor.

Study tools

Summary

In this chapter, audit tests were considered, and the types of tests and purposes for them were explained. Differences between *walk-through procedures, tests of controls* and *substantive tests* were explained and exampled. Test techniques that enable efficiencies include *sampling, dual testing* and *directional testing* were introduced.

Working paper purposes, ownership and protocols were discussed, although each audit firm will vary as to the detail. Working paper hierarchies and examples were also illustrated. This chapter also introduced IT technology tools used by the auditor, such as *automated working papers, audit software routines* and *AI expert systems* to improve audit quality. If used wisely, audit technology can enhance audit efficiency and effectiveness.

Case/resources link

CAATs for Classrooms

Accompanying this book is a series of data, integrated worksheets and exercises that are designed to support your learning and give you exposure to hands-on audit decision-making dilemmas faced by auditors in the planning elements of the audit process. Acquire the relevant material for this chapter from your instructor.

Review questions

8.1   Define 'testing'. How does this apply to audits?

8.2   What is the difference between the 'sufficiency' and 'nature' of audit evidence?

8.3   What is the difference between 'tracing' and 'vouching'?

8.4   What is a characteristic of 'confirmations' as to evidence quality?

8.5   What is the difference between the 'extent' and 'timing' of audit testing?

8.6   When would it be possible to rely on tests conducted only midway through the year?

8.7   What are the premises, implied or otherwise, that professionals test in an audit?

8.8   Define 'walk-through procedures'.

8.9   Define 'tests of controls'.

8.10   Define 'substantive tests'.

8.11   What does it mean to 'cast and cross-cast'?

8.12   What are the three major categories of audit tests?

8.13   What is the difference between 'dual' and 'directional' testing? Why are they used?

8.14   Provide an example of 'dual testing' and an example of 'directional testing'.

8.15   What is the meaning of a 'corollary test' and why is it useful?

8.16   What three conditions would be present to make audit sampling appropriate?

8.17   What is the difference between 'statistical' and 'non-statistical' sampling, and why is that difference important for an audit?

8.18   Why are audit working papers so important to the audit firm?

8.19 Name six purposes that working papers serve.

8.20 What are the ownership rights around working papers in Australia/New Zealand?

8.21 What is the difference between the 'current' and 'permanent' working papers?

8.22 Name and explain why three items are found in the permanent file.

8.23 Name and explain why three items are found in the current file.

8.24 What is 'computerised audit assistance'? It is owned and used by whom?

8.25 How do computerised audit assistance tools serve the auditor?

8.26 Why are LANs useful for the auditor in the field?

8.27 What is the difference between 'hard-coded' and 'template' working papers?

8.28 Name four audit tools and describe how they serve efficiency and effectiveness.

8.29 What aspects of the audit process would suggest the benefit of audit tools?

8.30 What do data-extraction tools do, and what are their benefits to the auditor?

8.31 Describe six different ways in which data-extraction tools can be used to test client data.

8.32 With what sampling functions can data-extraction tools assist?

8.33 How can auditors use 'expert systems'? Can they replace audit judgement?

Exercises

8.1 **TESTING:**

Required: Describe appropriate testing procedures for the following situations. Use audit-testing terms as much as is reasonable:

a Testing stock items for *existence* – the items are nails and screws in small boxes.

b Testing payroll expense adjusting journal entries conducted at the end of the year for *completeness*.

c Testing the last in, first out (LIFO) system to ensure that items in stock have been appropriately allocated to cost of sales.

d Testing to see whether there is any debt owed on expensive machinery purchased during the year.

8.2 **TESTING:**

Required: Describe the test of control you would use for each of the following and what management assertion you would be testing:

a The client claims that they have passwords giving only one employee access to the credit system.

b The doors on the warehouse are said to be locked any time the stock receiver is not there.

c The auditor is concerned that the client claims to do bank reconciliation but that they do not really know how to do it.

d The auditor is told that the cash is counted at each checkout counter at the beginning of each shift.

8.3 **TESTING:** Use the following case to answer the questions below:

R. Eka Ltd is a research and development lab whose primary assets are its employees. Controls over the manual payroll system include appropriate segregation of duties, reconciliations of the ledgers to journals, authorised pay rates and withholdings, separate signatures on payroll cheques (authorised by supporting documentation), and internal checks by the payroll department manager.

For each of these five procedures/controls, identify a:

a   walk-through test

b   pure compliance test

c   re-performance compliance test

d   direct test on balances (on gross payroll only)

e   test of transactions.

In combination, your series of tests would comprise a depth test. What are the benefits of a walk-through procedure? And of a depth test?

8.4   **TESTING:** Listed below are a number of audit procedures that are applied to supporting documentation, together with an indication of the purpose of the procedure.

a   A sales order is examined for evidence of credit approval.

b   A voucher is examined to see if supporting documentation is attached.

c   The amount on a cheque is compared with the amount in the cash book.

d   A sales invoice is traced to the debtor's ledger to see if it is properly posted.

e   A voucher is reviewed for evidence of a stamp indicating math re-performance.

f   A credit note is traced to the journal to determine if the account is correct.

g   The payment makers are compared with authorised payment makers.

h   A sale order is inspected for authorisation of prices and terms.

i   The sales journal is scanned to see if all invoices have been entered.

Required: Indicate whether each procedure is a test of control or a substantive test. What would make each a dual-purpose test?

8.5   **EVIDENCE:** The audit client, Rivets Ltd, manufactures nails, screws and similar products. The auditor wants to determine whether the inventory of nails and screws is *valid*. Answer the following questions:

a   Is the auditor concerned with *overstatement* or *understatement*?

b   If the auditor wishes to collect a sample, what sort of number sampled might be *sufficient*? Three? 100? 300?

c   If the auditor wishes to collect a sample of that in closing inventory, what might be an appropriate *timing* in which to conduct the test? Beginning of year? Mid-year? End of year?

d   If the auditor was collecting the sample to test the management assertion of *valuation*, should they examine: The number of nails? The location of the nails? Any damage to the nails?

8.6   **EVIDENCE AND RELIABILITY:** During your audit of Backlash Ltd, the following evidential matter has been included in your working papers:

a   flowcharts of the company's payroll routine prepared by your audit assistant and backed up by compliance tests

b   an oral statement by the production director that the expected working life of a plant acquired in January 2021 is ten years c   a letter to the managing director from the company bank manager indicating that the bank intends to extend overdraft facilities for a period of one year

d   a list of items of stock counted by a member of your firm of chartered accountants during observation of the company's stock count

e   a letter from a debtor to your firm in reply to a confirmation request indicating agreement with the balance as recorded in the books of Backlash Ltd.

For each of the above:

i   explain what specific audit objective could be achieved

ii   state, giving reasons, how reliable you judge the evidence to be.

8.7   **EXPERT SYSTEMS:** From the following list, choose where you think expert systems will be of most value in the future. See if you can deduce where expert systems were seen to be of most and least value, and why.

a   planning

b   internal control evaluation and compliance tests

c   substantive testing

d   completion and review, including going concern decisions, related party evaluations and the choice of the audit opinion.

8.8   **WORKING PAPERS:** The working trial balance (see **Table 8.8**) is filed in the auditor's completed working papers.

Required:

a   Prepare a working paper showing recommended AJEs and explanations. Assume adjustments > $5000 net profit or > $9000 in balance sheet accounts are material.

b   Explain what communications should occur as a result of these findings.

Table 8.8 Working trial balance

Account	Year: 2017 Debit	Year: 2017 Credit	Adjustments Debit	Adjustments Credit	Adj. balances Debit	Adj. balances Credit
Cash	1 700		0	0	1 700	
Accounts receivable	125 300		4 500	0	129 800	
Provision – doubtful debts		1 000	0	4 500	0	5 500
Inventory	416 040		0	10 000	406 040	
Notes receivable	21 000		0	0	21 000	
Equipment	358 200		0	3 000	355 200	
Accum. depreciation		175 600	0	4 500		180 100
Notes payable		16 000	0	0		16 000
Accounts payable		48 000	0	0		48 000
Interest payable		0	0	0		0
Long-term debts payable		180 000	0	0		180 000

169

→

	Year: 2017		Adjustments		Adj. balances	
Account	Debit	Credit	Debit	Credit	Debit	Credit
Share capital		200 000	0	0		200 000
Retained earnings		145 810	0	0		145 810
Sales revenue		582 000	4 500	0		577 500
Sales returns & allowances	12 000		0	0	12 000	
Cost of goods sold	257 360		10 000	0	267 360	
Wages expense	94 650		0	0	94 650	
Supplies expense	17 500		3 000	0	20 500	
Depreciation exp.	4 710			0	4 710	
Bad debt expense	1 500		0	0	1 500	
Interest expense	38 450		0	0	38 450	
Net profit		155 830	17 500	0		138 330
WTB total	1 348 410	1 348 410	22 000	22 000	1 352 910	1 352 910

8.9 **WORKING PAPERS:** The auditor is preparing working papers for tests completed and evidential matters collected on the client's accounts receivable account. Fill in the hierarchical framework in **Figure 8.6** with a reasonable set of working paper titles for this account. Use headings and codes as appropriate.

Working trial balance

A Cash	1 700
B Acc Recbl	125 300
R Capital	200 000
S Sales	582 000
T Cost of sales	341 000

Figure 8.6 Hierarchical framework

8.10 **WORKING PAPERS:** DeBoy Parts Ltd has prepared an accounts receivable schedule that you downloaded from their system (see **Table 8.9**). On confirmation of each account, you find the following:

a Pink Zebra claims that products were faulty, returned them and refused to pay.

b Blue's Drilling could not be located; they have left the country.

c Green Grocers is making small but consistent and regular payments.

Required: Complete the working paper set out below. Make determinations about results, advised AJEs and conclusion.

Table 8.9 DeBoy Parts Ltd accounts receivable schedule

Schedule of accounts receivable ageing DeBoy Parts Ltd – 30.6.22				Prepared by:	Reviewed by:
	Balance	**Days**			
Customer	30.6.22	0–30	31–60	61–90	Over 90
Amber Vineyard	14 289	7258	5031	2 000	
Blue's Drilling	6 700				6 700
Green Grocers	5 316	0	456	760	4 100
Lavender Farms	11 949	10 500	1 449		
Orange Appeal	2 356	2 356			
Pink Zebra Rentals	7 901	7 901			
Shades of Grey Apparel	12 553	2 553	10 000		
Violet Appliance	2 105	2 105			
Totals	63 169				

8.11 WORKING PAPERS

Required: Complete the working paper (see **Table 8.10**) by: Vouching and re-performing calculations. Note evidence of your re-performance with an 'x' in the boxes. During testing, you find that the equipment used as collateral is worth only a scrap value of $22 000. In spaces below, set out any recommended adjusting journal entries, and the 'results' and 'conclusion' you may reach as a result of your tests. That is, complete the working paper.

Table 8.10 Sample working paper

Notes payable schedule (including accrued interest)				Prepared by: Date:				Reviewed by: Date: N010.15			
	Dates			**Notes payable**				**Interest payable**			
Creditor	Made	Due	Collateral	Beg. Bal.	Addt'ns	Paymts	Ending Bal.	Beg. Bal.	Expense	Paymts	End Bal.
Local Bank 7%	30.6.00	30.6.24	Stock $20K	10 000	5 000		15 000	700	962.5		1 662.4
DB Credit 13%	30.9.01	30.9.25	Equip. $50K	0	30 000		30 000	0	2 250		2 250
NotiBank 6%	1.1.19	Annual	Stock $25K	20 000	35 000	20 000	0	3 000	600	2 600	1 000
Totals			$95 000	30 000	70 000	20 000	450 000	3 700	3 812.5	2 600	4 912.5

8.12   **TEST STRATEGY RESPONSES:** Each row in **Figure 8.7** sets out different overall, inherent and control risk assessments, and a corresponding test strategy response. Each response calls for some combination of 'high' and 'low' testing levels for substantive and control tests.

Required: Explain why each of the eight strategies may be reasonable in terms of the corresponding risk assessments. Start from the top and work to the bottom.

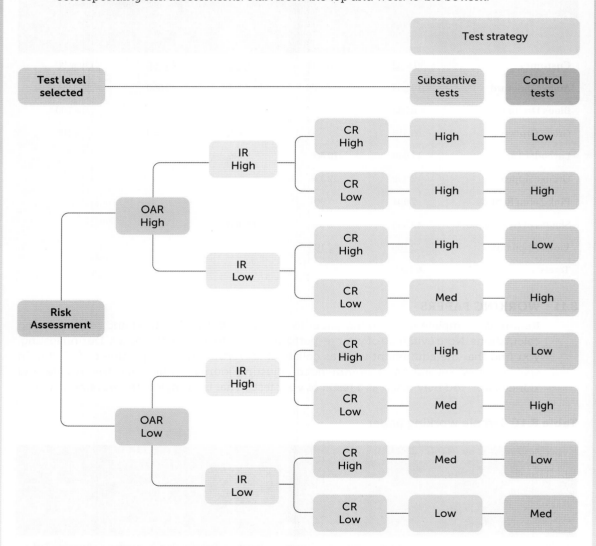

Figure 8.7 Risk assessments and corresponding test strategies

Audit process and analytical procedures

Learning objectives

After studying the material in this chapter, you should be able to:
- describe the risk approach to the audit process, how it came about, and its characteristics
- describe the different audit opinions and the circumstances in which the auditor issues different types of reports
- evaluate the value of evidence gained in analytical procedures
- identify the nature, extent and timing of analytical procedures that may be applied to account balances or transactions as a substantive test.

Introduction

This chapter begins our journey into the audit process by describing the overall audit approach, its processes and phases. While different audit firms will have different process elements, this chapter is designed to include the main steps, roughly in order, of an audit investigation (see **Figure 9.1**).

Initial planning	**Detailed planning**	**Audit test response**	**Completion**
• Preliminary engagement activities • Review client's business • Perform risk analysis • Form audit strategy	• Study accounting system • Evaluate internal controls • Develop detailed plan	• Tests of controls • Further develop plan • Substantive tests	• Completion and review • Management letter (introduced later) • Audit report and opinion • Client's AGM

Figure 9.1 Steps in an audit process

The second part of the chapter introduces analytical procedures (also referred to as AP), emphasising those that comprise a form of substantive tests of detail. We discuss how they are used and when, as well as follow-up investigations, and the implications for professional scepticism, possible confidence and risks. Let us begin with the audit process.

Audit approaches

Audits have been around for thousands of years, the modern audit for the past few centuries. Yet, enterprises have changed over time, as have the approaches to audit (see **Table 9.1**). The Australian and New Zealand auditing standards and guidelines, IFAC, CPA Australia, the PCAOB and AICPA (US), and CA ANZ, lay down certain expectations of today's *risk-based* approach. Some reflection on how this came to be, and why, may explain why it operates as it does today.

Table 9.1 Audit approaches: An evolution

	Transaction approach	Balance sheet approach	Systems approach	Risk analysis approach
Time	In the beginning!	1960s	1970s/early 1980s	1980s
Basis	Each transaction	Balance sheet accounts	Transaction systems	Risks around accounts/assertions
Sources of evidence	Vouching, re-perform	Verify, vouch, trace BS accounts	Tests of controls	Any, based on risk and materiality
Approach to risk/ materiality	All transactions = 'importance'	Smaller balances – less material	Not directly considered	Evidence guided by risk and materiality

The *transactions* approach required the vouching of all transactions to their origin. This was possible only where there were large but few transactions (although, to some extent, this is possible now using downloaded client data). However, the transactions approach should never be used alone because the *completeness* assertion cannot be tested. A transaction approach only examines what is 'there'. Furthermore, transactions tell us little about the *existence* or *rights-obligations* related to an asset. Accordingly, the transactions approach is appropriate as part of a more inclusive model.

The *balance sheet* approach involves (among other things) verifying all but the very smallest of balance sheet accounts. By so doing, the profit is automatically tested, subject to validating opening balances.[1] This was developed in an era in which users relied on balance sheets for their long-term investment decisions and less so on profit or price/earnings.

The *systems-based* audit became popular in the 1970s due to growth in the use of computers and accounting packages. By testing the system controls (only), it was assumed that the transactions would be correct. While testing systems is part of today's approach, doing so is not a standalone step. A systems test would not, for example, capture unusual or one-off transactions, nor a manager's override of the system.

The *risk analysis* approach is a combination of these methods, based on the auditor's evaluation of various audit risks (ASA 330; ISA NZ 330).

Regarding the risk analysis approach, ASA 330 (paras 5–6) explains:

> The auditor shall design and implement overall responses to address the assessed risks of material misstatement at the financial report level … [and] further audit procedures whose nature, timing and extent are based on and are responsive to the assessed risks of material misstatement at the assertion level.

---

[1] Opening balances are the beginning-of-period account balances. Ending balance sheet accounts are constructed from opening balances plus or minus current transactions. It is impossible to reach assurance on the ending balances unless it has been, or can be, reached on their beginning (or opening) amounts. When conducting an audit for the first time, correspondence with the previous auditor is advised (see ASA 510 and ISA NZ 510: Initial Audit Engagements – Opening Balances).

The 'response' referred to here consists of the evidence collected and decisions made in *response* to risks identified. The risk analysis approach is 40–50 years old now but continues to evolve. Even as business models change – such as operating virtually – it will continue to adapt. The risk analysis approach thus combines aspects of other approaches and adds a few of its own, mandating an individualised approach to each and every engagement. It is grounded in the theory of auditing that we introduced at the beginning of this book.

Audit process steps

Assuming a risk-based approach, the audit process can be divided into three phases: *planning*, *performing* and *completion*. The process is illustrated in **Figure 9.1** (and in chapters to come). Generally, the audit team will stick with their plan, but occasions could arise during the course of the audit that lead to changes.

Auditing in practice

Analysis of inventory

A plan to *not* test frozen goods' valuation may change on discovering that the client's freezer was turned off and stock spoiled. Or the auditor may increase a planned volume of testing for the *existence* of designer clothing stock on discovering that the stock was rarely in a secured room.

That said, typically, the following steps should proceed roughly in order.

Initial planning: Steps 1–4

A significant amount of audit time is spent on planning, as this forms the basis of an effective and efficient audit (see **Table 9.2**).

Table 9.2 Initial planning steps 1–4

Audit step	Purpose	Procedures	Working papers
1 Acquire appointment	Determine the appropriateness of appointment, clarify terms of the engagement	1 *Assess ethical issues* 2 *Assess continuance issues* 3 *Evaluate the scope* 4 *Attend site, meet key staff and directors, attend annual general meeting (AGM)*	✓ Engagement letter ✓ Processes and decisions
2 Review client's business	Understand the client's industry, structure, practices, key personnel, financial situation	1 *Visit the site* 2 *Review industry journals* 3 *Obtain prior financial statements* 4 *Review major documents* 5 *Management discussions*	✓ Copies of client documents ✓ Processes and decisions

→

3 Perform audit risk analysis	Provide an informed basis for risk-based approach and plan	1	*Analyse* • *Management integrity* • *Business and industry risk* • *Fundamental controls* • *Conduct analytical procedures* • *Determine materiality*	✓ Internal control questionnaires (ICQs) ✓ Processes and decisions
4 Develop audit strategy	Budget for resources, time and staffing	1	*Prepare budgets* • *Conduct team meetings* • *Obtain partner approvals*	✓ Budgets ✓ Agreements

1   Acquire appointment

The bidding process is likely to be highly competitive, pitting different firms against each other in trying to acquire the audit engagement. In an initial engagement, the auditor should evaluate the scope of the engagement and ensure they have appropriate resources. Prior to committing to a subsequent period of engagement, the firm should also consider whether there are significant changes to the scope of the audit or to the nature of the business. Guidance is provided in ASA 320 and 330, and ISA NZ 320 and 330.

2   Review client's business

In this stage, the auditor gains the information needed for their risk and materiality assessments. They would visit the sites; review industry journals; obtain prior financial statements, management forecasts and budgets; and review formation documents such as partnership agreements or articles of association.

This is all to understand the client's business, industry, key personnel and business operations. It is a step towards determining the client's industry and business risk, and obtaining an understanding of their structure and pressures on the business.

3   Perform an audit risk analysis

Having conducted a review of the client's industry and business, the auditor is ready to perform their risk analysis to develop a detailed audit plan. This process includes the risk and materiality assessments referred to earlier and also the performance of *overall analytical procedures* (see Chapter 10).

4   Develop an audit strategy

The risk schedule developed in step 3 provides the basis for the audit plan (also see ASA 300: Planning an Audit of a Financial Report and ISA NZ 300: Planning an Audit of Financial Statements). This process will clarify the approach, nature, timing and extent of audit tests. It will also produce a time and cost budget; that is, which staff will be on the audit, when, and doing what tasks.

CONCEPT QUESTION 1   Describe an 'audit strategy' and its purpose.

Detailed planning: Steps 5–7

With initial planning complete, the auditor starts examining their systems (see **Table 9.3**).

Table 9.3 Detailed planning

Audit step	Purpose	Procedures	Working papers
5 Study the accounting system	Document systems producing the statements, assess if there are adequate documents and records	1 *Review client manuals and system descriptions* 2 *Inquiries as to processes* 3 *Identify subsystems and transaction types* 4 *Walk-through procedures*	✓ ICQs ✓ Flowcharts ✓ Data flow diagrams (DFDs) ✓ Processes and decisions
6 Evaluate internal controls	Identify controls on which the auditor will rely, identify further risks	1 *Create flowcharts, DFDs* 2 *Review fundamental and comprehensive controls* 3 *Select controls to rely on*	✓ DFDs, flowcharts ✓ System strengths and weaknesses ✓ Processes & decisions
7 Develop detailed audit plan	Plan nature, timing and extent of response (all audit tests)	1 *Design* • *Tests of controls* • *Substantive tests* • *Completion tests* • *Obtain partner approval*	✓ Detailed audit program ✓ Approvals ✓ Processes and decisions

5 Study the accounting system

This step calls on the auditor to perform walk-through procedures and then document the accounting information system or the portion they potentially intend to rely on.

This is where the experience of having conducted previous audits for the same client can save time. This is because the auditor may only have to update, not create, information for flowcharts and DFDs, and the auditor would be familiar with the system.

6 Evaluate the system of internal control

The auditor now understands the accounting system and proceeds to evaluate the internal controls from the documentation prepared in step 5. The purpose is to determine client controls on which they rely to provide confidence in the account balances.

If the preliminary evaluation suggests that there are controls on which the auditor wishes to rely, then tests of controls are planned (steps 7 and 8). Where the preliminary evaluation discloses weaknesses in, or the absence of, internal controls, the auditor will have to increase the nature, timing and extent of their substantive tests (steps 7, 9 and 10).

7 Develop detailed audit plan

All detailed audit procedures and tests are designed in light of the audit strategy and evaluations made to date (steps 4 and 6). The *detailed audit plan* has far more particulars as to the nature (what tests), timing (when to perform them and by whom), and extent (how many) of the intended audit tests.[2] Hence, the detailed plan is individualised for each engagement based on the systems and risks now identified.

Most audit firms use master program 'outlines' that are adaptable to any client. The risk, as always, of pre-formatted decision-making tools is that they can stifle initiative, be subject to *anchoring and adjustment* bias, and replace personal decision making. They are useful and time-saving, however, so are invariably used (planning issues are covered in detail in Chapter 10).

Once the detailed audit plan has been developed, it is time for fieldwork in the form of audit testing for tests of controls and substantive tests of balances.

Audit test responses: Steps 8–10

The audit 'response' is effectively the 'fieldwork' responding to assessments of risk and materiality. It is the point at which the audit team conducts control and substantive tests, according to the detailed audit plan (see **Table 9.4**).

Table 9.4 Audit test response

Audit step	Purpose	Procedures	Working papers
8 Tests of control	Gather evidence on reliability of controls on which the auditor intends to rely	• Perform tests of controls	✓ Test results ✓ Add to draft of system weaknesses ✓ Processes and decisions
9 Develop the audit program	Evaluate the implications of control test results on the audit plan	• Assess results of tests of controls, revise plan accordingly • Partner approval	✓ Revised audit program (if revised) ✓ Processes and decisions

10 Substantive testing	To gather evidence on the financial account balances directly, or on the transactions that lead to those balances	• Substantive AP
		  • Detailed tests on balances
		  • Tests on transactions leading to balances
			✓ Test results
			✓ Processes and decisions

8 Tests of control

As their name implies, tests of control are designed to ensure that the internal controls on which the auditor wishes to rely are working properly throughout the period under review. The nature of the tests will depend on the control, but essentially they involve checking transactions for evidence of compliance. Sensibly enough, ASA 330 and ISA NZ 330: The Auditor's Responses to Assessed Risks point out that the more the auditor relies on the client's controls, the greater their tests of controls must be.

The auditor should no longer rely on a system or its controls based solely on a preliminary evaluation; the *systems* audit approach is not enough. The auditor should obtain evidence that the controls operate throughout the year. The Australian *Pacific Acceptance* (1970) case was particularly useful in highlighting this requirement.

---

[2] The detailed audit plan is referred to as the 'audit plan' in ASA 300 and ISA NZ 300.

That which is being tested by a test of control is subject to a 'yes' or 'no' question: they operate or they do not operate. The transaction itself is not tested. For this reason, the auditor must record and investigate all deviations revealed, regardless of the amount, because an error implies a system that does not work. If tests of control disclose no exceptions, the auditor's preliminary evaluation is confirmed, and reliance can be placed on it.

Auditing in practice

IT audit note

If there is the capacity to download the client's data into the auditor's system for testing, it may be less costly to conduct substantive tests on that data than to carry out some tests of controls which require the selection or flowcharting. Nonetheless, *completeness* may not be tested in this way, so tests of fundamental controls will usually be necessary.

---

9   Develop the audit program

Using the risk-based approach and considering risks, systems and OAR already analysed, tests of internal control may, or may not, be acceptable. If the former, then the detailed plan as set out in step 7 can be developed into an audit program. If tests of control reveal that they do *not* operate as expected, then step 9 is used to modify the detailed audit plan and develop it in accordance with those findings. This usually involves the approval of the audit senior-in-charge.

10   Substantive tests

Substantive tests are performed to determine whether the balances or transactions leading to balances indicate any material misstatements.[3] Substantive tests include:

* **analytical procedures risk** (termed APR in the audit risk model)
* tests of transactions leading to balances (part of your *depth tests*)
* direct tests on balances (refer to Chapter 8 for all test categories).

Analytical procedures for substantive testing are discussed later in this chapter. *Tests of transactions* and *direct tests on balances* directly test or **verify** an account balance.

By contrast, *tests of transactions leading to balances* are performed as part of the auditor's depth testing; that is, on the capture, processing or output of recorded transactions (which may include tests of control as well).

Let's also bring to mind the audit risk model in which the nature, timing and/or extent of substantive procedures (excluding APR) can be guided by the *risk model approach*, from inherent (IR), control (CR) and APR risks.

$$STR = OAR/(IR \times CR \times APR)$$

Prior to step 10 of the audit process, all except STR and APR have been determined; that is, all except the substantive test risks. Suppose the auditor decides that there is a low overall risk, a low inherent risk, a low control risk and a low risk indicated by APs. In that case, the risk acceptable from substantive procedures can be relatively 'high'.

analytical procedures risk (APR)
The risk that audit procedures to estimate an account balance will fail to identify a material misstatement in the account or the assertion being tested.

verification (to verify)
A type of direct test on balances. Examples include inspecting fixed assets for *existence*, inspecting purchase documents for *rights and obligations* over them, re-performing depreciation schedules on them for *accuracy*, or ascertaining what one can purchase them for as to *valuation*.

---

[3] Analytical procedures are sometimes referred to as 'data analytics'. We use 'overall analytical procedures' or 'substantive analytical procedures' in this text.

Auditing in practice

IT audit note

Equally, in an intensely online or virtual audit, where client data is downloaded, and the auditor's systems can test the data extensively, and control testing is expensive, it may be better to use the risk formula to determine the level of control testing that is necessary. In that case:

$$CR = OAR/(IR \times STR \times APR)$$

assuming fundamental controls are tested and that there are separate tests for *completeness*.

Therefore, the need for substantive testing will be dictated by the auditor's risk model assessment. At its conclusion, the auditor will be in a position to make a preliminary decision about whether the financial statements comply with GAAP.

Completion: Steps 11–13

The final audit response procedures ensure that all relevant issues have been considered by junior, management and senior staff. The aim is also to obtain evidence that is not available until other tests are complete. This is also the auditor's opportunity to obtain final evidence prior to coming to that all-important 'audit opinion' (see **Table 9.5**)

Table 9.5 Completion

Audit step	Purpose	Procedures	Working papers
11 Completion and review	Gather final evidence, review the process at all levels of the firm, consider the potential for fraud and other risks, draft opinion	1 Obtain evidence on: • Going concern • Post-balance sheet events • Related party events • Conduct AP (closure) • Review: disclosures, all working papers, legal issues, risks identified in testing	✓ Letter of representation ✓ Final checklists ✓ Review points ✓ Senior approvals ✓ Processes and decisions
12 Report and opinion	Produce the auditor's opinion and the audit report	• Form the audit opinion • Prepare draft audit report for partner review/approval • Prepare management advice for the forthcoming year	✓ Management letter ✓ Audit report and the audit opinion ✓ Process and decisions
13 Client AGM	To provide owners and other stakeholders with an opportunity to consider the auditor's opinion. To consider whether to approve re-appointment		

11   Completion and review

The auditors are responsible for the work of their staff members (again, reminding us of the *Pacific Acceptance* case ruling). Continuous and senior review of working papers to date should always be part of the audit process, to determine that:

- the work has been performed in accordance with professional standards
- that documentation of work performed, results obtained, and conclusions are complete.

High-risk discoveries should be carefully considered because this is an opportunity to collate information from all segments of the audit team and all findings they may have had.

Auditing in practice

Discretion over asset valuation

1   If managers have discretion over asset valuations (recalling *management risk*), they may be tempted to overstate (distort) their value.
2   If one member of the audit team discovers an unusual supplier and another finds cost of sales unusually high, these two findings can be collated at this point to conclude that the *validity* of suppliers is a risk that requires further evidence.

Therefore, a senior auditor should consider whether all significant audit matters have been identified and addressed, that the objectives of the audit have been achieved, and that the conclusions expressed are consistent with the results of the work performed. The audit manager of an engagement will normally perform a contemporaneous review of all working papers and, together with the partner-in-charge, address all major concerns and the following high-risk issues.

Going concern review

Normally, accounts are drawn on the assumption that the organisation is a 'going concern'. The auditor must test this assumption, however. The auditor thus obtains evidence, and remains alert during the audit for evidence that may cast doubt that the going concern assumption is appropriate.

If there is doubt, ASA 570 and ISA NZ 570: Going Concern recommend the auditor obtain further evidence to 'confirm or dispel if a material uncertainty exists'. The auditor should also review management plans based on the going concern assumption, and obtain written representations from management about their plans for future action.

A significant number of indicators should be reviewed to satisfy this requirement. This is covered later in this text (see Chapter 16).

Other information

An annual report will contain the notes and policies of the financial statement, all normally audited. However, there are other elements, such as the director's report and the governing board's report, short biographies and pictures of top management, graphs, tables, and general marketing material. It is noted that, while not required to audit this material, ASA 720 and ISA NZ 720: The Auditor's Responsibilities Relating to Other Information do set out some requirements for the auditor to scan this information, mainly for errors of a factual nature, even though it does not come under the scope of the audit itself. The completion period is a time when doing so is appropriate.

Post-balance date review (subsequent events)

A substantial period can elapse between the accounting year-end and the date the audit partner signs the audit report. Material events occurring after the year-end could substantially affect those accounts, and in extreme cases could render them totally meaningless. For this reason, the auditor must ensure that such events have been incorporated into their audit planning and program.

Cut-off tests – tests on transactions occurring a few days before or a few days after the balance date – may also be performed at this time to ensure the *completeness* and *occurrence-validity* of transactions that occur just before or after the year-end.

Letter of representation

Towards the end of the audit, a letter of representation should be obtained from the directors or governing body regarding their own responsibilities and claims. Such a letter does not relieve the auditor of their liability, but it does remind directors of their responsibilities. Further, it provides an opportunity to obtain written corroboration (evidence) of any representations that management may have made more casually during the audit. This is considered under ASA 580 and ISA NZ 580: Written Representations.

Final checklists

An *audit completion checklist* will be prepared by the auditor-in-charge, addressing a variety of issues. This will cover, for example:
- checking that the client's borrowing is within specified limits
- reviewing for compliance with memorandum, articles and contracts
- the proper completion of all working papers
- drafting reports and plans for next year
- review of the client's governing board's minutes for matters of interest, such as capital commitments, contingent liabilities, legal issues or customer complaints.

A *disclosure checklist* relates to addressing assertions around *presentation* in the financial statements. The auditor must ensure that disclosures are made in accordance with law and regulations. Most firms have pre-printed checklists that are updated for current disclosure requirements. For example, requirements may change for stock exchange disclosures as a condition of listing, so depending on the engagement, the auditor may need to ensure that this exists.

Senior reviews

The audit manager will perform a detailed review of the working papers after fieldwork is complete. In particular, they will ensure all programmed work has been completed, whether the conclusions reached are valid, whether supervision has been adequate, and whether outstanding issues have been addressed.

The audit partner in charge of the engagement will prepare a points-on-accounts schedule, including all outstanding issues or policy points requiring senior partners' judgement.

Before signing the accounts, a senior partner will review all the work that the audit staff has performed, to express an opinion on the accounts. The auditor's accountability in law and through the courts is a particular incentive to be careful in this process. Particular attention is paid to presentation, the appropriateness of the accounting policies used, and any points or concerns remaining. A second partner may be called on to review the situation for higher-risk engagements.

<table>
<tr><td>**CONCEPT QUESTION** 2</td><td>What is meant by 'points on accounts'?</td></tr>
</table>

12   Report and opinion

In Chapter 1, you learned that the auditor is required to express an opinion as to whether the accounts prepared by the client are a fair representation and comply with GAAP. The auditor can express an unmodified (or 'clean') opinion. The opinion will be included in the auditor's report, addressed to the owners/shareholders of the client. If the auditor is *not* satisfied with the adequacy or reliability of the client's accounting system, or if the accounts contain information that may materially mislead users, or fail to provide the information required in law, or the auditor has been unable to obtain all the information and explanations required, then the auditor must consider modifying the report, providing a qualified opinion. Under current standards, a modification will fall under one of the categories shown in **Table 9.6**.

Table 9.6 Audit modification matrix

	Material (but not fundamental)	**Fundamental**
Scope limitation	Qualified (scope)	Disclaimer
Disagreement	Qualified (disagreement)	Adverse

The categories are as follows:
- *Qualified (scope)* – The auditor cannot gather sufficient evidence on a material aspect of the statements, although as a whole they comply with GAAP.
- *Qualified (disagreement)* – The auditor disagrees with a material aspect of the financial statements, although they comply with GAAP as a whole.
- *Disclaimer* – The auditor is unable to form an opinion on the statements because of a fundamental limitation in the scope of the audit. It is, effectively, 'no' opinion.
- *Adverse* – The auditor expresses the opinion that the financial statements as a whole do *not* present a true and fair view. This is the most serious outcome.

13   Reappointment at the annual general meeting of shareholders

Finally, under most legislation, the auditor has the right to attend and speak at an AGM. They may be asked questions about what they found. The owners/shareholders can vote to continue the auditor's appointment for the next period. Continuance is usual unless the auditor withdraws. There are usually significant transaction costs for the client on a change of auditor, as it takes time to help the new auditor 'get up to speed'. However, a change of perspective can add value and reduce risks of complacency and familiarity. Any reason for withdrawal by the auditor, or non-recommendation by management for reappointment, should be explored as it may be due to an issue that should be disclosed to shareholders.

Analytical procedures

In this section we offer information about analytical procedures, defined by ASA 520 and ISA NZ 520 (paras A1–A3) as

> evaluations of financial information through analysis of plausible relationships among both financial and non-financial data.

References to these procedures were made earlier in this text. As a reminder, from Chapter 8 on audit testing: the auditor conducts analytical procedures (AP) to compare expected patterns or trends with actual disclosures in the statements. The purpose is to identify and subsequently investigate unusual variations that could potentially lead to material misstatements.

APs are thus a form of evidence, an overall form of audit 'testing', that can point to possible areas of concern. They do not identify *specific* sources of concern but can provide *indicators*, suggesting that something, somewhere within a system or accounts may be amiss.

Auditing in practice

Unusual payroll expense

A furniture maker's direct payroll expenses are usually 40–42 per cent of the cost of finished goods, and in the current year, that cost exceeds 46 per cent. While the auditor does not know the *source* of this variation, its existence indicates that something unusual has occurred, and the source of this variation thus requires further investigation.

When analytical procedures are used as a substantive test, they are referred to as *substantive analytical procedures*. These are concerned with assertions as to account *balances*.

> The auditor's substantive procedures at the assertion level may be derived from tests of details, from substantive analytical procedures, or from a combination of both. (ASA 520, para A4; ISA NZ 520, para A4)

For example, a 'gross margin' ratio observed over five years might help the auditor identify whether a specific account – cost of sales – appears reasonable in the current year. As per a previous chapter, this relates to audit risk and its relationship to AP. In AP we find a powerful tool with which to identify the general *location* of potential material errors, ones we are warned not to overlook. Contradictory evidence may only be discovered from analytical procedures, such as that unusual level of cost of sales, further emphasising the need for a sceptical approach to management's claims.

Professional scepticism

Professional scepticism is necessary to the critical assessment of audit evidence. This includes questioning contradictory audit evidence. (ASA 200, para A22; ISA NZ 200, para A22)

AP methods effectively highlight 'contradictory evidence' by emphasising inconsistencies in trends, ratios and known relationships that may reveal material misstatements. The availability of IT support systems and large client data gives the auditor a reason to make AP a growing element of their audit.

AP and the audit process

The auditor will normally apply APs in all three major phases of the audit process; that is, during the:

1 *planning* phase, which contributes to the auditor's assessment of risk and to identifying areas of particular concern. Using AP for risk analysis contributes by identifying concerns that will affect audit planning. The risks revealed by AP during the planning phase are the APR element of the audit risk model:

$$STR = OAR/(IR \times CR \times APR)$$

Performing AP is not *required* in standards at this stage; however, it is important. At the risk analysis stage, AP is termed *overall analytical procedures*, discussed in Chapter 10 on audit planning.

2 *performance* process, but specifically for *substantive testing*. This is where APs constitute a form of substantive testing by anticipating what a particular account balance should be. APs (or termed *specific analytical procedures* when used as a substantive test) can be commenced several months prior to the balance date if the data can be trusted. While not *required*, it is a standard recommended tool.

> The decision about which audit procedures to perform, including whether to use substantive analytical procedures, is based on the auditor's judgement about the expected effectiveness and efficiency of the available audit procedures to reduce audit risk at the assertion level to an acceptably low level. (ASA 315; ISA NZ 315)

We believe specific analytical procedures should be applied to all investigations because they are generally a low-cost method of providing considerable insight. Using the audit model logic, confidence in its results can reduce other forms of substantive testing. AP as a substantive test is covered later in this chapter.

3 *completion* phase of the audit, to find indications of material misstatements, or fraud, benefiting from the fact that we now have 'audited' balances. It is mandatory to

> design and perform analytical procedures near the end of the audit that assist the auditor when forming an overall conclusion as to whether the financial statements are consistent with the auditor's understanding of the entity. (ASA 315; ISA NZ 315)

There is also value in AP for the going concern analysis, which is brought together during the completion phase of the audit (ASA 570; ISA NZ 570).

In Australia and New Zealand, ASA 520 and ISA NZ 520: Analytical Procedures, and ASA 330 and ISA NZ 330: The Auditor's Responses to Assessed Risks, guide situations in which AP is applied. While mandated only during the completion stage, it is an important source of evidence, for different reasons, for all three phases of the audit process.

CONCEPT QUESTION 3	Define 'analytical procedure'.

Specific analytical procedures

The use of AP for substantive testing has grown because of digitised client data and the availability of data-extraction and audit software routines able to download and manipulate large volumes of client data.

Audit judgement applied

AP's value lies in providing a signal to the auditors – a flag, if you will – to provide a focus for additional audit effort. While there can be many possible reasons for variations, the financial auditor is mainly concerned with a material misstatement. **Figure 9.2** illustrates the process by which this focus, and logic, is applied to specific APs.

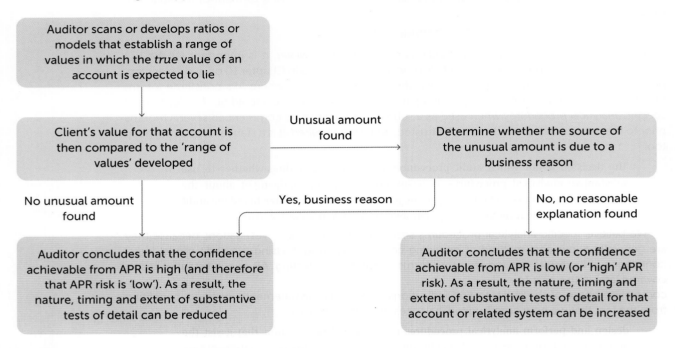

Figure 9.2 Specific AP process

Due to its cost and ease of use, specific analytical procedures should generally be performed before other substantive tests of detail.

Procedures used

Accounts in the Statement of Income are most likely to signal useful information, as we would expect patterns to occur in revenues and costs. Specific APs that can be performed will depend on the accessibility and relevance of the available data. Methods of obtaining evidence for this purpose include scanning, ratio development, graphs and models.

Scanning

The comparison of data by visual scanning (colloquially termed 'eyeballing') makes for a useful start to the analysis, but it is the least effective of all the analytical methods, providing only a low level of confidence. Examples of this technique are year-by-year comparisons of accruals or prepayments, and year-over-year comparisons of monthly sales data.

Ratio development

Ratios can provide a medium to high level of confidence, depending on the rigour of the test and the independence and quality of the data.

> **Auditing in practice**
>
> ### Ratios
>
> Weekly gross pay to hours charged to jobs is calculated. The average ratio over the last four years was, respectively, 22.5/1, 22.8/1 and 22.1/1, with the current period showing a ratio of 24/1. This could signal an increased wage rate, reduced efficiencies on the job, understated internal charge hours or overstated wages. The last possibility concerns the (financial statement) auditor, so the source should be investigated.

As this example reveals, the ratio may indicate a problem, but it would have to be explored further to determine whether or not there is audit significance.

Graphical analysis

Graphical analysis is useful for identifying relationships between datasets when the relationships are not immediately apparent or where large inconsistencies have been identified. In **Figure 9.3**, even a small increase in the sales-to-sales-returns pattern could signal an issue with, for example, understated sales or stock valuation.

The auditors can obtain a low-to-medium level of confidence from graphs and illustrate the issue to the audit team or client.

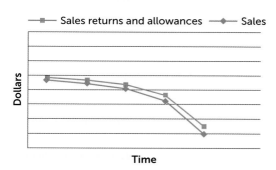

Figure 9.3 Sales-to-sales-returns pattern

Model construction

Model construction and analysis involve calculating the results anticipated by the auditors using alternative means to those used by the client. Depending on the quality of the variables, models can yield a medium-to-high level of confidence in indicating areas of potential risk.

Using data from outside the system or non-financial data (see **Table 9.7**) can add independence to the model. So, for example, sales revenue can be calculated from customer numbers, and hotel room revenue can be predicted from occupancy rates and average charges. Reasonably complex audit software routines can be applied, such as the following:

- *Neural networks*, recently applied to audit, incorporate relationship nodes and networks to model non-linear relationships among data. They can be a type of AI that can help the auditor anticipate events or account balances (e.g., see Koskivaara, 2004)
- *Regression analysis* can be used to identify variations in account balances. Regression uses multiple independent variables – nominal, financial or non-financial (such as in the examples in **Table 9.7**) – to estimate the dependent (account) variable. So, for example, sales can be a function of:

Sales = f (labour costs ($), average temperature, exchange rate, supply expense average)

Table 9.7 Industry data for analytical review

Industry	Balance tested	Some factors affecting size of balance
Bank	Interest received Interest paid	Average balance/days/rate
Car hire	Income Vehicle cost	Vehicles Mileage Vehicle cost
Hire-purchase	Deposit interest	Deposit balance Number of days Base rate
Hotel	Room income Meal income	Guest/night Occupancy ratio Number of guests Average price of a meal Capacity of restaurant
Insurance	Provision for claims outstanding	Premiums received Claims made in past
Investment institution	Yield Management expenses	Market average Other investment companies
Laundry or laundrette	Sales	Water used Utility costs
Leasing	Rental income	Number of units leased Rental charged
Lending institutions	Interest received	Loans outstanding Ruling interest rates
eBusiness	Sales Stock on approval	Dispatches Returns
Mining	Revenue expenditure	Tonnes produced
Professional service	Fees	Number of employees Changing rates
Property companies	Rent revenue Expenses	Value of portfolio Current yields Rent received
Public utility	Sales-credit	Units used to price Number of consumers Temperature
Retailer	Sales Gross profit margin	Number of employees Floor area Shelf footage Gross profit margin of other retailers

Shipping	Passage sales	Number of berths, days of cruise, fares
	Fuel costs	Tonnes fuel/price
	Wages	Complement pay rates
Stockbrokers	Commission	Total value of bargains
		Number of bargains
Transport	Revenue	Passenger/kilometres
		Tonnes/kilometres
		Fuel used
Rental business	Rental income	Number of items rented
		Rental charge

Source: Derived from Westwick (1981).

The advantages of regression analysis are its flexibility and the support of (scientific) statistical inference. Both the confidence in, and range of, true balances are formed, as can be the strengths of correlations among variables. Also, planning decisions about acceptable levels of confidence (such as 95 per cent) can be incorporated into the model. All of this adds to the rigour and independent support for the auditor's decisions about variations found in the client data.

As with any model, the reliability of the result also lies in the selection and measurement of the elements chosen. These are matters of auditor judgement. The benefits of AP as the substantive test are significant. At a minimum, we believe the auditor should:

1 compare financial information with
   a information from prior periods
   b anticipated results (e.g., budgets and forecasts)
   c other profit centres within the organisation
   d industry data.
2 examine relationships between
   a accounts expected to conform to a predictable pattern (gross margins, day's sales in debtors)
   b non-financial as well as financial information (wages to hours worked, salaries to employee numbers).
3 scan adjusting journal entries and accounts for unusual transactions that may be associated with *fraud* or *distortion*. Events that are intentionally 'left out of' or distorted by management can be particularly hard to catch. This is where substantive AP is particularly useful, as you are using various data from different sources to identify what it may want to hide. Should suspicions of fraud or distortion be raised, you must, as you will recall from case law, gather such evidence as can resolve the source of the problem.
4 scan documents on major debtors, creditors, items of stock and fixed assets: missing or major new items should be investigated. Significant elements of temporary control accounts should be compared from year to year. The latter is particularly useful when the system of internal control has not been tested.

Obtaining evidence on the completion assertion is often a challenge, and APs can be particularly insightful in this respect. However, the AP test is not complete once performed, as further investigation into any significant variation would be required.

Variations

APs are always a comparative procedure: the auditor compares what the client has in the accounts to what the auditor expects to see. APs are therefore a tool that enhances the opportunity for applying professional scepticism.

> **Professional scepticism**
>
> 'Professional scepticism includes being alert to, for example:
> - audit evidence that contradicts other audit evidence obtained
> - information that brings into question the reliability of documents and responses to inquiries to be used as audit evidence
> - conditions that may indicate possible fraud
> - circumstances that suggest the need for audit procedures in addition to those required by standards.
>
> Sources: ASA 200 (para A21); ISA NZ 200 (para A21).

Once the AP is complete, the auditor should go on to consider what could have caused any variations. Variations can be sourced from so-called 'innocent' sources such as:
- changes in macroeconomic conditions
- general inflation
- changes in the prices of specific goods and services used by the organisation
- seasonal factors affecting the organisation or the industry
- industrial disputes within the organisation or involving its major suppliers or customers
- changes in the general level of business activity in the economy as a whole
- technological advances rendering products or services obsolete
- planned expansion or contraction of the operations of the organisation
- government action affecting labour, taxes, energy usage or regulation.

> **Auditing in practice**
>
> ### High cost of sales
>
> Unexpectedly high cost of sales could be because supply chain expenses increased due to a global pandemic or because a low-cost supplier business closed (valid business reasons). Or it could have occurred because a manager's personal mortgage payments were included in cost of sales (of audit concern, as it is a misstatement and a possible management distortion).

That is, substantive analytical procedures can reveal variations for valid business reasons or they can lead to the discovery of an audit concern.

Confidence from analytical procedures

Factors influencing the confidence available from SpAR are drawn from ideas about the reliability of evidence generally, and it is suggested that the auditor should consider all of the following:
- The *source of the data*, such as whether it was independently developed or internally derived (or whether it is from external sources), and whether the source has been audited or is carefully controlled
- The *sensitivity of the techniques* used. Sometimes a slight variation in an expected ratio can be cause for concern. Scanning will normally provide a low level of sensitivity, whereas ratios, regression and other models can potentially provide a medium or high measure, depending on how precisely they measure underlying events.
- The *reliability of the relationship*, or the degree to which the relationships between the dependent and independent variables tend to be consistent. The client's relationship between sales and direct wages can, in some businesses, be very reliable.

Predicting sales

Predicting sales from an unaudited system is less *reliable*, and provides less confidence, than if it were from an audited and separate (*independent*) system. On the other hand, *sensitivity* occurs if there is a close and consistent relationship between sales and cost.

The quality of assurance available from specific AP is only as good as the lowest assurance available from any of the above factors (see **Table 9.8**).

Table 9.8 Confidence available from specific APs

Factors influencing confidence	Level of assurance		
	High	Medium	Low
Source of data	*Internal audited External data Independent data*	*External data Independent data*	*Internal unaudited data*
Sensitivity of evidence	*Ratio analysis Regression Model construction*	*Ratio analysis Graphical analysis*	*Scanning (low, except in small populations)*
Evidence of variable relationship strength	*Statistical Tests of detail*	*Historical analogy*	*Limited to subjective scanning-type analysis*

Risks of using APs

While AP can be a relatively straightforward technical procedure, interpreting the results can be more difficult. Suppose the auditor uses management's unaudited balances for AP. In that case, the results could be misleading as they may be anchored by erroneous opening balances.

Also, auditors should not necessarily attribute results to only one cause when several causes may be the source of variation. Schedules of trends, ratios and comparisons should be included in the auditor's working papers, along with follow-up investigations and reasons for the decisions reached.

CONCEPT QUESTION 4	What is the meaning of an 'unexpected variation' in specific analytical procedure results?

Study tools

Summary

This chapter looked at how audit approaches developed over time, and explained why the risk approach is the accepted method. We then outlined the audit process and procedures in a step-by-step manner. This concludes our introduction to the audit phases; you may wish to refer back to this as we delve into its component parts.

We also introduced analytical procedures, where they are applied (all phases!), and why. The focus then turned to APs performed during the *performance* phase and, in particular, as a type of substantive test. The chapter concluded with methods, processes, means of analysis, and sources of confidence from specific AP. Analytical procedures – overall or substantive – tend to be an 'indicator' of a potential problem that requires further investigation. The implications for professional scepticism were highlighted.

✎ Case/resources link

CAATs for Classrooms

Accompanying this book is a series of data, integrated worksheets and exercises that are designed to support your learning and give you exposure to hands-on audit decision-making dilemmas faced by auditors in the planning elements of the audit process. Acquire the relevant material for this chapter from your instructor.

Review questions

9.1　Distinguish between possible approaches to audit work.

9.2　Why does the risk approach serve today's audit?

9.3　Name and describe the steps in the initial planning process, and detailed planning processes.

9.4　What role do a company's shareholders play in these processes?

9.5　How is an understanding of the client acquired? Describe the type of information such methods may provide.

9.6　Describe an 'audit detailed plan' and its purpose.

9.7　Describe how the audit risk model serves decisions about substantive testing.

9.8　Define 'verification' as used for audit.

9.9　Name and describe activities in the completion process. Describe what each of these activities is intended to accomplish.

9.10　What is a 'letter of representation'? Describe its purpose for audit.

9.11　When is the audit report prepared, and what is its purpose?

9.12　Name the two types of 'modified' audit report that would be issued should a fundamental problem exist.

9.13　What is the difference between the two types of 'qualified' report?

9.14 Define substantive APs and explain their purpose. How are they distinct from the broader category of APs?

9.15 Where else in the audit process are APs used? Why?

9.16 List methods of performing substantive APs and sources of data for each.

9.17 What are 'neural networks', and how can they be used for specific APs?

9.18 How can 'regression' be used to model sales?

9.19 How can APs provide information not available elsewhere?

9.20 List basic recommended substantive APs for most audits (and reviews).

9.21 Confidence from APs can be determined from the data's source, sensitivity and reliability. Define each of those terms and provide examples.

9.22 What three characteristics would lead to the lowest level of assurance from a specific AP?

9.23 Describe how Australian/New Zealand auditing standards address the issue of APs for substantive testing and what they expect from the auditor.

Exercises

9.1 **AUDIT ACCEPTANCE:** You recently established an accounting practice with another chartered accountant whom you first met when you were both at university. Your partnership has been approached to take over the audit of a medium-sized manufacturing company. To decide whether you are capable of tackling a task of this nature, you resolve to list the steps necessary to undertake an audit.

Required: Identify and list in a logical, chronological order, the main steps involved in the audit process:

a   before the audit can be accepted

b   after the audit has been accepted.

For each audit objective give techniques commonly used to satisfy the objective.

9.2 **AUDIT STEPS:** A number of events have occurred during the recent audit of Shifty Ltd (a retailer). Your task is to put the following eight scenarios in the order in which they would have occurred, explain what each is trying to accomplish, and why.

a   The audit manager prepares a schedule detailing the timing and extent of audit visits.

b   The audit fee is confirmed.

c   A flowchart is drawn up detailing the sales and purchasing system.

d   The audit manager reviews industry journals and newspaper articles.

e   The audit junior tests 50 purchase orders for an authorising signature.

f   A report is sent to Shifty's management detailing internal control weaknesses.

g   The audit junior prepares a regression analysis on sales using variables such as floor space and shelf footage.

h   A letter of representation is requested from the directors of Shifty Ltd.

Consider each situation independently.

9.3 **AUDIT PROCESS COMMUNICATIONS:** Describe what potential effect each of the following events, considered independently, may have on the audit and discuss what conversations you would have, and with whom, when these events occur:

a   During the test-of-control process, it is discovered that controls assessed as 'very good' turn out not to exist.

b   During the appointment process, it is found that the partner-in-charge's spouse sits on the board of directors of the potential client.

c   Up until three months ago, you had an expert on your audit staff on the topic of property valuations. The upcoming bid process is on a larger FMC reporting entity that is a property developer.

d   Your client pulled out last year's audit report (unqualified) and gave it to you during discussions with them early in the audit engagement.

9.4 **AUDIT APPROACHES:** One of your senior audit partners insists on using the 'systems approach' to audit engagements. As he says, 'This is what we used in the 80s, and it's as good for complicated systems of today as it was then.' How might you tactfully respond to this claim?

9.5 **AUDIT PROCESS:** You are a new member of a small audit firm that has been run by its three senior partners for 30 years. The partners are looking forward to you sharing your knowledge of current practice and have asked you the following questions:

1   The firm has an ongoing audit client it has audited for the last six years without any problems encountered. It plans to take the client on again and, as it knows the client pretty well, it will use the same audit program as the year before. This online B2B (business-to-business) toy store client has not changed its business but has opened a new shop in Christchurch.

2   The same client has asked you to perform your tests before the year-end because they will have fewer staff available after the year-end.

Required: Answer the following questions for each situation and in combination:

a   Do you see any issues or problems with the situations described? What? Why are they an issue?

b   How would you address the issue(s) raised?

c   What is a solution you might seek for each issue?

9.6 **AUDIT PROCESS:** Describe at what point in the audit you would conduct each of the audit procedures shown in **Table 9.9** for an auto rental company and explain why.

Table 9.9 Conducting audit procedures

Objective	Audit procedure		
	Nature	**Timing**	**Extent**
To confirm that purchases over $100 are *authorised* by purchasing officer (compliance)	Inspect carbon copies of purchase orders over $100 for the signature of purchasing officer	Cover purchase orders for the whole year	Representative sample to provide a medium level of assurance
To confirm the *existence* of motor vehicles as represented by ledger account 'motor vehicles' (substantive)	1 *Reconcile asset register (or schedules) for vehicles to ledger account* 2 Inspect *vehicles recorded in the asset register*	At or close to the balance date	(Depending on fleet size) Representative sample to provide a high level of assurance
To confirm the *completeness, accuracy, existence, valuation* and *beneficial ownership* of the bank balances at balance date (substantive)	1 *Obtain independent* confirmation *from bank of account balances* 2 *Confirm to closing balance on bank statements* 3 *Review (or re-perform) reconciliation*	At balance date, when at least two weeks' post-balance date statements are available	For all bank accounts held by the client

9.7 **SPECIFIC AP:** Assume that you have been presented with the statements of profit and loss and the balance sheets for the past four years of a public company engaged in retailing. Your client has requested that you provide him with the relevant ratios and comparisons you used in SpAR procedures' performance. He hopes they can assist him in determining the company's progress (if any) over these four years.

Required: Explain to the client the purpose of your specific analytical review procedures and why it may not be relevant to use them to achieve his goals.

9.8 **VARIATIONS:** If an auditor discovers that there has been a significant change in a ratio when compared with the prior year(s), they should consider the possible causes. Give possible reasons for the following and determine which the auditor should investigate further.

a The ratio of cost of sales to average inventory has decreased from prior years.

b The number of days' sales in receivables (ratio of average daily accounts receivable to sales) has increased.

9.9 **RATIO ANALYSIS:** In connection with your analytic review of 2021 operations, you are presented with a summary of certain data prepared by an employee in your client's accounting department, as shown in **Table 9.10**.

Table 9.10 Analytical review of operations

Description	2022	2021	2020
Net profit on net sales	3.63%	6.4%	3.6%
Net profit on tangible net worth	7.62	7.70	5.20
Net profit on net working capital	17.64	23.00	21.30
Net sales to tangible net worth	2.10	1.03	0.95
Net sales to inventory (times)	8.8	7.84	6.93
Collection period (in days)	53	50	52
Current assets to current debt	2.46	2.39	2.60
Current debt to inventory (%)	120.8	120	151
Inventory to net working capital (%)	52.9	54.0	41.0

    a On the basis of this information, which ratios should the auditor investigate further?

    b Describe a potential cause for each trend that could indicate:

      i an audit problem

      ii a non-audit (business) situation.

9.10 **RATIO ANALYSIS:** Review Exercise 8.8, which has an extensive set of working papers before and after audit-recommended adjustments.

    Required: Carry out a substantive ratio analysis on both working trial balances and:

    a identify any issues of concern in both sets of WTBs

    b determine whether the AJEs will modify the concerns that were raised in the pre-adjusted WTB.

9.11 **SUBSTANTIVE AP:** Using the financials presented in **Table 9.11**, create a model to predict the expected:

    a costs of sales

    b sales returns and allowances

    c interest expense.

Table 9.11 Predicting financial outcome

Account	Adjusted balance	Account	Adjusted balance
Cash	2 300	Share capital	−200 000
Accounts receivable	100 000	Retained earnings	−130 000
Provision for bad debts	−1 000	Sales	−170 000
Inventory	200 000	Sales returns and allowances	13 000
Notes receivable	20 000	Cost of sales	101 000
Fixed assets	350 000	Wages	60 000
Accum. depreciation	−175 000	Income tax expense	15 000
Notes payable	−12 000	Bad debt expense	17 500
Accounts payable	−29 000	Interest expense	1 200
Payroll taxes payable	−19 000	Rent expense	18 000
Long-term debts payable	−180 000	Net profit	−73 700

Required: Design three different models for use as substantive APs. Specify what account(s) you are trying to predict. Explain the reason for your choice and identify the method you would use on the models. Identify four sources of possible variance that could result.

Audit planning

Learning objectives

After studying the material in this chapter, you should be able to:

- describe, evaluate and perform selective procedures used in the initial planning process, with an emphasis on
  - scope-defining issues
  - engagement letter
  - audit-related risk decisions
  - analytical procedures
- describe, evaluate, apply and document procedures used in the preparation of an audit plan within the detailed planning process.

Introduction

Planning is the first step in the audit process. Proper planning clarifies the scope and direction of the audit before testing begins. It is where initial decisions about risk and materiality are made and where the auditor determines how their audit plan will respond. As elsewhere, an attitude of professional scepticism accompanies the planning process. **Figure 10.1** was introduced in the previous chapter. In this chapter, we look at the audit planning stage in greater detail.

Initial planning	Detailed planning	Audit test response	Completion
• Preliminary engagement activities • Review client's business • Perform risk analysis • Form audit strategy	• Study accounting system • Evaluate internal controls • Develop detailed plan	• Tests of controls • Further develop plan • Substantive tests	• Completion and review • Management letter (introduced later) • Audit report and opinion • Client's AGM

Figure 10.1 Steps in an audit process

While we will discuss audit steps and stages in a step-by-step order, the audit process is far less straightforward in practice. It is essentially a circular process (see **Figure 10.2**). New or unexpected information may turn up at any stage, information which may require a reassessment of risk and of what type or volume of evidence is required.

Initial planning process

Important decisions are made in the planning of an audit. While the *audit manager* is typically responsible for planning and preparing working papers, the *audit partner* also takes an active role, as problems that occur here affect the rest of the audit (see ASA 330 and ISA NZ 330). The procedures discussed in the following sections explain how the planning is accomplished.

Initial planning: Preliminary activities

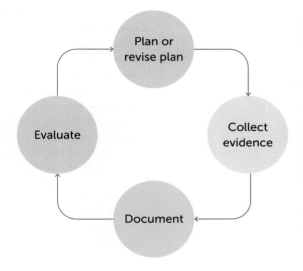

Figure 10.2 Audit's circular process

Preliminary engagement activities are those conducted *prior to* when the auditor contracts with the client. Steps are taken to determine whether it is appropriate to go forward with the audit, and how. Procedures include the following:

- *Assess ethical issues.* Consider the firm's independence, including personal and financial *relationships* between audit staff and the potential client. The impact of the audit fees should not lead to *fee dependence*, and auditor *rotation* should be considered. While it is tempting to acquire a new client, the firm should resist underbidding (*lowballing*) or having an *interest* in the client (see ASA 102 and ISA NZ 102).
- *Consider continuance issues.* For an ongoing client, this includes communicating whether there are new plans or changes to the scope of the engagement. If an initial audit, it is a time to obtain assurance from the previous auditor that there is no professional reason for declining the engagement. It is possible to get the information from the preceding auditor without breaking confidentiality boundaries for this purpose. This includes assessing that the firm's resources are sufficient and appropriate for the engagement (see ASA 220 and ISA NZ 220).
- *Clarify the scope of the engagement*, whether continuing or not. This includes discussing other matters to be included in the **engagement letter**, such as communicating the responsibility of management, agreement on the assistance that the client will provide, and the basis of the audit fee. Note that assistance from the client does not absolve the auditor of their responsibilities.
- *Agree as to the terms of the engagement.* This includes preparing an engagement letter and acquiring the appropriate signatures from the client's governing board and the audit firm partners/owners. In a statutory financial statement audit, and because law determines much of its criteria, the engagement letter may only be reviewed every three years or so (see ASA 210 and ISA NZ 210). Under most corporate

engagement letter
Contractual agreement between the auditor and the client to perform a professional service such as an audit, review or compilation.

articles of association, directors (the governing body) have the power to fill a vacancy in the position of auditor, usually ratified at the AGM (see ASA 320 and 330, and ISA NZ 320 and 330).

Identifying and documenting the engagement *scope* is now considered in further detail.

Scope of the financial audit

The audit scope – what is or is *not* being investigated – has direct consequences for how the audit proceeds. Evidence about issues outside the scope of the engagement is unlikely to be collected as it would be an unnecessary expense. Failing to collect evidence that is within the scope implies a negligent audit.

Clarifying the scope of the financial statement audit informs the strategy and plans to follow, and is influenced by the:

1 *jurisdiction* in which the organisation is registered. A large entity may be located in multiple jurisdictions, and determining the legal status and reporting requirements may require the advice of local experts.

2 *size and structure* of the organisation of the entity, increasing the engagement's complexity. The auditor will inquire as to:
   — whether there are subsidiaries, divisions, branches or stores
   — whether any 'group' of entities is associated with the organisation: holding companies, trusts, strategic partnerships or associated companies
   — which auditors will lead the group audit, and whether distant sites are reasonable to staff (see ASA 600 and ISA NZ 600 for more detail).

   The auditor may need to be aware of exchange rules, statutory law, common law and tax law from jurisdictions other than their own.

3 *auditable records*, which must be produced independently before the audit can begin. One of the authors recalls a small client whose employees claimed to have maintained a general ledger. An initial inspection indicated that this was true. An audit fee was agreed upon, and a contract was signed. During planning, it was found that the 'ledger' was a random list of cash transactions, not a real general ledger. It had to be externally reconstructed (by that point, at the auditors' expense).

4 *special expertise* that needs to be available for unique audit requirements, usually at a cost to the auditor. For example, the auditor of an insurance company client may require the expertise of a registered valuer, an actuary, a specialised solicitor or an environmental scientist.

Matters 1 to 4 should be investigated for all new clients and on a periodic basis for existing clients, as practices may change over time. Concerns of 'independence' may emerge, and ethical principles should be considered.

Auditing in practice

CSL Ltd

CSL Ltd, an Australia-based global biotechnology company, manufactures in three countries, operates in 35+ countries, and markets to over 100 countries. It thus requires the skills and knowledge of other jurisdictions for parent and subsidiary audits, and it requires qualified staff to be available at those locations for testing work.

Statutory financial auditors in Australia and New Zealand primarily look to law and standards to define aspects of the scope, such as what claims should be examined (those around the financial statements, policies and notes) and for what period (usually the 'year ending ...'). Other professional services may not be so clearly defined.

Scope of other assurance services

Audits may be requested pursuant to the sale of a business, the issuance of royalties, increased cost claims, union claims, or the sale of a partnership. Other reasons may include fraud audit investigations or performance reviews. Sole proprietors, partnerships, trusts, estates, clubs, and social, religious and welfare organisations, may need an assurance service on occasion should their lenders, or fund providers, require it.

The same quality of audit 'assurance' is required in these situations as in the statutory audit of financial statements (see AUASB, 2020a). However, the scope and the users for special-purpose audits can vary.

Scope of non-assurance services

A client could contract with an audit firm for other professional services, such as the compilation (preparation) of financial statements. Compiling statements, preparing tax reports, providing tax or budget advice, or offering system expertise offer no assurance from the professional because the *activity*, not the auditor's *independence*, is being provided. This does not excuse them from doing their job professionally; it simply means that you cannot provide assurance on your own work.

Documenting the scope may be even more important in non-assurance engagements. The scope is less defined in law and more subject to management's requirements. The auditors should identify what is required and arrange with the client what support will be provided by the client's staff (more guidance is provided later in this text; also see AUASB, 2020a).

Engagement letter

The engagement letter documents the scope of the engagement by setting out the goals, terms and conditions under which the audit firm is contracted. The engagement letter protects the auditor, the client and stakeholders by ensuring shared communication about the audit's scope and fees. It should normally include:

- details of the business and functions to be audited
- the period of time covered by the engagement
- independence and other ethical considerations
- the accounting policies, standards, regulations or laws to be applied
- special audit procedures to be used or omitted
- the audit timetable and reporting deadlines
- to whom the report is to be addressed.
    Usually, the contracted fees are included (or at least how they are calculated).

> **Auditing in practice**
>
> **Working paper notes**
>
> A copy of the engagement letter should be held in the permanent audit file.

With respect to the statutory financial audit, many of the 'terms' are set out under standards of due care (common law), statute and professional standards. See ASA and ISA NZ 210: Agreeing the Terms of Audit Engagements for examples. Standards require clarification of scope with the governing body of the client (see ISA 210; ISA NZ 210, paras 2, 10). Concerning non-statutory engagements, the letter of engagement becomes the primary document that sets out those conditions.

A copy of the engagement letter should be sent to the client:

- when the client is initially accepted, to ensure a clear understanding
- at regular periods, to remind all parties of this scope and of their responsibilities
- following significant changes in the client's management, ownership or any other factor that could influence the scope of the engagement
- when it appears that management misunderstood the purpose of the audit.

An example of a portion of an engagement letter is featured in **Figure 10.3**, although note that they will vary by company and situation.

Initial planning: Review the business

Becoming familiar with the client's business helps in planning the resources auditors need, and when and where they are required, and contributes to understanding the risks associated with the client's business and industry (part of IR). The auditor will observe or inspect:

- *practices unique to the industry* and the specific skills or techniques needed (an example is the skill of assessing the depletable assets of an oil exploration client)
- *circumstances that increase the likelihood of errors* being present, or which may add to the difficulties of audit verification (examples include poor managerial supervision and high staff turnover)
- *particular events, transactions or accounting practices* that have a significant impact on financial situations (such as the acquisition, or disposal, of a subsidiary)
- *the background* against which the evidence gathered can be evaluated to see if it 'makes sense' and 'looks right'. Clear trends in business activity should be reflected in the financial results (e.g., the entry of a major competitor may reduce profit margins).

This understanding of the client is acquired through:

- reviewing industry journals and newspaper articles
- visiting the client's site, touring the premises and meeting key personnel
- discussing with key personnel trading issues, financial challenges and changes
- reviewing legal documents such as articles of association, partnership agreements, major contracts, policy manuals and commercial agreements (such as franchises or employment agreements).

Auditing in practice

Working paper notes

'Integrity' and 'control' checklists should form part of the auditor's working papers, but they should not be made available to the client or the client's employees, as dishonest employees could adjust their behaviour to fit the questions asked and avoid being noticed.

Initial planning: Perform risk analysis

This is the point at which the risk analysis is performed, and initial risk model decisions are made. The risk decisions made at this point guide the procedures and decisions to follow. To recall the risk model's elements:

$$STR = OAR/(IR \times CR \times APR) \text{ or } STR = f(OAR, IR, CR, APR)$$

So, at this point, the auditor will:

- determine the overall audit risk (OAR)
- analyse risks associated with the client's context (inherent risk, or IR), including that to do with:
  — integrity of, and pressure on, management
  — the business and industry in which the client operates

To the (governing body),

You have requested that we accept appointments as auditors of (entity). This will include the audit of the general purpose financial statements (GPFS) for the (period) ended… We are pleased to confirm our acceptance and our understanding of this engagement by means of this letter. Our audit will be made in accordance with (detail appropriate legislation) to express an opinion on the financial report.

We will conduct our audit in accordance with the auditing standards issued by the Chartered Accountants Australia New Zealand (CA ANZ) that require us to plan and perform our audit to obtain all the information and explanations which we consider necessary to provide us with sufficient evidence to give reasonable assurance that the financial report is free from material misstatements, whether caused by fraud or error. We will also evaluate the overall adequacy of the presentation of information in the financial report.

An audit includes examining, on a test basis, evidence relevant to the amounts and disclosures in the financial report. An audit also includes assessing the significant estimates and judgements made by the (governing body) in preparing the financial report, and whether the accounting policies are appropriate to (entity's) circumstances, consistently applied and adequately disclosed.

Because of the nature of tests and other inherent limitations of an audit, together with the inherent limitations of any accounting and internal control system, there is an unavoidable risk that even some material misstatements may remain undiscovered.

We remind you that the responsibility for preparing the financial report, including adequate disclosure, is that of the (governing body) of (entity). This includes the maintenance of adequate accounting records and internal controls, the selection and application of accounting policies, and safeguarding the company's assets.

As part of our audit process, we will request from the (governing body) written confirmation concerning representations made to us in connection with the audit. In particular, we will seek confirmation from the (governing body) that adopting the going concern assumption is appropriate.

We look forward to the full cooperation of your staff, and we trust that they will make available to us whatever records, documentation and other information are requested in connection with our audit. Our fees, which will be billed as work proceeds, are based on the time required by the individuals assigned to the engagement plus out-of-pocket expenses. Individual hourly rates vary according to the degree of responsibility involved and the experience and skills required.

This letter will be effective for future years unless it is terminated, amended or superseded by either the auditor or the (governing body).

Please sign and return the attached copy of this letter to indicate that it is in accordance with your understanding of the arrangements for our audit of the financial report.

Yours faithfully
(signed)

Name of auditor and title

Date

Acknowledged on behalf of (the entity) by
(signed)

Name and title

Date

Figure 10.3 Letter of engagement example

Source: Adapted from NZICA (2017, AS-202). ISA NZ recommended formats are similar.

- conduct a preliminary review of internal control (CR) with a view to:
  — identifying whether **fundamental controls** exist to determine auditability
  — deciding whether the client's control system can be relied on.
- conduct overall analytical procedures (APR) to identify any patterns of concern.

It is also the stage at which materiality criteria are determined based on that which would be important, or 'material', to users and stakeholders. Risk assessment procedures are guided by ASA 315 and ISA NZ 315. Let us examine the procedures in terms of audit risks.

....
fundamental controls
The key controls necessary to ensure that accounting records are in an auditable state. Adequate segregation of duties, reasonably effective routine supervision and access controls (in IT systems) are usually among these controls.

Assess overall audit risk (OAR)

The auditor evaluates, at this point, the interests of the client's stakeholders, including shareholders, lenders, regulators or others, who are likely to rely on the financial statements.

There is a narrow range to consider for OAR. Overall, 'confidence' should not be lower than 95 per cent, and no audit can be a perfect 100 per cent. So, if the engagement is not particularly sensitive (of great concern to stakeholders), then the tolerable OAR can be relatively high (say 5 per cent) and the confidence required can be relatively low (95 per cent).

Auditing in practice

Examples: Sensitive engagements where OAR should be low (1–2 per cent)

1   The public has a strong interest in national airlines because they have a near-monopoly position (and can thus raise prices outside a competitive market), and because there are so many businesses and families that depend on such airlines operating safely and consistently. People in Australia and New Zealand have a particular sensitivity to this, as we are all aware of the 'tyranny of distance' under which businesses operate.
2   A client – a fruit export partnership – is taking on a new silent partner who will contribute significant funds to the client once the financial statements are considered. The new partner will not be part of management.
3   A client – a private corporation – is returning to their lending bank to obtain financing to expand their business; thus, there is a 'special relationship' between auditor and bank.

It is important to keep in mind that if the OAR is low, then the nature, timing and extent of the audit evidence required increases. That is, a low OAR leads to the need for more and/or more reliable testing and a higher-cost audit.

Auditing in practice

CAATs

The risk model exercises in the classroom CAATs program accompanying this text can be used to illustrate this relationship.

Assess inherent risk (IR)

IR is a function of the risks associated with management integrity – inherent or situational – and the business and industry.

Management integrity

Inquiry and background search are often used to obtain explanations about complex or critical issues. They are also used to obtain an understanding of management, their character and their incentives. Management that lacks integrity – as individuals or as a function of their organisational culture – may attempt to mislead the auditors.

Inherent integrity

The auditors should continually evaluate the quality of management's responses to requests for information and explanations. Should any response appear to be deliberately misleading, the matter should be referred to the partner in charge. Examples of inherent integrity concerns are shown in **Table 10.1**.

Table 10.1 Inherent integrity examples

Indicator of integrity risk	Potential misstatement	Implication
Management has not provided reliable responses to requests for information	Potential distortion where subjective evaluations made as part of the financial statements	Cannot rely on inquiries of management as audit evidence – check for manipulation in areas of subjective evaluation
Indications of past manipulation committed by management		
Evidence of tax evasion or cut-off distortion practices in client		
Evidence of management theft	Misstatement of assets	
Evidence of manager's misuse of business assets for personal use	Misstatement of assets	
Manager does not delegate or interfere in delegated responsibilities	Management override of internal controls	Cannot rely on client's internal control
Manager takes an unusually active interest in the system of internal control		
High turnover of accounting staff	Breakdown of controls	

The auditors should also be aware of the potential for tax evasion, asset theft or personal misuse of business assets, particularly where there is more than one owner-manager or where management is separated from the owners.

Situational integrity

Sometimes, a manager who has previously demonstrated integrity may be pressured into misleading the auditors. **Table 10.2** describes some warning signs.

Table 10.2 Situational management risk examples

Indicator of situational risk	Potential misstatement	Implication
Management appears to live beyond their means	Understated income	Increase nature, timing and extent of substantive tests in affected areas to have high reliability of evidence
Incentive schemes account for a significant portion of managers' remuneration	Overstated income	
Management's salary package appears non-competitive	Management integrity issue	
Budget variances require unusually detailed explanation	Management distortion	
Business requires additional finance in order to continue	Overstated assets, understated (hidden?) liabilities	
Business likely to be sold	Overstated assets, understated liabilities	

Evaluating business and industry

The auditor should evaluate the client's business and industry, and therefore, obtains an understanding of the client's business, industry and economy as a whole. The auditor should have knowledge of, at least, the client's:

- *governance structure* – director independence and experience, audit committees
- *corporate advisers* – including the client's lawyers, lenders and accounting firm
- *structure* – including operating divisions and management organisational structure
- *cycles* (or *subsystems*) of each major type of transaction
- *accounting policies* used by the organisation
- *sales practices* – major and potential markets, customer characteristics, distribution
- *production characteristics* – product range, supply chains, raw materials or components, methods of production, warehousing
- *finance practices* – banking relationships, plans, share or bond performance
- *strategy*, to understand the client's long-term intent, risk and planning
- *information technology* and implications for reliable onsite or offsite client data
- *internal audit* by the client, it's quality and independence
- *external services* and implications for acquiring and auditing external data of client.
  Each industry has its peculiarities and risk factors. The auditor should evaluate:
- *the products or services* environment, such as patterns in supply, demand and delivery
- *sales agreements* and influences of policy, exchange rates, consumer patterns
- *the production environment* – stresses in supply chains, union activity, production
- *the legal environment* – new laws that may impact sales, valuations, rights/ownership
- *the industry environment* – how the industry reacts to economic trends and regulation.
  Information about the industry can be obtained from a variety of sources, including:
- the client, through inquiry of knowledgeable members
- financial news media, such as the *Australian Financial Review* and the *Financial Times* in Australia, or the *National Business Review* in New Zealand
- industry publications that may be available to the public
- economic surveys by banking institutions
- accounting bodies; for example, industry guides of the ICAEW
- legal accounting and reporting requirements.
  Examples of such risks and potential audit implications are illustrated in **Table 10.3**.

Table 10.3 Business and industry risk examples

	Potential misstatement	Implication
Indicators of business risk		
Raw materials or supply chain cost increases	Understated cost of sales	Test classification, cost components, LIFO etc.
Client dependent on: trade receivables or trade payables	Overstated receivables, understated payables	Test valuation, debt allowances*
Patents, trademarks or franchises lose value or conclude	Intangibles overstated, depletion understated	Inspect 'rights' documents, valuation*
Indicators of industry risk		
Client's services or products are obsolete	Overstated inventories or receivables	Tests on valuation must remain at a high level*
Sales delayed due to pandemic	Sales recorded early	Check cut-off at year-end for sales overstatement*
Competitors in financial trouble	Stock or asset overvalued	Assess where subjective valuation is present*
Law, tax, regulation or price controls affect the industry	Unrecorded contingent and other liabilities	Re-perform tax liability and classifications, valuation
Changes in employment law, price controls or exchange rates	Unrecorded contingent liabilities, misstated sales	Review policy against valuation and presentation

* Going concern could also be an issue as a result of this event.

Each industry responds differently to economic events and may be subject to restrictive laws. Auditors should identify how the industry reacts to these events and what effect regulations or major market changes have had on the industry.

Assess client's control system (CR)

This is conducted to determine the extent to which the records are indeed auditable, and whether the auditor can rely on the client's system to reduce their substantive testing requirements.

As to whether the accounts are auditable, the auditor considers whether:
- the client's staff is sufficiently large to enable adequate segregation of duties
- there is adequate oversight in key areas within the system of internal control
- there are fundamental **controls** (these can be present as **control strengths** and **control weaknesses**).

And, furthermore, with respect to the possibility of relying on the client's internal controls to reduce their substantive tests, the auditor should consider whether the:
- volume of transactions is large enough to make it efficient for the auditor to test internal controls
- accessibility of the client's programs and file data retrieval systems makes it more efficient to increase the substantive tests than to test the client's controls.

At this point, the auditors may want to restrict their evaluation to a review of the client's fundamental controls and major transaction categories. The auditor in charge may be the person to manage this because what is found here leads to strategic decisions about how the audit proceeds (see ASA 315 and ISA NZ 315).

controls
'Checks' that are built into a system to prevent or detect errors and irregularities in the data. Those controls are designed to prevent or detect errors in financial and other cost reports in an accounting information system.

control strengths
Controls within the accounting system that, if operating properly, will prevent or detect errors and irregularities.

control weaknesses
Aspects of the system that are susceptible to unauthorised manipulation but lack control to prevent or detect such error or fraud.

The transaction cycle (subsystems) is understood by performing 'walk-through' procedures from the inception of a transaction (normally a commitment to disburse funds or change ownership) to its end (the disbursement or ownership change). The auditors attempt to identify risks associated with each phase of the transaction cycle and which activity generates costs, revenues or finance for the client's business (see **Table 10.4**).

Table 10.4 Transactions and risks for a trading concern

Transactions	Risk
Place order for stock	Cost price and thus selling price may decline before goods are delivered, or goods may never be delivered, and therefore no sale can take place
Receive goods into stock	Losses occurring as a result of theft, damage, deterioration or obsolescence while in stock, or a reduction in demand, such that stocks are not saleable or selling prices decline to below cost
Pay supplier	Misappropriation of payment
Sell to customer	Non-payment by a customer or illegitimate customer
Receive payment	Misappropriation of receipts

control systems
Integrated combinations of controls that, together, go towards meeting prevention and detection goals in a subsystem as a whole.

Some of these risks depend on the effectiveness of accounting **control systems**. Other risks relate to the product, suppliers or customers irrespective of the internal control system, and should be evaluated in their own right. The auditors should also determine when the sale earns profit; for example, if a right of return exists, a full allowance should be made for potential returns at each year-end.

The accounting transaction cycles usually include purchases, payroll, production, sales and the financing subsystems. Allowance should be made for differing controls used for the same subsystem. For example, cash sales are usually accounted for differently from credit sales and are treated as different accounting transaction types.

The CR of the engagement is the outcome of this process and is the basis for conducting tests of controls at a later stage of the audit.

> **CONCEPT QUESTION 1**   What is the meaning of 'transaction categories' (or subsystems)?

overall analytical procedures
Refer to analytics performed during planning. For example, major purchases, dispositions, related parties, new branches, or areas of concern as to material misstatements, could be indicated by the discovery of sales trends or profit ratios. (ASA 315, para A14; ISA NZ 315, para A14.)

Assess analytical procedures risk (APR)

Overall analytical procedures are also employed at this stage of the audit.

Common analytical procedures may include the use of scanning, ratios or models. They also point to indicators of concern that require further investigation. However, they are different in their concern with the *general* situation, and this is because they indicate the financial strength of the client *taken as a whole*. Generally, ratios calculated during this phase include, at the very least, those for:

- *liquidity* – can the business meet current obligations?
- *solvency* – can the business continue to operate for the foreseeable future?
- *profitability* – is the business profitable?

They may involve using (so-far-unaudited) financial or non-financial statement figures or comparisons to budgets, industries and over time (see **Figure 10.4**).

From the auditor's perspective, the most important ratios are:

Gross profit as a percentage of sales
Unusual patterns over time might indicate a genuine shift in trading conditions or could indicate the existence of material errors, distortions or frauds. If genuine trading factors cause the unusual pattern, we may expect to find either an improvement or decline in cost efficiency or a change in sales mix.

Net profit as a percentage of sales
The net profit margin may disclose variations in overhead expenses. The breakdown of expenses into groups of related items (e.g., selling, administration and finance), and the calculation of the percentage to sales of each group, is a valuable elaboration that may cause the auditors to examine individual items.

Sales to total assets
The ratio of sales to total assets indicates how intensively assets are utilised. Thus, if the ratio of return on assets is rising, and there is no comparable rise in the ratio of net profit to sales percentage, the ratio of sales to total assets must be rising (or there is a misstatement). The more intensive the use of total assets, the better – provided that it does not indicate that the business is running the risk of overtrading.

Sales to fixed assets
Changes in the ratio of sales to fixed assets will reflect changes in the level of the productive use of fixed assets. Significant decreases in the ratio may indicate that certain assets are no longer being used for productive purposes.

Sales to current assets
This ratio indicates how effectively management is utilising the client's working capital. A high ratio is desirable from a 'performance' point of view. However, too high a turnover rate can also indicate a shortage of working capital, and it may give early warning of strained credit and a potential going concern problem.

Current ratio
Current assets / current liabilities indicate the ability of the client to service their current obligations for the upcoming year. Consideration should be given to a situation in which the going concern ability of the client is questioned, as the value of assets and the collection date of liabilities may significantly change this ratio.

Acid test ratio
Current assets – stock / current liabilities also indicate the ability of the client to service their current obligations, giving some going concern comfort, even should their stock (inventory) be difficult to liquidate.

Figure 10.4 Useful ratios for APR analysis

Indicators of expected patterns contribute to an ability to reduce OAR.

Liquidity

The *quality* of the current assets and the nature of the current liabilities should be understood. The quality of the current assets relates to the value attributed to them in the financial statements. For example, are allowances for stock write-downs and doubtful debts conservative or the bare minimum? The nature of the liabilities concerns how quickly they have to be paid.

The *rate of turnover* of trade current assets and trade liabilities should also be analysed. This includes the average time needed to convert the assets into cash and the amount of time that can be taken to settle the liabilities. The net trade cycle of the client can be calculated as any one or more of the following:

- a day's purchases in raw materials (RM): purchases/365, divided into closing RM.
- a day's manufacturing costs in work in progress: manufacturing costs/365, divided into closing work in progress
- a day's cost of sales in finished stock: cost of sales/365, divided into closing finished stock
- a day's sales in debtors: sales/365, divided into debtors
- days to convert inventory to cash: total of above (gross trade cycle)
- a day's purchases in creditors: purchases/365, divided into trade creditors
- net trade cycle: gross trade cycle less day's purchases.

The resultant days can be compared against previous years or verified values. For example, if the standard credit terms are 30 days and the average debtors outstanding is 90 days, this warrants investigation. In this case, the auditor should consider the capacity of the company to borrow additional funds against its short-term assets to protect against bankruptcy. The dollar value of non-utilised borrowing capacity can be calculated as asset (including stock) values, which lenders will take as security, plus cash, less existing loans on those assets.

Solvency

The ability of the business to continue to operate over the long term depends on its ability to withstand extraordinary losses and maintain its solvency in adverse trading conditions. The key elements in the evaluation of long-term solvency are analysing the asset structure relative to the business' capital structure, and the business' ability to generate funds to meet its obligations and repay its borrowings (fixed charges).

Profitability

The starting point for comprehensive analytical procedures of profitability is ROA (return on assets), which is adjusted pretax income expressed as a percentage of total assets. Pretax income can be compared to an asset base that takes into account fully depreciated assets and leased assets. ROA ratios measure two aspects of profitability:

1   components of net income and the gross margin achieved for each product or sales line
2   the efficiency with which the business uses assets to generate sales; that is, 'asset utilisation'.

Determine materiality

In practical terms, materiality criteria assist the audit staff in determining:

- when accounting adjustments must be made
- which accounts do not require audit work because they are immaterial
- which accounts require a limited review
- the nature, extent and timing of substantive testing.

The auditors should calculate planning (overall) materiality during the planning process and disaggregate that to individual accounts or transactions. If the net aggregate of these differences exceeds the materiality limit, adjustments must be made to the financial statements.

The materiality model in the classroom CAATs program accompanying this text provides integrated examples and student exercises to select and allocate overall materiality and allocate it to particular accounts.

Auditing for material misstatements

Fundamentally, audit tests are designed to provide sufficient, appropriate evidence to determine whether financial statements are materially misstated. The auditors should identify the limit above which the cumulative net effect of errors is deemed to be material based on quantitative and qualitative criteria (discussed previously).

The audit program should be related to this materiality limit, and audit tests should not be designed to identify immaterial misstatements, either by size or importance. The resulting audit plan should concentrate the audit effort on significant assets and liabilities and areas containing the greatest misstatement risk.

Accounts requiring a basic review

The benefits of a risk approach are often lost through unnecessary testing should auditors fail to apply the concept of 'materiality' to their testing decisions. To address this, those account balances that are lower than the *tolerable error* can be subjected to a lesser, or 'basic', review at a lesser cost. A basic review requires the auditor to:
1 identify what the balance represents and what types of transactions give rise to the balance
2 agree the balance to the general ledger and scrutinise the relevant account
3 decide if, compared to previous years, the balance appears reasonable
4 conduct specific analytical procedures on the balance
5 consider whether any special qualitative attributes would make the item material (such as a management integrity risk of an understatement).

An understanding of 'materiality' can save the time and cost of unnecessary testing and guide the auditor towards what is most important for the audit.

Auditing in practice

CAATs

While all errors found should be documented in audit working papers, illustrated in the WTB section of your CAATs program, only those that are material, alone or in combination, call for the auditor to insist that the client correct them (see ASA 300, para 12; ISA NZ 300).

It should be noted that, if the potential error or irregularity is likely to result in omissions, substantive tests for completeness should be performed, as the true account balance may be material, and it is not known whether it may be understated or overstated.

Initial planning: Form audit strategy

The auditor now makes a strategic decision as to finding a balance between testing the controls of the client and performing substantive tests. This, together with the budget process, comprises the audit strategy (see ASA 330, paras A8–A10; ISA NZ 330, paras A8–A10). Concentrating on the 'budget', the process to determine it involves:

- allocating staff to oversight, management or tasks of which they are capable
- estimating the number of hours that will be necessary to complete the task
- preparing a timetable for completion of the audit tasks.

The bulk of the audit time and resources should be spent on areas with the highest potential for material misstatement. Once the reporting deadlines have been established, the audit partner can schedule and approve the exact timing of the specific audit tasks. The progress of the audit should be monitored against the budget so that cost overruns can be identified, and appropriate action can be taken.

Audit fees charged are typically determined on an estimated hourly charge-out rate. Different staff members will have different charge-out rates, with senior partners at the highest rates; therefore, the auditor will normally place junior staff on more routine and time-consuming tasks to keep the costs down. Some principles apply:

- Senior audit staff should lead the planning process and the detailed evaluation of internal control. In practice, managers and in-charge (senior) staff are usually responsible for planning processes and client interaction.
- Less-experienced audit staff should not be left unsupervised for any length of time. In practice, new staff members are usually involved with internal control and substantive testing procedures, but they should understand the risks involved.

Once the deadline has been established, the timing of evidence-collection activity can be scheduled, including tests prior to the balance date if the engagement is agreed early. Testing some controls and conducting some analytical reviews early on can save time later when deadlines are tight. A common ordering is shown in **Figure 10.5**.

Planning requires team involvement, and it can take a circular route for approval, staff buy-in and revision as evidence is evaluated (see ASA 300 and ISA NZ 300). Quality is under the firm's control, and if audit staff are insufficiently trained or under extreme time pressure, a low-quality audit can result. There is evidence to indicate that shortcuts tend to be taken by new staff under pressure. Irrespective of time pressures, in an audit, quality should not be compromised.

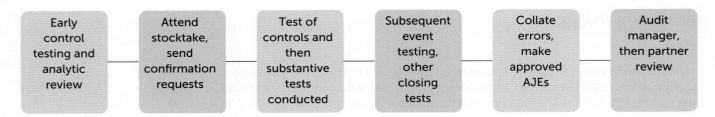

Figure 10.5 Timing of testing processes (early planning assumed)

Working paper notes

The decisions made during the planning process should be recorded, usually in the form of a planning document approved by the audit partner and/or other senior members of the audit team. All decisions agreed at the pre-audit meeting should be recorded in a planning memorandum, which can be stored in the current audit file so that it may be referred to by audit staff when necessary.

This concludes the initial planning procedures. Peer reviews have, in the past, shown a deficiency in firms' planning processes, and this is concerning in light of the importance of these processes to the success of the risk-based audit engagement.

Detailed planning process

There is now a commitment to the engagement. The framework for the work is clear, and there is a reasonable understanding of the business, transactions cycles, claimed controls and audit-related risks. Time is now dedicated to the design of an audit plan.

Detailed planning: Study the accounting system

To begin with, the portion of the client's control system on which the auditor tends to rely is the area of focus. Systems may be large or complex, so dividing the whole into *subsystems* or *cycles* is useful so as not to be overwhelmed – these usually include the purchases, wages, revenue, conversion and finance subsystems.

A record will be made of each subsystem of interest. The recommended approach with cloud, digitised or computerised client systems is to record and evaluate the control environment and accounting system controls. The auditor gains these understandings, and documents them, primarily through:

- *observation* of the client's accounting system
- *inquiry*: asking questions of client personnel
- *ICQs or evaluations* that the auditor completes
- *walk-through procedures* to see how each subsystem treats its transactions
- *flowcharts* or *DFDs* to illustrate the system.

These methods of documentation will be extensively detailed further in this text.

IT audit note

Automated working papers and *software routines* make this task easier, providing access to the audit firm's protocols, decision policies and pre-formatted working papers. They enable consistency and training, and give (senior) auditors the ability to modify the plan and changes if needed through software programs and firm-integrated networks.

CAATs

Relevant extracts of planning decisions and their bases should be obtained for the auditor's working papers as evidence of due care. Examples can be found in the Risk and the Materiality worksheets of your classroom CAATs program.

Detailed planning: Evaluate internal controls

After recording the client's control system, or that portion of it on which they will rely, the auditor puts their 'decision' hat on again to assess the implications of controls of interest to the auditor. This assessment concludes with decisions about those controls on which the auditors intend to rely, which are important in determining the role of 'tests of controls' in the detailed audit plan to follow. This is also extensively detailed later in this text.

Detailed planning: The audit plan

This is the detailed setting out of the nature, timing and extent of the planned audit tests. It will normally include information with which to create *depth tests* for each subsystem relative to risks of concern. It includes planned tests of control and substantive tests; that is, *all* tests. See **Table 10.5** for an example of a small portion of a detailed audit plan.

The plan may be modified should new or conflicting information be discovered, but otherwise, this is the guide to the rest of the audit. **Table 10.5** illustrates the level of detail required for each system, financial or assertion, and for each risk.

Table 10.5 Audit program: Example segment for accounts payable

Risk	Test of control	Test objective	Substantive tests
IR: low CR: low APR: high	Credit voucher, sample for approval: n = 10+0	Occurrence-validity, accuracy	Vouch sample x from WTB to purchase order; examine source of APR risk
IR: high CR: high APR: low	Purchase order, pre-numbered reconciliation test: n = 10 days	Completeness	Cut-off: 1–5 January, purchase orders trace to payables; review sample Y of payments to the supplier after year-end
IR: low CR: low APR: low	Payables test data, inspect exception report	Classification	Scan payables, inventory and cost of sales accounts
IR: low CR: low APR: med	Senior manager compares disclosures against GAAP	Presentation	Inspect disclosure: current and LT liabilities; accruals, depreciation, depletion policies

CONCEPT QUESTION 2   What is a 'detailed plan' and how is it achieved?

Planning should be completed before the commencement of audit testing so that risk assessments are incorporated into the audit. Planning can constitute a substantial part of the audit time (up to 25 per cent) and is the foundation of an effective and efficient audit. The risks of failing to do so include:

- spending time on a non-auditable set of accounts
- risk audit reputation and costs should the firm lack the necessary expertise
- failure to discover intentional wrongdoing by the client if risks unassessed
- testing omissions, or redundancies, if risk and materiality are not considered
- performing a negligent audit if the audit team is not qualified or is under too much pressure to carry it out with due care.

Study tools

Summary

This chapter described aspects of the audit planning process set against a background of comprehensive risk analysis. The focus of the planning stage is to determine the nature, extent and timing of the collection of audit evidence in the light of the auditor's assessment of materiality and taking account of identified audit risk. The chapter described how to evaluate and perform selective procedures used in the initial planning process, and discussed the detailed planning process.

🔗 Case/resources link

CAATs for Classrooms

Accompanying this book is a series of data, integrated worksheets and exercises that are designed to support your learning and give you exposure to hands-on audit decision-making dilemmas faced by auditors in the planning elements of the audit process. Acquire the relevant material for this chapter from your instructor.

Review questions

10.1　Distinguish between the role of the 'audit manager' and of the 'audit partner'.

10.2　Why is it important that the 'scope' of the engagement be clarified early in the engagement? What could happen if there are misunderstandings as to scope?

10.3　What three characteristics define the scope of an engagement?

10.4　Explain the purpose of the engagement letter. Who prepares it, and why should there be a copy of it in the audit working papers?

10.5　At what point should an engagement letter be prepared?

10.6　What points should be set out in the engagement letter?

10.7　Name types of 'risk' that should be evaluated during the initial planning stage.

10.8　Provide three examples for each of the potential misstatements that could arise from:

　　a　inherent integrity risk

　　b　situational integrity risk

　　c　management integrity risk.

10.9   Provide five examples or categories of business risk that could be reviewed at this point.

10.10 What is the purpose of 'overall analytical procedures' at this stage of the audit?

10.11 Provide two examples of each of the following categories of ratios appropriate to review at this stage of the audit, and explain how they may be useful to the auditor:

    a   liquidity ratios

    b   solvency ratios

    c   profitability ratios.

10.12 Define 'fundamental controls'. Explain why they are important.

10.13 Explain why 'materiality' determinations are needed at this stage of the audit.

10.14 What is the meaning of conducting a 'basic review' of accounts? Provide examples where doing so may be appropriate.

10.15 Why is the audit budget important for the firm and the client?

10.16 Explain:

    a   why tests of controls are not in the planning process

    b   where in the planning process it is particularly important for the senior partner to be involved, and why.

Exercises

10.1   **AUDIT PLANNING PROCESS:** Jerome, who is new to the audit practice, managed a small audit firm and decided – for cost reasons – to dispense with one of the planning processes. He is auditing a small clothing retail business. The business is an international franchise located on a busy Brisbane street, with much foot traffic and other shops nearby. Their profit margin has been 1–2 per cent for the last five years. Consider what could be the result should Jerome fail to:

    a   consider the audit firm's ability to have specific retail competencies

    b   fail to visit the site before accepting the engagement

    c   fail to find industry ratios for similar businesses

    d   fail to obtain a copy of the interim and previously audited financial statements.

10.2   **AUDIT PLANNING PROCESS:** Talia is the audit manager for a new client, Sleepbnb, a local online competitor to the international Airbnb practice. The client, a one-person sole trader, primarily arranges accommodation for international travellers. Sleepbnb has been operating for three years, taking a 1 per cent margin off the cost of accommodation, and has shown a profit each year. Sleepbnb expanded in the current year and is now seeking an audit to borrow funds for new accommodation. Consider what could be the result should Talia fail to:

    a   properly analyse management integrity of the sole trader

    b   select an overall materiality level that is greater than the size of the profit figure

    c   consider the effect of Airbnb competition

    d   look at fundamental controls before agreeing to the engagement.

10.3 **AUDIT PLANNING PROCESS:** Jerome is assigned to manage the financial statement audit of a local subsidiary of an international finance company. He is under pressure to keep audit costs down, so he is considering one of the following options.

Required: For each option, consider the implications on audit quality of 'shortcutting' this step:

a Reduce audit team meetings to *after* audit tests have been conducted to keep meeting costs down.

b Use last year's engagement letter without inquiring as to whether changes are required.

c Omit the examination of fundamental controls, and save that procedure for when other tests of control are conducted.

d Leave out the review of 'independence' issues, as this process was adequately carried out for last's year's audit and no problems were found.

e Focus only on a review of the *financing system* as, for this business, the other departments are immaterial.

10.4 **AUDIT PLANNING PROCESS:** The audit firm wishes to allocate functions to senior and junior staff members according to their complexity.

Required: Put the following events in order of 'most' complex to 'least' complex.

a Test client's finance derivatives.

b Conduct fixed asset *existence* procedures.

c Conduct the risk analysis in the planning stage.

d Formulate the audit opinion.

e Come to a planning materiality decision for the client.

f Come to a decision about whether the client has a going concern problem.

g Come to a decision about whether the client has recorded a contingent liability, now in the footnotes, appropriate in accordance with GAAP.

h Conduct a review of the client's bank-reconciliation procedures.

i Re-perform those bank reconciliations.

j Carry out overall analytical review procedures on revenue.

k Evaluate the results of the overall analytical review procedures on revenue.

l Inquire of the client whether there are any related party transactions.

Justify each decision you make.

10.5 **ENGAGEMENT LETTER:** You are preparing an engagement letter for the statutory financial statement audit of a government-owned Roads Division. The manager of the Roads Division also asked you to conduct an audit of their cost systems.

a Compare the scope of the two engagements.

b In what respect should statutory and non-statutory audit engagement letters differ?

c Identify possible 'independence' issues.

d Prepare an engagement letter.

10.6 **ENGAGEMENT LETTER:** Explain what modifications may be required, if any, to an engagement letter prepared for your client TopShelf Ltd, a limited liability company. TopShelf Ltd is a brand-new client, and you only agreed to the engagement two months after the 31 December 2023 (ending) balance date. They became a limited company in February 2022 and maintain all their records in a cloud database. The company has accounting, information systems, marketing and management departments.

10.7 **AUDITOR APPOINTMENT:** The directors of Loopy Ltd, a newly formed company, are seeking to secure your services as an auditor. Regarding their letter, you note the following comments:

'Your duties and rights as an auditor will be determined by the board of our company. In the main, these duties are in line with the requirements of companies' legislation, but in the event of conflict or exclusion, we will indemnify you against any legal action brought as a consequence of the position adopted. The board also retains the right to dismiss you at any time without necessarily disclosing the reasons for their action.'

a   Explain which rights and/or duties of auditors under current legislation the statement of the directors of Loopy Ltd contravenes.

b   Describe what steps you would take prior to accepting the appointment as auditor for the company.

10.8 **AUDIT PLANNING PROCESS:** Prepare, describe and justify a detailed audit plan for a listed company's audit for the current fiscal year. Prepare questions for management, where appropriate, and assume that you receive answers to them (so that you can proceed). Assume you have no knowledge of the events that may follow.

10.9 **OVERALL ANALYTICAL REVIEW:** You have discovered the information shown in **Table 10.6** by conducting an overall analytical review ratio analysis for your client. The current audit is for the year 2023.

Table 10.6 Overall analytical review ratio analysis

	2023	2022
Current ratio	2.0	4.5
Acid test ratio	0.8	1.2
Net profit (– loss)	–73 700	–123 700
Gross profit (– loss)	56 000	56 000
Debt/equity	0.94	1.16
Inventory turnover	570	445
Receivables turnover	181	75
Return on assets	–11.8%	–24.4%

Required: Consider what this information may imply about areas worthy of further evidence.

10.10 **OVERALL ANALYTICAL REVIEW:** Conduct an overall analytical review of the information on your client Dave's Caves Ltd, provided in **Table 10.7**. Identify the indicators of risk.

Table 10.7 Account balances of Dave's Caves Ltd

Account	Dr	Cr
Cash	3 200	
Accounts receivable	94 300	
Provision for BD		1 000
Inventory	264 600	
Notes receivable	20 000	
Fixed assets	358 200	
Accum. depreciation		167 500
Notes payable		12 000
Payroll taxes payable		79 200
Interest payable		15 400
LT debt payable		1 800
Note payable: Dave		168 800
Share capital		200 000
Retained earnings		32 200
Sales		411 400
Sales returns	8 000	
Cost of sales	233 600	
Wages	75 000	
Income tax expense	16 100	
Depreciation exp.	8 100	
Bad debt expense	3 500	
Interest expense	17 900	
Rent expense	18 000	
Net profit		31 200
WTB total	1 120 500	1 120 500

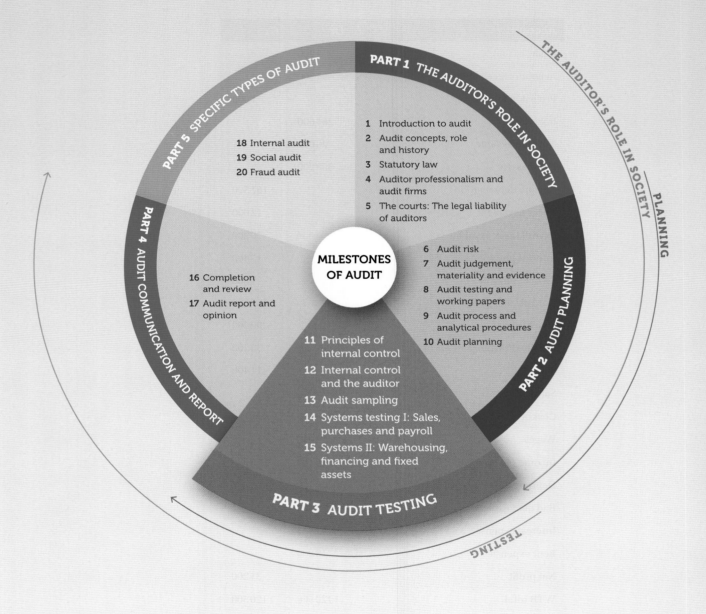

MILESTONES OF AUDIT

PART 5 SPECIFIC TYPES OF AUDIT

18 Internal audit
19 Social audit
20 Fraud audit

PART 1 THE AUDITOR'S ROLE IN SOCIETY

1 Introduction to audit
2 Audit concepts, role and history
3 Statutory law
4 Auditor professionalism and audit firms
5 The courts: The legal liability of auditors

PART 2 AUDIT PLANNING

6 Audit risk
7 Audit judgement, materiality and evidence
8 Audit testing and working papers
9 Audit process and analytical procedures
10 Audit planning

PART 4 AUDIT COMMUNICATION AND REPORT

16 Completion and review
17 Audit report and opinion

PART 3 AUDIT TESTING

11 Principles of internal control
12 Internal control and the auditor
13 Audit sampling
14 Systems testing I: Sales, purchases and payroll
15 Systems II: Warehousing, financing and fixed assets

THE AUDITOR'S ROLE IN SOCIETY

PLANNING

TESTING

Audit testing

Part 3 of the textbook focuses on audit testing and comprises five chapters. Chapter 11 introduces the principles of internal controls. The purpose of this chapter is to explain the process for documenting and assessing a client's system of internal control. Chapter 12 is concerned with when and how audit tests should be performed on internal controls. Audit sampling is covered in Chapter 13. The chapter sets out the principles of sampling practice and provides information on and illustrations of its application. Chapters 14 and 15 introduce the more common types of risks, controls and tests associated with audit depth testing within common accounting systems, such as sales, purchases, payroll (covered in Chapter 14), warehousing, finance and fixed assets (covered in Chapter 15).

Principles of internal control

Introduction

This chapter introduces internal control systems with a focus on computerised/digitised control systems of relevance to the financial auditor. Common terminology and control examples relevant to the auditor are detailed. The purpose is to prepare you for documenting and assessing a client's system of internal control.

You will recall that *controls* prevent and detect errors. *Internal control systems* are a combination of controls that can be computerised, embedded, manual and document-based, as well as physical such as locks and gates. They are of value to management and, for different reasons, to the auditor.

Internal controls can be found at all levels of an organisation, although we have selected a four-level structure that tends to include most controls of relevance to the financial auditor (see **Figure 11.1**). At the organisational level, they are to do with overall vision and oversight; at the management and systems levels, they pertain to management practice accountabilities. Accounting control systems, as logic dictates, relate to practices within and around an organisation's accounting information system.

As you will recall, planning includes an evaluation of the client's control system, and that evaluation, in turn, is part of assessing audit risk. In this chapter, we provide some essential tools to enable you to evaluate a client's control systems in preparation for the auditor's risk-assessment process and testing of controls.

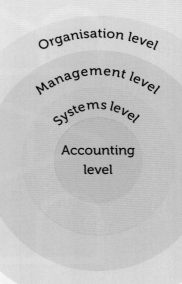

Organisation level

Management level

Systems level

Accounting level

Figure 11.1 Internal control systems

Control systems: Levels

Internal controls over financial reports (ICFR) is a useful concept for referring only to those controls of interest to the financial auditor. ICFR is defined by the US Securities and Exchange Commission (SEC, 2003) as a 'process, effected by an entity's board of directors, management and other personnel designed to provide reasonable assurance regarding the reliability of financial reporting'. ICFR includes controls and systems with which the external financial auditor is concerned.

> An entity's system of internal control contains manual elements and often contains automated elements. The characteristics of manual or automated elements are relevant to the auditor's risk assessment and further audit procedures based thereon. (ASA 315; ISA NZ 315)

There are so many possible controls within an information system that it may be useful to understand them in terms of categories, such as where they sit within an organisation. Here, we focus on ICFRs – although they are, of course, only part of a whole organisational system of control.

However, it is not the goal of a financial statement auditor to assess all controls, only those relevant to the audit of financial statements. The control system categories, or layers, with which we are concerned (see **Figure 11.2**) are suited to the internal control concerns of the external auditor; each is discussed below.

Figure 11.2 Levels of internal controls

Organisational layer

Control systems of interest to the financial auditor at the organisational level are business decisions made at the very top of the client's structure. These include the following:

- *Corporate strategy* – envisions a purpose and future for the organisation as a whole. For example, there may be a strategy to focus on two key services for a law firm, devolving or selling off other services and restructuring in line with that aim. The auditor would want to be aware of this to understand the potential for going concern issues, for revenue impacts, or for litigation risks such as those related to employment changes, anti-trust activities or professional liability.

- *Authorisation structures* – most readily known by organisational charts as well as formation documents, setting out levels of authority. Is the internal auditor accountable to the board (ideally) or to middle-level management (not ideal)? To whom are system developers accountable? External auditors may be concerned about a structure that allows management to overrule controls (see **Figure 11.3**).

- *Governance structures* – establish authority, and some segregation of duties, at the highest level of the entity. Who makes up the governing board? What are their skills or experience? How independent are they from management? The auditor will be interested should that structure be unclear (leading to accountability problems) or unreasonable in terms of ensuring the effective operation of accounting controls. The governance structure is a *control* because it clarifies responsibilities, and accountabilities, within the organisation.

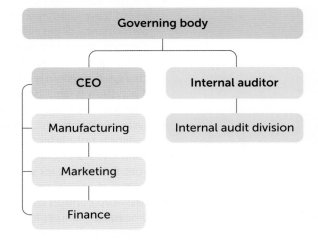

Figure 11.3 Corporate structure example

Management level

Management control systems, or certain portions of them, are also of concern to auditors. These pertain to the decisions made by senior and middle management, and the auditor will be interested in those relating to factors such as duty segregation, asset protection and employment policies.

- *Segregation of duties* – has to do with who is authorised to do what at the management level of operations. This is so important in assessing the quality of the client's ICFRs that it is considered in further detail later in this chapter.
- *Asset protection protocols* – an obvious area for control when it comes to physical assets – equipment, vehicles, tools, stock and so on – but also applies to data, or patent or copyright information. Controls can include:
  — locks on doors, controlled-entry gates and separated facilities
  — passwords
  — documented legal rights concerning, e.g., licensing, copyright, patents, warranties, forward contracts and clientele lists (if part of goodwill)
  — offsite locations, such as for storing construction equipment or backup data
- *Employment policies* – relate to the appropriate behaviour expected of employees in the organisation. Effective employment policies help reduce the likelihood of inappropriate behaviour by employees at work.

Systems level

The focus here is on *systems development*, as most system controls are established at this time. It's easy to overlook what goes on when systems are added or changed, such as when a system shuts down to add new apps, but this is important. Auditors should give this a great deal of thought because vulnerabilities exist during the time when changes occur.

System development controls govern the process of establishing a system, modifying it, or having access to the process of change. Systems development is an interplay of hardware, software and communication devices, and the procedures to establish a system. It can involve the use of experts within and outside an organisation, or a restructure of existing jobs, and lead to changes in the audit trail.

This is also a time when access may be available to unauthorised people, or unapproved transactions could occur. The following are of concern during system development:

- *internal audit oversight* of those situations, usually in the public sector or larger organisations, in which there is an internal audit function. The external auditor may be able to rely on, in part, the performance of the client's internal audit function; and where there are complex or frequent system changes, an internal audit function may be required to ensure controls are in place.
- *access, process and authorisation*, which here refer to the process of systems development or change. If a system is changed, then those who have access to its program can use it to their benefit. If a system is 'shut down' during change, then controls may not operate during that time, or the changes may simply not work. Duties should be segregated (more on this later) and tested.
- *systems testing*, which is important during and after any change to a client's system. If the external auditor is not present, then they may need to rely on the client's internal audit division and/or tests conducted later using dummy (fictitious) data.

Specific controls for systems development may include:

- *system change approval protocols* to ensure only authorised changes occur
- *password controls* over access to the process of change
- *procedure manuals* for conducting system changes or new development
- *authorisation controls* over access to the site or system during change

- *testing* performed during development processes
- *dummy data* to test how the system 'treats' different types or volumes of data
- *vulnerability assessment tools* that prevent unauthorised access during change
- *interrogation software* that makes intentional efforts to 'break into' the system
- *documentation* of the development or change so it won't be lost.

Accounting level

We're all familiar with the accounting cycle, but it bears further attention as it is so important to the external financial statement auditor. *Accounting* (or *procedural*) *controls* look to the processes by which financial information is captured by the system, input, processed, converted into output, and stored (see **Figure 11.4**).

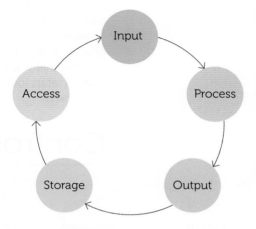

Recording and processing transactions form the heart of the accounting process. The elements will be familiar to you: access to financial systems; data input for a journal entry, processed into journals and ledgers; output as working trial balances, statements or reports; storage in-house or in cloud formats; and further access for adjusting and reversing journal entries – and then the process begins again. The recording cycle is fundamental to financial statement auditing. Control 'tools' can include:

Figure 11.4 Accounting cycle

- *field checks* to ensure all data fields are complete before processing
- *check digits* using calculations to compare data input to data output
- *record checks* that check the number of records entered to that authorised
- *limit checks* that prevent larger unauthorised amounts from being processed
- *batch checks* that ensure, e.g., that all records entered are accounted for
- *read-only terminals* for access to look at, but not change, data
- *keys* – manual or electronic – that can be used to unlock terminals or otherwise gain access
- *passwords and digital authorisation devices* for access to data or components
- *logs* that can record when a terminal is used, by whom and how, and which can issue exceptions reports or flag unauthorised entries.

Storage controls involve the protection of information and information assets that must be risk-managed. Data may be a type of asset or comprise confidential information. It may be accessed, but only with authority. Controls may include:

- password controls specific to storage
- data-management system controls
- offsite storage and concurrent backup
- recovery plans.

Transmission and interface

The transmission of data and its interface with a system's components permeate all levels. While we are mainly concerned with the accounting 'level' here, transmission occurs internally and externally at all levels.

Communication was revolutionised with the introduction of wireless media together with the ability to hold information assets and authorisations (i.e., bank payments). These can be held in tiny packages (mobile phones, tablets), but these are vulnerable to theft or casual loss. *Controls within transmission and interface* may include:

- *local area network* (LAN) server and wi-fi access controls
- *user logs*, usually embedded and with the potential to be audited
- *echo checks* that return data information to the source for comparison

- *encryption*, which is important to protect data accessed without authorisation during the transmission process
- *file labels,* including a label that indicates the 'end' of a transmission, looked for during output to ensure that the full transcription arrived
- *physical controls* over access to and the return of tablets, laptops, keys and mobile phones.

Interface controls ensure that the communication exchanged between the components of a network is complete, accurate and valid. There are appropriate access controls over terminals and components within the network. Interface controls can be susceptible to seemingly small system changes, which can, without anyone knowing it until errors are found, affect the entire network if not properly integrated.

Now that you have some knowledge of the type and range of controls that can exist within an ICFR system, let us look at what the auditor (and management) hopes those controls – working together – will achieve.

Control system: Objectives

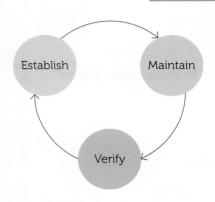

Figure 11.5 Control objectives

Three conditions should exist within each level of a client's organisational control system: each should be well established, maintained over time, and verifiable from evidence (see **Figure 11.5**). These objectives, and several control categories enabling them, are considered below.

- *Establishment controls* ensure that there is an appropriate authority structure and the responsible parties are named. Establishment controls should be appropriate to the corporate culture, risk-management plan and strategic intent. They should be established, reviewed and approved during the development or redevelopment of an information system.
- *Maintenance controls* include those from inception to the completion of a transaction, and which apply throughout the period in which assets are owned and maintained. Such controls ensure proper reporting stewardship and the prevention or detection of problems that may occur while the operations are processing data.
- *Verification controls* give an account of the successful operation of a control. They ensure that there is an audit trail by subjecting the system to physical notation, routine internal checks, embedded audit tests, and readouts.

Establishment

No organisation can design a control system that prevents all errors from occurring, nor is it cost-effective or practical to do so. Nonetheless, it is important to establish an environment in which material irregularities are less likely to occur. *Organisational, management* and *systems* controls, introduced earlier, establish an accountability framework for ICFR. However, some topics call for further discussion: namely, the segregation of duties, policy practices and employment practices.

Segregation of duties

An important administrative control is to structure and allocate accounting duties to staff so that no one employee has an opportunity to both perpetuate and conceal a transaction; that is, to make errors or commit fraud.

The **segregation of duties** is conducted by identifying duties that, if combined, could allow an employee to record or benefit from a transaction without oversight or accountability. For example, it may be risky to allow one employee to receive, record and bank the remittances from debtors because the employee might do none of the above – other than to bank it in their own account, of course.

For similar reasons, it is important that, should jobs be shared, there is a means for an internal check to identify who carried out what transaction. For example, should multiple restaurant employees each be able to record payments during the same shift, a control could identify which of them carried out which transaction. This may be accomplished through assignment (who will be the cashier) or electronically (input employee codes). The segregation of duties is important at all levels of an organisation. As an example, see **Figure 11.3**, which illustrates the role of the internal auditor as independent of middle management.

The segregation of duties, no matter how thorough, cannot guarantee error-free data. A segregation practice can be overridden by managers who oversee and have access to systems, or the controls can be ignored should employees not be held to account for them. Nor can very small businesses – those with one or two people in 'accounts' – fulfil the rigid requirements of a complete segregation of duties.

A further issue is agency considerations. There is an agency assumption in the segregation of duties; that is, employees are 'agents' managing on behalf of 'principals', and control 'monitors'. This arrangement would not be acceptable in flat organisations, where individuality and creativity may be fundamental to the entity's purpose and strategy.

Deciding whether the segregation of duties can be imposed on staff, and to what extent, is a risk-management decision to be made by considering the needs of the organisation and its staff, and the cost of the segregation itself. Usually, some level of segregation can be achieved. The sort of functions that, ideally, should be kept separate are illustrated in **Table 11.1**.

Table 11.1 Segregation of duties

Computerised information system (CIS)	Manual system
Systems development	Initiating the transaction
Computer programming and/or systems design	Recording the transaction (journals and ledgers further segregated)
Access	Control over assets (physical or online control)
Data input	
Operations (i.e., maintaining a LAN)	Conduct internal checks (e.g., re-performance, reconciliations, comparisons of work done)
Output control	
Data and file storage functions	Authorising transactions and processes
Internal audit functions	Internal audit of processes
Combined CIS and manual Segregation would depend on how that combination occurs	

Segregation can be extended to processes, databases and accounts, including, for example, intangible assets and liabilities (since the authority to set up a liability implies the authority to release assets). Contract employees may be brought in to conduct a stock count because they are independent of employees receiving stock and recording purchases, thus segregating *recording* and *asset control* from *internal checks*.

While adhering to control principles, the segregation of duties in a computerised system has different requirements because of the ability of a few individuals – such as programmers or database managers – to have access to many processes. So, for example, a programmer without oversight can design a payments system to send payments to their personal account. A person with access to data can delete records that implicate their actions. It is important to segregate such functions from each other and those operating or conducting internal checks over the system.

Policy practices

Accountability is improved where duties are defined in a way that all other staff can recognise. This may be achieved by producing organisational charts, procedural and quality-control manuals, job specifications, or special instructions.

The objective is to ensure that all employees know to whom they are accountable, about what, and who is responsible. This is more important than you may think because errors can easily result if clarity is lacking. Policy documents can also be a useful training tool – this is another type of *establishment control*.

Employment practices

The quality and commitment of employees determine whether an organisation's system vulnerabilities are likely to have been breached. To reduce such risks, human resource policies must be put in place so that:

- qualified and ethical staff are recruited
- there is a commitment to ongoing training and education
- integrated systems development and company-wide communication policies are in place.

Employment policies are an important part of the control system, as an employee who is motivated to sabotage a firm or who is ignorant of practice can cause a great deal of damage to the credibility of that firm.

A failure to account for people, and incentives, knowledge and access, is a major factor in system faults and asset loss. Auditors should pay attention to employment practices as much as they do to technical control elements to determine system vulnerabilities that may lead to material misstatement.

Maintenance

Maintenance controls help ensure that controls over transactions are effective throughout all stages of capturing, recording and processing a transaction. Each stage of a process provides opportunities for error or for 'uninvited guests'. It follows that a valid record must be maintained at each stage, from inception to completion.

Accounting controls (at the accounting level of subsystems) and asset-protection controls (at the organisational and management levels) can address these objectives. Examples aligned with the audit assertions can be found in **Table 11.2**.

Table 11.2 Accounting controls and audit assertion examples*

Controls over input
Compare arithmetical recalculations to original entry for *accuracy*.
Conduct record of document counts for *completeness* of input.
Limit controls on amounts recordable to reduce *occurrence-validity* errors.
Initiating and buyer vouchers matched before authorised for *occurrence-validity* (or *accuracy*).
Check figures comparing input to amounts received for *accuracy*.
Field checks of customer credit ratings before payment for *occurrence-validity*.
Reasonableness tests would set off an alarm if accounts payable is credited on payment for *classification*.
Batch numbers compared to entered numbers for *occurrence-validity* and *completeness*.
All except one person has read-only access to data entry for *occurrence-validity*.

$\rightarrow$

Controls over processing
Pre-numbered receipts checked for missing receipts, for *completeness*.
Cast and cross-cast function automatic check after daily journal entries for *accuracy*.
Check journal accounts are the same as those posted for ledgers, for *accuracy* and *classification*
Error messages occur if input is not in machine-readable form, for *completeness, accuracy*
Bank-to-books or accounts-to-ledger reconciliations for *occurrence, completeness* and *accuracy*

Controls for outputs
Error reports reveal debits to sales, for *occurrence-validity* or *classification*
Output printed and checked for unauthorised transaction, for *occurrence-validity*
Record compares input data with number of outputs for *occurrence-validity* and *completeness*
Output disruptions or interrogations yield error reports, for *occurrence-validity*
Record checks to ensure customer accounts cannot be deleted, for *completeness*

* Not including segregation of duties

Verification

The functioning of control – any control – should be indicated by some sort of record. That could be the initialisation of a document, a report write-up, register signatures or embedded data signatures. This evidence holds the employee concerned to account and provides control over others who might attempt to enter the system. Verification also provides an audit trail, which is crucial to the auditor. A specific example may prove useful, as provided in the 'Auditing in practice' box.

Auditing in practice

Purchase orders

When a purchase order is placed on a supplier, the buying officer can be made accountable by using a prenumbered purchase order, supported by an independently authorised goods requisition. When the goods are received, a prenumbered goods-received note can be created. An independent party later compares these documents, and the documents are cancelled once received.

None of these accounting controls will effectively discourage errors and irregularities unless management ensures that the controls are working in practice. Such assurance can be achieved partly through internal checks or by internal audits, and often a combination of the two can be used to advantage. Management normally incorporates checking procedures into the accounting process, and these are referred to as **internal checks**.

Internal checks should be made at each point where details are entered from documents onto subsequent records, and at any stage where significant action is based on the documents. For example, before cheques are signed, supporting documents should be checked to confirm validity and appropriateness.

internal checks
A re-performance or review activity enabled by segregating duties in such a way that no one person can initiate, authorise, conduct and record a transaction from start to finish without the work coming under the surveillance of at least one other person.

Routine checks

Routine checks of assets against accounting records include physically inspecting stock, investments and cash balances, and reconciling bank balances to bank statements. In addition to direct checks on the custody of assets, indirect checks can also prove useful. For example, employees' duties can be allocated in such a way that statements to customers are prepared and distributed by, and replies received are routed to, employees who do not usually handle remittances. In this way, those employees indirectly check the work of an employee who normally receives remittances.

Verification is conceptually similar but different in practice for a full CIS. In a manual or part-manual system, one can use initials or cancel documents to provide evidence that a process has taken place (see **Figure 11.6**).

Figure 11.6 Example: Internal check performed on customer invoice

Acme office supplies: customer invoice									
Invoice #	Date	Customer #	Item #	Description	Price	Payment	Credit approval	Cancel on data entry
2346	15.3.18	2834IDA	2346A	File cabinet	199.95	CR	*KVP*	*MP*
8311	15.3.18	2834IDA	2395D	Ergo chair	134.50	CR	*KVP*	*MP*

Evidence of independent checks on performance will be less obvious in a CIS since such checks are programmed (embedded) into the system, not performed manually by an employee. To verify that controls are in place and operating effectively, therefore, the auditor should typically review:

- *policy and program documentation*, including manuals, to obtain an understanding of the authorising and review structure and the protocols expected of users
- *exception reports* identifying problems that may have occurred over the year (it is important, of course, that the exception reports reveal problems of interest to the auditor, and a review of what the exception reports catch and what they do not catch may be as important as reviewing the output)
- *user access logs*, particularly where unauthorised access is suspected, to determine who obtained access to the system, when, and what rights they had or had used. (Read-only? Read-and-write? Update and delete functions? – the latter being of greatest concern, of course.)

In addition, internal (verification) checks can include comparing a sample of general ledger entries to source documents, or re-performing a bank reconciliation. The extent to which the client verifies their transactions is relevant to auditors.

Computer information systems (CIS)

Computer information systems (CIS) consist of components (hardware), software, data, and the people who develop, manage or use them. Systems can be document-based or electronic, or partially online and partially manual. Each requires its own unique range of protocols, controls and expertise. Incorporating LANs, cloud-based accounting and business networks can get complicated.

Documents are still used and (you might be surprised to hear) are reasonably common as they provide visibility, a backup, accountability and an audit trail. However, they are usually part of a computerised or digitised system. Most controls in a CIS are established during development and are invisible to the naked eye. External application programs may form a part of the system, such as payroll, stock or combined packages. The primary aim of an audit is the same as for a CIS system: to assess whether fundamental controls exist, and the extent to which they can be relied on to reduce substantive testing.

Controls and control systems will vary in practice. Auditors must be able to adapt to a client's system to be able to assess controls of importance to them. Let's start with CIS **components** and some terminology we will be using.

Components in CIS

While you will encounter many different terms and systems, some reasonably common ones follow.

A manual system looks to documents for evidence of transactions, processing, data, data storage, and security or control. In computerised systems, many of these functions are hidden. Therefore, the audit trail must also be made available in document form and/or accessible as incorporated within the databases and systems.

Systems that incorporate transmission functions, which is most of them, add further complexity. LANs (linked components and data) will control databases through **servers**. For example, a Google Gmail DNS (domain name system) provides and communicates usernames. Like other components, servers call for controls in transmission components and interface software to ensure completeness, accuracy and validity of communications. Another term used to refer to businesses is **ebusiness**.

An ebusiness may solicit customers online through pop-up ads, process orders online, or receive and make payments online. It may source its own products from a digital source, review stock online, meet its suppliers through Zoom or Skype, and/or sign purchase agreements online. Organisations may post the product or refer to the service provider without ever witnessing buyers, products or sellers.

While there are many forms that an ebusiness can take, essentially they all require some form of advanced software, external servers, marketing access, and the controls needed to ensure the protection of their assets and data. Some of the characteristics of these businesses, relevant to the audit, can be found in **Table 11.3**.

components
The hardware that comprises part of any computerised or partially computerised system. Fundamental components of a computer system are the units for input, output, storage, processing, transmission and control.

servers
Provide resources, data services or programs to other computers within a network. Servers can host, for example, web apps (applications), catalogues, communication or other computer resources. They may be owned by the client, hosted by a hosting services provider, or cloud-based.

ebusiness
Refers to the practice of carrying out a business online.

Table 11.3 Components common to CIS

System	Input/output/ storage	Processing and processing software	Servers	Transmit	Staffing
Manual	Paper	n/a	n/a	n/a	Personnel
Computer–manual mixed	Above + PC or mobile, printers, datastore	Mainframe, PCs, printers, monitors, application, licensing and security	Internet servers, browsers	Phone line or wi-fi, fibre	Electronic and requires fewer personnel but with greater expertise. Need for an internal audit is greater. May rely on contracted expertise
Local area (computer) network (LAN)	Above + cloud or other external	Above + central hardware; dedicated PCs, network management	Above + LAN file servers	Above + cabling	
Fully online ebusiness	Cloud or other external	Above + offsite algorithms, firewall security, encryption	Above + ISP (Internet service provider), offsite database	Above + direct external line	

enterprise risk management (ERM)
Sourced in the Committee of Sponsoring Organizations (COSO) model about an organisation's internal controls, ERM is carried out by management, working with internal auditors, to anticipate future events, opportunities and risks that could affect the entity's risks and opportunities (see https://www.coso.org).

Computerisation and the digital economy are having a growing, exciting and sometimes alarming impact on human resources, management decisions and contracting practices. **Enterprise risk management (ERM)** and enterprise data services have become all the more important in a digital economy.

CIS calls for a particular understanding of its functions, terminology and, for auditors especially, risks.

CONCEPT QUESTION 1   Define control system 'components' and identify four examples.

Characteristics of a CIS

A CIS can be partially or fully digitised. By definition, ebusinesses are online. From an audit perspective, the following situations should be considered in the design of the audit program for a CIS:

- *Rigorous security controls over access* to any part of the system are needed to protect the system from unauthorised interrogation. An ebusiness can be shut down temporarily or permanently by cyber-extortion, digital blackmail or the theft of customer information, creating going concern or contingent liability risks.
- *The existence of ebusiness assets may be difficult to determine*, as they could be offsite, intangible or temporary (e.g., influencer existence).
- *Valuation of business assets* is difficult to determine, and the value may change from day to day due to customer satisfaction, supply chain events, or fashion. In an ebusiness, changes can be expressed extensively and quickly, leading to reputational damage and revenue loss in no time.
- *Determining the completeness, accuracy and occurrence-validity* of data entered *or processed* in the system may require embedded audit testing. Understanding a virtual or external system may be time-consuming, if not impossible, and evaluating the client's control system impractical and costly.

Common to CIS or ebusiness systems are their real-time processing, use of database management systems, and embedded controls.

Real-time processing

Real-time processing refers to systems in which transactions data are created and/or updated immediately, sometimes from remote sites. If a system is fully online and real-time, then files are updated instantly on input. Unless intentionally introduced, there may be no documentation to provide an audit trail. Benefits to the business and society are the speed with which transactions can occur and the ability to rely on immediate information for management decision making.

Database management systems

XBRL (eXtensible Business Reporting Language)
A global framework used by businesses for recording, exchanging and disclosing business accounting information.

enterprise data services
Form a bridge between business applications and data sources, coordinating the integration of the data sources so they are accessible by the business.

Database management systems (DBMS) use and manipulate a pool of stored information that is an output of processing transactions. So, for example, a sale recorded in a DBMS may automatically update stock records, credit records, receivable ledgers, production records and internal sales analytics.

The use of **XBRL (eXtensible Business Reporting Language)**, **enterprise data services** and other platforms increase the flexibility and speed of management systems, which also affects the financial statements.

Any error in any input, from potentially any department, has wide repercussions because the data and its applications are widely integrated. Financial records can be distorted by mis-entries in the marketing or production departments. Therefore, greater care is required in the construction of a system that fits the institution and the authorisation and validation of input from any source.

Data stored on the organisation's site can be destroyed, lost or disappear due to component damage or theft. Loss of virtual storage or problems with uploading or replacing data could also affect offsite and cloud storage. Such risks have clear corporate and audit implications, particularly if the data is necessary for preparing financial statements. Of particular concern is the unauthorised interrogation of data by the client's employees, competitors or others (going concern and distortion or fraud risks).

Many of these problems can be overcome with advanced preparation prior to data-management system setup, using the system development and access or process controls referred to earlier. The auditor does not want to alert the client's staff to areas to be tested, so having predictable downloads is not advisable.

Embedded controls

Embedded controls are those 'built into' the CIS itself, usually at the development stage, and which would not be visible to the naked eye. To ensure that appropriate controls are embedded within a system, it is usually important for there to be:
1   an internal audit function to manage the systems development process, with an internal auditor, being an employee of the client, being part of the development
2   observation of the development, which, as long as they are not influential in that development, can be done by an external auditor (independence issues prevent them from being involved in management decisions); there are also likely to be embedded controls over LAN
3   an element of trust, or ability to test, in relation to a CIS purchased externally by the client.

Because controls can be invisible in a CIS, the auditor needs to be able to ensure their existence and quality for, at least, determining if fundamental controls are in place. Examples of embedded controls include the following:
*   *Buffer storage and batch processing* – Documents may be submitted or retained in batches or buffer storage for a short time prior to processing. Tests on data input can be performed early in the processing and on the entire batch or each transaction as it is entered.
*   *Data transmission controls* – The potential for data loss is significant during this process because of problems with server traffic or interference as it is being transmitted. Controls must therefore be embedded at each stage of the process. Your client may have to rely on controls installed by external providers, such as internet providers. In such cases, the auditors may have to evaluate the external provider's and client's capabilities through dummy variable testing.
*   *Direct access updating* – Datastores have the advantage (in terms of speed) of being accessible for updating, but this may result in information loss when data is deleted. An example is when settled (zero-balance) debtor accounts are permanently closed. For reconstruction purposes, the client will normally 'dump' closed-out files onto a separate store for the auditor. If this is not done, then a specific audit request will need to be made so that the auditor can test the entire population.
*   *Simultaneous updating controls* – These protect data when more than one party accesses the file or data at the same time.
*   *Error and exception reports* – Clients will probably need fewer printouts every month than they would have had in a manual system, and producing electronic exception reports will usually be more efficient.
*   *Computer-generated/transmitted calculation controls* – Related to the previous issue, the CIS may generate a total that is communicated and used as the input for a subsequent process, with no intermediate printout. This is a common problem, encountered frequently in practice. Data can be lost or accuracy problems missed because the processes cannot be checked. A control could include a printout, or a separate file, so that the auditor can conduct tests on it.

- *Password controls* – It is common to have a hierarchy of passwords in any system, IT or manual that allows some employees particular access to the system or its components. CIS-based passwords can be quite sophisticated and specifically for
  — each person, individualised and changed daily
  — read-only purposes
  — adding data only
  — adding or deleting data, but based on a limit
  — complex passwords or codes
  — restricting access to, e.g., 'office hours' to enable oversight
  — second-level authentication should someone unauthorised have code access
  — authorisation by fingerprint or eye/face-recognition devices
  — limiting tries to three or fewer attempts before being locked out or reported
  — linking to alarms should repeated attempts be made.
- *Virus-protection controls* – You will be familiar with downloadable cybersecurity for your mobile phones, tablets and home computers; some are free (and possibly worth what you pay). Security should be integrated throughout the network in a business as viruses and intruders may look for any vulnerabilities.

Without such controls, the auditor may have to resort to limited tests of controls, and/or they may have to rely heavily on substantive testing.

Auditing in practice

Calculating stock value

There may be no printout of stock figures, such as calculations for the weighted average cost of stock, even though it would have involved numerous calculations using a variety of databases. You may have to investigate this by estimating its balance (SpAR) or by testing the program itself with the test data.

Evolving technologies

Some discussion of advanced systems is also in order. In *AI (artificial intelligence)* systems or social/retail media systems, the controls would also have to address the algorithms which determine output decisions in, for example, finance or marketing. These may be impossible to determine, much less test, and difficult decisions may have to be made.

Blockchain technology is viewed by some as a foundational concept in future risk management. It can help de-risk transactions by reducing compliance costs, while increasing the transparency of contracts and transactions, and mitigating against fraud through encryption. However, it adds other types of risk to the enterprise due to enabling transactions to be outside regulated financial institutions (fraud). Where a client uses cryptocurrency (which is based on blockchain technology), this can give rise to often-unstable market values (valuation). Its power needs are also enormous and are of environmental and social concern.

As is often the case with new technology, the controls tend to be introduced later, once problems have emerged. While audit principles continue to apply, the techniques used to mitigate these risks are yet to fully emerge.

There are advantages to the auditor of a client with a well-managed CIS, but there are also risks and challenges. Audit implications of control systems are considered next.

CONCEPT QUESTION 2   What is a 'hierarchy of passwords'?

Internal controls: Audit implications

> Test of controls [are] an audit procedure designed to evaluate the operating effectiveness
> of controls in preventing, or detecting and correcting, material misstatements at the
> assertion level. (ASA 330, para 4(b); ISA NZ 330, para 4(b))

While clients may be excited about what a new technology 'can do for them', the auditor should view system developments from an attitude of care and professional scepticism about their value and the risks they may introduce to the audit.

Professional scepticism

'Maintaining professional scepticism requires an ongoing questioning ... [including] considering the reliability of the information to be used as audit evidence and the controls over its preparation and maintenance ...' (ASA 240, para A10; ISA NZ 240, para A10)

Material misstatements are often grounded in intentional acts, and if the client's control system has vulnerabilities, then they can be exploited. Internal control systems can neither solve nor prevent all misstatements.

> All internal control systems have inherent limitations, including the possibility of
> circumvention and overriding of controls, and, therefore, can provide only reasonable
> assurance as to the reliability of financial statement preparation and such asset
> safeguarding. (SEC, 2006)

This is because control systems are designed around events and transactions that tend to be frequent and regular. They are not designed to identify all events or all transactions. Material misstatements could be missed, therefore, if there is only a reliance on the client's controls for evidence. Events outside the system may include those that:

- occur at the end of the year, or the beginning of the next year, should they not be processed by the system on the correct day
- are adjusting journal entries or unusual transactions that, by their nature, bypass the internal control system
- occur while the system is being developed or modified
- require the client to make an estimate, such as depreciation or valuation
- pertain to 'disclosures', such as in the policies/footnotes section of the financial statements, or that involve classifying in accordance with GAAP
- involve the possibilities of litigation or going concern assessments
- involve new types of transactions, products or divisions that have not yet been integrated into the client's system
- for which management overrides the controls and makes them inoperable.

To this, ASA 315 (ISA NZ 315, Appendix 2) adds a number of other situations that could bypass the internal control system and indicate material misstatement.

Audit benefits of control systems

An internal control system may be adept at finding or correcting calculation errors, identifying omissions, flagging unusual entries, or correcting misclassifications. In keeping with the focus on 'assertions', examples of errors and misstatements, by assertion and in terms of their impact, are illustrated in **Table 11.4**.

Table 11.4 Classification of errors and irregularities

Audit test assertion	Possible errors or misstatements	Internal control possibilities	Error, distortion and/or fraud possible
Occurrence validity	Absence of supporting documentation that the transaction occurred and was authorised	Authorised 'signatures' on hardcopy or digitised	Manipulate support documentation to support unauthorised entry
Completeness	Failure to make a book entry or record the transaction; loss of a record; the system fails to record	Codes (e.g., barcodes) require processing or will set exception message or alarm when off-property	Suppress a book entry, interrogate or modify a computer program, or interrupt system
Accuracy	Inaccurate calculation of book entry, possibly involving computer program error	Controls that cast and cross-cast entries, exception reports, or notice if incorrect	Making erroneous entry or calculation or posting, potentially through computer program interrogation
Classification	Posting to an inappropriate ledger account	Protocol to review allocation algorithms	Make an improperly classified entry to hide the true purpose of cost
Existence	Losing stock, equipment or intangibles (e.g. copyright, patent)	Digitised control on stock, protocols to review ownership	Misappropriating stock, equipment or intangibles
Rights–obligations	Failure to record liabilities against assets, or recording non-owned assets as owned	Authorisation protocols for entry; reviewing unusual cash debits	Misclassifying non-owned assets or off-balance-sheet financing
Valuation	Failing to adjust for market changes in valuation	Protocols to check against values; reviews by (independent) internal auditor	Intentionally overstating (e.g., net accounts receivable) or understating (e.g., current portion of long-term debt) valuations
Presentation	Forgot to disclose methods as required by GAAP	Protocols to review presentation at year-end.	Omitting important information to distort, such as contingent liabilities or new debt

A client's CIS system could enhance the auditor's testing process. Digitised data and cloud databases allow clients to keep *extensive and detailed records* useful for the auditor's analytical procedures. For example, an analysis of detailed stock movements by location can establish the credibility of stock sales by location.

The auditor may be able to rely on a client's CIS for its *repetition* ability (so any correct calculation would *always* be correct), mathematical ability and embedded controls. For example, embedded exception reports will usually be reviewed by the auditor. While the auditor may need to test the program itself (such as by using test data), further tests on data may be reduced if reliable.

If embedded, the client's CIS can also perform *internal checks* for the auditor, such as downloading and comparing sales data and sales journal entries at cut-off. The auditors can use the client's *utility programs* (or apps) to select an audit sample and to download, sort and save it for use in testing.

CONCEPT QUESTION 3	Define 'internal check'.

Audit challenges from control systems

It is tempting for a business to acquire new apps, gadgets or platforms offered at – seemingly – low or no cost. It is perhaps too easy, however, to overlook the costs, and risks of, in particular, digitised information systems. These include the possible lack of an audit trail, software damage, or unauthorised access which goes undetected. So, there are also real audit risks associated with control systems. Here are a few examples of the challenges auditors can face:

- *External program:* An agent's online airline booking service electronically interrogates the airline's reservation file and books tickets for a travel agent's clients. A risk for the client is in relying on an external company's system and potential bias towards one airline. For example, the system may not process an agent's overseas client because they don't deal with the overseas airline. In audit terms, risks include that the client may not be able to install the desired controls, or that, without access to the external party's program, the auditor cannot test it.
- *Handling errors:* Barcodes (Universal Product Codes) on individual stock items can be read automatically and recorded immediately into the client's stock system to update stock and purchase ledgers. A risk may lie in the potential for errors made by those installing the barcodes, by programs or persons updating the purchase or sale prices, or, as always, in the potential for someone to over- or undervalue the product (distortion) through access to the program.
- *Authorisation codes, processing damages:* An automated teller machine (ATM) enables a bank's customers to withdraw or deposit cash without using bank hours or locations. Transfers can also be done online. Risks are errors in the bank's system (yes, it happens), lost or stolen cards or passwords, or unauthorised access to the program. Bad weather or poor networks can disable systems. Thieves can insert skimming machines (to steal passwords) or physically ram and steal the ATM.
- *Authorisation cards lost / no receipts:* The payWave method of paying for products means that customers do not have to recall or use passwords or carry cash to conduct transactions. They do, of course, have to carry a card, which is susceptible to theft or loss (the per-transaction maximum is, in fact, a limit check), and if the customer has no hardcopy receipt, system errors cannot be disproven. From an audit perspective, authentication of customers may be difficult to prove.
- *Data-input problems:* Payroll systems can be purchased such that manual or automated payroll authorisation entries are immediately recorded, classified and modified for tax withdrawal. Net amount (net pay) can be deposited directly into the employee's bank account. Risks include lack of access to external programs and controls for testing, errors in coding, input errors, dated withholding authorisation or, without updates, paying redundant employees. Audit trails may be inaccessible.

The auditor is responsible for including computerised systems in their assessments (ASA 330; ISA NZ 330), which is where many of the controls operate, but doing so can be complex and costly. CIS and ebusiness, while making exciting contributions to enterprise, pose traps for the unwary (see International Auditing Practice Statement 1013: Electronic commerce – Effect on the audit of financial statements). CIS, AI and network expertise are required for most audits today.

We cannot all be computer audit experts, just as we are not all tax experts, nor do we suggest any single approach to an audit, as systems vary. But all auditors should be aware of audit principles and CIS challenges and be able to assess them enough to know what is required, communicate with IT staff, and provide leadership as to what to collect, when, and why – and when to call for help.

Study tools

Summary

This chapter described internal controls and aspects of internal control systems important for the financial auditor. Control systems are classified by organisational level (organisational, management, systems and accounting) and objective (establishment, maintenance or verification). Control types (such as 'embedded', 'segregation of duties', 'internal checks' and 'passwords') were discussed. Examples of controls and audit situations were offered throughout.

The chapter concluded with implications for the auditor. There are many possible controls and control structures, all of which will vary from client to client. Principles and concepts covered in this, and the following chapter should be understood as those of primary concern to the external auditor of financial statements.

Case/resources link

CAATs for Classrooms

Accompanying this book is a series of data, integrated worksheets and exercises that are designed to support your learning and give you exposure to hands-on audit decision-making dilemmas faced by auditors in the planning elements of the audit process. Acquire the relevant material for this chapter from your instructor.

Review questions

11.1　Explain why internal control is significant to the auditor.

11.2　Explain how controls could potentially reduce distortion, fraud or error as to:
  a　occurrence-validity assertions
  b　completeness assertions
  c　accuracy assertions
  d　classification assertions.

11.3　Name the benefits to auditors of clients having computerised systems.

11.4　Identify the challenges to auditors of clients' computerised systems.

11.5　Define 'real time' processing.

11.6　Define ebusiness and explain the characteristics of it that the auditor should consider.

11.7　Distinguish between organisational, management, system development and accounting controls. Provide examples of each.

11.8　Identify five different ways in which passwords can restrict those who have access to components, software or data.

11.9　List the categories of duty that should be kept segregated and describe how they differ between a manual and a computerised system.

11.10　Define 'embedded controls' and provide three examples of types.

11.11　What is the difference between 'establishment', 'maintenance' and 'verification' controls, and how do each of these serve the business and the auditor?

11.12 Describe five ways in which the auditor may gain assistance from a client's computerised accounting system.

11.13 What is meant by a 'loss of audit trail'? Describe five ways in which such a loss could occur.

11.14 How can 'employment policies' be considered a control?

11.15 Name and describe five processing controls.

11.16 What are 'exception reports'? What are 'error reports'? What purpose do they serve?

Exercises

11.1 **CONTROL TYPES:** Distinguish between accounting controls and administrative controls in a properly coordinated system of internal control. Apply this general understanding to the operations of your local bookstore by preparing a list of administrative controls and a separate list of accounting controls that may be appropriate for this type of retail business.

11.2 **CONTROL TYPES:** Name three specific controls that would fall under each category of control listed in the accounting (procedural) controls section of this text for a travel agency client. The travel agency employs one manager, five agents and one bookkeeper, and it has a chartered accountancy firm prepare monthly statements.

11.3 **CONTROLS AND ASSERTIONS:** One of the examples of an accounting (procedural) control follows: 'Daily data batch number sent – batch numbers input for occurrence-validity and completeness.'

Required: Identify two different versions of this control, one of which would identify occurrence-validity problems and the other which would identify completeness problems.

11.4 **SEGREGATION OF DUTIES:** Lewis and Associates is considering whether to develop a manual purchases system or a computerised purchases system for its new division in property repair supplies. It anticipates over $1 million in annual purchases for the new division, and it plans to employ four staff (Jason, Jane, Justin and Jill) exclusively for it. Lewis plans to oversee the property repair supplies division, and he wants to authorise major purchases and review quarterly results.

Required:
a Suggest appropriate segregation of duties for a manual system.
b Suggest appropriate segregation of duties for a computerised system in which all orders are made from Jill's smartphone once authorised.
c Consider why the two systems need to be different.

11.5 **SEGREGATION OF DUTIES:** For the sales receipts system described below for SHS, a pharmacy and retail store, come to a conclusion as to the nature of 'risk' that could occur in this system in terms of the potential for misstatements in the financial statements. What could happen?

a Beth is the receptionist and cashier. She has worked at SHS for 10 years and is a model employee.
b Beth would collect SHS's copy 2 of the sales receipt (when pharmacy is finished) and match it with copy 1 (pre-pharmacy sales receipt) and cash.

    c Beth usually comes to work early, leaves late, and rarely takes time off, unless SHS is closed.

    d Beth recently helped the internal audit department switch to a fee-for-service system.

    e Paolo, who works in the same department, recounts, compares to receipts, deposits cash and signs off on completion.

    f Paolo also ensures that all prenumbered invoices are accounted for and filed at day's end.

11.6 ACCOUNTING CONTROLS: You are the auditor of a company that processes most of its accounting records on a computer. The business is medium-sized and employs a manager, a senior systems analyst, three junior systems analysts, three programmers, an operations supervisor, two operators and two control clerks. In conducting your review of the quality of the internal control over transactions, what are the main areas that you, as the auditor, would examine to satisfy yourself that accounting records are being processed in a controlled environment?

11.7 COMPUTERISED CONTROLS: Identify the internal controls (or the lack of a needed internal control) in each of the items listed below for a university health centre. For each, determine whether that control is: (1) an internal check; (2) segregation of duties; or (3) another type of control.

    a The campus student health service was small, with few employees.

    b Earnings were cash-only fees from medical and pharmacy services to students.

    c University policy requires managers to vet applications and contact references before employing.

    d In 2021, the university's internal audit department reviewed operations.

    e The auditors noted that there were few procedures for tracking revenue earned.

    f The internal auditors set up a system that used prenumbered multiple-copied receipts for all sales.

    g Copy 1 is kept and ensures receipts at the end of each shift are all present.

    h Copy 2 is attached to the doctor's prescription, sent to the pharmacy and used to distribute medications.

    i Copy 3 is pulled off and given to the student-patient if they ask for it.

11.8 COMPUTERISED ACCOUNTING SYSTEMS: Vita-Link Health Services is a business that uses Zoom to consult with customers as to their medical concerns. In the first stage, the customer enters their symptoms into Vita-Link's diagnostics, and a potential range of diagnoses are output to that customer. If the customer wishes to purchase the second layer of service, a medical practitioner will come online and discuss the symptoms with them. Customers pay via PayPal for each level of service and time online served.

Required: Answer the following:

    a Identify risks for the business related to its system that could be of concern to the auditor.

    b What duties should be segregated in a computerised accounting system for Vita-Link to ensure good internal control?

   c What online and other controls may be advised to:

     i establish controls over the customer's first-stage payment

     ii establish controls over the liability of the diagnostic program

     iii maintain controls over the receipt of payment through to its proper recording

     iv verify and enable the auditor to examine the payment system?

11.9 **ACCOUNTING CONTROLS:** Identify controls to prevent or detect the following unrelated computerised system problems.

   a A sales administrator enters the selling price as $46.90 instead of $469.00. No product for the company sells for less than $200.

   b Desk staff work three eight-hour shifts in a resort complex and make sales entries into its system. The internal auditor is concerned that accounts receivable records should be updated before successful reconciliation by the last shift.

   c Bank customers have access to their account balances but should not be able to change them.

   d We are not confident that the new program will manipulate data as authorised.

   e File data may be lost because of frequent access.

   f The client's main office is located in New Zealand's Chatham Islands, where power outages are common.

Internal control and the auditor

Learning objectives

After studying the material in this chapter, you should be able to:

- describe an appropriate strategy to evaluate a client's control system for audit
- prepare and evaluate documentation methods such as system flowcharts and data flow diagrams using the procedures introduced
- select and describe tests of controls in response to the auditor's evaluation of the client's internal control system.

Introduction

This chapter is about internal controls and when audit tests should be performed on them. Auditing standards define the frame of interest:

> For [these] purposes ... the system of internal control consists of five interrelated components: (i) Control environment; (ii) Entity's risk assessment process; (iii) Entity's process to monitor the system of internal control; (iv) Information system and communication; and (v) Control activities. (ASA 315, para 12m; ISA NZ 315, para 12m)

Here, we consider how to incorporate control-testing decisions into the audit strategy and plan (see **Figure 12.1**). We introduce fundamental controls and consider whether tests of the client's controls allow the auditor to reduce the nature, timing or extent of substantive testing.

This chapter introduces two documentation methods that we ask you to learn to use. Overall, the chapter introduces procedures to understand and evaluate that portion of the client's system of concern to the financial statement auditor.

Audit strategy and the client's system

As part of the audit risk analysis, the auditor should assess the risks of material statement at both the 'overall financial report level; and the assertion level for classes of transactions, account balances and disclosures' (ASA 315, para 2; ISA NZ 315, para 2). This, in effect, requires the auditor to assess the client's control systems around financial transactions and account balances to assess auditability and to reach an audit strategy.

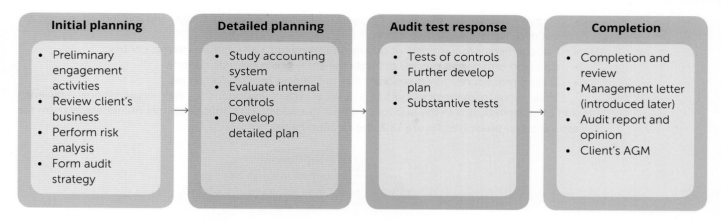

Figure 12.1 Steps in an audit process

Controls and auditability

As part of the planning phase of an audit engagement, the auditors will normally conduct a preliminary review of *essential* or *fundamental controls* with a view to determining whether they are adequate to provide the basis for the preparation of financial statements. Fundamental controls usually comprise, at a minimum:

- *policy* – formal systems, documents and records that are sufficiently documented (or in databases) to ensure that procedures are known and available
- *approvals* – authorisation protocols, particularly over initial recordings of transactions
- *independence* – segregation of incompatible functions, particularly in the raising of documentation for transactions.

The *completeness* assertion can be difficult to test if the client's system lacks essential elements of control. For example, in a retail business with cash sales, substantive tests may provide evidence of the accuracy and occurrence-validity of money deposited but cannot provide comfort in relation to whether all takings were deposited in the till if the clerk did not record them (completeness).

Suppose the preliminary review indicates an absence of fundamental controls. In that case, the auditors will need to consider whether to withdraw from the engagement until the accounting system has been rendered reliable or, alternatively, anticipate a qualified audit report (disclaimer). The client should be advised of this fact as early as possible so that they have a chance to find remedies. It is noted that the necessity for such extreme action would be comparatively rare.

CONCEPT QUESTION 1 What are 'fundamental controls' and why are they important?

Controls and process

As a reminder, internal control systems have inherent limitations. Internal control is a management tool and exists to serve the client organisation, whether that is to inform marketing, to improve pricing policies, to refine stock and supply chain practices, or to improve manufacturing efficiencies. The interests of the external auditor may be secondary. So, the auditor should select controls of interest so that:

- testing costs are proportional to the potential loss that may result from that control's absence
- controls tend to be directed at routine transactions, not unusual or adjusting transactions

- human carelessness, mistakes of judgement (such as in system design) and misunderstandings are not necessarily caught by controls
- management, programmers or others with 'oversight' can override internal controls
- collusion with parties outside or inside the entity could override controls
- control procedures may deteriorate due to business or system changes.

Thus, while management's interest is in a system important to their organisational efficiency and effectiveness, it is in the auditor's interest to evaluate only those controls of interest to them for assurance purposes (see **Figure 12.2**, the smallest circle).

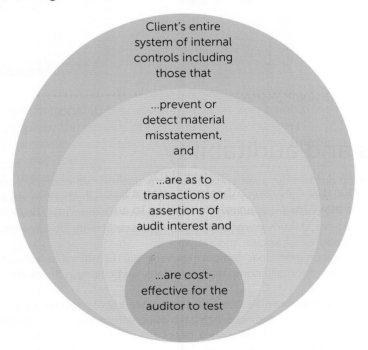

Client's entire system of internal controls including those that

...prevent or detect material misstatement, and

...are as to transactions or assertions of audit interest and

...are cost-effective for the auditor to test

Figure 12.2 Controls of interest to the auditor

Auditing in practice

Controls of interest

If there is an internal control regulating purchasing efficiencies in the client's system, the auditor will probably not examine it because it would not prevent or detect errors in the accounts. On the other hand, controls that ensure that large asset purchases are capitalised (classified) are of interest to the auditor because of the financial statement implications.

Case law has confirmed the value of testing controls in situations that have come before the courts. For example, Justice Moffitt (in the *Pacific Acceptance* case) confirmed that the auditors' examination should cover the whole of the financial year, and examining controls are an important means of accomplishing this. The *H E Kane* case, in which transactions were made up for (and others eliminated from) the system, confirms the importance of controls for *completeness* and *occurrence-validity*.

Practices will continue to evolve even as controls are externalised through, for example, enterprise resource planning (ERP) systems, blockchains, AI and cloud computing. Irrespective of the system, audit strategy decisions evolve from the nature of the client's internal control systems in the manner and process illustrated in **Figure 12.3**.

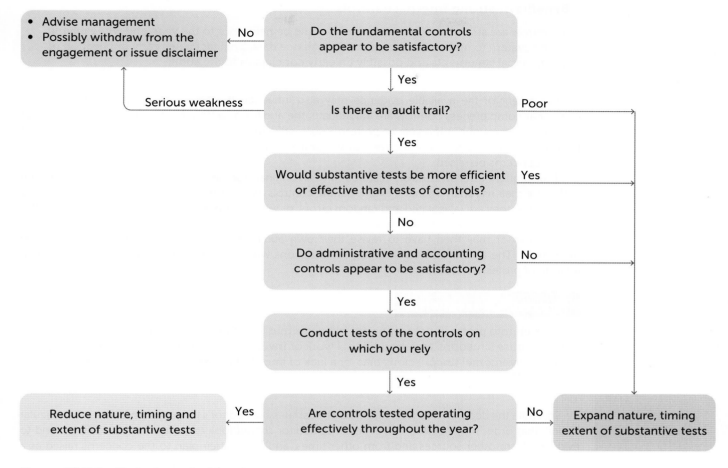

Figure 12.3 Audit strategy decision tree

The auditor must make strategic decisions about the balance to be achieved between the testing of controls and the conduct of substantive tests based on these decisions, always particular to each client and each audit year. We can also return to the audit risk model to illustrate the effects of each strategy:

$$STR = OAR/(IR \times CR \times APR)$$

So, assuming that overall audit risk must remain the same, less reliance on the client's controls means that substantive testing will have to be extended, and vice versa.

Controls and timing

Internal control reliance will also have a major influence on the *timing of tests of controls*. If the auditor is satisfied that the internal control system is working effectively throughout the year, then less end-period testing may be needed. The auditor may rely on the system to perform some verification procedures prior to the year-end.

The extent of the available evidence may also influence the *timing of substantive tests*. In the event that completeness controls are inadequate, the auditor may have to attend the client's premises early and/or throughout the year to perform substantive tests on transactions as they occur. It is also important to reconsider the effectiveness of controls during, before and/or after system changes or should concerns be raised.

If subsequent tests on controls fail to confirm an original assessment, the auditor may have to return and revise their risk analysis. In the event that the controls are no longer reliable, the auditor should find out whether they are (a) isolated and random errors, or whether there is (b) a pattern to them (the latter is more likely to have a material impact).

The auditor may then have to revise their own audit strategy and plan in light of unexpected discoveries. The auditor's ability to recognise situations which require revision are fundamental to an attitude of professional scepticism.

Professional scepticism

Research into professional scepticism indicates that to 'influence the ability of an auditor to recognise situations where additional work or investigation is required, [the auditor may have to overcome] unconscious bias, or a lack of knowledge, experience or expertise'. (Hurtt et al., 2013, p. 72)

So, while the decision tree (see **Figure 12.3**) illustrates the auditor's judgement process in a particular 'order', that order may need to be revised. The auditor should look to their own 'gut feelings', and to evidence from other sources and from other times, and adjust their plan to the concerns raised as a result.

Documentation: Studying the system

The process whereby controls are documented is the topic of the sections that follow. The client's control system, or parts of it, must be understood before tests can be chosen. Methods to document a client's control system for audit analysis can include the following:

- *Narrative notes:* The auditor's written notes are adaptable to different audit situations, but they can be cumbersome to use, inconsistent in form, and difficult to interpret and review. It is also challenging to identify from them whether any part of the system has been omitted. Narrative notes used alone may be appropriate for small business audits or to describe overall systems in larger enterprises.
- *Internal control questionnaires (ICQs):* These are pre-printed documents asking specific questions, as per a checklist, to which a negative answer normally implies a weakness in control. ICQs help ensure that all basic control points are considered, but they are not efficient, nor necessarily effective, because they can be very cumbersome and are not risk-adjusted to each particular client's system.
- *Flowcharts:* These are a graphic representation or a picture of the flow of documents and data through an accounting system. Flowcharts illustrate incomplete processes because a missed stage

results in the flow line simply stopping mid-page. The method also eliminates the need for a lengthy narrative and facilitates the identification of, in particular, segregation of duties among personnel. While the method can be cumbersome, flowcharts are widely regarded as an important tool in the evaluation of systems.

- *Data flow diagrams (DFDs):* DFDs or bubble charts are widely used in external auditing. They tend to be quicker to develop, prepared even while listening to an employee describe their system. They allow the auditor to concentrate on data flows of interest rather than all of the system's activities, and they are suited to IT and CIS.

You should not assume that these techniques are mutually exclusive. Indeed, all of them may be used for any one audit. Also, different audit firms adopt different policies about their use and style. We now introduce two relatively straightforward methods, both of which focus on audit interest, so that you can become familiar with the process for exercises that are yet to appear.

To begin any documentation, the auditor will perform *walk-through procedures* to find out how data is captured and processed. Remember, walk-throughs are for understanding, not testing – they are used to illustrate what *is claimed to have occurred*.

Auditing in practice

Computer audit issue

It may not be possible to trace an individual transaction in an IT system, but it will usually be sufficient to trace the items to batch inputs or computer-produced outputs, a process termed 'auditing around the computer'.

The auditor does not usually rewrite system descriptions each year, but their accuracy is important, so inquiries should be made as to any changes that may have occurred. The danger of performing an audit based on outdated understandings of the client's system should be avoided to prevent a negligent audit.

The following offers the basic knowledge needed to prepare flowcharts and DFDs. This will be used here and in later chapters to analyse accounting systems and controls.

Flowcharts

The type of flowchart style illustrated in the sections to follow is relatively simple, using fewer symbols than more complex flowchart methods (a complexity which we have found is not needed for audit purposes generally). To obtain value from it, you are advised to familiarise yourself with the symbols even if you are familiar with an alternative method. The symbols, together with the accompanying narrative and format, are similar to those used by at least one major audit firm.

Flowcharts will usually be prepared for any part of an accounting system that processes large volumes of transactions, and that can be segregated by management responsibility. Common segments include the sales 'cycle', the purchases 'cycle' or the wages 'cycle', but a segment can also be a subset of these systems.

For the convenience of preparation and review, it is necessary to prepare one section of a system independently of the others but to link them by cross-referencing, especially in such obvious areas of overlap as purchases/stock.

The information for the preparation of the charts will come from management, so it is necessary to confirm that the details are correct because you may be given wrong information – not necessarily because management wishes to deceive, but simply because managers themselves may have an incorrect understanding of how the systems actually work.

Without strong controls or system mapping (e.g., such as using Promapp digital applications), systems that are in use can be gradually changed without authorisation or awareness of managers. These changes can go unnoticed by senior officials, especially in the absence of an internal audit. Hence, it is important for the auditors to perform tests of controls.

Showing the separation of functions

If you look at the sample flowchart reproduced in **Figure 12.4**, you will see separate columns for each function, identified across the top of the page. These emphasise the division of responsibilities (segregation of duties). It may be sufficient to record the work of a whole department in one column, or it may be necessary to record the work of each individual within the department, depending on the client's authorisation structure and what the auditors want to know.

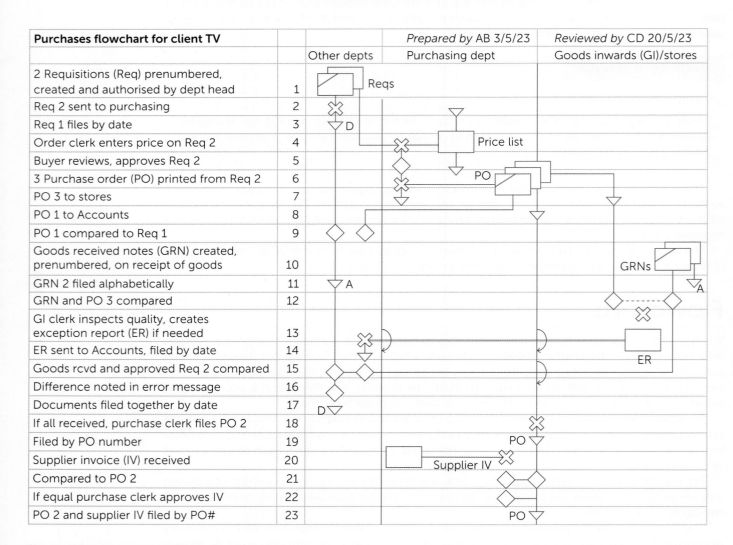

Purchases flowchart for client TV			*Prepared by* AB 3/5/23	*Reviewed by* CD 20/5/23
		Other depts	Purchasing dept	Goods inwards (GI)/stores
2 Requisitions (Req) prenumbered, created and authorised by dept head	1	Reqs		
Req 2 sent to purchasing	2			
Req 1 files by date	3	D		
Order clerk enters price on Req 2	4		Price list	
Buyer reviews, approves Req 2	5			
3 Purchase order (PO) printed from Req 2	6		PO	
PO 3 to stores	7			
PO 1 to Accounts	8			
PO 1 compared to Req 1	9			
Goods received notes (GRN) created, prenumbered, on receipt of goods	10			GRNs
GRN 2 filed alphabetically	11	A		
GRN and PO 3 compared	12			
GI clerk inspects quality, creates exception report (ER) if needed	13			
ER sent to Accounts, filed by date	14			ER
Goods rcvd and approved Req 2 compared	15			
Difference noted in error message	16			
Documents filed together by date	17	D		
If all received, purchase clerk files PO 2	18			
Filed by PO number	19		PO	
Supplier invoice (IV) received	20		Supplier IV	
Compared to PO 2	21			
If equal purchase clerk approves IV	22			
PO 2 and supplier IV filed by PO#	23		PO	

Figure 12.4 Flowchart example

Showing the flow and processing of documents

Continuous lines show document or data flow. Vertical lines indicate what occurs over time, whereas horizontal lines either show 'internal checks' or the movement of documents or data from one area to another.

Usual practice has the flow moving from top left down the page to lower right, though this can vary. Diagonal lines should *not* be used as they create confusion. You should also avoid having crossing document flow lines. If this cannot be avoided, crossings can be denoted by a 'bridge' symbol (see **Figure 12.4**).

A broken horizontal line can be used to show information flow or a comparison check. Some examples include preparing one document using the information contained in another, posting a ledger account, or checking one document against another. A 'lightning' symbol can be used to indicate non-manual data transmission, as shown here.

Showing the documents and books of account

Documents or books should only be shown once when they are first set up, and the title should be entered close alongside. Where documents are brought forward from previous charts, or where the charts have become very complicated, it may be appropriate to restate the document via 'ghosting', as in the second example:

It would not be appropriate to show an unbroken square again, for this would imply that a new document was being introduced. Where documents are transferred from one chart to another, the following connector symbol can be used (at the bottom of the page):

If multiple documents are prepared, this should be shown in the following way:

A 'diagonal' line in the corner indicates prenumbered documents. This is a type of 'internal check' if the prenumbered documents are regularly accounted for.

Showing operations and checks

An internal check is distinguished from an operation because it has special audit significance; that is, it is evidence of the existence of a control. For this reason, the 'diamond' should be used for when a check occurs and an 'X' should be used for an operation that does not include an internal check.

Operation ✕   Check (internal check) ◇

However, if the comparison checks only one document, then a combination (both a diamond and an 'X') may be appropriate. The 'filing' of a document is depicted by an inverted triangle, against which letters can be placed to symbolise filing by date, name, or invoice or order number (D, N, I/Iv, PO) (see **Figure 12.4**).

Where documents are received from, or sent, outside the client, an arrow can be used with a narrative description of the source destination. That is, the 'outside' data or document need not be specified except in a description, because the concern is with what happens to information when it arrives in your client's system. Where documents are destroyed, the word 'destroyed' is normally written at the end of the flow line (as it can indicate a loss of accountability).

You will note from the flowchart example in **Figure 12.4** that sufficient space has been left for a narrative down the left-hand side of the page. In the main, the symbols are sufficient to indicate the flow of documents or data, but a brief note for each action helps explain their precise nature, and details of the person performing the tasks could be included. The narrative must be made immediately opposite the relevant step on the chart and should be numbered accordingly. For this reason, you should write the narrative as you draw the chart.

In the purchasing system, we show that internal checks are illustrated with diamonds, whereas duty segregation is apparent by the use of columns. (Further diagrams are presented in the systems chapters later in this text.)

The flowchart, including the style taught here, illustrates what controls may be missing as well as those that may be present. For example, **Figure 12.4** may prompt the auditor to ask the following questions about concerns that it raises:

- Is the price list updated and accessible by password to authorised employees?
- What occurs if the PO and Req. do not match?
- Are exception reports, error messages and prenumbered documents checked for completeness or validity?
- Should the Purchasing Department be receiving the supplier invoice?

This is the format we will use throughout the text. Additional symbols can be added, but by combining the 'narrative' and the symbols, no more should be necessary.

Data flow diagrams (DFDs)

Flowcharts are acceptable for understanding the movement of pieces of paper, files and some data, but they are not ideal for all needs. Auditors who use flowcharts for analysis have to determine whether input or storage is data on paper, hard drives, off-site drives or the cloud. This forces the auditor to ask about components that may be audit-irrelevant. Nor do the flow lines identify the data structure or data that moves between processes. A most basic piece of data that cannot be broken into more detailed units is considered a **data item**. By contrast, each flow line in a DFD is labelled to identify the **data structure** moving from one process to another.

We recommend the DFD for documenting IT systems, particularly ebusiness systems in which transactions occur outside of any documentation.

Data flow diagram symbols and diagrams

Only four symbols are used in our DFD method, showing the flow of data through a system and identifying the system's **datastores** (see **Figure 12.5**).[1] An external entity (e.g., customers, suppliers, or other transaction divisions internal to the client) is the originator or receiver of data, but lying as they do outside the boundary, externals are not included in any one DFD. Source data may originate from, or go to, an external entity (including those external to this particular subsystem).

---

[1] For styles in addition to those shown here, see, for example, Bodnar and Hopwood (2001).

data item
The most basic piece of data that cannot be broken into more detailed units. It also may be called a *data element* or a *field*.

data structure
A meaningful combination of data items. Data structures also are referred to as *records*.

datastore
A temporary or permanent storage position for data structures and/or data items within a system. A datastore may be manual (physical) – e.g., the storage of a piece of paper or a form in a file cabinet; or it may be computerised (electronic) – e.g., the storage of data on a microcomputer diskette or a DBMS on a hard drive.

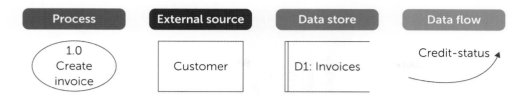

Figure 12.5 DFD symbols and examples

Evidence of payment and billing

Source data may be evidence of payment from the client's Finance Division to Sales, and outputs may be the billings to customers from the Sales Division.

Looking at the four symbols: The rectangular box identifies external entities, such as PURCHASING DEPARTMENT or CUSTOMER for a SALES DEPARTMENT.

A process is depicted by a circle. Processes portray the transformation of data, so they should always include a verb, such as 'VERIFY CUSTOMER CREDIT' or 'CREATE INVOICE'. The verb describes what *happens* to the data.

Each process symbol has a unique identification number (such as 1.0, 2.0 or 3.0) that can be used to distinguish it from all other processes in the DFD. Process numbering is done according to a decimal system to facilitate the layering or partitioning of the data-flow-diagram process.

A DFD starts to reveal the system's controls once it is layered into lower-level diagrams. Flowcharts force auditors to simultaneously document what is being done and how it is being done. DFDs show what is being done, at the macro level, first.

A datastore symbol represents a manual or computerised database in which data resides. This may be temporary or permanent storage. In manual systems, datastores may be paper reports, filing cabinets, microfiche, card files, rotary files, shelves or even 'George's in-tray'. Computerised systems may be computer drives, offline storage facilities, or a sophisticated relational DBMS.

Datastores are identified by alphanumeric designations (D1, D2 or D3), just as processes are numbered 1.0, 2.0, 3.0 etc. A meaningful name should be assigned that identifies the contents of the individual database, filing cabinet or paper in the datastore. For example, a datastore might be labelled D1: INVOICES. Another datastore might contain completed purchase orders and be named similarly; for example, D2: PURCHASE ORDERS, COMPLETED.

A data flow symbol (curved arrow) is used to show the flow of data between process bubbles, external entities or datastores. You should note that a data flow must always flow to or from a process. So, for example, CREDIT-STATUS is data to which some process (e.g., checking) is applied. The name or content of the data flow is indicated next to the flow line.

Data flows can be from physical sources, such as letters, invoices, purchase orders or credit requests, but they only refer to the 'data' of concern. So, for example, an invoice may include 'authorisation', 'numbers purchased', 'item prices' or 'total sales amount'. Data in a DFD should be specific and only refer to *one* of those at any one time.

Context diagrams

You start the DFDs by producing a context diagram. the context diagram (see **Figure 12.6**) provides a broad overview of the system and its boundary. Anything external to that system would be placed in

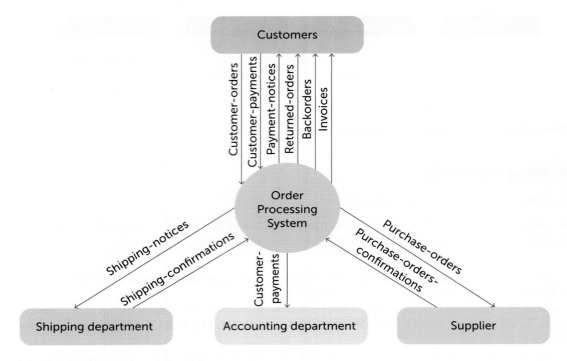

Figure 12.6 Context diagram for DFDs

the box. So, for example, CUSTOMERS, SHIPPING DEPARTMENT, ACCOUNTING DEPARTMENT and SUPPLIER are all external to our ORDER PROCESSING SYSTEM, but they should be shown to illustrate how this system is related to others. If the ACCOUNTING DEPARTMENT actually is part of the audited system, then it should be within one of the round bubbles.

Anyone who reviews a context diagram – such as your audit manager – can quickly see the name of the system that is being audited, the major data flows into and out of that system, and the external entities that interface with the audited system. It gives them context within a complicated system.

Layering or partitioning

Once the auditor has identified the system's boundary in the context diagram, *layering* is done to shift through the details. The first layer is a level 0 DFD (see **Figure 12.7**). A level 0 diagram shows the main processes that transform the data in some manner, and it also shows the storage or transfer of this data when it is processed. That is, this is a new *layer* partitioning the circle within context diagram. Bubbles in a level 0 DFD represent a subsystem that can also be layered, allowing them to show whatever level of detail is needed.

This is followed by level 1 DFDs and then level 2 DFDs, each focusing on one particular bubble of interest to the auditor. This layering is useful for the auditor, who has to focus only on certain aspects of the client's control system. So, while the context diagram and level 0 DFDs are useful for understanding the larger system, layering starts to reveal the controls. Take note of the following characteristics of DFDs:

- Each data flow line has the name of the data structure flowing through that part of the system. The data name can be related to a paper document, such as CUSTOMER-ORDER or, for example, a user's request for data (USER-REQUEST).

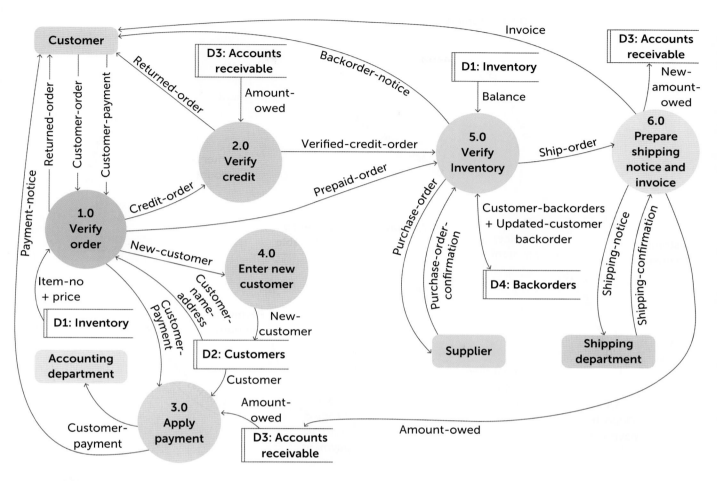

Figure 12.7 DFD diagram: Level 0

- Each process is numbered sequentially and identified using a verb and object. The auditor might wish to add the name of a responsible part within the process bubble.
- Each external entity is identified by a meaningful name.
- Each datastore is identified by letter and number (D1, D2 etc.) and name. A datastore may be computerised, cloud-based or in hardcopy (such as in a filing cabinet)

Figure 12.8 shows the next layer – a level 1 DFD – for a system having five processes.

Let us assume that the auditor needs more detail on process 3.2. The level 2 DFD (see **Figure 12.9**) is a further layering of what bubble 3.2 does, showing some controls and leading to questions as indicated.

Because this technique uses only four symbols and the data flow lines are curved (easy to draw), sketching a preliminary DFD while interviewing or during walk-throughs is possible; it can be 'tidied up' at a later time.

In summary, combining a context diagram and layering provides auditors with a cost-effective tool to document those parts of a client's control system on which the auditor may rely. Three levels of layering are described in **Table 12.1**.

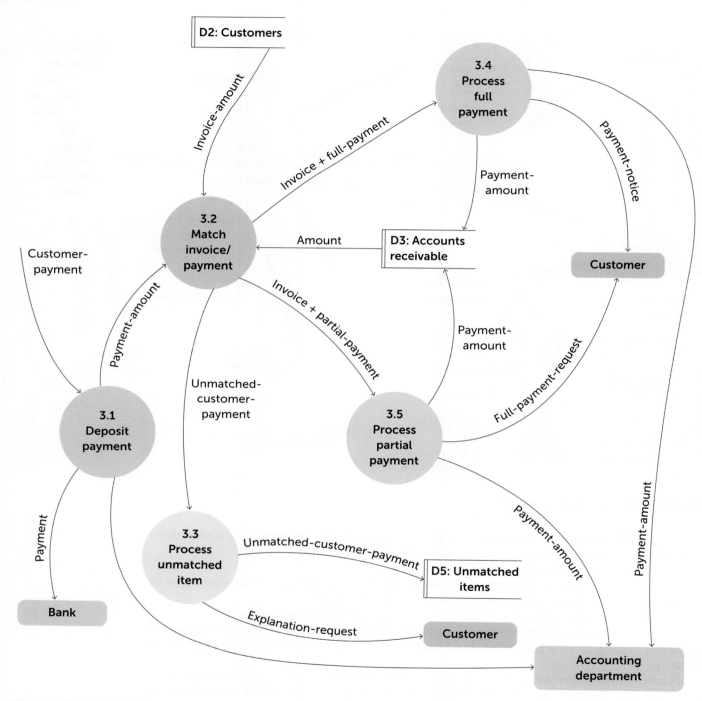

Figure 12.8 DFD diagram: Level 1

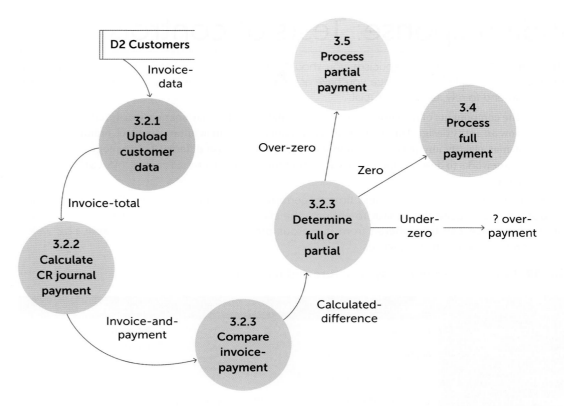

Figure 12.9 DFD diagram: Level 2

Table 12.1 Levels of detail in data flow diagramming

Type of DFD	Level of detail
Context diagram	Overview – represents the scope or boundary of the audit.
Level 0 diagram	System view – pictorially describes the entire system on a single sheet of paper. All 'major' processes, datastores and data flows are shown.
Levels 1, 2 etc.	Detailed – only processes as required for audit are partitioned to this level.

System documentation can take quite a bit of auditor time, particularly for a new client. Once you're into consecutive audits for the same client, however, it may be possible to update existing documents using inquiry and ICQs, and this usually takes less time. This is one reason the auditor hopes to retain their client from year to year, as documenting the systems of a new client can be time-consuming and expensive. Once the client's system is documented, it is possible for the auditor to test those controls on which they intend to rely.

CONCEPT QUESTION 2	In a data flow diagram, what is the meaning of 'partitioning' or 'layering'?

Audit response: Tests of controls

In the interest of professional scepticism, you should not assume that what a client *tells you* about a control is actually taking place. Once you have assessed the control risks and know the controls on which you intend to rely, testing is crucial.

> The components of the entity's system of internal control … may not necessarily reflect how an entity designs, implements and maintains its system of internal control, or how it may classify any particular component. Entities may use different terminology or frameworks to describe the various aspects of the system of internal control. (ASA 315, para A91)

Some tests of control may take less time to perform than a substantive test. Others take longer, particularly if they require the auditor to evaluate the client's programs. Audit evidence as to internal control compliance can be gathered from numerous procedures, as classified in **Table 12.2** within system structure and control objectives.

Table 12.2 Control categories by structure and purpose

	Establishment	Maintenance	Verification
Organisational	Governance		Internal audit and internal checks
Management	Segregation of duties		
Systems	Systems development		
Accounting	External services	Accounting process	

Each is discussed next, incorporating tests of controls and examples of controls in tables.

Governance: Testing and evidence

> To ensure audit quality, directors and audit committees may consider certain good practice matters when: recommending the appointment of an auditor to members, assessing potential and continuing auditors, facilitating the audit process, communicating with the auditor, maintaining auditor independence [and] assessing audit quality. (ASIC, 2021)

Cyber risk is increasing, and protecting an organisation's knowledge, personnel data and knowledge-based assets is a growing role of the governing body. The auditors can reasonably expect that an organisation's *Audit Committee* or *Audit Risk Committee* will have incorporated cyber risk policy into their practice. An organisational chart is also useful, to determine who is responsible for various authorisations.

In terms of testing, the auditor may – after inquiring – inspect board policy, board committee documents, minutes and cyber risk policy. Inquiry and inspection could include security software scope and contracts.

Segregation of duties: Tests of controls

The *flowchart*, *ICQs* and *DFDs* are tools to identify what segregation of duties is said to be in place. Audit tests of compliance with them could include observation (such as observing people doing tasks or operating in certain locations). Other tests of controls may be electronic, such as using *dummy data* or looking at *access logs* to attempt to access a function or system to which the user should not have access.

Separating authorisation functions – purchase order authorisation, bad debt write-offs or customer credit approvals – may be done manually by an employee or 'built into' the IT system. There should also be a segregation of those who handle assets (cash or bank, fixed assets or stock) from those who authorise input or handle output. Separating employment records and employment authorisation are other examples.

Tests of controls may involve reviewing 'approval' e-signatures or examining policies. Auditors may have to inspect passwords and digital readers, vouch or trace samples, or examine exception reports, employment policy or trial intrusions to test them (see **Table 12.3**).

Table 12.3 Tests of control examples over segregation of duties

Control said to exist	Evidence of control: Verification	Test of control possibility
Store-front staff cannot access stock	Password-protected digital entry card includes access approval for stock staff only	Review program authorisation; run dummy data Review exception reports
Sales staff cannot access journal input	Online access logs are used to show who was on the site and at what time	Examine a sample of logs for unusual entries Inspect exception reports
Management delegates system development tasks	Any system development tasks are signed off with e-signatures	Inspect development task sign-offs

Systems development: Tests of controls

Where there are comprehensive manual controls, the auditors may not examine the computer directly. In all cases, however, it will be necessary to review the systems development controls, including those over changes to the system. The auditor may need to be present during any change, or be able to trust the client's internal audit department to oversee control and risk management. Testing could include parallel runs of data, intrusion attempts or simply observation. Auditors will normally review all exception reports generated by the system as well, since this is where information is provided about unusual transactions.

External services: Tests of controls

External parties may provide database management, apps or other software. External parties may provide Internet access; server support; payroll, stock or tax system software; cloud computing; system development support; or off-site datastores. Clients may obtain complex services at a reasonable cost and obtain the benefit of external expertise.

Control issues do emerge. The services of any external provider could have, or lack, controls leading to a material effect on the financial statements. If so, the auditors should consider the following:

- *Ownership and stability* – Does the external provider have suitable financial backing to make using it a long-term, viable proposition? Is it regularly updated?
- *Location* – Is the location of the external party such that it guarantees the performance of processing within the time schedule under all conditions (e.g., bad weather, power failures, strikes etc.)? Is it accessible to the client?
- *Backup (stand-by)* – Has the external party got stand-by arrangements to ensure continuity of processing within the during communication or system failure?
- *Documentation, education and programs* – Does the external party provide the client with systems and program documentation and user manuals? It may be important to know who owns the programs, the extent to which they are reviewed, and how changes are authorised, made and documented.

Table 12.4 Tests of control examples over development and external services

Control said to exist	Evidence of control: Verification	Test of control possibility
Purchased payroll package is updated	Provider sends update information; payroll tests update before and after change	Review evidence for existence of before-after tests on payroll data; compare to update 'dates'
ERP system is protected by insurance	Insurance policy	Inspect insurance policy
Revisions to sales program tested	Parallel running for two weeks following any change	Inspect evidence of two weeks of parallel processing following any system changes
Systems changes only in controlled environment	Performed after 9 p.m., internal auditor present	Attend, or inspect evidence of these conditions existing

- *Liability* – What is the liability of the external provider for loss of data or fraud? The auditors may be concerned with the external provider's solvency or insurance coverage as well.
- *Control* – Is there evidence of controls that are designed to protect access to, and modifications of, data? What controls are there over stored data, and are error and exception reports produced? Similar concerns would exist over standard application packages as well as external provider-designed programs.

The use of externals by the auditor's client does not reduce the auditor's obligation to come to an opinion on them even where such systems are outside the client's direct control. ISA NZ 610: Using the work of an expert auditor applies to the use of a range of other and external experts.

The principles of audit testing are the same as for in-house installations, but there will be practical challenges. Those to whom the client is contracted have no obligation in law to give the auditor access to data or processes – this may have to be arranged ahead of time. Testing may be restricted to inquiry and inspection of outputs. Permission for audit testing may need to be prearranged. In one respect, of course, the auditors can rely on greater control – an external provider is more likely to be independent of the client. **Table 12.4** provides examples of tests of control over development and external services.

Accounting process: Tests of controls

> While emerging technologies may be seen to be more sophisticated or more complex compared to existing technologies, the auditor's responsibilities in relation to IT applications and identified general IT controls ... remain unchanged. (ASA 315, appendix 5, para 5)

You have been introduced to a multitude of controls, any of which may need to be tested. A few additional testing approaches are also important to the auditor and so are discussed here. They have to do with: utilities in the client's system, portable components, auditing through or around systems, and internal checks.

Using client utilities

The client's utility programs can be particularly useful for performing substantive tests. Data can be downloaded from client platforms, and calculations re-performed and compared to the client's results. The client's production of relevant *exception, error reports* or *logs* – themselves – can be subject to tests. The auditor should always review exception, error and limit check report logs in any case, as they can identify actions that lie outside that which is authorised – actions auditors would wish to know about. However, such reports will only catch what errors are programmed into them, as the 'Auditing in practice' box here shows.

Error in client's software

The credit manager relies on their app to produce a limited check of accounts unpaid after 90 days. The programmer made an error, however, and entered 120 days into the algorithm. This means that accounts between 91 and 120 days late were not flagged. The auditor reviewed the limit check listing but failed to identify $200 000 of debt that should have been expensed as 'bad debt'.

The client's use of continuous audit and testing modules can also be used by the external auditor. So, using continuous audit, client data is tested even as it is being processed. Embedded in the client program is the capacity to download data, re-perform the operation and/or confirm its reasonableness. Error or exception messages can be produced. Many large companies use continuous auditing so that they can respond to demands for continuous reporting and costing. An *internal audit* function can ensure that the client process includes reasonableness tests, limit tests, echo checks or other controls together with logs.

If trusted, and if relevant to financial statements, it may also be relied on by the external auditor to reduce their tests of control. The external auditor should determine the experience and skills of the internal audit team and the quality of its practices before relying on it. Testing procedures to do so may include inquiry, inspection of policies and backgrounds, and testing of the client's processes or log reviews. A qualified internal audit function, which is relatively independent of the organisation's own management, can potentially considerably reduce the external audit cost.

Small component testing

Laptops, tablets and mobile devices use application programs (apps) that tend to be flexible and easy to acquire and operate. Access and input are usually simple in the extreme, often determined or limited by the user, and output is immediately visible.

While this is convenient for the user, it can be a nightmare for the auditor. Business knowledge and assets can be in the back pocket of any employee, whether at work or at home. Because of small components' phone-like character (but computer-like capability), management may not realise the need for controls over them. As you know, however, the potential for information loss or fraud from their misuse is significant.

Access to organisational assets and personnel (private) information is a concern. Controls may involve careful records for mobile phone distribution and return, just like keys to a storeroom would be checked out and checked in on redundancy. App and data selection and use may need similar oversight.

Control testing may involve inspecting or testing physical component or app access policy and practice, and security software policy and practice, and log testing to see if those policies are being carried out. Computers can be tested using test packs and by reviewing exception or error reports (if produced). An examination of the browser history can be made, if necessary, for unusual types or timing of events. These tests can be costly, and privacy may be an issue, but equally they may be the only way to determine the *existence*, *rights/obligations* or *validity/occurrence* of some select transactions or assets.

Auditing 'through' or 'around'?

Auditors must also decide whether to audit 'through' or 'around' the client's system. Much of the data the auditors need may only be held in digital form (particularly if an internal auditor is not involved to ensure auditability.). The auditor must decide whether to test the client's internal controls (or data in a substantive test) by studying the client's programs and processes (*through*) or by auditing *around* the system. The latter involves re-performing transactions separately from the client's system and comparing results to the client's results, or using *test data* to see what the system will do with it (see **Figure 12.10**).

Figure 12.10 Auditing 'through' and 'around' the computer

In most cases, it may be more economical to audit *around* the computer, although it may be necessary to audit *through* studying the program, where system fraud is a concern.

Test packs consist of test data that, though not real client data, can be processed in the same way. The data may either be fictitious, invented by the auditors, or genuine data selected prior to processing. Test pack data will normally fall both outside the control parameters (to trigger an error report) and within parameters (to be processed normally). If the results are satisfactory, the auditors may then be satisfied that the controls are operating effectively.

Internal checks

The client's employees may perform internal checks, such as manually comparing sales pre-lists to sales data processed, verifying their action with initials or e-signatures. Testing is a process of inspecting the documents for signatures or cancellation marks.

Internal electronic checks are now common as well. To compensate for the loss of audit trails, alternative tests must be considered. The most valuable computerised controls are those that are well documented and installed during program development. For example, internal checks that re-perform input calculations ensure some *accuracy*.

With the advent of apps and cloud-based software, many of the internal check procedures will be embedded in the client's (or an external) program. It may be only substantive tests that can test their performance.

Table 12.5 offers examples of controls and tests over the accounting process.

Table 12.5 Tests of control examples for accounting process and communication

Control said to exist	Evidence of control: Verification	Test of control possibility
Cash reconciled daily to receipts	Reconciliations are printed and filed by date	Review for existence of reconciliations
Sales invoice price totals are re-performed	Sales clerk inserts √ at the base of each invoice re-performed	Look for √ on a sample of sales invoices
No sales over $300 by store-front staff	Program limit check prevents sale if over $300	Run dummy variables at $299 and $301 to test this control Inspect exception reports
All sales journalised and posted	Record counts before input and after posting compared	Inspect evidence of comparison made
No sales made outside store hours	Error reports issued if attempts made before 8 a.m. or after 5 p.m.	Try to make a sale before 8 p.m. or after 5 p.m.; review error reports

All sales invoices accounted for	Sales invoices prenumbered, counted and documented daily	Inspect sample of documents for evidence of these checks
Sales numbers all recorded	Record checks, compare entries to invoices processed	Dummy data for existence of record checks, or observe if manual
Sales price changes made after closure	Exception reports issued for changes made at other times	Examine exception reports Use test data to try changes early
Credit check data emailed from bank	Echo check confirms category sent is category received	Inspect sample of ledgers for evidence of transmission echo check
Receivables > 90 days of concern	Exception report discloses such debts; accounts manager contacts customer	Inspect exception reports Inspect evidence of customer follow-up

CONCEPT QUESTION 3   What are 'test packs' and how do they serve the auditor?

Study tools

Summary

This chapter drew on the understanding of control systems to show how the external financial statement auditor makes audit strategy decisions and becomes involved in documenting and testing the client's controls relevant to their work.

Techniques for constructing flowcharts and DFDs were presented. Categories related to the structure of organisations and the objectives of reports were used to introduce a range of audit-testing techniques. Examples of controls, and tests of controls, were provided. Analysing and testing a client's controls can be a time-consuming element of the audit process. Careful attention to 'cost' while retaining audit 'effectiveness' is the key to a non-negligent audit.

Case/resources link

CAATs for Classrooms

Accompanying this book is a series of data, integrated worksheets and exercises that are designed to support your learning and give you exposure to hands-on audit decision-making dilemmas faced by auditors in the planning elements of the audit process. Acquire the relevant material for this chapter from your instructor.

Review questions

12.1   What controls belonging to the client are of interest to the auditor?

12.2   What are the limitations to internal control?

12.3   Identify 2–3 fundamental controls and describe why they are fundamental.

12.4   Under what conditions are auditors likely to rely on the client's internal controls?

12.5 Define and describe the two strategy categories the auditor may employ, and state when one or the other is more likely to be employed.

12.6 Relative to all of the client's controls, what controls are of interest to the external auditor?

12.7 Explain how internal control influences audit testing.

12.8 Explain how a reliance on internal control can influence audit effectiveness.

12.9 Describe governing body controls about which auditors may be concerned.

12.10 Describe how each of the following methods of documenting a client's system of internal controls is conducted and when each might be used:

   a narrative notes

   b internal control questionnaires (ICQs)

   c flowcharts

   d data flow diagrams

12.11 What testing options are available to the auditor if they are unable to manually trace a transaction through a client's system because it is fully computerised?

12.12 What is the difference between a 'data item' and a 'data structure'?

12.13 What purpose do the 'columns' in the flowchart serve?

12.14 What is the difference between a context, level 0 and level 1 diagram?

12.15 Name and describe the ways in which a client's system can be used to test their controls.

12.16 What controls might be audit-useful for portable devices made available to staff such as mobile (smart) phones?

12.17 What does it mean for the auditor to be involved in 'system development testing'? Why might it be important to do so?

12.18 Most businesses today use externally developed and managed programs, or apps, algorithms or data storage. If material, what six issues should the auditor consider about them?

12.19 The client produces a log of data-entry attempts that were not successful. What risk concern(s) does this raise?

12.20 What procedures might the auditor use to conduct tests in a continuous audit?

12.21 What is the difference between auditing 'through' and auditing 'around' the computer? When would one or the other be employed?

12.22 Who owns the flowcharts and data flow diagrams?

Exercises

12.1 **DOCUMENTATION:** Look back to the flowchart partially pictured in **Figure 12.4** and do the following:

   a Identify four controls and what they may prevent.

   b Identify three ways in which the duties are usefully segregated.

c Identify the number of documents used in this system.

d Explain the circumstances in which the 'pre-numbering' control will operate effectively.

12.2 **DOCUMENTATION:** Look back to the context diagram for DFDs in **Figure 12.6** and do the following:

a Define the system being studied.

b Explain why customers and suppliers are outside the system.

c Explain why the accounting and shipping departments are outside the system.

d Explain whether the information on the data flow lines refers to what *happens* to the data or if it *describes* the data.

12.3 **DOCUMENTATION:** Look back to DFD diagrams for levels 0, 1 and 2 and answer the following questions about them:

a What is being explained in the circles? What do they have in common with each other?

b What in the level 0 diagram is drawn from the context diagram? How is it different?

c What circle from level 0 is highlighted in level 1. Why might the auditor choose to highlight that circle rather than any other?

d At what point do you find evidence of controls? Identify two controls.

12.4 **INTERNAL CONTROL WEAKNESS:** The purchase officer of an energy wholesaler authorises and orders oil and gas from qualified suppliers. Identify one possible way in which the purchase officer could carry out a fraud from which he financially benefits. Indicate how the auditor could potentially have found the problem and name one internal control that could be introduced to prevent this in the future.

12.5 **FUNDAMENTAL CONTROLS:** A school requires an audit. Its sales are from bake sales and local fundraisers, all primarily in cash. Identify a potential *fundamental control* that could be absent in such a situation, and offer ways by which the auditor could:

a prevent the situation from occurring if they were on the engagement at the beginning of the audited year

b address the situation if they were engaged after the year-end

c suggest ways in which the situation could be improved in the future if the client inserted a particular internal control.

12.6 **FUNDAMENTAL CONTROLS:** The client operates food concessions from caravans that they, or their employees, move from town to town. Customers pay with cash or direct debit. Most of the concessions are operated by a single person or by a married couple. Food supplies are purchased centrally, although those operating the concession purchase fresh products.

Required:

a Identify three fundamental controls that could be at risk here.

b What are the management assertions they could put at risk?

c What test by the auditor might help to uncover the problems they cause?

12.7 **CONTROL WEAKNESSES AND COMMUNICATION:** You have recently discussed the internal control weaknesses you observed in Biggles Aircraft Supplies Pty Ltd with senior management.

Required: For each of the weaknesses listed below, come up with and explain a recommendation to overcome the problem.

a Sales:
  i   credit notes not authorised
  ii no gate-check on goods leaving store to invoice
  iii no pricing and extension check on invoices
  iv no credit checks.
b Receipts:
  i   no checking digits on debtors' account numbers
  ii cash not banked intact daily.
c Payroll:
  i   no check on hours worked
  ii no authorisation of overtime
  iii inadequate records kept of sick leave and annual leave.
d Purchases and payments:
  i   no authorisation of orders
  ii goods received not checked to cart note
  iii vouchers prepared to support payments not always authorised.

12.8 **CONTROL TESTING:** Your client has a number of controls that you wish to test.

Required: For each situation below, describe how you would test that control and clarify what management assertion is being tested.

a The client's system performs a record check to ensure that no more than one payment is made to any single supplier within a monthly period. An error report is produced if more than one payment occurs, but all payments still go ahead.
b The head of the Human Resources Department approves all new employees by (manually) signing and dating their application forms. New employee names are not entered into the payroll system unless the data entry person sees and signs this signature.
c A staff member of the Human Resources Department reviews prenumbered notification forms from the (retail) floor manager daily. The notification reveals that an employee has left or been made redundant. HR completes an Employment Conclusion form, which is signed and, later, entered into the system by the data entry clerk.

12.9 **CONTROL EVALUATION:** Your audit client, LowGear Ltd, is a wholesaler and retailer of automotive parts. Eighty per cent of total annual sales of $2 000 000 are made to other retail outlets, and 20 per cent of sales are made directly to the public from the company's four warehouses. LowGear Ltd carries debtors of approximately $400 000 and usually writes off about $10 000 per annum in bad debts.

The mail is opened by Ms Brown, the computer operator, who prepares the bank deposit and debtors' journal. The debtors' ledger is kept on the computer. Mr Green, the office accountant, is handed the bank deposit, checks the details against money received, and does the banking. No receipts are issued for monies received through the mail unless specifically requested.

Each warehouse has prenumbered cash sale invoices, and at the middle of each day, cash received together with a reconciliation of the previous day's net sales and the relevant invoices are sent to Mr Green to include in the banking for that day. Petty cash expenditures and cash purchases averaging about $200 per week at each location are taken out of cash sales and recorded on the reconciliation forms.

In addition to the aforementioned functions, Mr Green reconciles the company's bank account between cash book and bank statements, and is a co-signatory of cheques with the managing director, Mr White. He is also frequently tasked with recommending to the sales manager the terms of credit given to customers. Account reconciliations and bad debt authorisations fall within his ambit subject to spasmodic review by Mr White.

Required:

a Document the system using a flowchart.

b Document the system using a data flow diagram.

c Summarise briefly what you consider to be the weaknesses in the system.

d Identify two controls and describe how you would test them.

12.10 **CONTROL EVALUATION:** You are new to your small firm and have been asked to design an internal control questionnaire for the sales cycle. Key questions are set out below. Go 'online' to find example formats and prepare an ICQ. Explain why each question may be important.

a Can any goods be despatched without being invoiced? Can services be rendered without being invoiced? (E.g., goods on consignment, goods to other branches, samples.)

b Can invoicing errors occur (sales invoiced but not recorded, or other errors)?

c Can monies from cash sales be improperly dealt with by:

　i persons initially receiving cash

　ii persons handling cash from initial receipt to final banking?

d Can debtors' accounts be improperly credited?

13 | Audit sampling

Learning objectives

....

After studying the material in this chapter, you should be able to:
- describe audit situations where sampling is appropriate and distinguish between types of sampling
- identify the judgements necessary to carry out audit sampling
- explain audit-sampling procedures
- perform tests of controls and substantive tests using these methods and evaluate the results.

Introduction

Auditors often conduct tests on samples. Audit sampling refers to:

> The application of audit procedures to less than 100% of items within a population of audit relevance such that all sampling units have a chance of selection in order to provide the auditor with a reasonable basis on which to draw conclusions about the entire population. (ASA 530, para 5(a); ISA NZ 530, para 5(a))

ASA 500: Audit Evidence (para A67; also ISA NZ 500) establishes that audit sampling is designed to enable conclusions to be drawn about an entire population on the basis of testing a sample drawn from it. Sampling is a useful technique if it saves audit costs without reducing audit quality. Testing a sample allows the auditor to form conclusions on the population taken as a whole from the examination of only a part of that population. As the size of audits and the risks they entail have grown, sampling has become a common practice.

This chapter is an introduction to sampling practices used in the audit. Its purpose is to set out the principles of sampling practice and to provide information and illustrations on its application. The use of sampling practice is part of tests of controls and substantive testing (see **Figure 13.1**).

Sampling: Audit applications

In sampling, the auditor applies a test of control or a substantive procedure to less than 100 per cent of the items within an audit population. Sampling may also be applied to risk-assessment procedures (ASA 330; ISA NZ 330). An audit 'population' can be that which makes up an account balance or a class of transactions, such as all sales invoices, all stock counts or all debtors' balances. Usually, a large population is needed to justify the costs of taking a random sample

Initial planning	**Detailed planning**	**Audit test response**	**Completion**
• Preliminary engagement activities • Review client's business • Perform risk analysis • Form audit strategy	• Study accounting system • Evaluate internal controls • Develop detailed plan	• Tests of controls • Further develop plan • Substantive tests	• Completion and review • Management letter (introduced later) • Audit report and opinion • Client's AGM

Figure 13.1 Steps in an audit process

Auditing in practice

Importance of sampling

A dairy store client raises thousands of sales invoices in a year, all of which are individually small. Yet, taken together, the invoices add up to a material amount (total sales). To test all invoices would strain the resources of the audit firm and expend too much on immaterial amounts. So a sample of items is taken and tested, and the result of that sample is generalised (extrapolated), so as to come to an opinion about the *accuracy* or *occurrence-validity* of *all* sales invoices.

In addition to 'sales', accounts receivable, inventory, purchase and wage records are often subject to sampling procedures.

Sampling for compliance and substantive tests

You will recall that compliance tests are performed to ensure that controls are working effectively throughout the year. Unless we wish to rely on a control procedure, there is no purpose in testing it, so testing all controls will not be necessary.

Where no controls exist, or where the auditor decides not to rely on a given control (e.g., Jackson, 2016), substantive tests must be increased to meet the auditor's test objectives. Virtually any control test or substantive test of detail may be conducted by either testing the whole population or sampling. Generally, the following audit procedures do *not* involve audit sampling:
- inquiry and observation, including walk-through procedures, which are used to understand a system
- analytical review procedures using ratios, trends and relationships
- tests of the population that, by definition, are not samples but examinations of all elements of concern
- balances, which do not require an audit, either because the potential for material misstatement is small (assuming a risk-analysis approach) or because the amounts themselves are immaterial (in the accounting sense).

It is important for the auditor to carefully plan the audit program to ensure that it is clear to the audit team what is to be sampled, why, how and for what purpose, so as to minimise the risk of auditor negligence.

Sampling and materiality

If an account balance is material (in terms of accounting materiality), but each individual element of the balance is not, then sampling may be appropriate. If sufficient assurance can only be provided through the performance of (often expensive) substantive tests, or if the cost of looking at the sample is less than the cost of testing the population, then *audit materiality* principles suggest that sampling may be appropriate. **Figure 13.2** illustrates the rationale followed by the auditor in deciding to use a sample (or not).

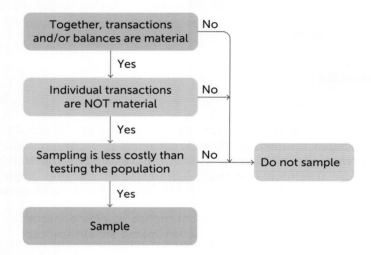

Figure 13.2 To sample or not to sample?

The 'Auditing in practice' box illustrates some of the judgements that have to be made by the auditor early in the process of reaching a sampling decision.

Auditing in practice

Judgements on audit sampling

The auditor is examining $2 million worth of receivable balances for overstatement. Their listing contains 50 balances that exceed the tolerable misstatement and which together total $1.6 million. Another 2000 smaller accounts make up the remaining $400 000 of book value. The auditor decides to verify the 50 material balances but is not sure what audit work needs to be performed on the remaining 2000. We should already have:
- evaluated and tested the related system of internal control
- reviewed entries in the sales account that revealed unusual items
- established through SpAR that the receivable balance is generally reasonable.

The auditor may either decide that sufficient evidence has been obtained and collected, or that any misstatement in them would not be material. In either case, no further tests would be necessary. Alternatively, the auditor may decide that additional substantive evidence is needed and select a random sample of those remaining accounts, test that sample, and extrapolate the results of that sample to the population of 2000.

Statistical and non-statistical sampling

Statistical sampling involves selecting the number of items to be tested in accordance with statistical 'rules'. Such rules include selecting the sample 'such that all sampling units have a chance of selection to provide the auditor with a reasonable basis on which to draw conclusions concerning the entire population' (ASA 530, para 5(a); ISA NZ 530, para 5(a)). These 'rules' enable the auditor to conclude the entire population from which the test is drawn. That is, a statistical test allows the auditor to *extrapolate* to the population.

Suppose you decide to perform a statistical sample. In that case, you will need to gather a random sample of items from the population, and you will be required to sample a sufficient number of items to permit you to draw probabilistic conclusions on the population taken as a whole.

Auditing in practice

Statistical sample

A statistical sample may be selected by using random number tables to select sales invoices. It may be necessary to test, for example, 100 of them to draw a conclusion on the population of all sales invoices with a confidence level of, for example, 95 per cent.

By contrast, *non-statistical sampling* does not require you to use such rigorous statistical techniques in selecting or evaluating the sample of items. You may decide to test very few items, and your selection of them need not be random.

Auditing in practice

Choosing an invoice sample

You may choose the 10 largest sales invoices because they are material. Or you may select the last 10 invoices in March because you have concerns about the client's cut-off procedures; hence, they are more likely to have errors.

Non-statistical sampling may be made more rigorous by following a carefully structured approach and using proven formulae for selecting the sample. On the other hand, statistical sampling calls on the auditor to follow more rigorous procedures and may be a costlier process. This raises an important question: Why would an auditor choose to use statistical sampling?

- Probability theory permits you to *quantify the confidence* used in your conclusion. For example, you may conclude that compliance errors are minimal, within a 95 per cent confidence level. With non-statistical sampling, confidence is not quantifiable, although you may have an intuitive feeling about whether the sample represents the population taken as a whole.
- Probability theory also allows you to *quantify the precision* of your conclusion. For example, you may be able to conclude that the true rate of non-compliance with control is between 0.5 per cent and 2 per cent. Or you may be able to conclude that total sales for the year lie between $900 000 and $1 100 000. Non-statistical sampling does not allow you to quantify results in this manner.
- Statistical sampling calls for collecting a random sample; that is, a sample that is not influenced by the preferences imposed by the auditor. *Random sampling reduces any bias* that an auditor's sample selection may introduce. The auditor may be tempted to select a sample from that part of the population that is most readily available, even if it is not the best sample to take in audit terms.

Random sampling

It is tempting to examine stock warehoused close to the client's workplace because it is easier for the auditor. Unfortunately, doing so may fail to uncover problems unique to other storage facilities. Random sampling methods force the auditor to reject such bias.

- Last but not least, the auditors must concern themselves with whether or not the evidence they have collected will stand up in a court of law, if they are called on to prove whether or not they have acted with reasonable care and skill. Using probability (and statistical sampling) is an accepted method of generalising to a population, and thus it provides stronger evidence than might be provided by non-statistical sampling.

  Of course, you can also use random selection methods without evaluating the sample statistically.

  Some statistical sampling plans allow the auditor to quantify other conclusions about the population, such as whether inherent risk makes the error more likely or whether an analytical review indicates a problem. This is useful because incorporating other evidence may justify reducing the size (and the cost) of the sample – 'how' will be discussed later in this chapter.

  Overall, no one rule guides the auditor in all circumstances. Statistical or non-statistical sampling may be appropriate under different situations of risk and cost-effectiveness. In fact, in Australia and New Zealand, most large audit firms apply a range of different policies, from virtually no use of statistical sampling to heavy reliance on its methods. Ultimately, the decision of whether, and to what extent, statistical sampling is appropriate must fall to those who make policy decisions and to the auditors. We again emphasise the importance of audit judgement when making these decisions.

> **CONCEPT QUESTION 1**
>
> Describe the conditions calling for statistical sampling as opposed to non-statistical sampling.

Sampling and judgement

Judgement plays an important role in the selection and evaluation of a sample. Sampling procedures require the auditor's judgement on the following matters:
- identifying the precise nature of the test *objective*
- identifying the *population*
- determining the *confidence level* required for minimum standards of care
- deriving the acceptable precision (*tolerable misstatement* or *rate of error*)
- estimating the total *expected error* in the population.

The objective

The audit objective of concern should be clearly determined before the sample is designed. We have already referred to audit test objectives via management assertions (OCAC-ERV – refer to the framework in **Table 7.4**). When a test is being developed, a precise definition of the purpose of the test is necessary. In particular, an auditor should determine what exactly constitutes a sample, an error, and where the error could occur. If the auditor fails to specify carefully what constitutes an error, the time spent in testing could be wasted, and a wrong test could be conducted.

Auditing in practice

Occurrence-validity and controls

Suppose an auditor is testing the occurrence-validity of credit vouchers, and a control is in place that calls for the authorisation of the vouchers. In that case, the auditor must be careful to test for that objective. If the auditor instead looks for the absence of prenumbered vouchers, the time taken for the examination will be wasted, and an important control may go unverified.

In *tests of controls*, an error will be a *rate of non-compliance* with the control being tested. For example, if casting and cross-casting of the daily inventory costs is the control of concern, then the test objective may be met by reviewing evidence that the casting and cross-casting occurred. If 50 days are examined, and on two of them there is no evidence of this control operating, then the sampling error is 4 per cent (2/50).

In contrast, an error *will be an amount or dollar-value discrepancy in an account balance for substantive testing purposes*. For example, if the auditor checks the amounts posted in journals against the general ledger, any mis-posted amounts will be given a specific dollar amount of difference. If any, the 'errors' will also be in dollar terms.

Do not forget that an error for:

- a test of control is the *rate of non-compliance* of that control
- substantive tests are the *amount of difference* between the book value and the audited value.

This difference between the two is important to audit planning and decisions covered later in this chapter.

The population

The *population* is the whole group from which the auditor wishes to sample. The individual items within a population are known as *sampling units*.

Auditing in practice

Sampling unit and population

In a sample for selecting items from the client's inventory categories for verification, a sampling unit may be defined as 'category of stock', and the number of all categories of stock comprise the population. This is different from a sampling unit in which each individual stock item is tested. The sampling unit would be the number of 'individual stock items', and the population would be all 'individual stock items'.

The definition of a population will always depend on the audit objective. If it is the dollar cost rather than the number of tested items, the sampling unit would be the 'cost of individual stock items' (or individual cost dollars). The population would comprise 'total cost of all stock'. The distinctions are important in ensuring that you are testing the right things.

One point to note is that testing for *overstatement* and *understatement* in an account may require different tests. For example, if testing for overstatement, the auditor might define the population as the list of transactions or balances in which the overstatement might lie. Understatement cannot be tested in this way, for sampling from a population can never identify understatement through omission. A reciprocal population would need to be identified and tested through directional testing. For example, to prove the completeness of sales invoicing, the auditor could select a sample of goods outwards notes (which have been proved as complete) and ensure that invoices were raised in relation to each of the sampled documents.

The confidence level

The confidence level required from an audit test relates to the idea of audit risk. Essentially, suppose the auditor is willing to accept a high overall audit risk on a particular engagement or account. In that case, the confidence required from related tests can be relatively low (but never below minimum standards of care). For example, if a misstatement in the investments account would have little impact on user decisions, then the auditor need not draw refined conclusions about the quality of that balance. A lower confidence level requirement permits the auditor to reduce testing; a high confidence level forces the auditor to increase the quantity and/or quality of evidence to meet standards of care.

Tolerable misstatement

Tolerable misstatement is the maximum error in a population that the auditor would be prepared to accept. It influences sample size (as does the confidence level) in that the smaller the tolerable misstatement, the larger the required sample size.

In tests of controls, tolerable misstatement is the maximum percentage *rate of deviation* that the auditor would be prepared to accept without altering the planned extent of reliance on the control being tested. Typically, auditors would not be prepared to rely on a control that may not work 5 per cent or more of the time. In substantive testing, tolerable misstatement can be converted to the maximum dollar error in an account balance or transaction series. It is the *amount* that the auditor would be prepared to accept such that, when the results of all audit procedures are evaluated, the auditor can conclude that the financial information is not materially misstated. For example, the auditor may be willing to 'tolerate' a $20 000 overstatement or understatement in fixed assets.

Tolerable misstatement will be related to, but typically will be less than, planning materiality. If the basic allowance method is used for disaggregation, the basic allowance itself is the tolerable misstatement that is required for the test being performed.

Expected error

A larger sample than normal will have to be examined if errors are anticipated in the population. This is because as sample errors increase, precision and/or confidence decreases. So, suppose that a minimum confidence level and a maximum tolerable misstatement have been determined. In that case, the discovery of a large number of errors in the sample is likely to result in rejection. This is a costly outcome as it is usually costly to go back to the work site and retest and gather new evidence – or worse, to qualify the audit opinion.

The level of expected error in a population will be influenced by error levels identified in previous audits, walk-through procedures, client inquiries, evidence available from internal control appraisal, and analytical review results.

CONCEPT QUESTION 2	Explain why an 'error' for a substantive test would be in a dollar amount.

Sampling procedures

Sampling plans are the different approaches used to perform sampling. **Figure 13.3** illustrates the relationship between various sampling plans.

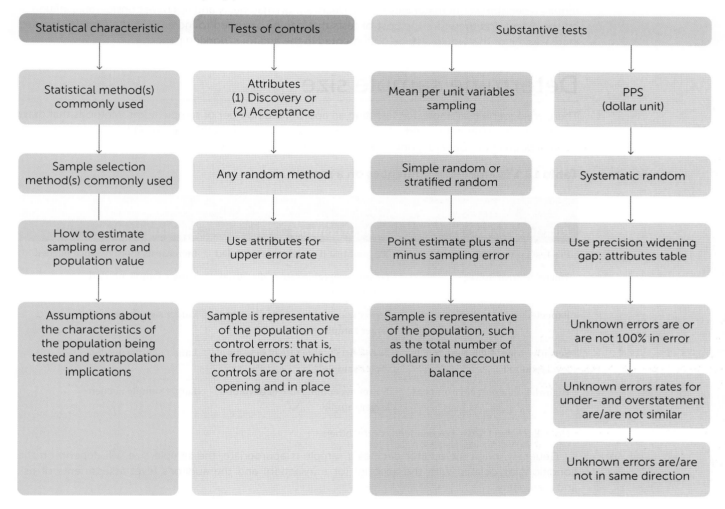

Figure 13.3 Statistical plans used in an audit

An appropriate sampling plan is used to test controls, and either variables or probability in proportion to size sampling (or similar) is used to test account balances. The reason for the different plans is to accommodate assumptions about the distribution of various populations. In tests of controls, we are looking for either the presence or absence of a control procedure. Hence, tests of controls require a sampling plan that analyses the attributes. On the other hand, substantive tests test dollar values or continuous data in statistical terms and require a sampling plan that accommodates that type of data.

Whether sampling is for controls or substantive purposes, the auditor generally performs the following procedures in roughly the order below:

1 Pre-sample judgements are made.
2 Appropriate sample size is determined.
3 Sample items are selected from the population.

4   Testing procedure is performed and errors are documented.
5   Errors are individually analysed.
6   Error rates or amounts are extrapolated (generalised) to the population.
7   Control or balance tested is accepted or rejected; implications are considered.

You will note that audit decisions 1, 2 and 3 are made prior to performing the test and that they require a decision about materiality or risk. Decisions on materiality and risk have considerable influence on the extent and therefore the cost of tests that can be assumed to increase as the sample size also increases. All of this would also be documented in the auditor's working papers.

Determine sample size

There are accepted methods for selecting an appropriate number of sample items. Methods that draw on probability assumptions and rely on particular sampling distributions are used to draw conclusions about a population. General principles are illustrated in **Table 13.1**.

Table 13.1 Examples of influences on a sample size

Risk assessment ...*	Effects on size of sample for:	
	Tests of controls	Substantive tests
Pre-test control risk 'higher'	May not test if no reliance intended	Increase as more reliance needed
Tolerable error 'lower'	Lower acceptable rate of deviation, larger sample	Larger sample needed
Expected error 'higher'	Lower acceptable rate of deviation, larger sample	Larger sample needed
Sensitive topic, high confidence level required	Lower acceptable rate of deviation, larger sample	Larger sample needed
High-risk-inherent environment	Lower acceptable rate of deviation, larger sample	Larger sample needed

* Note: Each issue taken independently of the others.

Generally, once the auditor decides a sample is appropriate, the sample size will depend on the conditions associated with the account (or transaction) and the auditor's level assessments of risk and materiality.

Auditing in practice

Computer audit note

An advantage of using a computer to download and select an audit sample is that the cost of selecting a large sample may be no greater than the cost of selecting a small sample.

Select the sample

Sample selection is an important part of the sampling process because poor selection can lead to wildly erroneous conclusions. The sampling unit should always be consistent with the objectives of the test. Sampling can either be random, non-random or haphazard.

Haphazard sampling

Haphazard selection is a process whereby the auditor selects a representative sample from the population with no intention of including or excluding specific units. However, as discussed, it is very difficult to minimise some bias in selecting samples.

Random sampling

Random selection ensures that all items in the population have an equal chance of selection. A random sample is required for statistical sampling to generate probability statements about the population. Random number tables may be used to select sample elements, or they can be generated from audit software (the standard Excel spreadsheet program can, for example, issue random numbers).

Auditing in practice

Random selection of sales invoices

The sales invoices for the current year may be numbered from 1000 to 2500. A random selection of 40 would call for choosing the sample size only from these invoices, and the auditor would be required to test those invoices that are randomly selected, all 40 of them, and no others (see **Table 13.2**).

Table 13.2 Random set of numbers generated between 1000 and 2500

Random set of numbers generated between 1000 and 2500				
1795	1569	1858	1710	1206
1742	1292	1956	1779	1455
1698	2130	1637	1147	2097
1941	1894	1156	2263	1256
1676	2206	2221	1106	1850
1817	1546	2122	1534	1372
1400	2222	1684	1447	1222
1972	1954	1865	1385	1830

In general, the auditor would usually use one of the following three methods to ensure that a random sample is taken (see also **Figure 13.3**):

- *Simple random sampling* – in which the auditor tests random numbers that are independently selected (such as in **Table 13.2** for a sample size of 40). A simple random sample would likely have a similar rate or the same relative amount of error as the population. It would contain large and small accounts/balances in roughly the same proportion. Simple random sampling can be unnecessarily expensive because of the difficulty of locating the invoices etc. that have been selected on a purely random basis. For this reason, systematic sampling is a useful alternative.
- *Systematic sampling* – involves selecting items using a constant interval between the selections. If a starting point is a random number within the first interval, and if errors within the population are not systematic, a random sample will result. So, for example, if the wage card number orders a population of wage cards, and if there are 10 000 wage cards and a sample of 200 is desired, then

every 50th card would be selected, and this would provide the sample. The interval, in this case, is 50. If the first wage card is randomly selected as a number between 1 and 50, and if the error rate is not itself systematic, then the sample should represent the population.

- *Stratified sampling* – appropriate to many audit tests because of the materiality concern. In a stratified sample, you divide the population into groups of similar items, or 'strata', and you then select sample units and apply tests independently to each stratum. It is possible to apply different tests or intensify the testing on any one stratum.

For example, in an audit population of accounts receivable, you may choose to divide all accounts into three strata: one contains large-balance accounts in excess of the tolerable error, one contains small-balance accounts that together are not material (in an accounting sense), and another contains medium-balance accounts. Since material errors are of concern in an audit, you may wisely decide to test the first stratum most heavily and the immaterially small stratum not at all. Since the purpose of the audit is to find material errors and not necessarily all errors, stratified sampling is a particularly useful method for reducing audit risk and audit cost at the same time. It is not relevant if the audit objective of concern is omission.

Non-random sampling

Non-random sampling is a way of identifying a sample that is not random. The auditor chooses sample elements for a specific purpose. It is not possible to arrive at probabilistic (statistical) statements if non-random samples are selected, but they may be useful under some circumstances. Some audit firms use non-random sampling almost exclusively because they believe that it is more important to incorporate the experienced auditor's judgement into selecting samples that are more likely to have errors than relying on a scientific process.

Our view is that non-random sampling is best restricted to situations where: (a) the test or balance is of low materiality from an accounting (amount) or auditing (risk-based) perspective; or (b) there is a suspicion that particular items are misstated or not controlled. This would occur if, for example, the auditor chose to sample only those payment invoices that they thought were fraudulently prepared.

Perform the test

Much of the sampling work does not involve work on the client's premises but back in the audit firm's office, where planning is undertaken and results are analysed.

Performing tests may involve checking whether the client's employees have given evidence of having carried out a control ('test of control') or recalculating or comparing numbers from a client's database (substantive test of detail). Once performed, the results and errors found should be recorded in the working papers.

Auditing in practice

Examining the wrong population

Untrained auditors may examine the wrong population by mistake. For example, the auditor may be examining the 'cost' of inventory when the test is actually meant to gather information on the 'value' of inventory. This makes the test invalid.

Sampling risk is the risk that an auditor will accept a control or balance that, in fact, is not in compliance; or that they will reject an account balance that is, in fact, not misstated. It is accepted (by the courts) and can be quantified in statistical sampling. It occurs by virtue of the fact that sampling does not look at the entire population. The confidence level, at say 95 per cent or 98 per cent, cannot be 100 per cent because of sampling risk: sometimes, through no fault of the auditor, the sample is simply not representative of the population. Sampling risk can only be reduced by increasing the sample size to increase confidence.

Non-sampling risk, as you will recall, is the risk that the auditor will (essentially) make a mistake. The audit firm will wish to reduce non-sampling risk, of course, and this is where quality-control procedures, peer review, auditor training, supervision, oversight, and ensuring the appropriate allocation of skilled staff, are important. Irrespective of the source, should the auditor come to an inappropriate conclusion, the result could either be an inefficient audit or audit failure, as illustrated in **Table 13.3**.

Table 13.3 Sampling and non-sampling risk costs

		Auditor's conclusion after testing	
		No material misstatement (substantive test) or control is operating and in place ('test of control')	Material misstatement (substantive test) or control is not operating or in place ('test of control')
Actual situation	Material misstatement (substantive test) or control is not operating or in place ('test of control')	Audit failure if oversight is material	Satisfactory audit
	No material misstatement (substantive test) or control is operating and in place ('test of control')	Satisfactory audit	Audit inefficiency (to continue testing unnecessarily)

Analyse individual errors

The auditor should have identified what constitutes an error during the planning stage of the audit. For each identified error/misstatement, the auditor must identify whether the client subsequently corrected the error. If so, then this is not a true error and it can be ignored as far as the auditor is concerned, provided it was identified during the course of the client's normal procedures. If the client did not discover the error, or if the discovery was purely by chance, then the auditor must consider the cause:

- *Carelessness* – The error may have arisen through carelessness or human error. If so, this should be considered in the evaluation of sample results, but it is not necessarily indicative of a larger problem.
- *Misunderstanding* – Suppose the cause of the error was a misunderstanding by the person performing the procedures. In that case, it is likely that all items within the population performed by that person or under that particular system will be incorrect. Consequently, the auditor will have to conduct additional audit procedures to determine the extent to which the errors may be material.
- *Irregularity* – Suppose the auditor concludes that the error identified during testing occurred as a result of distortion or misappropriation. In that case, the matter will have to be investigated further to determine its extent and to draw appropriate conclusions.

The impact of misunderstandings and irregularities on inherent or control risk, or the potential for fraud, should be considered. That is, the auditor should apply *professional scepticism* to explanations offered by management for errors found. If the number or value of estimated errors is caused by carelessness *and* is less than the acceptable number or value of errors, however, no further testing need be conducted.

Generalise (extrapolate) sample results to the population

Estimating the value (or rate) of errors in the *whole* population is important because auditors must determine whether estimated errors in the population exceed materiality levels. The *estimated errors in a population* consist of the amount or rate of error the auditor believes exists in the population tested and taken as a whole.

As only a sample of the population is observed, the population estimated error must come from that sample (see **Figure 13.4**). It is not possible to know the actual value/rate of errors from a sample, so, using statistical methods, a probability statement can be made. There are many ways to extrapolate from a sample, but there is no consensus (Barnett, Haworth and Smith, 2001), so methods vary.

Figure 13.4 Extrapolating test results to the population

Would you ask the client to correct errors found? Keep in mind that they cannot correct *all* the errors because only a few of them would have been identified in the sample. However, those found can be changed, and this can (sometimes) make a difference to the auditor's assessment of whether the accounts are 'true and fair'.

Auditing in practice

Tolerance error in sample

An error of $200 is discovered in a sample. If a tolerable error is $2000, and if the estimated total error is $2100, then correcting that one error found can spell the difference between 'accepting' and 'rejecting' the client's balance.

Generally, an auditor should reconsider inherent risk should management be unwilling to correct the errors found.

Professional scepticism

If management's resistance is indicative of a general lack of cooperation with the auditor, the quality of management's assertions, again applying professional scepticism, may be questionable. In some engagements, the cost of making corrections to the books may exceed their benefits. Where auditors are convinced that this is reasonable, no risk adjustment is necessary.

Misstatements may have audit implications if they indicate that fundamental controls are not working satisfactorily. In these circumstances, it may be necessary to change the nature, timing and/or extent of audit testing to provide confidence that no further misstatements exist. It is noted that it might not be appropriate to expand the same test, as this may well only confirm that errors exist without providing the basis for a further audit decision.

Compliance with controls may or may not indicate that fundamental misstatements have been occurring. For example, a purchase order may not be properly authorised for payment, but it still may be a valid purchase. In contrast, misstatements identified during substantive testing will have compliance implications; therefore, the discovery of a dollar-value error should be accompanied by consideration of the implications for the auditor's assessment of control risk.

Therefore, it is important to determine the impact of any sample errors found by the auditor on both the population and on the auditor's assessments of other risks.

Accept or reject the hypothesis

On the basis of the criteria set and extrapolated sample results found, it is now possible to accept (or reject) the hypothesis of concern. These hypotheses will be either that:
- the control being tested is operating throughout the year (test of control); or
- the true account balance is tolerably close to the amount in the financial statements (substantive test).

Therefore, the auditor's test on a sample must always conclude with an opinion on control or an account balance (see ASA 530; ISA NZ 530). It is easy to overlook the obvious and important role of coming to a firm opinion on the results of each audit test.

CONCEPT QUESTION 3	Non-sampling risks can result in one of two unwanted outcomes. Define and explain what they are.

Examples for audit sampling

We now apply the principles just introduced to two examples of audit sampling: one for a compliance test of controls and the other for a substantive test of balances.

Test of control example

In our first example, the objective of a test is to determine whether daily sales cash listings are being reconciled to deposit summary forms by the staff member on duty. The reconciliation ensures both the accuracy and the completeness of 'sales'. It is an important procedure; therefore, a 95 per cent confidence level is called for, and the auditor decides that non-compliance in excess of 6 per cent would be intolerable. The auditor expects a 1.5 per cent population deviation rate based on a pre-sample.

After identifying the objective and the population (of cash listings), and setting the confidence level and tolerable error criteria, the auditor then has to determine the appropriate sample size. Applying the criteria to a statistical distribution such as the one illustrated in **Table 13.4** does this. This table is designed to help the auditor select the sample size for a given confidence level (95 per cent in this table), a given expected population deviation rate (1.5 per cent in this example), and a tolerable deviation rate (6 per cent in this example). The sample size, therefore, should be no less than 103.

Table 13.4 Statistical tables for 'compliance tests'

Sample size for attributes sampling									
(95 per cent level of confidence)									
Expected population deviation rate (in %)	Tolerable deviation rate (in %)								
	2	3	4	5	6	7	8	9	10
.00	149	99	74	58	49	42	36	32	29
.25	238	157	117	93	78	66	58	51	48
.50	●	157	117	93	78	66	58	51	48
.75	●	208	117	93	78	66	58	51	48
1.00	●	●	156	93	78	66	58	51	48
1.25	●	●	158	124	78	66	58	51	48
1.50	●	●	192	124	**103**	66	58	51	48
1.75	●	●	227	153	103	66	77	51	48
2.00	●	●	●	181	127	88	77	68	48
2.25	●	●	●	208	127	88	77	68	61
2.50	●	●	●	●	150	109	77	68	61
2.75	●	●	●	●	173	109	95	68	61
3.00	●	●	●	●	195	129	95	84	61
3.25	●	●	●	●	●	148	112	84	61

3.50		•	•	•	•	•	167	112	84	78
3.75		•	•	•	•	•	185	129	100	78
4.00		•	•	•	•	•	•	146	100	89
5.00		•	•	•	•	•	•	•	158	116
8.00		•	•	•	•	•	•	•	•	179

Evaluating sample results using attributes sampling
[Five per cent risk of over-reliance = 95 per cent confidence level]

Sample size	Actual number of deviations found										
	0	1	2	3	4	5	6	7	8	9	10
25	11.3	17.6	•	•	•	•	•	•	•	•	•
30	9.5	14.9	19.5	•	•	•	•	•	•	•	•
35	8.2	12.9	16.9	•	•	•	•	•	•	•	•
40	7.2	11.3	14.9	18.3	•	•	•	•	•	•	•
45	6.4	10.1	13.3	16.3	19.2	•	•	•	•	•	•
50	5.8	9.1	12.1	14.8	17.4	19.9	•	•	•	•	•
55	5.3	8.3	11.0	13.5	15.9	18.1	•	•	•	•	•
60	4.9	7.7	10.1	12.4	14.6	16.7	18.8	•	•	•	•
65	4.5	7.1	9.4	11.5	13.5	15.5	17.4	19.3	•	•	•
70	4.2	6.6	8.7	10.7	12.6	14.4	16.2	18.0	19.7	•	•
75	3.9	6.2	8.2	10.0	11.8	13.5	15.2	16.9	18.4	20.0	•
80	3.7	5.8	7.7	9.4	11.1	12.7	14.3	15.8	17.3	18.8	•
90	3.3	5.2	6.8	8.4	9.9	11.3	12.7	14.1	15.5	16.8	18.1
100	3.0	4.7	6.2	**7.6**	8.9	10.2	11.5	12.7	14.0	15.2	16.4
125	2.4	3.7	4.9	6.1	7.2	8.2	9.3	10.3	11.3	12.2	13.2
150	2.0	3.1	4.1	5.1	6.0	6.9	7.7	8.6	9.4	10.2	11.0
200	1.5	2.3	3.1	3.8	4.5	5.2	5.8	6.5	7.1	7.7	8.3

The test is then performed by selecting 103 cash listings and related deposit summary forms at random and inspecting whether reconciliation has been performed on each of those 103 listings and forms. The inspection may only amount to looking for a signature that is used on completion of the reconciliation, by looking for evidence of vouching from one form to the other, or by looking for both.

If the item selected has been cancelled or is unused, a replacement item should be used in the sample. So, for example, the next item can be used as long as, where needed, that pattern is followed consistently. Normally, however, each 'random' item should be found and used for the audit test.

Let us assume that three errors were found in the sample. That is, of the 103 tested, three were found to have no evidence of reconciliation. The first analysis requires us to consider the source of those errors and whether they should have an effect on our risk assessments. If not, and if the misstatements appear to be due to error, then we may go on to generalise to the population.

To generalise the errors of the sample to the population taken as a whole, we may use the information provided by **Table 13.4**, which helps determine the upper error limit. By using this table, we can be 95 per cent confident that the population error rate (the rate of control failures) is no greater than the upper error limit or, in this case, 7.6 per cent. The true error lies, we believe with 95 per cent confidence, above zero, and is no greater than 7.6 per cent.

Since we decided prior to the test that any error rate above 6 per cent would be intolerable, we are forced to reject the hypothesis that the control is operating and in place throughout the entire year. The auditor may now conclude that this procedure's planned degree of reliance cannot be achieved and may have to be obtained from performing an increased number of substantive tests.

This test used a simple random sampling method to select the sample items and attributes sampling plan to draw conclusions from the results.

Substantive test example using PPS

Probability proportional to size (PPS) sampling uses attribute sampling theory to reach a conclusion about dollar-value balances or transaction series. In PPS sampling, the auditor defines the population in terms of the dollar units that make up the population, such that each individual dollar will have an equal opportunity of being selected. It is therefore usable for substantive testing.

The technique has gained widespread acceptance throughout the auditing profession because of its simplicity and the way in which it lends itself to use with risk trade-off models. Essentially, its *advantages* are as follows:
- It is easier to understand and implement than other substantive sampling plans.
- Systematic methods used with it automatically stratify the population and select material items more heavily, a distinct advantage as material accounts are of interest.
- Where anticipated error is low, PPS sampling will usually call for smaller sample sizes than other common sampling plans for substantive testing, saving audit costs.
- The process is built into automated working papers, so if data changes (i.e., adjustments to the client's accounts), this automatically flows through to adjust the test as well.
- It incorporates risk decisions made in the planning phase. Audit risk model may be solved for the required level of substantive tests (STR):

$$STR = OAR/(IR \times CR \times APR)$$

PPS sampling permits the auditor to incorporate assessments of inherent and control risk and confidence from analytical review in the formulation of the minimum sample size needed for substantive testing. Therefore, sample size is directly influenced by risk.

However, it is not advisable to use PPS sampling under some circumstances:
- When an anticipated error is high, PPS sampling may become less cost-efficient.
- Items that are understated (or missing) have less (zero) chance of selection – so, if understatement is a significant risk, other sampling plans may be more appropriate.
- The discovery of a number of errors in the sample is more likely to lead to rejection than when other plans are used. PPS sampling (usually) calls for smaller sample sizes, and smaller samples are less precise. Hence, it is more likely the results with errors will exceed tolerable limits.
  In such cases, it may be wise to use a means sampling approach (see **Figure 13.3**).
  The process to conduct a PPS sample involves the following steps:
1 Audit, inherent and control risks for the objective of concern can be estimated.
2 Confidence achieved from SpAR procedures is assessed. The population (book value) is determined.
3 The tolerable misstatement for the account balance is determined.

4 An assurance factor is calculated (see **Table 13.5**).
5 Sample is tested and errors found are recorded.
6 Individual errors are analysed.
7 Generalisation (or extrapolation) to the population occurs.
Most firms expect auditors to classify risks as being 'high', 'medium' or 'low' (see **Table 13.5**).

Table 13.5 Deriving the assurance factor to determine sample size: PPS

							Audit risk sensitivity		
1	**2**	**3**	**4**	**5**	**6**	**7**	**8**	**9**	**10**
Inherent risk	Internal control confidence	SpAR confidence	Inherent risk	Internal control confidence	SpAR confidence	Total confidence pre-t of d	Low 95% = 3.0	Medium 97.5% = 3.7	High 99% = 4.6
Risk assessments by auditor			Reliability (assurance) factors						
Hi	Hi	Hi	0.5	1.6	1.6	3.7	0.0	0.0	0.9
		Med	0.5	1.6	0.9	3.0	0.0	0.7	1.6
		Low	0.5	1.6	0.3	2.4	0.6	1.3	2.2
	Med	Hi	0.5	1.1	1.6	3.2	0.0	0.5	1.4
		Med	0.5	1.1	0.9	2.5	0.5	1.2	2.1
		Low	0.5	1.1	0.3	1.9	1.1	1.8	2.7
	Low	Hi	0.5	0.2	1.6	2.3	0.7	1.4	2.3
		Med	0.5	0.2	0.9	1.6	1.4	2.1	3.0
		Low	0.5	0.2	0.3	1.0	2.0	2.7	3.6
Med	Hi	Hi	0.7	1.6	1.6	3.9	0.0	0.0	0.7
		Med	0.7	1.6	0.9	3.2	0.0	0.5	1.4
		Low	0.7	1.6	0.3	2.6	0.4	1.1	2.0
	Med	Hi	0.7	1.1	1.6	3.4	0.0	0.3	1.2
		Med	0.7	1.1	0.9	2.7	0.3	1.0	1.9
		Low	0.7	1.1	0.3	2.1	0.9	1.6	2.5
	Low	Hi	0.7	0.2	1.6	2.5	0.5	1.2	2.1
		Med	0.7	0.2	0.9	1.8	1.2	1.9	2.8
		Low	0.7	0.2	0.3	1.2	1.8	2.5	3.4
Low	Hi	Hi	0.9	1.6	1.6	4.1	0.0	0.0	0.5
		Med	0.9	1.6	0.9	3.4	0.0	0.3	1.2
		Low	0.9	1.6	0.3	2.8	0.2	0.9	1.8
	Med	Hi	0.9	1.1	1.6	3.6	0.0	0.1	1.0
		Med	0.9	1.1	0.9	2.9	0.1	0.8	1.7
		Low	0.9	1.1	0.3	2.3	0.7	1.4	2.3
	Low	Hi	0.9	0.2	1.6	2.7	0.3	1.0	1.9
		Med	.0.9	0.2	0.9	2.0	1.0	1.7	2.3
		Low	0.9	0.2	0.3	1.4	1.6	2.3	3.2

The following formula should be used to calculate the minimum sample size (n) for PPS:

n = (Population × Assurance factor)/Tolerable misstatement

Let us use an accounts receivable balance example (see **Table 13.6**). The objective is to determine whether the accounts receivable balance of $450 000 is valid by asking a sample of debtors to confirm their balances. An estimate of total errors in excess of $90 000 would be a material misstatement.

Table 13.6 Example: Accounts receivable working paper for PPS

Customer	Book balance	Cumulative balances	#	Random start + sampling interval	Audited (tested and true) $ amount
Able	20 500	20 500			
Bailey	22 000	42 500	1	30 000	32 000 (so 10 000 understated)
Davis	2 750	45 250			
DeMerit	41 000	86 250	2	75 000	41 000
Fa'alua	2 000	88 250			
Gearin	30 050	118 300			
Lu	40 251	158 551	3	120 000	40 251
Mataira	300	160 651			
McKinley	1 800	160 351			
Naylor	16 300	176 951	4	165 000	16 300
O'Callahan	2 350	179 301			
Paula	22 505	203 781			
Peters	1 975	181 276			
Sharma	1 685	207 626			
Solomon	2 160	205 941			
Tai	20 000	227 626	5	210 000	20 000
Zale	29 005	256 631	6	255 000	29 005
(others)	193 369	450 000	7–10	(etc.)	
Totals	450 000		n = 10	n =10	

* Let $30 000 be the random start between 0 and 45 000. The sample is drawn and confirmations are sent.

It is a highly sensitive engagement; therefore, we set audit risk at 1 per cent (on a less sensitive engagement, we may go as high as 5 per cent). The management has gone through major changes, and its integrity or familiarity with the organisation is unclear; hence, we set inherent risk as medium.

Controls for recording and internal check appear to be in place; therefore, internal control confidence is high. However, tests on the relationship between accounts receivable and net credit sales appear to indicate a misstatement in one of the two accounts; therefore, confidence from SpAR is low. Using

Table 13.5, we can see that the assurance factor, given the decisions specified above, is 2.0. Placing this in the formula above results in the following sample size:

$$n = (450\,000/\,90\,000) \times 2.0 = 10$$

We must send at least 10 confirmations on a random basis.[1]

Usually, a systematic method is used to select the sample. Systematic samples are less costly to take (particularly where computers are involved) and still retain the benefits of a random sample as long as the selection in the first interval is random. A systematic sampling plan also conveniently allows us to consider each dollar as a sampling unit, with the population consisting, in this case, of the balance in accounts receivable. The sampling interval is $45\,000 ($450\,000/10) in our example. The first sample should be the account represented by a random number between $0 and $45\,000 ($30\,000 is chosen).

Generalising to the population (extrapolation)

We can only understand the population (of 'total dollars' in this case) by assuming that the sample tested is similar to what we would find if we had tested the whole population. That is, we *extrapolate* from the sample to the population.

We cannot have absolute knowledge about this population of accounts receivable dollars because we have not tested them all, but we may be able to estimate a relevant (or 'material') range around which we now believe that true population exists. That is, we can estimate from the sample that the true value is 'somewhere around' a certain amount.

Extrapolating from a PPS sample test result to a reliable conclusion about the population is not a totally agreed process. We apply a reasonably straightforward method to demonstrate the principles, but we acknowledge that it is not 'statistically' ideal.

This particular method of extrapolation assumes that the result found in the sample is *typical* of what we would find should we examine all of the amounts within that particular sampling interval. With this assumption, we can then apply any proportional error we may have found in the sample to the whole of that sampling interval.

So, for example, our test of the Bailey account (**Table 13.6**, sample 1) revealed that its book value is $10\,000 understated ($32\,000 − $22\,000). This is the only error found. Therefore, the distortion in this account is 45.45 per cent (10\,000/22\,000). We will assume that this same sort of distortion applies to the entire sampling interval of $45\,000 and extrapolate these results to the population via the following formula:

Estimated total misstatement = (10\,000/22\,000) × 45\,000 = 45.45% × 45\,000 = $20\,455

We conclude, therefore, that the accounts receivable is approximately $20\,455 overstated. As $20\,455 is less than the tolerable misstatement ($90\,000), we can accept that accounts receivable is 'true and fair'.

PPS sampling tends to lead to rejection decisions quite quickly. For example, it would have only taken two zero account balances that should have had a $1 balance each to conclude that tolerable misstatement had been exceeded. Furthermore, because systematic sampling selects large accounts, understated accounts are less likely to be selected (even though perhaps they should be). These are challenging decisions for the auditor to make in deciding whether and how to conduct a sample.

---

[1] We're keeping this sample unusually small for illustrative purposes.

Study tools

Summary

Statistical sampling provides a cost-effective way to make a probability statement about a population of account balances or controls, providing an important source of audit evidence. Sampling is used to perform a variety of control and substantive tests where conditions call for it. This chapter considered situations that called for sampling and weighed the benefits of statistical versus non-statistical methods. The importance of audit judgements in coming to sampling decisions was emphasised.

Case/resources link

CAATs for Classrooms

Accompanying this book is a series of data, integrated worksheets and exercises that are designed to support your learning and give you exposure to hands-on audit decision-making dilemmas faced by auditors in the planning elements of the audit process. Acquire the relevant material for this chapter from your instructor.

Review questions

13.1   On what types of tests can sampling be employed: tests of controls or substantive tests?

13.2   Would sampling be performed as part of:

a   walk-through procedures

b   analytical procedures

c   an examination of all items in the account?

For each, explain why or why not.

13.3   Name the three conditions in audit that, together, would suggest the need for sampling.

13.4   What does it mean to *extrapolate* to the population, and how is it used in sampling procedures?

13.5   How is 'tolerable misstatement' applied to the sampling process?

13.6   How is the 'confidence level' used in sampling, and how is it related to the risk model?

13.7   What 'statistical plans' are used for:

a   tests of controls

b   substantive tests?

13.8   What are the usual audit procedures?

13.9   Why is 'random' sampling important for statistical sampling? Name three types of random sampling used in an audit and explain how they differ.

13.10   How can sampling risk be reduced?

13.11 In what ways should the auditor be concerned about samples that reveal:

    a   carelessness

    b   misunderstanding

    c   irregularity?

13.12 Explain what it means to say that 'within a 95 per cent probability, the auditor rejects the hypothesis that the control is operating effectively'. What should the auditor do next?

13.13 Define each of the following:

a population	d expected error
b confidence level	e sampling risk.
c tolerable misstatement	

13.14 What is the 'assurance factor' and how is it used in audit sampling?

13.15 What does it mean to say that the audit is a particularly 'sensitive engagement'?

Exercises

13.1 **SAMPLE PURPOSE:** You are sampling data from the client's sales invoices. Distinguish between a sample that would be appropriate for a test of controls and a sample used for a substantive test, and explain how they would be different.

13.2 **TESTS OF CONTROLS SAMPLING:** Each day, all of the time card gross hours are compared against an authorised range. If the hours are within that range, the reviewer signs the card with their initials and the date. You are reviewing this control. Assume that an estimated error of 0.01 would be satisfactory, but that in excess of 0.04 would be unacceptable. Upon testing, you find five instances of non-performance, all of which appeared when one clerk was on duty.

    Required: Design a test of control, document your findings and conclusions in working paper format, and justify how they were reached.

13.3 **SUBSTANTIVE TEST SAMPLING:** Your client is a retailer with thousands of items in inventory and a management-calculated balance of $500 000. You are concerned that the cost of inventory items taken at stocktake should be correct, and you are particularly concerned with overstatement. This is a new client, and you believe a sale of the business may be in the plans. For the current portion of this test, you take a sample of stock items, recount them, and calculate their cost. Controls over stocktake are very good, as is your confidence in management. You are unable to perform an analytical review for this account. You have decided to use PPS sampling. Assume that on testing, you find one error on the second sample which overstates that stock item by $6000.

    Required: Design and perform the test and form your conclusions. Justify your decisions.

13.4 **TESTS OF CONTROLS SAMPLING:** The management of Whyfly claims that their credit officer reviews each new credit application prior to authorising the sale. The initialling of a copy of the sales invoice indicates this review. The auditor wishes to verify that this control has been operating throughout the year and, therefore, decides to sample a portion of the invoices and look for the initialisation. It is decided that any failure in excess of 4 per cent would be enough to warrant a decision not to rely on this control. It is anticipated that an actual non-compliance rate will likely be between 0 and 1 per cent.

Required:

a   You select and justify two sample sizes. The sample results in an actual failure rate of 1 per cent. What is your conclusion?

b   What would you do on finding the invoices lacking compliance?

c   Assuming simple errors, what conclusion/s would you draw?

13.5   TESTS OF CONTROLS SAMPLING: For the situations below, (1) describe the 'population' for this test; (2) describe the 'sample item'; (3) explain what you would do to conduct the test of control; (4) determine what (primary) management assertion is being tested.

a   On a monthly basis, as soon as the bank statement is received, the cash receipts journal (CRJ) and the cash disbursements journal (CDJ) are downloaded by staff in the accounting department. The CRJ and CDJ are reconciled to the bank statement, relying on the beginning (reconciled) balance. The documents are stapled together, signed and dated by the reconciling employee, and filed when the reconciliation is complete.

b   1000 prenumbered sales invoices are given to sales staff each week, with the accounting clerk signing off a control sheet setting out the beginning and ending numbers on the invoices. At the end of the week, the accounting clerk reviews online sales records and returned sales invoices to ensure that none are missing.

13.6   TESTS OF CONTROLS SAMPLING: The audit manager is helping the audit junior decide what type of sampling selection method should be used for a test of controls in each of the following situations:

a   The auditor is concerned whether the credit scores of customers whose purchases exceed $2000 within a month are checked before they are authorised. While the client's system issues a daily printed report of customers exceeding that limit, the credit check is done by hand, and – when complete – the checker dates and initials that part of the printed report.

b   The data of concern is the instances of pay raises that are shown on individual payroll records. The auditor will download the client's 4300 employees' payroll records to the auditor's own system. There is a mix of large and small items. The larger items are of particular interest, but the auditor does wish to estimate the total pay raises conducted during the period to compare it to their estimate for analytical review purposes.

c   Sampling the equipment of interest is expensive, so the auditor wishes to test all equipment worth more than $500 000 but only test 33 per cent of equipment worth $200 000 to $499 999, and only 10 per cent of equipment worth less than that. Statistical extrapolation is desired.

13.7   PPS SAMPLE: You are completing a PPS sample for the stock items listed in **Table 13.7**.

Required: Complete the table and identify the batches from which to select the sample.

Table 13.7 PPS sample for stock items

| Assume: tolerable error is $5000; assurance factor is 1.1 | | | | | |
Stk #	#Items	$ each	Total cost	Cum. cost	Selected?
1	117	24			
2	225	15			
3	25	5			
4	63	16			
5	41	94			
6	456	18			
7	855	2			
8	10	85			
9	22	34			
10	165	19			
11	295	4			
12	222	16			
13	195	74			
14	145	70			
15	28	55			
16	85	47			
17	66	17			
18	60	10			
Total					

13.8 **SAMPLING EXTRAPOLATION:** Assume that you took a sample of 27 for a PPS substantive test. The procedure you used was to identify the stock item on the stock list and vouch that to the existence of the item in the warehouse. In your sample alone, you found items worth $50 000 that may have been stolen. Extrapolating to the population, the potential loss was $150 000 to $180 000 (with a confidence level of 95 per cent). A tolerable misstatement has been decided at $160 000.

a List the questions that you would ask.
b Identify evidence procedures that you should carry out.
c If there is no new information, at what conclusion do you arrive?

13.9 **TESTS OF CONTROLS:** Assume that for the situation shown in the next exercise, one of the client's staff counts each category of items against the number of items recorded in stock records. Evidence of this check is via an electronic signature within the stock records of the client.

Required: Design a test of controls. Detail how you would make each sampling judgement decision. Assume that two issues of non-compliance are found. Perform your test and come to your results and conclusions.

Use the data in **Table 13.8** for the next five exercises.

Table 13.8 Sample data for monetary unit sampling (MUS) or PPS sampling

Stk #: up to	#Items	$ each	Total cost
372	372	$120.00	$44 640.00
518	146	$240.00	$35 040.00
622	104	$360.00	$37 440.00
736	114	$216.00	$24 624.00
761	25	$324.00	$8 100.00
792	31	$805.00	$24 955.00
1405	613	$96.00	$58 848.00
1985	580	$102.00	$59 160.00
2725	740	$72.00	$53 280.00
3483	758	$72.14	$54 682.12
4267	784	$65.52	$51 367.68
4457	190	$537.60	$102 144.00
4555	98	$430.25	$42 164.50
4635	80	$654.70	$52 376.00
4685	50	$85.40	$4 270.00
4728	42	$13.95	$753.90
4791	63	$137.68	$8 673.84
4901	110	$613.50	$67 485.00
Total	4901		$730 004.04

These data had been downloaded from the data files of your client, CarParts Ltd. While this is a full listing of their inventory (stock), note that all of the stock has multiple items. The auditor wishes to conduct a substantive test for occurrence-validity.

13.10 **PPS SAMPLE PROCESS:** Assume that you decide to collect a sample of 26 items.

    a Expand the data table to calculate and show the cumulative balance.

    b Assuming a random starting point of $15 000 (the first sample item), identify the batches from which your sample would be taken. (More than one sample may be taken from one batch.)

    c Would the sample tend to select 'larger' or 'smaller' items? Why?

    d Assuming the same random start, identify the batches from which a sample would be taken if you were only taking a sample of 20.

e   Given your decision to take a smaller sample size, what effect will this have on the confidence of your extrapolated findings?

f   Assume that sample #7 is 50 per cent overstated. Extrapolate to your conclusion.

13.11 **PPS SAMPLE SIZE:** Use **Table 13.8** and the information below to determine your sample size for this test:

a   The tolerable misstatement is $36 500.

b   Inherent risk is high, control risk is high, and SpAR confidence is low.

c   What would be the effect of doubling the tolerable misstatement? Why?

d   The auditor decided to double the tolerable misstatement after the tests were completed, as the test results indicated a rejection of the null hypothesis. Discuss this decision and whether or not it was appropriate.

13.12 **PPS SAMPLE RESULTS:** Use **Table 13.8** and the information below to complete a working paper on your sample results. You calculated your sample size from your risk assessments and tolerable misstatement to be 50. Before conducting the test, you discover that items 4636–4685 were miscounted. There are 350, not 50, items. Assume a random start of $10 000.

a   Calculate the effect of this discovery, if any, on your sample size assuming no change in tolerable misstatement.

b   Calculate the effect of this discovery, if any, on your tolerable misstatement, assuming you make no change in sample size.

c   Explain the implications of one decision over the other. What does this mean for audit quality and audit cost?

13.13 **PPS SAMPLING:** Use **Table 13.8** and the information below to answer the questions set out. Assume that with a sample size of 30, and a random start of $20 000, you find an overstatement in sample #5 of $13 000 and an overstatement in sample #16 of $28 500.

a   Calculate where those errors occurred, assuming an assurance factor of 2.0.

b   Determine whether the errors found exceed the tolerable misstatement.

c   Extrapolate those errors to the population using the method shown in the text.

d   Prepare a working paper showing your work, your results and your conclusions.

13.14 **PPS SAMPLING:** Use **Table 13.8** and the information below to answer the questions. Assume that with a sample size of 28, and a random start of $20 000, you found an overstatement in sample #5 of $53 000 and an understatement in sample #16 of $6000.

a   Calculate where those errors occurred, assuming an assurance factor of 1.8.

b   Determine whether the errors found exceed the tolerable misstatement.

c   Extrapolate those errors to the population. What are the implications?

d   Prepare a working paper showing your work, your results and your conclusions.

13.15 **RANDOM NUMBER SELECTION:** In Excel, the function to produce random numbers within a range is =RANDBETWEEN(x,y). The client's invoices being tested run from 1106–2305. Use your own Excel program to produce a random sample. Sixty items are required, and you should use the invoice numbers to identify the sample items.

Systems testing I: Sales, purchases and payroll

Learning objectives

After studying the material in this chapter, you should be able to:
- describe key transaction cycles and the subsystems of which they are composed
- apply your knowledge of documentation, risk analysis and internal controls to subsystem analysis
- identify substantive tests related to the accounting cycles associated with sales, purchases and payroll.

Introduction

The purpose of including this and the subsequent chapter in the text is to introduce you to some of the more common types of risks, controls and tests associated with audit depth testing within common accounting systems. Although we do not cover all audit procedures, we believe that it is important for you to familiarise yourself with the risks and tests usually associated with these subsystems.

An *accounting subsystem* (or cycle) comprises the processes by which accounting transactions are authorised, captured, recorded, manipulated and stored. It is one 'system' by virtue of the fact that the transactions within it are relatively contained within the system and are therefore somewhat independent of other transactions and other subsystems. An accounting cycle will also include accounting controls that lie within it.

The value of working with cycles is that they allow the auditor to compartmentalise complex processes into doable segments. That is, each cycle can be audited relatively separately, making the task less overwhelming. The principles for highly structured organisations also apply to less hierarchical organisations, so the lessons here can be used in a variety of different client situations.

Systems and structure

Accounting information systems (AIS) or enterprise resource planning (ERP) software link departments and sub-units of an organisation. Even a small business with only two or three office employees or one owner-manager will have a system structure of some kind. The approach of this chapter is thus to:
- *focus on service or retail enterprises* so as to include inventory
- *adopt a risk approach and identify the controls and tests* that follow
- *describe substantive procedures* common to the subsystem.

The use of computers and cloud technology is common; hence we tend to take a data-flow, rather than paper-flow, approach. Subsystems we cover include the:

- *sales cycle*, as to sales from inception to final payment by debtors
- *purchases cycle*, as to inventory from its request to order, delivery and payment
- *payroll cycle*, as to personnel, employment status and payroll liabilities
- *warehousing cycle*, as to information flows monitoring inventory
- *financing cycle*, including cash, debt and equity (see **Figure 14.1**)
- *fixed assets and intangibles cycle*, as to the acquisition, maintenance, valuation and disposal of long-term assets. (see **Figure 14.1**).

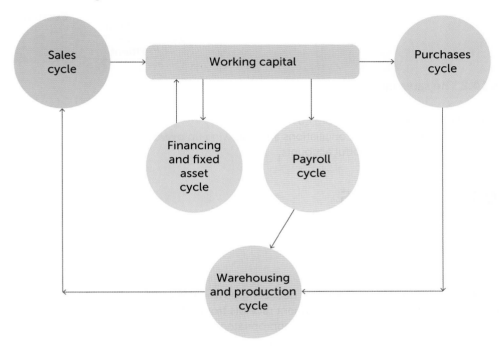

Figure 14.1 Five accounting cycles or subsystems

In this chapter, we focus on the *sales*, *purchases* and *payroll* cycles. Chapter 15 examines the *warehousing*, *financing* and *fixed asset* cycles. First, let's consider the sales cycle.

CONCEPT QUESTION 1	Describe the purpose of the five accounting subsystems introduced in this chapter.

Sales cycle

The *sales cycle* begins with an authorisation to make a sale and continues through to its representation in various financial statement accounts (see **Figure 14.2**). Keep in mind that we are dealing with sales prices only, not *costs*. Costs of stock are in the purchases cycle. Recording processes for sales include:

- making sales or receiving sales orders
- credit checks and sales authorisations
- recording the sales invoice on transfer of goods or service

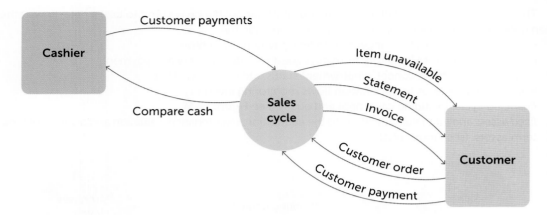

Figure 14.2 The sales cycle

- billing and recording payments from customers
- accounts receivable ledger reconciliations and following up overdue accounts
- assessing allowance for doubtful accounts.

Sales cycle risks

The following sections cover examples of fraud risks in this system, where controls are weak.

Teeming and lading

Teeming and lading involve an employee pocketing payment received from some credit customers and hiding the deficit by recording subsequent receipts from other customers against the accounts of those debtors whose receipts were first misappropriated. The accounts of the later customers will of course be overstated because their remittances have not been entered against their accounts. This type of fraud can occur when sales ledger clerks also have access to cash receipts (or are in collusion with the cashier). Even if only small amounts are removed at any one time, over a period of time, this fraud accumulates and can reach a substantial size.

The fraud is only likely to remain undiscovered if there is no regular independent (internal) check. If a system is poor, cash, cheques or direct payments could be misappropriated and the amount not credited to the debtor's account (or else credited, but the accounts are allowed to remain out of balance). It is likely, however, that sooner or later someone will check the account, possibly in response to a customer query, or the fraud-committing employee leaves and someone else discovers it. Normally, the perpetrator will become greedier and the system of interlocking frauds will become so complex that the edifice will collapse. Regularly sending statements to customers and independent reviews of customer queries can prevent or minimise this type of fraud.

Collusion between customer and sales invoicing

If employees collude with customers, invoices may not be raised for despatch or may be raised for a reduced amount. Such fraud can involve substantial sums of money but can be prevented by proper sequential control over despatch authorisation, supplier checks, and independent checks comparing despatch authorisations to invoices.

Failure to raise despatch documentation

Goods should not be allowed off the premises without proper despatch records. Unauthorised despatches could lead to losses that may not be discovered until the stocktake, when it is far too late. Therefore, the client should take precautions to prevent this possibility. This is best achieved by physical controls over the entry of personnel into the premises and the exit of goods from the premises.

The same principles apply to less tangible assets, such as database information, title documents and software assets. Controls may be in the form of computer access codes, communication encryption or data-storage controls. While this changes the substance of what the auditor has to assess, it does not modify the underlying principles or the need to assess the client's controls over assets.

Improperly raised credit notes

False credit notes can be used either to cover up the misappropriation of cash or reduce a customer's debts if the perpetrator colludes with the customer. The false writing off of bad debts can be used in the same way.

Misappropriated customer payments

Payments received, particularly if through the post, can be misappropriated even before they are recorded.[1] While in a controlled system this may call for the involvement (collusion) of two people, access to coding allocation in an IT system can enable one person to carry out this fraud. A clear segregation of duties, endorsement of cheques and program controls over the initial receipt of money may prevent theft.

If controls are weak, or difficult to test, an increase in substantive testing, such as confirmations to debtors, may need to be relied on. In systems where the direct deposit automatically updates the client's account, it is important that robust programs ensure that payments are directed to authorised accounts. Cash sales are always highly susceptible to fraud and almost impossible to eliminate entirely. However, procedures (discussed later) can be performed to reduce that risk as well.

Stock shrinkage

None of this can prevent out-and-out theft by customers or employees, although close supervision can go a long way to forestall it. Shoplifting is a multimillion-dollar 'business', and an allowance is commonly built into retail prices for what is politely known as 'stock shrinkage'. Evidence suggests that fraud/theft by employees is becoming just as much of a problem as shoplifting. As auditors, we have a part to play in assessing control procedures that can forestall such crime.

Sales cycle controls

Important controls in the sales cycle are often established in terms of duties that should be segregated. The principles of the systems described apply to either manual or IT systems, although particular issues for IT systems are noted. **Figure 14.3** illustrates some common controls in a sales system. Discussion of sales controls then follows.[2]

---

[1] Cash payment by post is not common these days. A similar kind of risk exists in retail sales.
[2] Flowchart examples for sales, purchases and payroll cycles appear at the end of this chapter – see Exercise 14.8.

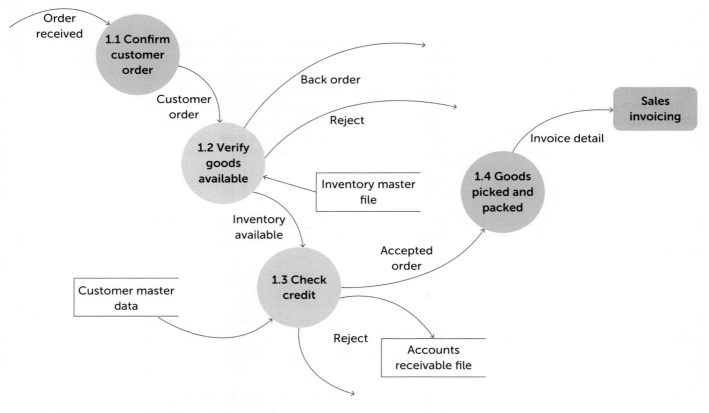

Figure 14.3 Data flow (level 0) example of a sales cycle

Sales department

The sales department should acknowledge orders received on sequence-controlled databases/documents (such as prenumbered receipts/orders) to initiate the 'accounting trail' and to enable reconciliation between orders issued and orders made. The sales department should also be responsible for agreeing selling prices and delivery dates, and an independent employee should approve any discounts.

Credit control

Before an order is processed, the credit-control department reviews and *authorises* (or fails to authorise) the sale based on the customer's creditworthiness. If the order is from an existing credit customer, the new order should not put the account over any predetermined credit limit. If the customer has not had previous dealings with the organisation, bank or trade references and credit checks may be needed.

Despatch and transport department

The despatch department will be responsible for packing ordered goods on the basis of authorisations from the sales department and credit control. A *goods outward note/record (GON)* should be raised for each consignment, either by the despatch department or by the gatekeeper. Later, this can be reconciled to sales stock records. Despatch documents can be sent with the goods to the customer, who signs off on receipt and returns it to the organisation as proof of delivery by the transporter.

Accounts

To ensure that all goods leaving the premises are invoiced, a GON sequence should be checked prior to raising invoices, and the system should include a check to ensure that each GON has an invoice raised for it. Electronic requirements are the same, although data may be online and stored, requiring more embedded controls with stop rules or error notifications.

Auditing in practice

IT audit note

Data may be in hardcopy or electronic forms. So, for example, the GON may be a paper prepared by the stock department, or it could be electronically authorised and sent. IT controls include limit or access controls, automated internal checks (reconciliations) to compare GON data to sales order data, and/or error reports when unusual data is found.

Sales ledger

Postings to sales ledgers are usually part of accounting packages or are developed by larger organisations. Controls in such systems may include batch testing to ensure that all invoices are included and that unauthorised 'sales' are disallowed. The ledgers should have frequent (or ongoing) reconciliations between entries and the accounts receivable control account.

The client should send statements to their customers on a regular basis. As customers are external independent parties, their review provides an independent check, particularly as to the overstatement of debtors or understatement of remittances received. Customers will complain if they think they are being overcharged. Statement sending may be part of the IT system, but it should at least be independent of data entry and after reconciliation to orders and GONs.

Queries from customers are an important control and should be reviewed by independent staff such as the client's internal auditor. The external auditor should usually review all 'complaint' files because they can point to audit concerns, such as the presence of teeming and lading or misappropriations of receipts.

Auditing in practice

IT audit note

In a paperless system, controls for completeness and occurrence-validity may include:
- batch control testing to ensure that the number of sales made is the same number actually input into the system
- validity checks to ensure that amounts entered appear to be reasonable (e.g., not exceeding sales prices) and are appropriate (e.g., are now allowed for customers whose credit has expired)
- processing internal checks, such as the reconciliation procedures for this system.

Credit control

The authority to write off bad debts or grant credit is a powerful one, as it enables customers (or fraudsters.) to avoid payment for services rendered. Granting credit of all types should be client-controlled. Credit-control people or processes should review accounts regularly to ensure that none have exceeded their credit limits, to find overdue balances, and to issue exception and error reports. IT approvals should be controlled at the programming level and reviewed regularly. Overdue balances should be followed up using standardised procedures such as warning letters with references to solicitors or debt-collection agencies if other efforts fail.

Sales cycle: Substantive tests

A sales cycle audit program would normally consist of the assertion risk-related audit test objectives, as shown in **Figure 14.4**.

Figure 14.5 shows the procedures that would normally be performed in the audit of a sales cycle.

Occurrence-validity
Sales captured by the accounting system represent true and authorised transactions.

Completeness
All sales, returns and adjustments that should be recorded are recorded.

Accuracy
Mathematical correctness is asserted, requiring re-performance or tracing amounts from inception through to the financial statements.

Classification
Recorded sales and trade accounts receivable are disclosed in the appropriate asset or expense accounts.

Existence
Customers recorded are actual trade customers.

Rights and obligations
Recorded accounts receivable is owned by the business.

Valuation
Trade accounts receivable is included, net of doubtful accounts, at an appropriately estimated amount in the financial statements.

Presentation
Sales and accounts receivable are disclosed in accordance with GAAP. This includes classification within the accounts and how notes to the financial statements set out the applied sales accounting policies.

Figure 14.4 Assertions: Sales subsystem, to confirm

Circularisation of trade accounts receivable on or before the year-end

Sales cut-off procedures correlated with inventory cut-off procedures

Title document inspection and comparison to invoices and terms of trade

Investigation of material credit balances and reclassification as accounts payable

Specific analytical procedures with respect to the completeness objective

Figure 14.5 Essential procedures: Sales cycle

Analytical procedures (SpAR)

SpAR has a particular application to debtors. If the percentage of debtors to credit sales is plotted over time, useful patterns may emerge. The quality of the internal control, combined with the results of the analytical procedures, will determine the extent to which the debtor balances need to be substantiated by tests of detail. The tests of detail may be accomplished by either tests of transaction (part of depth testing) or direct tests on balances such as sending confirmations. It will normally be appropriate to test for understatement by means of transaction tests from the despatch records through to the sales ledger (tracing), and for overstatement by balance testing (vouching) from the financial balance to the source documents.

Confirmations/circularisation

Confirmations involve the auditor communicating directly with external parties such as the client's debtors to independently confirm client receivable balances. Confirmations will almost always reveal the overstatement of debtor balances, because this would be of client concern. They may also reveal understatement, but they cannot be relied on to do so as this would not be in the debtor's interest. Independent confirmation provides reliable evidence, although in some cases supporting documents (delivery notes, orders or invoices) may have to be substituted if direct communication is not possible. Checking subsequent receipts can also be useful.

Communicating directly with the client's customers, with the client's permission of course, has been common practice since the 1960s. Two methods are used:

- *Positive method* – where debtors are asked to reply, stating whether they agree or disagree with the amounts claimed to be owed. The positive method is preferred if there is a high risk of material error because it requires a response: auditors must follow up on non-respondents. The positive method also allows the auditors to make statistical conclusions should a random sample of the population be tested. **Figure 14.6** provides an example of a positive circularisation request.
- *Negative method* – where customers are asked to reply only if they disagree with the client's record of their balance. While less expensive, because the auditor does not have to follow up on

---

Fundamentals Ltd
Melbourne, Australia

Fundamentals Ltd
Melbourne, Australia
Xrossrite Supply
Sydney, Australia

To the Administrator

In connection with the statutory examination of our financial statements, please confirm
directly to our auditors – COVEY AND FOLLY, CAs, Melbourne – the correctness of
the balance of your account with us as of 31 March 2022 as shown below.

This is not a request for payment; please do not send your remittance to our
auditors. Your prompt attention to this request will be appreciated. An envelope is
enclosed for your reply.

Graeme Covey
Manager, Fundamentals Ltd

Balance at 31 March 2022 is **$3079.00**

Confirmed by

Date:

Figure 14.6 Positive confirmation example

non-respondents, the negative method gives no proof as to whether the request has been received
or considered. It is, therefore, less reliable and should be used if assurance can be provided from
other sources. **Figure 14.7** provides an example of a negative request.

Note that auditors have no right to contact a client's debtors directly. This must be done *by the
client*, although it follows that, for the test to have value, there must be audit control.

Auditing in practice

Confirmation testing

The US 1930s *McKesson & Robbins* case is a well-known example of poor confirmation
testing. Confirmations were prepared by the auditor but 'posted' by the client. The letters
were never posted but were 'completed' by the client's employees for non-existent
'customers' and returned to the auditors again via post. There was, in fact, an entire
department dedicated to creating false sales. Unfortunately, the activity was discovered only
after many years of overstated sales and receivables. Lawsuits ensued.

Fundamentals Ltd
Melbourne, Australia

Fundamentals Ltd
Melbourne, Australia
Xrossrite Supply
Sydney, Australia

Administrator
In connection with the statutory examination of our financial statements, please directly
contact our auditors – COVEY AND FOLLY, CAs, Melbourne – should the balance of
your account with us as of 31 March 2022 (shown below) be incorrect in any way.

  NB: This is not a request for payment.

Graeme Covey
Manager, Fundamentals Ltd

Balance at 31 March 2022 is **$3079.00**

Confirmed by

Date:

Figure 14.7 Negative confirmation example

If the client is reluctant to allow a confirmation, or there are indications that they may interfere with it, doubt is cast on the validity of their debtor balances. Evidence about it may need to be collected in other ways.

Systematic sampling and PPS sampling are particularly useful for debtor confirmation, as a higher proportion of high-value accounts (i.e., more material in account) tend to be selected. Stratified sampling can also be used to treat different samples more or less intensely. So, for example, one 'strata' may be treated differently than strata in which random sampling is applied. Such strata could include accounts that should always be tested; for example:

- *Old unpaid accounts* – These may be fictitious balances to conceal defalcation, or there may be a genuine dispute, both of which could cause overstatement.
- *Accounts with round sum payments* – This may indicate teeming and lading, or that the debtor cannot pay the full amount. Note that, in the latter case, conclusive evidence in support of the validity of the debt may not be obtained from direct confirmation, as the debtor may confirm the amount due but be unable to pay it.
- *Accounts with nil balances* – These would be left out of a cumulative monetary sample, but it may be appropriate to select some in the event of weak control. In such circumstances, there could be the possibility of a duplicate (concealed) set of books with genuine balances being maintained by company employees or management to perpetrate fraud. The circularisation may reveal such understatement.
- *Credit (or negative) balances on the sales ledger* – Such balances could have been fraudulently set up with a view to subsequent fraudulent payments.

When selecting a sample using non-statistical methods, auditors should be conscious that they are introducing bias: results cannot be extrapolated to the population. The auditors should also consider whether the control failures are so significant as to cast doubt on the reliability of the accounting records as a whole. If so, then the auditors may need to extend the sample of debtors to obtain the confidence required. Practical problems may be encountered as well, as a further circularisation may delay the publication of the financial statements.

Other substantive tests

Tests for sales are largely designed to prove *occurrence-validity* and *existence* of debtors, but they do not necessarily prove their *valuation*. One test for this is to review the sales ledger for the existence of bad and doubtful debts, because bad debts should be written off and doubtful debts should be included in any provision calculation.

We also note that *prepayments* are susceptible to error because they may lie outside the usual double-entry system. Auditors should ensure that last year's prepayments are adjusted, and this is a good place to begin the cut-off tests of those of the current year.

Factoring, or invoice financing, is when a business sells its accounts receivable to a finance company at a discount. The business receives needed cash right away (sometimes at a severe discount) and the financial institution collects (and keeps) the debt. It is a common practice. For example, New Zealand exporters discount (factor) up to 95 per cent of their overseas debt. Factoring can be done with or without recourse to the client. At issue here is *valuation* as well as *ownership-obligation*. Testing may include document inspection and confirmation to the factoring financial institution.

> **CONCEPT QUESTION 2**   What is stock shrinkage?

Purchases cycle

The purchases cycle (see **Figure 14.8**) consists of accounting for transactions to authorise, order, receive and pay for inventory. Do keep in mind that it is the *cost* aspect with which this cycle is concerned, not the *sales price*. The purchases cycle can be divided into the following operations:
- requesting: or 'requisitioning' goods
- purchasing: ordering goods
- receiving: checking and storing goods (or returning goods)
- recording: processing the vendor's invoice, including review and approval
- payment: to the vendor and posting payment.

Purchases cycle risks

Risks of misstatement relate primarily to the potential for false or unauthorised suppliers, supplies not reaching the warehouse, or supplier overpayment. Purchases made around the balance date tend to be subject to error or manipulation. Internal controls, in the absence of collusion, are usually quite effective in preventing or detecting such problems.

Figure 14.8 The purchases cycle

Purchases cycle controls

A strict segregation of duties, carefully followed, gives the auditor some assurance in this cycle. Common controls for this cycle are set out in terms of those duties usually segregated and some are illustrated in the data flow diagram; see (**Figure 14.9**).

Requisitions

Authorised employees, guided by company policy and authorised limits, should ideally have the sole power to requisition goods. All requisitions should be serially numbered and sequence-checked, manually or by embedded controls, to ensure *completeness* and *occurrence-validity* prior to forwarding to the purchasing department.

Purchasing

Buyers are responsible for negotiating the best price and delivery dates from suppliers. A buyer department (or function) separated from requisitions, warehousing or users reduces the risk of ordering (and misappropriating) unauthorised goods. Buying authority may be supplemented by, for example, economic order quantities, and buyers may check requisitions against such limits. The user department can also act as a check on purchasing if inappropriate stock is received. Orders may include automated account numbers, reducing the chance of misclassification errors.

Supply chain problems are relatively recent and are in part created by global shifts to just-in-time (JIT) stock practices. They have been recently exacerbated by the COVID-19 pandemic disruptions. Thus, stock may not arrive at all or not on time. While this is fundamentally a management problem, it is a business risk and the external auditors may wish to assess the potential for unrecorded shipping costs, late-delivery penalties or warranty contraventions that could result. Such costs should be recognised, disclosed, classified and valued in the accounts in accordance with GAAP.

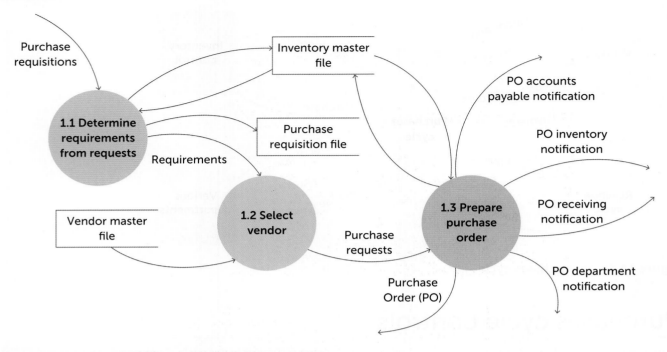

Figure 14.9 Data flow examples for a purchases cycle

Receiving

Goods should be received in designated protected areas. Control can be established at the gate by raising goods received notes (GRNs) there. GRNs should be serially numbered to facilitate reconciliations against orders and cut-off procedures. These controls can be embedded into a barcode and an online signature IT system as well.

GRN information should *exclude* the 'number' of items ordered. This is so that receiving department staff are forced to count the materials received and not just tick a box indicating what 'should' be there. A copy of completed and signed-off GRNs should be sent to the accounts department for reconciliation to requisition and order data. Error or exception reports should be conveyed to someone independent of receiving and made available to the auditor for review.

Recording

Accounts will receive invoices from the client's suppliers, dating and prenumbering them to provide a basis for control. Relevant supporting documents (requisitions, orders, GRNs and inspection reports) should be collated, manually or by the client's IT system, prior to allowing any authorisation of payment.

Auditing in practice

IT audit note

IT controls over some of these procedures may include:
* embedded reconciliation to ensure that requisitions authorised, ordered, received and paid are in amounts that are in accordance with authorised invoice data

→
- reconciliation, which can also be useful if linked to the cash book expenditure records
- batch and digit checks to ensure that all of the above authorisations have been made
- validity checks and access controls (e.g., passwords) for employee authorisation
- error reports or messages to disclose authorisation breaches or repeated access attempts
- ongoing tests of how data moves through the system as it is being processed.

It is unwise to use suppliers' statements as the sole authorisation for payment or recording. Not all suppliers send statements, as they could have errors, or suppliers may not be authorised or totally fictitious. This points to the importance of internally developed authorisation-control practices for the purchase process.

Payment

Most payments are automatically deposited into the supplier's account from a barcoded direct entry or transfer from the purchaser. If purchases are made by cheque, the cashier usually prepares them and records payments in the cash journal. Irrespective of the form, authorisation from ordering and receiving data is important.

The IT system may include embedded tests to ensure the *validity* of payees or payee accounts and under what circumstances. Cheques should be signed by someone independent of this recording function; in some cases, more than one signature is required. The other side to the double entry (either a debit to supplier payable or straight to expense) will normally be made on the basis of the entry.

Payments made directly into client's bank account also rely on the quality of the bank's procedures, the client's own program controls and independent reconciliations. Accounting records are normally updated at the same time that payment is made. Small cash payments may be via petty cash, and this is best controlled by employing the 'imprest system' (more on this in the next chapter).

Unauthorised payments are probably best guarded by controlled ordering and authorisation systems so that payments go to a legitimate party. Questions around the audit of *cryptocurrency* transactions are very far from being addressed, much less resolved, but it may be fair to say that new audit techniques will be needed to account for their use in the future.

Purchases cycle: Substantive procedures

Risks about which the auditor is concerned may consider any or all of the management assertions in the audit of a purchases subsystem shown in **Figure 14.10**.

Creditors may be substantiated either by tests of transactions or by direct tests on balances. So, for example, transaction depth testing can check for both over- and understatement, depending on the direction taken (*vouching* or *tracing*). However, it is often difficult to obtain sufficient confidence about understatement from suppliers because they may not wish to inform you of this. Controls over acquisitions would have to be strong, with little opportunity for management override.

Confirmations can test for existence, occurrence-validity and completeness, and may be necessary in the event of a limited period between the year-end and signing off the audit report. For this reason, it is now common practice among larger auditing firms to circularise creditors in a similar way to debtors. Traditionally, this practice has been resisted by clients because the process could reveal to suppliers any overstatement in the client's records, to which the supplier would happily agree. This objection can be addressed by omitting the balance from the request and asking the creditor to insert the amount due.

Occurrence-validity
Trade purchases are valid and authorised purchases of the organisation.

Completeness
Trade purchases, returns and adjustments that should be recorded, are recorded.

Accuracy
Accounting records and schedules are mathematically correct.

Classification
Costs of sales are not capitalised as fixed assets.

Existence
Recorded liabilities exist and recorded purchase transactions are valid.

Rights and obligations
Recorded liabilities represent valid claims on the business.

Valuation
Recorded liabilities are fairly stated.

Presentation
Purchases and trade accounts payable information has been appropriately disclosed in the financial statements.

Figure 14.10 Audit of a purchases subsystem

Step 1
Review documentation after year-end to identify unrecorded liabilities for goods and services. Such documentation may include creditors' invoices, purchase journals, unprocessed documents, payment vouchers and cash books.

Step 2
Perform cut-off procedures in correlation with inventory cut-off procedures.

Step 3
Convert liabilities in foreign currencies at rates in forward cover contracts or year-end rates.

Step 4
Perform specific analytical procedures with special attention to the completeness objective.

Figure 14.11 Essential procedures: Purchases cycle

Alternatively, many auditors rely on an analysis of supplier statements unless there is reason to believe they may be fraudulent. At a minimum, reviewing suppliers' statements received within a month or so after the balance date (a cut-off test) is common practice, to indicate the presence of any attempts to understate expenses.

Auditing in practice

Cut-off tests

Cut-off tests are the auditor's control and substantive tests for transactions occurring just before and just after the balance (year-end) date. They are intended to uncover transactions that were recorded but should not have been (*occurrence-validity*), and transactions that were not recorded but should have been (*completeness*). For example, the auditor may examine receiving reports just before and just after the balance date to determine if stock costs and payables are appropriate.

Attention should always be paid to *accruals and adjusting entries* made, often manually, at year-end. These entries may not be part of usual system transactions, so they are highly susceptible to error. This is also where senior management may be able to distort the accounts, a practice that will almost always lead to material misstatement. One simple adjusting entry, such as whether goods are 'costed' or 'capitalised' in stock, can have a material effect on the profit and financial ratios.

It is also essential to ensure that last year's *accruals are reversed* in the current period, and this is a good basis for examining the credibility of entries made in the current year. Accruals do not ordinarily alter much from year to year, so any missing or unusual entries can be a 'flag' to the auditor and call for investigation.

Accruals in relation to trade creditors should be checked by reference to those end-of-year GRNs that are unmatched with supplier invoices. This is, of course, another type of cut-off test.

SpAR procedures are also an important form of testing for this system. SpAR can test expected relationships between cost of sales and revenue (over time, by product or by department), or expected relationships between cost of sales/inventory and usage. For example, equipment run time may be related to production output. Such tests give the auditor indications of misstatement.

CONCEPT QUESTION 3   What is the importance of cut-off tests?

Payroll cycle

The payroll cycle can be surprisingly complex (See **Figure 14.12**.) It involves authorisations and accounts related to a variety of employment conditions and contracts, benefits, redundancies and hiring policy. It is concerned with fringe benefits, payroll taxes and insurance premiums.

End-of-year accruals can be complicated, as they involve both pay for employees on different contracts, and agreements, as well as external liabilities and accruals. Numerous IT packages are used for payroll; those both used and reviewable may be the more reliable. It is important that they be nation-specific and kept up to date with tax and employee regulations (see MacPherson, 2021, pp. 61–5 for examples).

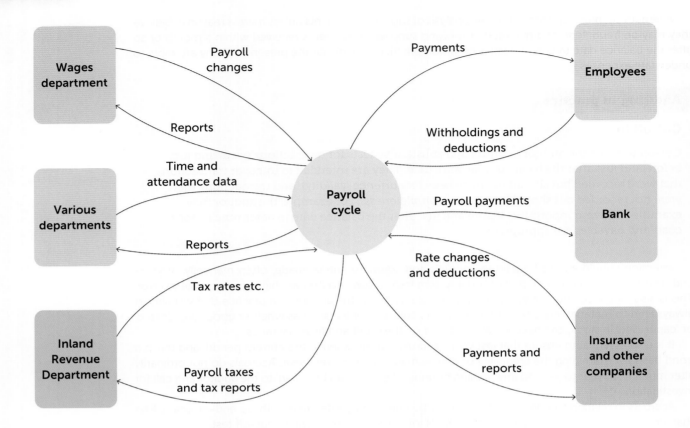

Figure 14.12 The payroll cycle

The payroll cycle consists of the following operations:

- employment policy and personnel record management
- employment and redundancy practices
- recording the work done or hours worked during the period
- calculation of gross pay and payroll deductions
- journalising payroll payments and payroll liabilities
- paying employees, collecting withholdings and paying payroll liabilities
- posting payroll summaries in the accounting records.

Original data in a payroll system would include:

- personnel records and personnel policies
- employee-agreed authorisations for withholdings
- PAYE withholding authorisation
- wage rate, salary and fringe benefit policy and contracts
- employee-prepared time cards.

Usually, the steps from the calculation of gross pay onwards are performed, to a greater or lesser extent, by the client's payroll package. If so, the auditors may wish to assure themselves that the software captures information correctly and applies rates and withholdings according to current law. Payroll may be the subsystem most susceptible to changes. Errors here have legal implications, as do misstatements in the financial statements, due to the possibility of, for example, a client withholding too much or too little tax from an employee's wages.

Auditing in practice

IT audit note

Auditors should also ensure that the payroll software and access to the software is controlled, since the insertion of non-existent employees (occurrence-validity) is no less possible than in the case of a manual system. Organisations with a large number of employees are most susceptible to this risk.

Payroll cycle risks

In the absence of controls, different types of misstatements become possible. We note that while payroll fraud may be of concern to your client's management, it will not necessarily, or even usually, lead to *material* misstatement. Nonetheless, suspicions uncovered are deemed 'material' in the sense that they should be investigated, and reported if found at an appropriate level of client management, and it could indicate problems elsewhere in the organisation.

Dummy names

If an independent record of employees is not maintained, someone could create 'dummy names' (an *occurrence-validity* problem if 'they' are paid). Fictitious names may be invented, or employees who have left employment may be retained on the payroll. Often, this fraud is perpetrated by wages office staff, but managers or supervisors may also be in a position to commit fraud in this way, though they will only be able to do so if there is no independent check on the payout.

Overstatement of gross pay

If the wages clerk colludes with an employee on the shop floor, it is possible for the gross pay to be overstated and overpaid. The wages clerk could receive a share of the overpayment, and if the amounts involved are not excessive, such a fraud is difficult to trace. Some frauds are revealed by **whistleblowers** who observe the unfairness, so corporate minutes and employee complaints should be reviewed. Collusion is surprisingly hard to maintain, however, as it asks fraudsters to work cooperatively.

whistleblower
A person, usually an employee or an insider, who reveals information on wrongdoing occurring within an organisation.

Overstating the payroll

A very simple fraud can involve the overstatement of payroll by committing deliberate errors in the arithmetic of the pay listing. It can, however, be prevented by an independent check, casting and cross-casting the payroll at the time of approval. In practice, this is usually performed as part of a standard payroll software program.

Overstating hours worked

Depending on the system, there are many ways to overstate hours worked (or sales made if the employee is paid on commission). If the fraud is widespread or continues for a long time, it can result in a considerable sum of money, and, of course, employee fraud is of concern to management. If employees are paid on the basis of 'output', an independent check on the quantity produced/sold/serviced may be required.

Deductions

These are also susceptible to fraudulent activity. It is difficult to manipulate payments to government tax authorities unless the controls over payees are weak. However, deductions for superannuation, insurance premiums or trade union fees can be misappropriated, especially if the perpetrator also has dealings with those funds or access to the payroll program. Overpayments can then simply be requested and the excess removed before payment into the fund. Ideally, no-one in accounts or the personnel department should control payroll funds, and reimbursement requests in respect of deductions should be scrutinised.

Payroll cycle controls

Controls should exist for all forms of remuneration, from directors to shop-floor employees, from salaried managers to piece-rate workers, and commissioned sales staff. Numerous IT packages are available for clients who do not have their own programs to accommodate this, all with some levels of control. It is important that they be reviewed and jurisdiction-specific, however, and kept up to date with the newest tax and employee regulation (again, see MacPherson, 2021, pp. 61–5 for examples). The data flows pictured in **Figure 14.13** illustrate the relationships among a sample of controls in a payroll system.

We again look at the more common controls for this system in terms of how the various payroll recording duties may be distinguished.

Authorisation

The HR department is usually responsible for employment and redundancies, and for carrying out authorised alterations to rates of pay and benefits. The existence of a separate department negotiating

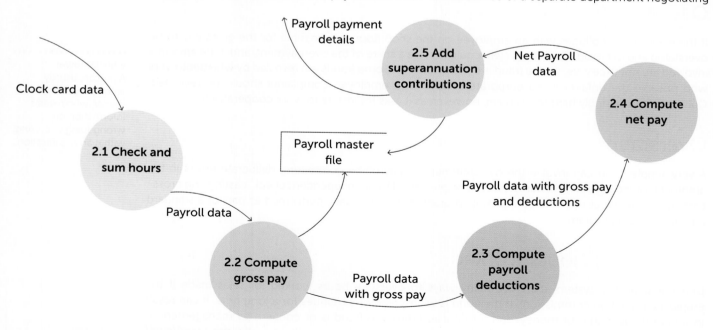

Figure 14.13 Payroll subsystem DFD example

these matters is important from the auditor's point of view because its members are independent of those likely to benefit from payroll distortion or theft. Serially numbered change authorisations should always be used, and the HR department should retain a copy for subsequent review.

Gross wages should be authorised in policy (and law). Commissioned staff salaries should be based on independently prepared sales data. Clock cards or time sheets may be used to record hours worked for hourly wage earners. Salaried staff should have authorised pay agreements. Piece-rate workers' pay (those paid on the basis of production) should be authorised by independently approved information on output.

Recording and payment

There are usually embedded internal checks in payroll packages for inputs and calculations. Common would be access and validity embedded checks together with reconciliation procedures, such as casting and cross-casting payroll journals and ledgers. The usual segregation of duty protocols should be followed.

Once the payroll has been approved, and as, or after, recording has taken place, cheques can be drawn or automatic deposits can be authorised. Often, the person approving the payroll will be independent of the HR and payroll department, and payment can be made only on approval after verification of supporting data or documentation.

Payroll cycle: Substantive procedures

Audit objectives in terms of management's assertions are summarised in **Figure 14.14**.

Payroll cycle depth tests for substantive testing are similar to those for the sales and purchases subsystems (see **Figure 14.15**).

Tracing for *completeness* would normally move forward towards the ledger and account balances; *occurrence-validity* tests would go (vouch) the other way to payroll-authorising documents.

Government payroll forms, such as those prepared for the relevant tax authority, are useful for reconciliation to payroll records and to verify gross pay and liability accounts. End-of-year adjusting entries, which can be significant, should be reviewed. Essentially, tests on all of the following balances are involved in this cycle:

- *payroll or wages expense* – gross amount of wages
- *payroll payable* – for end-of-period net wages not yet paid
- *tax withholding payable* – collected on behalf of the employee but not yet paid
- *payroll expenses* – such as insurance, partially or fully funded by the employer
- *payroll tax (and other) expense* – non-wage employer expenses for employee.

Auditing in practice

IT audit note

Online audit test packages for payroll records normally involve:
- performing SpAR procedures by downloading client data and subjecting it to models to determine the reasonableness of payroll expenses
- applying test data to the system to test accuracy and occurrence-validity
- performing cut-off tests to ensure end-of-year expenses and liabilities are captured
- reviewing adjusting entries made and seeing how they were authorised and calculated
- comparing personnel records with employees paid (occurrence-validity, existence).

Occurrence-validity
Wage and salary rates and withholdings are authorised by the organisation, by the employee and in law.

Completeness
Payroll transactions that should be recorded, are recorded, and material payroll liabilities are accrued.

Accuracy
Accounting records and supporting schedules such as wage cards, payroll journals and ledgers are mathematically correct.

Classification
Accruals record appropriate current payroll liabilities.

Existence
Payroll payments and accrued liabilities are for actual employees.

Rights and obligations
Payroll liabilities represent valid claims on the organisation.

Valuation
Payroll liabilities are fairly stated.

Presentation
Payroll cycle information has been appropriately disclosed in the financial statements.

Figure 14.14 Substantive procedures for payroll cycle

As many concerns about payroll fraud have to do with unauthorised or non-existent employees, substantive tests may include a surprise payroll cut-off in which, on an unnotified date, the auditor requires the personal handing out of pay cheques. Any unclaimed cheques may indicate unauthorised employees and should be investigated. Although usually payroll errors are found to be immaterial, studying this system can lead to a reassessment of risk elsewhere.

CONCEPT QUESTION 4   What are the main payroll cycle risks?

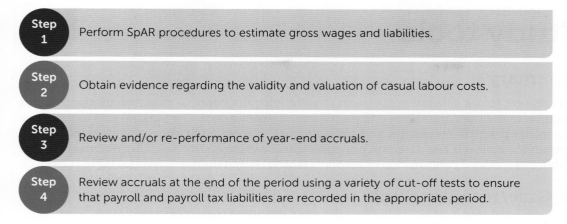

Step 1 Perform SpAR procedures to estimate gross wages and liabilities.

Step 2 Obtain evidence regarding the validity and valuation of casual labour costs.

Step 3 Review and/or re-performance of year-end accruals.

Step 4 Review accruals at the end of the period using a variety of cut-off tests to ensure that payroll and payroll tax liabilities are recorded in the appropriate period.

Figure 14.15 Essential procedures for payroll cycle

Study tools

Summary

This chapter took a subsystem approach to identifying the controls, risks and substantive tests common to the sales, purchases and payroll cycles (subsystems). The purpose was to introduce you to the practical procedures and tests adopted in most audit engagements, explained in terms of the concepts and assertion principles discussed previously. Key substantive procedures introduced included confirmation of accounts receivable and the depth tests for these cycles.

🔗 Case/resources link

CAATs for Classrooms

Accompanying this book is a series of data, integrated worksheets and exercises that are designed to support your learning and give you exposure to hands-on audit decision-making dilemmas faced by auditors in the planning elements of the audit process. Acquire the relevant material for this chapter from your instructor.

Review questions

14.1   Identify significant risks in each cycle and explain why they are a risk:

    a   sales cycle

    b   purchases cycle

    c   payroll cycle.

14.2   Describe the essential substantive procedures for the:

    a   sales cycle

    b   purchases cycle

    c   payroll cycle.

14.3   Define two *authorisation* controls that would be expected to exist in each of the:

    a   sales cycle

    b   purchases cycle

    c   payroll cycle.

14.4   Define 2–3 *completeness* controls that would be expected to exist in each of the:

    a   sales cycle

    b   purchases cycle

    c   payroll cycle.

14.5   Explain why the sales and purchases cycles should be separated.

14.6   Define 2–3 *validity* controls that would be expected to exist in each of the:

    a   sales cycle

    b   purchases cycle

    c   payroll cycle.

14.7 Define 2–3 *accuracy* controls that would be expected to exist in each of the:

    a   sales cycle

    b   purchases cycle

    c   payroll cycle.

14.8 Explain the role of prenumbered documents for shipping and sales invoices in preventing errors in the value of sales.

14.9 What duties should be segregated in the:

    a   sales cycle

    b   purchases cycle

    c   payroll cycle?

Exercises

14.1 **CONTROLS – EFFECTS:** A small medical practice consisted of the general practitioner (i.e., doctor), his wife (a nurse) and a practice administrator. The trusted practice administrator handled all of the appointments and patient payments. However, the GP discovered that she was not recording all the payments received for consultations and prescription scripts. The administrator was also responsible for banking the transactions.

    Required:

    a   What risks does this case raise for the audit of the financial statements?

    b   What internal controls would you recommend should be put in place?

14.2 **ANALYTICAL PROCEDURES – SALES:** Analytical procedures can highlight material misstatements in the sales cycle. What do each of the following analytical procedures potentially highlight in an audit of a retail organisation?

    a   sales commissions divided by net sales

    b   sales returns and allowances divided by gross sales

    c   accounts receivable as a percentage of credit sales.

14.3 **ANALYTICAL PROCEDURES – PURCHASES:** Analytical procedures can highlight material misstatements in the purchases cycle. What do each of the following potentially highlight in an audit of a retail organisation?

    a   purchases for the year broken down by month and compared to similar periods in prior years

    b   value of cost of goods sold (COGS) as a percentage of gross sales

    c   average wages divided by the number of employees

    d   Analyse the financial statements of a retailer. From your analysis, state the specific purchases cycle assertions requiring special audit effort to ensure material misstatements do not exist.

14.4 **PURCHASES:** FitOutz Limited manufactures kitchen fittings for domestic use. The production process involves raw materials such as plastics, wood, metal and various fabrics. Mahe, the warehouse department's inventory clerk, is responsible for all purchasing activity. He reviews the inventory records within the warehouse department and decides when certain materials need to be purchased.

Mahe prepares a purchase order, which he sends electronically to a supplier. The PO includes all the necessary information (materials to be purchased, the prices of the goods, the quantity needed and the requested delivery date). This PO is also sent to the receiving department.

The receiving clerk, Jackie, creates a receiving report once the materials are received. This report is based on the suppliers' packing slip and PO information. The receiving department files the packing slip, PO and receiving report.

The accounts payable department receives a copy of the receiving report. This report is matched to the invoice from the vendor, and Amanda, the accounts payable clerk, records the liability in the creditors account and the schedule for month-end payments. Any invoice problems are referred back to Mahe in the warehouse.

Required: With reference to the case study material above, respond to the questions below:

a   Draw a context diagram to show the purchasing cycle at FitOutz Limited.

b   List two internal control issues that arise in the purchasing system at FitOutz Limited and identify how these could be addressed (including who should take on the task).

c   Following evaluation of the internal controls, what substantive procedures would you recommend be part of the audit program?

d   In the audit of FitOutz Limited, the audit team runs test data through the purchases system. In two or three paragraphs, explain why the audit team would perform this test and state the drawbacks of this technique.

14.5   **CONTROL EFFECTS:** In 2020, a university students' association comes under investigation owing to missing funds in excess of $600 000. The association charged students $125 a year to belong in 2019 and $100 in 2018. Misappropriation examples included the following:

i   A student requested a hardship grant of $350 and received it in two envelopes, one containing $200 and one containing $150. She demanded to see the records and they said she had been paid $980. The student hardship fund paid no-one out in 2018 but $69 700 in 2019.

ii   The president's rent and other expenses were paid by the association and she is under police investigation.

iii   No financial accounts are available eight months after the end of the financial year, and the treasurer has resigned. Your audit firm has been asked to assist with assessing and auditing the financial position of the association.

Required:

a   What process should you go through in order to decide if your audit firm would take on the preparation and auditing of the association's accounts?

b   What are the key internal controls that you would recommend for ensuring that the payments from the association are appropriately authorised?

c   Draw a DFD and flowchart to show how a hardship grant application should be authorised and paid out.

14.6   **SALES:** Your client, Fitzherbert Shopping Centre, has 30 shop tenants. All leases with the shop tenants provide for a fixed rent plus a percentage of sales, net of GST, in excess of a fixed-dollar amount computed on an annual basis. Each lease also provides that the landlord may engage a chartered accountant to audit all records of the tenant for assurance that sales are being properly reported to the landlord.

Your client has requested you to audit the records of the Southern Star Restaurant to determine that the sales, totalling $390 000 for the year ended 30 June 2022, have been properly reported to the landlord. The restaurant and the shopping centre entered into a five-year lease on 1 July 2019. The Southern Star Restaurant is BYO and offers only table service. There are four or five servers in attendance who prepare handwritten prenumbered restaurant invoices for the customers during meal times. Payment is made at a cash register, manned by the proprietor, as the customer leaves. The proprietor is also the bookkeeper. Complete files are kept of restaurant invoices and cash register tapes. A daily sales book and general ledger are also maintained.

Required:

a   List the auditing procedures that you would employ to verify the total annual sales of Southern Star Restaurant.

b   Identify the primary control risks in this system from the information provided above and the implications of those risks for potential misstatement.

14.7   **PAYROLL:** Consider the following errors independently of each other.

i   Tom receives pay for working in a company in the building industry. He submits his time card on a weekly basis. While Jane in the HR department continues to approve his time cards, Tom has never been officially approved for employment due to his prior poor employment history.

ii   A payroll cheque is mistakenly made out for $670 instead of $6700.

iii   Amounts withheld for employee health insurance premiums are misappropriated to an account owned by an HR employee. The premiums are never paid. No-one has (as yet) made a claim on the insurance.

Required:

a   Are these events likely to lead to material error? Explain.

b   What control would have prevented or detected this problem?

c   How might the auditor have discovered it?

14.8   **PAYROLL:** Consider the following errors independently of each other:

i   Gary was employed by Smith Industries but left in May last year. His foreman did not notify management of his departure and instead completed time cards for him and approved them. The foreman then opened an account in Gary's name and deposited the cheques.

ii   A payroll cheque is mistakenly made out for $6700 instead of $670.

iii   An extra 0.10 is deducted from each employee's weekly pay cheque for tax withholding. The correct amount is paid to the relevant tax authority, and the difference is paid into an account controlled by the payroll clerk.

Required: Answer the following:

a   Are any of these events likely to lead to material error? Explain.

b   What control would have prevented or detected each problem identified?

c   How might the auditor have discovered it?

14.9 **SALES – ACCOUNTS RECEIVABLE:** Your firm has been engaged to audit the financial statements of RST Ltd for the year ending 31 December. RST Ltd is a medium-sized manufacturing company. The company has approximately 400 open trade accounts receivable and does not prepare monthly statements.

The audit manager assigned to the engagement has decided to circularise the trade accounts receivable as of 30 September (three months before year-end). The senior on the job asks you to be at the company headquarters on the morning of Wednesday 1 October, to mail requests for confirmation. He tells you to ask the company's personnel to prepare 25 positive confirmation requests and 100 negative confirmation requests.

He further asks you to obtain an aged trial balance as of 30 September, to trace the balances of the open accounts to the trial balance from the subsidiary ledgers, to test the ageing, to foot the trial balance, and to compare the total of the trial balance with the accounts receivable control account in the general ledger. The senior also informs you that detailed tests of the sales and credit journals will be made for September.

Required:

a How would you select the accounts to be circularised by the positive method?

b How would you select the accounts to be circularised by the negative method?

c Outline a plan for maintaining adequate control over confirmation requests.

14.10 **FLOWCHART EXAMPLES FOR SALES, PURCHASES AND PAYROLL:** For each of the three flowcharts in **Figure 14.16**, **Figure 14.17** and **Figure 14.18**:[3]

a identify existing controls and their purpose, and what they may prevent

b identify one or two controls that could exist but do not, and what they would serve.

---

[3] Our thanks to Carolyn Cordery for her support with portions of the documents in these figures.

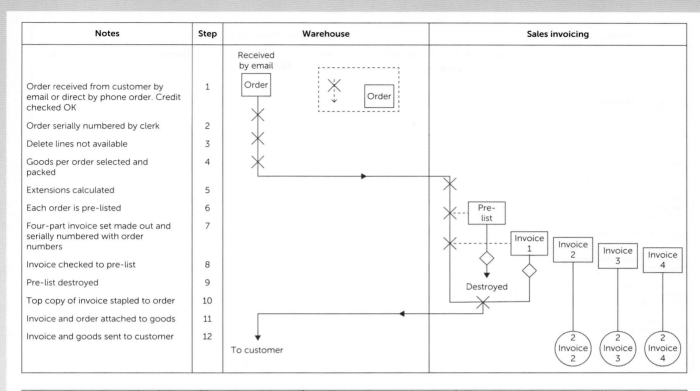

Notes	Step	Warehouse	Sales invoicing
Order received from customer by email or direct by phone order. Credit checked OK	1		
Order serially numbered by clerk	2		
Delete lines not available	3		
Goods per order selected and packed	4		
Extensions calculated	5		
Each order is pre-listed	6		
Four-part invoice set made out and serially numbered with order numbers	7		
Invoice checked to pre-list	8		
Pre-list destroyed	9		
Top copy of invoice stapled to order	10		
Invoice and order attached to goods	11		
Invoice and goods sent to customer	12		

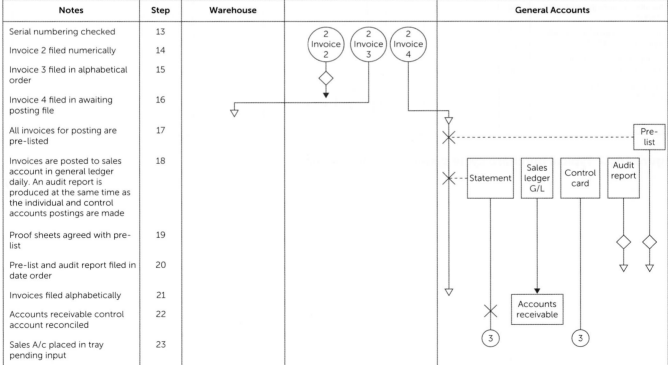

Notes	Step	Warehouse	General Accounts
Serial numbering checked	13		
Invoice 2 filed numerically	14		
Invoice 3 filed in alphabetical order	15		
Invoice 4 filed in awaiting posting file	16		
All invoices for posting are pre-listed	17		
Invoices are posted to sales account in general ledger daily. An audit report is produced at the same time as the individual and control accounts postings are made	18		
Proof sheets agreed with pre-list	19		
Pre-list and audit report filed in date order	20		
Invoices filed alphabetically	21		
Accounts receivable control account reconciled	22		
Sales A/c placed in tray pending input	23		

Figure 14.16 Typical sales cycle system: Partial flowchart

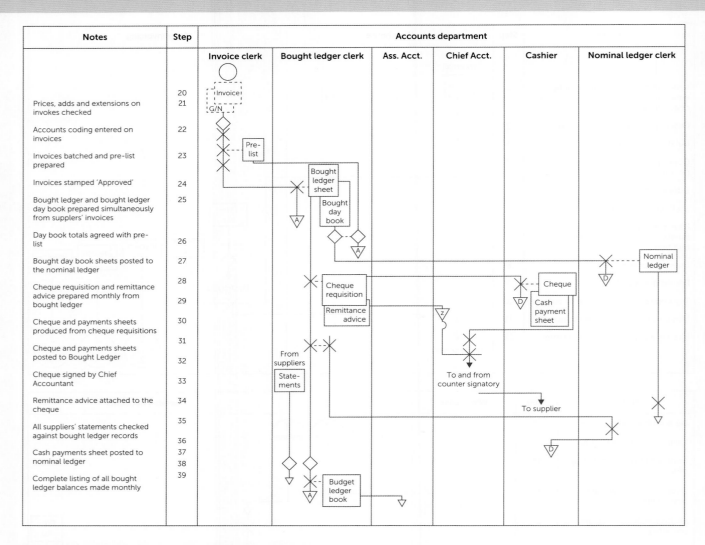

Notes	Step	Accounts department					
		Invoice clerk	**Bought ledger clerk**	**Ass. Acct.**	**Chief Acct.**	**Cashier**	**Nominal ledger clerk**
	20						
Prices, adds and extensions on invokes checked	21						
Accounts coding entered on invoices	22						
Invoices batched and pre-list prepared	23						
Invoices stamped 'Approved'	24						
Bought ledger and bought ledger day book prepared simultaneously from supplers' invoices	25						
Day book totals agreed with pre-list	26						
Bought day book sheets posted to the nominal ledger	27						
Cheque requisition and remittance advice prepared monthly from bought ledger	28 29						
Cheque and payments sheets produced from cheque requisitions	30						
Cheque and payments sheets posted to Bought Ledger	31 32						
Cheque signed by Chief Accountant	33						
Remittance advice attached to the cheque	34						
All suppliers' statements checked against bought ledger records	35 36						
Cash payments sheet posted to nominal ledger	37 38						
Complete listing of all bought ledger balances made monthly	39						

Figure 14.17 Typical purchase cycle system: Partial flowchart

→

→

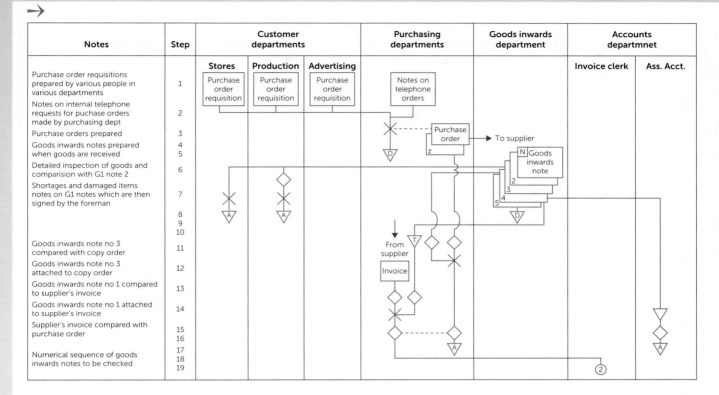

Notes	Step	Customer departments			Purchasing departments		Goods inwards department	Accounts departmnet	
		Stores	Production	Advertising				Invoice clerk	Ass. Acct.
Purchase order requisitions prepared by various people in various departments	1	Purchase order requisition	Purchase order requisition	Purchase order requisition	Notes on telephone orders				
Notes on internal telephone requests for puchase orders made by purchasing dept	2								
Purchase orders prepared	3					Purchase order			
Goods inwards notes prepared	4						N Goods inwards note		
when goods are received	5								
Detailed inspection of goods and comparision with G1 note 2	6								
Shortages and damaged items notes on G1 notes which are then signed by the foreman	7								
	8								
	9								
	10								
Goods inwards note no 3 compared with copy order	11				From supplier				
Goods inwards note no 3 attached to copy order	12								
Goods inwards note no 1 compared to supplier's invoice	13				Invoice				
Goods inwards note no 1 attached to supplier's invoice	14								
Supplier's invoice compared with purchase order	15								
	16								
	17								
Numerical sequence of goods inwards notes to be checked	18								
	19								

Figure 14.17 continued

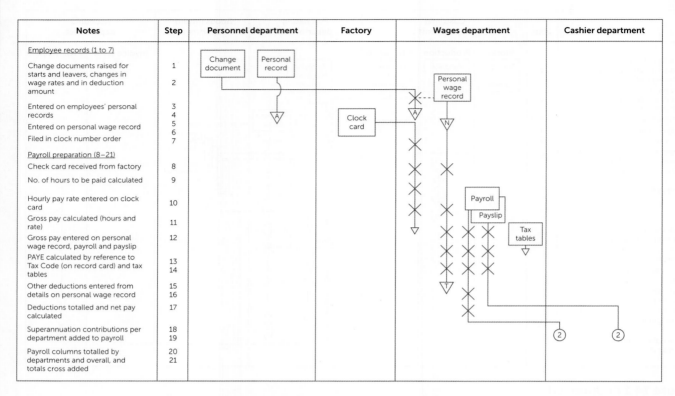

Notes	Step	Personnel department	Factory	Wages department	Cashier department
Employee records (1 to 7)		Change document Personal record		Personal wage record	
Change documents raised for starts and leavers, changes in wage rates and in deduction amount	1 2				
Entered on employees' personal records	3 4		Clock card		
Entered on personal wage record	5 6				
Filed in clock number order	7				
Payroll preparation (8–21)					
Check card received from factory	8				
No. of hours to be paid calculated	9			Payroll	
Hourly pay rate entered on clock card	10			Payslip	
Gross pay calculated (hours and rate)	11			Tax tables	
Gross pay entered on personal wage record, payroll and payslip	12				
PAYE calculated by reference to Tax Code (on record card) and tax tables	13 14				
Other deductions entered from details on personal wage record	15 16				
Deductions totalled and net pay calculated	17				
Superannuation contributions per department added to payroll	18 19				
Payroll columns totalled by departments and overall, and totals cross added	20 21				

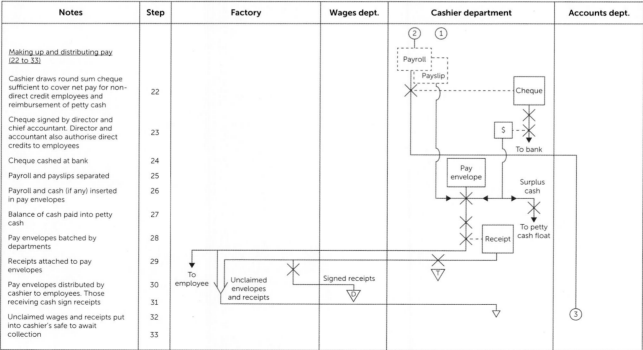

Notes	Step	Factory	Wages dept.	Cashier department	Accounts dept.
Making up and distributing pay (22 to 33)				Payroll Payslip	
Cashier draws round sum cheque sufficient to cover net pay for non-direct credit employees and reimbursement of petty cash	22			Cheque	
Cheque signed by director and chief accountant. Director and accountant also authorise direct credits to employees	23			$ To bank	
Cheque cashed at bank	24				
Payroll and payslips separated	25			Pay envelope Surplus cash	
Payroll and cash (if any) inserted in pay envelopes	26				
Balance of cash paid into petty cash	27			To petty cash float	
Pay envelopes batched by departments	28			Receipt	
Receipts attached to pay envelopes	29	To employee			
Pay envelopes distributed by cashier to employees. Those receiving cash sign receipts	30 31	Unclaimed envelopes and receipts	Signed receipts		
Unclaimed wages and receipts put into cashier's safe to await collection	32 33				

Figure 14.18 Typical payroll cycle system: Partial flowchart

Systems II: Warehousing, financing and fixed assets

Introduction

This chapter continues our introduction to audit risks, controls and substantive tests for commonly encountered client subsystems from Chapter 14. The following cycles are discussed in this chapter:

- *Warehousing cycle* – deals with where and how inventory is received and later shipped out to customers.
- *Financing cycle* – deals with processes to acquire and use funds and other financial resources.
- *Fixed assets and intangibles cycle* – deals with the acquisition, maintenance, valuation and disposal of long-term assets.

The transactions in these cycles – with the notable exception of cash – tend to be fewer in number and larger in size than in sales, purchases or payroll subsystems. Purchasing a building may be expensive but likely infrequent. Hence, random sampling may be less common, while original document examination is highly common. Year-end adjustments for accounts can often be material and, as they may involve long-term assets or liabilities 'opening balances', they can take on significance.

Systems tests for warehousing, financing and fixed assets is part of tests of controls and substantive testing (see **Figure 15.1**).

Professional scepticism

Professional scepticism 'is about asking the right questions, not simply a lot of them, and about not accepting the first answer. It is also clearly about having the experience to recognise what can go wrong' (ICAEW, 2018).

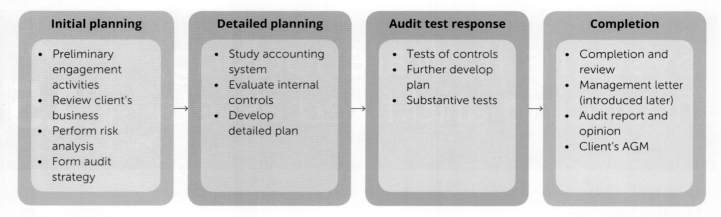

Figure 15.1 Steps in an audit process

Warehousing (inventory) subsystem

The *warehousing cycle* is the subsystem dealing with inventory, which is received into the organisation and then on-sold to customers. Inventory that is warehoused may comprise consumer goods ready for sale or goods to which the organisation will add value, such as raw materials or work in progress. In retail organisations, this could even include, for example, value added to food at a café. While the previous chapter considered the costs relating to inventory flowing in and out, this chapter focuses on the risks and tests around warehoused inventory.

Risks in warehousing

Inventory presents the greatest verification problems of any asset, largely because the amounts involved are invariably material, directly affect profit, and are subject to misappropriation and distortion. Stock shrinkage can occur. Inventory may be correct in amount but difficult to locate. Complex costing systems and supply chains increase error, theft and distortion risks.

Stock shrinkage

The major cause of overstatement of inventory is stock shrinkage (theft). It is estimated that shrinkage accounts for between 1.75 per cent and 4 per cent of total sales in retail, and over 0.5 per cent in manufacturing (de Kok, von Donselaar and van Woensel, 2008). Shoplifting is a multimillion-dollar industry, and an allowance is commonly built into retail prices for its likelihood.

Fraud or theft by employees is becoming just as common. If custody procedures are weak, employees may remove stock and hide the deficiency by falsifying stock records. Although some 'stock shrinkage' is almost inevitable, it can be kept to a minimum with the use of controlled storerooms and automated security measures.

None of this can, of course, prevent out-and-out theft, although barcode security can go a long way to forestalling it. As auditors, we must consider the reasonableness of the client's loss estimates and advise them as to controls to forestall future crime.

Multiple warehouses

Inventory may be at a number of different locations, which requires controls in each location and when shipping between locations. Having inventory close to customers reduces delivery times, but multiple warehouses increase the risks of error. Complex supply chains do as well. While inventory may be correctly logged, if it is difficult to locate at year-end, then *valuation*, *existence* and even *ownership* (*rights-obligation*) can be difficult to prove.

Distorted inventory value

Senior management may be motivated to distort stock values to achieve the appearance of a better profit or asset picture. Stock can also be stolen and accounts distorted to cover up the theft. Obsolescence or damage can be missed.

> **Auditing in practice**
>
> ### Inventory distortion at Fortex
>
> Fortex, a New Zealand meat-processing company, illustrates how distortion in inventory is possible. Low-value lamb ribs were classified as high-value products in its year-end stock. It is understood this error was not detected by the external auditors.
>
> Source: Owusu-Ansah et al. (2002).

Some type of inventory products are difficult to value and may require the services of an outside expert.

Warehousing controls

Procedures for recording stock movements to and from the warehouse for purchases and sales were considered previously, so they are not repeated here. Controls over custody and stock count are distinct, however. Therefore, they are divided into controls over 'custody', which should operate throughout the year; and over 'stock count', which may only occur on an annual or semiannual basis.

Controls over custody

Tests of controls over custody are required throughout the year. These tests involve six major steps to ensure proper accounting for stock: ordering goods, physical controls, checking of controls at the stage of issuing stock, maintenance of stock records, reconciling of physical quantities, and the recording of any stock write-offs:

1 *Ordering goods:* Stock should be ordered from approved suppliers, and receiving, checking and recording goods inwards should be instituted.
2 *Physical controls:* Custody procedures are normally achieved using segregated, lockable areas under the control of a store person who is held accountable by means of stock records. Electronic locks and layered password protection can also be useful to enable specific authority over access.
3 *Store-person issuing stock:* Properly authorised inventory requisitions should precede any release of stock. Goods should not be allowed out of the premises without proper despatch documentation.

(Unauthorised despatches may not be discovered until the stocktake, when it will be too late.) Warehouses should have physical controls over people entering the premises. Normally, one person should be in charge to ensure there is a clear line of accountability.

4 *Maintenance of stock records:* Stock records should be kept by someone who has no access to physical stock and is not responsible for sales or purchases records.

5 *Reconciling:* Physical quantities should be reconciled to stock records. This internal check may be managed by an independent internal auditor.

6 *Write-offs:* Any writing-off or provisioning for damaged, slow-moving and obsolete stock should be performed by an independent official on the authorisation of appropriate evidence.

Note how the principles of segregation apply. Asset custody is separate from recording, and recording from reconciliation is distinct from the right to authorise write-offs and changes to the general ledger. In the absence of segregation, the auditors should reconsider their own analysis of control risk and the subsequent implications for substantive audit testing.

The same principles apply, of course, to less tangible stock such as customer data or design illustrations kept in a database. Controls may be in the form of computer access codes, communication encryption and data-storage controls. **Figure 15.2** provides the warehousing DFD context.

While the nature of a system changes the type of test, it does not modify the underlying principles of control. **Figure 15.3** presents the warehousing data flow level 0 example.

Controls over stock count: What the auditor does on New Year's Eve

Significant controls in this cycle are carried out when the (usually annual) stocktake is conducted. It may be essential for the auditors to be present while a stocktake is on; their tests are discussed later. Controls should, at a minimum, have the following characteristics:

- The person checking the stock should be independent of those controlling stock in other ways. Usually, stocktakers are employed on a temporary basis.
- The instructions given to stocktakers are clear and are followed.

Figure 15.2 Warehousing: DFD context

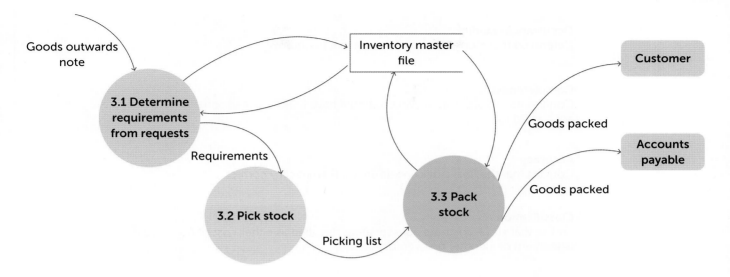

Figure 15.3 Warehousing data flow: Level 0 example

- The instructions include procedures for dealing with exceptions. Exceptions may occur, for example, when a stock item is missing or is in an inappropriate location.
- There is adequate supervision of stocktaking at all times. It is good practice to have stocktakers working in pairs.
- Test counts are an internal check by the client on the stocktakers (the auditors will also perform test counts independently of the client's procedures).
- Stock records are controlled, prenumbered or access-restricted to ensure that none disappear (understatement) or are fabricated (overstatement).
- The counting process is observed to ensure that stocktakers follow processes, including over exceptions, and identify damaged or obsolete stock.
- The process is orderly, and sufficient time is available for the count.
- Information is recorded in ink or in data files that cannot be modified.
- Adequate physical security is provided. For example, doors should be secured, and access is given only to authorised individuals.

    Organisations now use *radio frequency identification* (*RFID*) tags to track stock through a warehouse. Chips inserted into goods or pallets are scanned by hand-held devices, improving efficiency and offering segregation of duties between assets (stock) and recording (RFID). Risks include double-counting, missing items and poor programming.[1]

    Overall, the purpose of the auditor observing the stocktake is to ensure that management procedures for this process are being followed.

Warehousing substantive procedures

Tests for this system centre on warehoused stock, tests over their entry and exit, and recording. Direct labour costs for manufactured goods may be tested in the payroll cycle. To identify risks related to the custody of stock and its count, an auditor will usually address management assertions (see **Figure 15.4**).

---

[1] More on IT audits can be found in the internal audit section of this text: see Chapter 18.

Occurrence-validity
Determine that stock listed is of the current period.

Completeness
Confirm that all stock items which should have been counted actually have been accounted for.

Accuracy
Confirm that the final stock sheets are mathematically correct.

Classification
Ensure that stock costs are appropriately classified as either cost of goods sold (statement of income) or inventory (asset).

Existence
Confirm that stock on hand exists, including owned in-transit items.

Rights-Obligations
Determine ownership of stock on hand.

Valuation
Determine that the valuations on the stock are appropriate.

Presentation
Confirm that inventory has been appropriately recognised in the financial statements and disclosed in the notes to the account.

Figure 15.4 Assertions for the warehousing subsystem

With respect to *presentation*, inventory and work in progress should be subclassified on the face of the balance sheet in accordance with GAAP. GAAP also determines appropriate disclosure for stock valuation, cost of sales, writedowns, and inventories pledged as security (AASB 102; NZ IAS 2: Inventories, para 36).[2]

Rights and obligations are of particular concern for the stock. The consignment of goods may require contract inspections to determine ownership. Cut-off tests may be needed for overstatement (occurrence-validity), and completeness ownership should be determined.

The so-called Romalpa or 'reservation of title' clause is of interest in Australia and New Zealand. In the absence of a specific contract specifying otherwise, the title to goods passes to the buyer on delivery (as it does when goods are sold freight on board (FOB destination)).

---

[2] Note that AASB and NZ IAS are accounting standards, not *auditing* standards.

Auditing in practice

The Romalpa concept

The famous case of *Aluminium Industrie Vaassen BV v. Romalpa Aluminium Ltd* (1976, 2 552, QBD and CA) involved a transaction that was made subject to a reservation of title clause. It stipulated that until the purchaser had paid for the raw materials, ownership remained with the seller. Subsequent development of the Romalpa concept extended the seller's ownership claims to manufactured goods.

Thus, if the buyer goes into liquidation after delivery but before payment, then the seller could lose the stock and the money. The auditor should inspect major contracts for any title reservations or their absence.

Specific analytical review procedures

An analytical review of inventory will highlight possible misstatements in stock records. At a minimum, the ratio of inventory to cost of sales for each type of inventory, each location, and over time or comparatively should be performed for:
- steady patterns (suggesting no obvious problems)
- steady build-up of inventory, suggesting possible overstocking or obsolescence
- inventory reduction, suggesting possible liquidity problems
- missing inventory, suggesting error or fraud
- a dramatic build-up of inventory, suggesting possible management distortion.

Of course, unusual patterns could indicate normal industry, legal or business events. The auditor must determine whether a material misstatement is or is not the source.

Substantive tests of detail/transactions

Auditing standards make it clear that the external auditor has a role in ensuring that inventory is not misstated in the client's accounts.

> If inventory is material to the financial statements, the auditor shall obtain sufficient appropriate audit evidence regarding [its] existence and condition by: (a) Attendance at physical inventory counting, unless impracticable ... (iv) Perform[ing] test counts; and (b) Performing the audit procedures over the entity's final inventory records ...
> (ASA 501, para 4; ISA NZ 501)

These standards recognise that if an auditor is unable to attend the year-end stocktake, alternative procedures should be undertaken. In addition, the auditor should normally perform the substantive tests outlined in **Figure 15.5**.

If a periodic inventory system is used, stocktaking may require the auditors to be on the premises at odd hours and at unusual times (i.e., New Year's Eve), as the count is the only way to verify what is sold and what stock remains.

Sample plans, and their randomness, depending on the situation. The auditor may need to observe the stock count at specific locations or select them for their risk or value. Test data and dummy variables should not interfere with the client's data or processes, so it is best to inform the internal auditor about what an external auditor needs to do so that they can work together on it.

CONCEPT QUESTION 1   Explain the concept of cut-off tests and why these are necessary.

Check the stock programs, or run test data to ensure that:
- stock item data within a reasonable range is all captured *(completeness)*
- journal counts, such as entry additions and withdrawal subtractions, are handled appropriately by the program *(accuracy)*
- updating of continuous (perpetual) stock records appears to be performed appropriately *(classification primarily)*
- data storage cannot be uploaded, modified or deleted without authority *(occurrence/validity)*.

Vouch stock recorded back to original input, invoices, overhead costs or documents.
Pay particular attention to unusual amounts, items or adjusting entries *(occurrence/validity)*.

Perform cut-off tests on transactions just before *(occurrence-validity)* and just after the balance date *(completeness)* to ensure that entries are recorded in the correct period. This may require examining evidence of goods-in-shipment, particularly if they are shipped FOB shipping point (when the title changes).

Compare stock cost calculations with the valuation method used, such as LIFO, FIFO or weighted average.

Check a sample of stock against market values, particularly those in which there may have been obsolescence or stock damage.

Consider whether the client has followed GAAP as to *valuation* (lower of cost or market) or whether a valuation specialist is needed.

Agree sales and purchases at year-end to accrual schedules and supporting documentation for *existence* and *ownership*.

Be present for and review the stocktaking process:
- to ensure authorised procedures are being applied
- to take test samples and recount
- to ensure that amounts counted are those entered into the records.

Pay particular attention to large or unusual items, or any adjusting entries made outside the usual system or at year-end.

Inspect error and exception reports to identify unauthorised entries.

Figure 15.5 Essential substantive procedures: Warehousing

Finance subsystem

The *finance cycle* includes the processes used to acquire, use and hold financial resources. These include:
- cash and other liquid assets
- investments such as company shares, art and other valuables
- derivatives and financial instruments, bitcoin and virtual assets
- liabilities such as short- and long-term loans, debentures, contingent liabilities, provisions and deferred expenses

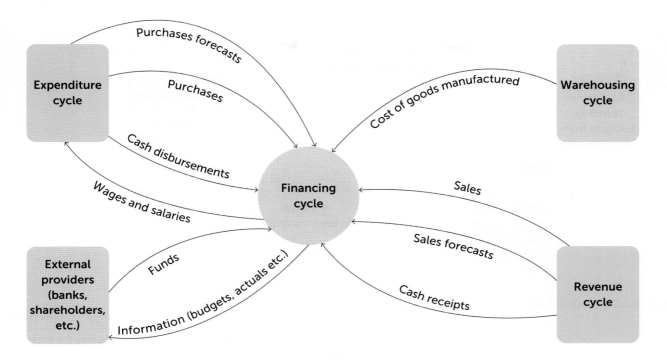

Figure 15.6 Context for a financing subsystem

- equity accounts, such as share, partner or owner capital, and retained earnings.

If individually material but infrequent, *existence* and *rights-obligations* may require verification from their original documents. GAAP may provide a guide as to how they are to be *presented*. It is incumbent upon the auditor to remain current with accounting standards to ensure that *presentation*, *classification* and *valuation* are compliant.

While these assets may not be visible, if they are not safeguarded, there will be opportunities for theft. So, for example, it may be important for the client to ensure that only authorised staff can uplift financial assets, that investments are only made within authorised policies, and that an independent check (e.g., reconciliation) occurs at regular intervals. This section will consider cash, investments, derivatives and financial instruments, then equity and liabilities. Broadly, this subsystem can be illustrated by the DFDs in **Figure 15.6** and **Figure 15.7**.

Cash and liquid assets

Cash is always susceptible to fraud, and it is almost impossible to eliminate this risk entirely. The following control principles may keep problems below a material level.

Controls for cash

Controls over the handling of cash normally include the following:
- The best control over cash lies in an *independent reconciliation*, comparing, for example, records of cash receipts with amounts deposited. Frequent reconciliation of cash control accounts to the independently produced bank statement is essential for effective cash control.

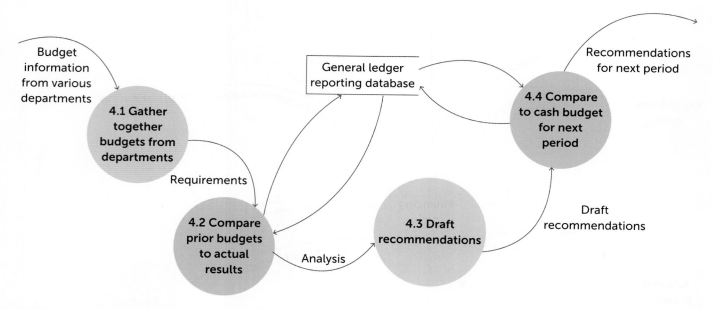

Figure 15.7 Level 0 diagram for a financing subsystem

- A *cash imprest system* can be useful to control small amounts of cash on hand used to pay for small items ('petty cash'). A cash imprest system calls for petty cash payments only when receipts are tendered for expenditure.
- Whenever possible, there should be an *independent record of monies received*. The best method is to segregate the point of sale/loan from the point of cash receipt. This may be done by one person electronically if, on recording a sale via barcode, it captures the correct price without intervention by the cashier.
- Arrangements should be made for senior officials to take over the function of authorising cash payments or recording receipts when the person responsible is on leave. Requiring staff to *take leave* is an important control, and a number of organisations require staff to take a minimum of two weeks in a row. This reduces the likelihood of schemes involving timing such as teeming and lading.
- Large payments can be *authorised by two officials* to control expenditure, with supporting evidence of dual approval. Internal checks or the auditor's random checks can identify non-dual-approved payments.
- Minimum controls might include reconciliation between the bank and accounting records, controlled authorisations over access, internal checks to ensure correct coding, and data-storage control over records and controls.

Substantive tests for cash

Audit procedures to substantiate cash balances may include the following:
- The auditor reviews the client's year-end reconciliation of the cash receipts journal to bank statements as a matter of course, with particular attention paid to unpresented cheques and uncleared lodgements, to ensure *completeness*.
- The auditors should *obtain a bank certificate* directly from any institution known to have a relationship with the client (see **Figure 15.8**). The bank certificate authenticates balances as at the year-end and may uncover unknown accounts or liabilities. Independent confirmation is important because, without it, a client could create artificial evidence of assets to conceal defalcations.

Bank certificate

To: [Bank or lender] Manager

Date: [Today]

Dear ...

Request for Bank Confirmation for R. Client [account number]

We are writing to request and to authorise you to complete a standard Auditors' Confirmation form as to accounts, loans, financial instruments and/or other arrangements held with us in any branch of your institution.

To facilitate the timely completion of our financial statement audit, it would be most appreciated if you could complete and return via secure email to [address] by [date] directly to our auditor Princeton Carlson Ltd [address], and a duplicate copy to us at [address].

We assume that the report will be completed honestly and with the best knowledge available to the branch at the time it is prepared. Any charge for providing this information can be charged to our account. We thank you for your time and efforts in this regard.

Yours sincerely,

R. Client

Please include any and all of the following held by us:

- Bank accounts
- Promissory notes
- Loans, short- or long-term
- Financial instruments
- Accounts open or closed, when, and amounts
- Foreign currency contracts
- Offset arrangements
- Insurance or surety arrangements, beneficiaries
- Other arrangements

Please include the following information for each arrangement.

- Account name and number
- Interest rate and repayment terms
- Accrued interest
- Currency held
- Any restrictions or withdrawals
- Items held for security
- Money-laundering issues raised during the year

Figure 15.8 Bank certificate: Reduced example

However, this may not bring to light bank accounts which are held but which the auditors do not know about, so any indication of a client's relationship with new or unknown lenders should be investigated further – particularly if it is hidden, it is likely to be material.

- The *review of endorsements* on the back of cheques, or *authorisations* on electronic disbursements, can provide assurance that payments were made to authorised individuals (*validity*). A relatively common fraud is to issue a cheque/payment to an authorised individual only to have it diverted, through endorsement on the cheque, to another account. In Australia and New Zealand, cashed cheques are not usually provided with the bank statement, and an auditor's request will incur a bank fee for the client. Although this has cost implications, auditors' need for assurance may call for this sometimes-unpopular request, as identifying unusual payees can be indicative of fraud.

- *Petty-cash balances* will often be counted by the auditor, although they will seldom be material. They are counted because of their susceptibility to fraud and because management often expects the auditors to perform this function. If possible, all cash holdings should be counted at the same time to prevent the possibility of substitution.
- Inspect *error and exception reports* for, for example, invalid transactions or access at unusual times or places.

In addition to these substantive procedures, analytical procedures can serve cash and other liquid asset reviews. This can include quick ratio to ensure that the organisation has sufficient funds to repay current debt (a going concern issue). The organisation's budget can be useful in assessing cash-management projections.

Traditional investments

Traditional investments include share ownership, cash deposits, tradeable government or company bonds, property and the like. In order to ensure that the risks present in any audit are minimised, an auditor may look for the following controls and undertake specific audit tests for investments, as noted here:

- To ensure *accuracy and occurrence-validity*, the cost of investments acquired during the year should be vouched to contract notes and brokers' statements.
- The *valuation* of investments should be at the lower end of cost or market and *classified* as current or long-term assets, as appropriate.
- Share registry reports or broker statements should be inspected for *existence* and *rights-obligations*. A circularisation of the share registries confirming their ownership and value may be appropriate.
- Some investments are difficult to value – such as superannuation schemes valued at a net market value (under AASB 1056: Superannuation Entities and NZ IAS 26: Accounting and Reporting by Retirement Benefit Plans) – and guidance, where available, should be used to assess the client's estimate.

According to the organisation's liquidity needs, tax goals and long-term strategies, investment assets will change, and change carries audit risk. Auditors should review formation documents, minutes and other legal documents to understand the *rights/ownership*, *valuation* and *validity* of the client's investments. For example, outsourcing, knowledge sharing, the Romalpa clause and other alliance agreements may replace simple share-ownership *rights*. Board minutes can also draw attention to 'investments' misclassified as 'revenue' and other distortion or omission risks.

Auditing in practice

Bernard Madoff

Bernard Madoff was convicted in June 2010 and sentenced to 150 years in prison. He ran a Ponzi scheme to attract new investors, using the funds from new investors to pay the older ones. Madoff courted investors by promising ever-increasing returns, apparently picking stocks that would always rise (Jackson, 2010). While this was logically impossible, Madoff fleeced 'investors' for many years.

Frauds such as those perpetrated by Madoff, the collapse of Greensill Capital, and failures in Australia and New Zealand's finance companies between 2008 and 2010, reinforce the need for independent valuations of an organisation's investments.

Derivatives and financial instruments

The value of derivatives, a high-risk investment, has been under discussion for many years. The current requirements are incorporated in AASB 132 and NZ IAS 32: Financial Instruments: Presentation. It is challenging for the professional to keep up with new standards, yet where they concern a material asset, the determination of their value may be guided by GAAP. Implications for going concern, related parties and contingent liabilities should always be considered.

A **financial instrument** is any contract that gives rise to a (recognised or unrecognised) financial asset of one entity and a (recognised or unrecognised) financial liability or equity instrument of another entity (AASB 132; NZ IAS 32, para 11).

This is a broad definition indeed and includes, for example, commodity-linked arrangements whereby the holder receives something (cash, shares) contingent on the value or occurrence of something occurring in the future. It is difficult to come up with an objective value as it depends on future events. Managers are known to give optimistic values or idealised likelihoods of future events. To that end, AASB 132 and NZ IAS 32 attempt to provide some guidance:

> For each class of financial asset ... liability and equity instrument ... disclose:
>
> - information about the extent and nature of the financial instruments
> - the accounting policies and methods adopted, including the criteria for recognition and the basis of measurement applied.

Following the financial crisis, the IFRS 9 (AASB 9; NZ IAS 9) was introduced by the IASB to recognise expected loan losses, as the expected loss impairment model is considered to allow more timely recognition of anticipated credit losses than is possible using the incurred loss method (Kutubi et al., 2021). Auditors need to carefully examine the application of the change in the standard and evaluate the impact of the forward-looking expected credit loss model that should result in more timely recognition of loan losses.

The auditor's task is to ensure that such disclosures have been made. The risk of overstatement is most likely when the client owns the instrument; the risk of understatement (or omission) is most likely when the client issues the instrument. It will be necessary to assess management's assumptions of discount ratios, specific markets and risks (as laid out in ASA 540 and ISA NZ 540: Auditing Accounting Estimates and Related Disclosures). This is a specialist area where it may be pertinent for auditors to obtain expert advice.

financial instrument
Any contract that gives rise to a (recognised or unrecognised) financial asset of one entity and a (recognised or unrecognised) financial liability or equity instrument of another entity. (AASB 132; NZ IAS 32, para 11)

Equity and liability accounts

The other side of the balance sheet also deserves a careful review, as discussed next.

Equity and debenture accounts

A number of audit risks emerge in the area of equity and debenture accounts. Distortion is a risk, particularly in owner-controlled companies where loans and changes of equity may be difficult to differentiate from each other and where the owner-manager may seek to show one as the other for tax or lending purposes.

Court cases even as far back as, for example, *London and General Bank* [1895], involve inappropriate distributions of equity, reminding us of their materiality to potential users and the litigation that could result from their misuse. The greatest risks arise due to the possibility of fraud by senior management. For this reason, auditors need to reflect on their assessments of management integrity as well as the strength of their controls.

Common audit-testing procedures include:

- reviewing the allocation between equity and debt for *occurrence-validity* and *classification*, as to, for example, convertible debt and financial instruments
- reviewing any accounts that form a part of distributable retained earnings (specifically dividends), as unauthorised distributions can lead to lawsuits, particularly should company failure occur
- looking for the directors' sign-off that the organisation meets the solvency test at the time of the distribution (it is not an auditor's task to complete a solvency test)
- vouching any issue of shares during the period against board minutes for authority, and against the memorandum of association, to ensure that the authorised share capital has not been exceeded
- the reverse – tracing from the minutes to issue – so as to provide assurance of *completeness*; disclosure should align with the appropriate GAAP
- checking debenture issues for authorisation by reference to the board minutes and the articles of association. Premiums and discounts should be disclosed in accordance with GAAP.

Contingencies and estimates

A contingent liability is defined in AASB 137 and NZ IAS 37: Provisions, Contingent Liabilities and Contingent Assets, as a 'possible obligation that arises from past events and whose existence will be confirmed only by the occurrence of uncertain future events' (para 10).

As has long been the practice, contingent liabilities are generally disclosed, but not in the body of the financial statements. It is assumed that they are 'assessed continually to determine whether [they qualify as a contingent liability]' (AASB 137, para 30; NZ IAS 37, para 30). The auditor should, therefore, carefully review evidence of that assessment and the appropriateness of the disclosure, as well as the appropriateness of any provisions needed to settle them.

There is a significant risk of inadequate disclosure in this area, as management may be reluctant to inform shareholders about uncertain, potentially costly events, or to raise hopes by projecting positive uncertain events. A review of these accounts is also important for partnerships, cooperatives and public sector organisations.

> The auditor is to obtain sufficient appropriate audit evidence about whether: (a) accounting estimates, including fair value accounting estimates, in the financial statements ... are reasonable; and (b) related disclosure in the financial statements are adequate, in the context of the applicable financial reporting framework. (ASA 540, para 6; ISA NZ 540, para 6)

Evidence of estimates, with respect to contingencies, will usually involve:

- confirmation from the client's solicitor that there is no pending litigation against the client, or if there is, what the terms and anticipated costs are (*completeness* or *presentation*) (see ASA 501 and ISA NZ 501: Audit Evidence – Specific Considerations for Inventory and Segment Information)
- reviews of the board's minutes, revealing potential liabilities (*completeness*)
- letters of representation signed by the client towards the end of the audit
- observations and discussions with management and staff generally.

Loans and other liabilities

The greatest risk here is that *off-balance-sheet financing* is an inappropriate classification of debt and hides the true value of liabilities. An organisation may conceal debt in order not to breach a lending covenant or to improve the financial picture generally to reduce their own risk of losing necessary finance. The result would be an overstatement of net assets.

Auditing in practice

Incorrectly recorded loans at Fortex

A New Zealand company – Fortex, a meat processor – illustrates the problems that can occur if loans are not recorded properly. In the few years prior to its failure, Fortex recorded loans as 'sales' and, by doing so, substantially overstated net income and net asset value.

Off-balance-sheet financing may include traditional debt arrangements or could arise from, for example, undisclosed public–private partnerships, commitments to defined benefit plans, or guarantees on behalf of related organisations. Solicitor confirmations and bank confirmations, along with general awareness and attention to unusual transactions or unknown lenders, may be the only ways in which auditors can identify unrecorded liabilities if management intentionally conceals their source.

Minimum testing in the area of loans should include:

- reviews of board minutes (*completeness*)
- reviews of original loan documents (*occurrence-validity: classification, accuracy*)
- confirmations to lenders (both *completeness* and *occurrence-validity*)
- analytical procedures as to loan expenditures or unusual relationships (*completeness* or *classification*)
- reviews of interest payment patterns or solvency patterns
- re-performance or reviews of the loans payable schedule
- reviews for proper *presentation* and being sensitive to any preoccupation by management on the selection of specific accounting disclosures.

Deferred taxes

Because directors are allowed to omit a provision for deferred taxation in some circumstances, auditors must satisfy themselves as to whether those circumstances exist. A deferred taxes audit involves re-performance of the calculations used to reach the balance, a review of the assumptions taken to carry out those calculations, and an inspection of how they are disclosed in the financial statements. This includes checking calculations for timing differences and allocations. Appropriate accounting standards include AASB 112 and NZ IAS 12): Income Taxes.

CONCEPT QUESTION 2	What distinguishes a contingent liability from liability in terms of audit risk?

Fixed assets and intangibles

The *fixed assets cycle* comprises the purchasing, maintenance, valuation and disposal of long-term assets. Other long-term assets include intangibles. Property, plant and equipment are subject to similar risks as those to stock (see **Figure 15.9**).

We expect an authorised purchase requisition, a competitive selection of a vendor, and order preparation on purchase. Asset delivery notes should match those that are ordered. Asset values may increase once onsite; so for example, a movable building cost, once established, may be increased for the cost of the foundation, plumbing and electrical infrastructure. A *segregation of duties* specific to their control may include:

- authorisation of capital expenditures performed by a senior member of management, or by the board if material

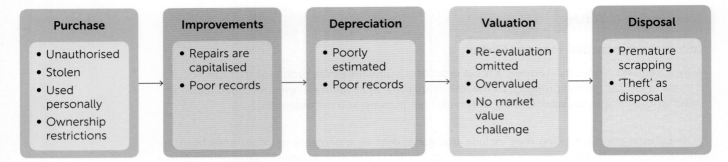

Figure 15.9 Fixed asset misstatement risks

- accounting records, which should be maintained by someone, or a system, unassociated with the purchase, disposition or warehousing of fixed assets
- plant and property registers, which are maintained separately from control over the asset itself, so that reconciliations between the two will constitute a meaningful control
- ownership restrictions, such as if the title is limited under the Romalpa clause, lease arrangements, in-transit supply chain arrangements, or other debt obligations.

Many organisations have separate fixed asset registers for recording long-term assets and determining depreciation, but these are often simple PC-based systems with poor controls (King, 2005), which staff may fail to maintain. Other concerns include valuation and revaluation if the asset is modified, and authorisation for disposal. Fixed assets may, in particular, be susceptible to fraud or distortion.

Fraud

Misappropriation is a significant risk for an organisation that owns small or online but valuable, fixed assets. The following situations present the greatest risk of fixed asset fraud:

- *Theft* – small portable items can be easily stolen from the premises. This can be prevented by ensuring that someone is accountable for all items of equipment and by providing access controls. If the thief also has access to accounting records or a plant register, they will be able to conceal the misappropriation.
- *Online assets* – these should be subject to IT controls to prevent unauthorised use.
- *Premature scrapping* of an asset by an employee who then sells it for cash. The same can occur with assets sold prior to retirement and being written off.
- *Company assets that can be used for private purposes*. This practice will inevitably happen to some degree, but major frauds can also occur in this way. It can be difficult to prevent if senior management is involved. Still, the internal audit department can play a useful role by making spot checks on the location and by examining the condition of assets.

Distortion

The auditor's task may also include ensuring that the client hasn't overestimated the value of a fixed asset, as doing so would lead to overstatement. AASB 116 and NZ IAS 16: Property, Plant and Equipment, set out the principle that the carrying amount should not be greater than the recoverable amount. This can occur from a failure to:

- depreciate the assets using an acceptable method or over an appropriate life
- disclose liabilities or ownership restrictions related to the assets
- write down asset values where the asset's recoverable amount differs from the carrying value (this may occur where the asset is obsolete or damaged)

- omit recording non-owned assets, such as those in transit or on consignment
- capitalise repairs, interest expense, research or development as assets.

Audit of fixed assets

The auditor's task is to ensure that there are no material misstatements in recording fixed assets, including depreciation. A sample may be taken, either random or – often for this asset – a selection of the higher-risk assets.

Auditing in practice

Avoiding material misstatements

An auditor examined 16 of 200 hospital equipment assets to find that four were missing or damaged. The client's manager was not concerned, saying: 'That's only four out of 200 with a problem.' It was, of course, four of 16 tested or 25 per cent, suggesting that the misstatement may be material. More testing was conducted.

Substantive procedures

Land and buildings, fixtures and fittings, plant and machinery, and motor vehicles are the most common assets. The verification procedures will be similar in all four and may include tests for assertions, as per **Figure 15.10**.

Checking the entire fixed-asset register is time-consuming and is unlikely to be necessary if good internal controls are in place. However, the auditor needs to test large-value items as noted. It may also be worthwhile to prepare a working paper to reconcile the client's records to the auditor's inspection and calculations (see **Table 15.1**).

Occurrence-validity
Capitalised assets recordings are supported by underlying transactions.

Completeness and accuracy
The cost of land and buildings acquired should be vouched to appropriate documentation, such as contracts of sale. Smaller assets should also be vouched, at least on a sample basis if the total amount is material.

Classification
Freight inwards, installation charges and other related expenditures should be reviewed for proper classification in the accounts. The cost of land should be distinguished (as it is not depreciable) to comply with GAAP provisions.

Figure 15.10 Substantive procedures for long-term assets

Valuation

All fixed assets purchased for use will normally be valued on the basis of carrying value or depreciated historical cost, and depreciated over their useful life in accordance with GAAP. Since estimation is involved in determining the depreciated value of assets, the assumptions and calculations used to reach this value should be carefully reviewed. (In Australia and New Zealand, the auditor should be guided by ASA 540 and ISA NZ 540: Auditing Accounting Estimates and Related Disclosures, and ASA 620 and ISA NZ 620: Using the Work of an Auditor's Expert.)

Existence

The existence of nearby land, buildings and individually material assets should not be difficult to prove, but the auditor may have to rely on associates to verify assets located overseas.

Rights-obligations

Most land and buildings are subject to a mortgage, so the auditor should review mortgage documents and expense calculations. Reference can be made to the certificate of title in the land registry office if material.

Presentation

Disclosure involves the allocation of fixed assets into appropriate classes and disclosure of depreciation methods. (Current Australian and New Zealand guidance can be found in AASB 116 and NZ IAS 16: Property, Plant and Equipment, and in AASB 101 and NZ IAS 1: Presentation of Financial Statements.)

Figure 15.10 (continued)

Table 15.1 Working paper (partial) for fixed assets reconciliation

	Purchase		Improvements		Depreciation			Disposition or writedown				Carrying value
	Date	Cost	Date	Cost	Date	Expense	Accumulated	Date	Code	Amount	G/L	
Ford 4W	3.21	53 000	3.21	7 000	3.23	10 000	20 000	–	–	–		40 000
Conveyor	3.22	126 000	–	–	9.22	12 600	12 600	9.22	xy	110 000	(3 400)	0
Building	9.13	750 000	9.13	50 000	3.23	40 000	380 000	–	–	–	–	420 000
Totals		929 000		57 000		62 600	412 600			110 000	(3 400)	460 000

Intangible assets

Some types of transactions are not part of a regular cycle, or they may occur outside the business's usual day-to-day operations. They may not result in the existence of physical or tangible assets. The assets and liabilities that result from such activities are highly vulnerable to overstatement distortion and theft. These include, for example, intangibles such as research and development (R&D), goodwill, brands and intellectual capital (see AASB 138 and NZ IAS 38: Intangible Assets). Professional scepticism can usefully be applied to intangibles and fixed assets given the potential distortions that can take place with just one adjusting entry.

Research and development (R&D)

There are examples of company collapse that can be partially attributable to overindulgent research and development costs on unprofitable products. However, the financial statements may not reflect the underlying value if research is capitalised. For example, in the collapse of the UK company Rolls-Royce, significant amounts of R&D were capitalised, despite the slim chance of cost recovery.

The auditors should ensure that organisations comply with GAAP regarding R&D. Currently, AASB 138 and NZ IAS 38 draw a distinction between pure research on the one hand and development work on the other. The former should be written off against income, and the latter can potentially be capitalised if the development outgoings meet the requirements of the accounting standard.

Goodwill

Goodwill is perhaps the most peculiar of all assets, for it cannot be distinguished from an organisation. It is thus difficult to ascribe a value to it except under situations of a business sale or business consolidation where an arm's-length agreement has been reached. Standards on goodwill are developed with the intent to achieve consistency and conservatism in its recognition, though in practice they often allow goodwill to either be unrecognised, or, if recognised, to remain on the books for considerably longer than their value would justify.

Management might try to allocate goodwill in a new purchase to other assets by overvaluing these other assets. In practice, goodwill problems are not considered to be too serious, for investment analysts tend to ignore goodwill value in their decisions. The auditors must ensure that any goodwill is properly and separately disclosed in accordance with accounting standards (AASB 101; NZ IAS 1).

Brands or mastheads

The adoption of international accounting standards in Australia and New Zealand confirmed that so-called unique intangibles (e.g., internally generated), such as brands or mastheads, do not qualify for capitalisation. This is because 'subsequent expenditure on brands, mastheads, publishing titles, customer lists and items similar in substance … is always recognised in profit or loss as incurred [and]… such expenditure cannot be distinguished from expenditure to develop the business as a whole' (AASB 138; NZ IAS 38, para 20). So, with respect to such assets, the auditor should be aware of any changes to accepted accounting standards.

Intellectual capital

A challenge for accountants and auditors is the growing call to recognise intellectual capital (IC) and knowledge-based assets in financial statements. Sometimes simply known as the employees' 'raw talent', IC consists of the loyalty, knowledge and efforts of the employees of the organisation. IC has been used to explain why a company's market value is greater than the value of its tangible assets. Intellectual capital is of value to the company only if it is organisationally embedded and can't walk out the door when an employee leaves. This might be achieved through knowledge-management systems, patents, trademarks, or a strong organisational culture sustaining tacit knowledge.

Increasingly, an organisation's success (or failure) depends on its intellectual capital and ability to innovate. Even if auditors are not yet called upon to attest to the value of intellectual capital, the implications for their client's success could be significant in a competitive environment, and the auditors would be wise to incorporate this risk into their analysis.

CONCEPT QUESTION 3	Explain how goodwill is different to tangible assets in terms of audit risks.

Study tools

Summary

This chapter identified audit risks and controls common to the warehousing, finance and fixed assets subsystems. Audit procedures rely heavily on source documentation and external verification of transactions that are frequently individually material. Direct tests on balances are common.

Auditors should rely on accounting as well as auditing guidance in estimating value and determining disclosure where, for example, fixed assets, intangible assets, contingent liabilities, or deferred taxes, form part of the financial statements. Transactions for equity and debt accounts may require inspection and reference to original formation documents.

Case/resources link

CAATs for Classrooms

Accompanying this book is a series of data, integrated worksheets and exercises that are designed to support your learning and give you exposure to hands-on audit decision-making dilemmas faced by auditors in the planning elements of the audit process. Acquire the relevant material for this chapter from your instructor.

Review questions

15.1 Describe 1–2 authorisation controls that would be expected to exist in the
   a   warehousing subsystem
   b   finance subsystem
   c   fixed asset subsystem.

15.2 Identify the risks in the warehousing cycle with respect to:
   a   custody of assets
   b   stock counts.

15.3 Explain the role of the auditor in attending stock counts. Why is their participation important?

15.4 What duties should be segregated in the:

    a   warehousing cycle with respect to custody

    b   warehousing cycle with respect to stock count.

15.5 Describe and justify essential procedures to verify amounts related to:

    a   warehousing

    b   finance accounts

    c   fixed assets.

15.6 Identify the greatest risks in each of the following, and explain why:

    a   cash system

    b   other finance accounts

    c   fixed assets (particularly with respect to fraud and distortion).

15.7 Describe and justify the audit procedures used for a cash system.

15.8 Describe and justify audit procedures that should be used for:

    a   investments

    b   goodwill

    c   research and development

    d   equity accounts.

15.9 Define a bank certificate and its purpose.

15.10 Define a financial instrument and why it can create valuation problems.

Exercises

15.1 **WAREHOUSING – STOCK COUNT:** The directors of AB Ltd inform you that the board does not wish to count the raw material inventory at the balance date because a count to verify the perpetual stock records was made two months prior to the balance date.

    Required:

    a   State the factors you would consider in determining whether the preliminary count could be accepted in lieu of a count made at the balance date.

    b   If the stock count two months prior raised issues, how would your answer to (a) above be different?

15.2 **WAREHOUSING – CUT-OFF:** Sketch a timeline for an organisation's year-end of 31 March 2022. Against this timeline, plot the four different scenarios noted below for goods shipped to the client prior to year-end. Describe how the auditor would determine the ownership of the goods from each scenario and whether they should be included in the client's financial statements. The scenarios are as follows:

    a   Goods shipped FOB origin on 15 March 2022. They are expected to arrive on 15 April.

    b   Goods received on consignment by the organisation on 25 March 2022. Half of the goods have been sold at 31 March.

    c   Goods are held in-store to be sold on commission. None have sold at year-end.

    d   Goods shipped FOB destination on 20 March 2022. They are expected to arrive on 15 April.

15.3 WAREHOUSING – ANALYTICAL PROCEDURES: Analytical procedures are useful to signal misstatements in the warehousing cycle.

Required:

a   What do the following analytical procedures highlight in an audit of an organisation that carries large stocks of inventory?

   i   inventory turnover compared to gross profit

   ii   ratio of inventory to COGS (this is also applicable to Chapter 20)

   iii value of inventory at specific seasonal or monthly periods in the business cycle, compared to prior years.

b   Why might differences in these ratios between periods not signal potential distortions in the inventory balance?

15.4 WAREHOUSING – ASSERTIONS: Analyse the financial statements of a retailer. From your analysis, state the specific warehousing cycle assertions requiring special audit effort to ensure material misstatements do not exist.

15.5 INVENTORY AND WAREHOUSING: Below are a number of independent inventory situations.

a   The audit client sells high-fashion garments. The organisation's accountant tells you that everything has been valued at net realisable value.

b   HV Jewellers Ltd manufactures necklaces, earrings and rings for mid-range customers. HV Jewellers also operates a number of retail outlets. One inventory item is a large roll of wire that is used in jewellery manufacturing. The CEO advises you the wire is gold and estimates the value by taking the average quotes from two gold buyers' websites.

Required: For each of the independent issues outlined above, describe the audit procedures that you would undertake. Ensure you outline the internal controls you believe you should be able to rely on, the substantive procedures you would undertake, and any assistance you would need in ensuring there were no material discrepancies in the value of inventory.

15.6 INVENTORY AND WAREHOUSING: Below are two independent inventory situations.

a   EzyFoods supplies its shops from a number of different warehouses. They import preserved (canned, bottled and frozen) food goods from many overseas countries. Their customers are restaurants and large caterers. Often, goods are required to be shipped overnight to different locations from where they are stored.

b   Your audit client is a winemaker with a large warehouse full of bottled wine and contracts to buy more grapes in the next season. The market price for wine has recently fallen, and the winemaker is in poor financial health.

Required: For each of the independent issues outlined above, describe the audit procedures that you would undertake. Ensure you outline the internal controls you believe you should be able to rely on, the substantive procedures you would undertake, and any assistance you would need in ensuring there were no material discrepancies in the value of inventory.

15.7 CASH – BANK CERTIFICATE: Your client's bank returned the bank certificate sent to you. In the information they provided, you discover that your client has a cheque account you were unaware of and a loan outstanding with a higher balance than the books indicate. What are the implications, and what procedures would you now carry out?

15.8   **FIXED ASSET – DEPRECIATION:** Your client prepares a depreciation expense, accumulated depreciation schedule at the balance date. All fixed assets are straight-line and no revaluations are done.

Required: Describe and justify internal controls that you would look for and substantive procedures that you would use to identify misstatements that are most likely to occur in respect of the depreciation expense schedule.

15.9   **CASH – RECONCILIATIONS:** Your client performs reconciliations of their cash receipts and cash payments journals against the monthly bank statements. However, the reconciliation at balance date is shown in **Table 15.2**.

Table 15.2 Reconciliation at balance date

Balance per bank statement	$2 350	Cash journal beginning balance	1 000
Deposits in transit	4 000	Cash receipts	13 700
Unpresented cheques	1 650	Cash disbursements	10 000
Adjusted balance at month-end	8 000	Ending balance at month-end	4 700

The client thinks it is fine. Do you? Why or why not? Does this provide confidence in their reconciliation controls? Why or why not? What would you do next?

15.10   **INTANGIBLES:** N. Real, your client, carries on a boat-design business. He has the following assets on his books:

Cash	$300
Goodwill (net)	$50 000
Leasehold improvements	$30 000
Research and development	$110 000

Required: Design the substantive tests you would perform in an audit program for these accounts. You should consider all appropriate audit objectives.

15.11   **FIXED ASSET VALUATION:** Your audit client is a large retail chain that owns a number of its stores but leases a number of others. All fixed assets are listed on a register, and there are a number of controls over the purchase and disposal of these assets. The organisation has a regular cycle of revaluation of its assets and employs an independent valuer to value large assets at replacement cost. Despite an economic downturn, the assets' values have remained the same in the current year.

Required:

a   Describe the audit procedures you would recommend as part of the audit program to assess the valuations of this organisation's fixed assets.

b   How would your procedures differ if the valuations had been performed by management rather than by an accredited valuer?

c   Explain how you would audit the depreciation in both (a) and (b)?

15.12 **FIXED ASSETS AND SpAR:** Analytical procedures are useful for highlighting material misstatements.

Required:

a What might the following analytical procedures highlight in an audit of a service-related organisation with a large fixed-asset portfolio?

   i ratio of equipment repairs and maintenance to total equipment (this year and compared to prior years)

   ii ratio of depreciation expense to assets (broken down by major asset classes)

   iii analysis of interest expense and loans due.

b Design a model to estimate the value of the business' stock of farm trucks, which they lease to local farmers, charging a daily rate.

15.13 **FINANCE, FIXED ASSETS AND INTANGIBLES: PRESENTATION**

Required: Look up the annual report of a large Australian or New Zealand company, such as JB Hi-Fi or Fisher & Paykel Healthcare. Identify whether there are sufficient disclosures for each of the following (refer to accounting standards). Think about how those disclosures could be erroneously combined, omitted or overstated, and, if they were, how you may identify them in an audit:

a fixed assets

b investments

c contingent liabilities

d financial instruments

e goodwill or brand values or other intangibles

f long-term debt versus short-term debt

g ownership (equity, partner or sole trader) accounts

h consolidation entries, if any.

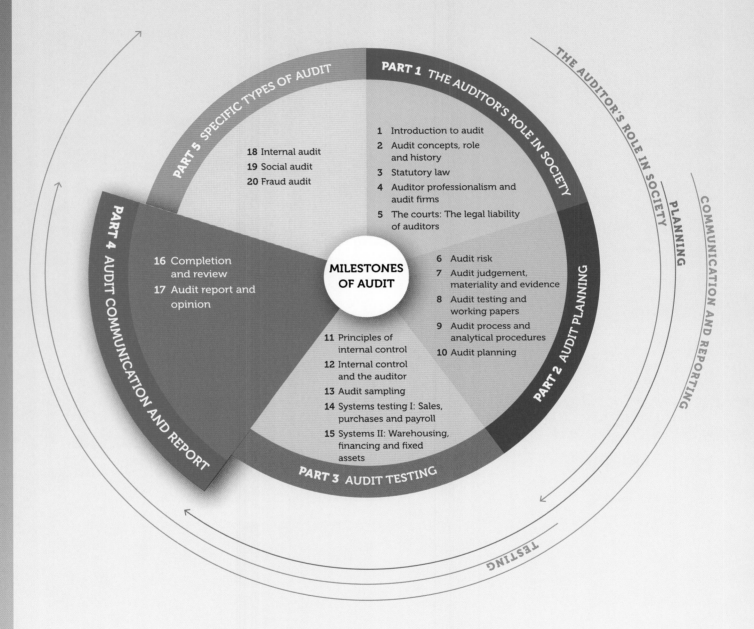

MILESTONES OF AUDIT

PART 5 SPECIFIC TYPES OF AUDIT
18 Internal audit
19 Social audit
20 Fraud audit

PART 1 THE AUDITOR'S ROLE IN SOCIETY
1 Introduction to audit
2 Audit concepts, role and history
3 Statutory law
4 Auditor professionalism and audit firms
5 The courts: The legal liability of auditors

PART 4 AUDIT COMMUNICATION AND REPORT
16 Completion and review
17 Audit report and opinion

PART 2 AUDIT PLANNING
6 Audit risk
7 Audit judgement, materiality and evidence
8 Audit testing and working papers
9 Audit process and analytical procedures
10 Audit planning

PART 3 AUDIT TESTING
11 Principles of internal control
12 Internal control and the auditor
13 Audit sampling
14 Systems testing I: Sales, purchases and payroll
15 Systems II: Warehousing, financing and fixed assets

THE AUDITOR'S ROLE IN SOCIETY

PLANNING

COMMUNICATION AND REPORTING

TESTING

Audit communication and report

Chapter 16	Completion and review
Chapter 17	Audit report and opinion

Part 4 of the textbook comprises two chapters, on completion and review, and audit report and opinion. In Chapter 16, the final steps and decisions needed to complete the audit engagement are discussed. The chapter includes a review of key issues such as subsequent events, related party transactions, and going concern, and expands on the evidence gathered on these issues. Chapter 17 introduces the communication required between auditors and their clients and others during the course of an engagement. The chapter discusses the means by which auditors communicate, both in formal and informal ways.

PART 4

Completion and review

Learning objectives
. . . .

After studying the material in this chapter, you should be able to:
- explain letters of representation, their purpose, content and use
- explain going concern reviews and how they are conducted
- explain subsequent events reviews, their audit purpose and process
- explain disclosure and checklist reviews, their nature and content
- explain related party transactions, and the auditor's role in their discovery and disclosure
- explain management letters, their development, purpose and content
- explain final review processes conducted by the audit manager and partner(s).

Introduction

We identified three phases of the audit: planning, conducting and completion. The completion phase is where senior members of the audit team review all aspects of the audit, all the evidence collected to date, and – after discussion, deliberation and some final testing – come to an opinion as to whether there is truth to the claim that the financial statements are 'true and fair'. The audit opinion will be communicated widely in the audit report (see Chapter 17). This chapter looks at those final processes that lead to forming that opinion as conducted during completion and review.

Of importance at this stage is the letter of representation, going concern review, post-balance sheet (subsequent) events review, disclosure requirements, related party transactions, and the audit-completion process. This chapter relates to the completion and review of audit, which is the last set of steps in an audit process (see **Figure 16.1**).

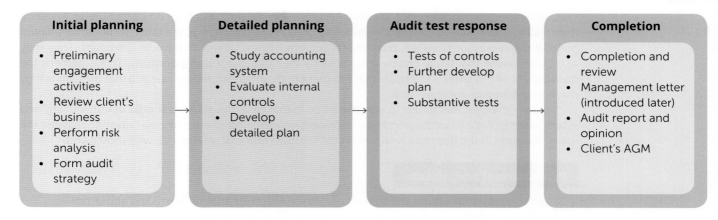

Figure 16.1 Steps in an audit process

Letter of representation

A *letter of representation* will be sought by the auditor from the directors at the concluding stage of the audit (see **Figure 16.2**).

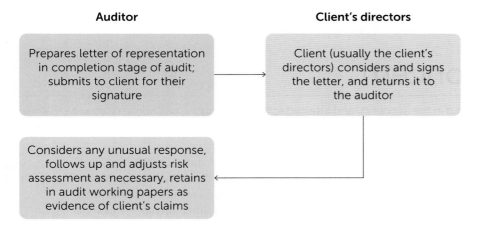

Figure 16.2 Letter of representation

While the letter of representation is an attestation by the client, it is drawn up by the auditor. Its purpose is confirmation, from the client, of certain matters stated in the accounts. It will particularly be about matters for which it has been difficult for the auditor to obtain evidence.

Auditing in practice

Letter of representation for unknown event

Firm A's letter of representation did not ask about the client's bank balance because the firm acquired that from independent bank records. They did seek confirmation as to whether the client had litigation in process, whether management had restructuring plans, or whether there was known but undisclosed fraud. Such events, all potentially material, are difficult to determine from other sources.

Client representations are not the strongest form of evidence, but they do contribute to evidence from testing and inquiry. If the client's governing body is reluctant to sign the letter, it should be pointed out that the representations are primarily to confirm matters already known or discussed. They may also be reminded that the accounts are ultimately their (the client's) responsibility. This is perhaps the main benefit of this letter – to ensure that the client both understands their role and that the claims they made to the auditor are important.

Suppose the directors refuse to sign the letter. In that case, the auditors should determine why and assess whether it is a misunderstanding or, concerningly, whether there may be a reason to reassess the risk of the audit. If the directors won't attest to their own financial statements, why should you?

Professional scepticism

'Scepticism is about asking the right questions, not simply a lot of them, and about not accepting the first answer. It is also clearly about having the experience to recognise what can go wrong.' (ICAEW, 2018)

If a refusal to sign off the letter indicates a potential misstatement or dishonesty, the auditors will have to:
*   carry out extra work to discover the nature of the reservations; and/or
*   modify their opinion, probably stating that they are unable to express an opinion because they have not received all the necessary information and explanations.

As is clear, failing to agree to the claims of this letter can signal a serious risk.

A letter of representation may include items such as those set out in **Figure 16.3**.

As you can see, concerns about fraud occupy a strong position within the letter of representation, as do a number of matters introduced later in this chapter.

Going concern

Valuation bases adopted in the accounts, and attested to by the directors, will normally assume that the client organisation is a going concern for the next year. It follows that auditors must carry out sufficient work to ensure that this premise can be supported.

> Under the going concern basis of accounting, the financial statements are prepared on the assumption that the entity is a going concern and will continue its operations for the foreseeable future. General purpose financial statements are prepared using the going concern basis of accounting, unless management either intends to liquidate the entity or to cease operations or has no realistic alternative but to do so. (ASA 570, para 2; ISA NZ 570, para 2)

This means seeking evidence that the organisation is likely to continue trading. Under current standards, this period refers to at least 12 months from the date of the auditor's current report (ASA 570, para 13.2; ISA NZ 570, para 13.2). In the past, the audit report date would stretch out to as much as 18–24 months after the client's year-end (balance date). Hence, coming out as late as that made it a poor tool of accountability.

Current obligations are that the auditor should review the client's own assessment of their going concern situation or perform it themselves if not available (see **Figure 16.4**).

In practice, the auditor essentially performs a going concern review irrespective of how much assessment the client has done. On completion of their going concern review, the audit manager or partner should discuss the results with management or the client's governing board, as appropriate, in order to

> determine whether management has identified events or conditions that, individually or collectively, may cast significant doubt on the entity's ability to continue as a going concern and, if so, management's plans to address them. (ASA 570, para 10; ISA NZ 570, para 10)

Letter of representation

Financial report content

We have fulfilled our responsibilities … in accordance with [standards] and [statute(s)]; in particular [that] the financial report gives a true and fair view …

The methods, the data and the significant assumptions used in making accounting estimates, and their related disclosures are appropriate …

Related party relationships and transactions have been appropriately accounted for and disclosed in accordance with [standards].

Subsequent events … have been adjusted or disclosed as required under [law].

The effects of *uncorrected misstatements* [as disclosed] are immaterial, both individually and in the aggregate, to the financial report as a whole.

Information provided

We have provided you with … access to all information of which we are aware that is relevant to the preparation of the financial report … additional information that you have requested and … unrestricted access … to obtain audit evidence.

All transactions have been recorded … and are reflected in the financial report.

We acknowledge our responsibility for … internal control to *prevent and detect fraud.*

We have disclosed to you … our assessment of the risk that the financial report may be materially misstated as a result of *fraud.*

We have disclosed to you all information in relation to fraud or *suspected fraud* …

We have disclosed to you all known instances of non-compliance or suspected non-compliance with *laws and regulations* [relevant to] the financial report.

We have disclosed to you all known actual or possible *litigation and claims* whose effects should be considered when preparing the financial report.

We have disclosed to you the identity of the entity's [known] *related parties*.

Figure 16.3 Letter of representation: Topics and phrasing

Source: Derived from extended example in ASA 580 (App. 2) and ISA NZ 580 (App. 2) (emphasis added).

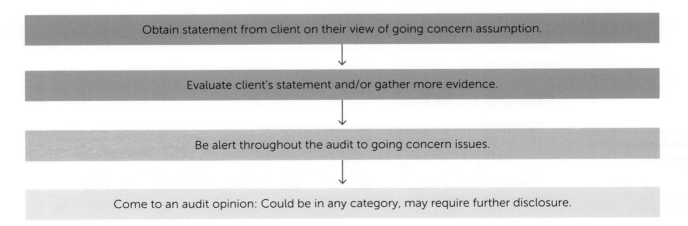

Obtain statement from client on their view of going concern assumption.

↓

Evaluate client's statement and/or gather more evidence.

↓

Be alert throughout the audit to going concern issues.

↓

Come to an audit opinion: Could be in any category, may require further disclosure.

Figure 16.4 Auditor's going concern analysis

Traditional practice would suggest that auditors

> plan and perform procedures specifically designed to identify material matters that could indicate concern about management's view that the adoption of the going concern assumption is appropriate in the preparation of the financial report. (ASA 520, para 30)

The auditor is further expected to remain alert to the possibility of a going concern problem throughout the engagement. In other words, it should be on the auditors' mind as they perform other tests and inspect other documents.

A going concern review does not begin in the completion stage, but issues around it are kept in mind from the very beginning of the audit.

> The auditor shall remain 'alert' throughout the audit for audit evidence of events or conditions that may cast significant doubt on the entity's ability to continue as a going concern. (ASA 570, para 11; ISA NZ 570, para 11)

The following are the sorts of indicators to which auditors should remain alert:
- downward trend in sales and/or profitability
- liquidity problems and/or a weak or falling current ratio
- vulnerability to legislative changes, economic pressures or a highly competitive market
- supply chain problems or labour disruption
- overdependence on a few suppliers, customers or finance providers
- substantial research and development not yet justified by the possibility of the product's success
- reductions in, or cancellations of, capital projects
- large capital investment with unrealistic returns.

If problems are identified, the auditor would be expected to conduct an investigation of the client's plans to mitigate the risk of business failure. This may include:
- examining cash-flow forecasts, profit forecasts and budgets for the ensuing period – the assumptions contained should be scrutinised and corroborated by independent evidence, if possible, and through discussions with the client
- examining the cash budget to ensure sufficient credit is available to cover short-term requirements
- bank confirmations to assess the availability of overdraft or similar facilities.

In the absence of forecasts, or should they reveal risks, the auditor will have to reconsider whether it is appropriate to adopt the going concern assumption. Indeed, the very absence of a budgetary process suggests that the client could struggle to survive a financial crisis.

In the event that the auditor does *not* consider the client to be a going concern, the governing body should be advised. The auditor should also ensure that the accounts are prepared on a market value or 'break-up' basis. This may involve reducing the value of assets or stock to 'liquidation' prices. It may involve reporting long-term liabilities as current should lenders have the right to collect. So, if the directors fail to do these actions when requested, the auditor may have to express (or more likely, threaten) an adverse opinion. Even if the directors comply with the request, disclosure is still required (see Chapter 17).

Auditing in practice

Self-fulfilling prophecy

A going concern disclosure in the audit report is of concern to the client and users. It may influence the client's ability to raise finance, or bring forward an inevitable bankruptcy; that is, disclosure of a going concern problem may create its own **self-fulfilling prophecy**. This is certainly not always the case, but it can occur.

It is thus clear why the client may be reluctant to see the auditor require going concern disclosures. If they are needed, difficult conversations could ensue.

While predicting client failure a year in advance may not seem possible, evidence shows that it is usually possible (e.g., Van Peursem and Pratt, 2006). Doing so is important. Many of the court cases against auditors follow on from losses generated by a client that has gone into liquidation.

CONCEPT QUESTION 1	Why might going concern analysis require experienced audit judgement?

Subsequent events

Subsequent events (also called *post-balance sheet events*) are those actions, transactions and recordings that occur, or can be identified, in the time following the 'balance date' of the statements under review. The auditor is expected to perform procedures during this time, and about events occurring during this time, to obtain evidence about either unknown or misclassified transactions.

Normally, this involves applying audit procedures after the balance date up through and including the report date (see ASA 560 and ISA NZ 560: Subsequent Events). These are therefore important dates to understand, namely the following:

- The *date of the financial statements (date of FS)*, or the *balance date*, is the last date in the period under review. If client A's fiscal year-end for their annual financial statement audit is 31 March, then 31 March is their balance date.
- The *report date* is when the auditor's report is signed off after fieldwork is complete.
- The *issue date* is when the audited financial statements are distributed.

This means that the auditor cannot ignore events that occur subsequent to the balance date. Indeed, events that occur after the year-end can reveal the effects of distortion or fraud, teeming and lading, or unexpected transactions such as major expenses delayed until the new year. Collecting evidence on some events, and carrying out most cut-off tests, is only possible post-balance date (see **Figure 16.5**).

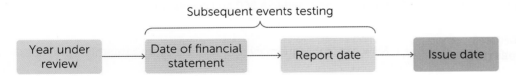

Figure 16.5 Timing of subsequent events and subsequent events testing

Events discovered during a subsequent event's review may, in some circumstances, lead to the need for adjustments:

> The objectives of the auditor are: (a) to obtain sufficient appropriate audit evidence about whether events occurring between the date of the financial statements and the date of the auditor's report that require adjustment of, or disclosure in, the financial statements are appropriately reflected in those financial statements ... and (b) to respond appropriately. (ASA 560, para 4; ISA NZ 560, para 4)

While not clarified in current standards, prior standards usefully identified subsequent events – those occurring between the *date of financial statement* and the *report date* that would call for such adjustment. This guidance continues to be used:

- *Adjustable events* are conditions that existed at the balance date and would normally require an adjusting entry. An example is if an insurance settlement was resolved after the balance date but before the report date for an event (say a 'fire') that occurred during the year under review. Because the amount was not determinable at the balance date, it was reported as a contingent liability, but it should now be adjusted thanks to a subsequent event review.
- *Non-adjustable events* are those discovered after the balance date that indicate conditions that also arose subsequent to the balance date. An example is where a client's major customer went into bankruptcy as a result of storm damage that occurred after the balance date of the client. No adjustment is necessary.

Some events are difficult to classify. For example, suppose it transpires that the net realisable value of year-end stock fell materially below cost. It may be hard to determine whether that valuation change occurred *before* or *after* the balance date. Nonetheless, the auditor must gather the best evidence reasonable under the conditions and come to their own opinion on the matter.

The period between the report date and the issue date is also significant to the audit. Suppose the auditor becomes aware of the client's liquidation *after* the report date, even though it occurred two days *before* the balance date. In that case, every effort must be made to ensure that the accounts (and opinions) are adjusted before they are distributed to the shareholders (ASA 560; ISA NZ 560). Somewhat unhelpfully, standards advise the auditor to consult a solicitor should this occur.

Because of their importance, it is standard practice to conduct a *subsequent events program*, including:

- a comparison of significant accounting ratios before and after year-end to identify cut-off or going concern problems
- a review of governing board minutes and notes looking for changes in contracts, customers, capital commitments, accounting policy, finance agreements, market conditions or products, and contingent liabilities
- a review of transactions occurring just before and just after the balance date, looking for specific cut-off problems or unexpected transactions
- solicitor confirmations which, like bank confirmations, offer independent evidence of events about which the auditor may be unaware.

All evidence should be documented and the necessary adjustments disclosed. Further guidance may be found in ASA 540 and ISA NZ 540, and ASA 560 and ISA NZ 560.

| CONCEPT QUESTION 2 | How can 'subsequent events' reveal a client's unethical practices? |

Disclosure (presentation) review

Disclosure (*presentation*) issues to which the auditor must pay attention include:

- *classification of accounts* on the financial statements, such as the classification of the current portion of loans as a current asset
- *aggregation or disaggregation* of accounts, such as having a separate account for such assets as goodwill and brand names, so that the user can incorporate (or exclude) their value from financing decisions
- *legal and regulatory disclosures* guided in standards and arising from the growth in, and concerns about, the client's legal responsibilities
- disclosure in the *footnotes* and in *accounting policy* information
- *recognition of business events or conditions* required, such as directors' salaries and contingent liabilities

- ensuring that issues required to be disclosed are *complete*, that important elements or events are not missing, and that they are disclosed in the manner set out by accounting standards (GAAP).

Successive statutes have required more disclosures, and this trend is certain to continue. While clients may argue that too much disclosure is also a problem (they can be mis- or overinterpreted, causing overreaction by stakeholders), the auditor is usually concerned with ensuring that they have disclosed enough.

An extensive range of disclosure requirements can be found in accounting standards, some on 'disclosure' only (such as AASB 7 and NZ IFRS 7), and others on specific issues. Auditors must decide whether the requirements of accounting standards have been interpreted appropriately, whether accounting policies have been followed, and whether there has been consistent compliance with the relevant standards. Normally, client organisations will comply with these provisions, but occasionally the auditor may discover exceptions. This may be a mistake by the client and is resolved by correcting the treatment and ensuring that the financial statements are changed.

However, much of the litigation against auditors is found to come from failures to disclose related party events, going concern questions or questionable asset valuations. Even a small disclosure problem can lead to inappropriate reliance by a user and audit failure. The risk of this occurring creates a material misstatement for what may seem to be small transgressions. Unless the auditor agrees that the non-compliance is 'true and fair' (a reasonably rare event), the auditor should consider qualifying the opinion when the client refuses to provide appropriate disclosure.

The New Zealand *Feltex* case (2010–11) is an example of where a failure to disclose loan arrangements and banking covenants led to problems. This oversight is probably now met with profound regret, though there are many others (e.g., see Mong and Roebuck, 2005). We note that ASA 705 and ISA NZ 705: Modifications to the Opinion in the Independent Auditor's Report, and ASA 706 and ISA NZ 706: Emphasis of Matter Paragraphs, now regulate these matters.

Stock exchange disclosures

All companies listed on the securities (or stock) exchange must comply with the listing requirements published by the relevant exchange (e.g., the Australian Securities Exchange or ASX, New Zealand's Exchange or NZX, and the New York Stock Exchange or NYSE). The requirements are that certain information must be circulated with the directors' annual report. These requirements themselves should present few audit problems, other than checking for compliance. ASX Listing Rule 3.1 requires a listed entity to disclose information 'concerning it' that 'a reasonable person would expect to have a material effect on the price or value of the entity's securities'.

Legal and regulatory disclosures

Corporations and market authorities have numerous legal obligations that may be directly or indirectly related to accounting disclosures. Hence, it is not surprising to see this point now being made in the standards:

> It is the responsibility of management, with the oversight of those charged with governance, to ensure that the entity's operations are conducted in accordance with the provisions of laws and regulations, including compliance with the provisions of laws and regulations that determine the reported amounts and disclosures in an entity's financial statements. (ASA 250, para 3; ISA NZ 250, para 3)

This does not, of course, replace the requirement on the auditor to apply their judgement, ethics, scepticism and due care to each and every audit situation.

> **Professional scepticism**
>
> 'ISA's require you to exercise both professional scepticism ... and professional judgement in planning and performing an audit of financial statements.' (CA ANZ, 2016, p. 5)

Overseas disclosure mandates

It would certainly be common in Australia and New Zealand to audit the subsidiary or parent of an international company. In such cases, the auditor needs to acquire reasonable knowledge about relevant international requirements, as may be necessary. The US *Sarbanes–Oxley Act 2002* is pointed to frequently in this respect as it has added to disclosure requirements, particularly as to information about governance and internal controls. The consolidated accounts audit is discussed in the chapter on social audit – see Chapter 19.

Other disclosure requirements

The auditor's task is to ensure that disclosure requirements of other professional and legal bodies for the financial statements are met. This will usually be a routine matter that the use of checklists can best achieve through requests for a written representation from the client's solicitor (see ASA 501 and ISA NZ 501: Audit Evidence – Specific Considerations for Inventory and Segment Information).

Related party transactions

> ... the nature of related party relationships and transactions may, in some circumstances, give rise to higher risks of material misstatement of the financial report than transactions with unrelated parties. (ASA 550, para 2; ISA NZ 550, para 2)

Related parties can come about in many ways. Related party transactions occur between businesses (or persons engaging in business) who are associated with each other in more than one way. Transactions between related parties are of particular concern to accountants (and to auditors) because such exchanges are more susceptible to being misstated due to pressures having to do with these multiple relationships. Related party transactions may fail to be arm's-length, and disclosures provided about them could distort the financial statements or place the client at going concern risk.

> **Auditing in practice**
>
> ### Examples of related parties
>
> Examples of related parties include the following:
> - A tourism operator is part-owner of that business' lending company.
> - Business owners rent their premises from a company that controls their supply.
> - Sales are made to a company part-owned by the seller.

The following 'non-arm's-length' transactions are the sorts of concerns that accompany related party transactions:
- sales/purchases at other than normal prices
- granting of loans at other than normal terms of interest or repayment
- exchange of assets at other than market value.

The auditor's primary concern is identifying the existence of related party transactions and ensuring that they are appropriately *disclosed*. The auditor is *not* responsible for deciding whether or not related party transactions are at market value. That is up to the reader (user) of financial statements to decide. The user should, however, be informed of the related party relationships through disclosure.

Auditing in practice

Risk of temptation to inflate profit

The managing director of retail client Alpha Ltd also owns the company Beta Ltd, which supplies inventory for Alpha Ltd. There is the concern – and the risk – that Beta's director would be tempted to pad their revenue by charging above market value for stock sold to Alpha Ltd. Conversely, if they want to 'improve' Alpha's accounts for a pending loan, they may be tempted to underprice goods sold to it and distort the gross margin.

AASB 124: Related Party Disclosures (or NZ IAS 24) requires auditors to:

- obtain an understanding of the client's related party relationships and transactions – this would include transactions that the client knows about and discloses, and those that may exist but are either unknown or undisclosed
- ensure that such parties and transactions are disclosed in accordance with GAAP in the financial statements (*incompleteness* is a particular risk)
- determine whether they involve risk factors, such as fraud risk.

The following audit procedures may identify related parties as yet undisclosed:

1 Examine the register of shareholders for substantial holdings.
2 Review the annual return for evidence of other cross-directorships.
3 Review financial records for evidence of associated companies or funds.
4 Review the register of directors' shareholdings.
5 Examine directors' minutes and solicitor's correspondence.
6 Examine the terms of any significant loans.
7 Confirm the nature of any guarantees given.

For known related parties, the following should ensure appropriate disclosure:

1 Collect evidence of any significant transactions and confirm that they are on a normal commercial basis.
2 Investigate the client's ledgers for material debts from them and ensure that they are collectable. This could involve obtaining information from credit agencies or banks.

In particular, the auditor should consider the collectability of debts with related parties. It is a vulnerable area as, if there is intent, it would not be difficult to carry out a material misstatement through a related party transaction

---

CONCEPT QUESTION 3   Explain why 'related parties' offer a unique audit risk.

Management letter

While the statutory audit aims to allow the auditor to come to an opinion on the 'true and fair' nature of financial statements, it is normal practice to also issue a *letter to management* (management letter). The letter to management is prepared by the auditor for the client (see **Figure 16.6**).

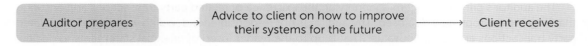

Figure 16.6 Management letter

It is completed near the end of the audit, based on discoveries made during the audit, and provides advice about how that client may improve their systems or practices in the future.

It does *not* change what has happened in the past, nor does it change the auditor's opinion on the current engagement. However, the client can use the advice to improve their systems in the future. While previously optional, the following is now expected:

> The objective of the auditor is to communicate appropriately to those charged with governance and management, deficiencies in internal control that the auditor has identified during the audit and that, in the auditor's professional judgement, are of sufficient importance to merit their respective attentions. (ASA 265, para 5; ISA NZ 265, para 5)

There is no standard format for this letter, as it would vary by situation and organisation. However, it would not be uncommon to include an extensive list of issues such as:

- weaknesses in the client's internal controls or internal control systems
- breakdowns in the accounting systems
- fraud or material errors that could (or did) occur as a result of such problems
- explanations as to why, as a result, more audit time was needed
- poor accounting procedures or policies
- inefficiencies created by poor systems, and for each item listed
- recommendations and constructive suggestions to improve the system.

The management letter also clarifies who is responsible for such systems and is an effective 'warning' that significant problems should be resolved to prepare for the next assurance engagement.

It is an important communication. Usually addressed to the governing body or managing director, it is intended to be useful to the client, and they usually appreciate getting it. The matters it contains should be discussed with management at an appropriate level before the report is written in order to avoid misunderstandings.

The final review

Before audit partners would be prepared to express an opinion on the accounts, senior members of the firm review the adequacy of the work performed, the presentation, and the content of the statements. Discussions between and among audit staff are particularly important to clarify issues risks and plan ways forward together as an audit team. Firms will differ – smaller firms may not have multiple partners – but most closing process roles are as shown in **Figure 16.7**.

The junior and managing audit personnel in charge of the day-to-day audit work should ensure that it is ready for review by:

1   ensuring that all the stages in the audit are complete and documented
2   performing final analytical procedures and documenting issues

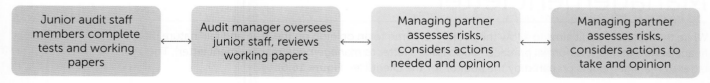

Figure 16.7 Closing stage audit firm roles and discussions

3 ensuring that working papers are complete, ordered and updated
4 reviewing the accounts for presentation, including notes and policies
5 reviewing audit risk schedules to ensure the issues identified are addressed
6 reviewing legal and regulatory issues and their impact
7 reviewing non-audited portions of the client's annual report[1]
8 preparing final comments on points requiring partner-level decisions
9 drafting a letter to management
10 completing the audit time schedule and budget, explaining variances.

These procedures may be part of a detailed *audit completion checklist* to ensure that audit personnel do not overlook processes when under pressure at the concluding stages of the audit. The audit personnel in charge will carry out any necessary extra work to answer questions raised by the manager's review, and the work will then undergo a final partner review. These reviews, and their implications for audit risk and further audit testing, are illustrated in **Table 16.1**.

Table 16.1 Manager and partner review

	Implications for:	
	Risk assessment	**Further testing/action**
Audit manager's review		
Is any evidence unobtainable?	Insufficient level of assurance?	Add to letter of representation; consider the potential for disclaimer (opinion)
Working papers incomplete?	Evidence collection incomplete or non-sampling risk?	Discuss with audit staff to resolve
Reliance on oral representations?	Insufficient level of assurance?	Gather more reliable evidence
Any concerns with the reliability of management?	Reassess inherent risk	Gather further evidence or issue a disclaimer
Unusual policies or estimates found?	Misstatement undiscovered	Probe to obtain evidence as to why
Does evidence from different audit-testing sources add up to material misstatement?	Minor misstatements in different systems may add up to material misstatement	Collate audit test findings and assess the combined effect
Are any disclosure problems apparent?	Potential distortion or oversight	Probe to determine why and resolve
Audit partner's review		
Issues raised by the manager?	Audit failure through negligence	Resolve; consider the effect on opinion
Representations by client incomplete?	Misrepresentations or distortion	Resolve; consider the effect on opinion
Overview to identify significant or unusual events	Implications for material misstatement	Obtain evidence to assure as to the business reason
Opinion formulation	Audit failure	–

As any additional work at this point will probably relate to problems or sensitive areas, it is important that senior members of the audit team are involved and that their decisions are documented. The partners' review also ensures an experienced and independent assessment of the audit process and may reduce any bias introduced by a team becoming too familiar with the client's management or their systems.

---

[1] See ASA 720 and ISA NZ 720: The Auditor's Responsibilities Relating to Other Information, which sets out the auditor's responsibilities in identifying inconsistencies or misstatements in respect to non-audited portions of the annual report.

Study tools

Summary

This chapter considered the final steps and decisions needed to complete the audit engagement. A review of key issues such as subsequent events, related party transactions, and going concern expanded on the evidence gathered on these issues to date and focused the auditor's attention on them. Several layers of review ensure that independent consideration of the issues is made and that no key points are missed. The letter of representation is also important in this regard and provides, as well, an opportunity for further communication with the client.

Case/resources link

CAATs for Classrooms

Accompanying this book is a series of data, integrated worksheets and exercises that are designed to support your learning and give you exposure to hands-on audit decision-making dilemmas faced by auditors in the planning elements of the audit process. Acquire the relevant material for this chapter from your instructor.

Review questions

16.1   What is the purpose of the letter of representation? Who prepares it? Who agrees to it and why? Why is it prepared only during the completion phase of the audit?

16.2   List 10 issues that should be included within a Letter of Representation.

16.3   Who is responsible for originally making the going concern assumption? What role does the auditor have, according to auditing standards?

16.4   When does the auditor become involved in a going concern analysis for their client? When do they come to a conclusion about it?

16.5   List symptoms of going concern problems.

16.6   What sorts of actions should the auditor take if a going concern problem is identified?

16.7   What is 'subsequent events testing'? What is its purpose?

16.8   Distinguish between the 'date of the financial statement' (balance date), 'report date' and 'issue date'. What do each of them mean? Why is each of them important to the auditor?

16.9   Describe ways of testing for subsequent events.

16.10   Distinguish between 'adjustable' and 'non-adjustable' events.

16.11   How is the New Zealand *Feltex* case an example of what can occur when presentation problems exist? How are auditing standards attempting to address such concerns?

16.12   What is the relationship between 'accounting' standards for disclosure and 'auditing' standards related to disclosure? That is, how are the accountant and auditor roles distinguished in terms of disclosure?

16.13   In addition to statutes affecting governing bodies and auditors, identify statute and disclosure requirements required for companies listed on the ASX or NZX.

16.14 Why are related parties and related party transactions important to the auditor?

16.15 By disclosing 'related party' transactions, is evidence thus provided of non-arms'-length transactions? If so, why? If not, why not?

16.16 Name seven audit procedures for identifying related party transactions.

16.17 Explain what Australian/New Zealand auditing standards require of the auditor with respect to related party transactions.

16.18 Describe the purpose of the management letter and who it benefits, and explain why it is prepared in the completion phase of the audit.

16.19 What sorts of issues might appear in the management letter?

16.19 List processes for the final review of audit working papers.

16.20 Distinguish between the purpose of an 'audit manager' review and an 'audit partner' review.

Exercises

16.1 **SENIOR REVIEW:** Three levels of supervision and review are often performed on audit work:

   a On those engagements where the audit team comprises more than one staff member, the audit personnel in charge will do an initial review of each assistant's work papers before they are placed in the audit file on completion of that segment of the audit.

   b On major engagements, the audit manager will perform a detailed review of the working papers prior to their submission to the partner.

   c The partner in charge of the engagement will review the working papers.

   Describe the apparent purpose of the review work that will be performed at each of the above levels.

16.2 **SUBSEQUENT EVENTS:** Before completing the audit, the auditor is required to conduct a review for subsequent events. The client is a beauty parlour franchise experiencing pressure to retain a certain level of sales each year. They have occasionally had to borrow from non-bank finance companies to meet their billing needs.

   a Give one specific example of a subsequent event you might want to perform in terms of the risk related to the sales pressure. Explain how you would perform it, what you would look for and what would comprise a concerning find.

   b Give one specific example of a subsequent event you may want to perform on risk related to the lending issue, what you would look for and what would comprise a concerning find.

   c Determine for both (a) and (b) the management assertion of primary concern and whether the event is more likely to yield an overstatement or understatement, and of what account(s).

16.3   **GOING CONCERN COMMUNICATIONS:** The audit partner in charge becomes concerned about the going concern assessment of two different clients. Their situations are described below.

   a Valevale Ltd adopted the going concern assumption, but they also failed to reclassify half of their $2 000 000 debt as current. Valevale argued that their personal banker had, in a phone conversation, agreed to reclassify the whole debt as long-term. An increase of this size in short-term debt would cause all liquidity ratios to be −1 or smaller. How would you address this issue?

   b While the CEO of Wallace Ltd acknowledged that they might have a going concern problem, they resisted disclosing the fact because they believed that, by doing so, there would be a self-fulfilling prophecy. What did they mean by this? What might be the auditor's response?

   Required: Explain how the audit partner should address these issues: to whom they should communicate them and why, and what resolution they would seek.

16.4   **RELATED PARTIES:** The managing director of Paua Ltd has a 20 per cent shareholding in Smithers Printing Ltd. Smithers owes Paua Ltd a considerable amount, which has been converted to a short-term note. The note is supported with adequate documentation, and a positive confirmation was received from Smithers, showing no exceptions. Describe and justify the procedures you would take for verification. What are the implications for the auditor?

16.5   **GOING CONCERN:** The auditor has collected or created the following evidence for going concern review for a financial adviser client. The client assumed a going concern situation.

   i   beginning-year capital budgets

   ii   sales forecast made and submitted to the client's bank for an impending loan

   iii five years of prior financial statements for the client

   iv gross profit margins, and net profit margins, for the last five years

   v   macroeconomic indicators showing expected cost-to-revenue ratios

   vi accounts receivable ageing schedule

   vii cost savings from the departure of the CFO, who left mid-year unexpectedly and has not yet been replaced

   viii sales figures for each type of product line, including the one for derivatives, opened mid-year.

   Required:

   a For each item listed, explain how it may (or does) provide important information for the going concern analysis.

   b Given the indicators above and the general need for information, provide a list of 3–4 items that you might request from the client to complete your going concern analysis.

16.6   **GOING CONCERN:** Assume that you are auditing a wholesale distributor of locks, safes, alarms and other security devices. Your overall analytical procedures reveal a recent and significant drop in consumer sales for these products; nonetheless, solvency and liquidity ratios remain positive and stable. While there is no negative publicity about your client, you are aware that there may be some engineering problems with the alarms that have been sold recently. The owner-manager, who has been a steady client for four years and has had a profitable business for over 20 years, remains stable. Your client's insurance should cover any warranty problems, and the owner-manager has confirmed an effort to look into this further. Other information about the client includes the fact that a competitor security products provider has opened up in your client's larger sales district.

Required: Using a scale of 1 (low risk) to 3 (high risk), identify potential going concern issues and rank their risk for this client. Justify your decisions.

16.7 **COMMUNICATION WITH MANAGEMENT:** During the completion stage of the audit of Ace Manufacturing Ltd (an unlisted public company), you have identified that the company has not provided for depreciation on its factory buildings. You inform Mr Beta (the managing director) that you would have to qualify your opinion if he does not allow the adjustment of the financials for depreciation. Discussions become heated and Mr Beta demands your resignation, even though you have been the company's auditor for many years.

Required:

a   Discuss whether you may resign before issuing your opinion.

b   Discuss whether you would be entitled to refuse to resign and what steps would have to be taken by the company to remove you as an auditor.

16.8 **RELATED PARTIES:** An auditor discovers the following three events during the course of the audit of BurgerMash, a New Zealand food service franchise for schools. The business is doing well, showing a 6 per cent profit margin and growing.

i   Paul is BurgerMash's CEO. Paul's sister Eileen purchased kitchen equipment from BurgerMash for her own (separate) catering business.

ii   BurgerMash purchases all its fresh raw material from a farm in mid-Canterbury. The farm's owner lent BurgerMash start-up funds of $50 000 five years ago and has extended that loan by $10 000 each year. The farmer expects to be repaid next year.

iii   Daphne is on BurgerMash's board of directors, and she also sits on the board of BurgerMash's local bank. A total of $17 000 is owed to the local bank by BurgerMash.

Required:

a   Identify the auditor's responsibility to find each of these occurrences.

b   Suggest how the auditor may have identified each of these. Your suggestion should include a specific evidence-collection procedure.

c   Once found, the auditor discusses this with BurgerMash's audit committee and explains that they needed to be disclosed. The audit committee resists doing so, stating that 'There is nothing untoward in our actions'. How would you explain to the committee your – and their – responsibilities with respect to related party transactions?

16.9 **SUBSEQUENT EVENTS:** Consider each of the following events independently of the others for Latham Ltd, with a balance date (date of financial statement) of 31 March 2023. Assume, unless noted otherwise, that all costs are material:

a Latham had a fire in its warehouse on 23 February 2023, incurring repair costs of $210 000. The insurance company was contacted and Latham recorded the event as a contingent liability. Settlement was reached at $110 000 in June 2023.

b In its March 21 annual meeting, the board considered a recommendation from one of the shareholders that they expand into the Australian market. The board followed through with this suggestion by taking out a $100 000 short-term loan on 15 April 2023 to secure facilities and acquire inventory for a Melbourne office, which was opened on 1 May 2023.

c During the auditor's cut-off tests, they found that Latham had recorded a purchase made on 27 March that was FOB departure; that is, the title changed at the point at which the purchase was shipped from the seller. It was shipped on the day purchased; however, as it was not received until 2 April, it was recorded in payables/inventory on the date received.

Required: For each of the above situations, determine whether an 'adjustable' or 'non-adjustable' event has occurred and why. Explain what should have occurred had the auditor discovered any of these events after the 'issue date'.

16.10 **SUBSEQUENT EVENTS:** Assume that your client, EverReady, has a 31 March 2023 balance date. They had a customer who owed $95 500 for a 15 December 2022 purchase. As the debt was current, no provision for doubtful debts was allocated to this account. In May 2023, the auditor needed to perform subsequent events procedures.

Required:

a What subsequent event procedures would you perform to address the management assertions for accounts receivable, including this debt?

b Assume that this customer went into liquidation in January, and no debtors are likely to recover their amounts. Determine whether this is an 'adjustable' event or not and what should be done next.

16.11 **MANAGEMENT LETTER:** You have completed the audit for Tirau Sheet Metal Works Ltd. During your investigation, you found that an HR employee, Samuel, falsified several employee records and, as no prenumbered approval documents were required, they resulted in $53 500 being paid into a bank account of Samuel. It also seems that there was no internal check to ensure that only one bank account was authorised for each employee. Samuel was also able to divert funds to his account by preparing year-end accrual entries that paid a small portion of PAYE withholdings for other employees to his account. You discovered these events by accident: one of Samuel's co-employees, whom Samuel had made redundant (again without authority), blew the whistle on him. On discovery of this, Tirau did make Samuel redundant, although, because poor records were kept on Samuel's own employment application, he is proceeding against Tirau in employment court.

In all respects, the audit was completed to the auditor's satisfaction, and an unqualified opinion was provided.

Required: Prepare a management letter for the governing board of Tirau Sheet Metal Works Ltd.

Audit report and opinion

Learning objectives

After studying the material in this chapter, you should be able to:
- explain audit communication history and context
- prepare an audit report and understand the reasons for its elements
- explain various audit opinions and the reasons for them.

Introduction

For information to be of value to others, it must be communicated in a way that can be understood. Audit communications are no different. The auditor tries to ensure that their concerns and opinions are clear so that knowledgeable, if not expert, readers can understand their meaning. This chapter looks at communication principles, audit report and opinion, and other engagement communication practices that audit professionals use. An audit report and opinion is the last step of the auditor's work (see **Figure 17.1**).

Initial planning	Detailed planning	Audit test response	Completion
• Preliminary engagement activities • Review client's business • Perform risk analysis • Form audit strategy	• Study accounting system • Evaluate internal controls • Develop detailed plan	• Tests of controls • Further develop plan • Substantive tests	• Completion and review • Management letter (introduced later) • Audit report and opinion • Client's AGM

Figure 17.1 Steps in an audit process

Audit communications

In writing a memo or preparing a report, the auditor seeks to share knowledge, make an inquiry or express a view. Following communication principles, communications should not be ambiguous or contradictory. There should be sufficient information for the reader to understand and respond to that information, and the language should be targeted to the receiver's skills and knowledge. The speaker/writer should reflect on their own role with those to whom they are speaking and consider how their views or comments may be received (see **Figure 17.2**).

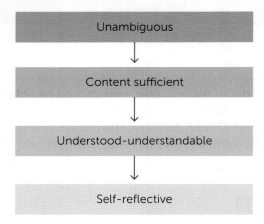

Figure 17.2 Qualities of good communication

Essentially, the speaker's message does not serve its purpose if the receiver fails to understand their role concerning that content. In linguistic terms, it becomes as important for the auditor to

> focus on how speech acts are received and how meaning is inferred as well as how meaning is conveyed. If the ... reader understands the ... intent behind the utterance in a way similar to that intended by the speaker ... then the ... effect is seen to be achieved ... (Van Peursem, Locke and Harnisch, 2005, p. 116)

The success of an auditor's communication effort can be measured by whether the reader *understands* it. This is why, over time, there has been a great deal of effort to assess and revise the audit report in an attempt to improve this communication.

Many communications occur during an audit to which these principles apply. Some are informal, such as discussions with the client about the industry or how the business is operating. Others are intended to follow up on concerns or ask questions. Delicate issues may need to be raised, such as whether there is a likelihood of fraud, or unreasonable going concern assumptions or poor staff cooperation.

Professional scepticism

'The ever-present doubt of the classical skeptic is to be replaced [in audit] by a call to recognise when doubt should be raised and to enquire as to areas of risk.' (Van Peursem, 2020, p. 300)

How to communicate in particular situations cannot be easily addressed in standards. They are unique to the situation; they require an awareness of the interests of the person being addressed and an understanding of the auditor's obligations to them. Experience and relationship building play a role in effective communication.

Some communications are standardised and follow rigid formats. ICQs and letters of engagement for statutory engagements are usually standard, attested to, and retained in working papers. The audit firm may use the information as they conduct the engagement and, of course, on (hopefully rare) occasions when courts look to them for evidence. Formal communications include but are not limited to:

1   recommendations prepared by the auditor for the client for them to consider in the future, such as those expressed in the *management letter*
2   matters agreed between the auditor and the client as to the scope, user and level of assurance required, such as what is found in the *engagement letter* prepared in the opening stages of the audit
3   claims made by the client but which are difficult to evidence, such as what may appear in the *letter of representation*
4   correspondence seeking evidentiary matter, such as *circularisation* to the client's customers, suppliers, bankers or lawyers
5   discussions with the client's governing body – see ASA 260 and ISA NZ 260 as to the auditor's responsibility for communicating with the client's most senior leadership
6   finally, and in the closing phases to the audit, the *audit report*, which is appended to the financial report and includes the *auditor's opinion*.

A growing number of standards on audit report communication also exist:

- ASA 260 and ISA NZ 260: Communication with Those Charged with Governance
- ASA 265 and ISA NZ 265: Communicating Deficiencies in Internal Control to Those Charged with Governance and Management
- ASA 700 and ISA NZ 700: Forming an Opinion and Reporting on a Financial Report
- ASA 701 and ISA NZ 701: Communicating Key Audit Matters in the Independent Auditor's Report
- ASA 705 and ISA NZ 705: Modifications to the Opinion in the Independent Auditor's Report
- ASA 706 and ISA NZ 706: Emphasis of Matter Paragraphs and Other Matter Paragraphs in the Independent Auditor's Report
- ASA 710 and ISA NZ 710: Comparative Information – Corresponding Figures and Comparative Financial Statements.

Communication guidance for the auditor can also be found within most audit/assurance standards. Communication is a skill calling for sensitivity, intuition, and that sense of professional scepticism which usually develops over time.

Professional scepticism

'The ancient teachings of the philosophical skeptic offer ways forward [for the auditor] by focussing on the nature of enquiry and by encouraging investigations which are more sensitive to the social, integrative and subjective nature of audit decision making ... reveal[ing] the importance of a free-form sort of search that looks deeply into each individual situation and that uncovers the concerns about which users and auditors wish to know.' (Van Peursem, 2020, p. 311)

Audit report

The audit report is the apogee of the auditor's effort. The formation, expression and communication of the auditor's opinion is the purpose and outcome of what can be a lengthy and expensive engagement process. While having changed over time, it tends to follow a rigid format intended to be consistent and clear to a wide variety of potential readers. Ensuring that there is clarity around the opinion being provided is crucial so that the report can serve its purpose as a sometimes-public communication document.

Purpose and history

The audit report and opinion is no secret: for statutory audits, it becomes widely available to shareholders, competitors and the public. It is 'presented' at an annual meeting for corporate entities and to stakeholders in other cases.

Prior to 1994 in Australia and New Zealand, the report was in a 'short form', or precise, and less than half a page long. It included only the identification of the users (e.g., shareholders), the scope, a statement of compliance with the statute, the opinion, auditor's signature and the report date. Short-form reports did not explain the audit process or the role of the client in producing GAAP-compliant financial statements. It did not explain that the auditor provides 'assurance' but not a 'guarantee' of the statements' quality. Nor did the short-form report express much about the organisation's major events or future viability.

The short form was applauded for its conciseness and clarity (following communication principles) but was criticised for failing to provide adequate information to readers who may not be as familiar with the audit as the auditor. Some non-accountants placed little reliability on the audit opinion. Other users showed little understanding of the auditor's work or the meaning of the terms used, such as 'unqualified' or 'modified'. Many were not comfortable understanding issues around internal controls or going concern. Others simply had unrealistic expectations of what the auditor was doing: there was an expectation gap.

As a result, expansion of the report was advised. Probably the most significant catalyst for change was a 1977–78 report commissioned by the AICPA titled the *Cohen Report*, which asserted the following:

- Standard report *language had become symbolic*. Since the wording was always the same, the report was rarely 'read' but had become a rubber stamp: looked 'for' but not carefully looked 'at'. Subtle changes could easily be missed.
- The user may not have understood that *the auditor used judgement* in coming to an opinion, and that the auditor neither guaranteed nor examined all transactions.
- *Technical terminology* such as 'present fairly' ('true and fair' in Australia and New Zealand) was not defined for the reader.

The recommendations of the *Cohen Report* were, for the most part, taken up (e.g., America's SAS 58). The UK's ASB made related changes in 1989, while both Australia and New Zealand followed suit with AUP3 (1990) and AS 10 (1994), respectively. The 'long form' is used today, although discussions about it, and changes to it, are ongoing (e.g., see Li, Hay and Lau, 2019; Turner et al., 2010). For example, by December 2017, key audit matters and auditor's responsibility details were added (see ASA (NZICA) 570, 700 and 701 on going concern).

Linguistically, we can say that the auditor preparing an audit report incorporates both text and language to convey their own self-understanding. The report employs

> a discourse as it arises from an association's own social practice and history … and comprises its own particular construct of social identity. Such discourse … provides an intimate expression of how people within institutions go about structuring knowledge.
> (Mataira and Van Peursem, 2010, p. 114)

Furthermore, using consistent language and looking to objective facts in the audit report speak to the professional and serious nature of the task. Together, they convey the auditor's (intended) objectivity and independence from the matter under investigation. Language is thus a means to achieve both clarity as to the auditor's opinion and explanation as to the source, nature and responsibilities of the various parties involved.

Structure and content

The audit report and opinion receive attention because of their importance to the audit. Elements of the audit report are derived from ASA 700 (paras 20–45) and ISA NZ 700 (paras 20–45) and illustrations. From this guidance, the audit report structure and content is set out as exampled in **Table 17.1**.

Table 17.1 Audit report example

Purpose	Example
Addressee	**INDEPENDENT AUDITOR'S REPORT** [Appropriate addressee]
Scope	**Report on the Audit of the Financial Report** We have audited the financial report of ABC Company Ltd (the Company), which comprises the statement of financial position as at 30 June 2023, the statement of comprehensive income, statement of changes in equity and statement of cash flows for the year then ended, and notes to the financial statements, including a summary of significant accounting policies, and the directors' declaration.
Opinion	In our opinion, the accompanying financial report of ABC Company Ltd is in accordance with the *Corporations Act 2001*, including: (a) *giving a true and fair view of the company's financial position as at 30 June 2023 and of its financial performance for the year then ended; and* (b) *complying with Australian Accounting Standards and the Corporations Regulations 2001.*
Basis for opinion	We conducted our audit in accordance with Australian Auditing Standards. Our responsibilities under those standards are further described in the Auditor's Responsibilities for the Audit of the Financial Report section of our report. We are independent of the Company in accordance with the auditor independence requirements of the *Corporations Act 2001* and the ethical requirements of the Accounting Professional & Ethical Standards Board's APES 110 Code of Ethics for Professional Accountants (including Independence Standards) (the Code) that are relevant to our audit of the financial report in Australia. We have also fulfilled our other ethical responsibilities in accordance with the Code. We confirm that the independence declaration required by the *Corporations Act 2001*, which has been given to the directors of the Company, would be in the same terms if given to the directors as at the time of this auditor's report. We believe that the audit evidence we have obtained is sufficient and appropriate to provide a basis for our opinion.
Key audit matters	Key audit matters are those matters that, in our professional judgement, were of most significance in our audit of the financial report of the current period. These matters were addressed in the context of our audit of the financial report as a whole, and in forming our opinion thereon, and we do not provide a separate opinion on these matters. [Description of each key audit matter in accordance with ASA 701.]
Responsibilities of the directors for the financial report	The directors of the Company are responsible for the preparation of the financial report that gives a true and fair view in accordance with Australian Accounting Standards and the *Corporations Act 2001*, and for such internal control as the directors determine is necessary to enable the preparation of the financial report that gives a true and fair view and is free from material misstatement, whether due to fraud or error. In preparing the financial report, the directors are responsible for assessing the Company's ability to continue as a going concern, disclosing, as applicable, matters related to going concern and using the going concern basis of accounting unless the directors either intend to liquidate the Company or to cease operations, or have no realistic alternative but to do so.
Auditor's responsibilities for the audit of the financial report	Our objectives are to obtain reasonable assurance about whether the financial report as a whole is free from material misstatement, whether due to fraud or error, and to issue an auditor's report that includes our opinion. Reasonable assurance is a high level of assurance, but it is not a guarantee that an audit conducted in accordance with the Australian Auditing Standards will always detect a material misstatement when it exists. Misstatements can arise from fraud or error and are considered material if, individually or in the aggregate, they could reasonably be expected to influence the economic decisions of users taken on the basis of this financial report.

$\rightarrow$

Report on the remuneration report	*Opinion on the Remuneration Report* We have audited the Remuneration Report included in [paragraphs a to b or pages x to y] of the directors' report for the year ended 30 June 2023. In our opinion, the Remuneration Report of ABC Company Ltd for the year [period] ended 30 June 2023 complies with section 300A of the *Corporations Act 2001*. *Responsibilities* The directors of the Company are responsible for the preparation and presentation of the Remuneration Report in accordance with section 300A of the *Corporations Act 2001*. Our responsibility is to express an opinion on the Remuneration Report, based on our audit conducted in accordance with Australian Auditing Standards.
Closure	[Auditor's name and signature][1] [Name of firm] [Date of the auditor's report][2] [Auditor's address]

Source: Derived from ASA 700 (paras 36–9).

The language used in audit reports, as in other communications, should avoid ambiguity. So, there should be clarity as to what category of opinion is being provided. In this light, some have argued that the 'emphasis of matter' creates confusion because – even though the opinion may be unmodified ('clean') – this additional paragraph can give an impression that 'something is wrong'. The language used in (unmodified) statutory financial audit reports now tends to look identical from one engagement to the next, except, of course, as to the scope issues.

Scope

Early sections of the report establish the scope of the engagement and clarify the source of the opinion and the level of assurance. This is important as the reader should understand that on which an opinion has been formed. A later section to the report – auditor's other responsibilities – may include issues of scope as well, as they pertain to legal obligations or additional services performed in relation to the audit (examples are in ASA 700 and ISA NZ 700). Finally, should comparative statements be presented, the auditor's opinion should refer, as appropriate, to each period about which an audit opinion is addressed (ASA 710; ISA NZ 710).

Opinion

The auditor's opinion is stated early in the report. It is, of course, the purpose of producing the report and expresses either an 'unmodified' (clean) or 'modified' opinion (more on this later).

Basis for opinion

This represents the profession's effort to reduce that part of the expectation gap in which the users of financial statements (and users of audit assurance) may misunderstand what the audit is about. Also, reference to any other relationship the auditor may have with the client can be found here.

---

[1] The auditor is required, under the *Corporations Act 2001*, to sign the auditor's report in both their own name and the name of their firm (section 324AB(3)) or the name of the audit company (section 324AD(1)), as applicable.
[2] The date of the auditor's report is the date when the auditor signs the report.

Key audit matters

This is a new and evolving element of the auditor's report. Key audit matters (KAMs) are:

> Matters that, in the auditor's professional judgement, were of most significance in the audit of the financial statements of the current period. (ASA 701, para 8; ISA NZ 701, para 8)

The KAMs should not be confused with a modification made to the auditor's opinion — a KAM is not a modification. Nor should it be confused with the 'Emphasis of matter', which may also be included in the audit report. KAMs are intended to identify issues that created particular challenges experienced during the audit and about which the reader may wish to be advised.

A KAM may include the effect of significant events or transactions on the financial statements, such as, perhaps, the effect of selling a major division of the business. It may be matters that were found to be of higher risk in the engagement or that required significant estimations or judgements, such as the valuation of assets that are not valued in the market.

While standards on KAMs now exist, their selection and inclusion are left up to the auditor's judgement. It could cause confusion: Will the reader know to distinguish KAMs from other issues? Will they understand that it is not a modification of the opinion? It may be a controversial issue for some time to come.

Directors' responsibilities for the financial statements

Also termed the 'Responsibilities of those charged with governance …', this section to the auditor's report sets out the legal framework under which the governing authority (or senior management in some cases) must comply. It may include the applicable financial reporting framework used — such as GAAP or 'true and fair view' — and should include the client's responsibility for preparing the statements in accordance with that framework. So, for example, it also includes the governing body's responsibility to come to a going concern view.

Auditor's responsibilities for the audit of the financial statements

This sets out the auditor's objectives in conducting the service, the nature of reasonable assurance, and the issuance of an opinion. There would be comments on their responsibility to identify misstatements, if any, from fraud as well as errors and limitations to those responsibilities. There may be a comment about how 'materiality' is defined for the particular engagement.

There would be an explanation of the meaning of audit *risk* and *materiality* for the engagement, the auditor's role with respect to the client's internal controls, and their view on the management's use of policies and going concern assumptions.

Much of the section thus sets out the *limitations* to what the auditor can do or does. There is also an acknowledgement that the auditor is responsible for the audit opinion, and a description of the process used to come to that opinion.

Other reporting responsibilities

This section would be included in the auditor's report should the auditor also conduct other services, such as, for example, management advisory services. It may include reporting on legal or regulatory requirements other than that referred to earlier in the report. Essentially, this section clarifies whether and how the auditor is engaged with the client and further clarifies the scope of the engagement.

Closure

The auditor's signature indicates their personal obligation for the quality of the engagement. You will recall that it is signed on the report date, which is the day on which evidential matter is no longer collected. This is important because the auditor's obligations are different *before* that date than they are *after* that date. More detail can be found in the standards referred to above.

The audit report is now reasonably long and, to some readers, may be overly complex. It is important to explain the limitations and the contribution of the audit opinion, however, to ensure the reader has reasonable expectations of the auditor's role. It is important to distinguish between the auditor's role and the governing body's role for the same reasons. This report does that now, more than in the past. Time will tell whether it reduces the expectation gap between audit professionals and users of the audit report.

CONCEPT QUESTION 1	Explain why KAMs and emphases of matters do not communicate 'opinions'.

Audit opinion

It is now time to consider the type of audit opinion appropriate under different circumstances. First, we consider the 'unqualified' opinion followed by situations that would lead the auditor to modify that opinion. We also consider what situations would lead to 'qualifying' the auditor's opinion, in what form, and why (see **Figure 17.3**).

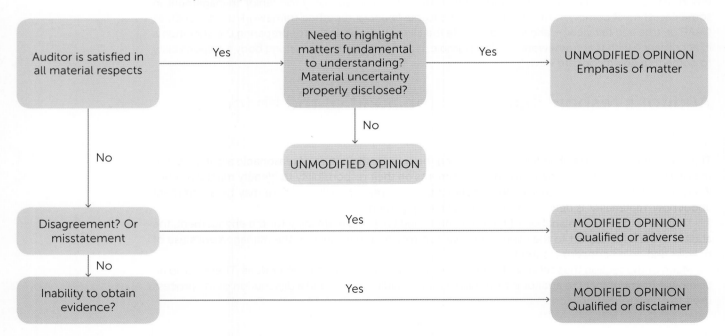

Figure 17.3 Which audit opinion is appropriate?

Note: A modified opinion would be qualified if the problem is 'material', and either a disclaimer or adverse if the problem is pervasive (ASA 705, para 5; ISA NZ 705, para 5).

Unqualified audit opinions

Unqualified opinions are granted when the auditor concludes that the financial statements comply with GAAP.

> The auditor shall express an unmodified opinion when the auditor concludes that the financial statements are prepared, in all material respects, in accordance with the applicable financial reporting framework. (ASA 700, para 16; ISA NZ 700, para 16)

An unqualified opinion is sometimes called a 'clean' opinion, and it is the opinion that everyone hopes the financial statements will achieve. If unqualified, then the auditor has concluded that acceptable accounting policies have been consistently applied, GAAP and relevant legislation were followed, and relevant information is disclosed (see **Figure 17.3**).

Australia, New Zealand and other jurisdictions allow the auditor to add information to the auditor's report in the form of KAMs, and for an 'Emphasis of matter', which allows the auditor to comment on an unusual matter that may be of particular importance to the user. It is *not* a qualification to the opinion. It should be used on relatively rare occasions, including situations in which:

1   an uncertainty exists (see below for more on this)
2   a new accounting standard could create confusion for the reader
3   a catastrophe or other event may have an ongoing effect on the entity's financial position (examples derived from ASA 706; ISA NZ 706, p. 608).

A common error made by students new to audit is to assume that adding an 'Emphasis of matter' (or 'Other matter' or KAM) qualifies an opinion: this is *not* correct. To give you some comfort, users of financial statements often make the same mistake. They provide additional information for the reader within the long-form report.

Qualified audit opinions

Qualified opinions are given by the auditor when there is a problem with the financial statements, and the client refuses or cannot resolve that problem prior to the report. If qualified, the auditor effectively states that the statements, or some aspect of them, do *not* or are *not known to* 'comply with GAAP'. The problem – or qualification – may be classified as to the *degree* of the problem (material or pervasive) and to its *source* (scope or disagreement) (see **Table 17.2**).

Table 17.2 Types of qualifications to the audit opinion

	Affects financial statements:	
	Material[3]	Material and pervasive
Scope limitation	Modified	Disclaimer
Disagreement	Modified	Adverse

Qualifications: Degrees of significance

Where it is seen to be appropriate to render a qualified opinion, the auditors must determine the degree of the problem:

* *Material* – A matter may be considered to be important, or *material*, if the misstatement, or restriction to the scope of the investigation, is specific to certain (but not substantial) elements of

the statements but is not fundamental to the users' understanding of the statements (derived from ASA 705, para 5; ISA NZ 705, para 5).

- *Material and pervasive* – A disagreement or restriction on the scope that is seen to be *material* and *pervasive* has the additional characteristic of being either not confined to specific elements of the financial statements, or, if confined, substantial or fundamental to users' understandings of the accounts (derived from ASA 705, paras 5, 16–17; ISA NZ 705, paras 5, 16–17).

General practice would suggest that a fundamental ('material and pervasive') disagreement or limitation is indicated by:

- the dollar magnitude of the items affected or potentially affected
- the significance of the items to the interpretation of the accounts; for example, a distortion that results in a net loss being disclosed as a net income, even if small, seems pervasive and fundamental, while a failure to disclose stock-flow policies in the footnotes is material because it does not render the interpretation of the accounts unfeasible
- the departure being significant to the accounts taken as a whole, such as may be caused by the use of the cash-based system rather than accrual
- the number of accounts affected or potentially affected being substantial
- a combination of material errors or uncertainties that occurs.

ASA 706 and ISA NZ 706 add a further condition: if the auditor wishes to communicate with readers about matters other than the financial statements, the auditor can include a separate paragraph entitled 'Other matters', following the opinion and any 'Emphasis of matter' paragraphs (ASA 706, paras 4–8; ISA NZ 706, paras 4–8). Our view is that, while this may be useful under some circumstances, it may also confuse the reader. We think KAMs are likely to replace the use of most 'Other matter' paragraphs, but time will tell.

While the new Australian and New Zealand standards are detailed, it is unclear whether they provide greater clarity for the reader on matters of the report. However, there are a few hard and fast rules, and it is up to the auditor as to what is or is not 'material' versus 'material and pervasive'. KAMs are generally expected, but it is also up to the auditor what they may be and whether to add additional non-opinion paragraphs to the audit report.

Qualifications: Source of the issue

The following circumstances distinguish one source for a qualification from another:

- *limitation of scope:* where there is a restriction on the scope of the auditor's examination so that it is not possible to obtain sufficient evidence to 'conclude that the financial statements as a whole are free from material misstatement' (ASA 700, para 17; ISA NZ 700, para 17)
- *disagreement:* where the auditor disagrees with the client's financial statements, generally as a result of a departure from GAAP, or non-compliance with statute, and therefore they are *not* free from material misstatement.

Disagreement

A disagreement occurs if the auditor finds that 'the financial statements are not free from material misstatement' despite their efforts to encourage the client to comply with the required framework (GAAP, in our case). It may be due to problems with:

- the acceptability of the selected accounting policies
- the application of the selected accounting policies
- the adequacy of disclosures in the financial statements.

Such a disagreement may be either material or material and pervasive. For example, the client may insist on disclosing stock at cost, despite material reductions in its market value. This is both in contravention of GAAP and does not reflect a 'true and fair' view with respect to the value of inventory.

If the matter can be isolated to a few accounts, and if the impact of stock overstatement is fundamental to the statements taken as a whole, this may be seen as a 'material' circumstance.

The auditor should provide the reasons for the modification in the audit report with a 'Basis for modification' paragraph. This paragraph is to be distinguished from the 'Emphasis of matter' paragraph because the former accompanies qualified opinions and the latter accompanies unqualified opinions.

The 'Basis for modification' normally provides a description of the reason for the modification or omitted disclosure, and its effect on the financial statements if determinable. The paragraph normally precedes the opinion paragraph (ASA 705, para 16; ISA (NZ 705, para 16). An example of a qualified opinion from the standards is provided in **Table 17.3**.

Table 17.3 Qualification for disagreement

Purpose	Example
Audit opinion qualified: Except for disagreement	We have audited the financial report of ABC Company Ltd (the Company), which comprises the statement of financial position as at 30 June 2023, the statement of comprehensive income, statement of changes in equity, and statement of cash flows for the year then ended, and notes to the financial statements, including a summary of significant accounting policies, and the directors' declaration. In our opinion, except for the effects of the matter described in the Basis for Qualified Opinion section of our report, the accompanying financial report of ABC Company Ltd is in accordance with the *Corporations Act 2001*, including: *(a) giving a true and fair view of the company's financial position as at 30 June 2023 and of its financial performance for the year then ended; and* *(b) complying with Australian Accounting Standards and the Corporations Regulations 2001.*

An *adverse opinion* (see **Table 17.4**, from the standards) should be issued when the effect of a disagreement renders the financial report fundamentally misleading.

Table 17.4 Adverse opinion

Purpose	Example
Audit opinion: Adverse	We have audited the financial report of ABC Company Ltd (the Company), and its subsidiaries (the Group), which comprises the consolidated statement of financial position as at 30 June 2023, the consolidated statement of comprehensive income, the consolidated statement of changes in equity and the consolidated statement of cash flows for the year then ended, notes comprising a summary of significant accounting policies, and the directors' declaration. In our opinion, because of the significance of the matter discussed in the Basis for Adverse Opinion section of our report, the accompanying financial report of the Group is not in accordance with the *Corporations Act 2001*, including: *(a) giving a true and fair view of the Group's financial position as at 30 June 2023 and of its financial performance for the year then ended; and* *(b) complying with Australian Accounting Standards and the Corporations Regulations 2001.*

Sources: Derived from ASA 705 and ISA NZ 705 (illustrations 1A and 2A).

The auditor must set out the circumstances giving rise to the adverse opinion under a separate heading and state that the financial report does not give a true and fair view. An adverse opinion would be rare in practice, but it is an important incentive available to the auditor to convince the client to conform with GAAP.

If the auditor concludes that financial statements do not comply with GAAP, then every effort should be made to persuade the client to change the statements. If the client insists on presenting financial statements with which the auditor disagrees, the auditor will be forced to modify their opinion.

Limitation in scope

A limitation on the scope of the audit exists when the auditor has been unable to obtain 'sufficient appropriate evidence to conclude that the financial statements are free from material misstatement' (ASA 705, para 17(a); ISA NZ 705, para 17(a)). For example, if the client's record systems have been destroyed by fire, then it is impossible to test transactions against vouchers or database records that no longer exist. When the likely effect is material but not pervasive, the auditor should issue a qualified opinion. The auditor should disclose the effect of disagreement or limitation on the financial statements in monetary terms wherever possible.

Scope limitations arise when factors outside the client's (or the auditor's) control limit the auditor's work. This may occur should records simply not be available at all or should the auditor be contracted after the important stocktake process occurs. The auditor should discuss the reasons for the scope limitation in the *basis for the modification* paragraph and qualify the opinion so that users can understand why it occurred and assess the client's role in creating the limitation.

The auditor should not voluntarily accept scope limitations, and every attempt must be made to overcome any that are imposed. The previous Australian and New Zealand standards specified that if, prior to acceptance, it was apparent that a fundamental scope limitation would exist, the engagement should be declined. While the current internationally led standards do not address this issue, it remains sound advice. As elsewhere, the auditor would need to exercise judgement.

Professional scepticism

'The modern skeptic allows space to explore truth's proxy based on indirect knowledge of the phenomenon of concern. The concept of mitigated skepticism ... demonstrating that while we cannot understand the substance of a phenomenon [such as misstatements where there is a limitation in scope] there may be ways of evaluating its presence, its absence or its trajectory ... if one can understand a representation or an association, then some level of truth-pattern can be revealed.' (Van Peursem, 2020, p. 312)

A disclaimer of opinion should be issued when the effect of a limitation of scope prevents the auditor from collecting sufficient appropriate audit evidence to express an opinion on the financial statements taken as a whole. If, for example, the client maintained no fundamental controls, a disclaimer would be called for (see **Table 17.5**).

Table 17.5 Qualified for a material limitation in scope

Purpose	Example
Audit opinion qualified: Scope limitation	'ENZ Co Ltd's management was unable to produce reliable inventory records for the period 1 June to 31 August 2005. Any misstatement of these balances would affect the results for the year ended 31 March 2006.' 'In this respect alone, we have not obtained all of the information and explanations that we have required or determined whether proper accounting records were kept.' 'In our opinion, except for adjustments that might have been found to be necessary had we been able to obtain sufficient evidence concerning inventory, the financial report complies with generally accepted accounting practice in New Zealand and gives a true and fair view.'

Sources: Format from NZICA AGS-1002 (2003); some terminology from ISA NZ 700 and ISA NZ 705.

An inherent uncertainty is defined under previous standards as a situation in which the 'resolution is dependent on uncertain future events outside the entity's management' (ASA 702, para 6). This may occur if the outcome of a lawsuit against the client is unknown or if warranty obligations will increase substantially due to the unknowable costs of a natural disaster.

An inherent uncertainty is *pervasive* if the magnitude of its impact is so great that the financial reports would be seriously misleading were it is not adequately disclosed. It is *material* if the financial statements, including disclosure of the uncertainties, still give a fair presentation. Questions of *going concern* tend to be significant and thus deserve special reporting treatment. The practice traditionally adopted, and as advised by ASA 570 and ISA NZ 570: Going Concern, is as follows:

- If the going concern uncertainty exists, but disclosure about it is adequate, then there should be *no qualification* to the audit report. This is a situation when an 'Emphasis of matter' paragraph should be added to the audit report.
- If the financial statements have been prepared on a going concern basis – so, for example, the client has not written down assets to liquidation prices, and they should be – then ASA 570 (para 21) and ISA NZ 570 (para 21) would suggest that an *adverse* opinion should be given if no adjustment is made, as it would be both material and pervasive.

Suppose that a material and pervasive uncertainty exists with respect to going concern, and the auditor has been unable to collect sufficient information about it, so disclosure is inadequate. In that case, the auditor may consider whether a disclaimer is appropriate (ASA 570; ISA NZ 570) based on the degree of the problem (see **Table 17.6**).

Table 17.6 Disclaimer of opinion (limitation of scope)

Purpose	Example
Audit opinion: Disclaimer	We were engaged to audit the financial report of ABC Company Ltd (the Company), which comprises the statement of financial position as at 30 June 2023, the statement of comprehensive income, statement of changes in equity and statement of cash flows for the year then ended, and notes to the financial statements, including a summary of significant accounting policies, and the directors' declaration. We do not express an opinion on the accompanying financial report of the Company. Because of the significance of the matter described in the Basis for Disclaimer of Opinion section of our report, we have not been able to obtain sufficient appropriate audit evidence to provide a basis for an audit opinion on this financial report.

Source: Derived from ASA 570.

CONCEPT QUESTION 2 What is the relationship between a 'qualified' opinion and professional ethics?

Other engagements

In addition to historical financial statement audits, the professional may be called on to perform other types of assurance, non-assurance and advisory services. Auditing standards for such other services are provided either by an independent standard-setting authority or by the auditors' professional body.

Standards and rules for these engagements are under constant review, and they are issued by a multitude of different organisations and committees. They may be inspired by international standards or by unique local situations, such as standards for New Zealand's 'service performance' disclosures. Topics covered in other standards may therefore include but are not limited to:

- review (assurance) engagements (ASREs Australia, ISREs New Zealand)
- compilations (APESB Australia, profession-issued in New Zealand)

- single financial statements, or single elements of a financial statement
- summary financial statements
- special purpose frameworks
- audits or reviews of accounting forecasts or projections
- agreed-upon procedures, factual findings or the like
- accounting and auditing professional, ethical standards
- audits or reviews of any other type of claim for which assurance is sought.

Particularly for 'other' engagements, professional members should ensure that the scope is very clear in the engagement letter. The engagement letter becomes both guide and reference when evaluating what is or is not important to investigate. It is crucial that the scope, assurance and users are consistent with what is produced in the final report and opinion (see **Figure 17.4**). Should that not occur, there are circumstances indicating that any resultant misunderstandings can lead to both loss and lawsuit.

Some audit communication guidance is found in law (e.g., ASX listing rule; NZX exchange rules). Appropriate overseas legislation needs to be understood for companies (or subsidiaries) listed on foreign exchanges.

A challenge for the profession today is in communicating the meaning of other levels of assurance and the purpose of their other engagements. These engagements will continue to influence standards and practice even as assurance practices reach into more and more activities in which accountability is required.

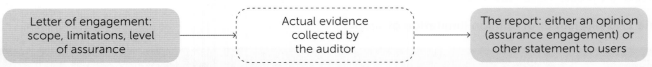

Consistency needed through to final report of the audit professional

Figure 17.4 Communication: Consistency for non-financial audit engagements

Study tools

Summary

This chapter explained the value of unambiguous communication between auditors and users of financial reports. During the course of an engagement, the auditor will be communicating with many different people for different reasons. This chapter discussed the means by which professionals do so in both formal and informal ways.

How auditors express themselves is important not only to convey content but also to add to their evidence and provide assurance to others. The auditor's credibility is manifested in a professional code, situated within an associational membership and grounded in normative foundations of integrity and objectivity.

The history of audit report was reviewed, including the rationale for long-form reports. We evaluated the auditor's report and the audit opinion. We introduced the 'Emphasis of matter' and key audit matters, and explained how opinions are modified in depth and in scope. The significance of the report and opinion was emphasised.

Case/resources link

CAATs for Classrooms

Accompanying this book is a series of data, integrated worksheets and exercises that are designed to support your learning and give you exposure to hands-on audit decision-making dilemmas faced by auditors in the planning elements of the audit process. Acquire the relevant material for this chapter from your instructor.

Review questions

17.1   What is the purpose of the audit report?

17.2   Why is audit opinion important?

17.3   What characteristics should good 'communication' have?

17.4   What does it mean to say that report language is 'symbolic'?

17.5   Name and define the eight sections of the standard audit report.

17.6   Name and define five types of audit communication (other than the audit report) and whether they are formal or not.

17.7   How may professional and philosophical scepticism apply to the audit communication with the client?

17.8   Provide an example of a key audit matter, and answer the question of whether its presence modifies the audit opinion or not.

17.9   Define 'Emphasis of matter', provide an example, and answer the question of whether its presence modifies the audit opinion or not.

17.10 Why is it important to convey the 'report date' in the audit report?

17.11 Define a 'limitation of scope'.

17.12 Define 'disagreement' as the basis for a modification.

17.13 What is the difference between a 'material' qualification and a 'material and pervasive' qualification?

17.14 When should a 'modification due to a limitation in scope' be issued?

17.15 When should a 'modification due to disagreement' be issued?

17.16 When should a 'disclaimer' be issued?

17.17 When should an 'adverse' opinion be issued?

17.18 Name two different types of 'uncertainties' as defined for the audit report.

17.19 Define the circumstances under which the following opinion may be given for a going concern problem:

   a   'Emphasis of matter' only

   b   adverse opinion

   c   disclaimer.

17.20 Identify other assurance standards and their purpose, as currently promulgated.

Exercises

17.1   **AUDIT REPORT:** Your experienced audit senior prefers the 'short-form' report, which does not include information about the 'Basis for the opinion' or the 'Auditor's responsibilities'.

   Required: Explain to the auditor the purpose of these sections and how they may help reduce the expectation gap.

17.2   **EMPHASIS OF MATTER:** Your junior audit staff member cannot decide whether the following matters should lead to a 'qualification' of the opinion or an 'Emphasis of matter'. What do you think? Treat each independently of the other.

   a   The potential for company failure within six months of the report date exists, but this has been appropriately disclosed in the client's financial statements.

   b   The client has refused to disclose in accordance with the GAAP requirement that their inventory is valued at the lower of cost or market because, in their business' case, the inventory is likely to be sold at a higher market value. While you agree with the client in principle, you believe that the information should be disclosed in accordance with GAAP.

   c   The client plans to reduce their building operations business by 50 per cent in the coming year and replace it with a division that provides finance to customers.

17.3   **EMPHASIS OF MATTER AND KAMs**

   Required: For each of the circumstances below, suggest whether the item would be more likely shown as either an 'Emphasis of matter' or a KAM. Consider each situation independently.

   a   A subsequent event occurs that is so material that the reader should be made aware of it, such as an intent to change the nature of the business.

   b   The analysis of opening balances is made particularly difficult due to the fact that the previous financial statements were reviewed but not audited.

   c   Infrastructural assets are listed and depreciated, but they are not owned, such as can occur in government.

   d   A challenge for the now-completed audit was in obtaining information about the value of intangible assets. This was ultimately acquired through obtaining the opinion of a registered valuer.

17.4 **AUDIT OPINION:** What type of audit opinion would you expect to see in the following circumstances and why? Consider each independently.

   a Inventory was valued at higher of cost or market, which is not a true and fair representation.

   b A payroll fraud was discovered, but the amount was immaterial and had no other apparent effects.

   c The client kept inadequate documents and records.

   d Inventory was valued at higher of cost or market, and the auditor concludes that this represents a true and fair value.

17.5 **AUDIT OPINION:** What types of audit opinion would you expect to see in the following circumstances and why? Consider each independently.

   a A takeover bid could have a major effect on the company's share price. This is disclosed in the footnotes to the financial statements.

   b Same as (a), but this is not disclosed.

   c The outcome of existing litigation could result in company dissolution. This is disclosed in the footnotes.

   d A related party is one of the company's suppliers. This is not disclosed.

   e A material misstatement of stock is undiscovered by the auditor.

   f A fire destroyed much of the warehouse building, a major asset of the client, and the inventory therein. There was no insurance. A large volume of sales recorded in the current year was for items destroyed in the fire, and many of these sales were subsequently cancelled before year-end. The client refused to reduce the value of either the fixed assets or the stock in accordance with GAAP, refused to adjust the volume of sales, and refused to make any further disclosures.

17.6 **OPINION AND CASE LAW:** If an auditor gives an unqualified opinion on a company's financial statements and that company goes into liquidation six months later, the auditor might face an action for negligence. Explain:

   a to whom auditors owe a 'duty of care'

   b the significance of the following cases in the extension of the auditor's liability to third parties:

      i   *Donoghue v. Stevenson* (1932)

     ii *Hedley Byrne and Co. Ltd v. Heller and Partners* (1963)

    iii *Scott Group Ltd v. McFarlane* (1978)

    iv *Twomax Ltd and Goode v. Dickson, McFarlane and Robinson* (1983)

     v *Caparo Industries PLC v Dickman* (1990).

17.7 **AUDIT REPORT:** The financial report gives a true and fair view, except that debtor records were destroyed in a flood. The possible effect of this is material but not fundamental. Write an appropriate audit report.

17.8 **OPINION AND GOING CONCERN:** Your audit firm ranks each going concern issue on a scale of 1 (low concern) to 3 (high concern) on a number of matters.

     You are auditing a wholesale distributor of locks, safes, alarms and other security devices. Assume that industry patterns show a recent, significant drop in consumer sales. While there is no negative publicity about your client, you are aware that they have had engineering problems with the alarms that were sold, and warranty costs are likely to go up significantly. Furthermore, a new competitor has recently opened up in their sales district, and they have more modern equipment. Ownership and management have had no changes in recent years.

Required: For the situation described, derive a ranking of each of the issues named (see Table 17.7). Conclude as to whether you believe this situation requires a going concern qualification and, assuming appropriate disclosure (or not), what type.

Table 17.7 Ranking of going concern issues

	Materiality*	Risk*	(Weighting × risk)
Liquidity ratios			
Media reports			
Litigation			
Business risk			
Board changes			
Internal control risk			
Industry risk			
Competition issues			
Solvency ratios			
Market effects			
Ranking (max. 30 each)			
Total ranking (maximum 90)			

* Use a scale of 1–3, with 3 denoting greatest importance (weighting) and highest risk.

17.9 **COMPLETION AND AUDIT REPORT:** The financial statements for the period ending 31 March 2022 for Agris Ltd, a New Zealand company, are being audited by Bongart & Bongart CAs. Bongart is the audit partner in charge. Alan is Agris's CEO.

Required: For each situation (i)–(iii):

a name the type of opinion the auditor should provide (or should have provided)

b name the issue of concern raised here

c explain what should be (or what should have been) done by the auditor.

Assume, unless specified otherwise, that all amounts are material. Also assume that each situation is independent of the others. The report date is at the statutory limit of five months from the date of the financial statements.

i This is the first year Agris has been audited, so Bongart has no audited beginning balances. All beginning balances were confirmed except inventory (due to periodic inventory method use), so Bongart uses the amount shown in the compiled statement prepared by management as at 31 March 2022 and conducts some (non-convincing) SpAR. No further evidence is reasonably obtainable about this beginning balance.

ii After issuing an unqualified audit opinion in the audit report, Bongart was socialising with friends, and one of those friends told him that the financial manager of Agris was carrying out foreign exchange transactions with a prohibited country, an action not allowed under New Zealand law. The values and transactions related to these events were audited and reported fairly, and their value was, taken together, *not* material. Even though he had already issued the audit report, Bongart discussed this concern with Agris's CEO (Alan) and with Agris's audit committee, but did nothing further. Neither Alan nor the audit committee took any further action, and the transactions are probably still going on.

iii On 15 May 2021, Alan sold used construction equipment to Cameras Inc. for $450 000. The transaction is recorded as a credit to equipment (net of accumulated depreciation) which is appropriately calculated and as a debit to long-term assets, although it is a short-term Notes Receivable.

17.10 **COMPLETION AND AUDIT REPORT:** The financial statements for the period ending 31 March 2022 for Agris Ltd, a New Zealand company, are being audited by Bongart & Bongart CAs. Bongart is the audit partner in charge. Alan is Agris's CEO.

Required: For each situation (i)–(iii):

a name the issue of concern raised here

b explain what should be (or what should have been) done by the auditor

c explain the opinion the auditor should provide, assuming no further changes are made.

Assume, unless specified otherwise, that all amounts are material. Also assume that each situation is independent of others. The report date is at the statutory limit of five months from the date of the financial statements.

i   A $470 000 sale in October 2021 to Cameras Inc. was recorded. Cameras Inc. had only paid $20 000 of this by the report date. Alan personally spoke to his brother, the CEO of Cameras Inc., about this. Alan then informed Bongart not to worry: Agris will receive the entire $450 000 within the year. Bongart asked Agris to document his conversation with Cameras Inc.'s CEO and disclose information about this transaction in the footnotes to the financial statements. Agris does the former (documents the conversation), but declines to add a footnote to the financial statements. This does *not* put Agris in an insolvency financial position.

ii During Bongart's subsequent events review, he discovers that Alan has plans to invest Agris's spare cash – about $1 100 000 – in financial futures on the Kenyan stockmarket. Bongart warns Alan against such a risky investment in writing, stating that the loss of this amount would send the company into liquidation, but Alan ignores this advice and withdraws the funds in May 2021. No disclosures of these plans are made in the March statements.

iii Bongart was also asked to carry out an efficiency review engagement of the Purchasing Division of Agris Ltd. Bongart combined his opinions of the financial and efficiency engagement into one audit report, as both of them could be 'unqualified'.

MILESTONES OF AUDIT

PART 1 THE AUDITOR'S ROLE IN SOCIETY

1 Introduction to audit
2 Audit concepts, role and history
3 Statutory law
4 Auditor professionalism and audit firms
5 The courts: The legal liability of auditors

PART 2 AUDIT PLANNING

6 Audit risk
7 Audit judgement, materiality and evidence
8 Audit testing and working papers
9 Audit process and analytical procedures
10 Audit planning

PART 3 AUDIT TESTING

11 Principles of internal control
12 Internal control and the auditor
13 Audit sampling
14 Systems testing I: Sales, purchases and payroll
15 Systems II: Warehousing, financing and fixed assets

PART 4 AUDIT COMMUNICATION AND REPORT

16 Completion and review
17 Audit report and opinion

PART 5 SPECIFIC TYPES OF AUDIT

18 Internal audit
19 Social audit
20 Fraud audit

THE AUDITOR'S ROLE IN SOCIETY

PLANNING

COMMUNICATION AND REPORTING

TESTING

Specific types of audit

Part 5 of the textbook is on specific type of audit and comprises three chapters. Chapter 18 is on internal audit, its role and risk, and covers the role of internal auditors, their professional and legal obligations, and the functions and processes employed by internal auditors. Chapter 19 is on social audit, its purpose and conceptual application. Aspects of public sector audit, non-profit charitable, small business and environmental audits are also covered in this chapter. The purpose of fraud and forensic audits, and the fraud audit process and approaches, are covered in Chapter 20.

PART 5

Internal audit

Learning objectives

After studying the material in this chapter, you should be able to:
- Understand the role of other assurance engagements
- explain the role of internal auditor
- describe the functions of internal audit
- document and conduct inquiry as to audits of cloud and virtual systems.

Introduction

This chapter is the first in a series of three introducing professional assurance engagements *other than* the statutory financial statement audit. It is important to focus on the financial statement audit up to this point because of the demand for it and because it is a pinnacle of professional work. The statutory financial audit requires experienced auditors grounded in the knowledge of their obligation to society at large. However, other forms of assurance do exist and are growing in number. It is timely to turn our attention to these other engagements.

We first consider internal audits, followed by chapters that describe the social audit (environmental, public sector, non-profits and SMEs) and the audit of fraud. We return to the *conceptual framework for audit* (refer back to **Figure 2.6**) to explain how the assumptions, concepts and standards apply to these different types of engagements. We also look at what 'makes' a professional, to understand why some may have higher status or credibility in the eyes of the public than others.

These engagements are agreed under contract or in employment agreements between an assurance provider (auditor) and a client or employer. Agreements will be specific and unique. Given their distinctiveness, guidance can be difficult to provide, although a nod has been given to this dilemma in the standards. Tax, cash or specially regulated bases of accounting, or auditors for bond indentures, loan agreements or project grants, are all examples in the standards (ASA 800 and ISA NZ 800: Special Considerations – Audits of Financial Statements Prepared in Accordance with Special Purpose Frameworks, A1-A2). We look at how the audit concepts and professional principles apply.

'Other' assurance engagements

Irrespective of the *type* of assurance sought, the auditor's credibility and work are important if their opinion is to be trusted. The fundamental postulates of the audit professional – accountability, evidence, access to information, standards, and economic or social benefit – remain. The concepts – risk, materiality, evidence, independence, communication and others – are relevant in other professional assurance engagements, although they may take different forms.

The terms of a financial statement audit contract are, in good part, determined in law. The auditing standards (ASA in Australia, ISA NZ in New Zealand) are mandated, and most are specific to the financial statement engagement. Law and court precedent addresses content, issues of materiality, disclosure, going concern, related parties, negligence and so on (a segment of the framework is reproduced in **Figure 18.1**).

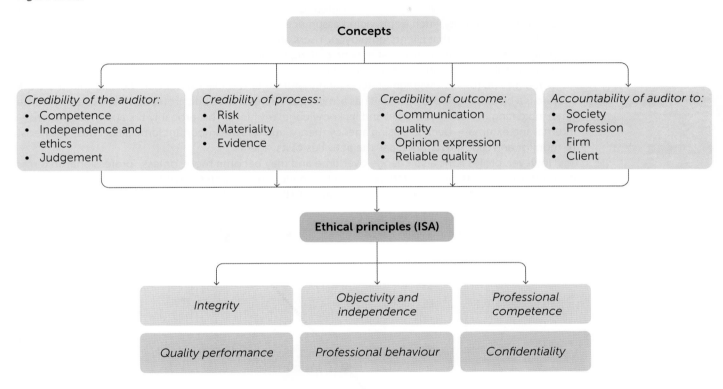

Figure 18.1 Segment of the conceptual framework for audit

This is less the case in other types of assurance engagements. There is room for variation when agreeing to an audit of public sector performance or a fraud search. There are also different professional associations. While accounting associations such as CA ANZ, CPA Australia, ICAEW and the AICPA are established, some since the 1850s, a look at professional norms informs what is expected of professional engagements.

Auditing in practice

CAATs

The CAATs program associated with this text offers an exercise to produce and evaluate a variety of assurance engagements that could be encountered.

A 'list' is not the only way to understand what it means to be a professional association. That which distinguishes a 'profession' may be that it has standards for entry and performance, ethical codes, and some accountability for its members. So, for example, if a chartered accountant behaves in a way that brings the profession into disrepute, their name may be published or they may be censured.

Burns, Greenspan and Hartwell (1994), basing their work on the internal auditor, offer an 'intimidation' model in which the influence and expertise of the association are what gives it status. That is, what makes an association a 'profession' that its members have:

- *high cruciality* – or that they are considered to be, as a group, critical to the prosperity, welfare or survival of an activity, such as providing assurance
- *high mystique* – or that clients/employers, users and other external parties believe members of that profession possess expertise that may be baffling to them but which is important and 'sublime'; that is, their skills are challenging to understand.

Given an auditor's knowledge of accounting (and other disciplines), it could be said that the work they do is a bit baffling to others, that it has a 'mystique'. Indeed, the audit profession has existed for some time, indicating it is seen as crucial and its knowledge 'mystical'. This probably fits audit associations – internal and external – because, using agency theory, auditors are important (crucial) because they exist to monitor and report to a 'principal' the activities of its 'agent'.

However, professions also change over time and may become more, or less, 'professional' in terms of the Burns, Greenspan and Hartwell model. The idea that a professional form evolves and changes over time is reflected in McNamee and McNamee's (1995) 'Transformation theory' (see **Figure 18.2**).

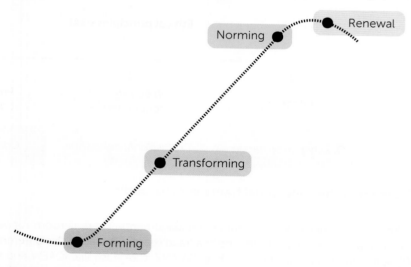

Figure 18.2 Transformation theory and professions

Source: McNamee and McNamee (1995).

In Australia and New Zealand, chartered associations were originally small and dispersed, forming in Australian states and in New Zealand in the early 1900s. Over time and with legislative support, they were *transformed* into accepted institutions with some monopoly privileges. Ethical codes, standards and the tightening of restrictions to entry occurred in the mid-to-late 20th century. Members' roles became, to some extent, empowered and 'normalised' through these events.

CPA Australia arose in the 1980s and is growing, focusing on international connections, and may be in an earlier stage of formation. More recently, other accounting professions have emerged, some challenging established 'norms'. The very act of combining the Australian and New Zealand chartered accounting associations in 2006, for the first time, gives a sense of 'renewal' in these more established professions by offering a more globally connected profession.

The older professions have also been pressed into *renewal* by increasing their range of consulting and technical practices. The challenge is in retaining audit 'independence' while continuing to provide consulting services, a concern that has led to careful reconstructions of ethical codes and practices. Renewal is also needed to cope with changes in global business, digital, cloud-based systems, online fraud and even professional competition.

Formation and transformation are likely to continue. In this and the next two chapters, we will be discussing associations of internal auditors (IIA), fraud auditors (ACFE) and environmental auditors (CES), all of which are relatively new and in 'formative' or possibly 'transformative' stages. The stage an association finds itself within gives us some understanding of its challenges and opportunities.

Internal audit role

Internal audit is an appraisal function performed within and for an organisation. An internal audit can play a very significant role in the testing of the efficiency of an internal control system as well as provide important information for the purpose of performing required changes. Internal audits can be conducted for various reasons, one of which is compliance testing of the internal control system. Internal audits can also be conducted for the purpose of providing assurance and advice on health and safety, regulatory and legal compliance, and environmental issues. Large organisations and government departments frequently have an internal audit division. Alternatively, a professional may be contracted to carry out an internal audit function.

Internal audit profession

The Institute of Internal Auditors (IIA) is the recognised professional association for internal auditors. The IIA was formed in 1941 in the United States, and the Australian and New Zealand branches are members of this international association. The IIA has a code of ethics, membership entry and retention requirements, though an accounting degree is not needed. Internal auditors tend to come from all walks of life. Also, unlike external auditors, internal auditors are accountable to an organisation's governing board or audit committee, not (usually) to shareholders directly or to external parties.

IIA cooperates with national accounting professions. The IIA is a member of the United Nations as a non-governmental organisation, is part of the International Consortium on Government Financial Management (ICGFM), the International Organization of Supreme Audit Institutions (INTOSAI) and the International Federation of Accountants (IFAC) – all of which are other professional associations, of course. It is also a charter member of the Committee of Sponsoring Organizations (COSO) group of the Treadway Commission.

Unlike CA ANZ or CPA Australia, however, the IIA does not provide a monopoly service and, as such, it is often viewed as being in a more supportive role for senior management. This is reflected by its own website:

> Internal auditing is an independent, objective assurance and consulting activity designed to add value and improve an organization's operations. It helps an organization accomplish its objectives by bringing a systematic, disciplined approach to evaluate and improve the effectiveness of risk management, control, and governance processes.
> (IIA, 2022)

In terms of the auditing conceptual framework, the IIA's vision, and internal focus, are illustrated by the topics listed in their standards (see **Table 18.1**).

Table 18.1 Concepts of auditing and IIA codes and standards

Credibility and ethics	Auditor competence	AS300: Proficiency and due professional care Code of ethics: professional competence
	Audit judgement	PS100: Manage the internal auditing activity
	Independence	AS200: Independence and objectivity
Process	Risk	PS210: Risk management process
	Materiality	AS410: Objectives of a quality assurance system
	Evidence	PS400: Perform the engagement
Auditor's accountability	To the public	n/a
	To the profession	via the Code of Ethics
	To the firm	AS100: Purpose, authority and responsibility PS600: Monitor progress PS230: Governance process
Communication	Internal	PS500: Communicate results AS400: Compliance – quality assurance system
	External	n/a

Note that accountability to external parties is not strictly part of the IIA's role. 'Independence' is from middle (and/or upper) management within the organisation, but not from the governing body. Some concerns have been raised over how internal auditors can retain their 'independence' from managers with whom they work daily, but that is the goal they try to achieve.

There is also growth in internal audit work by external audit firms. Care should be taken, or the situation should be avoided, in cases where the firm conducts both external and internal audit work, as their independence could be at risk. The presence of certain features may help internal auditors preserve a professional 'distance', including:

- *IIA membership*, as they incorporate independence issues into their code of ethics
- *audit charters*, a pseudo-contractual document setting out the role of the auditor and those to whom they can and should report
- *follow-up procedures* that call management to account for the extent to which they responded to auditor recommendations
- *control self-assessment procedures*, in which managers and internal auditors assess their own control environment.

The external auditor may be employed for a singularly defined purpose, such as to improve a payroll system or identify a suspected fraud. Internal auditors have become important participants in an increasingly regulated systems environment and in preventing or detecting fraud.

Regulation and authority

The growth in internal audit is inspired by growing global trading risks, including international bribery, money laundering and cross-border corruption. US legislators responded to some risks under the *Foreign Corrupt Practices Act 1977*. Further legislation includes the *Sarbanes-Oxley Act 2002*, which requires the disclosure of internal control quality for certain large entities. The *Cadbury Report* in the United Kingdom and Australia's *Corporations Act 2001* are also influential. Much of this legislation was inspired by scandals occurring due to a lack of quality internal controls (see the 'Auditing in practice' box on the WorldCom case).

Auditing in practice

WorldCom case

WorldCom, a telecommunications business, became the second-largest provider of long-distance phone services in the United States. Bernard Ebbers, its founder, loved deal-making, and as a result of his efforts, the company grew to dominate the market by the late 1990s. A competitive market and the rise of mobile phones put stress on its profits, however, and these were eventually overstated to the amount of US$3.8 billion.

The company's internal auditor, Cynthia Cooper, was a certified public accountant (US) and a certified fraud examiner, and had major accounting firm experience. During a meeting, the finance director explained that one of the capital expenditure items was for 'prepaid capacity'. While accepted by others, Cooper inquired further about what 'prepaid capacity' meant and how it was used.

She and her team discovered that amounts would flow into and out of this account in an unusual manner. Further investigation revealed expenditures ending up on the balance sheet as 'investments', or being transferred from one year (2001) to the next (2002), all with the assistance of the company's CFO, Scott Sullivan. It was difficult to study as the system had complex, obscure transactions.

The external audit firm (Arthur Andersen) and the SEC eventually revealed the problem (though WorldCom replaced Arthur Andersen with KPMG). This courageous internal auditor, who stood up to her governing board and senior members of management, prompted the discovery and disclosure of one of the largest frauds in US history.

This case was one of several that inspired the *Sarbanes-Oxley Act 2002* and COSO practices that raised the internal auditor's importance and independence to public attention. The profits from Cynthia Cooper's book on the case – *Extraordinary Circumstances: The Journey of a Corporate Whistleblower* (2008) – were contributed to universities for the purposes of ethics education.

This legislation has transformed the IIA and the international attention it receives as a result. In particular, the Treadway Commission – a joint initiative by the AICPA, the American Accounting Association (AAA), Financial Executives International (FEI), the IIA and the Institute of Management Accountants (IMA) – formed what came to be known as COSO. Its purpose is to address concerns raised by scandals on an ongoing basis.

COSO aims to encourage internal control improvements in risk management and to reduce corrupt practices and fraud. This is a direct nod to the importance of an internal audit function.

Due to the publicity surrounding such events, interest in the internal auditor has grown. The internal auditor plays an ethical role in advising management and is expected to use their skills to reduce risk at the highest levels within an organisation. The role and authority of internal auditors is illustrated in **Figure 18.3**.

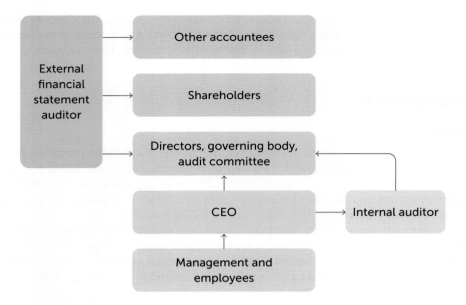

Figure 18.3 Internal auditor's accountability

Problems can occur in these arrangements, of course. Suppose the CEO sits on the governing board. In that case, the internal auditor is advised to negotiate an audit charter that ensures their independence from all levels of management, so that no-one escapes oversight. If the auditor is accountable to the CEO, not the governing board, they will find it difficult to hold the CEO to account.

CONCEPT QUESTION	1	How does the internal auditor's traditional role differ from their current role in terms of independence or professionalism?

Internal audit functions

Internal audit function is a good monitoring process; in the absence of it, management would need to apply other monitoring processes in order to assure itself that the system of internal control is functioning as per objectives. The need for internal audit and the extent of the internal audit function depend on several factors, such as the size of the organisation, types and complexity of operations, number of employees, the risks faced by the organisation, various compliance requirements, and organisational objectives.

The internal audit profession has a traditional role in developing, testing and overseeing control systems. These may occur through all of the client's systems: financial, managerial, production, environmental, marketing and so on. Internal auditors may carry out value-for-money audits to safeguard public assets, or fraud audits to identify intrusions. Their role is already extensive in many respects – it was even before governing board support became more common. However, we first look at that traditional role, which many internal auditors (particularly of smaller entities) find themselves to be in.

Developing effective control systems

The internal auditor was traditionally concerned with all processes forming an internal control system (**Figure 18.4**).

Systems development	Program design	Systems operation
• Establish risk management criteria • Monitor controls used	• Guide and test the program during design • Oversee embedded control design	• Manage control tests and access protocols

Data sharing	Data input-output	Data storage
• Establish controls over data transmission • Oversee transmission controls	• Establish controls for authorised entry and access • Establish controls over input or output data use	• Ensure controls over access and management • Monitor unauthorised access, manipulation or loss review • Oversee backup storage system

Figure 18.4 Internal auditor and control systems

They embed controls that could be performed and monitored while transactions were ongoing; that is, in a *continuous audit*. The internal auditor, then and now, may still be involved in these processes. For them, maintaining a sound system remains at the core of their work.

COSO has advanced this thinking by identifying five components of an effective internal control system involving the internal auditor:

1 *Control environments* – setting the tone of an organisation and including ethical values, operational style, personnel development and delegation practices.
2 *Risk assessment* – analysing risks relative to the organisational goals for achievement and determining how to manage them.
3 *Control activities* – policies and procedures that enable controls to occur, including the processes and checks we illustrated earlier in this text.
4 *Information systems* – including their ability to effectively pass information down, up and across internally, and to externals including customers, shareholders, suppliers, regulators and the community.
5 *Monitoring* – as discussed earlier, and by which the system, and those involved within it, are held to account.

These responsibilities may be delegated to the internal audit team or external firms via contract. A *transforming* role now places the internal auditor closer to governance.

Transforming role

Expectations from COSO and legislative attention to systems inspire companies to involve internal auditors in all aspects of management and governance to better ensure a risk-management regime. The relevant functions are detailed in **Table 18.2**.

Table 18.2 Internal audit roles and functions

Role type	Description
Communication role	Communication on issues such as the purpose of investigations and the audit plan, working with information technology staff, report and follow-up
Systems auditor	Conduct follow-up investigations, report to highest levels in an organisation, and work with external auditors
Technical role	Knowledge and application of particular audit or computer techniques
Risk management	Jack-of-all-trades support in helping management evaluate corporate strategy, identify risks and oversee system control issues
Control oversight	Low-level control testing, data processing and output testing, determining legal compliance and engaging in control self-assessment
Decision support	Participating with management in making decisions on systems issues
Systems involvement	Direct participation in systems revisions, development and oversight, including technical oversight

Source: Van Peursem (2004).

The internal auditor, in a strategic support capacity, works with the governing board to incorporate controls and other forms of risk management into new projects. While there is less involvement in 'testing', the internal auditor may retain oversight. We now consider a selection of these evolving functions.

Risk management

risk management
The idea that risk should be anticipated by management and incorporated into business planning, sometimes but not always controlled, so as to be the plan for organisational changes or unexpected events.

The auditor, and in particular the internal auditor, will be involved in **risk management**. Risk management treats controls as but one response to risk. The internal auditor is part of the management team, part of moving the organisation forward, not just restricting them:

> Internal auditing and risk management are so closely interlinked that it has become impossible to separate. Audit has to provide the frameworks for risk management and should also oversee business continuity and legislative compliance. (Van Peursem, 2005)

The risk-management process is pictured in **Figure 18.5**.

Controls can slow things down, increase costs, reduce efficiencies and lower the flexibility managers may seek in a business. Risk management engages with risk at a more strategic level so that risk can be reduced, mitigated or accepted by the following actions:
- *Avoiding risk* – changing the nature of the organisation or process such that the danger is avoided, including, for example, refusing to purchase from high-risk suppliers.
- *Diversifying risk* – reducing the chance of loss when all the 'eggs are in one basket'. A business with a variety of suppliers or customers helps ensure that the failure of one will not result in a major cost to the organisation.

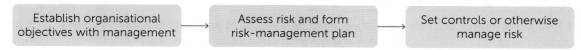

Figure 18.5 Sequence for risk auditing by COSO

- *Transferring risk* – ensuring that the organisation does not adopt the full weight of the risk. Transfer can occur through bonding, insurance and legal arrangements. Directors and officers can insure against negligence, fraud and professional indemnity.
- *Accepting risk* – acknowledging that some risk is part of doing business, and that in trying out new products or services or diversifying into new markets, there will always be some risk that things will go wrong. Accepting risk is not traditional in audit practice, but where flat organisations change and innovate constantly, then only the most important risks can be controlled.
- *Controlling* risk, instituting such measures that will prevent or detect errors, is but one option. It is not the only one in the process of managing risk.

Oversight and testing processes

The internal auditor should be independent of departmental managers whose systems are reviewed to carry out oversight and audit testing. Once tested, the internal auditor communicates their concerns and makes recommendations to the governing body.

After a while, the internal auditor may authorise a follow-up investigation. *Follow-up investigations* are unique to the internal auditor role. They involve returning to the system previously analysed to see if the changes recommended have been carried out and appropriately applied (see **Figure 18.6**).

Figure 18.6 Systems testing for the internal audit department

Communication

One of the internal auditor's most 'essential' functions derives from their obligation to share and communicate their views and findings. While the prominence of 'communication' may be surprising to you, it is a cornerstone of the internal auditor's work to facilitate solutions and find agreed balances between risk and control (e.g., see IIA performance standards 2020, 2400, 2410 and 2420).

Communication responsibilities include sharing knowledge and understandings as a member of the management team and the governing body. It is about agreeing with managers on the approach to risk management and conducting self-assessments. Communications are needed between the internal auditor and technical staff as to implementation. Knowledge of the system (and technical language) aids this process, as do a willingness and interest in ongoing communication with others.

Fraud deterrence

> Preventing fraud consists of those actions taken to discourage the perpetration of fraud and limit the exposure if fraud does occur. Internal auditing is responsible for assisting in the deterrence of fraud by examining ... controls, commensurate with the extent of ... risk ... of the entity's operations. (Vanasco, 1998, p. 24)

Internal audit can function as a form of fraud deterrence. Security-based control frameworks may protect the organisation in terms of its:

- information security
- access security

- physical security
- operations security
- developmental security.

Fraud audit is covered in Chapter 20, but suffice to say at this point that the most enduring role of the internal auditor has been to identify, prevent, detect or mitigate fraud in the organisation. This does not mean they are always effective in doing so, however:

> Most frauds are discovered by accident or by a whistleblower, not by audit or accounting system design. The search for a generally accepted methodology [to detect fraud before it becomes material] goes on. (Davia, 2000)

Nonetheless, the importance of fraud prevention to the internal auditor cannot be diminished. It is discussed later in this text.

External auditor relationship

The external financial auditor is concerned primarily with the internal auditor's role of managing risk and the testing and oversight of operations, procedures and records. External auditors would be wise to inform themselves of the role of the client's internal auditor because it may influence the extent to which the internal audit functions can be relied on to reduce their own tests of controls or substantive tests.

It is useful here to comment on the relationship between the external and internal auditor to justify this reduction in testing. Both internal and external auditors have a common interest in ascertaining whether there is an effective system of internal checks and ensuring that the system is working satisfactorily. Their responsibilities are prescribed respectively by statute (external audit) and management (internal audit). However, there is a fundamental difference between the two roles. Because the internal auditor is part of management, the external auditor must be cautious before relying on their work due to natural loyalties internal auditors may have to their employer – the client.

Nevertheless, there is a similarity between the two types of work. Both sets of auditors will examine internal control and accounting records, verify assets and liabilities, and pursue similar lines of observation and inquiry. It follows, therefore, that there are possible areas for coordination between the work of internal and external auditors. The internal auditor's work may include spot cash counts and visits to branches, and the external auditor may rely on such checks to reduce their costs.

Internal auditors can also assist external auditors in familiarising themselves with the accounting system, and they can act as a liaison between external auditors and other members of the client's staff. At year-end, internal auditors can assist by providing detailed scheduling procedures.

The internal audit function can also be effective when properly carried out in preventing fraudulent activities, and it can strengthen the system of internal control. The following factors should be considered in determining the extent to which the internal auditor contributes towards control reliability:

- *Qualifications of the appointed staff* – In themselves, qualifications may mean little, but their absence can be significant.
- *Experience of the appointed staff* – Newly appointed staff may have insufficient knowledge of the system to be of much assistance; on the other hand, long-term staff may think the systems are wonderful simply because they do not know anything else.
- *Internal audit programs* – These can give an indication of the abilities of the internal auditors, and the extent to which they have been completed will give an idea of the audit effectiveness.
- *Influence of the internal auditor on senior management* – The internal audit reports will provide a good idea of the quality of the audit staff, and in this context, it may be appropriate to note what action (if any) has been taken on the reports by management. If management takes little notice of internal auditors, this could weaken an external auditor's opinion of their effectiveness.
- *Level of internal audit reporting* – The reports should be made to the highest level of management or governance, for only at this level can independent action towards management be taken.

For example, it may be inappropriate for reports to be made to the chief accountant, who would have a vested interest in ensuring that inadequacies in the systems of control are not made public.

Even if all of these points prove satisfactory, you should remember that the external auditor can only rely on the internal auditor as one feature in their analysis of the internal control system. Internal audit is not a substitute for the external auditor's evaluation of the overall controls present as they are not focused on statutory law around financial audit, and internal auditors are not independent of the client. These principles are set out in ASA 610 and ISA NZ 610: Using the Work of Internal Auditors.

> Irrespective of the degree of autonomy and objectivity of the internal audit function, such function is not independent of the entity as is required of the external auditor when expressing an opinion on financial statements. The external auditor has sole responsibility for the audit opinion expressed, and that responsibility is not reduced by the external auditor's use of the work of the internal auditors. (ASA 610, para 4; ISA NZ 610, para 4)

Internal auditors also provide a little check on upper management and the governing body, as their work does not allow external auditors to omit substantive testing. There may be justification in reducing such testing should reliance on the work of the internal audit division be reasonable, but not eliminating it.

Professional scepticism

Auditing standards recognise the importance of professional scepticism in the collection of or in problems collecting evidence, including that around management or internal audit activities: 'Audit evidence comprises both information that supports and corroborates management's assertions and any information that contradicts such assertions. In addition, in some cases, the absence of information (for example, management's refusal to provide a requested representation) is used by the auditor, and therefore, also constitutes audit evidence.' (ASA 500, para 87)

Nor does relying on the internal auditor's fraud-prevention activities replace the external auditor's search (see ASA 240; ISA NZ 240). The external auditor has a specific responsibility to search for material misstatements caused by error *or* fraud.

CONCEPT QUESTION 2   How is 'independence' different for external and internal auditors?

Cloud and virtual system audits

Auditing standards for external auditors recognise the dilemma of dealing with systems, including virtual systems, that lack clear audit trails:

> The nature of the particular control influences the type of procedure required to obtain audit evidence about whether the control was operating effectively. For example, if operating effectiveness is evidenced by documentation, the auditor may decide to inspect it to obtain audit evidence about operating effectiveness. For other controls, however, documentation may not be available or relevant. For example, documentation of operation may not exist for some factors in the control environment, such as assignment of authority and responsibility, or for some types of control activities, such as control activities performed by a computer. In such circumstances, audit evidence about operating effectiveness

may be obtained through enquiry in combination with other audit procedures such as observation or the use of CAATs. (ASA 330, para A27; ISA NZ 330, para A27)

Part of the growth in internal and continuous audits is due to the need to respond to system invisibility and complexity. Systems, **networks**, servers and online or virtual **platforms** may lack even the most basic audit trails. The auditor may not be able to trace what has occurred in such systems.

The use of external service providers, blockchains, AI and robotics has highlighted the need for auditors to better understand and evaluate the implications for accountability. Data, applications, platforms and servers may be offsite and cloud-based; networks may be real or virtual. Expectations are clear that the auditor should

> obtain an understanding of the nature and significance of the services provided ... and their effect on the user entity's system of internal control, sufficient to provide an appropriate basis for the identification and assessment of the risks of material misstatement; and ... to design and perform audit procedures responsive to those risks. (ASA 402, para 7; ISA NZ 402, para 7)

Cloud-based systems can be very enticing to the manager because they can reduce the need for expensive hardware components, speed up recording practices, and offer complex data and analysis services. However, the auditor – external and internal – may find that they create new risks to do with lost or diverted information and assets. The **virtualisation** of systems is likely to present even more challenges.

The internal auditor is likely to be involved in developing such systems, but the external auditor may not even be aware of them until long after they have been formed. If the client modifies a system without audit support, the financial accounts are not auditable or otherwise faulty and increases the risk for the auditor. Auditing standards reinforce this point:

> The auditor shall perform risk assessment procedures to obtain an understanding of ... the entity's organisational structure, ownership, and governance, and its business model, including the extent to which the business model integrates the use of I.T. (ASA 315, para 19(a))

Today, employer/clients' systems may be composed of almost any combination of components and software: holistic accounting applications, commercial applications with customisation, integrated platforms of multiple applications, or individualised systems combining internally developed and purchased subsystems. Some are more straightforward and can be addressed, as was advised in earlier chapters (also see ASA 315; ISA NZ 315). In other situations, however, the auditor may be dealing with a *type* of system in which each of the elements is decoupled, or separated, from the others, or, at best, loosely linked together.

In an online system, there is direct entry of data or individual transactions via terminals that result in an immediate updating of computer files. Six important controls are required in an online system: access control, control over passwords, maintenance and development of system control, programming control, transaction logs and application controls. In an e-commerce environment, an entity should have appropriate controls over security, storage, and confidentiality of the information transaction integrity and process alignment of e-commerce activities with the organisation's business strategy. Appropriate security measures to prevent any cybercrime, such as cybersquatting or hacking, and protection from virus attacks are very important.

To understand how such individualised systems work, think of buying a car. The traditional method was to walk to a car dealership and choose a car from a limited choice of vehicle models, colours and features. In an individualised car-buying environment, you could choose the type of steering wheel, the tyre and piston size, dashboard styles and seating types. In other words, you can design a unique car (or system) to fit your particular interests.

Having these choices seems ideal from a management point of view, but they offer new risks from an audit point of view. The unique system has not benefited from being tested in its current form over

---

network
Consists of all the computers (or virtual machines) to access and share resources, including printers, databases and software.

platform
A technological foundation on which software and applications are developed. Apple's operating system is essentially a 'platform'.

virtualisation
Virtualisation systems replace multiple physical workstations, computers and printers with a single computer, creating a virtual layer that can act as independent 'computers' or virtual machines.

time or under stress. It has not benefited from the feedback of other users as there have been no other users. The auditor must consider these unique risks in any organisation.

> In obtaining an understanding of the I.T. environment relevant to the flows of transactions and information ... the auditor gathers information about the nature and characteristics of the I.T. applications used, as well as the supporting I.T. infrastructure ... (ASA 315, app. 5; ISA NZ 315, app. 5).

We offer a framework as a starting point to illustrate the fundamental nature of auditing a unique system. As such systems are often created in cloud-based and outsourced accounting for commercial use, we will focus on that likelihood. In our framework, we separate *components*, *activities* and *characteristics*, so that the auditor can piece together each client's system from these elements (see **Figure 18.7**).

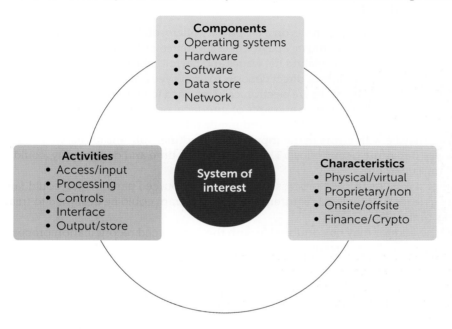

Figure 18.7 A system framework

The first challenge is to define the system boundaries. What is the system of concern, and what does it include? What does it *not* include? Is it the entire accounting system? Is it the communication system? Tax reporting system? Sales control system? In the example that follows, it is the payroll subsystem, including HR. Once identified, the *components*, *activities* and *characteristics* can be used to understand the exact system you are examining.

Activities refer to the nature of the accounting process, whether capturing pay and HR data, or modifying data through calculation, or controlling it via authorisation checks. It may include payable system calculations, net payroll payment, data storage and managed historical records. It will include how elements are **interfaced**.

Characteristics relate to features, which may include their physical or non-physical nature, ownership status, location or status. *Components* are the elements – hardware and software – of a system that can, in some cases, include the people who operate them as they are also part of an information (and control) network.

Once classified, the architecture of each particular system can illustrate where greater risks exist. So, for example, a *sales output's data management system* may be *virtual* and use a blockchain that accepts *bitcoin* for payments. This opens up risks of authorising and valuing such payments, data protection and

interface
A term used in IT to describe the exchange of information across a shared boundary, such as an internal network. An interface can occur between software, people or hardware and devices such as USBs and cables. An interface can send only (e.g., a microphone), receive only, or receive and send (e.g., firewall with alarm).

the need for embedded controls. Special expertise may be required, but at least the auditor now has a sense of *where* and *why* such expertise may be needed:

> The auditor's determination of whether to use the work of an auditor's expert and, if so, when and to what extent assists the auditor in meeting … requirements. (ASA 620, para A6)

The point is to understand each system in its 'uniqueness' so as to be able to identify the areas of greatest risk prior to testing. An example is provided in the 'Auditing in practice' box to illustrate how the framework may be used to obtain a basic understanding of a system for this purpose.

Auditing in practice

Partially virtual system

Assume that a payroll subsystem sits on a proprietary Microsoft XP platform but uses virtual (cloud-based) software to capture raw payroll data submitted by line managers. This is outsourced to Xero Ltd for calculating net wages and payroll liabilities. An HR manager manually reviews the results and authorises direct deposits to employee accounts from a subsequent printout. Once processed, results are electronically returned to an HR department temporary file.

Risks of such systems often lie at points of interface: originally capturing raw payroll data (and pay rates), outsourcing it to Xero, handling its return and authorising it for payment. Other risks may lie with errors in the input data: personnel authorisations, wage/salary rates or employee departure occurrences. These errors, over time and consistently, could yield material misstatement.

Another risk is the unseen process used by the outsourced party, which could fail to meet the client's needs or their legal requirements. The program could be designed to treat wages as salaries or the like.

While the auditor may be comfortable with the outsourced reconciliation process, the reasonableness of the end result should be checked using 'data analytics' – essentially, SpAR, to estimate net wages and payroll expenses. Finally, while bank accounts are used to make wage payments in this example, the use of cryptocurrencies for transactions raises questions about the reliability of the measure and value of net wages and payroll expenses.

Some controls, and tests of controls, may be more or less relevant in such systems. Let us look at some of those that may be worthy of consideration:

- *Outsourced vendor documentation* – Inspect it and compare it to the needs of your employer/client, reinforced in auditing guidelines for external auditors:

  > The … auditor shall enquire of management of the user entity … whether the user entity is otherwise aware of any fraud, non-compliance with laws and regulations or uncorrected misstatements affecting the financial statements of the user entity. (ASA 402, para 19, ref A41; ISA NZ 402, para 19, ref A41)

- *Access to unauthorised resources* – Controls to do with access are particularly vulnerable in such systems. Problems can occur by intent or (often) default, where software is purchased or where the interface is not well managed:
  - *Access architecture* should be checked, including what aspects of the system individuals can access. Also review logs and error reports for unauthorised access and programs for appropriate exceptions (such as noting after-hours access).
  - *Extending access privileges* adds risk because it allows the user to access multiple elements of that system – input, authorisation, output, storage – making traditional lines of duty segregation difficult.

- *Patching* procedures should be reviewed, such as updates to the software for security reasons.
- *Boundary definitions*, such as firewalls or antivirus software, should be checked to ensure they are appropriate for the network.
- *Employee departure* – account and password authorisations should be disabled when someone changes their position or leaves, and the new password may need to have a new architecture (layers) to limit their access to specific activities or data.
- *Communicating changes* is particularly important in a virtual environment. This is because partially virtual and cloud-based systems are, by their nature, ever-evolving. Access changes should be carefully considered and independently approved when systems grow or expand.

- *Multiple software programs* – A mix of software programs can lead to the use of incompatible controls or simply poor interfaces. In our payroll scenario, an example is where a contracted and internal program must work together. A review of interface processes may identify problems.
- *Unnecessary or outdated procedures* – Look for these as carried out by the employer's/client's system, as they add unnecessary complexity and risk exposure.
- *Storage capacity problems* – Data storage, processing capability and the like should be monitored as overloading can lead to loss of data or processing error.
- *Data management* – This is important, particularly if offsite, as its structure (data configuration) should be appropriate to the organisation. Access to data viewing, printing or changes should be limited to authorised parties.
- *Offsite data storage* – This is strongly advised. Australia's challenging physical environment around its mining industries makes its software and hardware subject to natural as well as human damage.
- *Digital analytics* – Performing SpAR and analytical review procedures to anticipate relevant ranges can replace the loss of manual reconciliation or casting and cross-casting.
- *Continuous audit* – Implementation or review if this should occur, including what and when test data is used, and ensuring that tests and concurrent running don't create errors.
- *Sampling for audit tests* – This creates interesting challenges, as a non-random selection may be most appropriate. This is because a non-random method can test the riskiest transactions, such as those immediately following a platform revision, a programming change, or around interface processes. Continuous auditing can be designed to select and test random or non-random samples if necessary.
- *Maintaining an audit trail* – This may require the direct involvement of the internal auditor to ensure that data summaries and details are downloadable for audit.
- *Social media or open-source coding* – Where this occurs on an employer's platform, it is a security risk. It provides fraudsters with opportunities to access soft assets (i.e., data), knowledge structures and operations. Malware or ransomware can put a complete stop to business.

CONCEPT QUESTION 3 How does a cloud-based system fundamentally change the nature of audit evidence?

Study tools

Summary

This chapter began by returning to our auditing conceptual framework and professional concepts. While practices and goals may differ, concepts remain. This is because audits introduced in these last chapters are different from the external financial audit, and concepts may be interpreted differently.

So 'independence' may now be as to the relationship between the internal auditor and middle management, not between the external auditor and the client. However, this does not diminish the importance of 'independence' or the need for 'ethics'; it simply highlights how it can take a different form. Audit judgements may be on different issues, evidence may come in different forms, and risk may be as to different concerns. Still, they all remain fundamental to providing an assurance service.

An internal auditor may be involved in any of these and may be employed or under contract. Firms may contract on a fixed-term basis for internal audit services. However, their primary accountability is to the organisation, less so to the larger public or the external financial auditor.

We closed the chapter with some introductory concepts providing an audit perspective on the virtual and cloud-based systems that are becoming common. Methods to address this in detail cannot be presented here, but it is intended that the approach offered and the risks identified will give the reader a sense of what it takes to perform an assurance engagement on such complex and unique systems.

Review questions

18.1   Describe the purpose and elements of the Burns, Greenspan and Hartwell (1994) intimidation model of professionalism.

18.2   Define the transformation model and what it describes.

18.3   What are the procedures used in an internal auditor's systems testing process?

18.4   Name the sources of (a) COSO and (b) the *Sarbanes-Oxley Act 2002* and why they are relevant to internal audit in Australia and New Zealand.

18.5   Describe the internal auditor role and six usual functions in current times.

18.6   From what or whom should the internal auditor be independent? Why?

18.7   Use seven points to explain the relationship between the 'external' and 'internal' auditors.

18.8   Name internal auditor characteristics that may help the external auditor to rely on them.

18.9   Define the following IT terms:

a platform

b server

c network

d virtualisation

e interface.

18.10   Identify twelve system control or testing vulnerabilities present in a virtual IT system.

18.11 Explain the purpose of the system framework shown in **Figure 18.7**.

18.12 Identify two risks related to an audit of cloud-based or virtualisation systems.

Exercises

18.1 **PROFESSIONS:** Answer each of the following:

  a Describe how the Burns, Greenspan and Hartwell (1994) model of intimidation is different to the 'list' model. Identify why one model may have more credibility than the other. Explain your reasoning.

  b Identify a professional association to which you could aspire to be a member. How would you describe it in terms of transformation theory? Why?

18.2 **INTERNAL AUDIT AND FRAUD:** Evaluate implications for the internal auditor of each of the following 'findings' made by a major accounting firm:

  a Approximately 50 per cent of organisations experience intrusions into their internal systems, most from outside hackers.

  b More than half of all security breaches involve computer viruses.

  c COSO has found that 'fraud' tends to be more prevalent in SMEs.

  d Management inquiry and letters of representation from management are an important part of identifying fraud in a company.

  e Deterrence of fraud is the responsibility of management. Internal auditors are responsible for examining actions taken by management to fulfil this obligation.

18.3 **INTERNAL VS EXTERNAL AUDIT:** Evaluate the implications for the *external* financial statement auditor of the findings listed in Exercise 18.2.

18.4 **INTERNAL AUDIT:** For each statement below from the IIA, identify both the 'pros' and 'cons' of these policies for their employer, for society or even for themselves.

  a The IIA believes that the internal auditor should actively seek out indicators of fraud representations.

  b Per the IIA, internal auditors are expected to have knowledge equivalent to that of a person whose primary responsibility is to detect and investigate fraud.

  c The IIA believes that the external auditor should inform the internal auditor if potential or actual fraud exists.

18.5 **PROFESSIONS:** In terms of Burns, Greenspan and Hartwell's (1994) professional (a) 'mystique' and (b) 'cruciality', rank each of the following on a scale of 1 (high) to 3 (low), and explain why and/or under what conditions. What is the most important ethical issue for a member in each of these?

  a general practitioner: medicine
  b plumber
  c health ministry manager
  d accountant (no audit work done)
  e airline pilot
  f scientist
  g solicitor or barrister
  h nuclear physicist
  i minister of parliament
  j automobile mechanic.

18.6 **INTERNAL AUDITOR ROLE:** Review the case set out in this chapter on WorldCom, then investigate it further (online). Discuss the following implications for the internal auditor:

a What was the nature of the fraud? What type of transactions caused it, and who authorised those transactions?

b What could have occurred had the internal auditor been within a structure that held their division accountable to middle management? Might this have affected the outcome? How?

c Why are professional 'ethics' of relevance to this case? Or to the role of the internal auditor in this case?

18.7 **VIRTUAL SYSTEMS:** Use the payroll example in this chapter to:

a classify each element within the framework (**Figure 18.7**)

b distinguish issues of concern to the external financial auditor from those of interest to management

c for the vulnerabilities identified, describe controls that could protect them

d for the vulnerabilities identified, and assuming no controls are in place for them, offer substantive tests that might test each appropriate balance.

Social audit

Learning objectives

After studying the material in this chapter, you should be able to:
- describe the purpose of, and conceptual applications to, public sector audit
- describe the unique requirements of a consolidated accounts audit
- identify the distinguishing features of non-profit, charitable and small business audits
- describe the nature, purpose and regulatory environment of environmental audits.

Introduction

The professional auditor may be called on to be part of a team that evaluates claims regarding the impact of an organisation's emissions, the efficiency of public services, or controls over a charity's receipts. The auditor may be called on to review whether or not the spirit of the Australian *Environment Protection and Biodiversity Conservation Act 1999* or New Zealand's *Resource Management Act 1991* has been met. Sometimes, the assurance required can be as straightforward as providing confidence that ticket sales are handled well.

Essentially, auditors contribute their skills to whatever task is before them in audit, review, compilation or *agreed-upon procedures*. Those skills may be applied to corporations and partnerships, but they can also be applied to the non-commercial sector, to very small (SMEs) or very large (consolidated accounts) entities. This chapter looks at the principles, standards and practices that guide such services, with an emphasis on:
- public sector audits and the legislative audit bodies that select and perform them
- public sector standard-setters and the growing role of consolidated account audits in the public (and private) sector
- non-profit entities, particularly small charities, and small enterprises (or SMEs)
- environmental audits for compliance or as a public good.

What non-profit entities share in common is their concern with a social good such as environmental protection or public service. What makes non-commercial entities fundamentally different from their commercial counterparts is that 'inputs' (taxes, donations) are not directly related to 'outputs' (services provided) in terms of a singular financial measure of profit on increased equity. In the commercial sector, expanding 'inputs' (costs) ideally yield proportionally larger 'outputs' (revenue) (see **Figure 19.1**, left) and a financial return on investment. If you spend more and employ more people, you anticipate greater sales. In the non-commercial sector, that direct relationship may not exist (see **Figure 19.1**, right). For this reason, large charities in New Zealand are required by the XRB's PBE FRS 48 Service Performance Reporting to provide Statements of Service Performance that explain their purpose and goals, and achievements in relation thereto. This information may be descriptive and quantitative and must be audited if the entity is required to have a financial audit.

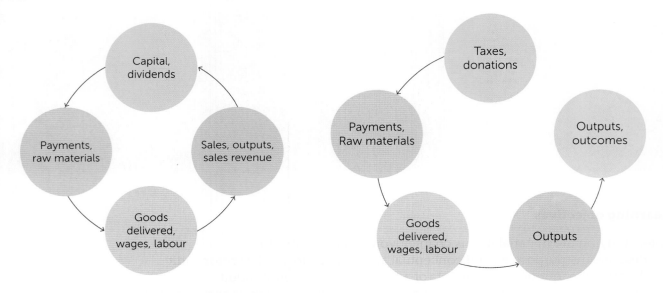

Figure 19.1 Social vs commercial sectors: Resource flows

Source: Van Peursem and Harnisch (2009).

Politics and law directly influence inputs (tax levies and government budgets). 'Profit' is less meaningful in the social sector but financial probity remains important. Capital appreciation becomes a political achievement, not a commercial one. Social measures tend to be in non-financial performance indicators. Examples are the number of 'students graduating' from a university or 'patient survival rates' in health care. In law, achievements may also be required, such as pollution levels or fish catch limits.

Analytical procedures may not be useful to anticipate 'output-to-input' patterns because such patterns may not exist. As a result, audits and reviews tend to focus on 'compliance' and on the 'non-financial' aspects of an organisation. Applying our conceptual framework is revealing (see **Table 19.1**).[1]

Table 19.1 Conceptual elements compared to the commercial sector

Credibility/ethics	Public sector, non-profit, environmental audit elements
Audit competence	Similar to commercial, although auditor may need to access scientific, legal or other specialist skills
Audit judgement	Public interest, legal compliance
Independence	From those parties or entities investigated
Process	
Risk	Failure to identify non-compliance in law
Materiality	Any non-compliance, any measure of public interest
Evidence	Analytical procedures are applied differently: non-financial, contract access

---

[1] AASB Staff Paper Improving Financial Reporting for Australian Charities (November 2017) suggested various forms an Australian differential reporting framework could take. Some of the alternative frameworks contemplated a differential reporting framework similar to the framework applying to New Zealand NFP public benefit entities (PBEs). Service Performance Reporting (SPR) requirements are integrated parts of the Tier 3 and Tier 4 NZ PBEs standards.

Auditor's accountability	
To the public	A primary interest, possibly enforceable in law
To the profession	Yes, but may be different professional associations
To the client	Depends on the contract: may be only for the user
Communication – *letter of engagement very important to set scope, assurance, users*	
Internal	May be extensive, contract scope dependent
External	Depends on contract or law/regulation

Non-profit engagements may require competencies in science (i.e., for environmental audits) or the law. Independence may be needed from line managers but not necessarily from the CEO, depending on the scope of the engagement. Risks of fraud may not be measured in currency but in instances: risks in environmental engagements may be assessed relative to scientific calibrations, complaints or noise levels. Concepts and ethical principles are applied in a unique way to this sector, a point reinforced in the standards:

- *Confidentiality*: 'The auditor's duty of confidentiality would normally preclude reporting fraud or error to a 3rd party. However, in certain circumstances, the duty of confidentiality is overridden by statute, law or the courts of law.' (ASA 240)
- *Materiality*: 'The use of public monies tends to impose a higher profile on fraud issues, and auditors may need to be responsive to public "expectations" regarding the expectation of [any] fraud ...' (AUS 210 (January 2002)) – such expectations may be expressed in legislation, regulation, ordinances or directives.
- *Evidence*: 'The auditor must plan and conduct the audit so as to have a reasonable expectation of detecting misstatements that have a material impact on the financial report arising as a result of non-compliance by the entity with laws and regulations.' (ASA 315)

Engagements vary widely. Hence, while audit concepts remain, social engagements are audited using different priorities and measures. Each engagement must be considered individually in terms of its *scope*, *assurance level* and *accountees* (*users*). In this sector, we do note the emphasis on **public good**.

There is movement in the non-profit sectors of both Australia and New Zealand towards re-framing the sector as 'For Purpose' in contrast with 'For Profit'. We refer this nomenclature as it is descriptive of the sector rather than defining it by what it is not. We now look at three types of entities that are concerned with the public good: public sector audit, for purpose (non-profit) audit and environmental audit.

public good
Is both non-excludable and non-rival. A public park is an example: the public should not be excluded from it, and its use by one party does not affect its use, or the quality of its use, by another.

Public sector audit

The public sector consists of a wide variety of organisations, distinguished by their close association with, or complete reliance on, the government of a nation or its states. Elected officials or their representatives may govern such entities. They may be relatively independent of government but funded by taxpayers, such as schools and hospitals.

By definition, public sector entities are not (as a rule) commercial enterprises. Their primary interest is public good, not profit or an increase in capital wealth. Generally, they are formed to carry out functions overlooked or disincentivised by the commercial market. Hence, they are sometimes described as interventionist: they intervene in the market to serve social outcomes. Such outcomes may be to:

- stabilise a market, such as to resolve the crisis created by housing booms or inflation
- allocate public resources for public good assets such as parks, roads and waterways
- distribute or collect resources, including the collection and redistribution of taxes for social welfare: recently unemployed, children or the elderly
- regulate and oversee, for example, the capital market via reserve banks, road and transport via traffic wardens, crime response via police, and international relations via government
- see that insurance protection is provided for, as an example, disaster relief.

They may be classified along the lines of the extent to which they are governed internally or externally. Their means of intervention can include:

- taxation
- redistribution, such as through social welfare
- regulation via laws and statute
- physical intervention such as by public roadworks or the police
- macroeconomic regulation via, for example, interest rate controls, market regulation or bank reserve requirements.

It is important to clarify the scope of an assurance engagement before the engagement begins. Even if the 'entity' to be audited is clear, what is the auditor *attesting* to? They may have to come to an opinion about the client's (or employer's):

- compliance with law
- stewardship over public assets, in conformance with an agency theory of auditing
- financials or budgetary compliance
- social performance indicator claims
- inter-period equity (i.e., taxing the public for the cost of a bridge over the life of the bridge)
- organisational objectives, specifically their reasonableness
- efficiencies
- equity across demographic boundaries
- effectiveness in achieving a program's objective or policy
- quality, appropriateness or extent in terms of services provided.

That is, in terms of the 'scope' of the audit, the sorts of claims being investigated, the engagement can be about anything reasonable.

Government auditors

Government auditors exist in both Australia and New Zealand. Their presence raises a number of questions. Should they support or evaluate the public sector? How can they retain 'independence' if they do both? Are public auditors 'internal' to the entity or 'external'? Are they directly accountable to the public? How are such offices held to account? Should the office be charged with protecting the 'client's' confidentiality, or – in the public interest – disclose all they find? There are no easy answers, but models for government audit office structures attempt to address their form.

An *integrated model* expects the auditor to set out policies for the auditor-general's office *and* undertake audit work, including financial audits and performance reviews (see **Figure 19.2**). The challenge here is that it lacks accountability to the government (or public) for the decisions made.

A *segmented model* separates the roles of *setting policy* and *performing* audit. This is what occurs in Australia and New Zealand. The Auditor-General for Australia is an independent officer of the Parliament with responsibility under the *Auditor-General Act 1997* for auditing Commonwealth entities and reporting to the Australian Parliament. The Auditor-General is supported by the Australian National Audit Office (ANAO). In New Zealand, the Office of the Controller and Auditor-General sets policies and contracts for private (or semi-private) firms to conduct the audits. Doing so may be less efficient,

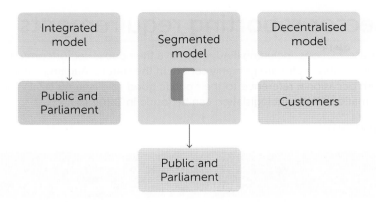

Figure 19.2 Model for public audit delivery

Source: Houghton and Jubb (1998).

because two parties are involved in each audit, but it is important to ensure that each institution is independent of the other's decisions. A *decentralised model* shifts focus and sets the entity being audited as the primary client. Advice and support for the public sector entity must be contracted elsewhere, usually at public cost.

Both Australia's and New Zealand's public audit functions (Fiji as well) are influenced by their association with the states (and territories), in which the government auditor's office is an independent entity. They are led by a politically appointed officer of parliament for a set period of time and enjoy considerable independence as to what they choose to examine.

Not all nations are the same – for example, the United States has a General Accounting Office at the behest of the Senate at the federal level, and state offices. The following sets out how the two governments with which we're concerned are set up and how they serve the public interest.

In New Zealand, the role of the Office of the Controller and Auditor-General is determined by the *Public Audit Act 2001*, which follows the *segmented model*. This was not always the case. The office previously carried out audits, provided advice to government organisations, and developed audit policy, reporting to parliament. Now, under the 2001 Act, there is a clear separation between the Office of the Controller and Auditor-General (policy setting) and Audit New Zealand (audit service provider). The Controller and Auditor-General is accountable to parliament for audit policy and may authorise audit on any aspect of any public sector entity.

Access to information is guaranteed under the Act, as New Zealand's Auditor-General

> may inquire, either on request or on the Auditor-General's own initiative, into any matter concerning a public entity's use of resources [s. 18/1] ... [and] may require a public entity or any person to produce a document in the person's custody, or provide the AG with information or an explanation about any information. (s. 25)

The Auditor-General also has significant authority to 'disclose such information as the AG considers appropriate to disclose in the exercise of his/her functions ... [and] must consider the public interest, professional obligations' (s. 30).

The office is charged with independent oversight led by a government-appointed Auditor-General. Each Auditor-General produces an annual report submitted to the House of Representatives on a wide range of issues selected and disclosed as 'appropriate' for inclusion in the report by the Auditor-General (see ss. 21–30).

Audit New Zealand is a business unit of the office and is the largest provider of public sector audits. Other NZ Government audit services include the Inland Revenue Department (tax), the Serious Fraud Office (with significant authority to investigate fraud) and the police investigations unit.

Public sector reporting requirements

While professional associations, including IFAC, may have their public sector committees, the reporting and audit obligations of this sector are primarily set out in the statute. Auditing standards recognise the sector's needs, with occasional reference to their public good role (see AS NZ 1: The Audit of Service Performance Information). Relevant legislation can be found in **Table 19.2**.

Table 19.2 Selective public sector legislation

Australia		New Zealand	
Statute	**Regarding**	**Statute**	**Regarding**
Auditor-General Act 1997	This Act establishes an office of Auditor-General for the Commonwealth and sets out the Auditor-General's functions	*Public Audit Act 2001*	Controller and Auditor-General role and responsibilities
Public Governance, Performance and Accountability Act 2013	An Act about the governance, performance and accountability of, and the use and management of, public resources by the Commonwealth, Commonwealth entities and Commonwealth companies	*Crown Entities Act 2004*	Requirements for all Crown entities
State-level public finance Acts	Various states have their own equivalent public finance Act (e.g., NSW *Government Sector Finance Act 2018*; *Public Finance and Audit Act 1987* of South Australia)	*Public Finance Act 1989*	Principles of public sector reporting
State-owned enterprise Acts	Various states have their own equivalent state-owned enterprise Act (e.g., *State Owned Enterprises Act 1992* of Victoria; *State Owned Corporations Act 1989* of NSW)	*SOE Act 1986*	Commercial government-owned entities

Australia

When the first Commonwealth Parliament assembled in Melbourne in May 1901, its immediate task was to begin building the necessary institutions of national government. The fourth Act passed by the parliament was the *Audit Act 1901*, which created the office of the Auditor-General. The Auditor-General was intended to be an independent and impartial public official who could scrutinise Commonwealth administration and give true assessments on the state of the public accounts without intimidation by government or other vested interests. The role of the Auditor-General was seen as fundamental to good government. The Auditor-General provides the Legislative Assembly, and public sector entities, independent professional opinions. The opinions may be on matters related to financial management, compliance with legislative requirements, and comments on performance-management systems in place at public sector entities. Individual states and territories have their own Auditor-General: for example, the Northern Territory Auditor-General's Office, Victorian Auditor-General's Office, and Audit Office of New South Wales. In South Australia, auditors-general have been responsible for auditing SA Government finances, systems and processes since 1839. The Queensland Audit Office is the independent auditor of the public sector in that state.

The *Auditor-General Act 1997* took effect on 1 January 1998, replacing the *Audit Act 1901*. The office of Auditor-General is a 10-year statutory appointment made by the Governor-General on the advice of the prime minister. In recognition of the Auditor-General's status as an officer of the parliament, the Australian Parliament's Joint Committee of Public Accounts and Audit (JCPAA) must approve any proposed recommendation for appointment.

Under the *Auditor-General Act 1997*, the Auditor-General's functions include:

- auditing the financial statements of Commonwealth entities, Commonwealth companies and their subsidiaries
- auditing annual performance statements of Commonwealth entities
- conducting performance audits, assurance reviews and audits of the performance measures, of Commonwealth entities and Commonwealth companies and their subsidiaries
- conducting a performance audit of a Commonwealth partner as described in section 18B of the Act
- providing other audit services as required by other legislation or allowed under section 20 of the Act
- reporting directly to the parliament on any matter or to a minister on any important matter.

There are four types of governance structures in Australia:

1   Primary bodies are part of the Commonwealth or have a separate legal status.
2   Secondary statutory structures are established within a primary body by legislation.
3   Secondary non-statutory structures are established within a primary body without legislation.
4   Other governance relationships are established by Commonwealth involvement through membership or investment.

All primary bodies are subject to the *Public Governance, Performance and Accountability Act 2013*. Non-corporate Commonwealth entities are legally and financially part of the Commonwealth and include:

- departments of state
- parliamentary departments.

New Zealand

In New Zealand, the Office of the Controller and Auditor-General originated as a government function in 1840. After restructuring in the early 1990s which separated the operational and parliamentary reporting functions of the office, there were calls to make the controller and Auditor-General independent of executive government. The Auditor-General became an officer of parliament under the *Public Audit Act 2001*, which came into force on 1 July 2001. The purpose of this Act was to establish the controller and Auditor-General as an officer of parliament and to reform and restate the law relating to the audit of public sector organisations. The controller and Auditor-General is appointed by the Governor-General on the recommendation of the House of Representatives.

New Zealand's public sector accounts for over 40 per cent of New Zealand's economy (GDP), defined under the *Public Audit Act 2001* as:

- local and regional authorities
- infrastructural entities, such as roadworks
- regulating (i.e., Inland Revenue Department) and policing authorities
- educational institutions
- health institutions, such as district health boards
- central government departments.

Given their size and impact, it is understandable why there is interest in ensuring accountability for these organisations. Statute law, in particular the *Public Finance Act 1989, the Local Government Amendment Act (No. 2) 1979*, and others related to each sector, together with Treasury requirements, has instituted financial-management reporting practices throughout this sector.

The assurance and advisory services performed may include contract or project management, capital projects, non-financial performance, sensitive expenditures, sensitive activities, tendering processes, information systems, corporate governance arrangements, organisational change processes, consultations and costs of services – and more.

New Zealand public sector organisations, are subject to financial and other audit requirements under statute broadly and for each entity established in statute. For example, under the *Crown Entities Act 2004*, independent audit is required for qualifying entities. The *State Owned Enterprise (SOE) Act 1986* relates to commercial companies owned by the New Zealand Government. It is a significant sector of society, guided by extensive statutory law. Under the *Public Finance Act 1989*, public sector entities must produce budgetary and performance information. Sizeable entities must follow GAAP and/or file reports of strategic intent, submit information about their plans and public obligations, and/or prepare and have audited statements of service performance.

Value for money

performance auditing
In the public sector, VFM, or value for money auditing, is the practice of auditing against such goals.

new public management
Tends to focus on the economy, efficiency and effectiveness of government policy and programs, and less on meeting annual line-item budgets.

In the public sector, the importance of **performance auditing** (also called value for money or VFM audit) and **new public management** is significant.

The scope of most VFM audits centres on the economy, efficiency, effectiveness or equity. VFM audits are of primary interest in this sector, possibly being more important than financial audits because they measure the stewardship of public assets. The general aims of VFM are to measure economy, efficiency, equity and effectiveness, as described in the following, and in **Figure 19.3**.

- *Economy:* the measure of resources consumed vis-à-vis planned consumption – 'doing things cheaply'. This is a measure of how liquid resources such as cash have been converted into raw materials (in the case of a manufacturing company) or personnel (in the case of a service company).
- *Efficiency:* the relationship between resources consumed (inputs) and benefits produced (outputs), providing an indication of how the conversion process is carried out.
- *Effectiveness:* the measure of actual output to planned output that achieves the right results. What 'right' is will vary from one organisation to another, of course, so these audits are dependent on knowing the aims and objectives of organisational strategy so that effectiveness can be understood and measured.
- *Equity:* the distribution of resources or benefits deriving from public enterprise. So, for example, information on equity may reveal how resources are geographically distributed or distributed among various age groups (of particular interest in the public sector).

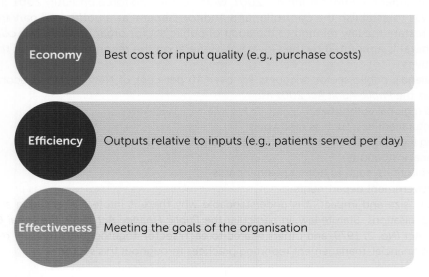

Figure 19.3 Value for money audit benchmarks

We cannot rule out the possibility that the level of assurance required for either the financial or strictly VFM audit may differ among services, particularly where assurance is required for forecasts (for which it is hard to provide an 'audit' level of assurance) or for non-financial information. Concepts such as *materiality* and *evidence* may serve in other forms than those found in the commercial finance sector.

Note that the responsibility to report any fraud in a public sector entity and to evaluate management systems suggests to us that agency interests (the principal–public concerned with the agent–bureaucrat/elected official) and social accountability interests (especially stewardship of public monies) are dominant paradigms influencing the auditor's role in this sector.

We are likely to be seeing further changes in both the nature of, and mandate for, public sector audit. Public sector audit is a separate study in itself. Suffice to say that, while audit concepts remain, conducting an audit for a public sector organisation calls for a consideration of different forms of independence, different types of risks given its public good and tax costs, and different understandings of materiality and evidence.

CONCEPT QUESTION 1	How do public sector entities differ from private commercial enterprises?

Consolidated accounts audit for the public sector

There is growing discussion about the question of whether consolidated accounts, or some equivalent, are appropriate for the public sector.

> The public sector consolidated financial statements represent a challenging topic of worldwide research and also became a debated issue both for international regulatory bodies (IPASB) and for governments. (Cirstea, 2014)

Indeed, the IFAC subcommittee for the public sector, the International Public Sector Accounting Standards Board (IPSASB), has introduced standards which address consolidation – joint ventures; joint arrangements, such as sovereign wealth and some pensions; and interests in other entities – and its relevance to the public sector. In particular, IPSAS 35: Consolidated Financial Statements makes such requirements.

The AASB is required by the *Australian Securities and Investments Commission Act 2001*, section 227(1)(d), to participate in and contribute to the development of a single set of accounting standards for worldwide use. Accordingly, the AASB uses the IFRS standards set by the IASB as a basis for accounting standards covering the for-profit sector and the not-for-profit sector, which includes the public sector. The AASB's *Approach to International Public Sector Accounting Standards* replaces the previous document, *Australian Accounting Standards and IPSAS*, issued in October 2011. The AASB intends that the conditions necessary for the adoption of IPSAS would be reviewed periodically (at least every five years) and the results of that assessment made public.

Notably, New Zealand has used IPSAS as a basis for developing accounting standards for its 'public benefits entities', known as PBE standards. The PBE standards are primarily based on IPSAS, with some modifications where necessary to make the IPSAS requirements appropriate for New Zealand, including modifications to enable application to the private not-for-profit sector. The PBE standards also include other standards (based on IFRS or domestic standards) to address topics not covered in IPSAS, and reduced disclosure requirements for tier 2 entities.

IFAC is not a national association, so public sectors need not follow New Zealand standards. Nonetheless, it does indicate a move towards consolidating some entities whose governing authority controls another. For that reason, and because the consolidation is common in the private sector as well, we look here at those audit processes useful in the audit of the **consolidated financial statement**.

Challenges for the auditor in engagements involving group (or consolidated) accounts include determining the entity's scope and complying with current (and frequently changing) GAAP with respect to valuation and disclosure.

Consolidated financial statements are the financial statements of a group presented as those of a single economic entity (AASB 127 and NZ IAS 27: Consolidated and Separate Financial Statements). Group financial statements generally consist of consolidated balance sheets, profit and loss statements, and cash flow statements for an entire group of companies. Group financial statements usually must be prepared by companies which own subsidiaries.

The challenge often lies in determining whether a group of organisations should, or should not, be combined for the purposes of disclosure, and, if so, how. Under most circumstances, and depending on ownership proportions, either the purchase method or the equity method is used for consolidated accounts. A limited number of circumstances may justify the pooling-of-interests method. Several misrepresentations can occur if an inappropriate method is chosen or applied incorrectly.

Auditing in practice

Over-aggregation and under-aggregation

1   If the over-aggregation of accounts occurs as a result of combining the accounts of several companies, the consolidated accounts can show 'profits' when, in fact, the parent company is experiencing profitability problems, and a smaller or unrelated entity contributes to the profit.
2   If the under-aggregation of accounts occurs, and subsidiaries are not consolidated as they should be, then the process can hide the creation of separate companies formed solely to absorb losses or to reflect unacceptable practices.

An organisation must not take credit for the profits (or losses) of other entities to which it does not have a right. It is an area of high audit risk, particularly where the management integrity risk is high. Therefore, the first audit task is to determine whether or not the client is a 'parent' to subsidiaries. The following substantive procedures may be appropriate in most such circumstances:

- inquiries and reviews of board minutes, which should reveal whether organisational subsidiaries exist – if they do exist, but they are not revealed in this way, you may have considerable concern over the risk of off-balance-sheet financing
- inspection of original documentation of investments in group company shares and debentures, or certificates received from the custodian
- confirmation of all loans to and from group organisations not audited by the firm, as well as sales, purchases and other transactions
- consideration of any trading transactions with group organisations, and whether they should be separately recorded
- examination of documentation on items required by legislation.

A second challenge is to ensure that consolidated working papers are correct (accurate) and in compliance with GAAP. In checking consolidation working papers, pay attention to:

- goodwill or reserves arising on acquisitions made during the year
- pre-acquisition and post-acquisition profits
- minority interests
- adjustments for inter-company profits in the stock

- agreements of inter-company indebtedness
- cut-off for inter-company transactions
- inter-group trading and turnover
- adjustments for different accounting periods by different group members
- taxation accruals
- foreign exchange calculations and the exchange rates used.

Finally, disclosure and valuation are crucial, particularly where management integrity is of concern. At a minimum, the following, some required in corporate law, should be reviewed:

- changes in accounting policy
- changes in the interests register
- directors' remuneration and other benefits
- donations
- officer names
- audit fees and other fees paid to the same firm
- valuations of assets and liabilities of the subsidiaries
- financial statements of the subsidiaries, including policies used in them.

An audit program of consolidated accounts should consider the following audit assertions:

- accuracy – to confirm that the accounting records and supporting schedules are mathematically correct.
- completeness – to confirm that all transactions related to group company shares and loans that should have been recorded, have been recorded
- existence and occurrence-validity – to confirm that group company investments/obligations exist and that related income statement transactions have occurred
- rights-obligations – to confirm the business owns the recorded group company investments/obligations
- valuation – to confirm that the cost and book value of group company investments/obligations and related income statement transactions are fairly stated
- presentation – to confirm that all information relating to group company investments and obligations has been appropriately disclosed in the financial statements.

Australian and New Zealand branches of international audit firms often find themselves involved in the audit of international subsidiaries, with the results of their investigations and reports being transmitted to corporate headquarters overseas.

CONCEPT QUESTION 2	What are the main considerations in the audit program of consolidated accounts with regards to completeness and existence?

Non-profit and small business (SMEs)

There are thousands of non-profit organisations and sole traders. They are easy to form and can involve their owners/managers in more complexity than they may originally expect. In this section, we look at small non-profit charitable organisations and small businesses, which share some characteristics and audit challenges. There are also many large non-profit organisations, some of which are larger than many listed companies. However, the process for auditing these is not significantly different from that described in earlier chapters, except that they require Statements of Service Performance (in the case of New Zealand) which must be audited.

Non-profit charities

Most large non-profit organisations are now professionalised and rely less, or not at all, on volunteers at least in so far as governance or management are concerned. Documents to advise their governing bodies and/or managers may be produced by audit firms, and this may include audit or review support. There are specific reporting obligations for charities that require compliance so as to allow them to retain their tax-beneficial 'charitable' status. These requirements change and may vary based on the organisation's size.

The Australian Parliament recognises the unique nature and diversity of not-for-profit entities and the distinctive role they play in Australia. The Australian Charities and Not-for-profits Commission (ACNC) is the principal regulator of charities at the Commonwealth level. The ACNC was established in December 2012 under the *Australian Charities and Not-for-profits Commission Act 2012*. Its establishment followed a series of reviews and inquiries into the not-for-profit sector since the mid-1990s. Some charities reporting to the ACNC must submit financial reports that have either been reviewed or audited. Medium-sized charities (with annual revenue of more than $250 000 but less than $1 million) are required to submit financial reports that have either been reviewed or audited, while large charities (with annual revenue over $1 million) must submit audited financial reports. The *Australian Charities and Not-for-profits Commission Act 2012* sets out who can audit reports that must be provided to the ACNC.

In New Zealand, 'large' is measured in expense dollars. Some standards have been issued (or are in train at the time of publication), giving further guidance to, and expectations of, these managers.[2] Legislation that establishes non-profits in New Zealand usually requires an annual report and an independent audit or review. A case in point is New Zealand's *Charities Act 2005*, which requires such reporting; for example:

> ... tier 3 [larger] not-for-profit (NFP) public benefit entities (PBEs) will be required to prepare a performance report [including] entity information and a statement of service performance, together with historical financial information. Depending on [its] size or type ... the performance report may be required by law to be audited or reviewed. (XRB, 2015)

The non-profit sector includes many very small organisations. They may be run by a few volunteers with little in-house financial experience. In these respects, they resemble 'small businesses', or SMEs. We combine our consideration of them in the sections following.

Small and medium enterprises (SMEs)

There are standards for auditors of small businesses. They have an application to small charitable non-profit entities as well. The following debate applies to both:

> One of the key audit debates in recent years has been whether one size of auditing standards fits all – in other words, do the clarified Auditing Standards work equally well for entities defined as listed companies in Australia, and entities defined as issuers in New Zealand, as for SMEs? ... Preparers, businesses and organisations of companies indicat[e] that Auditing Standards should be further developed to be better suited for ... SMEs. (AUASB, 2012a)

---

[2] For example, 'Explanatory Guide Au9: Guidance on the audit or review of the performance report of Tier 3 not-for-profit public benefit entities', issued December 2015 by XRB.

Reduced reporting, GAAP and audit requirements may apply to very small entities. We will continue to see more standardisation as societies pivot from large, centrally controlled incorporated entities to more online, owner-led, virtual, entrepreneurial and smaller enterprises for both profit and charity.

Audit challenges

By virtue of their size, small charities and SMEs may struggle to manage an administrative load well in areas with which they are unfamiliar.

Auditing in practice

When you don't manage administrative load

One of the authors worked for a roofing company run by three brothers. They had excellent and long-term construction and trade skills, but no financial experience. They struggled to set budgets, achieve profits and keep costs under control. Due to their weak management, costing finance and tax skills, the business eventually failed and went into liquidation. They went back to their trade as employees for others.

A small business owner may often enjoy skills that put them into business, but struggle with the financial side. Equally, and from an audit perspective, they may struggle to provide the IT expertise to establish, or manage, a system of internal control. Furthermore, achieving segregation of duties is difficult. For example, if there is only one office staff and an owner-manager, then controls over authorisation, asset control and recording are almost impossible to separate.

As a result, the auditor may not be able to place reliance on internal controls. Therefore, it is common for the auditor to rely less on control tests and more on substantive procedures – re-performance, checking input, reconciling bank accounts – in such audits. Analytical procedures to 'estimate' certain balances – such as sales or profit – can be highly useful as well to identify risk areas.

Audit standard-setters have heard the challenges of small organisations; see, for example, responses to SME concerns found in the 2012 *Explanatory Guide Au9: Applying the Auditing Standards on Audits of Smaller Entities in Australia and New Zealand*. Smaller, less complex entities (LCEs) make a critical contribution to the world economy and account for the great majority of audits globally. At the same time, increasingly complex structures and transactions need to be addressed through the development and revision of the ISAs. The IAASB recognises that reflecting this complexity in the ISAs could pose challenges for audits of less complex entities.[3]

These engagements also require an understanding of the assurance concepts so as to apply them to different situations. What is *material* may depend on the client's bank's needs. *Risks* may have to place greater weight on the possibility of failure and so consider current ratios and going concern. *Evidence*, as mentioned, may rely on substantive procedures. Small charities and SMEs provide new types of audit challenges.

CONCEPT QUESTION 3	Why do non-profit entities differ from commercial enterprises from an audit perspective?

---

[3] The IAASB developed the exposure draft of the proposed International Standard on Auditing for Audits of Financial Statements of Less Complex Entities (ED-ISA for LCE) on an accelerated basis. The IAASB approved ED-ISA for LCE in June 2021.

Environmental audits

Environmental, or sustainable, audits also come under the umbrella of 'social audit', because they have at their core an interest beyond the growth of capital and profit. An environmental audit assesses actions or reporting practices against standards. Such standards are often set in law, hence the environmental audit becomes a 'compliance' audit. There may be a range of reporting obligations: to managers, the client's/employer's governing board, regulatory bodies, or the public. The investigation may also involve providing recommendations to improve future practices or detect and report direct violations of environmental regulations. In the broader sense, sustainability or environmental audit may include a considerable 'scope', as it could involve, for example, examinations of emissions, water quality, resource constraints, community impacts or ecology.

In Australia, a federation of six self-governing states and two self-governing mainland territories, responsibility for the protection and conservation of the environment is shared across governments. The Commonwealth Government is primarily responsible for the protection of matters of national environmental significance. The states and territories are responsible for a broad range of environmental matters, including the regulation of pollution, approval of certain types of development activity, and regulation of natural resources management.

An environmental audit provides advice on risks of harm to human health or the environment and may consider the suitability of site uses. Each state and territory has its own environmental regulation. For example, in Victoria, the Environmental Protection Authority (EPA) appoints environmental auditors to perform audits; the auditors give an independent assessment of site conditions and risks. As per the recommendation of AASB/IASB Practice Statement 2: Making Materiality Judgements (APS/PS 2), auditors of the financial statements may consider

> climate-related risk and other emerging risks as part of their risk assessment applying ASA 315 Identifying and Assessing Risks of Material ... [and] whether climate-related risk and other emerging risks are relevant for... under ASA 540 Auditing Accounting Estimates and Related Disclosures.

In regards to New Zealand:

> In October 2021, the Financial Sector (Climate-related Disclosures and Other Matters) Amendment Bill was passed and received Royal Assent. As a result, the XRB now has a mandate to issue climate standards as part of a climate-related disclosures framework, and guidance on environmental, social and governance (ESG) matters. (XRB, 2022)

While regulations tend to play a large role, a sustainability audit need not be restricted to legal requirements:

> Environmental audit does not stop at compliance with legislation. Nor is it a 'green-washing' public relations exercise. Rather it is a total strategic approach to the organization's activities. (International Chamber of Commerce, 2007, in Ozbirecikli, 2007, p. 115)

It is a growing field. Studies have shown that, for example, of 13 major countries surveyed (Holland and Foo, 2003, cited in Ozbirecikli, 2007, p. 118):

- Nearly 3 of 4 include environmental information
- One in 4 separate environmental reports

While the conditions of an assurance engagement with the environment in mind can comprise almost any combination of fauna, flora or the people that occupy it, a category framework of different types of environmental report can be useful to understand the sort of moral and ethical problems one may have in reporting for events (outside of legally required disclosures). Gray, Owen and Maunders offer an approach to such decisions based on the scope and structure of an engagement (see **Table 19.3**).

Table 19.3 Structure for ethical environmental reporting

Report for ...	Report compiled by ...	
	Internals	Externals
Internals	Social accounts, program evaluation, attitudes audit, compliance, environmental	Quango reports (government compliance), environmental consultants, waste and energy audits
External	Social accounts and reports, compliance audits, mission statements, environmental	Social audit, association (e.g., Greenpeace), journalists, external environmental audits

Source: Gray, Owen and Maunders (1987).

In Gray, Owen and Maunders's (1987) rendition, those who prepare the report – and those for whom they are prepared – guide certain communication actions to follow. Reports compiled by internals for internals should probably be audited, or overseen, by internal auditors. Also, reports by contracted 'externals' for internal use may also be reasonably kept out of the public eye.

However, producing reports for 'externals' offers a different landscape, as this creates a gap between those who have 'prepared' and those for whom they prepare it, potentially calling for an external, client-independent professional to conduct the assurance service.

Regulations are not the only incentive to disclose sustainability issues, therefore. Blumenfeld (1989) also sets out an ethical framework for the organisation itself and for the internal or external auditor (see Table 19.4), guiding the sorts of ethical circumstances in which it may be appropriate to disclose environmental concerns.

Table 19.4 Conditions for ethical environment reporting

To disclose or not to disclose: An important audit judgement issue		
Assumption	Underlying principles	
	Fundamental duty	Consequences
1 Failure to disclose would potentially cause serious harm to health/ environment	There exists a fundamental moral duty to protect innocent third parties from harm	Disclosure of the hazard might prevent significant human health or environmental damage
2 Failure to protect employer confidentiality is unethical	Auditor has a fundamental moral obligation not to disclose company information intended to be confidential	Disclosure of confidential information jeopardises the trust which underlies all current and future audits

Source: Blumenfeld (1989).

There is a cost to the auditor in doing so, as the requirements for keeping client information confidential are fundamental to the auditor's ethical context. However, in Blumenfeld's framework, disclosing confidential information is a risk personally and professionally balanced against a personal moral obligation to disclose when the consequences of not doing so may be great, such as permanent damage to forests or the sea.

Some of the same challenges introduced earlier for non-profits and the public sector apply here as well; much on which assurance must be reached is likely to be non-financial. In particular, audits related to the earth, sea and air are more likely to require astronomical, meteorological, biological or marine biology experts. Audit as to cultural achievement, or appropriation, also requires recognised experts of yet more disciplines and legal considerations. Knowledge of environmental management systems such as ISO 14001 on wastewater management and related accounting issues could be helpful.

Furthermore, because of the cost of an audit, it is not surprising that environmental reports tend to be produced more consistently in situations where they are required in law, in regulation, for certification or for funding. The focus on compliance is simply more likely to yield actual audits.

Areas of audit *risk* with respect to the environment may encompass any of the following (derived in part from Dixon, Mousa and Woodhead, 2004, in Ozbirecikli, 2007, p. 117):

- whether 'provisions' for existing liabilities are disclosed
- contingent liabilities should certain events occur in the future, their identification and likelihood
- asset valuations, which are a challenge when there is no 'market' value for qualities of life or the environment
- whether an expenditure is an 'asset' or an 'expense': When a business spends money to return a mining site to its original condition, is that a cost of doing current business or an asset for the future? When an organisation is obligated to return salmon fishing stocks to the original farm, is that liability or a source of future revenue or an asset (a prepaid expense)?
- going concern assessments can be difficult: What is being measured? What is the scope of that being measured – the future of an organisation or of the planet?

The Certified Environmental Auditor (CEA) is one recognised professional association. Although membership in it is not necessarily required for carrying out a sustainability audit, its value may grow. In terms of 'professional' locations, it appears to be in a 'formative' stage, still ironing out its mission with a growing membership. CEA includes the elements and rules we might expect (relevant degree requirement, standards and codes, relevant work experience, and examination on environmental law, programs, science and technology).

The internal auditor may also increasingly play a role in producing environmental audit reports. IFAC acknowledges that environmental, social and sustainability reports are growing. External auditors also have a role. In 2004, IFAC's IAASB issued a standard (Assurance Engagements Other than Audits or Reviews of Historical Financial Information) setting out some principles and procedures for all [other] assurance engagements (IFAC, 2004, cited in Ozbirecikli, 2007, p. 121). (New Zealand had a similar standard issued in 2009: ISA NZ 3000). There was an express call to evaluate against set criteria (3A(a)/1).

The use of a letter of engagement (as with all non-statutory audits) should be carefully considered for each investigation, as the level of assurance and intended users are not a 'given' for these unique contracts. Full access and communication expectations should also be expressed in letters of engagement.

As to planning and conducting an environmental audit, the auditor would probably need to gather information about relevant regulations and standards to which the claim pertains. Special expertise may be needed to strengthen evidence analysis. The audit program can be modified in accordance with those needs and objectives.

| CONCEPT QUESTION 4 | What are the main objectives of environmental audit? |

Study tools

Summary

This chapter introduced the purpose, shared characteristics, and practices associated with the social assurance services. Social audits attest to claims that may be non-financial or which may be established in statute and require assessments as to performance indicators. VFM audits for the public sector, and substantive testing-oriented audits for small enterprises, were discussed. Economy, efficiency, effectiveness and equity concepts were introduced. The role of governmental auditors, professional associations, auditing standards and international frameworks were reviewed. The importance of a clear letter of engagement to include access and communication expectations was emphasised. The auditing conceptual framework was used to illustrate how concepts of *risk*, *materiality*, *evidence*, *independence* and *communication* may apply to these social audits.

Review Questions

19.1 What primary characteristic do non-profit entities have in common?

19.2 How are non-commercial entities fundamentally different from commercial entities?

19.3 How do the audit conceptual framework 'concepts' apply to this sector?

19.4 Identify five possible outcomes from public sector entity intervention in the market.

19.5 Compare and contrast the 'segmented' and 'integrated' models of public audit delivery.

19.6 Name and describe three key pieces of legislation over your nation's public sector audit.

19.7 Describe the differences between 'economy', 'efficiency' and 'effectiveness' with respect to the Value for Money (VFM) government audit.

19.8 When and how is the consolidated financial statement 'put together'?

19.9 Describe challenges for the auditor in group (consolidated) account engagements.

19.10 How are non-profit charities different from other entities with respect to 'employees/ volunteers' and 'tax treatments'?

19.11 Identify three unique audit risks to Small and Medium Enterprises (SMEs).

19.12 Explain why environmental audits may be described as 'compliance' audits.

19.13 Name one example each of a report compiled by (a) internals for externals; (b) externals for internals; (c) internals for internals and (d) externals for externals.

19.14 Ethics and environmental audit: Name the characteristics that Blumenfeld (1989) says should influence the disclosure, or non-disclosure, of an environmental issue.

Exercises

19.1 **PUBLIC SECTOR:** In terms of the public sector's interventionist role, and considering the six categories, where would you classify each of the following organisations as audit clients?

  a cemetery boards

  b Australian National Audit Office (ANAO)

  c Customs and Immigration

  d Earthquake and War Damage Commission

  e children, family services

  f Accident Compensation Corporation/Transport Accident Commission

  g Australian Taxation Office

  h Reserve Bank of Australia/New Zealand.

19.2 **PUBLIC SECTOR – ACCOUNTABILITY:**

  a Should the opinion on an investigative audit by the government auditor be publicly available:

    i for an individual

    ii for a private estate agency business

    iii for a local authority?

  b Should local council audits be contracted out to the lowest bidder for:

    i financial audit

    ii compliance with laws

    iii equity?

19.3 **PUBLIC SECTOR – SCOPE:** Name a circumstance in the case of local (or district) council whether the audit should be for:

  a the whole council

  b only a part

  c the council and the advisory (or equivalent) board together.

In addition, what do you think are the assurance issues related to local (or district) council audits?

19.4 **PUBLIC SECTOR – ASSURANCE:** Can you come to a high level of assurance on the:

  a effectiveness of policy set by the Reserve Bank

  b equity of hospital services distribution to rural and urban patients

  c stewardship of native flora and fauna, bush tracks and huts

In addition:

  d How can a diverse public best be provided with assurance?

  e Auditor as oversight or in support?

  f Which decisions should be left to the auditor-general's discretion?

  g How wide should the auditor's authority be drawn?

19.5   SUSTAINABILITY – RIGHTS AND OBLIGATIONS:

i   In carrying out a financial engagement, the auditor suspects that the company is emitting super-heated water into the local water system. There is no specific law or regulation in New Zealand referring to super-heated water, although studies overseas indicate that it can affect water quality.

ii   BizzyBee Ltd manufactures plastic 'construction' kits for children under eight. While they can't be swallowed and there are no sharp points, it is possible that one of the toys could injure a child if in more unusual circumstances.

Required: Using Preuss (1998), which ethical principle would you choose first to follow in each of the above events:

a   ethical obligations: a decision framework

b   utilitarianism, which roughly equals consequentialism

c   deontology, which has to do with fundamental duty

d   environmental audit and sampling.

Fraud audit

Introduction

This chapter continues to introduce non-financial assurance services, detailing the fraud investigation. Like other professional assurance engagements, it is informed by the conceptual framework for audit and its principles and concepts. Fraud investigations are distinguished in terms of where efforts are directed and why, as well as in terms of what is expected and to whom to report. References are made to *forensic audit*. Implications for the professional auditor are considered throughout.

Fraud defined

'Fraud' encompasses a multitude of activities: deception, concealment, distortion, bribery, corruption and outright theft. The IIA (Australia) defines it as the

> misuse of entrusted power for personal gain including bribery, conflict of interest, extortion, embezzlement and fraud. (IIA, 2021)

A consistent element is that 'fraud' involves a considered or *intentional* act:

> The distinguishing factor between fraud and error is whether the underlying action that results in the misstatement of the financial report is intentional or unintentional. (ASA 240, para 2)

This may be *intent* to deceive, *intent* to conceal facts, and/or *intent* to obtain assets unlawfully. Proving 'intent' is difficult in the courtroom because the mindset of a fraudster (their 'intent') is hard to know 'beyond reasonable doubt'. So, even though fraud is costly, those who commit it may not be easily held to account. The existence of fraud threatens the use of resources and the viability of business itself.

Fraud is ever-present. In early 2021, KPMG surveyed over 70 senior executives to explore the impact COVID-19 had on fraud and corruption risk faced by Australian organisations both here and abroad. The survey found that 72 per cent reported that the risk of fraud and corruption had increased during the COVID-19 pandemic, and 85 per cent said they did not expect the risk to reduce in 2021. Ninety-two per cent of the respondents believed the risk of cyberfraud had increased during the COVID-19 era (KPMG, 2021b).

An annual analysis of fraud in New Zealand (2020–21) found the following:

> The value of large fraud cases (over $100 000) totalled $72 million. Two exceeded $3 million each, with the largest fraud case a $45 million Ponzi scheme. Business owners were the most common perpetrators of fraud, followed by financial advisors; 23% of business fraudsters were known to falsify invoices. (KPMG, 2021a)

The Treadway Commission's COSO made recommendations on the principles around which an internal control system can be designed to prevent fraud (see **Figure 20.1**)

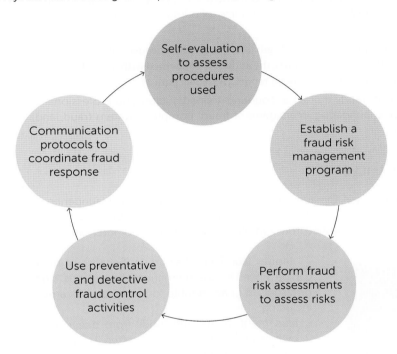

Figure 20.1 COSO-based fraud internal-control principles

Sources: Derived from COSO (2016). Information also sourced from NCFFR (1987).

Fraud is of ongoing concern to management, shareholders, customers and governing boards. Fraud concerns those who rely on the viability of financial statements and those who have invested time and money in a business. Auditors have always operated under some expectation that they will find or prevent material financial fraud, and internal auditors may be specifically tasked with doing so. Hence, understanding why it exists, and where and how to find it, is of direct concern to auditors – internal and external.

Fraud types

Fraud can appear in many contexts and take many forms. Types of fraud include:
- *tax fraud*, such as claiming unlawful tax deductions or hiding taxable revenue – in tax fraud, managers may overstate costs or understate revenue to reduce tax liabilities, which runs counter to likely financial distortion, leading to understated liabilities or expenses and overstated assets or revenue
- *corruption*, including syndicated activities, kickbacks or influence schemes

- *web-aided frauds* against individuals, such as advance-fee frauds (Nigerian frauds), affinity frauds (pretending to be a member of a known group), Ponzi schemes, identity theft, credit card theft, falsifying authorisation through e-signature, unauthorised data access, and ransomware
- *plagiarism*, including using someone else's published research or creations
- *contract fraud*, including poor work or kickbacks; for example, a contractor may have agreed to three coats of house paint but only performed one
- *insider trading*, or the buying or selling of the securities of a company by a person who, by virtue of some connection with the company, has the benefit of information not generally available – a director or senior manager is the person most likely to possess significant inside information
- *management fraud*, in which an organisational manager uses their position to obtain unauthorised access or outcomes, sometimes through the use of *system* or *computer* fraud
- *financial statement fraud*, which is, of course, of primary interest to the statutory financial statement auditor.

> Although fraud is a broad legal concept, for the purposes of the Australian [and New Zealand] Auditing Standards, the auditor is concerned with fraud that causes a material misstatement in the financial report. (ASA 240, para 3)

We now look at frauds that an accounting-trained auditor and professional may be most likely to encounter: money laundering, management fraud, computer system fraud, and, of course, financial statement fraud.

Money laundering

Wherever fraud results in the acquisition of ill-gotten gains, money laundering may be the means by which such gains are hidden and, ultimately, spent. Money laundering occurs where (usually) illegal funds are 'laundered' or 'washed' through other enterprises and/or international movements of finance so as to appear legal.

Money laundering has grown because of the ease by which assets can be moved across international boundaries, hidden in cryptocurrency or disguised in acceptable forms. It can be carried out in several ways, including:

- *placement*, or moving funds from direct association with a crime by banking the illegal money, often in amounts less than $10 000, in multiple locations
- *layering*, or disguising the trail by splitting the funds within the institution and/or moving parts out – money launderers may buy gold, bonds or insurance with the illegal funds and redeem or sell them overseas
- *integration*, or pulling seemingly legitimate money out and making it available to the criminal. (See **Figure 20.2**.)

Money-laundering activity is a concern for professionals, including accountants and auditors. This is because, under current law, professional accountants, together with financial institutions and legal professionals, must conduct procedures to ensure they know their customers or clients, make certain disclosures about them to legal authorities, and provide assurance that their clients are not involved in money-laundering schemes. As identifying laundered funds prevents their use by a fraudster, identifying and disclosing money laundering is important.

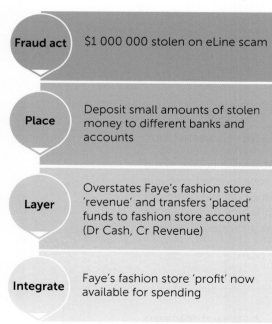

Fraud act — $1 000 000 stolen on eLine scam

Place — Deposit small amounts of stolen money to different banks and accounts

Layer — Overstates Faye's fashion store 'revenue' and transfers 'placed' funds to fashion store account (Dr Cash, Cr Revenue)

Integrate — Faye's fashion store 'profit' now available for spending

Figure 20.2 Example of a money-laundering scheme

Management fraud

Management fraud is any unauthorised, intentional activity carried out by someone in a management position to the detriment of their organisation. As a manager may have access to systems and authority not available to other employees, and because they may be evaluated on indicators of 'performance' such as profit margins, managers have both the *opportunity* and possibly the *incentive* to perform a fraudulent act.

So, for example, a manager may use distortion, such as removing stock receipt records, to carry out the theft of that stock. It has been found that fraud and unusually good financial results exist together. One study found that

> fraud firms are more likely to meet or beat analyst forecasts and inflate revenue than non-fraud firms are even when there is no evidence of prior earnings management.
> (Perols and Lougee, 2011)

Some of the more common types of management fraud are:

- *asset misappropriation* – simply stealing assets and removing records
- *inflated asset values* – in which a liability or equity account is credited, resulting in a deceptively good statement of financial position (balance sheet)
- *increasing remuneration* – through, for example, unauthorised fringe benefits or by abusing access to personnel files or wage systems
- *enhancing shareholdings* – if there is access to authorisation
- *improper use of assets* – in which organisational assets such as cars or homes are used for personal purposes
- *use of affiliated companies* – which can absorb the original organisation's liabilities or which can create inflated 'sales' transactions
- *kickbacks* – in which someone receives personal funds in exchange for providing a 'favour', such as agreeing to contract work with the person providing the kickback.

Auditing in practice

Bill Papas vs big banks

The investigation by liquidators suggesting Bill Papas's alleged fraud involving the siphoning of more than $500 million from Westpac Banking Corporation and other major Australian banks began in 2013. The findings of the liquidators are based on analysis of more than 110 000 transactions across approximately 150 bank accounts held by Bill Papas's business Forum Finance and its related entities and beneficiaries. Westpac and two other lenders, Société Générale and Sumitomo, filed Federal Court civil action charging Bill and his company with orchestrating fraud against the banks by forging signatures of executives at the banks' blue-chip clients. Westpac won approval from an Australian court to launch legal action in Greece to execute freezing orders over the international assets of Bill Papas – Bill left Australia in June 2021 and is currently residing in the Greek seaside city of Thessaloniki.

Source: Derived from Chau (2021).

All types of fraud usually involve unauthorised access to and use of systems, computers, communication or data storage.

System access fraud

Systems and computer fraud can be carried out by someone outside or inside an organisation. Those external to the organisation may attempt to acquire access by:

- *browsing*, which is essentially searching for means of access to someone's private account, whether that be looking over someone's shoulder, searching waste bins or other means
- *masquerading* or impersonating legitimate users or a legitimate entry to the system which then accepts that the masquerade is authorised
- *piggybacking* by intercepting communication lines or access
- *between-lines entry* activities involving a penetrator taking advantage of the time during which a legit user is still connected, perhaps just before they log out but after they have left the site
- *spoofing*, in which the penetrator fools the user into thinking the interaction is with an authorised system or person – spoofing may even involve simulating a system crash so that they can observe how the user logs on again
- *Trojan horses*, essentially an app or utility program that appears to be authentic but which is not and provides access to the perpetrator.

Insiders, including those in governance, may have access to an organisation's systems, or portions of it.

> Those charged with governance of an entity oversee the entity's systems for monitoring risk, financial control and compliance with the law. In many circumstances, corporate governance practices are well developed and those charged with governance play an active role in oversight of the entity's assessment of the risks of fraud and the controls that address such risks. (ASA 240, para A20)

This is where the appropriate system development protocols, segregations of duty, internal checks and internal audit functions, discussed previously, help prevent fraud.

Financial statement fraud

The external auditor, as you know, has an obligation to search for material fraud:

> The [financial statement] auditor is concerned with fraud that causes a material misstatement in the financial statements. Two types of intentional misstatements are relevant ... misstatements resulting from fraudulent financial reporting and misstatements resulting from misappropriation of assets. (ISA NZ 240, para 3)

Types of fraud affecting financial statements are many and varied. Some of these are illustrated in **Table 20.1**, together with examples of the types of internal controls, internal audit protocols, and external audit tests and procedures that could prevent or detect them.

In the ordinary course of a financial statement audit, there are some activities that can be carried out by the organisation's internal audit division or the external auditor, including the following:

- analytical review procedures to reveal unusual patterns in expenses, revenues or even the number of events (e.g., sales) that occurred in a period of time
- testing internal controls over higher-risk activities, such as where there is poor duty segregation between receiving and recording payments
- vulnerabilities can occur with system or business changes, so audit inquiries should include asking about such events and how they were managed. Selective sampling can focus audit testing on that vulnerable period of time.

Keep in mind, however, that the role of the external financial statement auditor is distinct from the fraud auditor. The fraud auditor may have far more narrow and focused responsibilities.

Table 20.1 Examples of financial fraud and potential means of detection

Employee or management fraud performed	Detection with ...
Duplicate payment fraud occurs when duplicate payments are made for the same debt. *Multiple payee* is similar, except the amounts paid are unequal.	Payee authorisation controls; duplicate payments checks
Defective delivery involves the shipment or delivery of goods of inferior quality or to illegitimate addresses.	Analytical procedures; controls over payees
Defective shipment defrauds the seller by shipping higher-quality goods than ordered or paid for.	QR code cost entry integrated to shipment and sales
Defective pricing is when overpricing (or underpricing) margins go to illegitimate recipients.	Controls over price authorisation
Shell games or *shell fraud* occurs on the payment of alleged debts to fictitious companies or for unperformed services. The fraudster overbills and thereby steals assets. Shell companies such as holding companies can be legitimate, or they can be used to hide liabilities.	Related party evidence gathered by auditor
Teeming and lading is when customer receipts are stolen (i.e., credited to a personal account) and the customer's accounts are credited with the next series of payments from other customers. The funds stolen usually grow in volume over time.	Customer complaint or should the employee take leave
Unrecorded sales, particularly cash sales when the customer fails to ask for a receipt.	Controls over cash sales (usually small amounts)
Asset misappropriation or their improper use may be easier for managers if they can override internal controls.	Observation; indicators of fraud
Inflated asset values occur through adjusting journal entries.	Inspect AJEs
Illegitimate remuneration may be possible if controls over, for example, fringe benefits can be overridden.	Analytical procedures; personnel policy tests
Enhanced shareholdings can occur should assets or liabilities be misclassified.	Auditor review of material transactions
Complex schemes can involve multiple companies, false addresses, multiple financial accounts and overseas accounts.	Related party evidence gathered by auditor

CONCEPT QUESTION 1   Define 'fraud'. What distinguishes it from 'errors'?

Incentives for committing fraud and fraud indicators

Incentives for committing fraud

It is said that understanding the mind of the fraudster can help the investigator find occurrences of fraud. So, for example, a senior manager with significant control may have access and the motivation to commit financial fraud. The fraud triangle (see **Figure 20.3**) is frequently offered as a way of understanding such incentives (Mintchik and Riley, 2019).

Originating in 1973, the fraud triangle explains the likelihood of fraud in terms of what motivates the fraudster:

- *pressure* – such as pressure to achieve certain goals, or personal pressure to pay a home mortgage or medical bills
- *opportunity* – the opportunity offered by, for example, weak internal controls or inappropriate access through poor segregation of duties
- *rationalisation* – a personality and behavioural characteristic associated with justifying to oneself the perpetration of a fraud.

Use caution, however, as the auditor should only use these observations to identify whether they indicate a *risk*, not whether fraud actually occurred. Standing alone, they do not provide evidence of fraud, but they can direct the auditor to the relevant evidence.

Fraud indicators

Situations that tend to increase the risk of financial statement fraud were introduced in earlier chapters. Indications that it may exist include any of the following, some of which are derived from ASA 240: Business Rationale for Significant Transactions (para A49):

- *overly complex (client) transactions* – using multiple entities to create revenue streams that may be from related parties is one example; complex processes or programs can offer opportunities for fraudsters, particularly if no-one else understands what they are doing, or, worse, if the employee takes the knowledge of the program with them when they leave the organisation
- *unusual adjusting entries* – particularly if not authorised by the governing body
- *related party transactions* at all or with non-consolidated entities – off-balance-sheet financing (or debt) can hide the financial position or real profit of an organisation
- *poor internal controls* – may give employees access to assets and record-keeping (essentially, a poor segregation of duties)
- *characteristics in keeping with the fraud triangle* – such as where a manager exhibits excessive ambition or excessive personal spending, or puts excessive pressure on managers due to a reliance on their financial performance (although keep in mind that these are also the characteristics of an ambitious management, which can be a very good thing)
    - *absence of, or reluctance to take, holidays* – giving the employee an opportunity to continue covering up fraudulent activity; this may occur in combination with a poor segregation of duties, or, as in 'teeming and lading', fraud can occur with good controls but only if the fraudster is always there to keep it hidden
    - *an overheated economic environment* – it may be such that fraudulent transactions go unnoticed.

More red flags particularly associated with management fraud include:

- management failure to display the appropriate attitude towards internal control, as well as operating and financial stability, management characteristics and industry characteristics (in that order)
- management lying, being aggressive, or emphasising earnings projections and complex or difficult-to-audit transactions
- management's effort to convince you of an accounting treatment that may not represent the economic reality (adapted from Smith et al., 2005).

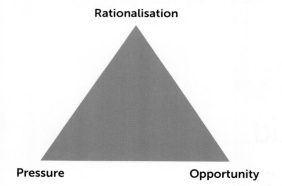

Figure 20.3 Fraud triangle

Source: Cressey (1973), p. 30.

US Enron case

The US Enron case provided, in retrospect, classic indications of fraud occurring, such as:

- unduly aggressive earnings targets, and management bonus compensation based on those targets
- excessive interest by management in maintaining stock price or earnings trends through the use of unusually aggressive accounting practices
- management setting unduly aggressive financial targets and expectations for operating personnel
- the inability to generate sufficient cash flow from operations while reporting earnings and earnings growth
- assets, liabilities, revenues or expenses based on significant estimates that involve unusually subjective judgements
- significant related party transactions.

Source: Thomas (2002).

This emphasises the importance of establishing an internal control environment and systems, as introduced by COSO, that take into consideration the possibility of fraud.

CONCEPT QUESTION 2	What are the three elements of a 'fraud triangle' and what do they attempt to explain?

Fraud audit purpose

Fraud audits are one response to fraud's proliferation. It 'involves the use of auditing techniques... for the sole purpose of detecting evidence of fraud' (Davia, 2001). A fraud investigation may call for forensic skills, computer program competencies, or system interrogation skills. We begin with a reminder of the financial statement (statutory) auditor's responsibilities with respect to fraud, and then go on to consider the more focused 'fraud' and 'forensic' audit types.

Financial (statutory) audit

Standards for the audit of statutory financial statements are set out in ASA 240 and ISA NZ 240:

> An auditor conducting an audit in accordance with Australian Auditing Standards is responsible for obtaining reasonable assurance that the financial report taken as a whole is free from material misstatement, whether caused by fraud or error. Owing to the inherent limitations of an audit, there is an unavoidable risk that some material misstatements of the financial report may not be detected, even though the audit is properly planned and performed in accordance with Australian Auditing Standards.
> (ASA 240, para 5; ISA NZ, para 5)

Australian Standard AS 8001: Fraud and Corruption Control sets out this process further. Clearly, there is a responsibility to plan and perform a financial audit with the expectation of identifying material fraud. The statutory financial statement auditor may conduct a non-negligent audit even if they fail to discover existing fraud.

Fraud audit (non-statutory)

A non-statutory fraud audit may be conducted regularly by an internal auditor, carried out under statute as part of the financial audit, or contracted to assess a specific situation.

> Fraud auditing is a unique auditing speciality that involves the use of auditing techniques for the sole purpose of detecting evidence of fraud. (Davia, 2000, p. 32)

That sole purpose distinguishes it from a financial statement audit (see **Table 20.2**).

Table 20.2 Conceptual framework and the fraud audit

Concept	Financial statement audit	Fraud audit
Independence from ...	Client (governing body, management)	Potential fraudster; Otherwise contract-dependent
Risk of ...	Material financial misstatement	Failure to identify fraud
Materiality refers to ...	Material misstatements in the accounts	Not probabilities of fraud, but the existence of any fraud
Evidence ...	Needed to form an opinion; sample may be based on likely location of fraud	Identify vulnerability (proactive) or follow up indicia (reactive); if forensic, legal standard met
Judgement	Opinion formed from evidence	Identify indicators, imagine fraud scenarios, puzzle-solving
Opinion expressed	... in audit report to public	Contract-dependent; may be for governing body or manager
Accountability to	... users, stakeholders	Contract-dependent
Ethical principles	Always apply to any engagement	

In either a financial statement or fraud audit, any occurrence of fraud found may be material because of that 'intent' on the part of someone to deceive. Nonetheless, neither the fraud nor financial auditor is qualified to determine the 'guilt' in law of a suspected fraudster:

> Although the auditor may suspect or, in rare cases, identify the occurrence of fraud, the auditor does not make legal determinations of whether fraud has actually occurred. (ISA NZ 240, para 3)

So, the fraud auditor applies their professionalism to determining and disclosing facts, not judgements. Litigation and, ultimately, a judgment in law, is the aim of a different type of investigation, however – the *forensic audit*.

Forensic audit

> Forensic Accountants combine their accounting knowledge with investigative skills, using this unique combination in litigation support and investigative accounting settings. (CA ANZ, 2021)

The Forensic Accounting Special Interest Group of CA ANZ was founded in 2006. Forensic investigators may investigate fraud or fraud suspicions that end up in a courtroom, such as an insolvency or bankruptcy court, or through the resolution of marital or partnership property. Forensic investigations draw from many professional skills, including, of course, accounting but also law enforcement, legal knowledge, science and insurance.

The forensic auditor (or accountant) may be employed by the prosecution, defence, court, insurance companies, law enforcement agencies or financial institutions. As obtaining convictions can be difficult to achieve, imposing a penalty on the fraudster is often not possible. Asset recovery of items stolen may be achievable, however, as may be the identification of vulnerabilities which can lead to actions that prevent such frauds in the future.

Auditing in practice

A fraud auditing scenario

A fraud auditor may be contracted to identify the source of unusually high employment costs. On discovery of duplicate payments, the organisation may choose to bring the action to court. Still, more often, the situation will be handled internally by improving controls or even by relocating the employee.

Any public disclosure of a fraudulent event, no matter how small, can cause image problems for the organisation, so management may choose to deal with it privately.

Is forensic accounting important to the financial and fraud auditor? History would suggest this is so:

> In the early years of the accounting profession, when fraud discovery was acknowledged as being one of the principal objectives of the financial audit, forensic accounting was an integral part of mainstream accounting. During subsequent decades as the accounting profession attempted to distance itself from fraud discovery responsibilities, forensic accounting became identified as a specialized subset of the profession. Now, on the heels of many embarrassing corporate failures and passage of the Sarbanes-Oxley Act, forensic accounting is being reunited with the profession. Fraud discovery is again acknowledged as one of the principal responsibilities of the auditor and the tools of the forensic accountant are now being rediscovered. (Gray and Moussalli, 2006)

Forensic audit, while relying on the investigator's accounting and auditing skills, also looks to a variety of professionals to pursue instances of concern.

Fraud audit process

Fraud investigations can be very expensive, and sometimes they lead to nothing because the source cannot be found. If the benefits of finding fraud are small, and other methods to prevent or mitigate it are possible, then it may be more cost-effective to modify controls or functions where gaps exist. If not required in law or statute, the decision to look for the *source* of fraud may be based on particular criteria (see **Figure 20.4**).

Legal, economic or social consequence of finding source is crucial for:
- Compliance
- Prevention
- Mitigation and/or
- Accountability, and

You're likely to be able to find the source of the fraud, *and*

It is cost-beneficial to do so.

Figure 20.4 When to look for the source of fraud

Investigation types

On concluding that an investigation should be initiated into the existence, or cause, of fraud, one of two types of investigation will occur:

1 proactive investigation
2 reactive investigation

Proactive investigations

Proactive investigations are referred to as searching for a 'needle in the haystack'. This is because the professional searches for evidence of fraud, but it is not known whether or not, or what kind of fraud, may exist. Proactive investigations can be a 'deterrence' technique not unlike the medical practitioner's practice of examining their patients for signs of malignancies even though the patients appear to be in good health. Such searches may be due to a general risk of fraud occurring and can be part of an effort to deter fraud before it occurs.

Normally, there will be a *stop rule* in any proactive investigation, which is a specific point at which to stop looking; time 'runs out'. Without a stop rule, investigations can be interminable, pointless (as at some point they're less likely to uncover fraud) and costly. Proactive investigations will normally consist of a:

- *prediscovery stage*, in which the auditor selects areas to search and procedures to use while being alert to fraud indicators
- *post-discovery stage*, in which the auditor *envisions* the nature of possible fraudulent acts that could have occurred given indicators identified in the *prediscovery* stage. The auditor then acquires evidence to either support or refute the potential for that envisioned fraud.

Reactive investigations

In contrast, *reactive investigations* are when the auditor reacts or responds to specific suspicions of a fraudulent event. The task then becomes one of finding evidence to support that suspicion. The search is easier than a proactive search because the auditor knows where to focus their investigation.

Auditing in practice

Reactive fraud audit

One of the authors conducted a reactive fraud audit for a property investment partnership. The partners suspected their manager overcharged them for maintenance. Given this suspicion, the investigation focused on analytical procedures to identify likely areas of risk, examining the occurrence-validity of invoices and comparisons to the control account, and investigating the validity of suppliers. Some inflated costs by one supplier were identified, and procedures to approve costs were changed.

A reactive audit already benefits from known indicators of fraud, which turns the investigation from a blind search (proactive audit) into a specific search for the suspected misappropriation (see **Figure 20.5**).

CAATs

Use your CAATs Learning Toolbox to suggest different types of fraud situations which can be 'imagined'.

Fraud audit approaches

The fraud audit decision process thus differs from a financial audit (see **Figure 20.5**).

Fraud investigations pose new challenges for the auditor. The fraud auditor is advised to:

- avoid entanglement in endless facts
- distinguish between 'indicative' and 'validating' evidence
- be 'creative' and 'unpredictable' in gathering evidence, which can help detect fraud involving those expecting more traditional activities in the investigation
- consider the effects of collusion
- determine whether proving 'intent' or 'legal evidence' is necessary.

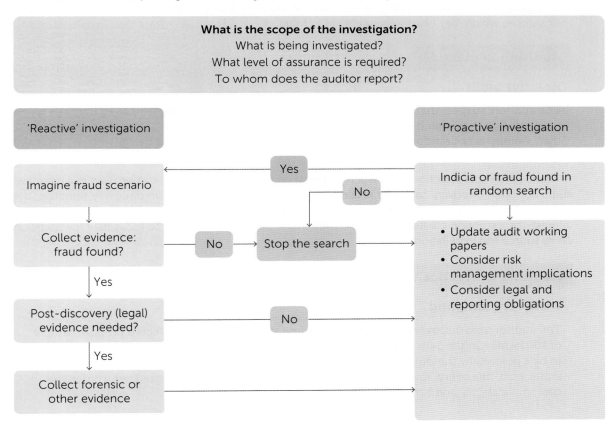

Figure 20.5 Fraud audit process flowchart

Paul's entanglement error

Paul, a staff member unaccustomed to fraud audit, spent days reviewing and confirming all invoices with spelling errors. This entanglement was unnecessary as one confirmation would have revealed that these were simple input errors. Furthermore, they distracted Paul from an indicative situation: duplicate invoices. If he had noticed them, he could have validated the fraud by determining that they were authorised but prepared by one employee, Sheryl. Paul may have found evidence if he had imagined what caused the duplicates and had, for example, examined the bank account holder to whom payments had been made. He could have considered the possibility that Sheryl was in collusion with the usual authoriser or if the authorising process had control weaknesses.

Sampling for fraud audit

The *sampling procedures* used for fraud investigations may call for non-random sampling, particularly in a *reactive* audit, as extrapolating to a population would not be relevant. That is, the auditor selects their sample, which may be more susceptible to fraud.

Reactive audit

The auditors suspect that one of the input clerks, Jay, may be creating false sales invoices for products that their watch-manufacturer is making. The sample of invoices chosen to test for their validity is not random but chosen from those invoices authorised by Jay.

Random sample selection plans (such as simple, systematic or stratified) can be used in a *proactive* audit, but often *discovery sampling* is used because it creates a stop-rule. In discovery sampling, the auditor stops sampling as soon as one exception is found. As the source of the exception is what is of interest, the exception creates a post-discovery event, allowing the auditor to focus their investigation on its source and implications.

Discovery sampling

The auditor uses discovery sampling to examine stock costing and selects a random sample of 100 items. On the 34th sample, a miscoding is discovered and, on investigation, found to be a potentially fraudulent modification to the program's coding. The investigation then shifts (post-discovery) towards finding how that coding problem occurred, who did it, the cost implications, and how it should be pursued.

Discovery sampling thus enables the auditor to focus on fraud without wasting time, by
- looking for incidence of fraud (a proactive search)
- being conscious of unusual events
- following up suspicions.
  In the example above, the search is now 'reactive'.

Cluster sampling can also be useful in fraud investigation. *Cluster sampling* is a sample selection plan which can be random but within a common 'cluster'. A cluster may be a sub-population in a particular location or as prepared by a particular office branch. Cluster sampling usefully avoids costly testing at multiple locations. It is also useful to the fraud investigator in a 'reactive' audit because it enables the auditor to concentrate on a location or similar grouping of items, or even people who are more likely to have committed the fraud.

Auditing in practice

Reactive audit and cluster sample

Analytical procedures reveal that credits for damaged stock, held on-site, are unusually high in one of 10 client-owned storage facilities. The suspicion is that stock is being stolen. Applying discovery sampling and a stop rule, the auditor makes a surprise visit to this location (cluster) and takes a random sample. They compare so-called 'damaged' stock against the credit notes. Any missing 'damaged' stock is then investigated.

There is no point in wasting time looking at events without any apparent problems.

CONCEPT QUESTION 3	Under what circumstances may a fraud auditor decide not to pursue the source of fraud any further?

Fraud audit: Regulatory environment

Legislators and regulators have attempted to reduce fraud through rules and regulations, sometimes creating enormous amounts of detailed paperwork in the process. Their efforts have had an impact and, with that in mind, we consider selected professional and legal actions in Australia and New Zealand relevant to financial and management fraud.

Professional associations

CA ANZ and the Association of Certified Fraud Examiners (ACFE) are the focus, although we note that the IIA also offers guidance on fraud-detection matters. CA ANZ has guidance for any professional on any type of professional engagement:

> Where a member, in the course of the member's professional work, discovers evidence of fraudulent or illegal activities, the member must ... where appropriate, raise the matter with the appropriate level of management of the client or employer, and consider the member's legal and professional rights and duties to disclose the information to other parties. (ASA Code of Ethics, appendix 2, para 7)

The first step, on the discovery, is to recommend that the client fix the problem and disclose information fairly. They may be guided towards how it could be prevented in the future. This is not normally a problem if the fraud has been committed by non-management employees. Management would want to solve the problem. It can be much more challenging if the fraud occurs at the governance or upper-management level because the auditor may be dealing directly with the fraudster.

Confidentiality obligations can also be raised. Unless there is a specific legal or statutory obligation to disclose a fraud to third parties, the professional must work within the organisation and, if this proves impossible, consider withdrawing from it. Withdrawing from an organisation may be a message in itself.

Cooking the books

A cost accountant and employee of a food distributor, Kay, discovered that her owner-manager boss was 'cooking the books' to obtain bank loans. This occurred on a regular basis. Kay spoke with him on multiple occasions, informing him that she would not be a part of it and trying to convince him to desist. He would not, but he did take her off the accounts. Kay eventually left the company. She had no external reporting rights or obligations, so she could not disclose the situation. A high turnover of employees raised bank concerns which eventually brought him to the attention of the law. He was arrested for fraud while attempting to leave the country.

The ACFE was formed in 1988 by a former Federal Bureau of Investigation (FBI) agent from Texas. Its objective is set out on its website:

> The proliferation of technology in the modern-day workplace presents a world of opportunity for fraudsters – and a complex challenge for fraud examiners and investigators. Anti-fraud professionals must know how to combat cyber fraud and how to use technology in fraud examinations. Learning the basics of digital forensics is crucial to uncovering fraud in the 21st century. (ACFE, 2022)

The ACFE aims to reduce fraud and white-collar crime via nurturing qualified individuals through specific training and development programs. It was inspired by the massive growth in fraudulent opportunities offered by modern technology access. As with other associations, it establishes qualification (via examination), continuing education, a code of conduct, ethics, and disciplinary procedures. As with other fraud audit activities, ACFE members should collect evidence for the purposes of forming an *opinion*, not a *judgement*, the latter of which should be reserved for the courts.

Legislation

Statutory law has been used to prevent fraud or at least make its perpetrators – on conviction – more accountable. However, it tends to emerge only after a public outcry and so is not timely nor always effective in preventing fraud. Nonetheless, legislation may provide prevention because, if caught, consequences can be severe. Australian and New Zealand legislation of interest is set out in **Table 20.3**.

Legislation has more recently turned to issues around data access and abuse. In New Zealand, legislation was led by the 1998 hacking of ISP ihug and Telecom's Xtra, in which Andrew Garrett (of Xtra) was charged with obtaining credit from Telecom without revealing that he was bankrupt, and using software for personal gain. Subsequently, ihug lobbied for an amendment to the *1961 Crimes Act* which was passed into law in 2003, drawing from the *American Computer Abuse and Fraud Act*. Securities legislation, such as the *Financial Markets Conduct Act*, (NZ), also provides some protection for investors against fraudsters.

Table 20.3 Australian and New Zealand: Select fraud-impacting statute

Purpose	Australia	New Zealand
Criminal activity, including fraud, theft	*Criminal Code Amendment (Theft, Fraud, Bribery and Related Offences) Act 2000*	*Crimes Act 1961, Crimes Amendment Act 2003*
Hacking, malware, unauthorised access	*Cybercrime Act 2001* (Cth)	*Crimes Amendment Act 2003*
Whistleblower protection	*Treasury Laws Amendment (Enhancing Whistleblower Protections) Act 2019*	*Whistleblowers Protection Act 1996* (and amendments)
Investigation of fraud	*Criminal Code Amendment (Theft, Fraud, Bribery and Related Offences) Act 2000*	Serious Fraud Office Police Investigations Unit
Financial markets regulation	Financial Transaction Reports Regulations 2019	*Financial Markets Authority Act 2011*
Banks and financial institutions	*Financial Transaction Reports Act 1988*	*Reserve Bank Act* regarding banking, prudential supervision, money laundering
Money laundering	*Anti-Money Laundering and Counter-Terrorism Financing Act 2006*	*Anti-Money Laundering and Countering Financing of Terrorism Act 2009*

CONCEPT QUESTION 4 Compare and contrast the professional accounting associations (such as CA ANZ and CPA Australia) and the ACFE.

Study tools

Summary

This chapter defined 'fraud' and introduced the nature, characteristics and practices used in fraud audit. The fraud auditor's role was compared to the statutory financial statement auditor role. Forensic auditing, indicators of fraud, and fraud approaches and methods were introduced and exampled. Professional leadership practices and legislative control over financial and white-collar crime were outlined.

Review questions

20.1   Name and define the six different types of fraud.

20.2   Why should the professional auditor/accountant be concerned with 'money laundering'? What are their responsibilities regarding discovering and/or reporting it?

20.3   Name four means by which outsiders may gain unauthorised access to an organisation's computer information system.

20.4 Name and describe different types of management fraud.

20.5 Can a manager commit management fraud that does not involve direct theft? What would it be, and how?

20.6 Describe the (statutory) auditor's responsibility to identify fraud in the conduct of a financial statement audit.

20.7 Can a statutory financial statement auditor fail to find fraud and still conduct a non-negligent audit? How?

20.8 Describe the four steps in a money-laundering scheme.

20.9 Name six different indicators of fraud.

20.10 Distinguish between the responsibilities of the auditor in the:

    a statutory financial statement audit

    b fraud audit

    c forensic audit.

20.11 Name some reasonable responses to the discovery of fraud and why they may be reasonable under different circumstances.

20.12 Describe the difference between a proactive and a reactive fraud investigation.

    a Under what circumstances might you use one over the other?

    b How would the 'stop rule' differ for each type of approach?

20.13 Name and describe how sampling in a proactive fraud situation would be distinct. Discuss both sampling methods and decisions.

20.14 Identify fraud legislation in Australia or New Zealand and detail what type of fraud it may prevent, detect or discourage through sanction.

Exercises

20.1 **FRAUD DILEMMAS (EXTERNAL FS AUDITOR):** Auditors discovered, through following up SpAR procedures, that $8 million in stock was misappropriated. Senior management carried out the fraud by inappropriately authorising write-offs for 'damaged' stock that was actually unsold. Auditors required an adjustment, but corporate management refused. There was no audit committee, and the board refused to take it up. What is likely to happen now? How might a dishonest and determined board continue to deceive?

20.2 **PROACTIVE FRAUD:**

    Required: Decide what you would do next in a fraud investigation should any of the following occur. Treat each situation independently of the others:

    a A bank-to-cash reconciliation reveals no indicia of fraud.

    b There is no segregation of duties between the development of a system for sales recordings and actually recording sales when they occur.

    c A potential new partner is concerned with how existing partner withdrawals are actually authorised in the form of loans or salary.

20.3   **REACTIVE FRAUD**:

Required: Decide what you would do next in a fraud investigation should any of the following occur. Treat each situation independently of the others:

a   The fraud investigation reveals no indicia of fraud.

b   Evidence is obtained demonstrating an instance of employee theft.

c   Evidence is obtained showing an instance of management overriding controls.

d   Evidence is obtained that the data system has been accessed by an external party.

e   Evidence is obtained which shows that an employee theft is one-off and small.

f   Evidence of fraud shows that money laundering has been carried out by a member of the governing board using the organisation's system.

20.4   **COLLUSION AND INDICATOR ALERTS:** Office supply brokers conspired with the stock manager of Company X. Ordered merchandise was not delivered, but the stock manager would issue false receiving reports and thereby authorise payment. The stock manager left the company before the end-of-year stocktake. The brokers and stock manager on-sold the stock and split the revenues. What might be an 'indicator' of the problem to a fraud auditor?

20.5   **SUSPICIONS OF FRAUD:** The auditor wanted to verify $450 000 in renovations to an old medical clinic building. While normally procedures would be limited to document checks, the auditor visited the site and observed a brand-new medical building.

a   What seems odd here?

b   What do you suspect?

c   How would you obtain evidence to support your suspicions?

20.6   **EMPLOYEE VS MANAGEMENT FRAUD:** Fraud designed to benefit the organisation generally also benefits the employee, and fraud perpetrated to the detriment of the organisation usually deceives an outside party as well.

Required: Provide one possible example of each of these two situations.

20.7   **FRAUD IDENTIFICATION:** Below is a list of events carried out in OurBusiness.

Required: Identify which of them, if any, are 'fraudulent' events and which are not. Why or why not?

a   sale of fictitious assets

b   related party transactions, which are conducted at arm's-length

c   kickbacks

d   concealing data

e   failing to meet deadlines

f   unintended violation of government statutory law

g   understated transfer pricing costs between related companies A and B to increase profit on the financial statement.

20.8   **PROACTIVE AND REACTIVE FRAUD:** Belle is a bookkeeper for PromoType, a small business in which the owner, Cheryl, creates and sells marketing plans. Belle records and processes all accounts. The business has no cash sales – customers deposit payments directly into PromoType's bank account. Payment is due on invoice.

Because segregation of duties is difficult, other methods are used to reduce fraud risk, including the following:

i   Cheryl issues and sends the online invoices, which she prenumbers. Monthly, she compares invoices sent that month to deposits made and contacts non-paying customers.

ii   Cheryl also reviews all bank receipts and disbursements at the end of each month, looking for anything unusual.

Required:

a   Describe procedures you might carry out for a proactive audit. Be specific. Cheryl can only pay for 20 hours of investigation, so keep costs in mind.

b   Assume that your investigation reveals a possible unauthorised payee. What procedures would you now perform in this reactive audit? Be specific.

20.9   **FRAUD AUDIT METHODS:** Choosing from the list provided here, what would you classify as the five most useful, and five least useful, methods for detecting warehousing fraud?

a   Account for items in transit, compare counts with stock records and reconcile differences.

b   Compare classification (WIP, raw materials) to auditor's test counts.

c   Examine receiving area for stock that should be included in the count.

d   Follow up all exceptions and exception reports.

e   Determine whether costs should be included in the valuation of items (e.g., freight, storage).

f   Review physical security.

g   Review major adjustments made.

h   Examine stock descriptions on tags and compare them to actual stock.

i   Draw a flowchart of an internal control system and compare it with policy.

j   Agree stock sheet schedule and perpetual ledger with physical counts.
     Explain your choices.

20.10 **SYSTEM OR COMPUTER FRAUD:**

Required: Describe a control that could prevent each of the following frauds from occurring:

a   A data-entry clerk enters a 'selling price' for a product that exceeds the price and allocates the difference to a personal account.

b   A programmer takes the stock system program with them when they resign.

c   A hotel front desk operates 24 hours per day in three eight-hour shifts. The evening shift person logged on and authorised several disbursements before the morning person logged off.

d   A bank customer was able to log on to their account and change the balance.

e   A manager instigated a power outage during which they 'conveniently' added false sales, which led to their meeting their mandatory sales goal.

f   While school system records were being updated, the systems developer stole some personal student data.

g A payroll clerk was able to increase the wage rate of their husband, who worked for the same company.

h A false supplier was created and invoices from this supplier were shown as received and were authorised for payment.

Conclusion

This chapter concludes our text on auditing theory and practice in Australia and New Zealand. We hope that you found the subject of audit to be engaging. We also hope that you will feel both able and willing to use your assurance skills to contribute to society and the economy in a useful, professional and ethical way. We believe that society will be enhanced by you bringing your knowledge, skills and professionalism to bear on this important field. We close with some thoughts on professional scepticism:

> There is an economy to the professional-sceptical mindset, which recognises an endpoint to enquiry ... More care could be given to the nature of improvisational enquiry and less to dogmatic structures. A freer search should be encouraged in audit practice if skepticism is to be the guide. The elements of the sceptical regress [including] the constant search ... non-dogmatism, mitigated scepticism, and instruments of truth – provide a platform on which better audit can be based. (Van Peursem, 2020)

GLOSSARY

A

accountee the person or entity to whom information is owed.

assurance 'Refers to the expression of a conclusion by an assurance practitioner that is intended to increase the confidence that users can place in a given subject matter.' (CPA Australia, 2019, p. 5)

assurance engagement 'An engagement in which an assurance practitioner aims to obtain sufficient appropriate evidence in order to express a conclusion designed to enhance the degree of confidence of the intended users other than the responsible party about the outcome of the measurement or evaluation of an underlying subject matter against criteria.' (AUASB, 2014)

assurance practitioner an individual, company or other organisation, whether in public practice, industry or commerce, or the public sector, conducting assurance engagements or related services engagements. (AUASB, 2017)

attestation engagement a party *other than* the assurance practitioner measures, offers and usually presents the subject matter to the assurance practitioner (the auditor). The assurance practitioner addresses whether (it) is free from material misstatement. (AUASB, 2014)

audit/auditing 'A systematic process of objectively obtaining and evaluating evidence regarding assertions about economic actions and events to ascertain the degree of correspondence between those assertions and established criteria and communicating the results to interested users.' (AAA, 1973)

audit committee subcommittee of a governing board. Despite its title, it is the client, *not* the external auditor. Audit committees represent shareholders' interests and liaise with auditors on issues of strategy, governance and audit. They are usually composed of 3–7 members, some or all of whom are independent of management.

audit risk model a mathematical expression of the relationship between an acceptable level of overall audit risk (OAR) and the risk particulars of an organisation, system, industry or economy that increase or reduce that risk.

audit trail the ability to determine the source, the processing and/or the conclusion of a transaction by referring to accounting records.

audit working papers a 'record of audit procedures performed, relevant audit evidence obtained, and conclusions the auditor reached'. (ASA 230, para 5; ISA NZ 230, para 5)

C

components the hardware that comprises part of any computerised or partially computerised system. Fundamental components of a computer system are the units for input, output, storage, processing, transmission and control.

confidentiality 'To respect the confidentiality of information acquired as a result of professional and business relationships [and therefore not disclose such] information outside the firm or employing organisation without proper and specific authority ... to disclose, nor use, the information for the personal advantage of the assurance practitioner or third parties.' (APES 110, para 114; PES 1, para 100.5d)

conflicts of interest 'Occurs when an entity or individual becomes unreliable because of a clash between personal (or self-serving) interests and professional duties or responsibilities.' (Segal, 2022)

consolidated financial statement a combined set of financial statements comprising the accounts of two or more organisations. A consolidated statement is collated only at the end of an accounting period. A number of adjustments are made to eliminate transactions between the companies consolidated and to represent their combined net assets. As a result, the consolidated entity exists only insofar as the accounts are created to comply with GAAP.

continuous audit refers to a situation in which audit functions are ongoing and where audit tests are carried out on a system as that system is operating. A continuous audit usually employs automated procedures that test, and report, whether data is being captured, processed and stored appropriately throughout the year.

control strengths controls within the accounting system that, if operating properly, will prevent or detect errors and irregularities.

control systems integrated combinations of controls that, together, go towards meeting prevention and detection goals in a subsystem as a whole.

control weaknesses aspects of the system that are susceptible to unauthorised manipulation but lack control to prevent or detect such error or fraud.

controls 'checks' that are built into a system to prevent or detect errors and irregularities in the data. Those controls are designed to prevent or detect errors in financial and other cost reports in an accounting information system.

D

data item the most basic piece of data that cannot be broken into more detailed units. It also may be called a *data element* or a *field*.

data structure a meaningful combination of data items. Data structures also are referred to as *records*.

datastore a temporary or permanent storage position for data structures and/or data items within a system. A datastore may be manual (physical) – e.g., the storage of a piece of paper or a form in a file cabinet; or it may be computerised (electronic) – e.g., the storage of data on a microcomputer diskette or a DBMS on a hard drive.

defendant the person or other party about which a complaint is being made in a court of law.

direct engagement the assurance practitioner measures or evaluates the subject matter against criteria, obtains appropriate evidence, and evaluates the subject matter against the criteria. (AUASB, 2020a, paras 12–13; NZAuASB, 2014, paras 12–13)

directors' declaration a declaration by the directors on the financial statements and the notes.

E

ebusiness refers to the practice of carrying out a business online.

engagement letter contractual agreement between the auditor and the client to perform a professional service such as an audit, review or compilation.

enterprise data services (ERM) form a bridge between business applications and data sources, coordinating the integration of the data sources so they are accessible by the business.

enterprise risk management (ERM) sourced in the Committee of Sponsoring Organizations (COSO) model about an organisation's internal controls, ERM is carried out by management, working with internal auditors, to anticipate future events, opportunities and risks that could affect the entity's risks and opportunities (see https://www.coso.org).

F

fee dependence if the fees from one audit client make up a large proportion of an audit firm's revenue, then that audit firm may have – or may be seen to have – a vested interest in the outcome of the audit.

financial instrument any contract that gives rise to a (recognised or unrecognised) financial asset of one entity and a (recognised or unrecognised) financial liability or equity instrument of another entity. (AASB 132; NZ IAS 32, para 11)

financial interest a situation in which there is a financial interest between the auditor or audit firm and the client's organisation, other than the current fee for the audit engagement.

fundamental controls the key controls necessary to ensure that accounting records are in an auditable state. Adequate segregation of duties, reasonably effective routine supervision and access controls (in IT systems) are usually among these controls.

G

going concern an entity that has the ability to pay its debts as they fall due and that is solvent (assets exceed liabilities).

I

integrity risk the risk that a manager may be inclined to distort the financial statements.

interface a term used in IT to describe the exchange of information across a shared boundary, such as an internal network. An interface can occur between software, people or hardware and devices such as USBs and cables. An interface can send only (e.g., a microphone), receive only, or receive and send (e.g., firewall with alarm).

internal checks a re-performance or review activity enabled by segregating duties in such a way that no one person can initiate, authorise, conduct and record a transaction from start to finish without the work coming under the surveillance of at least one other person.

J

joint and several liability arises in contract 'when two or more persons jointly promise in the same contract to do the same thing, but also separately promise to do the same thing'. (Thomson Reuters, 2022)

L

limited assurance engagement 'An assurance engagement where the assurance practitioner's objective is a reduction in assurance engagement risk to a level that is acceptable in the circumstances of the assurance engagement, but where that risk is greater than that for a reasonable assurance engagement, as the basis for a negative form of expression of the assurance practitioner's conclusion. A limited assurance engagement is commonly referred to as a review.' (IAASB, 2008)

lowballing occurs where the audit contract price is cut to such an extent that the fees received are less than the costs incurred by the professional. Auditors are willing to do this because they expect to earn 'quasi-rents' (lower costs resulting from auditing a previously audited client) by keeping the engagement for a number of years. In addition, they may anticipate lucrative consultancy projects as a spin-off from the audit.

M

management advisory services (MAS) refers to the practice of performing non-assurance services for an assurance client.

management fraud an intentional act by one or more individuals among management – those charged with governance, or employees or third parties – involving the use of deception to obtain an unjust or illegal advantage. (ISA NZ 240, para 12(a))

management risk the potential for material misstatement resulting from the intentional actions of management.

misstatement 'The act of expressing a fact that is not correct.' (Cambridge Dictionary, 2022)

N

network consists of all the computers (or virtual machines) to access and share resources, including printers, databases and software.

new public management tends to focus on the economy, efficiency and effectiveness of government policy and programs, and less on meeting annual line-item budgets.

non-sampling risk the risk that the auditor uses inappropriate procedures or misinterprets evidence and, as a result, fails to recognise an error.

O

overall analytical procedures refer to analytics performed during planning. For example, major purchases, dispositions, related parties, new branches, or areas of concern as to material misstatements, could be indicated by the discovery of sales trends or profit ratios. (ASA 315, para A14; ISA NZ 315, para A14.)

overall audit risk (OAR) the impact of an inappropriate audit opinion – that is, of audit failure – and the costly outcomes that could occur as a result. Such an outcome could be, for example, a third party's unjustified reliance on an opinion to purchase a business that, had that opinion been appropriate, they would not have bought.

P

performance auditing in the public sector, VFM, or value for money auditing, is the practice of auditing against such goals.

plaintiff a party or person that brings a case against another in a court of law.

platform a technological foundation on which software and applications are developed. Apple's operating system is essentially a 'platform'.

professional liability refers to how the auditor is or can be legally held to account for the quality of their work.

professional scepticism an 'attitude that enhances the auditor's ability to identify and respond to conditions that may indicate possible misstatement ... This critical assessment is necessary in order for the auditor to draw appropriate conclusions'. (IAASB, 2012, Foreword)

public good is both non-excludable and non-rival. A public park is an example: the public should not be excluded from it, and its use by one party does not affect its use, or the quality of its use, by another.

R

reasonable assurance the highest level of assurance possible, obtained through an audit engagement where the professional acquires sufficient appropriate evidence to reduce the risk of misstatement to a low level. (ISA NZ 200, para 5)

regulations authoritative rules or orders, usually dealing with details or procedures. They may, or may not, have the force of law, but when established under statute, they are likely to be required in law.

risk management the idea that risk should be anticipated by management and incorporated into business planning, sometimes but not always controlled, so as to be the plan for organisational changes or unexpected events.

role senders those who influence auditors' behaviour and can have legal, contractual or cooperative relationships with the auditor.

S

safeguards actions, taken individually or in combination, that effectively reduce threats to compliance with the fundamental principles to an acceptable level. (APES 110, para 100.2(c))

sampling risk the risk that the auditor's conclusion, based on a sample, may be different from the conclusion that would be reached if the entire population were tested.

segregation of duties 'An internal control designed to prevent error and fraud by ensuring that at least two individuals are responsible for the separate parts of any task.' (CA ANZ, 2016, p. 7)

self-fulfilling prophecy a prediction or expectation that causes itself to become true.

servers provide resources, data services or programs to other computers within a network. Servers can host, for example, web apps (applications), catalogues, communication or other computer resources. They may be owned by the client, hosted by a hosting services provider, or cloud-based.

situational pressure the risk that management will misstate the financials as a result of pressure they may be under.

small and medium enterprises (SMEs) businesses whose personnel numbers fall below a certain threshold.

special relationship occurs when the auditor knows the purpose involved, and the specific person or class of people who will be relying on their opinion.

statutory audit engagements in which an audit is conducted primarily because it is imposed under Australian or New Zealand statutory requirements.

substantive tests the audit evidence-collection procedures that determine whether account balances, or transactions that lead to account balances, comply with GAAP.

T

tolerable misstatement the amount of error or omission the auditor is willing to tolerate and still conclude that the account (or account group) shows a true and fair view.

V

verification (to verify) a type of direct test on balances. Examples include inspecting fixed assets for *existence*, inspecting purchase documents for *rights and obligations* over them, re-performing depreciation schedules on them for *accuracy*, or ascertaining what one can purchase them for as to *valuation*.

virtualisation virtualisation systems replace multiple physical workstations, computers and printers with a single computer, creating a virtual layer that can act as independent 'computers' or virtual machines.

W

whistleblower a person, usually an employee or an insider, who reveals information on wrongdoing occurring within an organisation.

working papers auditor's documentation for each engagement. It is evidence of the auditor's work and describes what occurred and what decisions were made.

X

XBRL (eXtensible Business Reporting Language) A global framework used by businesses for recording, exchanging and disclosing business accounting information.

REFERENCES

Abernethy, M.A., and J.U. Stoelwinder. 1995. The role of professional control in the management of complex organizations. *Accounting, Organizations and Society*, 20(1): 1–17.

Abernethy, M.A., and P. Brownwell. 1997. Management control systems in research and development organizations: The role of accounting, behavior and personnel controls. *Accounting, Organizations and Society*, 22(3,4): 233–48.

Accountancy. 1992. Big Six join forces to fight 'epidemic', 110(1190): 11.

Accountancy. 1997. Cadbury Schweppes, 120(1250): 55.

Accounting Professional & Ethical Standards Board (APESB). 2018. APES 110: Code of ethics for professional accountants (including independence standards). November.

Alles, M.G., A. Kogan and M.A. Vasarhelyi. 2008. Putting continuous auditing theory into practice: Lessons from two pilot implementations. *Journal of Information Systems*, 22(2): 195–214.

American Accounting Association (AAA) Committee on Basic Auditing Concepts. 1973. *A Statement of Basic Auditing Concepts*. Sarasota, FL: AAA.

American Institute of Certified Public Accountants (AICPA). 1950. *Audits By Certified Public Accountants: Their Nature and Significance*. New York: AICPA.

Amir, E., L. Kirschenheiter and K. Willard. 1997. The valuation of deferred taxes. *Contemporary Accounting Research*, 14(4): 597–622.

Anderson, G.D. 1987. News and views. *The CPA Journal*, 57(11): 4–9.

Anderson, R.J. 1977. *The External Audit*. Toronto: Pitman.

Anderson, U., and L. Koonce. 1998. Evaluating the sufficiency of causes in audit analytical procedures. *Auditing: A Journal of Practice and Theory*, 17(1): 1–12.

Anonymous. 1994. Turning the tide. *Chartered Accountants Journal of New Zealand*, 73(9): 7–9.

Archer, S. 1997. The ASB's exposure draft statement of principles: A comment. *Accounting and Business Research*, 27(3): 229–41.

Arens, A.A., and J.K. Loebbecke. 1981. *Applications of Statistical Sampling to Auditing*. New Jersey: Prentice-Hall.

Arkin, H. 1984. *Handbook of Sampling for Auditing and Accounting*, 3rd edn. New York: McGraw-Hill.

Asare, S.K. 1992. The auditor's going concern decision: Interaction of task variables and the sequential processing of evidence. *The Accounting Review*, 67(2): 379–93.

Association of Certified Fraud Examiners (ACFE). 2010. *2010 Report to the Nations*. Austin, TX: ACFE.

Association of Certified Fraud Examiners (ACFE). 2022. Computers and technology. https://www.acfe.com/fraud-resources/computers-and-technology

Auditing and Assurance Standards Board (AUASB). 2012a. *AUASB Bulletin: Applying the Auditing Standards on Audits of Smaller Entities in Australia and New Zealand*. June. https://www.auasb.gov.au/admin/file/content102/c3/AUASB_Bulletin_Audits_of_Smaller_Entities.pdf

Auditing and Assurance Standards Board (AUASB). 2012b. *AUASB Bulletin: Professional Scepticism in an Audit of a Financial Report*. August. https://www.charteredaccountantsanz.com/-/media/f9bae272e7d74df188f27f8db81cee31.ashx

Auditing and Assurance Standards Board (AUASB). 2014. Framework for assurance engagement. June. https://www.auasb.gov.au/admin/file/content102/c3/Jun14_Framework_for_Assurance_Engagements.pdf

Auditing and Assurance Standards Board (AUASB). 2017. Definitions. https://standards.auasb.gov.au/node/479

Auditing and Assurance Standards Board (AUASB). 2020a. Framework for assurance engagements. May. https://www.auasb.gov.au/admin/file/content102/c3/Framework_AssuranceEngagements_May20_FINAL.pdf

Auditing and Assurance Standards Board (AUASB). 2020b. Application and other explanatory material. June. https://standards.auasb.gov.au/node/560

Auditor's Report, The. 1999. Staff director of the public oversight board's panel on audit effectiveness speaks to auditing academics at annual meeting, 23(1): 9–21.

Australian Securities and Investments Commission (ASIC). 2021. Audit quality: The role of directors and audit committees – How can directors and audit committees promote audit quality? Information sheet no. 196. October. https://asic.gov.au/regulatory-resources/financial-reporting-and-audit/auditors/audit-quality-the-role-of-directors-and-audit-committees/#promote-quality

Baber, W.R., E.H. Brooks and W.E. Ricks. 1987. An empirical investigation of the market for audit services. *Journal of Accounting Research*, 25(2): 293–305.

Baldwin, A., S. Shiu and Y. Beres. 2008. *Auditing in shared virtualized environments*. 16 January. Palo Alto, CA: HP Laboratories.

Bamber, E.M., R.J. Ramsey and R.M. Tubbs. 1997. An examination of the descriptive validity of the belief-adjustment model and alternative attitudes to evidence in auditing. *Accounting, Organizations and Society*, 22(3,4): 249–68.

Barnes, P. 1987. The analysis and use of financial ratios: A review article. *Journal of Business Finance & Accounting*, 14(4): 449–61.

Barnett, V., J. Haworth and T.M.F. Smith. 2001. A two-phase sampling scheme with applications to auditing. *Journal of the Royal Statistical Society*, 164(2): 407–22.

Barr, A., and I.J. Galpeer. 1987. McKesson and Robbins. *Journal of Accountancy*, 163(5): 159–62.

Beach, L.R., and J.R. Frederickson. 1989. Image theory: An alternative description of audit decisions. *Accounting, Organizations and Society*, 14(1,2): 101–12.

Beasley, M.S. 1998. Boards of directors and fraud. *The CPA Journal*, 68(4): 56–8.

Beattie, V., and S. Fearnley. 1998. Auditor changes and tendering: UK interview evidence. *Accounting, Auditing & Accountability Journal*, 11(1).

Becker, E.A. 1980. The evolution of financial auditing in the United States. *Baylor Business Studies*, 11(2): 37–54.

Bedard, J., T.J. Mock and J.E. Boritz. 1992. Expert and novice problem-solving behavior in audit planning; discussion. *Auditing: A Journal of Practice and Theory*, 11(Supplement): 1–32.

Behn, B.K., J.V. Carcello, D.R. Hermanson and R.H. Hermanson. 1997. The determinants of audit client satisfaction among clients of Big 6 firms. *Accounting Horizons*, 11(1): 7–24.

Bell, T. B., J.C. Bedard, K.M. Johnstone and E.F. Smith. 2002. KRiskSM: A computerized decision aid for client acceptance and continuance risk assessments. *Auditing: A Journal of Practice & Theory*, 21(2): 97–113.

Bell, T.B., and A.M. Wright. 1997. When judgment counts. *Journal of Accountancy*, 184(5): 73–7.

Benson, H. 1980. The profession and the community. *The Australian Accountant*, 50(4): 239–44.

Bernardi, R.A. 1994. Fraud detection: The effect of client integrity and competence and auditor cognitive style. *Auditing: A Journal of Practice and Theory*, 13 (Auditing Symposium): 68–84.

Bessell, M., L. Powell and G. Richardson. 2014. *The Demand for Registered Company Auditor Services in Australia*. CA ANZ.

Biss, T. 1997. Solicitors' trust accounts. *Chartered Accountants Journal of New Zealand*, 76(7): 46.

Bloom, R., and H.Q. Heymann. 1986. The concept of 'social accountability' in accounting literature. *Journal of Accounting Literature*, 5: 167–82.

Blumenfeld, K. 1989. Dilemmas of disclosure: Issues in environmental auditing. *Business and Professional Ethics Journal*, 8(3): 5–28.

Bodnar, G.H., and W.S. Hopwood. 2001. *Accounting Information Systems*, 8th edn. New Jersey: Prentice Hall.

Boffa, M.P., and M. Miller. 1997. Audit automation with lotus notes. *The Internal Auditor*, 54(3): 15–17.

Bones, S. 1988. How to impress the switched-on client. *Accountancy*, 101(1138): 116.

Bonner, S.E., R. Libby and M.W. Nelson. 1997. Audit category knowledge as a precondition to learning from experience. *Accounting, Organizations and Society*, 22(5): 387–410.

Booth, C., and J. Land. 1992. Illegal acts: The auditor's responsibility. *The Accountants' Journal*, 71(1): 48–9.

Botica Redmayne, N., M.E. Bradbury and S.F. Cahan. 2010. The effect of political visibility on audit effort and audit pricing. *Accounting & Finance*, 50(4): 921–39.

Boyle, C. 1995. Factors to consider. *Chartered Accountant*, 9–12.

Bradshaw, W. 1996. Enquiring into enquiry. *CA Magazine*, 129(7): 42–3.

Bremser, W.G., and L.J. Gramling. 1988. CPA firm peer reviews: Do they improve quality? *The CPA Journal*, 58(5): 75–7.

Brennan, I. 1995. The future of public sector internal audit. *Chartered Accountant*, 4: 30–1.

Briloff, A.J. 1986. 'Corporate governance and accountability: Whose responsibility?' Address in April 1986, at the University of Connecticut, Storrs, Connecticut.

Brody, R.G., S.P. Golen and P.M.J Reckers. 1998. An empirical investigation of the interface between internal and external auditors. *Accounting and Business Research*, 28(3): 160–71.

Brown, D.L., S. Shu and G.M. Trompeter. 2009. The insurance hypothesis: The case of KPMG's audit clients. 10 February.

Brown, J. 1998. December 1998: The season of goodwill. *Accountancy*, 121(1253): 61.

Brown, R., ed. 1905. *History of Accounting and Accountants*. Edinburgh: T.C. & E.C. Jack.

Burn, A. 1991. The equity of limited liability. *The Accountants' Journal*, 70(June): 2–3.

Burns, D.C., J.W. Greenspan and C. Hartwell. 1994. The state of professionalism in internal auditing. *The Accounting Historians Journal*, 21(2): 85–116.

Burton, J.C. 1972. Corporate financial reporting: Ethical and other problems. Symposium held in Absecon, NJ, 17–19 November, 1971.

Cadbury Committee. 1992. *The Financial Aspects of Corporate Governance*. Committee on the Financial Aspects of Corporate Governance, Chair Sir Adrian Adbury. London: Financial Reporting Council.

Cambridge Dictionary. 2022. Misstatement. Cambridge University Press. https://dictionary. cambridge.org/dictionary/english/misstatement

Canadian Institute of Chartered Accountants (CICA). 1980. *Extent of Audit Testing*. Toronto: CICA.

Canadian Institute of Chartered Accountants (CICA). 1981. *Audit Committees: A Research Study*. Toronto: CICA.

Canadian Institute of Chartered Accountants (CICA). 1988. *Auditibility: Audit of a Small Business*. Toronto: CICA.

Carey, P.J., M.A. Geiger and B.T. O'Connell. 2008. Costs associated with going-concern-modified audit opinions: An analysis of the Australian audit market. *Abacus*, 44(1): 61–81.

Caster, P., and K.V. Pincus. 1996. An empirical test of Bentham's theory of the persuasiveness of evidence. *Auditing: A Journal of Practice and Theory*, 15 (University of Waterloo Symposium on Auditing Research Supplement): 1–22.

Chaffey, J., K.A. Van Peursem and M. Low. 2011. Audit education for the profession: Perceptions of New Zealand auditors. *Accounting Education*, 20(2): 153–85.

Chambers, R.J. 1966. *Accounting, Evaluation and Economic Behavior*. Englewood Cliffs, NJ: Prentice-Hall.

Chan, K.H. 1996. Estimating accounting errors in audit sampling: Extensions and empirical tests of a decomposition approach. *Journal of Accounting, Auditing & Finance*, 11(2): 153–61.

Chandler, R. 1985. Materiality: Does it need to be a guessing game? *Accountancy*, 96(1098): 84–6.

Chartered Accountants Australia and New Zealand (CA ANZ). 2016. The art of professional scepticism: An overview of the series. https://www. charteredaccountantsanz.com/-/media/cf40ecd7a886 423598280423b2197652.ashx

Chartered Accountants Australia and New Zealand (CA ANZ). 2021. Forensic accounting. https://www. charteredaccountantsanz.com/member-services/ technical/forensic-accounting

Chartered Accountants Australia and New Zealand (CA ANZ). 2022. Professional scepticism. https://www. charteredaccountantsanz.com/member-services/ technical/audit-and-assurance/professional-scepticism

Chartered Accountants Journal of New Zealand. 1994. Turning the tide. 73(9): 7–9.

Chartered Accountants Journal of New Zealand. 1995. Liability progress. 74(3): 28.

Chartered Accountants Journal of New Zealand. 1996. Letters: Discipline. 75(June): 46–7.

Chartered Accountants Journal of New Zealand. 1998a. Member struck off for bringing profession into disrepute. 77(9): 86.

Chartered Accountants Journal of New Zealand. 1998b. New solicitors' trust account regulations. 77(2): 46.

Chau, D. 2021. Bill Papas's companies earned $500 million from fraud, liquidators allege. *ABC News*. 14 October.

Christenson, C. 1983. The methodology of positive accounting. *The Accounting Review*, 58(1): 1–22.

Chua, W.F. 1986. Radical developments in accounting thought. *The Accounting Review*, 61(4): 601–32.

Chung, J., J. Farrar, P. Puri and L. Thorne. 2010. Auditor liability to third parties after Sarbanes-Oxley: An international comparison of regulatory and legal reforms. *Journal of International Accounting, Auditing and Taxation*, 19(2010): 66–78.

Cirstea, A. 2014. The need for public sector consolidated financial statements. *Procedia Economics and Finance*, 15: 1289–96.

Coderre, D.G. 1994. Seven easy CAATT. *The Internal Auditor*, 51(4): 28–32.

Coderre, D.G. 1996. Data integrity and CAATTs. *The Internal Auditor*, 53(1):18–20.

Cohen, M.F. 1978. *The commission on auditors' responsibilities: Report, conclusions and recommendations (The Cohen Report)*. New York: AICPA.

Committee of Sponsoring Organizations (COSO). 2010. COSO announces project to modernize internal control integrated framework. COSO news release, 18 November Altamonte Springs, FL.

Committee of Sponsoring Organizations (COSO). 2016. *Fraud Risk Management Guide*. https://www.coso.org/SitePages/Fraud-Risk-Management-Guide.aspx?web=1

Consultative Committee of Accountancy Bodies (CCAB). 1990. *The Auditor's Responsibility in Relation to Illegal Acts*. London: Auditing Practices Committee of CCAB Ltd.

Cook, J.M., and H.G. Robinson. 1979. Peer review: The accounting profession's program. *The CPA Journal*, 49(3): 11–16.

Cooper, D.J., and M.J. Sherer. 1984. The value of corporate accounting reports: Arguments for a political economy of accounting. *Accounting, Organizations and Society*, 9(3,4): 207–32.

Cordery, C. 2007. NAFTs 'annus horribilis': Fraud and corporate governance. *Australian Accounting Review*, 17: 62–70.

Cordery, C., and R. Sinclair. 2013. Measuring performance in the third sector. *Qualitative Research in Accounting & Management*, November.

Cordery, C., B. Baskerville and B.F. Porter. 2010. Control or collaboration? Contrasting accountability relationships in the primary health sector. *Accounting, Auditing & Accountability Journal*, 23(6): 793–813.

Cosserat, G. 1997. Consistently inconsistent on accounting for value. *Accountancy*, 119(1245): 66.

Cousins, J., A. Mitchell, P. Sikka and H. Willmott. 1998. *Auditors: Holding the Public to Ransom*. Basildon, Essex: Association for Accountancy & Business Affairs.

Cox, R. 2000. Auditor independence becomes hot international topic. *Chartered Accountants Journal of New Zealand*, September: 7–10.

Coyne, M.P., S.F. Biggs and J.S. Rich. 2010. Priming/reaction-time evidence of the structure of auditors' knowledge of financial statement errors. *Auditing: A Journal of Practice and Theory*, 29(1): 99–123.

CPA Australia. 2019. *A Guide to Understanding Auditing and Assurance: Australian Listed Companies*. November. Southbank, Vic.: CPA Australia.

CPA Journal, The. 1994. IAPC issues codification of worldwide auditing standards, 64(12): 11.

Cressey, D.R. 1973. *Other People's Money: A Study in the Social Psychology of Embezzlement*. Montclair, NJ: Patterson Smith.

Curtis, G. 1995. Process analysis and modelling. In *Business Information Systems: Analysis, Design and Practice*, 2nd edn, pp. 351–400. Essex: Longman Group United Kingdom Ltd.

Dalziel, A. 1996. Whistleblowing. *Chartered Accountants Journal of New Zealand*, 75(10): 12–13.

Davia, H.R. 2000. *Fraud 101: Techniques and Strategies for Detection*. Toronto: John Wiley.

Davidson, L. 1975. The role and the responsibilities of the auditor: Perspectives, expectations and analysis. Background paper for the American Institute of Certified Public Accountants (AICPA) Commission on Auditors' Responsibilities.

Davidson, R.A., and W.E. Gist. 1996. Empirical evidence on the functional relation between audit planning and total audit effort. *Journal of Accounting Research*, 34(1): 111–24.

Davis, D. 1991. Audit risk or risky audits? *The Accountants' Journal*, 70(10): 23–6.

De Kok, A.G., K.H. van Donselaar and T. van Woensel. 2008. A break-even analysis of RFID technology for inventory sensitive to shrinkage. *International Journal of Production Economics*, 112: 521–31.

De Paula, F.R.M. 1948. *Developments in Accounting*. London: Sir Isaac Pitman and Sons Ltd. Reprinted 1978, Arno Press, New York.

DeStefano, D. 1989. Using computer assisted audit techniques in public sector audits. *The Government Accountants Journal*, 38(3): 43–50.

Dilton-Hill, K.G. 1986. Quality control in the smaller audit practice. Available from author.

Dilton-Hill, K.G., and M.J. Pratt. 1982. Experiences in quality control review. *The South African Chartered Accountant*, (June): 249–51.

Dixon, R., G.A. Mousa and A.D. Woodhead. 2004. The necessary characteristics of environmental auditors: A review of the contribution of the financial auditing profession. *Accounting Forum*, 28(2): 119–38.

Dopuch, N., R. King and J. Berg. 1991. The impact of MAS on auditors' independence: An experimental markets study; discussion. *Journal of Accounting Research*, 29: 60.

Drucker, P. 1995. *Managing in a Time of Great Change*. New York: Truman Talley Books/Dutton.

Dutta, S.K., and L.E. Graham. 1998. Considering multiple materialities for accounting combinations in audit planning and evaluation: A cost efficient approach. *Journal of Accounting, Auditing & Finance*, 13(2): 151–71.

EDs are on track. 1998. *Accountancy*, 121(1254): 8.

Eilifsen, A., W.R. Knechel and P. Wallage. 2001. Application of the business risk audit model: A field study. *Accounting Horizons*, 15(3): 193–207.

Eining, M.M., D.R. Jones and J.K. Loebbecke. 1997. Reliance on decision aids: An examination of auditors' assessment of management fraud. *Auditing: A Journal of Practice and Theory*, 16(2): 1–19.

Elliott, R.K., and J.J. Willingham. 1980. *Management Fraud: Detection and Deterrence*. New York: Petrocelli Books Inc.

Epstein, J.H. 1998. Knowledge as capital. *Futurist*, 32(4): 6.

Ewbank, E.E. 1932. *The Concepts of Sociology*. New York: D.C. Health & Co.

Exposure drafts on provisions and contingencies and fixed assets and goodwill. 1997. *Management Accounting – London*, 75(8): 3–4.

External Reporting Board (XRB). 2013. Explanatory guide Au7. https://www.xrb.govt.nz/dmsdocument/1870

External Reporting Board (XRB). 2015. Explanatory guide Au9. https://www.xrb.govt.nz/dmsdocument/1872

External Reporting Board (XRB). 2021. PES 1: Code of ethics for assurance practitioners.

External Reporting Board (XRB). 2022. Climate-related disclosures. https://www.xrb.govt.nz/standards/climate-related-disclosures/

Fama, E.F. 1970. Efficient capital markets: A review of theory and empirical work. *The Journal of Finance*, 25(2): 383–417.

Fisher, C. 2002. Auditors under the microscope. *Chartered Accountants Journal of New Zealand*, 81(4): 50–1.

Fisher, S.W. 1997. In defense of double entry accounting. *National Public Accountant*, 42(3): 33–4.

Flint, D. 1971. The role of the auditor in modern society: An exploratory essay. *Accounting and Business Research*, 1(4): 287–93.

Flint, D. 1982. *A True and Fair View in Company Accounts*. London: Institute of Chartered Accountants of Scotland.

Flint, D. 1988. *The Philosophy and Principles of Auditing: An Introduction*. Basingstoke, UK: Macmillan Education.

Foulds, M. 1998. Fraud and the role of the auditors. *Accounting & Business*, 1(6): 38–40.

Fowler, C. 2010. Financing, accounting and accountability in colonial New Zealand: The case of the Nelson School Society (1842–52). *Accounting History*, 15(3): 337–69.

Friedman, M., ed. 1953. The methodology of positive economics. In *Essays in Positive Economics*. Chicago: University of Chicago.

Galpin, S., and K. Van Peursem. 1994. Management fraud: Inherent risk sign posts. *Chartered Accountants Journal of New Zealand*, 73(4): 40–2.

Gascoyne, R.J.N. 1992. CAATs it if you can. *The CA Magazine*, 125(6): 38–40.

Gaston, S.J. 1986. *Controlling and Auditing Small Computer Systems*. Toronto: CICA.

Geller, L. 1990. PC audit tools. *Computers in Accounting*, 6(2): 16–21.

Geuss, R. 1981. *The Idea of a Critical Theory: Habermas and the Frankfurt School*. Cambridge: Cambridge University Press.

Gibbins, M. 1984. Propositions about the psychology of professional judgement in public accounting. *Journal of Accounting Research*, 22(1): 103–25.

Giddens, A. 1984. *The Constitution of Society: Outline of the Theory of Structuration*. Cambridge: Polity Press.

Gilling, D.M. 1978. The role of the auditor in modern society: Towards a conceptual analysis. Ph.D. diss., University of Newcastle, Australia.

Glover, S.M. 1997. The influence of time pressure and accountability on auditors' processing of nondiagnostic information. *Journal of Accounting Research*, 35(2): 213–26.

Godsell, D. 1991. Auditors' legal liability and the expectation gap. *The Australian Accountant*, 61(1): 22–8.

Godsell, D. 1993. *Auditors' Legal Duties and Liabilities in Australia*. South Melbourne: Longman Professional.

Goldman, A., and B. Barlev. 1974. The auditor-firm conflict of interests: Its implications for independence. *The Accounting Review*, 49(4): 707–12.

Graham, A. 1998. It's the thought that counts. *The Internal Auditor*, 55(2): 6.

Grant, J. 1998. A principled approach to providing assurance. *Accountancy*, 121(1256): 74.

Gray, O.R., and S.D. Moussalli. 2006. Forensic accounting and auditing united again: A historical perspective. *Journal of Business Issues*, 2: 15–25.

Gray R., D. Owen and K. Maunders. 1987. *Corporate Social Reporting: Accounting and Accountability*. London: Prentice-Hall International.

Greenawalt, M.M. 1997. The internal auditor and the critical thinking process: A closer look. *Managerial Auditing Journal*, 12(2): 80–6.

Gregor, K. 2010. Audit partner guilty of Feltex-books breach. *The New Zealand Herald*, 28 September, B003.

Groomer, S.M., and U.S. Murthy. 1992. Assessments of control risk for computer-based systems. *Internal Auditing*, 7(3): 27–37.

Gul, F. 1991. Size of audit fees and perceptions of auditors' ability to resist management pressure in audit conflict situations. *Abacus*, 27(2): 162–72.

Gul, F., H. Teoh and B. Andrew. 1991. *Theory and Practice of Australian Auditing*, 2nd edn. South Melbourne: Nelson.

Gurganus, F.E., and C.A. Smith. 1994. Is reciprocity possible between the US and the UK? A look at the auditing environment. *International Journal of Management*, 11(4): 909–16.

Gwilliam, D. 1985. Assessment and evaluation of internal control: Judgments relating internal control to audit program planning. In *A Survey of Auditing Research*, chapter 15. London: ICAEW.

Gwilliam, D. 1987a. What does reasonable care and skill entail? *Accountancy*, 100(1131): 124–6.

Gwilliam, D. 1987b. A contribution the negligent should make. *Accountancy*, 100(1132): 109–13.

Gwilliam, D. 1988. Making mountains out of molehills. *Accountancy*, 103(1135): 22–3.

Hackenbrack, K., and W.R. Knechel. 1997. Resource allocation decisions in audit engagements. *Contemporary Accounting Research*, 14(3): 481–99.

Hand, J.R.M. 1990. A test of the extended functional fixation hypothesis. *The Accounting Review*, 65(4): 740–63.

Hardcastle, A. 1988. Going to the government, cap in hand. *Accountancy*, 101(1133): 15–16.

Harris, I., and R. Spannier. 1976. Accountability: Answerability and liability. *Journal for the Theory of Social Behavior*, 6(2): 253–9.

Hasan, M., P.J. Roebuck and R. Simnett. 2003. An investigation of alternative report formats for communicating moderate levels of assurance. *Auditing: A Journal of Practice & Theory*, 22.

Hatherly, D.J. 1985. Evaluating the effects of interrelated evidence sources. *Accounting and Business Research*, 16(61): 35–46.

Hay, D., and C. Cordery. 2018. The value of public sector audit: Literature and history. *Journal of Accounting Literature*, 40(June): 1–15.

Heazlewood, T. 1998. Bean counter!!? Been there, done that, what next … *Accounting & Business*, 1(7,8): 19–21.

Hendriksen, E.S. 1982. *Accounting Theory*. Homewood, IL: Irwin.

Henry, L. 1997. A study of the nature and security of accounting information systems: The case of Hampton Roads, Virginia. *Mid-Atlantic Journal of Business*, 33(3): 171–89.

Higson, A. 1995. Corporate communication: A conceptual framework for financial reporting (a potential outline). Paper presented to the Financial Accounting and Auditing Research Conference, London Business School.

Hillison, W., and M. Kennelley. 1988. The economics of non-audit services. *Accounting Horizons*, 2(3): 32–40.

Hoffman, V.B., and J.M. Patton. 1997. Accountability, the dilution effect and conservatism in auditors' fraud judgments. *Journal of Accounting Research*, 35(2): 227–37.

Holland, L., and Y.B. Foo. 2003. Differences in environmental reporting practices in the UK and the US: The legal and regulatory context. *The British Accounting Review*, 35(1): 1–18.

Hollingshead, R.T. 1996. Discussion of an empirical test of Bentham's theory of the persuasiveness of evidence. *Auditing: A Journal of Practice and Theory*, 15 (University of Waterloo Symposium on Auditing Research Supplement): 33–6.

Holstrum, G.L., and T.J. Mock. 1985. Audit judgement and evidence evaluation: A synopsis of issues and research papers. *Auditing: A Journal of Practice and Theory*, 5(1): 101–8.

Holt, G., and P. Moizer. 1990. The meaning of audit reports. *Accounting and Business Research*, 20(78): 111–21.

Hoover, D.C., and G.A. Roberts. 1996. Avoiding peer review findings: Part 2. *Ohio CPA Journal*, 55(1): 42–4.

Horgan, J.M. 1997. Stabilising the sieve sample size using PPS. *Auditing: A Journal of Practice and Theory*, 16(2): 40–51.

Houghton, K. A., and C.A. Jubb. 1998. The function of the auditor-general: Independence, competence and outsourcing – the policy implications. *Australian Accounting Review*, 8(15): 30–5.

Humphrey, C., P. Moizer and S. Turley. 1993. The audit expectations gap in Britain: An empirical investigation. *Accounting and Business Research*, 23(91a): 395–411.

Hurtt, R.K., H. Brown-Liburd, C.D. Earley and G. Krishnamoorthy. 2013. Research on auditor professional scepticism: Literature synthesis and opportunities for future research. *Auditing: A Journal of Practice & Theory*, 32(1): 45–97.

Icerman, R.C., and W. Hillison. 1989. Risk and materiality in governmental audits. *Association of Government Accountants Journal*, fall: 51–61.

Institute of Chartered Accountants of England and Wales (ICAEW). 2008. Auditors liability conundrum. August. https://www.icaew.com/regulation/working-in-the-regulated-area-of-audit/audit-liability/auditors-liability-conundrum

Institute of Chartered Accountants of England and Wales (ICAEW). 2018. *Scepticism: The Practitioners' Take*. London: ICAEW Thought Leadership: Audit & Assurance Facility.

Institute of Chartered Accountants of New Zealand (ICANZ). 1998. *New Zealand Codified Auditing Standards and Audit Guidance Statements, Exposure Drafts, and Other Documents*. July. Wellington: ICANZ.

Institute of Internal Auditors (IIA). 2021. Factsheet: Fraud and corruption. https://iia.org.au/sf_docs/default-source/technical-resources/2018-fact-sheets/factsheet-fraud-and-corruption.pdf?sfvrsn=2

Institute of Internal Auditors (IIA). 2022. About internal audit. https://www.theiia.org/en/about-us/about-internal-audit/

International Accounting Education Standards Board (IAESB). 2017. Basis of conclusions: 2017–2021 IAESB strategy and 2017–2018 work plan. March. https://www.ifac.org/system/files/publications/files/IAESB-Strategy-and-Work-Plan-Basis-of-Conclusions.pdf

International Auditing and Assurance Standards Board (IAASB). 2008. *International Framework for Assurance Engagements*. March. New York: International Federation of Accountants.

International Auditing and Assurance Standards Board (IAASB). 2012. Staff questions & answers: Professional skepticism in an audit of financial statements. February. https://www.iaasb.org/publications/staff-questions-answers-professional-skepticism-audit-financial-statements-2

International Auditing and Assurance Standards Board (IAASB). 2019. PS focus, professional scepticism lies at the heart of quality audit.

International Federation of Accountants (IFAC). 2005. *Handbook of International Auditing, Assurance and Ethics Pronouncements*. New York: IFAC.

Jackson, A.B., M. Moldrich and P. Roebuck. 2008. Mandatory audit firm rotation and audit quality. *Managerial Auditing Journal*, 23(5): 420–37.

Jackson, G.T. 2016. The auditor's sampling decision in the presence of redundant internal controls. *Journal of Accounting and Finance*, 16/3: 88–95.

Jackson, R.A. 2010. Fighting the good fight: Henry Markopolos … Ponzi schemes in history. *Internal Auditor*, 67(3): 44–6.

Jacobs, J.J. 2001. Materiality: It's not the same old concept anymore. *Pennsylvania CPA Journal*, 72(2): 36–40.

Jacoby, J., and H.B. Levy. 2016. The materiality mystery. *The CPA Journal*, 86(7): 14–18.

Jenkin, E., and K. Van Peursem. 1996a. Expert systems. *Chartered Accountants Journal of New Zealand*, 75(8): 30–1.

Jenkin, E., and K. Van Peursem. 1996b. Audit: Expert systems (part 2). *Chartered Accountants Journal of New Zealand*, 75(9): 30–2.

Jensen, M.C., and W.H. Meckling. 1976. Theory of the firm: Managerial behaviour, agency costs and ownership structure. *Journal of Financial Economics*, 3(4): 305–60.

Johnson, J.A. 1985. Automated work papers: A new audit tool. *Journal of Accountancy*, 160(2): 123–6.

Johnstone, K.M. 2000. Client-acceptance decisions: Simultaneous effects of client business risk, audit risk, auditor business risk, and risk adaptation. *Auditing: A Journal of Practice & Theory*, 19(1), 1–25.

Joint Committee of Public Accounts and Audit. 2002. Report 391: *Review of Independent Auditing by Registered Company Auditors*.

Jones, C.S., and I.P. Dewing. 1997. The attitudes of NHS clinicians and medical managers towards changes in accounting controls. *Financial Accountability & Management*, 13(3): 261–80.

Joshi, Kailash. 2016. Chapter 11: Expert systems and applied artificial intelligence. Management Information Systems, College of Business Administration, University of Missouri, St Louis. https://www.umsl.edu/~joshik/msis480/chapt11.htm

Kaplan, S., and P.M.J. Reckers. 1995. Auditor's reporting decisions for accounting estimates: the effect of assessments of the risk of fraudulent financial reporting. *Managerial Auditing Journal*, 10(5): 27–36.

Kasparek, W. 1987. Applying computer-assisted audit techniques overseas. *Internal Auditing*, (2): 64–8.

Katz, E.M. 1998a. Keys to an effective audit committee. *Credit World*, 86(4): 21–3.

Katz, E.M. 1998b. Characteristics of an effective audit committee. *The Banking Law Journal*, 115(1): 37–41.

Keeper, T. 2014. The new financial reporting regime. *New Zealand Law Journal*: 248–50.

Kenley, W.J. 1971. Legal decisions affecting auditors: Comments on the Pacific Acceptance Corporation case. *The Australian Accountant*, 41(4): 153–61.

Kennedy, J., and M.E. Peecher. 1997. Judging auditors' technical knowledge. *Journal of Accounting Research*, 35(2): 279–93.

Kent, P., and R. Weber. 1998. Auditor expertise and the estimation of dollar error in accounts. *Abacus*, 34(1): 120–39.

King, A.M. 2005. Do you know where your financial assets are? How to revamp PP&E records so internal controls comply with Sarbanes-Oxley. *Strategic Finance*, 86(8): 24–9.

Kinne, D. 1994. Local area networks: A realistic audit approach. *Managerial Auditing Journal*, 9(5): 8–15.

Kissinger, J.N. 1977. A general theory of evidence as the conceptual foundation in auditing theory: Some comments and extensions. *The Accounting Review*, 52(2): 322.

Koh, H.C., and E. Woo. 1998. The expectation gap in auditing. *Managerial Auditing Journal*, 13(3): 147–54.

Koskivaara, E. 2004. Artificial neural networks in analytical review procedures. *Managerial Auditing Journal*, 19(2): 191–223.

KPMG. 2021a. Fraud barometer update: A snapshot of fraud in New Zealand. October. https://home.kpmg/nz/en/home/insights/2021/10/fraud-barometer-2021.html

KPMG. 2021b. Fraud survey 2021. 22 March. https://home.kpmg/au/en/home/insights/2021/03/fraud-risk-survey-2021.html

Krishnan, J., and J. Krishnan. 1997. Litigation risk and auditor resignations. *The Accounting Review*, 72(4): 539–60.

Kutubi, S.S., K. Ahmed, H. Khan and M. Garg. 2021. Multiple directorships and the extent of loan loss provisions: Evidence from banks in South Asia. *Journal of Contemporary Accounting & Economics*, 17(3).

Lee, T.A. 1984. *Audit Brief*. London: Auditing Practices Committee.

Lee, T.A. 1986a. *Company Auditing*, 3rd edn. London: Van Nostrand Reinhold International.

Lee, T.A. 1986b. The nature of auditing and its objectives. *Accountancy*, April: 292–6.

Leeuw, F.L. 1996. Performance auditing new public management and performance improvement: Questions and answers. *Accounting, Auditing & Accountability Journal*, 9(2): 92–102.

Leslie, D.A., A.D. Teitlebaum and R.J. Anderson. 1979. *Dollar-Unit Sampling: A Practical Guide for Auditors*. Toronto: Copp Clark Pitman.

Levi, P.C. 1997. Make audits effective and efficient. *Accounting Technology*, 13(3): 45–52.

Lewis, M.T. et al. 1983. Evaluation of audit evidence in the audit planning process: A multiple criteria approach. In J.J. Schult and L.E. Brown, eds. *Symposium on Auditing Research*. University of Illinois.

Li, H., D. Hay and D. Lau. 2019. Assessing the impact of the new auditor's report. *Pacific Accounting Review*, 31(1): 110–32.

Limperg, T. 1985. *The Social Responsibility of the Auditor*. Amsterdam: Limperg Institute.

Lin, W.T., T.J. Mock and A. Wright. 1984. Use of the analytic hierarchy process as an aid in planning the nature and extent of audit procedures. *Auditing: A Journal of Practice and Theory*, 4(1): 89–99.

Linton, R. 1936. *The Study of Man*. New York: D Appleton – Century Company.

Linton, R. 1945. *The Cultural Background of Personality*. New York: D Appleton – Century Company.

Lochner, Jr., P.R. 1993. Accountants' legal liability: A crisis that must be addressed. *Accounting Horizons*, 7(2): 92–6.

Loeb, S. 1978. *Ethics in the Accounting Profession*. Santa Barbara, CA: Wiley.

Loughman, T.P., R.A. Fleck and R. Snipes. 2000. A cross-disciplinary model for improved information systems analysis. *Industrial Management and Data Systems*, 100(89): 359–69.

Low, C.K., and H.C. Koh. 1997. Concepts associated with the 'true and fair view': Evidence from Singapore. *Accounting and Business Research*, 27(3): 195–202.

Lys, T., and R.L. Watts. 1994. Lawsuits against auditors. *Journal of Accounting Research*, 32(Supplement): 65–93.

MacDonald Commission. 1988. *Report of the Commission to Study the Public's Expectation of Audits*. Toronto: CICA.

MacPherson, S. 2021. What's the best payroll solution for your business? *Acuity Magazine*, August–September: 61–5.

Mak, T., K. Cooper, H. Deo and W. Funnell. 2005. Audit, accountability and an auditor's ethical dilemma: A case study of HIH Insurance. *Asian Review of Accounting*, 13(2): 18–35.

Malthus, S., and C. Fowler. 2009. Perceptions of accounting: A qualitative New Zealand study. *Pacific Accounting Review*, (21)1: 26–47.

Management Accounting – London. 1997. Auditors' liability: The deep-pockets syndrome, 75(6): 62.

Marshall, J. 1991. CPAs as consultants: Conflict of interests? *US Banker*, 101(11): 23–4, 66.

Mataira, K., and K.A. Van Peursem. 2010. An examination of disciplinary culture: Two professional accounting associations in New Zealand. *Accounting Forum*, 34: 109–22.

Matthews, J., and T. MacAvoy. 1997. Securities Act. *Chartered Accountants Journal of New Zealand*, 76(8): 12–13.

Matthews, P. 2021. 1988: Unemployment hits. Stuff. https://www.stuff.co.nz/the-press/christchurch-life/124978508/1988-unemployment-hits?rm=a

Mautz, R.K. 1983. Self regulation: Perils and problems. *Journal of Accountancy*, 155(5): 76–84.

Mautz, R.K., and H.A. Sharaf. 1961. *The Philosophy of Auditing*. Monograph no. 6, American Accounting Association.

McElveen, M. 2002. New rules: New challenges. *Internal Auditor*, December: 41–7.

McNamee, D., and T. McNamee. 1995. The transformation of internal auditing. *Managerial Auditing Journal*, 10(2): 34–7.

McNamee, D., and G. Selim. 1999. The next step in risk management. *Internal Auditor*, June: 36–8.

McRae, T.W. 1971. Applying statistical sampling to auditing: Some practical problems. *The Accountant's Magazine*, July: 376.

McRae, T.W. 1982. *A Study of the Application of Statistical Sampling to External Auditing*. London: ICAEW.

Mednick, R. 1990. Independence: Let's get back to basics. *Journal of Accountancy*, 169(1): 86–93.

Mednick, R. 1991. Reinventing the audit. *Journal of Accountancy*, 172(2): 71–8.

Mintchik, N., and J. Riley. 2019. Rationalizing fraud: How thinking like a crook can help prevent fraud. *The CPA Journal*, 89(3): 44–50.

Mock, T., and M. Washington. 1989. Risk concepts and risk assessment in auditing. *Advances in International Accounting*, 1(Supplement): 105–18.

Mong, S., and P. Roebuck. 2005. Effect of audit report disclosure on auditor litigation risk. *Accounting and Finance*, 45: 145–69.

Monti-Belkaoui, J., and A. Riahi-Belkaoui. 1996. *Fairness in Accounting*. UK: Quorum Books.

Moroney, R. 2007. Does industry expertise improve the efficiency of audit judgment? *Auditing: A Journal of Practice & Theory*, 26(2): 69–94.

Murray, Z. 2012. Professional scepticism. *Chartered Accountants Journal*, 91(11): 36–8.

Napier, C.J. 1998. Intersections of law and accountancy: Unlimited auditor liability in the United Kingdom. *Accounting, Organizations and Society*, 23(1): 105–28.

Nash, R. 1988. Auditing related party transactions. *The CPA Journal*, 58(4): 84–90.

Nath, N., K.A. Van Peursem and A. Lowe. 2006. Emergence of public sector performance auditing: A historical perspective. *Malaysian Accounting Review*, 4(2).

National Commission on Fraudulent Financial Reporting (NCFFR). 1987. *Report of the National Commission on Fraudulent Financial Reporting*. Washington, DC: NCFFR.

Needleman, T., and R.H. Bellone. 1997. Making payroll pay off. *Accounting Technology*, 13(3): 36–41.

Nelson, M.W. 1993. The effects of error frequency and accounting knowledge on error diagnosis in analytical review. *The Accounting Review*, 68(4): 804–24.

New Zealand Auditing and Assurance Standards Board (NZAuASB). 2014. Explanatory guide Au1A: Framework for assurance engagements. July. https://www.xrb.govt.nz/dmsdocument/1864

New Zealand Institute of Chartered Accountants (NZICA). 2010a. *Auditing and Assurance Standards*. Wellington: NZICA.

New Zealand Institute of Chartered Accountants (NZICA). 2010b. *International Standards on Auditing (ISA) Implementation in New Zealand*. Wellington: NZICA.

New Zealand Society of Accountants (NZSA). 1990. *New Zealand Auditing Standards and Guidelines*. Wellington: NZSA.

New Zealand Society of Accountants (NZSA). 1996. *New Zealand Auditing Standards and Guidelines*. Wellington: NZSA.

Newberry, S. 2007. The Feltex debacle: New Zealand's ENRON? Press release: CAFCA 05-12.

Newsroom. 2018. PwC to lose lucrative Fonterra audit contract. December. https://www.newsroom.co.nz/pwc-to-lose-lucrative-fonterra-audit-contract

Nigrini, M.J., and L.J. Mittermaier. 1997. The use of Benford's Law as an aid in analytical procedures. *Auditing: A Journal of Practice and Theory*, 16(2): 52–67.

Nobes, C. 1998. The continuing merger of UK and IASC standard setting. *Accounting & Business*, 1(5): 24–5.

Normanton, E.L. 1966. *The Accountability and Audit of Governments*. Manchester: Manchester University Press.

O'Brien, J.A. 1996. *Introduction to Information Systems*, 8th edn. London: Irwin.

O'Hagan, E.T. 1997. Important new legislation. *Chartered Accountants Journal of New Zealand*, 76(8): 4.

Owusu-Ansah, S., G.D. Moyes, B.P. Oyelere and D. Hay. 2002. An empirical analysis of fraud detection likelihood. *Managerial Auditing Journal*, 17(4): 192–204.

Ozbirecikli, M. 2007. A review on how CPAs should be involved in environmental auditing and reporting for the core aim of IT. *Problems and Perspectives in Management*, 5(2): 113–26.

Pallot, J. 1992. Elements of a theoretical framework for public sector accounting. *Accounting, Auditing and Accountability Journal*, 5(1): 38–59.

Palmrose, Z. 1987. Litigation and independent auditors: The role of business failures and management fraud. *Auditing: A Journal of Practice and Theory*, 6(2): 90–103.

Pany, K., O.R. Whittington and W.P. Lam. 1996. *Auditing: Revised Canadian Edition*. Toronto: McGraw-Hill Ryerson.

Parker, L.D. 1986. *Value-for-Money Auditing: Conceptual, Development and Operational Issues*. Caulfield, Vic.: Australian Accounting Research Foundation.

Parker, L.D. 1990. Towards value-for-money audit policy. In J. Guthrie, L. Parker and D. Strand, eds. *The Public Sector: Contemporary Readings in Accounting and Auditing*. Sydney: Harcourt Brace Jovanovich.

Pasewark, W.R., R.A. Shockley and J.E. Wilkerson, Jr. 1995. Legitimacy claims of the auditing profession vis-à-vis the behaviour of its members: An empirical examination. *Critical Perspectives on Accounting*, 6(1): 77–94.

Paterson, R. 1998. Will FRS 10 hit the target? *Accountancy*, 121(1254): 124–5.

Paukowits, F. 1998. Mainstreaming CAATs. *The Internal Auditor*, 55(1): 19–21.

Perkins, A. 1996. Put it in writing. *Accountancy*, 117(1232): 68–71.

Perols, J.L., and B.A. Lougee. 2011. The relationship between earnings management and financial statement fraud. *Advances in Accounting*, 27(1): 39–53

Plumlee, R. 1985. The standard of objectivity for independent auditors: Memory and bias effects. *Journal of Accounting Research*, 23(2): 683–99.

Porter, B., C. Ó hÓgartaigh and R. Baskerville. 2012. Audit expectation-performance gap revisited: Evidence from New Zealand and the United Kingdom. Part 2: Changes in the Gap in New Zealand 1989–2008 and in the United Kingdom 1999–2008. *International Journal of Auditing*, 16(3): 215–47.

Porter, B.A. 1987. *Study Guide for 10.275: Principles of Auditing and Taxation*. Palmerston North: Department of Accounting, Massey University.

Porter, B.A. 1988. Towards a theory of the role of the external auditor in society. Research monograph no. 1, Department of Accounting, Massey University, New Zealand.

Porter, B.A. 1990. The audit expectation-performance gap and the role of external auditors in society. Ph.D. diss., Massey University, New Zealand.

Power, M. 1998. Auditor liability in context. *Accounting, Organizations and Society*, 23(1): 77–9.

Pratt, M.J. 1990. *External Auditing: Theory and Practice*. New Zealand: Addison Wesley Longman.

Pratt, M.J. 1991. Auditors' liability and the public interest. *The Accountants' Journal*, 70(9): 41–4.

Pratt, M.J. 1993. Going concern qualifications in audit reports of New Zealand listed companies which failed after the 1987 stock exchange crash. Proceedings of the April 1993 British Accounting Association Conference.

Pratt, M.J., and K.G. Dilton-Hill. 1986. Microcomputer assistance for audit planning in small practices. Available from authors.

Pratt, M.J., and K.A. Van Peursem. 1993. Towards a conceptual framework of auditing. *Accounting Education*, 2(1): 11–32.

Pratt, M.J., and K.A. Van Peursem. 1996. Auditing risk, materiality and judgment standards: An international comparison. *Managerial Finance*, 22(9): 86–99.

Prawitt, D.F., and M.B. Romney. 1997. Emerging business technologies. *The Internal Auditor*, 54(1): 24–32.

Presutti, A. H. 1995. Anchor and adjustment heuristic effect on audit judgement. *Managerial Auditing Journal*, 10(9): 13–21.

Preuss, L. 1998. On ethical theory in auditing. *Managerial Auditing Journal*, 13(9): 500–8.

Pryde, D. 1996. Our day has come. *Chartered Accountants Journal of New Zealand*, 75(6): 5.

Puxty, A.G., H.C. Wilmott, D.J. Cooper and T. Lowe. 1987. Modes of regulation in advanced capitalism:

Locating accountancy in four countries. *Accounting, Organizations and Society*, 12(3): 273–91.

Pyzik, K.P. 1997. Building a better toolbox. *The Internal Auditor*, 54(2): 32–5.

Ramsay, I. 2001. *Independence of Australian Company Auditors: Review of Current Australian Requirements and Proposals for Reform*. Department of Treasury, Australian Government. https://treasury.gov.au/sites/default/files/2019-03/ramsay2.pdf

Ravlic, T. 2001. Adopt standard, warts and all: Experts. *The Age*, 10 September.

Ridley, A.J., and L. Burnham. 1998. Where are the auditors? *Directors and Boards*, 22(2): 61–3.

Ro, B.T. 1982. An analytical approach to accounting materiality. *Journal of Business Finance & Accounting*, 9(3): 397–412.

Robb, A.J. 2002. Fonterra illustrates audit-law weakness. *New Zealand Herald*, 21 August.

Robertson, B. 1997. Flexibility for exempt companies. *Chartered Accountants Journal of New Zealand*, 76(7): 56.

Roebuck, P., and K.T. Trotman. 1990. A field study of the review process. Working paper series 100, University of New South Wales School of Accounting.

Rosenfield, P. 1973. Stewardship. In J.J. Cramer and G.H. Sorter, eds. *Objectives of Financial Statements*, chapter 2. New York: AICPA.

Ross, M. 1992. Financial control failure: Sharing the blame. *The Accountants' Journal*, 71(9): 64–7.

Ross, M. 1998a. Audit negligence. *Chartered Accountants Journal of New Zealand*, 77(2): 21.

Ross, M. 1998b. Audit: Expert's report. *Chartered Accountants Journal of New Zealand*, 77(9): 76–7.

Rutherford, B.A. 1983. *Financial Reporting in the Public Sector*. London: Butterworths.

Saint, O. 2004. The view of an investor. *Chartered Accountants Journal*, December: 64–6.

Satov, T. 1995. Computer audit update. *CA Magazine*, 128(5): 10–11.

Scarbrough, D.P., D.V. Rama and K. Raghunandan. 1998. Audit committee composition and interaction with internal auditing: Canadian evidence. *Accounting Horizons*, 12(1): 51–62.

Schandl, C.W. 1978. *Theory of Auditing*. Houston: Scholars Book Co.

Schwartz, D.A. 1997. Audit sampling: A practical approach. *The CPA Journal*, 67(2): 56–9.

Segal, Troy. 2022. Conflict of interest. *Investopedia*. 24 March. https://www.investopedia.com/terms/c/conflict-of-interest.asp

Sherwin, D. 1998. Ernst & Young fraud report points finger at the enemy within. *Accounting & Business*, 1(June): 8.

Shilts, J., 2017. A framework for continuous auditing: Why companies don't need to spend big money. *Journal of Accountancy*, March: 3–4.

Sikka, P. 1997. Regulating the auditing profession. In M. Sherer and S. Turley, eds. *Current Issues in Auditing*, 3rd edn, pp. 129–45. London: Paul Chapman.

Sikka, P., and H.C. Willmott. 1995. The power of 'independence': Defending and extending the jurisdiction of accounting in the United Kingdom. *Critical Perspectives on Accounting*, 6(4): 341–69.

Sikka, P., A. Puxty, H. Wilmott and C. Cooper. 1992. *Eliminating the Expectations Gap?* Canada: Chartered Association of Certified Accountants.

Simon, D., and J. Francis. 1988. The effects of auditor change on auditor fees: Tests of price cutting and price recovery. *The Accounting Review*, 63(2): 255–69.

Sinason, D., and P.J. Hector. 2001. *The Impact on the Internal Audit Department When an Entity Implements a New Accounting System or New Accounting Software*. 17 December. DeKalb, IL.

Singleton-Green, B. 1990. Audit independence: Dodging Mr Davies. *Accountancy*, 106(1168): 22.

Skinnon, J., and L. Brown. 1993. Regulation of auditors. *The Accountants' Journal*, 72(11): 40–5.

Slade, Maria. 2019. How not to do it: Disgraced Fuji Xerox warns others as part of its redemption. *The Spinoff*, 11 May. https://thespinoff.co.nz/business/11-05-2019/how-not-to-do-it-disgraced-fuji-xerox-warns-others-as-part-of-its-redemption/

Smith, M., B. Fiedler, B. Brown and J. Kestel. 2001. Structure versus judgement in the audit process: A test of Kinney's classification. *Managerial Auditing Journal*, 16(1): 40–9.

Smith, M., N.H. Omar, S.I.Z.S. Idris and I. Baharuddin. 2005. Auditors' perception of fraud risk indicators: Malaysian evidence. *Managerial Auditing Journal*, 20(1), 73–85.

Stair, R.M., and G.W. Reynolds. 1998. Systems investigation and analysis. *Principles of Information Systems*, 3rd edn, pp. 509–66. Cambridge: MA Course Technology.

Staubus, G.J. 1977. *Making Accounting Decisions*. Houston: Scholars Book Company.

Stephens, R.G. 1983. Investigation of the descriptiveness of the general theory of evidence and auditing. *Auditing: A Journal of Practice and Theory*, 3(1): 55–74.

Stevens, M. 1985. *The Accounting Wars*. New York: Macmillan.

Stevens, M. 1991. *The Big Six*. New York: Simon & Schuster.

Stewart, R. 1977. Independence: The auditor's cornerstone. *The Accountants' Journal*, 56(9): 333–7.

Sutton, S.G., and J.R. Byington. 1993. An analysis of ethical and epistemological issues in the development and implementation of audit expert systems. *Advances in Public Interest Accounting*, 5: 231–43.

Tabor, R.H., and J.T. Willis. 1985. Empirical evidence on the changing role of analytical review procedures. *Auditing: A Journal of Practice and Theory*, 4(2): 93–109.

Takacs, J. 1993. Attestation engagements on internal control structure over financial reporting. *The CPA Journal*, 63(8): 48–53.

Taylor, John (The Australian National University/ASSA), and Tahu Kukutai (Te Whare Wānanga o Waikato/The University of Waikato). 2015. *Report to the Academy of the Social Sciences in Australia on the Workshop Data Sovereignty for Indigenous Peoples: Current Practice and Future Needs*. 9–10 July. https://socialsciences.org.au/publications/data-sovereignty-for-indigenous-peoples-current-practice-and-future-needs

The responsibility rests on you. 1981. *The Accountants' Journal*, 60(7): 265.

Thomas, C.W. 2002. The rise and fall of Enron. *Journal of Accountancy*, New York, 193(4): 41–52.

Thomson Reuters. 2022. Glossary: Joint and several liability. *Practical Law*. https://uk.practicallaw.thomsonreuters.com/8-200-1391?transitionType=Default&contextData=(sc.Default)&firstPage=true

Thornhill, W.T. 1989. Computers: Auditors' friend or foe? *Internal Auditing*, 4(3): 86–94.

Tinker, A.M. 1980. Towards a political economy of accounting: An empirical illustration of the Cambridge controversies. *Accounting, Organizations and Society*, 5(1): 147–60.

Tinker, T., M. Neimark and C. Lehman. 1991. Falling down the hole in the middle of the road: Political quietism in corporate social reporting. *Accounting, Auditing and Accountability Journal*, 4(2): 28–54.

Toba, Y. 1975. A general theory of evidence as the conceptual foundation in auditing theory. *The Accounting Review*, 50(1): 7–24.

Toms, J.S. 1998. The supply and demand for accounting information in an unregulated market: Examples from the Lancashire Cotton Mills, 1855–1914. *Accounting, Organizations and Society*, 23(2): 217–38.

Tower, G., and M. Kelly. 1989. The financial accounting standard setting process: An agency theory perspective. Discussion paper series no. 94 (June), Massey University Accountancy Department, New Zealand.

Tucker, R.R., and E.M. Matsumura. 1997. Second partner review: An experimental economics investigation. *Auditing: A Journal of Practice and Theory*, 16(1): 79–98.

Turner, J.L., T.J. Mock, P.J. Coram and G.L. Gray. 2010. Improving transparency and relevance of auditor communications with financial statement users. *Current Issues in Auditing*, 4(1): A1–A8.

Tversky, A., and D. Kahneman. 1974. Judgement under uncertainty: Heuristics and biases. *Science*, 185(4157): 1124–31.

U.S. Securities and Exchange Commission (SEC). 2003. *Management's Report on Internal Control over Financial Reporting and Certification of Disclosure in Exchange Act Periodic Reports*. August. https://www.sec.gov/rules/final/33-8238.htm#iia

U.S. Securities and Exchange Commission (SEC). 2006. *Management's Report on Internal Control over Financial Reporting Report*. February. https://www.sec.gov/Archives/edgar/data/55785/000119312506252528/dex995.htm

Van Peursem, K.A. 2004. Internal auditors' role and authority: New Zealand evidence. *Managerial Auditing Journal*, 19(3): 378–93.

Van Peursem, K.A. 2005a. Conversations with internal auditors: The power of ambiguity. *Managerial Auditing Journal*, 20(5), 489–512.

Van Peursem, K.A. 2005b. Public dialogue toward social policy: A methodology for accounting research. *Accounting and the Public Interest (US)*, 5: 56–87.

Van Peursem, K.A. 2010. Public sector vs private entities: A fresh look at accounting principles. *Financial Reporting, Regulation and Governance Journal*, 8(1), 1–30.

Van Peursem, K.A. 2020. Audit professional scepticism and the classics: Does pyrrhonism serve the practitioner? *International Journal of Economics and Accounting*, 9(4): 294–314.

Van Peursem, K.A., and A. Balme. 2010. Threats to the New Zealand Serious Fraud Office: An institutional perspective. *Qualitative Research in Accounting & Management*, 7(3): 304–28.

Van Peursem, K., and R.A. Brook. 1990. Audit risk model: An analysis. Paper presented at the Asia Pacific Conference, October, Hawaii.

Van Peursem, K.A., and S. Galpin. 1994. Management fraud: Inherent risk sign posts. *Chartered Accountants Journal of New Zealand*, 73(4): 40–2.

Van Peursem, K.A., and N. Harnisch. 2009a. Auditors' legal liability: New Zealand and Australian case law patterns. Paper presented at the American Accounting Association Conference, 1–5 August, New York.

Van Peursem, K.A., and N. Harnisch. 2009b. Conceptual framework for PBE reporting: Meaningful basis for 'sector neutrality'. *Financial Reporting, Regulation and Governance*, 8(1): 1–30.

Van Peursem, K.A., and A. Hauriasi. 1999. Auditors' reputation: An analysis of public exposure and perceptions in New Zealand. *Accounting Forum (UK)*, 23(1): 93–108.

Van Peursem, K.A., and L. Jiang. 2008. Internal audit outsourcing practice and rationales: SME evidence from New Zealand. *Asian Review of Accounting*, 16(3): 219–45.

Van Peursem, K.A., and A. Julian. 2005. Ethics research: An accounting educator's perspective. *Australian Accounting Review*, 38, 16(1): 13–29.

Van Peursem, K.A., and L. Pumphrey. 2005. Internal auditors and independence: An agency lens on corporate practice. *Financial Reporting, Regulation and Governance*, 4(2): 1–33.

Van Peursem, K.A., and M.J. Pratt. 1993. Difficult and critical audit procedures: New Zealand auditor perceptions. *Accounting Forum*, 16(4): 43–66.

Van Peursem, K.A., and M.J. Pratt. 1998. Are private sector standards enough? An example from public sector hospitals in New Zealand. *Financial Accountability and Management*, 14(2): 123–40.

Van Peursem, K.A., and M.J. Pratt. 2002a. A New Zealand failure prediction model: Development and international implications. *International Advances in Accounting*, 15: 229–47.

Van Peursem, K.A., and M.J. Pratt. 2002b. Going concern prediction model for New Zealand companies. *Advances in International Accounting*, 15.

Van Peursem, K.A., and M.J. Pratt. 2006. Failure prediction in New Zealand SMEs: Measuring signs of trouble. *International Journal of Business Performance Management*, 8(2/3): 259–69.

Van Peursem, K.A., and P. Wells. 2000. Contracting services in SMEs: A case of New Zealand professional accounting firms. *International Small Business Journal*, 72: 68–82.

Van Peursem, K.A., J.L Locke. and N.P. Harnisch. 2005. Going concern guidance for New Zealand auditors: Transitions in communicative acts. *Critical Perspectives on Accounting*, 17: 109–37.

Vanasco, R.R. 1998. Fraud auditing. *Managerial Auditing Journal*, 13(1): 4–71.

Vasil, A. 1995. Lawyers suing Renshaw auditors. *The Dominion*, 15 November: 1.

Velasquez, M. 1988. *Business ethics: Concepts and cases*. Englewood Cliffs, NJ: Prentice Hall.

Wallace, W. 1980. *The Economic Role of the Audit in Free and Regulated Markets*. New York: Graduate School of Management, University of Rochester.

Wallace, W. 1988. Why have firms withdrawn from an AICPA section? *The CPA Journal*, 58(1): 26–32.

Ward, G.M., and J.D. Harris. 1987. Managing computer risk: The vital link. *Price Waterhouse Review*, 31(2): 2–8.

Watne, D.A., and P.B.B. Turney. 1990. *Auditing EDP Systems*. Englewood Cliffs, NJ: Prentice-Hall Inc.

Watts, R.L., and J.L. Zimmerman. 1979. The demand for and supply of accounting theories: The market for excuses. *The Accounting Review*, 54(2): 273–305.

Watts, R.L., and J.L. Zimmerman. 1986. *Positive Accounting Theory*. Englewood Cliffs, NJ: Prentice-Hall.

Watts, R.L., and J.L. Zimmerman. 1990. Positive accounting theory: A ten-year perspective. *The Accounting Review*, 65(1): 131–56.

Westwick, C.A. 1981. *Do the Figures Make Sense?* London: ICAEW.

Wide Format Online Magazine, n.d. Fuji Xerox NZ expands civil case, adds former accountant EY. https://wideformatonline.com/ news/wide-format-news/10151-fuji-xerox-nz-expands-civil-case-adds-former-accountant-ey.html

Willekens, M., A. Steele and D. Miltz. 1996. Audit standards and auditor liability: A theoretical model. *Accounting and Business Research*, 26(3): 249–64.

Williams, H.J. 1990. What do auditors really consider in making going-concern judgments? *The Practical Accountant*, 23(8): 64–9.

Willingham, J.J., and D.R. Carmichael. 1968. The professional auditing subculture. *Abacus*, 4(2): 153–63.

Woolf, E. 1987. The Financial Services Act and the auditor. *Accountancy*, 100(1130): 96–8.

Woolf, E. 1992. Whose fault is it anyway? *Accountancy*, 102(1139): 115–17.

Wright, A., and S. Wright. 1996. Relationship between assessments of internal control strength and error occurrence, impact and cause. *Accounting and Business Research*, 27(1): 58–71.

Wright, I. 1998. The changing shape of materiality. *Accountancy International*, 122(1259): 69.

Yates, D. 1997. A practical view of fixed asset impairment. *Management Accounting – London*, 75(5): 44.

Zeff, S. 1988. The business of being a CPA. *Accountancy*, 102(1134): 110–11.

Zwass, V. 1997. *Foundations of Information Systems*. Boston: McGraw-Hill.

List of Australian Auditing Standards

Auditing Standards created under section 336 of the *Corporations Act 2001*:

ASQM 1 Quality Management for Firms that Perform Audits or Reviews of Financial Reports and Other Financial Information, or Other Assurance or Related Services Engagements

ASQM 2 Engagement Quality Reviews

ASQC 1 Auditing Standard ASQC 1 Quality Control for Firms that Perform Audits and Reviews of Financial Reports and Other Financial Information, Other Assurance Engagements and Related Services Engagements (Compiled)

ASA 100 Preamble to AUASB Standards (Compiled)

ASA 101 Preamble to Australian Auditing Standards (Compiled)

ASA 102 Compliance with Ethical Requirements when Performing Audits, Reviews and Other Assurance Engagements

ASA 200 Overall Objectives of the Independent Auditor and the Conduct of an Audit in Accordance with Australian Auditing Standards (Compiled)

ASA 210 Agreeing the Terms of Audit Engagements (Compiled)

ASA 210 Agreeing the Terms of Audit Engagements (Compiled)

ASA 210 Agreeing the Terms of Audit Engagements (Compiled)

ASA 220 Quality Control for an Audit of a Financial Report and Other Historical Financial Information (Compiled)

ASA 230 Audit Documentation (Compiled)

ASA 240 The Auditor's Responsibilities Relating to Fraud in an Audit of a Financial Report (Compiled)

ASA 250 Consideration of Laws and Regulations in an Audit of a Financial Report (Compiled)

ASA 260 Communication With Those Charged With Governance (Compiled)

ASA 265 Communicating Deficiencies in Internal Control to Those Charged with Governance and Management (Compiled)

ASA 300 Planning an Audit of a Financial Report (Compiled)

ASA 315 Identifying and Assessing the Risks of Material Misstatement through Understanding the Entity and Its Environment (Compiled)

ASA 320 Materiality in Planning and Performing an Audit (Compiled)

ASA 330 The Auditor's Responses to Assessed Risks (Compiled)

ASA 402 Audit Considerations Relating to an Entity Using a Service Organisation (Compiled)

ASA 450 Evaluation of Misstatements Identified during the Audit (Compiled)

ASA 500 Audit Evidence (Compiled)

ASA 501 Audit Evidence – Specific Considerations for Inventory and Segment Information (Compiled)

ASA 502 Audit Evidence – Specific Considerations for Litigation and Claims (Compiled)

ASA 505 External Confirmations (Compiled)

ASA 510 Initial Audit Engagements – Opening Balances (Compiled)

ASA 520 Analytical Procedures (Compiled)

ASA 530 Audit Sampling (Compiled)

ASA 540 Auditing Accounting Estimates, Including Fair Value Accounting Estimates, and Related Disclosures (Compiled)

ASA 550 Related Parties (Compiled)

ASA 560 Subsequent Events (Compiled)

ASA 570 Going Concern (Compiled)

ASA 580 Written Representations (Compiled)

ASA 600 Special Considerations – Audits of a Group Financial Report (Compiled)

ASA 610 Using the Work of Internal Auditors (Compiled)

ASA 620 Using the Work of an Auditor's Expert (Compiled)

ASA 700 Forming an Opinion and Reporting on a Financial Report (Compiled)

ASA 701 Communicating Key Audit Matters in the Independent Auditor's Report (Compiled)

ASA 705 Modifications to the Opinion in the Independent Auditor's Report (Compiled)

ASA 706 Emphasis of Matter Paragraphs and Other Matter Paragraphs in the Independent Auditor's Report (Compiled)

ASA 710 Comparative Information – Corresponding Figures and Comparative Financial Reports (Compiled)

ASA 720 The Auditor's Responsibilities Relating to Other Information (Compiled)

ASA 800 Special Considerations – Audits of Financial Reports Prepared in Accordance with Special Purpose Frameworks (Compiled)

ASRE 2410 Review of a Financial Report Performed by the Independent Auditor of the Entity (Compiled)

ASRE 2415 Review of a Financial Report – Company Limited by Guarantee or an Entity Reporting under the ACNC Act or Other Applicable Legislation or Regulation (Compiled)

Auditing standards not made under the *Corporations Act 2001*:

ASA 805 Special Considerations – Audits of Single Financial Statements and Specific Elements, Accounts or Items of a Financial Statement (Compiled)

ASA 810 Engagements to Report on Summary Financial Statements

List of New Zealand auditing standards

ISA NZ Standards (as at November 2017) issued by the External Reporting Board subcommittee, the Auditing and Assurance Standards Board, Wellington:

XRB Au1 Application of Auditing and Assurance Standards

ISA NZ 200 Overall Objective of the Independent Auditor and the Conduct of an Audit in Accordance with International Standards on Auditing (New Zealand)

ISA NZ 210 Agreeing the Terms of Audit Engagements

ISA NZ 220 Quality Control for an Audit of Financial Statements

ISA NZ 230 Audit Documentation

ISA NZ 240 The Auditor's Responsibilities Relating to Fraud in an Audit of Financial Statements

ISA NZ 250 Consideration of Laws and Regulations in the Audit of Financial Statements

ISA NZ 260 Communication with Those Charged with Governance

ISA NZ 265 Communicating Deficiencies in Internal Control to those Charged with Governance and Management

ISA NZ 300 Planning an Audit of Financial Statements

ISA NZ 315 Identifying and Assessing the Risks of Material Misstatement through Understanding the Entity and its Environment

ISA NZ 320 Materiality in Planning and Performing an Audit

ISA NZ 330 The Auditor's Responses to Assessed Risks

ISA NZ 402 Audit Considerations Relating to an Entity Using a Service Organisation

ISA NZ 450 Evaluation of Misstatements Identified During the Audit

ISA NZ 500 Audit Evidence

ISA NZ 501 Audit Evidence – Specific Considerations for Selected Items

ISA NZ 505 External Confirmations

ISA NZ 510 Initial Audit Engagements – Opening Balances

ISA NZ 520 Analytical Procedures

ISA NZ 530 Audit Sampling

ISA NZ 540 Auditing Accounting Estimates, Including Fair Value Accounting Estimates, and Related Disclosures

ISA NZ 550 Related Parties

ISA NZ 560 Subsequent Events

ISA NZ 570 Going Concern

ISA NZ 580 Written Representations

ISA NZ 600 Special Considerations – Audits of Group Financial Statements (Including the Work of Component Auditors)

ISA NZ 610 Using the Work of Internal Auditors

ISA NZ 620 Using the Work of an Auditor's Expert

ISA NZ 700 Forming an Opinion and Reporting on Financial Statements

ISA NZ 701 Communicating Key Audit Matters in the Independent Auditor's Report

ISA NZ 706 Emphasis of Matter Paragraphs and Other Matter Paragraphs in the Independent Auditor's Report

ISA NZ 710 Comparative Information – Corresponding Figures and Comparative Financial Statements

ISA NZ 720 The Auditor's Responsibility Relating to Other Information

ISA NZ 800 Special Considerations – Audits of Financial Statements Prepared in Accordance with Special Purpose Frameworks

ISA NZ 805 Special Considerations – Audits of Single Financial Statements and Specific Elements, Accounts or Items of a Financial Statement

ISA NZ 810 Engagements to Report on Summary Financial Statements

PES 1 Code of Ethics for Assurance Practitioners

PES 3 Quality Control for Firms that Perform Audits and Reviews of Financial Statements and Other Assurance Engagements

ISRE NZ 2400 Review of Historical Financial Statements Performed by an Assurance Practitioner

NZ SRE 2410 Review of Financial Statements Performed by the Independent Auditor of the Entity

ISAE NZ 3000 Assurance Engagements Other than Audits or Reviews of Historical Financial Information

SAE 3100 Assurance Engagements on Compliance

SAE 3150 Assurance Engagements on Controls

ISAE NZ 3402 Assurance Reports on Controls at a Service Organisation

ISAE NZ 3410 Assurance Engagements on Greenhouse Gas Statements

ISAE NZ 3420 Assurance Engagements to Report on the Compilation of Pro Forma Financial Information Included in a Prospectus

Accounting Standards issued by the New Zealand Accounting Standards Board of the External Reporting Board as at October 2017:

NZ IAS 1 Presentation of Financial Statements

NZ IAS 2 Inventories (effective for reporting periods beginning 1 January 2018)

NZ IAS 12 Income Tax

NZ IAS 16 Property, Plant and Equipment

NZ IAS 24 Related Party Disclosures

NZ IAS 26 Accounting and Reporting By Retirement Benefit Plans

NZ IAS 27 Consolidated and Separate Financial Statements

NZ IAS 32 Financial Instruments – Disclosure and Presentation

NZ IAS 37 Provisions, Contingent Liabilities and Contingent Assets

NZ IAS 38 Intangible Assets

Previous standards:

NZ IAS 1 Presentation of Financial Statements (2012)

NZ IAS 10 Events after the Reporting Period (2012)

INDEX